OXFORD STUDIES IN SOC

GENERAL EDITOR: KEIT

THE RISE OF THE BA

THE RISE OF THE
BARRISTERS

A SOCIAL HISTORY OF THE
ENGLISH BAR 1590–1640

WILFRID R. PREST

CLARENDON PRESS · OXFORD

Oxford University Press, Walton Street, Oxford OX2 6DP
Oxford New York Toronto Melbourne Auckland
Delhi Bombay Calcutta Madras Karachi
Petaling Jaya Singapore Hong Kong Tokyo
Nairobi Dar es Salaam Cape Town

Associated companies in Beirut Berlin Ibadan Nicosia

OXFORD is a trade mark of Oxford University Press

Published in the United States
by Oxford University Press, New York

First published 1986
First issued in paperback (with corrections) 1991

British Library Cataloguing in Publication Data
Prest, Wilfrid R.
The rise of the barristers: a social history of
the English bar, 1590–1640.
1. Lawyers—England—History—16th century
2. Lawyers—England—History—17th century
I. Title
344.2'0023   KD463
ISBN 0–19–821764–1
ISBN 0–19–820258–X (Pbk)

Library of Congress Cataloging in Publication Data
Prest, Wilfrid R.
The rise of the barristers.
Bibliography: p.
Includes index.
1. Lawyers—Great Britain—History.   I. Title.
KD463.P74 1986   340'.023'42   86–2238
ISBN 0–19–821764–1
ISBN 0–19–820258–X (Pbk)

Printed and bound in
Great Britain by Biddles Ltd,
Guildford and King's Lynn

TO MY MOTHER
AND
IN MEMORY OF MY FATHER

PREFACE

'What made English history in the seventeenth century was the legal profession.'

> Ernest Barker, foreword to I. D. Jones,
> *The English Revolution* (1931).

'The *social* history of the bar . . . has never been written.'

> G. Sawer, *Law In Society* (Oxford, 1965), 121.

HISTORIANS often acknowledge, if only in passing, the remarkable all-round prominence of common lawyers in early modern England. Yet we still lack adequate biographical accounts of such central figures as Edward Coke, Thomas Coventry, and John Selden, let alone much sense of how far these eminent individuals were typical of their professional colleagues at large. Even a preliminary exploration of that theme must come to terms with both the internal and external histories of the bar. In other words, it must consider not only the various roles which barristers played out of court, but also the nature and patterns of their working lives, at a time when the legal profession was growing rapidly, and undergoing profound structural change. Ideally, one would also like to show how these two histories were interrelated.

This book is a sequel—albeit somewhat delayed—to *The Inns of Court under Elizabeth I and the Early Stuarts, 1590–1640*, which I published in 1972. That work did not attempt a sustained account of the lawyer-members of the inns, an obvious deficiency which I envisaged supplying quite promptly. Now slightly older and a little more experienced in historical research, I have come to realize that a comprehensive study of the English bar in the half-century before the Long Parliament could easily take several lifetimes.

Although something of a renaissance in legal-historical studies has occurred over the last two decades, we still lack thorough, archivally based studies of most central courts, and know only in broad outline the body of rules and doctrines which they administered. The most serious and challenging deficiency, however, is in our understanding of the ways in which the law and its institutions affected and were used by ordinary people. Although a start has been made on filling some of these gaps, they all urgently require more single-minded attention than I have been able to give them here.

Considering the current vogue for micro-history, fine-grained interpretative reconstructions of particular individuals and small communities, a study which is national in scope, not rigidly confined to a nominal fifty-year span, and based on the quantitative analysis of a large set of biographical data may seem to require a word or two of methodological justification. By concentrating on the barristers of, say, two or three counties at one or two given points in time, or indeed on a handful of particularly well-documented individual counsellors, it might well have been possible to achieve greater depth and thoroughness. On the other hand, a narrow focus, by definition, includes only part of the total view; this may not matter much if the general outlines are fairly clear, or the particular detail more or less self-contained, but neither condition holds in the present case. The broad conclusions advanced below obviously will not provide full or final answers to all the questions historians might conceivably ask about early modern common lawyers; but I hope that they may prove to be of some general interest, as well as constituting a reasonably firm point of departure for future investigation of what is still potentially a very fruitful field of research. In any case, the history of the bar in the later sixteenth and early seventeenth centuries is surely of sufficient significance to warrant at least an initial overview.

With the aim of countering the tendency towards excessive statistical abstraction inherent in the prosopographical approach, as well as making it easier for readers to follow and check my workings, abbreviated biographical outlines with full supporting references for all the lawyers in my sample groups appear as appendices. Unfortunately, it is almost impossible to eliminate error from such compilations, and I can only hope that I have corrected more from other sources than I have passed on or perpetrated myself. These last would have been far more numerous without the kind assistance of Mr J. P. Ferris and his colleagues from the History of Parliament Trust, as well as a number of specialists on particular families, groups and places—none of whom, however, should be held responsible for any remaining mistakes or omissions. Mass-biographical

research is a peculiarly frustrating activity; one can rarely claim to
have exhausted all possible lines of inquiry, especially when dealing
with the more obscure individuals. Although I have worked in more
than seventy record offices and archival repositories during the
twelve years it has taken to write this book, there can be no doubt
that I have still overlooked relevant material, especially among
papers in private hands and those held by municipal corporations.

A lot of people have helped put this book together, and while I
cannot mention each one by name, I thank them all nonetheless. My
prime debt is to Irene Cassidy, who has once again enabled an
Adelaide historian to pursue a project based on distant sources;
without her assiduous and informed aid this book simply could not
have been written. Research assistance, for which I am also grateful,
was given in Adelaide by Gillian Erskine and Cherry Walker, with
support from departmental and university funds. The initial phases
of the project were supported by the Australian Research Grants
Committee (as it then was), and I acknowledge with thanks travel
funds provided by the Australian-American Educational Foundation and the Myer Foundation.

Over the past decade I have held visiting fellowships at All Souls
College, Oxford; the Huntington Library, San Marino, California;
the Shelby Cullom Davis Center for Historical Study at Princeton
University; the Humanities Research Centre of the Australian
National University; and Clare Hall, Cambridge. I thank all those in
and around these institutions who encouraged and facilitated my
work, especially John Simmons, Mary Robertson, Lawrence Stone,
Ian Donaldson, and Geoffrey Elton. Archivists, librarians, and
computing scientists in England, North America, and Australia
helped me to gather and analyse the manuscript and printed sources
on which this book is based; it is impossible to enumerate all their
individual acts of kindness, but I should like to express particular
gratitude to Miss M. Cash, formerly Hampshire County Archivist,
Mr P. I. King, Chief Archivist at Delapre Abbey, Northampton, and
the staff of the Barr Smith Library, University of Adelaide, and the
Institute of Historical Research, University of London.

Many scholars have been good enough to encourage me with
questions, references, and other incentives to persevere; I thank
them all most warmly, and trust they will find their specific
contributions appropriately acknowledged. I am also grateful to the
editors of the La Trobe University journal *Law in Context* for

permission to reproduce in Chapter Six material which first appeared in that publication; to the various owners who have allowed me to consult their manuscripts, especially the Marquess of Bath, the Rt. Hon. Lady Lucas, Mrs H. Henderson, and Mr J. L. Jervoise; and to the authors of the unpublished theses cited in Appendix I, from whose work I have learnt a great deal.

Finally, I should like to express my thanks to several generations of colleagues, secretaries, and students at the University of Adelaide; to my sons Richard and James, who have lived with this book most of their lives; and to John and Veronica Baker, Tom and Jeanne-Marie Barnes, Chris and Sharyn Brooks, Trish Crawford, Sabina Flanagan, Chris and Amanda Helm, Christopher Hill, and Keith Thomas, for their friendship and many kindnesses.

W. R. P.

CONTENTS

LIST OF TABLES

ABBREVIATIONS

All works cited were published in London, unless otherwise noted. Spelling and punctuation have been modernized in quotations from primary sources, but not in the titles of books. Dates are New Style, with the year beginning on 1 January.

Additional	Additional MSS, British Library
AHR	*American Historical Review*
AJLH	*American Journal of Legal History*
Al. Cant.	*Alumni Cantabrigienses ... Part I*, comp. J. and J. A. Venn (Cambridge, 1922–7)
Al. Ox.	*Alumni Oxonienses ... 1500–1714*, comp. J. Foster (1891–2)
AO	Archives Office
AOI	*Acts and Ordinances of the Interregnum 1642–1660*, ed. C. H. Firth and R. S. Rait (1911)
APC	*Acts of the Privy Council of England*, ed. J. R. Dasent *et al.* (1890–)
Arch. Cant.	*Archaeologia Cantiana*
Benn, 'Essays'	Beds. RO, L28/46 ('Essays of Anth. Benn, Rec. of London')
BIHR	*Bulletin of the Institute of Historical Research*
BL	British Library
Bodl.	Bodleian Library
Borthwick	Borthwick Institute of Historical Research, York
C	Chancery group, PRO
CCAM	*Calendar of the Proceedings of the Committee for Advancement of Money, 1642–1656*, ed. M. A. E. Green (1888)
CCC	*Calendar of the Proceedings of the Committee for Compounding, &c., 1643–60*, ed. M. A. E. Green (1889–92)
CD 1621	*Commons Debates 1621*, ed. W. Notestein *et al.* (New Haven, 1935)
CD 1628	*Proceedings in Parliament 1628*, ed. M. F. Keeler *et al.* (New Haven, 1977–83)
Chicago	Joseph Regenstein Library, University of Chicago
CJ	*Journals of the House of Commons 1547–1714* (1742)

Clendinnen	T. B. Clendinnen, 'The Common Lawyers in Parliament and Society: A Social and Political Study of the Common Lawyers in the First Jacobean Parliament', Ph.D. thesis, University of North Carolina at Chapel Hill, 1975
CLJ	*Cambridge Law Journal*
Cottonian	Cottonian MSS, BL
CP	Court of Common Pleas group, PRO
Croke, 'Diurnall'	Account book of Paul Ambrose Croke, Rare Books Room, Library of the University of Illinois, Urbana-Champaign
CS	Camden Society or Camden Series
CSPD	*Calendar of State Papers, Domestic Series*, various editors (1858–)
CSPIre	*Calendar of State Papers ... Ireland*, various editors (1869–)
CUL	Cambridge University Library
DL	Duchy of Lancaster group, PRO
DLLA	J. Fortescue, *De Laudibus Legum Anglie*, ed. S. B. Chrimes (Cambridge, 1949)
DNB	*Dictionary of National Biography*, ed. L. Stephen and S. Lee (1885–1900)
DWB	*The Dictionary of Welsh Biography Down to 1940*, ed. J. E. Lloyd and R. T. Jenkins (1959)
E	Exchequer group, PRO
Egerton	Egerton MSS, BL
EHR	*English Historical Review*
Ellesmere	Ellesmere MSS, Henry E. Huntington Library
Folger	Folger Shakespeare Library
Foss	E. Foss, *The Judges of England* (1848–64)
GI	Gray's Inn
GIAdmR	*The Register of Admissions to Gray's Inn, 1521–1889*, ed. J. Foster (1889)
GIPB	*The Pension Book of Gray's Inn, 1569–1800*, ed. R. J. Fletcher (1901–10)
Hargrave	Hargrave MSS, BL
Harleian	Harleian MSS, BL
Haward, *Reports*	*Les Reportes del Cases in Camera Stellata 1593 to 1609*, ed. W. P. Baildon (1894)
HEL	W. S. Holdsworth, *A History of English Law* (1922–66)
HC	House of Commons
HL	House of Lords

HLQ	*Huntington Library Quarterly*
HLS	Harvard Law School
HMC	Historical Manuscripts Commission
H. of P.	*The House of Commons 1558–1603*, ed. P. W. Hasler (1981)
HS	Publications of the Harleian Society
Inns of Court	W. R. Prest, *The Inns of Court under Elizabeth I and the Early Stuarts 1590–1640* (1972)
IT	Inner Temple
IT AdmR	'Admissions to the Inner Temple to 1659', comp. R. L. Lloyd, typescript, Inner Temple Library
ITR	*A Calendar of the Inner Temple Records*, ed. F. A. Inderwick and R. A. Roberts (1896–1936)
JBS	*Journal of British Studies*
JLH	*Journal of Legal History*
KB	Court of King's (Queen's) Bench group, PRO
Keeler	M. F. Keeler, *The Long Parliament, 1640–1641* (Philadelphia, 1954)
Knowler	*The Earl of Strafforde's Letters and Despatches . . .*, ed. W. Knowler (1739)
Lansdowne	Lansdowne MSS, BL
Lawyers	*Lawyers in Early Modern Europe and America*, ed. W. R. Prest (1981)
LI	Lincoln's Inn
LIAdmR	*The Records of the Honourable Society of Lincoln's Inn . . . Admissions . . . 1420 to A.D. 1799*, ed. W. P. Baildon (1896)
LIBB	*The Records of the Honourable Society of Lincoln's Inn. The Black Books*, ed. W. P. Baildon (1897–1969)
LJ	*Journals of the House of Lords, 1578–1714* (1767–)
Lloyd, 'Welsh benchers'	R. L. Lloyd, 'Welsh Masters of the Bench of the Inner Temple from Early Times until the End of the Eighteenth Century', *Trans. Hon. Soc. of Cymmrodorion 1937* (1938), 145–200
Lowther, 'Autobiography'	'Sir John Lowther (1)'s Autobiography', Cumbria RO D/Lons/L, A/1, fols. 335–61, printed in *Surtees Soc.*, cxci (1979)
LQR	*Law Quarterly Review*
LRH	*Legal Records and the Historian*, ed. J. H. Baker (1978)
MT	Middle Temple

MT AdmR	*Register of Admissions to the Honourable Society of the Middle Temple, from the Fifteenth Century to the Year 1944*, ed. H. A. C. Sturgess (1949)
MTR	*Minutes of Parliament of the Middle Temple*, ed. C. T. Martin (1904–5)
N & Q	*Notes and Queries*
NLW	National Library of Wales
OJ	W. Dugdale, *Origines Juridiciales* (1663)
P & P	*Past and Present*
PCC	Will registered in Prerogative Court of Canterbury (now at PRO, PROB11)
PRO	Public Record Office, London
PROB	Probate group, PRO
Radicals	*Biographical Dictionary of British Radicals in the Seventeenth Century*, ed. R. L. Greaves and R. Zaller (Brighton, 1982–4)
REQ	Court of Requests group, PRO
RO	Record Office
Sloane	Sloane MSS, BL
SP	State Papers group, PRO
SS	Selden Society
STAC	Court of Star Chamber group, PRO
Stowe	Stowe MSS, BL
TRHS	*Transactions of the Royal Historical Society*
UCNW	University College of North Wales, Bangor
VCH	*The Victoria History of the Counties of England (1900–)*
WAM	*Wiltshire Archaeological Magazine*
WARD	Court of Wards and Liveries group, PRO
Whitelocke, *Lib. Fam.*	*Liber Famelicus of Sir James Whitelocke*, ed. J. Bruce (CS, 1858)

CHAPTER ONE

INTRODUCTION

i. Profession and society

THE social history of the bar in early modern England is (among other things) part of the history of the professions. This statement may well appear entirely uncontroversial, not to say banal. Yet, strangely enough, until recently, historians and social theorists seemed agreed in assuming that the professions hardly existed as significant historical entities before the Industrial Revolution. This odd notion was sustained by a mixture of ignorance and ideology. It could hardly be denied that some professions—the Church, law, medicine, for a start—had flourished before the coming of industrial society. That awkward fact was explained away, however, by discounting these 'old' or 'traditional' professions as mere parasitic appendages of the ancien regime's landed ruling élite. Modern professions, professions properly so-called, came into being (so it was claimed) only when industrialization created a much-expanded market for professional services, which proliferated step by step with the specialization of labour and the increasing range of scientific knowledge.[1]

Besides conforming to that sociological tenet which holds the modern world to be essentially the product of industrialization (rather than, say, renaissance individualism, the scientific revolution, democracy, or capitalism, to name a few possible alternatives), such an interpretative schema had the overwhelming practical advantage of absolving scholars from investigating the pre-industrial history of the professions. This was particularly helpful in view of the paucity of published work on the professions before 1800, and the fact that hardly any of what was available transcended merely anecdotal, biographical, or narrowly institutional approaches.

[1] Cf. T. Parsons, 'The Professions and Social Structure', in *idem, Essays in Sociological Theory* (Glencoe, Ill., 1954), 34–49; W. J. Reader, *Professional Men: The Rise of the Professional Classes in Victorian England* (1966), 9–10; M. S. Larson, *The Rise of Professionalism: A Sociological Analysis* (Berkeley, 1977), xvi, chs. 1–2; H. Perkin, *The Origins of Modern English Society 1780–1880* (1969), 252–5; *idem, Professionalism, Property and English Society since 1880* (Reading, 1981), 13.

Over the last decade or so, however, there has been a perceptible growth of interest in the history of the professions, both before and since the classical period of industrialization. The term 'profession' is now more widely recognized as a subjective, value-laden concept, not a precise analytical category, while the futility of attempting to 'establish a natural history of the professions or an ideal chronology of professionalization'[2] has also become increasingly apparent. As scholars shed their ideological and chronological blinkers, the impact of industrialization upon the development of the professions (broadly characterized as non-manual, non-commercial occupations sharing some measure of institutional self-regulation and reliance upon bookish skills or training) is seen as far from unique or unprecedented; previous eras of sustained economic growth produced, *pari passu*, effects similar in kind (and perhaps even in degree, on a per capita basis). There were several such phases in English history from the twelfth century onwards, although so far only one of them, that described in Geoffrey Holmes's *Augustan England: Professions, State and Society 1680–1730* (1983) has been the subject of a synoptic overview.

Whether or not we accept Holmes's claim that this 'Augustan' half-century saw changes 'more remarkable in themselves and far-reaching in their implications' than any previous period, it is quite clear that a fundamental transformation of the professional sector occurred between the mid-sixteenth and mid-seventeenth centuries. During those years the legal profession was in effect reconstituted along modern lines, while there was also a partial revival in the economic fortunes and a major advance in the academic qualifications of the clergy. This same period saw the appearance of 'a university-educated élite at the head of a nascent medical profession' and the rise of several new professional groups, most notably architects, schoolteachers, and university dons. At its close, during the late 1640s and 50s, when private property rights were effectively secured against both monarchical absolutism and popular radicalism, the privileges and status of the professional classes encountered perhaps the most searching critique they have yet sustained in the long course of English history.[3]

---

[2] D. Duman, *The English and Colonial Bars in the Nineteenth Century* (1983), 205, and ch. 7, *passim*.

[3] R. O'Day, *The English Clergy: The Emergence and Consolidation of a Profession 1558–1642* (Leicester, 1979); C. W. Brooks, 'Common Lawyers in England, *c.*1558–

Clergymen, lawyers, and physicians came under fire for various reasons during the revolutionary decades, not least because laymen resented the growing cultural, economic, and social aloofness of these learned professions. The professional man's heightened self-esteem and status contributed significantly to that 'enhancement of the extent and the complexity of social differentiation' which has come to be seen as a distinguishing characteristic of the century 1580–1680.[4] The early modern legal profession also exemplifies the second general tendency identified by Keith Wrightson, towards the integration of local communities into a national socio-economic order, as London-trained lawyers became increasingly prominent in the provinces and litigants flocked in ever greater numbers from the shires to Westminster Hall.

One of the main purposes of this book is to clarify the social identity of barristers during the half-century before the Long Parliament. But first we need to understand how barristers fitted into the complex structure of the early modern legal profession, and the nature of their vocational duties. Who they were is actually somewhat easier to establish than what they did; this latter topic has been so neglected, despite its obvious importance, as to merit separate treatment in Chapter Two below. Fortunately the institutional development of the bar during the sixteenth and early seventeenth centuries has received a good deal of attention in recent years, so its main outlines, at least, are fairly clear.

ii. Varieties of lawyers

There were, in fact, not one but several legal professions in early modern England. The main split within the lawyers' ranks divided practitioners of common law (common because received throughout the realm) from those who professed the civil law (civil because derived and adapted from Justinian's *Corpus Juris Civilis*, the great sixth-century codification of Roman law). As befitted the heirs of a still vigorous classical tradition, the civilians were graduates of Oxford or Cambridge and sometimes held higher degrees from

1642', in *Lawyers*, 42–64; M. Pelling and C. Webster, 'Medical Practitioners', in *Health, Medicine and Mortality in the Sixteenth Century*, ed. C. Webster (Cambridge, 1979), 235; K. Charlton, 'The Professions in Sixteenth-Century England', *U. of Birmingham Hist. J.*, xii (1969–70), 20–41; C. Hill, *Change and Continuity in Seventeenth-Century England* (1974), pt. III.

[4] K. Wrightson, *English Society 1580–1680* (1982), 13.

Continental universities. Those who carried their studies as far as the LLD were eligible to join Doctors' Commons, a corporate society of London-based practitioners set up in the later fifteenth century to provide senior members of the profession with facilities similar to those which common lawyers had enjoyed, at their inns of court and chancery, since at least the mid-fourteenth century. After Henry VIII prohibited the teaching or practice of canon law in England, the civilians inherited the business of the ecclesiastical courts, which maintained an extensive jurisdiction, especially over probate of wills, matrimonial causes, and a wide variety of moral and sexual offences. Civilians also held office and practised in various more recently established conciliar jurisdictions, notably the Court of Chancery, the High Court of Admiralty, and the Court of Requests in London, as well as the Council in the North at York and the Council in the Marches of Wales at Ludlow. Some also assisted the state in diplomatic negotiations and provided advice on matters of international law. Nevertheless, their career opportunities were distinctly fewer than those of the more numerous, and on the whole wealthier and more influential, common lawyers.[5]

The common law of England and its practitioners emerged during the two centuries following the Norman Conquest. The two leading and representative types of medieval common lawyer were the serjeant at law and the attorney; serjeants, created (not appointed) by the Crown, monopolized the esoteric science of pleading at the bar of the Court of Common Pleas, the busiest central court, while attorneys took responsibility on behalf of litigants for the various procedures required to initiate and pursue a suit in this and other common-law courts, both at Westminster Hall and in the provinces. Serjeants and attorneys kept up a connection with the inns of court and chancery in London, as did the 'apprentices' from whose ranks serjeants were drawn, men who worked as advocates or pleaders in central courts other than Common Pleas, notably King's Bench and the Exchequer. In addition, numerous men on the fringes of the profession, especially in the countryside, who had few or no formal links with the courts and inns of the London-based legal system, nevertheless practised law in one capacity or another, as manorial stewards and court-keepers, attorneys in borough courts, scriveners, town clerks, and under-sheriffs.[6]

    [5] B. P. Levack, 'The English Civilians, 1500–1700', in *Lawyers*, 108–28, and references cited therein.
    [6] J. H. Baker, 'The English Legal Profession 1450–1550', in *Lawyers*, 16–41; *idem*,

So far barristers have not been mentioned in this context, for the good reason that when the term 'utter-barrister' first occurs in the mid-fifteenth-century records of Lincoln's Inn, it lacked any overt professional significance. Utter-barristers were merely student members of the inns of court and chancery who had achieved enough proficiency in the inns' aural 'learning exercises' (modelled on the scholastic disputations of the medieval university) to be entrusted to argue their cases 'ouster le barre' (outside the bar) of their inn. (The precise nature of this bar remains obscure, but it was evidently part of the seating arrangements for learning exercises in the hall of each inn, perhaps intended to replicate the layout of the Court of Common Pleas.)[7]

The utter-barrister's transformation from mootman to advocate was a slow and tentative process. Barristers were for the first time officially recognized as men 'learned in the law' by a parliamentary statute of 1532, but not until 1590 did the case of Broughton v. Prince effectively establish call to the bar of an inn of court as the minimum necessary qualification for audience as a counsellor before the superior common-law courts. Some utter-barristers may have practised as pleaders in Westminster Hall or on the assize circuits from the early sixteenth century or even before. Yet it is significant that the title 'barrister' was less generally used during our period (except in the domestic records of the inns) than the vaguer terms 'counsellor', 'counsellor-at-law', 'professor of the law', 'professor and practiser of the law', the Latin *causidicus*, or even merely 'lawyer'. In other words, until about the eve of the Civil War, barristers were not generally recognized as constituting a distinct order of legal practitioners in the same way as attorneys or serjeants.[8]

This conceptual and semantic lag is best explained by the haphazard manner of the utter-barrister's emergence as an advocate during the sixteenth century. The main force which opened up the central courts to barristers was a massive expansion in the volume of litigation during the second half of the century, when the amount of

---

An Introduction to English Legal History (1979), ch. 10; *idem, The Order of Serjeants At Law* (SS, 1984): E. W. Ives, *The Common Lawyers of Pre-Reformation England* (Cambridge, 1983), ch. 1; R. C. Palmer, *The County Courts of Medieval England 1150–1350* (Princeton, 1982), ch. 4.

[7] Baker, 'Legal Profession', 29–30; W. R. Prest, 'The English Bar, 1550–1700', in *Lawyers*, 65–7.

[8] Ibid.; for further examples, see J. B. Gribble, *Memorials of Barnstaple* (Barnstaple, 1830), 290–1, and H. Fishwick, *History of Preston* (1900), 323.

business handled by the two major central courts of Common Pleas and King's Bench appears to have more than trebled.[9] Presumably because their seniors, the serjeants and apprentices, could not themselves meet a vastly increased demand for legal expertise, mere barristers began to appear as pleaders in Westminster Hall. Our knowledge of their presence comes initially from the judges' efforts to restrict it to men who had continued their studies and learning exercises for several years after call to the bar. The judges also attempted to rationalize procedures and qualifications for call. From the beginning of the seventeenth century at least, seven years' membership of an inn of court, plus the performance of learning exercises during the three years after call, were the basic minimum requirement.[10]

Deficiencies in the surviving records make it difficult to chart the timing of the barristers' rise as reflected by the numbers of students called to the bar. The names of those promoted to the rank of utter-barrister are listed in the minutes of the governing body of Lincoln's Inn from 1518 onwards, but this practice was not adopted at the other three inns of court until the middle of Elizabeth's reign; indeed, a complete record of bar calls at Gray's Inn does not become available until the 1630s. However, if the Lincoln's Inn experience is representative, the number of calls remained fairly stable from the second decade of the sixteenth century until the late 1550s, and then began to rise sharply as shown in Table 1.1. The previous Lincoln's Inn average of two or three calls a year doubled in the 1560s, and nearly doubled again during the 1580s; we now have a fairly comprehensive overview of all four houses, which shows that the combined totals remained on a high plateau through the next two decades, rising sharply again in the early 1610s. This peak was followed by a slight drop in the 1620s, from which a strong recovery led to a still higher level just before the Civil War; during the 1630s an average of over fifty men joined the pool of barristers each year.[11]

---

[9] C. W. Brooks, 'Litigants and Attorneys in the King's Bench and Common Pleas, 1560–1640', in *LRH*, 42–5, and Table 4.1 of Dr Brooks's forthcoming monograph on attorneys during the period 1560–1640, chs. 4–5 of which I have benefited from reading in draft.

[10] *Inns of Court*, 51–5.

[11] These figures supersede those given in Table 8 of *Inns of Court*, 52. Besides errors of counting, addition, and proof-reading, the 1972 data took no account of GI barristers called during learning vacations by individual readers, rather than the governing body of the house. Such calls were frequently not minuted in the pension

Table 1.1. Bar calls 1518–1639 (decennial totals)

	Gray's Inn	Inner Temple	Lincoln's Inn	Middle Temple	Total
1510–19	—	—	10*	—	10
1520–29	—	—	27	—	27
1530–39	—	—	28	—	28
1540–49	—	—	20	—	20
1550–59	—	—	24	—	24
1560–69	11*	9*	65	—	85
1570–79	51	30	66	37*	184
1580–89	126	62	113	82	383
1590–99	117	97	102	95	411
1600–09	117	92	98	109	416
1610–19	157	97	133	123	510
1620–29	97	88	146	110	441
1630–39	102	148	149	116	515
Total, 1590–1639	590	522	628	553	2,293

Sources: Inns' printed records; GI MS Pension Order Book, vol. 1; Harleian 1912.
* Part-decade only.

Contemporary opinion, both lay and legal, was well aware and, on the whole, disapproving of the bar's mushroom growth, although the efforts of the profession's senior members, the Westminster Hall judges and the benchers or readers who governed the inns of court, to limit the numbers called to the bar, met with little success. While the bar's size during our period is not easily measured, the total membership of the 'upper branch'—serjeants, benchers, and barristers—may have reached five hundred plus by the middle of James I's reign. If so, this means not only that the bar had grown about tenfold since the early sixteenth century, but also that the number of barristers per head of population was close to that in England and Wales during the late 1970s.[12]

order book, but may be inferred from other lists, notably those of men promoted to the more senior rank of 'ancient'. Such lists are generally arranged in order of seniority, making it possible to determine at least the decade, if not the year, in which a particular individual was called to the bar. By the time this practice ended in 1629, at least 168 barristers had been called at readings but not recorded in the first order book, which commences in 1569. These calls have been distributed among the GI decennial totals as follows: 1560–9, 11; 1570–9, 19; 1580–9, 20; 1590–9, 21; 1600–9, 30; 1610–19, 26; 1620–9, 41.

[12] See Appendix A below.

The dramatic numerical expansion of the bar was the most visible sign of a fundamental restructuring of legal practice during the sixteenth and early seventeenth centuries. The small medieval profession had protected the livelihood of its members by restricting both their numbers and the fees they charged. But the emergence and proliferation of the utter-barristers as advocates and counsellors opened up a rapidly expanding market to fiercely individualistic competition. Fixed scales of fees were abandoned, except perhaps in the Court of Common Pleas, where the profession's traditional leaders, the serjeants at law, continued to share a monopoly of diminishing value relative to the total volume of litigation handled by the central courts. The long decline of their order preceding its eventual extinction in the later nineteenth century had already begun, even though there were still many eminent and wealthy serjeants practising during our period.[13]

Meanwhile, the lower echelons of the profession were also being transformed in a recognizably modern direction, with the proliferation of London-based attorneys at the expense of provincial semi-professional practitioners, and the emergence of solicitors, who performed functions similar to those of attorneys, especially in the Court of Chancery, but were not formally enrolled as officers of any court. Solicitors survived and multiplied despite judicial fulminations against these 'caterpillars del common weale', but their history is of all lawyers in pre-Civil War England likely to remain the most obscure. Their names are nowhere recorded systematically; indeed, soliciting was often a casual, part-time occupation, undertaken by inns of court students and newly called barristers among others, together with such intriguingly marginal figures as one 'Finch, a cutler and solicitor', who was 'found dead in Purpool Lane, with his neck broke' in 1638.[14]

The subordinate status of these 'ministerial persons of an inferior nature' was increasingly insisted upon by the judges and benchers of the inns of court. From the mid-sixteenth century onwards, regula-

[13] Cf. Prest, 'English Bar', 71–2; for lawyers' fees and wealth, see ch. 5 below. Bodl. MS Rawlinson D 1123, 'The Certificate of the fees taken in the Common Pleas. Hil. 3. Car. I', lists the 'auncient and accustomed' fees of serjeants practising at the Common Pleas bar (fol. 2).

[14] Brooks, 'Common Lawyers in England', 51–3; *The Obituary of Richard Smyth*, ed. H. Ellis (CS, 1849), 15. Cf. the 'attorney & husbandman' buried 7 Oct. 1655 at Barwell, Leics. (*East Anglian*, NS iv. 251.)

tions prohibited the admission of attorneys and solicitors to the inns, and the inns forbade their members to practise in either capacity.[15] The central organizing principle of the modern, divided, English legal profession thus achieved institutional expression. The lines of demarcation between what eventually came to be known as its upper and lower branches, composed of barristers and solicitors respectively, were primarily social, not vocational. Membership of the inns of court was the sole avenue of entrance to the bar, and membership in these 'honourable societies' was itself a token of gentility; attorneys and solicitors, on the other hand, were theoretically confined to the subordinate *hospitia minora*, the inns of chancery. A relative lack of occupational specialization meant that barristers handled various tasks, most notably conveyancing, which were to be largely taken over by attorneys and solicitors after the Civil War, besides dealing directly with their own clients. The niceties of professional etiquette prescribing an exact division of work between upper and lower branches seem not to have been fully worked out until the later nineteenth century. The basic distinction between the counsellor's honorarium and the attorney's or solicitor's fee, however, had been widely accepted by the end of our period, lending further force to the disjunction between the *officium ingenii* of the upper branch and the *officium laboris* below the bar.[16]

Hence the organization of the modern legal profession was well established by the middle of the seventeenth century. Yet although that institutional framework plainly existed for more than its own sake, the working world it encompassed has received little notice from historians. Those interested in the development of the English legal system have made some effort to explore the allocation of tasks between attorneys and barristers, and the occupational self-interest of early Stuart common lawyers is traditionally invoked to explain away their political behaviour. But the precise nature of the work performed by early modern common lawyers, the way they went about it, the clienteles they served, the attitudes they brought to their work, and those which it imprinted on their daily lives—all these matters remain unexplored. This is not entirely surprising. Historians have often tended to regard work as an unproblematic and

---

[15] *OJ*, 311–21, conveniently sets out the main legislation.
[16] Brooks, 'Common Lawyers in England', 54–5; D. Duman, 'The English Bar in the Georgian Era', in *Lawyers*, 101–3.

rather uninteresting topic, marginal to both the public-political and private-domestic spheres, either mere mindless struggle for existence or an oppressive form of class exploitation. Yet the manner in which men and women earn their daily bread must always have considerable bearing on other facets of their lives, especially when the nature of the occupation sets those who pursue it somewhat apart from the rest of the community.

CHAPTER TWO

THE BUSINESS OF THE BAR

CAUSIDICUS. If you have any business you may impart it to me.
LOGICUS. Business? Then I perceive you are all for business, you
 have but little entertainment for a friend; well, sir, are not you a
 lawyer?
CAUSIDICUS. I may not deny my profession sir.

> Barten Holyday, Τεχνογαμία. Or the Marriages of the Arts
> (1618), sig. D2ᵛ

'I will a little relate unto thee the travail and pains of a lawyer, of
whom I may say this, that as he is generally a mover in other mens
cumbers and an author of them too if he be not a very honest man, so
hath he this recompense, that he never hath rest but is always in
cumber himself. For in riding to term, at term forenoon he goes to the
Hall, in summer in heat, winter in wet and cold, stands there
bareheaded at the bar ... after dinner he is tied to his chair and to
read evidences while he can see, and to advise and be advised, without
rest if he be in great practice and if in mean it is not worth following
abroad and term being done he returns to circuit and country practice
and so never hath rest and is most a stranger at home.'

> Sir John Lowther, 'Autobiography', in Lowther Family
> Estate Books, 1617–1675, ed. C. B. Phillips (Surtees Soc.,
> cxci, 1979), 213

EARLY modern common lawyers were notoriously hard-working.
According to one of Thomas Middleton's characters, a lawyer's
death could only occur during vacation, since 'he has no leisure to
die in the term'. Barristers themselves accepted and internalized this
popular image. In the 1620s Sir John Lowther protested that he
could hardly write his memoirs as an 'orderly composed treatise, for
that ... I am at this present exercised in the practice of the law,
which requireth a whole man and all his time.'[1] This was a slight
exaggeration; like many of his colleagues, Lowther evidently did
find time for family, friends, recreation, worship, scholarly pursuits,
the duties of local ruler and member of parliament, despite all the

---

[1] T. Middleton, Michaelmas Term (1607), I. i. 27–32; Lowther, 'Autobiography',
202.

pressures of his working life. Yet we shall not properly understand
these wider aspects of the lawyer's role until we have grasped at least
the main patterns of that busy existence.

i. Advocacy and counselling

Advocacy—the oral argument of a litigant's case in court—is rightly
thought of as the barrister's chief and distinctive professional
function. But even today, when vocational specialization within the
legal profession is far more highly developed than it was four
hundred years ago, many barristers spend much of their working
time out of court, while solicitors appear as advocates before courts
of limited jurisdiction. What distinguishes the barrister's professional sphere from that of other practitioners, now as then, is not
so much the nature of the tasks he performs as the presumed
capacities he brings to them. In the early modern legal hierarchy, the
barrister or counsellor with his bookish learning was the 'principal
person next unto serjeants and judges in the administration of
justice', whereas the formally untrained attorneys and solicitors
exercised a mere mechanic trade. On one famous occasion James I
was informed that 'causes which concern the life or inheritance or
goods or fortunes of his subjects are not to be decided by natural
reason, but by the artificial reason and judgement of law, which law
is an art which requires long study and experience, before that a man
can attain to the cognizance of it'. Sir Edward Coke was asserting
here not just a constitutional principle, but also the right of his own
learned order to pre-eminence in 'the administration of justice'.[2]

The early modern barrister's honourable and superior standing
did not, however, imply immediate or total segregation of his
vocational activities from those of the attorney and solicitor. Having
acquired the right of audience in the superior courts, men called to
the bar of an inn of court had no need to abandon all other kinds of
legal work and devote themselves exclusively to advocacy. On the
contrary, as their usual title 'counsellor-at-law' suggests, barristers
remained directly accessible to clients seeking expert legal advice
and, accordingly, continued to busy themselves with a wide variety
of out-of-court 'counselling'. Only gradually did many of the tasks
they had performed come to be regarded as mere routine matters,
and hence the proper province of the lower branch. The fluid
situation which prevailed well into the seventeenth century is

[2] *Reports of Sir E. Coke . . .* , ed. G. Wilson (1777), xii. 65. *OJ*, 317.

epitomized by a late Elizabethan treatise on the legal system: having assigned matters of 'practice' to attorneys and solicitors, while distinguishing 'judgement' as the proper realm of 'learned serjeants and counsellors at law', the author goes on to note, without apparent sense of anomaly, that in the Court of Chancery the 'common solicitors' were 'gentlemen barristers of the inns of court which are seen in the laws ... and by right information of their suitor's case doth the better instruct the serjeants and counsellors-at-law therein'.[3]

The professional prerogatives of the early modern barrister were defined, albeit negatively, in a series of decrees issued by the common-law judges. In 1574 they proclaimed that no utter-barrister under five years' standing might appear to plead at the bar of any Westminster court. This post-call probation period was reduced in 1614 to three years for barristers seeking to 'practice publicly' in the central courts.[4] But throughout our period and long afterwards, mere barristers were excluded from the Court of Common Pleas, where serjeants alone could practise; attempts were also made to confine the right of audience in the Court of Star Chamber to inns of court benchers or readers.[5] Conversely, even in the superior courts, advocacy was not yet the exclusive preserve of barristers, benchers, or serjeants. In Common Pleas and King's Bench, routine procedural decisions, or 'common rules', were granted in response to motions pleaded by attorneys, who, together with solicitors, presented similar interlocutory motions on behalf of their clients before Chancery.[6] Still wider opportunities for attorneys to act as advocates were offered by lesser provincial jurisdictions, such as quarter sessions and the multifarious municipal courts.[7]

[3] Cf. J. H. Baker, 'Counsellors and Barristers: An Historical Study', *CLJ*, xxvii (1969), 205–29; *idem*, 'Solicitors and the Law of Maintenance, 1590–1640', *CLJ*, xxxii (1973), 56–80; R. Robinson, 'A Briefe Collection of the Queens Majesties ... Courtes of Recordes', ed. R. L. Rickard, *Camden Miscellany*, xx (1953), 1–2, 13. HMC, *Salisbury*, xvii. 627, refers to an utter-barrister of six years' standing who 'follows the Lord Norrys his causes'.

[4] Cf. *OJ*, 312, 317–18.

[5] Cf. *GIPB*, i. 43; *ITR*, i. 306; *MTR*, i. 234.

[6] The practice of attorneys moving rules at the side-bar is mentioned by Roger North, *The Lives of ... Francis North ... Sir Dudley North and ... Rev. Dr. John North*, ed. A. Jessopp (1890), i. 132. (I am indebted to Dr Baker for helpful discussion of this point.) W. J. Jones, *The Elizabethan Court of Chancery* (Oxford, 1967), 311, 318. See also C. W. Brooks, 'Some Aspects of Attorneys in Late Sixteenth-and Early Seventeenth-Century England', University of Oxford D.Phil. thesis, 1978, 9.

[7] Ibid., 163.

Nor did the judges address themselves solely to controlling the barrister's activities as advocate. The five-year restriction laid down in 1574 applied equally to his right to 'subscribe any action, bill or plea'. Pre-trial pleading, when the precise points in dispute between litigants were refined and settled for judicial determination, had changed from oral to written form well before the beginning of our period. But as a relic of the days when pleading was the supreme test of a lawyer's skill, special pleas (which sought to distinguish one particular issue of fact or law as the crux of a case) were supposed to bear counsel's signature. So too were the written pleadings exhibited before Chancery and other 'English-bill' courts. While the ostensible reason for these rules was to avoid wasting the courts' time with insufficient pleadings drafted by ignorant men, they also reinforced the barristers' claim to exclusive possession of all but the most elementary and mechanical legal learning.

If the formal parameters of the early modern barrister's functions, as laid down collectively by the judges, make it clear that in-court advocacy was far from his sole concern, a more comprehensive picture is given in the treatise of an individual judge, Sir John Dodderidge. His manual for law students, published posthumously in 1631, includes the plan of a foreshadowed 'Treatise touching the Counsellor or Practitioner of the Laws'.[8] Unfortunately, all that survives of this work are three headings. These classify the barrister's duties as follows: first, 'private counsel given at home in his chamber to his client'; second, 'the drawing of assurances and conveyances'; and finally, 'his pleadings for his client'.

This last category contains four subdivisions. Of these, 'pleading in point of law' has just been discussed. Only in the preparation of the more complex special pleadings was it necessary or desirable to seek a barrister's assistance. The drafting of general pleas, which followed a stereotyped common form, could be safely left to an attorney, or to the clerks of the prothonotaries of Common Pleas or King's Bench, who may also have drawn up a good many special pleas, despite the formal requirement that these documents should only be exhibited in Common Pleas under a serjeant at law's signature.[9] Counsel's signature was not required in King's Bench

---

[8] J. Dodderidge, *The English Lawyer* (1632), sig. [A3ʳ].

[9] *HEL*, iii. 651–3; vi. 439–40, 445–6; Baker, 'Solicitors', 59. Sir Sampson Eure (d. 1659), in his *Doctrina Placitandi, ou l'art & Science De Bon Pleading* (1677), says [sig. A2] that 'in ancient times serjeants and others wrote and made their pleadings

until 1666, by which time the rise of the expert special pleader may have made the barrister's role in the actual drawing of pleadings little more than nominal. Special pleaders were usually not called to the bar, although they practised from chambers at the inns of court; by the mid-eighteenth century, when the art of special pleading had acquired a quite Byzantine complexity, they constituted a distinct coterie within the profession. It would be surprising if some such specialists had not already emerged during our period, although there is no direct evidence of their existence.[10]

So in Dodderidge's first subcategory of pleading, counsel had been largely superseded by other practitioners, and their diminishing role contained no element of oral advocacy. His second and third subdivisions, pleading 'in argument of demurrers' and 'in matter of fact, as in giving or delivering of evidence', did, however, refer to advocacy as such. Arguments on demurrers were made by counsel at hearings before the judges in Westminster Hall after special pleading had reached issue on a disputed point of law, or when the verdict of a trial was challenged on legal grounds. As the emphasis in litigation was shifting from pre-trial pleading to argument in court during and after trial, this branch of the barrister's work must have been more buoyant during our period than ever before. The same is probably true of his role on the assize circuits, where pleading 'in matter of fact' occurred when suits brought by writ of *nisi prius* were tried before a circuit judge and jury, following pre-trial pleadings at Westminster Hall of the general issue or special pleadings which reached issue in a disputed matter of fact.[11]

The three varieties of pleading discussed so far were all part of the procedures of the ancient common-law courts, with whose workings Dodderidge, a long-serving justice of King's Bench, was undoubtedly very familiar. But the proliferation in the late fifteenth and early sixteenth centuries of various 'conciliar', 'English-bill', or 'equity'

themselves . . . and to this day in the Great Sessions of Wales (where the most ancient form and practice of the common law is still used), the practisers of law not only make and write their pleadings themselves, but also the original brief and plaint. And it is a necessary attribute of a counsellor to be a good prothonotary' (my translation). T. Powell, *The Attourney's Academy* (1623), 114–16.

[10] *HEL*, vi. 445–6. Note, however, that in 1635 Henry Calthorpe, a barrister of 20 years' standing, sought to decline the recordership of London on the grounds that he was 'unused to plead at bars'. (Knowler, i. 506.) E. Leach, *The Downfall of the Unjust Lawyers* (1652), 5, refers to clerks or attorneys drafting special pleadings.

[11] Cf. J. S. Cockburn, *A History of English Assizes 1558–1714* (Cambridge, 1972), 140–4.

jurisdictions had given lawyers a further range of employment, to which Dodderidge referred (in appropriately generalized and perhaps even grudging terms) as his fourth and final sub-category of 'pleadings for the client': 'patronage of causes in courts of equity'. These courts—Chancery, Requests, Star Chamber, Wards, the equity side of the Exchequer, Duchy Chamber, the Council of the North, the Council in the Marches of Wales, and various smaller provincial jurisdictions—employed a common procedure, initiated not by Latin writ and law-French pleadings, but by petition or bill written in English.

We have already noticed a reference to barristers 'soliciting' cases in Chancery. While the English-bill courts lacked the large cohorts of attorneys serving Common Pleas and King's Bench, members of the bar, as well as men lacking formal professional qualifications, were not slow to supply this deficiency. But in addition to the overall direction and following of litigants' causes, the English 'pleadings' of these courts, unlike the bulk of written pleadings in the common-law courts, were also often drafted by barristers. An anonymous early seventeenth-century treatise, clearly the work of a person well acquainted with the mechanics of legal practice, asserted that one reason why 'the Court of Chancery of late is so frequented above the other common-law courts at Westminster' was that

> most of the young lawyers nowadays, in respect of the present gain is made in that court by drawing bills and answers, do begin their practice in that court, whereas the declaration and pleadings in the common-law courts yield them no profit, they all passing through the hands of prothonotaries, clerks and attorneys (whereof there are thousands), the lawyer never called thereunto [except] in some causes of special difficulty.[12]

English-bill courts usually had a rule that pleadings should not be accepted for filing unless signed by counsel.[13] Some litigants nevertheless drafted the documents themselves, or gave the job to an

---

[12] SP 14/199/177; another copy is Beds. RO, L28/47.

[13] Jones, *Chancery*, 192–3; W. Hudson, 'A Treatise on the Court of Star Chamber', in *Collectanea Juridica* (1792), ed. F. Hargreave, ii. 150–1; J. A. Guy, *The Cardinal's Court* (Hassocks, 1977), 81; W. H. Bryson, *The Equity Side of the Exchequer* (Cambridge, 1975), 104; W. J. Jones, 'The Exchequer of Chester in the last years of Elizabeth I', in *Tudor Men and Institutions*, ed. A. J. Slavin (Baton Rouge, La., 1972), 129; H. E. Bell, *An Introduction to the History of the Court of Wards and Liveries* (Cambridge, 1953), 91; Ellesmere 2916; *Select Pleas in the Court of Requests, 1497–1569*, ed. I. S. Leadam (SS, 1898), xcvi; P. Williams, *The Council in the Marches of Wales under Elizabeth I* (Cardiff, 1958), 67; R. R. Reid, *The King's Council in the North* (1921), 265.

attorney or clerk; in a few reported cases such pleadings tendered without counsel's signature were rejected by Chancery.[14] An unknown, but possibly sizeable, proportion of those accepted under counsel's hand had not actually been drawn up by the lawyer whose signature they bore. William Hudson, the leading Star Chamber practitioner in the early seventeenth century, complained that although defendants' answers in that court were supposed to be drafted by counsel, 'of late (such is the abuse) a careless answer is drawn by an ignorant clerk, and more simple counsellor's hand gained to it, for half fee'.[15] It is impossible to tell how far Hudson's wounded professional *amour-propre* and nostalgia for the good old days under Chancellor Ellesmere colour this claim, or to translate its generality into specific percentages. The same goes for the identical charge which Hudson makes with regard to the preparation of interrogatories, the written questions used to elicit evidence from parties and witnesses prior to trial.[16] However, counsel were certainly signing Star Chamber pleadings drafted by others before Ellesmere's demise; indeed Ellesmere himself implicitly sanctioned the practice when he decreed (unsuccessfully) that no Star Chamber pleading should be exhibited unless 'allowed and subscribed by a grave professor of the law [who] had been a reader in some of the inns of court or chancery'.[17] Finally, to conclude this long çatalogue, the progression of English-bill suits to hearing, judgement, and verdict was governed by rules, orders, and decrees issued in response to 'motions' argued at the bar by members of the upper branch (or, in routine procedural matters, by attorneys or solicitors). This last

[14] G. Cary, *Reports or Causes in Chancery* (1650), 40, 90, 113; C. Monro, *Acta Cancellariæ* (1847), 81–2, 211, 216–17.

[15] Hudson, 'Treatise', 161; Additional 25232, fol. 133. In one Chancery case, however, a bill drafted by a non-barrister was then submitted to Sir William Denny of GI for polishing, while Denny in turn undertook to seek his colleague Sir Thomas Crew's opinion on the final product. (*The Correspondence of Lady Katherine Paston, 1603–1627*, ed. R. Hughey (Norfolk Rec. Soc., 1941), 60.) The 'base fee' for merely signing a document was still paid in the nineteenth century. (Cf. S. Robinson, *Bench and Bar* (1891), 46.)

[16] Hudson, 'Treatise', 169. An anonymous interregnum commentator implied that in all courts counsel's role was normally limited to the perusal and subscription of pleadings, arguing that while limitation of counsel's fees to 30s. for signing bills or pleadings was reasonable, 'in case any serjeant or barrister draw any bills or pleadings that he may be paid *quantuum meruit* . . . for that in such cases his pains may be great though his writing but small'. (Philostratus Philodemus, *Seasonable Observations on a Late Book Intituled A System of the Law* (1653), 34.)

[17] STAC 8/49/6; Haward, *Reports*, 32; random instances of bills signed by non-readers during Ellesmere's chancellorship are STAC 8/255/5, 6, and 282/5.

form of pleading closely resembled the oral argument of barristers in the ancient common-law courts and on the assize circuits.

Dodderidge's analysis of counsel's role as pleader may seem rather clumsy. But despite the temptation to reduce his four subdivisions to a simple dichotomy between pleading in the sense of oral advocacy at the bar and pleading by the preparation and tender of written documents, his scheme is not without merit. As he rightly says, all pleading may be properly regarded as belonging to the barrister's duties '*agendo*, by way of public action'.[18] The signature authorizing a bill or plea which would form part of the official record of a suit was as much a public act as the oral argument of a demurrer or a special verdict in open court. By contrast, all the barrister's other professional doings had a private quality, in that they involved directly only client and lawyer, whether taking place at the latter's home or at the client's house, in an assize-town tavern or a chamber at the inns of court.

Across this broad field of 'counselling' (with which we may conveniently lump Dodderidge's second category, the drafting of legal instruments other than pleadings), barristers enjoyed no special vocational privilege. In consequence, their work overlapped with that of attorneys, solicitors, scriveners, and laymen lacking any formal qualifications. Barristers still could and did advise clients about their legal rights, and how best to enforce or defend them without the mediation of an attorney or solicitor, although John Hoskyns's remark that 'to go abroad is not our order, it is the office of a solicitor' suggests perhaps the beginnings of a convention against actively seeking out such work.[19] These consultations, whether in person or by letter, often entailed the drafting or perusal of various legal instruments—assurances, bonds, conveyances, indentures, marriage settlements, wills, and so on.[20] In many instances such tasks could certainly have been tackled equally efficiently, and perhaps for a lower fee, by any reasonably experienced attorney equipped with a formulary book like William West's *Symbolaeographia*.[21]

[18] Dodderidge, *The English Lawyer*, sig. [A3ᵛ].
[19] *The Life, Letters and Writings of John Hoskyns, 1566–1638*, ed. L. B. Osborn (New Haven, 1937), 73.
[20] For typical examples, see Additional 41654, fol. 7; Ellesmere 87, 890, 895; Stowe 2367; Glos. RO, D1571/E428; Kent AO, U350/C2/31; Som. RO, DD/PH 225/66; Longleat House, Thynne Papers, vii, fol. 332; Chicago, MS Bacon 4253.
[21] Cf. Brooks, thesis, 126, 183.

Yet barristers claimed to possess a theoretical, as distinct from a merely practical or procedural, knowledge of law. It was this which supposedly justified the higher fees charged by the counsellor at law, and helped account for the barrister's elevated professional and social standing. Hence clients who wanted and could afford the assurance that they were obtaining the best possible advice, especially where title to land or large sums of money were at stake, brought their problems to a barrister in preference to a less qualified man. Most junior members of the bar certainly undertook a good deal of very routine counselling work for immediate family, friends, and neighbours, often in conjunction with soliciting their causes in London during term.[22] The older and better-practised lawyer, however, was likely to gain a significant proportion of his business from strangers, referred by an attorney or some other third party, and the points on which his advice was requested might often involve fairly complex and difficult questions of law.[23] He could also on occasion be asked to peruse evidences or a prepared outline of the main facts of a case and deliver his written opinion, which might subsequently be incorporated into the briefs drawn up to inform counsel retained to argue the suit in court.[24] A further function often discharged by barristers, more rarely by other practitioners, was that of arbitration, when contending parties agreed to submit their dispute to the judgement of one or more lawyers.[25] Arbitrators, whether appointed by a court or chosen by the parties concerned, were not invariably men learned in the law; all those in positions of authority had an obligation to help settle differences among their neighbours and inferiors. In 1592 a disputant announced his determination to nominate any 'gentlemen and not lawyers, in study or in practice'— an exception which goes to prove the general rule.[26]

Finally, barristers also became involved in various activities

[22] See below, sect. iii of this chapter.

[23] See, e.g., the professional correspondence of Henry Sherfield (Hants RO, 44M69/xxx, esp. nos. 2, 35) and William Booth (William Salt Library, SMS 28, 'Clients Cases', esp. fols. 184ᵛ–185ᵛ, 211–12). See also sect. iii below.

[24] E.g. Herefs. RO, F76/iv/6; SP16/290/112; Beds. RO, MS St John J 1218; HMC, *De L'Isle and Dudley*, vi. 224; Egerton 1074, fols. 28–9; Additional 25079, fols. 91, 100, 108; Anon., *Reasons against the Bill Entituled An Act for County Registers* (1653), 12.

[25] E.g. STAC 8/142/5; WARD 9/530, fol. 563ᵛ; *APC 1617–19*, 40–1; Hunts. RO, dd M 28/2; Beds. RO, TW 1032; NLW, MS Chirke Castle F14059; Ellesmere 771; HMC, *Fifteenth Rep.*, viii. 22; H. Horneyhold, *Genealogical Memoirs of The Family of Strickland* (Kendal, 1928), 102.

[26] E. K. Berry, 'Henry Ferrers, an early Warwickshire antiquary 1550–1633', *Dugdale Soc.*, Occasional Papers 16 (1965), 14; cf. Additional 44846, fol. 70.

ancillary to their major preoccupations of advocacy and counselling. They officiated as stewards of manorial courts, commissioners of bankruptcy, recorders and town clerks for municipal corporations; held offices attached to the Westminster and provincial courts; served on *ad hoc* commissions appointed by the Privy Council; acted as agents and principals in land transactions, and as money lenders, often on a very large scale. Many barristers held landed estates and took a keen interest in their management; they were also prominent 'projectors' in overseas trading and colonizing companies, mining ventures, and fen-draining and other more or less speculative schemes.[27] While most of these pursuits were in no way unique to members of the bar, all were likely to benefit from the skills and contacts brought to them by the practising barrister.

ii. Clients

Having described in a bare and formal fashion the main constituents of the early modern barrister's work-load, we must now turn to consider the clientele for whom this work was done. It has been widely assumed by social historians and sociologists that all pre-industrial professions were 'dependent upon the power and prestige of élite patrons'.[28] Thus Harold Perkin asserts that in the era of the Industrial Revolution, 'with urbanisation and the rise of living standards, doctors, lawyers, writers and even the clergy . . . found an enlarged demand for their services, which reduced their dependence upon the few rich'.[29] Apart from possible quibbles about definitions of 'few' and 'rich', such judgements rely too heavily on the special case of the medical profession, and certainly underestimate the extent to which common lawyers had succeeded in establishing a broad national market for their services before the eighteenth century.

Despite widespread and traditional complaints about both the exorbitance of lawyers' fees and the legal system's overall discrimination against the poorer sort, it was not usually claimed during our period that the poor were actually priced out of the courts. If

---

[27] See further below, ch. 5, sect. iv. For barristers as stewards, see HMC, *Rutland*, i. 256; HMC, *Various Collections*, ii. 21–2; Chicago, MSS Bacon 3827, 4163, 4225, 4447; Huntington Library, MSS Stowe 2367–9; and as commissioners of bankruptcy, W. J. Jones, *The Foundations of English Bankruptcy: Statutes and Commissions in the Early Modern Period* (Philadelphia, 1979), 25–6.

[28] Larson, *Rise of Professionalism*, 4.

[29] Perkin, *Origins of Modern English Society*, 254.

artisans, craftsmen, merchants, shopkeepers, and peasants had not ample personal experience of the common-law's defects, it would be hard to understand why law reform became such a pressing concern for radical sectaries and other non-gentry social critics during and after the Civil War. Certainly their superiors were very conscious of what the barrister John Smyth of Nibley disparaged as 'the country malice and envy that rageth in this age with the inferior sort, [who] recourse to Westminster Hall (our cockpit of revenge) upon each poor action and occasion'.[30] Smyth's censure may have been a trifle disingenuous; in 1626 the legal profession in general was attacked on the grounds that, 'although they have in their law a maxim *De minimis non curat lex*, yet they admit every trifling action for gain, even of such poor clients also, as have scarcely bread to give their children . . .'. One early seventeenth-century satirist saw lawyers as godlike figures to whom 'all countrys [i.e. countrymen] crouching do for counsel come'; another wrote of country clients bringing their bags of gold to the lawyers of the Temple, while a third, depicts the 'pettifogging lawyer' as one who 'crams up crowns,/From hob-nailed boors and sheepskin country clowns'.[31] The number of such poorer clients may well have been significantly increased during the sixteenth century both by the effects of inflation, which eroded the statutory forty-shillings minimum limit on suits heard in Westminster Hall, and the proliferation of new legal fictions and forms of action designed to expand the business of the common-law courts. The consequent pressure, both within and outside parliament, for measures which purported to have the effect of 'avoiding trifling suits', arose as much from fear of the potential for social disruption inherent in unrestricted access to the central courts as from a paternalistic concern to protect the poor from the hazards of litigation.[32]

Given the common law's overriding concern with property, such protection was obviously of little relevance to the very poor and

[30] *The Lives of the Berkeleys . . . By John Smyth, of Nibley*, ed. J. MacLean (Gloucester, 1883–85), i. 242. Cf. the comments of Thomas Powell in 'The breath of an unfee'd lawyer', CUL MS Dd. 3.88 (10), 17, 42–3, 48–52, and of Maurice Griffin in Ellesmere 2029, fol. 11.

[31] W. Carey, 'The Present State of England', in *Harleian Miscellany*, ed. T. Park (1808–13), iii. 210. H. Fitzgeffrey, *Satyres* (1617), epigram 61, sig. E3; J. Heath, *The House of Correction* (1619), sig. C4ᵛ; J. Taylor, *Taylor's Water-worke* (1614), sig. F2. See also J. Earle, *Microcosmographie* (1628), sig. F6ᵛ.

[32] Cf. Brooks, thesis, 76–80. Relevant statutes include 18 Eliz., c. 14; 43 Eliz., c. 6; 3 Jac. I, c. 7; 4 Jac. I, c. 3; and 21 Jac. I, c. 16.

property-less. The only roles they usually played in legal proceedings were as witnesses in civil suits or defendants in criminal cases at assizes or quarter sessions. The poor man's need for legal counsel in the latter circumstances, however desperate, was effectively denied by the absence of any comprehensive legal-aid system as much as by the procedural rule which permitted counsel only to plead legal exceptions to the indictment or in charges of misdemeanour rather than felony.[33] In Westminster Hall, on the other hand, those who claimed inability to meet the costs of following civil suits could apply to sue *in forma pauperis*, on the production of a counsellor's or JP's certificate of good character, worthy cause, and slender means. If this application were approved, the court would assign the litigant attorney and counsel to act without fee.[34] Such grants were not uncommon, and the practitioners involved were by no means the most junior or inexperienced members of the bar, even if hostile contemporary comment suggests that the lack of a fee made pauper clients 'as welcome as Lazarus to Dives' as far as most lawyers were concerned.[35]

But quite apart from the occasional unpaid representation of such (at least technically) impoverished suitors, the professional market served by Elizabethan and early Stuart barristers extended far beyond what might roughly be termed the landed ruling class. Despite the very uneven distribution of wealth and privilege in pre-industrial England, it is important to remember that the middling sort, neither gentle nor destitute, constituted a stratum of considerable size, internal differentiation, and socio-economic importance. Christopher Brooks has suggested that this broad group—yeomen, husbandmen, tradesmen, small merchants, retailers, and so forth—was largely responsible for the great increase in litigation handled by the

[33] J. H. Baker, 'Criminal Courts and Procedure at Common Law 1500–1800', in *Crime in England 1550–1800*, ed. J. S. Cockburn (1977), 36–8; cf. J. Samaha, *Law and Order in Historical Perspective: The Case of Elizabethan Essex* (New York, 1974), 58; J. Langbein, 'The Criminal Trial before the Lawyers', *U. of Chicago Law Rev.*, xlv (1978), 307–9; *Calendar of Assize Records: Home Circuit Indictments Elizabeth I and James I. Introduction*, ed. J. S. Cockburn (1985), 108.

[34] Folger, MS V.b.186, p. 343, is an example of a petition to sue *in forma pauperis*. Cf. Jones, *Chancery*, 323–8; W. Style, *Practical Register* . . . (1694, first published 1657), 264.

[35] E. Hake, *Newes out of Powles Churchyarde* (1579), sig. [B7ʳ]; T. Scot, *Vox Dei: Injustice cast and condemned. In a sermon preached the twentieth of March 1622. At the Assizes holden in St. Bury in Suffolke* (1623), 40; W. Fennor, *The Compters Commonwealth* (1617), 13; E. F. J. Tucker, '"Ignoramus" and Seventeenth-Century Satire of the Law', *Harvard Lib. Bull.*, xix (1971), 327–8.

courts of Common Pleas and King's Bench between 1560 and 1640. During that period 'between 70 and 80 per cent ... of those who utilised these courts were not members of what, for the sake of convenience, is generally called the landed gentry'.[36] Comparable figures for the Jacobean Star Chamber, where litigation has been characterized as 'gentlemen's business first and foremost', show that even here about half the litigants were non-gentlemen (merchants, yeomen, husbandmen, artisans, labourers, and those of unknown, but presumably non-gentle, status).[37]

These figures of course relate only to some, though not the least, of the central superior courts. Outside Westminster Hall, especially in the many local customary jurisdictions, the proportion of middle- and lower-class litigants was much higher, even if the business transacted in these courts provided fewer opportunities for the employment of learned counsel. A similar qualification applies to the statistics just quoted, for we have already seen that the initial stages of most litigation, and indeed the entirety of most straightforward actions, could be managed by an attorney without the assistance of counsel. Nevertheless, parties to civil suits were not generally permitted at this time to act as advocates on their own behalf, so all those whose actions reached the stage of hearing *in banc* before the judges to determine points of law, let alone a trial at *nisi prius* on circuit, must have been obliged to retain counsel to plead for them.[38]

Given the wide availability of alternative, and presumably cheaper, sources of legal advice and assistance, the less well-to-do may have had relatively little incentive or need to utilize the *out-of-court* services of barristers. This point perhaps underlies a contemporary joke about the 'plain country fellow coming to the Temple for counsel in some point of law', who naïvely enquired for 'my Lord Coke's shop'.[39] It is also to some extent corroborated by the nature of the surviving evidence about consultations between barristers and

---

[36] Brooks, 'Litigants and Attorneys', 46–8.

[37] T. G. Barnes, 'Star Chamber Litigants and their Counsel, 1596–1641', in *LRH*, 10.

[38] For criticism and defence of the rule against litigants speaking in their own cause, see T. Reeve, *Moses Old Square for Judges* (1632), 84–5; Benn, 'Essays', fol. 26ᵛ; D. Gotherson, *An Alarm ...* (1660), printed in G. D. Scull, *Dorothea Scott* (Oxford, 1883), 45. The rule itself is stated in Style, *Practical Register*, 355, citing a case of 1650, but must already have been well established by that date. (I am again indebted to Dr Baker for his help with this point.)

[39] *'Merry Passages and Jeasts': A Manuscript Notebook of Sir Nicholas L'Estrange (1603–1655)*, ed. H. F. Lippincott (Salzburg, 1974), 49.

their clients, which mainly takes the form of correspondence in the estate and personal papers of landed gentry and noble families. Yet since the abilities to read and write were closely correlated with social rank, the less socially exalted client may well have made greater use of oral, face-to-face consultations, which by their very nature would have left little mark on the surviving records, except— as we shall see—in barristers' fee books. At all events, the evidence is quite clear that the early modern bar catered for a much less exclusive market than has hitherto been supposed, or than was served by, say, the upper reaches of the medical profession, which may have relied upon the patronage of a largely aristocratic clientele until the nineteenth century.[40] This fact alone clearly ranks among the most important reasons for the soaring numbers, influence, and prosperity of the common lawyers in early modern England; it also suggests that Notestein's memorable characterization of the bar as 'a class that interlocked with the gentry, or were its retainers' may be no more than a half-truth.[41]

Of course, even if early modern barristers worked for a socially mixed clientele, their relations with the upper ranks of the landed classes might still have been entirely deferential, and their careers largely dependent upon aristocratic patronage. In a society where so much power and wealth was concentrated in the hands of a landed élite, it is hardly surprising to find lawyers receiving annual retainers from knights and peers, publicly acknowledging their dependence on a good lord's favour, or seeking office through the influence of a noble patron.[42]

Yet the significance of these practices must not be exaggerated. Barristers also took retaining fees from town corporations, university colleges, and ecclesiastical bodies, but retainers constituted only a

[40] Cf. N. D. Jewson, 'Medical Knowledge and the Patronage System in Eighteenth-Century England', *Sociology*, viii (1974), 375–80.

[41] W. Notestein, *The Winning of the Initiative by the House of Commons* (Oxford, 1924), 50. Aylmer's conclusion that the largest share of the fees paid by litigants to lawyers was probably contributed by the landed classes, of whom the majority were gentry, is also open to question. (G. E. Aylmer, *The King's Servants. The Civil Service of Charles I, 1625–1642* (1961), 251.)

[42] For retainers, see Chicago, MS Bacon 4446; *Sussex Arch. Colls.*, xxxvii. 48–9; C. B. Phillips, 'The Gentry in Cumberland and Westmorland, 1600–1665', University of Lancaster Ph.D. thesis, 1974, 218; *CSPD 1603–10*, 633. On dependence, see *A Calendar of the Shrewsbury and Talbot Papers*, ed. G. R. Batho (HMC Joint Publn., 1966–71), ii. 147; *The Life and Original Correspondence of Sir George Radcliffe*, ed. T. D. Whitaker (1810), 97; Baker, *Serjeants*, 93–4. On seeking office, see below, ch. 5, sect. ii.

very small proportion of most lawyers' professional income, far less
than the casual fees paid for particular services by a multitude of
individual clients.[43] Their dealings with great men, either at court or
in the country, were not typically marked by lordly hauteur on one
side or grovelling subservience on the other, at least if we can
generalize from the apparently easy and cordial relations existing
between William Noy and the earl of Bridgewater, Robert Barnard
and the earl of Manchester, or John Haward and Sir Nicholas
Carew, to mention only a few examples. Sufficiently eminent lawyers
could expect a good deal of deference from gentry suitors seeking
their professional services; thus in the early 1620s Sir Richard
Grosvenor, Bt., 'most humbly desire[d]' the 'right worshipful' Sir
Thomas Coventry to 'be pleased to be of counsel with me in a law
cause', assuring him that as 'I may crave your patronage . . . so shall
I ever acknowledge your favour'. Rubbing shoulders with the
county élite (to whom they were often related by blood or marriage)
at assizes and quarter sessions, many barristers also shared the
emergent classical culture and educational background of the upper
classes; meanwhile their own developing professional ideology
emphasized both the worthiness of their calling and the client's
reliance on his counsellor's independent judgement.[44] Finally,
patronage was certainly an important, perhaps nearly indispensable,
asset in the competition for legal and every other kind of office; but
success in a career at the early modern bar actually depended rather
more on the support of powerful patrons within, than outside, the
profession.

iii. Friends and Neighbours, Patrons and Specialists

In building and maintaining a practice at the bar, kinship and
neighbourhood ties were of primary importance. Most practising
barristers lived outside London, riding up to town (or to one of the
provincial legal centres, notably Ludlow and York) only for the

[43] *Chetham Soc.*, xiii (1847), 118; *Arch. Cant.*, x (1876), 200; Whitelocke, *Lib. Fam.*,
15, 18; HMC, *Wells*, ii. 461; Harleian 2106, fol. 322.
[44] W. J. Jones, '"The Great Gamaliel of the Law": Mr Attorney Noye', *HLQ*, xl
(1977), 221; Hunts. RO, M/28/1/33-4; Berks. RO, D/ELı Cı/21, 24, 27, 31, etc.; Som.
RO, DD/PH 225/64. Chester City RO, Papers of Sir Richard Grosvenor, Memoranda book c.1627-39, pp. 5-6 (this letter, addressed to Coventry as attorney-general,
must have been written between 1621 and 1625); cf. Ellesmere 2894. P. Clark, *English
Provincial Society . . . Kent 1500-1640* (Hassocks, 1977), 287-90; Haward, *Reports*,
134; and see below, ch. 9, sect. iii.

terms, and following their regional assize circuit twice a year.[45] Much of their work, therefore, tended to come from relatives, acquaintances, and country neighbours. This localized pattern of practice, set during the early stages of a barrister's career, usually continued more or less throughout his working life.

Even before call to the bar, inns of court students were often entrusted with a variety of legal errands—soliciting in the broadest sense—along with other miscellaneous commissions undertaken in London for family and friends. Thus Sir Henry Slingsby of Knaresborough regularly employed his nephew James Metcalfe, who entered Lincoln's Inn in 1626, to sue out writs, retain counsel, and send down copies of judgements and decrees arising from his various lawsuits, together with fashionable clothes, domestic implements, and gastronomic delicacies unobtainable in the provinces.[46] This convenient arrangement doubtless continued after Metcalfe was called to the bar in 1633, since there was obviously much to be said for having a kinsman manage one's legal business. Thomas Knyvett of Ashwellthorpe, Norfolk, relied on a distant relative and namesake of the Middle Temple as his counsellor during a Chancery suit in the 1620s. While his solicitor grumbled that this barrister 'must be often put in mind . . . because he loves to defer things to the utmost limit of time', it was clearly some considerable compensation, after the rigours of his journey to London for the term, to be 'very kindly entertained of my cousin Knyvett and his wife with good cheer and lodging'.[47] As it happened, cousin Knyvett was a Londoner by birth and residence, but in general ties of kinship and region were closely entwined. So far as practice at the bar was concerned, they tended both to reflect and to sustain the marked sense of provincial identity which characterized early modern English society. Appearances before the local assize and quarter sessions sittings, together with the holding of local office, ranging from stewardship of a manorial court to the dignity of a place as county JP or borough recorder, naturally

---

[45] See below, sect. iv of this chapter, and ch. 4, sect. iii. N. L. Matthews, *William Sheppard, Cromwell's Law Reformer* (Cambridge, 1984), 13–15, documents the remarkable career of a barrister who apparently concentrated his efforts on a largely, if not wholly, provincial practice.

[46] Yorkshire Archaeological Society, Leeds, MS DD 56 J 3/5; cf. *The Oxinden Letters, 1607–42*, ed. D. Gardiner (1933), 7–8.

[47] *The Knyvett Letters 1620–1644*, ed. B. Schofield (Norfolk Rec. Soc., 1949), 25, 58. On the regional character of barristers' practices, see also Clendinnen, 153–4, and Barnes, 'Star Chamber Litigants', 26–7.

strengthened these connections by advertising a barrister's professional standing to potential clients in his neighbourhood.

The predominance of kinship and regional ties in moulding client–counsel relations was qualified, however, by patronage and specialization. A barrister known or believed to enjoy a judge's special favour inevitably attracted clients from outside his family or locale, who sought to exploit this privileged relationship for their own ends. The judge's favourite, often son, brother, nephew, cousin, or relative by marriage, was a familiar figure in the courts of Elizabethan and Stuart England.[48] From the litigant's viewpoint, the advantage of retaining a favourite was, according to the barrister Bulstrode Whitelocke, 'for no other end, but because they hope thereby to have more favour than otherwise they ought to have, a kind of close intention to bribery'. Whitelocke spoke with understandable bitterness, having seen his own earnings at the bar drop from over £300 in the last year of his father's life as a justice of King's Bench to under £50 following his father's death in 1632, although (as he claimed) Sir James 'far from showing him that countenance which some judges do to their favourites ... was no otherwise to his son than to the rest of his profession'.[49] It is conceivable that, as Whitelocke implies, suitors were mistaken in supposing that they would gain improper advantage (or at least avoid disadvantage) by retaining a judge's favourite. However, in most (perhaps all) central courts, favourites quite openly enjoyed the privilege of pre-audience, or priority in moving at the bar, with the result that barristers outside this charmed circle might find it very difficult indeed to get a hearing for their clients' cases. Hence a large proportion of the total volume of litigation naturally fell into the hands of these 'great counsel and favourites ..., a term fitter for kings than judges', according to Francis Bacon, one of many lawyers and laymen who criticized the consequent inflation of fees at the expense both of clients and those other lawyers who, at least in Chancery, 'have not been heard sometimes scarce once or twice in a term'.[50]

[48] Cf. *Inns of Court*, 51; R. Callis, *The Case and Argument against Sir Ignoramus* (1648), 5; D. Veall, *The Popular Movement for Law Reform 1640–1660* (Oxford, 1970), 46.

[49] R. H. Whitelocke, *Memoirs, Biographical and Historical of Bulstrode Whitelocke* (1860), 90–1; Additional 53726, fols. 53, 86ᵛ; R. Spalding, *The Improbable Puritan* (1975), 38.

[50] *The Works of Francis Bacon*, ed. J. Spedding, R. Ellis, and D. Heath (1857–74),

Jurisdictions in which cases were heard before a single judge, like Chancery and the majority of English-bill courts, may have provided the most hospitable environment for favourites; in the Court of Requests, for example, where the masters took it in turns to sit, it was suggested that as a result 'the client finds the way more easy for obtaining favour in the hearing of his cause'.[51] Such courts, proceeding largely by motion and without juries, may also have had slightly more flexible arrangements for bringing cases to trial, hence offering more opportunities for the exercise of judicial (and official) discretion to advance or retard the progress of a suit.[52] Yet favouritism was hardly unknown in the common-law courts, with the possible exception of Common Pleas, which Sir William Jones left in 1624 after three years as a puisne justice, transferring to King's Bench because (it was said) he wished to favour his son Charles and son-in-law Edward Littleton, who as mere barristers could not appear in Common Pleas. Favourites also flourished on the assize circuits, where civil litigation brought on writs of *nisi prius* was conducted before a single judge. Thus Nathaniel Finch stands out among the leading counsel on the Western circuit, during the time that his elder brother Sir John presided over that court in the later 1630s, because, unlike almost every other barrister riding the circuit, he possessed no West Country connections, being a Kentishman born and bred. Likewise when Sir William Jones rode the Oxford circuit in the 1620s and 30s, he naturally extended to his son and son-in-law the same mutually beneficial courtesies which they enjoyed when he sat at the Court of King's Bench in Westminster Hall.[53]

Barristers without the head start of close kinship to a judge or senior court bureaucrat could still hope to gain favour through the intercession of a mutual friend. In 1594 Paul Croke (who hardly

---

xiii. 192. The most comprehensive published criticism of 'favourites at the bar of justice' before the Civil War appears in a tract published anonymously as *The Iust Lawyer, his Conscionable Complaint* (1631), reissued in 1642 as W. L., *The Courts of Justice Corrected and Amended*, where the author is described as a practising lawyer 'many years sithence' (sig. A2).

[51] Leadam, ed., *Requests*, xcvii.

[52] See Appendix B.

[53] NLW MS Add. 466 (Wynn of Gwydir, no. 1254); *Western Circuit Assize Orders 1629–1648*, ed. J. S. Cockburn (CS, 1976), 83, 95, 99–101, 104, 109, 118–22, 125, 130, 133, 146, 175; *idem, History of English Assizes*, 134, 141–2; G. D. Hall, 'An Assize Book of the Seventeenth Century', *AJLH*, vii (1963), 236–45. For complaints against 'judges . . . that have favourites, sons, etc. down with them in their circuits', see *CD 1621*, iii. 101, iv. 105; for a more detailed denunciation, see Anon., *The Anti-Levellers Antidote* (1652), 6, 24, 37–8.

lacked legal connections, being the grandson of a master in Chancery and younger brother of two Inner Templars destined to rise to the bench themselves), persuaded his aunt, Lady Harington, to write to her friend Lady Puckering, wife of the lord keeper, as follows:

His [Croke's] practice his most desire is to follow in the Court of Chancery, and finding as well by some little experience of his own, as also by the advice of his experienced friends, that the favour and countenance of those before whom he is to plead in that place (and especially of my Lord Keeper) may much both advantage him in his causes and encourage him in his practice, to which end therefore his earnest suit unto me is for my letter to your Ladyship on his behalf that it would please you to do him that favour as to make him known unto my Lord Keeper and by your commendations he may be furthered unto my Lord's favourable good opinions.[54]

The immediate effects of this appeal are unknown, but Croke's subsequent career, if less distinguished than his brothers', was certainly far from a failure in financial terms.[55]

There were other, somewhat cruder ways to acquire the privileges of a favourite. James Whitelocke praised the judicial integrity of Sir Edward Coke, because he did not exact yearly 'pensions' from counsellors as the price of his favour. The 'cherishing of favourites, draweth the favourer into suspicion of corrupt partiality', according to a contemporary colleague; favourites, 'by alliances or yearly presents, gratuities or new year's gifts ... have ingrossed up all or the most part of the gains in every cause', claimed a well-informed Interregnum critic. The full extent of corrupt collusion during our period between judge, counsel, and litigants willing to pay cash for judicial favour is impossible to determine, but the same source also asserts that before the Civil War, Lord Keeper Coventry and Sir Henry Montagu, earl of Manchester (who presided over the courts of Chancery and Requests respectively) were experts in extracting bribes from suitors, either directly or via 'their favourites and creatures'.[56]

[54] Harleian 286, fol. 226; cf. Additional 38170, fol. 333, Francis Eure to Sir Julius Caesar, master of the Rolls, in 1619, requesting 'that you would be pleased to take notice of the bearer my son and to cast your favourable eye upon him in his practice before you'.

[55] P. Kopperman, 'Sir Robert Heath 1575–1649: A Biography', University of Illinois at Urbana-Champaign, Ph.D. thesis, 1972, 87–8; see also below, pp. 119, 353–4.

[56] Whitelocke, *Lib. Fam.*, 50; W. L., *Courts of Justice*, 14; *Anti-Levellers Antidote*, 38. For lists of presents made by counsellors to assize judges on the Western circuit in

Favourites naturally tended to build up specialized practices centred on the court or courts of their patron. But opportunities for specialization also depended upon the size of the market served. Since practice at the bar in every court of which we have knowledge appears to have been quite unevenly distributed, with a few leading counsel handling a disproportionately large share of the available business, it follows that these 'great impropriators' must have depended upon a clientele drawn from all over the country.[57] Of course, even they usually retained some attachment to their native soil, or at least to their eventual place of settlement, as has been emphasized in the case of the Jacobean Star Chamber, where 'among the fifty-four leaders half . . . had practices built principally on the county-regional base of their residence'.[58] Some courts had a more specialized and smaller bar than Star Chamber. Wards and Duchy Chamber are two examples, although in the latter, specialization was also regionally based, both on account of the court's equitable jurisdiction over the (mainly Northern) estates of the Duchy of Lancaster and the location of its offices at Gray's Inn (*par excellence* the Northerners' society), whence came most of the court's officials, as well as the barristers practising before it.[59] But, by and large, the busier and more eminent pleaders drew their clients from a correspondingly wider geographical area than their less well-practised colleagues.

The potential of patronage in enabling barristers to tap a national, rather than a merely local or regional market is strikingly exemplified by the career of Henry Sherfield of Wiltshire and Lincoln's Inn (*c*.1574–1634). Sherfield was called to the bar in 1607, and within a decade emerged as the leading counsel practising in the Court of Wards. This meteoric ascent was evidently a result of an intimate business and professional relationship with the county neighbour whom he addressed in 1611 as 'the very strength of mine existence', Sir James Ley, who had returned from service as chief baron of the Exchequer in Ireland in 1608 to take up the lucrative and influential place of attorney in the Court of Wards.[60]

the late 1590s, see 'The Expenses of the Justices of Assize . . . 1596–1601', ed. W. D. Cooper, *Camden Miscellany*, iv (1859), 3–4, *passim*.

[57] See below, ch. 3, sect. ii.

[58] Barnes, 'Star Chamber Litigants', 26.

[59] R. Somerville, *Office Holders in the Duchy and County Palatine of Lancaster from 1603* (1972), xxxiv.

[60] Hants RO, 44M69/xl/3; Bell, *Court of Wards*, 22–3; on the authority of the

Shortly after embarking on his career at the bar, Sherfield began
to enter the names of clients and the amounts they paid him in a
small vellum-covered notebook.[61] Some of his clients and their cases
can be identified from letters and other papers surviving in the
massive collection of Sherfield manuscripts, although it would be a
long and difficult task to reconstruct his clientele in full.[62] Moreover,
as his career advanced, the quantity and quality of information
recorded, other than the amounts of fees received, becomes progressively thinner, and is intermingled with miscellaneous financial
memoranda; further, a seven-year gap separates notebook 'A',
which runs from Lent vacation 1608 to the end of Trinity term 1613,
from the next surviving book, 'D', which begins in Easter term 1620.
Nevertheless, for our purposes it will be sufficient to examine some
of the earlier entries, which show how, thanks to Ley, Sherfield's
practice expanded from its original regional base.

For the greater part of the first year recorded in notebook A,
Sherfield's earnings in vacation time consistently exceeded his gains
taken during the law terms in London. But from Hilary term 1609
this pattern was decisively reversed, and henceforth vacation earnings contributed only a small fraction of Sherfield's annual professional income, as shown in Table 2.1. Until then, Henry Sherfield's practice had probably differed little from that of many other
young barristers who started their careers without the sponsorship
of a well-placed patron. Most of his business was generated and
discharged locally, for a socially mixed clientele. This is apparent
from the careful manner in which the fee-book entries distinguish
clients of gentle birth or standing, who are styled by title as well as
name: for instance, 'Mr Wm. Hammond', or 'The Lady Stapleton'.
Three of the twelve persons from whom Sherfield received fees in
Lent vacation 1608 are listed by name alone. Among them was
'Thomas Batwell, endited for a glover's trade', presumably the
defendant in an action brought by a common informer under the
Statute of Artificers, and tried at Salisbury assizes, where Sherfield
also represented Henry and Thomas Long, members of a prominent,
if economically decayed, Wiltshire county family into which he was

attorney of the Wards, see G. Goodman, *The Court of King James I*, ed. J. S. Brewer
(1839), i. 310.
  [61] Hants RO, 44M69/xxv/1.
  [62] The Sherfield papers, which were first kindly brought to my attention by Dr P.
Slack, are part of the Jervoise of Herriard Park collection; a mimeographed interim
list has been produced by the National Register of Archives (no. 74/78, 1974).

Table 2.1. *Henry Sherfield's Fees, 1608–10*

1608:	Lent vacation	£7 1s. 8d.	1609:	Lent vacation	£10 6s. 8d.
	Easter term	£6 11s. 6d.		Easter term	£36 3s. 6d.
	Easter vacation	£3 0s. 0d.		Easter vacation	£2 10s. 0d.
	Trinity term	£2 10s. 0d.		Trinity term	£51 13s. 0d.
	Summer vacation	£12 1s. 8d.		Summer vacation	£10 13s. 4d.
	Michaelmas term	£10 6s. 8d.		Michaelmas term	£61 2s. 0d.
	Vacation following	£4 10s. 0d.		Vacation following	£3 0s. 0d.
1609:	Hilary term	£30 9s. 0d.	1610:	Hilary term	£59 15s. 0d.

Source: Hants RO, 44M69/xxv/i (unfoliated).

to marry after the death of his first wife, the daughter of a
Winchester clothier. Other Salisbury clients were Mr Roger Gaunt-
lett, later an alderman of the city, Mr Thomas Elliott, a burgess of
Old Sarum, and Anthony Brickett, a Salisbury ironmonger.[63]

In the next assize vacation, from July to October 1608, Sherfield
was noticeably busier than before, and more than half his work
seems to have come from non-gentry clients, mostly Salisbury
tradesmen. They included the Salisbury guild of shoemakers, 'Christopher Griste the chandler', the linen-draper Thomas Hills, the
baker Giles Morgan, the victualler Richard Symes, the innkeeper
Henry Bull (who was dignified with the addition 'Mr'), and Bennet
or Benedict Swayne, a substantial Salisbury householder.[64]

In Easter, Trinity, and Michaelmas terms 1608, Sherfield received
fees in London from a numerically smaller but more select clientele,
drawn from a somewhat wider geographical area, including Sir John
Sammes of Essex, 'the Lady Hastings' (probably Mary, second wife
of Sir Francis Hastings of Somerset), Lady Stapleton of Laycock in
Yorkshire, Mr William Noyes (probably of Urchfont in North
Wiltshire), and Mr William Zouche (of Pitton, just to the east of
Salisbury, who is described as 'esquire' in the 1623 Wiltshire
visitation).[65] Whereas a third of Sherfield's vacation fees were
amounts of less than ten shillings, only two of his term-time fees fell
below this figure. The only clients from these three terms whom
Sherfield did not grace with the addition of at least 'Mr' were 'the

---

[63] Cf. *Tradesmen in Early Stuart Wiltshire*, ed. N. J. Williams (Wilts. Rec. Soc.,
1959), 40; Hants RO, 44M69/iv/1; *Poverty in Early Stuart Salisbury*, ed. P. Slack
(Wilts. Rec. Soc., 1975), 56.

[64] Williams, *Tradesmen*, 7, 10, 40; Slack, *Poverty*, 41, 66; *HS*, cv. 58.

[65] *HS*, xiii. 284; *Letters of Sir Francis Hastings*, ed. C. Cross (Som. Rec. Soc., 1969),
xxiv; *WAM*, ii. 184; *HS*, cv. 225.

burgesses of Wellington' (in Somerset), who had sought his assistance in connection with a dispute about their market rights, and who wrote on 17 November 1608 commending his 'great pains' on their behalf.[66] (Sherfield must have continued to give satisfaction, for he received several more fees from Wellington over the next few terms.) Unfortunately, little further indication is given of what Sherfield did to earn his term-time fees; single motions in King's Bench and Requests are specifically mentioned, but otherwise the entries merely list the client's name and the amount paid. There is as yet no sign, however, that Sherfield had established a significant presence in the field of wardship litigation.[67]

The effect on Sherfield's fortunes of Ley's patronage as attorney of the Wards did not become fully apparent until Hilary term 1609. In the preceding vacation Sherfield continued to be retained by near-neighbours such as 'Mr Drake of Wallop', 'Mr John Moggeridge', and 'Fonthill men' (probably tenants from a hamlet on the outskirts of Salisbury).[68] One client, 'Christopher Hibberd brought by Mr Barnes', subsequently figures in Sherfield's Wards practice; Barnes was probably an attorney or solicitor, and Sherfield later returned part of a ten-shilling fee Barnes had brought him for drafting an answer in Hibberd's suit. But after the first two entries for Hilary term, Sherfield began to enumerate his new clients; of the seventeen he had acquired by its end, no less than twelve were involved in wardship cases.[69] The first was a very substantial catch: Francis Clifford, fourth earl of Cumberland, who had a Wards suit with his sister-in-law over her efforts to protect the inheritance of her daughter Lady Anne Clifford.[70] Moreover, a significant proportion of clients and fees listed seem to have been brought to Sherfield by other lawyers, such as the diarist John Manningham of the Middle Temple and Thomas Thornton of Lincoln's Inn (of whom we shall

[66] Hants RO, 44M69/xxx/2.

[67] The Court of Wards entry book names Sherfield only once as counsel for the entire year 1608, and in this case he appeared for his brother Roger. (WARD 9/530, fol. 61.)

[68] Cf. *WAM*, xix. 263; *HS*, cv. 121–2.

[69] The entry books record the following appearances by Sherfield as counsel in 1609: Hilary term, 10; Easter term, 13; Trinity term, 18; Michaelmas term, 28: WARD 9/530, fols. 434–556, and WARD 9/531, fols. 12–481ᵛ. Further Wards matters in which Sherfield provided advice or drafted pleadings may be identified as such either from specific references in his fee book or from case papers in Hants RO, 44M69/xlix, lix–lxi, *passim*.

[70] G. C. Williamson, *Lady Anne Clifford* (Kendal, 1922), 78–9. For notes and papers on this case, see Hants RO, 44M69/xlix, 31–4.

hear more shortly), presumably in recognition of his newly won standing in wardship matters. In these instances it seems unlikely that Sherfield was previously known to the clients who retained him. This supposition is strengthened by the additional information which the fee book begins to provide during Hilary term 1612, when the names of new clients are accompanied by a marginal annotation giving their county of residence (or, possibly, the county where the *post-mortem* inquisition relevant to their case was taken). Of the twenty-six new cases listed in this way for the following Easter term, only one appears to have come from Wiltshire, and few from the surrounding counties.[71]

While the total size and geographical range of Sherfield's term-time clientele expanded with his growing prominence in the Court of Wards, his vacation practice remained virtually static, and indeed showed some tendency to contract into the two assize vacations. Yet success in London did not cause Sherfield to lose touch with his home base in Wiltshire, for he played a central part in Salisbury's political and religious affairs during the next two decades. Farming and other business interests, friendships and intermarriage with representatives of prominent gentry families, responsibilities as steward of the earl of Salisbury's West Country estates, and the representation of suitors from the area also kept Sherfield closely in touch with the concerns of provincial life.[72] In short, while his career shows how the support of a powerful patron could lift a barrister's practice from a merely regional to a national plane, it also demonstrates the durability of the ties which bound early modern Englishmen to their place of birth and residence.

Another barrister whose surviving papers enable us to analyse the development of his practice in some detail is Thomas Thornton (1553–1632), also of Lincoln's Inn, who was born and lived nearly all his life at Newnham, a small village on the outskirts of Daventry in Northamptonshire. Thornton's family background, while less obscure than that of Henry Sherfield, was likewise by no means

[71] The counties listed are Berks., Beds. (2), Essex, Glos., Kent, Lancs., Leics. (2), London-Middx. (2), Northants, Notts., Salop (2), Suffolk (2), Surrey (2), Sussex and Wilts. Two cases are unannotated, and two are given joint locales.

[72] Cf. P. Slack, 'Religious Protest and Urban Authority', in *Schism, Heresy and Religious Protest*, ed. L. D. G. Baker (Cambridge, 1972), 295–302; L. Stone, *Family and Fortune* (Oxford, 1973), 126–7. Professor Barnes informs me that all but one of the nine Star Chamber bills signed by Sherfield during James I's reign came from Dorset, Hants, or Wilts.

exalted. His grandfather was probably the first of the family to live and farm at Newnham, and although his father styled himself 'gent', the man who became his stepfather after his father's death in 1556 was a local yeoman, Richard Chaplin. On his mother's side, however, Thomas was connected with two substantial gentry families, the Spencers of Everton and Althorp, and the Temples of Stowe, Buckinghamshire, and Burton Dasset, Warwickshire, and also more distantly with a plethora of Midlands gentry, who figure prominently among Thornton's clients.[73]

Although he spent at least a year as a member of New Inn, the inn of chancery associated with Lincoln's Inn, before entering that society in 1575, Thornton was not called to the bar until 1584, two years after reaching the minimum necessary seniority. By this time he had married Elizabeth, daughter and coheiress of Henry Dacres of Chilvers Coton, Warwickshire, who bore him eight children before her death in 1604. In 1582, just before his marriage, Thomas began to keep a fairly detailed record of his income and expenditure, which he continued until a month or so before his death half a century later.[74] From these accounts it is clear that legal practice was by no means his sole source of income. Thus in the twelve months ending 25 March 1594, his tenth year at the bar, Thornton's fees amounted to only £68. 10s, whereas his own rents brought in £40, and his wife's another £47. 6s. His annual income from the law did not reach £100 until 1597, and only rose above £200 in four out of a total of nearly fifty years of active legal practice.[75] Yet Thornton was hardly a professional failure; he served as recorder to the corporation of Daventry from c.1591, and was elected associate bencher of Lincoln's Inn in 1620.[76] He also added to the estates he had inherited around Newnham by a succession of small purchases, culminating in 1625 with the manor and advowson of Brockhall, where his descendants remained for the next three centuries. In later years he developed a profitable money-lending business, and the post-1600

[73] *The Visitations of Northamptonshire Made in 1564 and 1618–19*, ed. W. C. Metcalfe (1887), 142; O. Barron, *Northamptonshire Families* (1906), 303–4; Northants RO, ZA 4668 (P. N. Skelton, 'The Chronicles of Newnham, Northants, Ad Annum 1799 A.D.', typescript, c.1970); E. F. Gay, 'The Temples of Stowe and their Debts', *HLQ*, ii (1938–9), 413–14.

[74] Northants RO, Thornton 2251, unfoliated (microfilm).

[75] Cf. *LRH*, 183.

[76] Northants RO, Thornton 2251: 24 March 1590/1, 'Pd. to Mr. Chamberlain's man by the appointment of the Burgesses of Daventry . . . xvi li for the recordership of Daventry.'

accounts include a regular line of receipts from money out at use. But by comparison with many of his colleagues, Thornton did not make spectacular financial gains from the law.

He began to practise, although not as an advocate, while still a student under the bar. His accounts show that he received his first fee before the start of Michaelmas term 1583 'from the tenants of Napton [presumably Napton-on-the-Hill, some six miles west of Daventry on the Leamington Road] for their leases'. Similar out-of-court counselling and drafting work for neighbours and relatives provided the bulk of his small gains from the law over the next few years. Thus, for example, between March 1584 and February 1585 Thornton earned six shillings 'of my cousin Temple for Mr Tracye and the rest for drawing of their indentures', ten shillings 'of John Keble for a replication in the Chancery', and three pounds 'of my cousin Anthony Spencer for Mr Rowley his bill which I procured from my cousin Thomas Wilmer' (presumably the fellow Lincoln's Inn student who had been called to the bar just after Thornton in the summer of 1584).[77] Over the next twelve months he notes fourteen separate fees: six of these were from his Pulteney, Saunders, and Temple cousins, and five from clients in nearby Leamington, Gaydon, Badby, and Newnham itself, while the remaining three were paid by 'Goodman Capenhurst' and one Thomas Nutt, in each case for the preparation of Chancery pleadings.

As the size of Thornton's practice slowly increased, the amount of identifying detail recorded about clients and their cases unfortunately tends to diminish. Nevertheless, his work seems to have retained a predominantly familial and regional character. So far as one can see, very few of his clients were referred by other lawyers, and there is no evidence that Thornton developed a specialized practice in any of the Westminster courts, although he regularly rode up to London for the terms, as well as attending Northampton and Warwick assizes. A large fraction of his work evidently continued to be non-contentious conveyancing and general counselling.[78] Thornton also regularly kept manorial courts for his cousin Edward Saunders at Brixworth, just out of Northampton, and for Mr Roger Pendleton, of Shenley, near Bletchley, in Buckinghamshire. But he was far from being just a landlord's lawyer. The majority of his clients are listed in

[77] *LIAdmR*, i. 83; *LIBB*, i. 434, 435.
[78] Cf. Thornton's correspondence with his Temple relations, in Huntington Library, Stowe MSS 2367–77.

the accounts by name alone, without any title, and he frequently acted for the tenants of neighbouring manors, as well as taking a leading part in the struggle of his fellow villagers against the Knightley family, lords of the manor of Newnham.[79]

Another perspective is provided by the fee book of a barrister who rose to higher professional dignity than either of our two previous examples. Serjeant Arthur Turner (?1589–1651) was the second son of a Middle Temple barrister who died in 1623, ten years after Arthur himself was called to the bar of his father's inn. His mother was the daughter of James Morice, attorney of the Wards, also an Essex man and Middle Templar, while Arthur married the daughter of yet another Middle Temple lawyer, the bencher John Jermyn of Norfolk. These formidable legal connections were sustained through the next generation, for Arthur's son and heir Edward also entered the Middle Temple, and rose to become a baron of the Exchequer under Charles II.[80]

Arthur Turner's sole surviving fee book does not indicate how his practice was originally built up, since it begins only in Hilary term 1642, when Turner was already a serjeant at law of five years' standing.[81] Yet, for this very reason, it provides an illuminating contrast with the Sherfield and Thornton accounts (which become increasingly less informative as the careers of their compilers advance), especially since Turner records not only the amount of each fee he received, the client's name, and that of his adversary, but also the venue in which the matter was proceeding. Throughout the period covered by the fee book, which runs to Hilary term 1651, albeit with a three-year break between Hilary term 1643 and Easter term 1646, Turner's legal income was derived almost exclusively from litigation in the central courts of Westminster Hall. There is no indication that he rode the circuits as a counsellor, although on at least three occasions between 1646 and 1648 he was commissioned as an assize judge.[82] The only vacation earnings noted are between Michaelmas term 1647 and Hilary term 1648, and after Easter term

[79] Cf. Northants RO, Thornton 1614–20, and ZA 4668, pp. 48 seq.

[80] See below, Appendix E. Turner was said to have been 'born a lawyer' by the bencher who compiled notes for a congratulatory speech following his Middle Temple reading. (CUL MS Dd. 5. 51(i), fol. 64ᵛ.)

[81] In a holograph law report, Turner does refer, however, to the death in 1640 of 'my honourable and true Maecenas', Thomas Coventry, lord keeper from 1625. (HLS MS 106, fol. 1ᵛ.) Coventry had appointed Turner as a trustee for lands leased to Lady Coventry's use shortly before his own will was made in July 1638. (PCC 1 Coventry.)

[82] Cockburn, *History of English Assizes*, 272–3; HLS MS 137 (unfoliated).

1649. The overwhelming bulk of his work was in Common Pleas, plus a small, but not insignificant, fraction in Chancery and before the master of the Rolls. He also appeared occasionally in King's Bench, Exchequer, Duchy Chamber, the House of Lords, and even the Court of Delegates (the highest court of appeal in ecclesiastical matters).[83] Advice to clients out of court constituted a very small fraction of his total business (see Table 2.2).

Turner provides little information about the social standing of his clients, who are mostly listed by surname alone (for example, 'Searle *ad* [*versus*] Woodford'). Although knights, peers, and army officers are given their titles, it would be dangerous to assume that all who appear without these adornments would not have claimed even that most modest mark of gentility, the prefix 'Mr'. In fact Turner probably did not know many of his clients personally. Although on one page of his list for Trinity term 1646 eighteen cases are annotated by county (presumably that in which the suit was laid), all

Table 2.2. *Arthur Turner's Practice; Venues and Fees, 1642–51*

	Common Pleas	Chancery	King's Bench	Exchequer	Advice	Other and unspecified	Total
1642[1]	93	74	9	3	4	15	198
1643[2]	14	—	6	—	2	2	24
1646[3]	193	81	18	1	—	8	301
1647	356	74	12	3	9	6	460
[Vacation][4]	5	9	—	—	—	3	17
1648	459	42	6	1	—	2	510
1649	354	42	8	1	—	3	408
[Vacation][5]	5	2	—	—	—	—	7
1650	358	52	6	1	1	6	424
1651[6]	50	3	—	—	—	—	53
Total	1,887	379	65	10	16	45	2,402
Percent	78.5	15.8	2.7	0.4	0.7	1.9	

[1] Hilary to Trinity terms; 6 motions listed for Michaelmas term, courts not specified.
[2] Hilary term only.
[3] Easter to Michaelmas terms.
[4] Vacation following Michaelmas term 1647.
[5] Vacation following Easter term 1649.
[6] Hilary term only.

[83] G. Cock, *England's Law Judge* (1656), 13, notes that common lawyers appeared 'both in the Admiralty and Court of Probates, in case a question upon any statute or other point of the common law comes into question'.

but four being from East Anglia, it is apparent from other notes both here and elsewhere in the fee book that most of Turner's clients were referred to him by attorneys or solicitors. Even in the first set of entries, for Hilary term 1642, we find one Common Pleas case listed simply as 'pro Mr Ingram's client—xs.', and Ingram's name recurs several times, together with many others written in the right-hand margin after each fee. While not all these third parties were necessarily attorneys, it seems that Turner's dealings with clients were generally mediated through members of the lower branch; indeed, about two-thirds of the sixty-odd names can be matched with the surnames of attorneys in the Common Pleas and King's Bench docket rolls from 1640.[84] Lord Keeper Finch had good reason to admonish Turner and other newly called serjeants in 1637 not to 'hug an attorney nor make an attorney's feast and so draw them by those base means to bring them clients'.[85]

Henry Sherfield, the favoured specialist; Thomas Thornton, the locally based all-rounder, and Arthur Turner, the successful Westminster Hall advocate, represent three distinct modes of practice at the early modern bar. Nonetheless, each of these individuals worked within a common matrix of opportunities and constraints imposed by the institutional and social characteristics of the legal system. The exploitation of familial and local connections was necessary in order to establish a practice; going much further required access to a broader clientele, which was unlikely to be achieved without unusual abilities, the sponsorship of an influential patron from within the profession, or—perhaps most commonly—a combination of both.

iv. Ways and means

Whether minor provincial counsel or great Westminster Hall pleader, every common lawyer faced certain practical problems of

[84] I am indebted to Dr Brooks for this information. 'Mr Cuttes' and 'J. Gosnold', two of those named by Turner, may be tentatively identified with members of MT listed as practising common attorneys in 1634. (*MTR*, ii. 837.) Cuttes is probably the Henry Cuttes admitted to the house in 1633; Gosnold was admitted in 1619, with Edward and Arthur Turner as sureties. (*MTR*, ii. 646, 808.)

[85] CUL MS Add. 6863, fol. 83ᵛ. Cf. Brooks, thesis, 179; Ellesmere 5912; STAC 8/90/20. The growing power of attorneys exercised through their retention of barristers did not end the regional basis of practice at the bar. In 1688 William Lowther, son-in-law of Serjeant Sir William Rawlinson, wrote: 'I am now removed from the Temple to Gray's Inn, the serjeant has put me in very good chambers. . . . It was his pleasure that I should remove, it lying more convenient for business with the Northern attorneys.' ('Letters of Lady Lowther of Ackworth 1682–1692', typed transcript in possession of

logistics and organization. The distinction between 'country' and 'city' lawyers will not bear too much emphasis, for the simple reason that a great many, perhaps most, practitioners maintained both a provincial base and a metropolitan presence. Lacking all the appurtenances of the twentieth-century office, from typewriters to paperclips, and especially access to modern means of communications, working barristers still had to maintain contact with clients and to transport themselves, their clerical assistants, servants, and paperwork backwards and forwards from London, around an assize circuit, and home to their wives and families.

Barristers today still operate out of chambers, not offices, but very few actually live there. In the period with which we are concerned, however, barristers, like most other people, lived by or above their work-place. There was as yet no rule of etiquette to prescribe that a practising barrister must be 'in chambers' at the inns of court, and many barristers never acquired a chamber, or held one for only a few years after call to the bar. Chambers were expensive either to buy or rent, and a man who had only occasional business in London during term could always arrange temporary accommodation with friends or kinsfolk, or put up in a Holborn tavern.[86] According to Roger North, 'practising chambers' should be no more than two stories high: 'The ground chamber is not so well esteemed as one pair of stairs but yet better than two; and the price is according.'[87] Although varying a good deal in size and amenities, the accommodation typically consisted of a general-purpose sitting-room, a partitioned study (sometimes little more than a wooden cupboard with a shelf for books and a writing table), and a bedchamber or two leading off it. Clients were interviewed either in the main chamber or a separate ante-room. Chambers were usually shared between at least two barristers and their servants, although benchers had the privilege of occupying a whole chamber by themselves.[88]

Sir William Pennington-Ramsden, Bt., Muncaster Castle, Cumbria; I am indebted to Dr D. R. Hainsworth for this reference.)

[86] Cf. *Inns of Court*, 12–14. REQ 2/199/2, 203/30: two examples of barristers staying at nearby taverns rather than their inn of court while in London during term.

[87] North, *Lives*, i. 41–2.

[88] *ITR*, i. 411, describes the newly built chambers of Sir Julius Caesar as containing 'on the first floor or storey thereof, two fair large chambers with chimneys in them, one study, one room for clients to attend in, one large woodhouse, one house of office, and a place thereto adjoining to lay things in . . .'. (*Inns of Court*, 84.) Cf. the description of Robert Kympton's GI chamber, in *Abstracts of Inquisitions Post-Mortem for The City of London, Part III, 1577–1603*, ed. E. A. Fry (Index Library, 1908), 31–2.

Yet most barristers were intermittent visitors to London, not permanent residents. The four law terms put together lasted little more than three months; as Sir Thomas Smith observed, 'The law is not open at all times, no, not the third part of the year.'[89] In 1588 Thomas Thornton spent a total of only just over fourteen weeks in residence at Lincoln's Inn, his longest stay being from 17 October to 22 November for Michaelmas term. Otherwise he lived at home in Newnham, travelling to the Warwick and Northampton assizes for a few days in March and August, with a brief excursion in mid-July to look over some land near Birmingham for a client, day trips to Northampton, Daventry, and Banbury to buy household goods, cattle and seed for his farm, and visits to relatives' houses nearby.[90]

Even while Paul Croke was living at Hackney, a mere three-mile ride from his Inner Temple chamber, he seems rarely to have spent more than half the year in London. After acquiring the manor of Cottesmore in Rutland during the early 1620s, Croke still commuted to London for the terms four times a year, but his stays were much briefer than before: during the year from Michaelmas term 1627 for example, he appears to have spent only nineteen weeks in the capital.[91] While we cannot reconstruct the annual itineraries of other barristers even to this limited extent, it seems likely that, with the exception of perhaps a few leading practitioners in the central courts, barristers picked up the greater part of their business out of term and outside London. Those whose practices were largely, or exclusively, confined to provincial courts, such as the councils of the North and the Marches, or to Ireland, obviously had even less reason to visit the capital.

Attorneys and clients showed no inhibitions about calling on barristers at home to discuss business. John Lowther noted that 'for the convenience of my practice [I] tied myself to a great inconvenience, that is to keep two houses, one at Meaburn . . . where I live in summer; another I take in Kendal where I live in winter . . . (attending the market day in my house for the resort that come to me for my profession)'.[92]

But if consultations about a tradesman's debt or a farmer's lease

---

[89] *De Republica Anglorum* (1583), ed. L. Alston (Cambridge, 1906), 52. Cf. C. R. Cheney, *Handbook of Dates for Students of English History* (1961), 66–8.

[90] Northants RO, Thornton 2251; however, John Smyth of Nibley and the MT appears to have spent as much as 7 months in London during the year dating from Michaelmas term 1605. (Bodl. MS Eng. misc. E 6, fols. 26ᵛ–30ᵛ.)

[91] Croke, 'Diurnall', *passion*.

[92] Lowther, 'Autobiography', 213.

might very well occur in a counsellor's drawing room or parlour,[93] the gentry and nobility were more likely to expect their lawyers to wait upon them, or to conduct their business largely by correspondence and through servants. The long run of letters in the papers of Sir Nicholas Carew of Beddington, Surrey, from his legal adviser, John Haward of Tandridge and the Inner Temple, show that Haward frequently waited upon Carew but not vice versa; on 13 July 1621 Haward wrote, 'My purpose was to have been with you this day but that Sir Thomas Gresham sent to me last night when I was in my bed to come to him this morning.'[94] The first earl of Bridgewater relied heavily on his steward, David Evans, as intermediary in his many dealings with lawyers, among whom William Noy was the most prominent. Evans's journal shows him continually attending Noy at the latter's Lincoln's Inn chamber during term in the late 1620s for opinions on deeds and other legal matters, while Noy also came to several working suppers with his master at Bridgewater House in the Barbican.[95] Yet despite their close and long-standing association, the earl never seems to have returned the compliment by visiting Noy. Perhaps this was not merely on account of Bridgewater's sense of what was becoming to his station; Noy was a very busy man, with a well-deserved reputation for brusque incivility towards anyone who wasted his time.[96] There is a story told by a fellow barrister about Noy's being summoned one morning to attend on the countess of Suffolk:

At last came in Mr Noy, passed clear through the with-drawing chamber . . . and knocked at my lady's chamber door. A maid came to him and said, what would you have? My lady, quoth he, sent for me and I am now come to know what she would with me. My lady, said she, is a little busy, I pray have

[93] Cf. PCC 81 Ridley, the will of John Barkesdale (1629), which contains a reference to a 'drawing room and my study within it'; also Norfolk RO, INV/38, no. 54, an inventory of Elias Brantingham (1632), whose 'study by the parlour' contained a chest, a table, two stools, a desk, an old carpet, and 'a frame with divers books'.

[94] Berks. RO, D/ELi Ci/117.

[95] Ellesmere 6310; 6477, *passim*. However, in 1600 Sir George Booth 'came to Manchester to visit Mr. Humphrey Damport [Davenport], counsellor of Gray's Inn'. (J. O. Halliwell, *The Private Diary of John Dee* (CS, 1842), 63.) In 1618 Sir Arthur Throckmorton wrote to Thomas Crew asking 'when I might find him best at leisure to confer with him'; Crew responded by agreeing to call upon Throckmorton, because 'he knew I loved not to take journeys'. (Northants RO, Montagu Letters 1553–1600 [*sic*], fols. 77ᵛ–78.) Cf. Birmingham Reference Lib., MS 66074/11; G. S. Thomson, *Life in a Noble Household, 1641–1700* (1937), 59.

[96] Jones, '"The Great Gamaliel of the Law"', 219–21.

a little patience and stay there. Other folk have business too, said he, and so went his way.[97]

Depending on the scale of his practice, a barrister would need one or more clerks to run messages and handle paperwork, especially outward correspondence and the drafting or engrossing of documents. Clerks were often more or less distant kinsmen, taken on straight from grammar or writing school and bound to serve their master for a period of years by articles of apprenticeship, on which substantial premiums were payable. Under this arrangement a clerk would be fed and clothed at his master's expense, living in his house and accompanying him to the inns of court each term, where he would eat with his fellow clerks at a separate table in hall and sleep either on a truckle bed in his master's chamber or in nearby lodgings.[98] He received no wages during this apprenticeship, and even clerks whose indentures had expired seem to have derived their incomes directly from fees paid by their master's clients.[99] But an able young man bound to a rising barrister had good prospects: 'if his master thrives, he cannot do amiss'.[100]

The practical experience gained from writing in a barrister's chamber and accompanying him to Westminster Hall and the assize circuits, riding on his own horse, a cloak bag full of briefs and evidences on his back, could provide an excellent introduction to the world of law, especially if supplemented by following one conscientious master's advice, 'when you are weary of writing, to read and study Littleton, West's precedents and the book of entries'.[101] So

[97] Staffs. RO, D661/11/1/17, fol. 27.
[98] Cf. the agreement between Thomas Thornton and Henry Buckby in 1581, whereby Buckby was to pay Thornton £39 over a 5-year period for his son's indentures. (Northants RO, Thornton 2251.) Buckby disappears from Thornton's expenditure accounts after 1584, apparently replaced by one Thomas Hauslopp, Thornton's cousin, and presumably a relative of the Richard Hauslopp, of Warwickshire and Clement's Inn, admitted to LI in 1598. (*LIAdmR*, i. 126.) See also Brooks, thesis, 96–9; J. Stephens, *Essayes and Characters* (1615), 329–35 ('A Lawyer's simple Clarke'); *A Brief Memoir of Mr. Justice Rokeby*, ed. J. Raine (Surtees Soc., 1860), 14.
[99] Barrister's accounts contain frequent entries of reckonings with their clerks, but not the payment of wages. Cf. Northants RO, Thornton 2251; Croke, 'Diurnall'; CUL MS EDC 3/1/1, fol. 5ᵛ, in which is recorded payment of 10s. to Francis Bracken for drawing a bill plus 3s. 4d. 'to his man for engrossing the same'. Stephens, *Essayes*, 334, says the clerk 'is a follower; for he wears a livery, but no servant, for he pays his own wages'.
[100] Stephens, *Essayes*, 335.
[101] HMC, *Cowper*, i. 450: 'Your letter to Mr. Gilbert I gave to my clerk to put up safe in the cloak bag'; Osborn, *Hoskyns*, 66.

many barristers' clerks went on to become practising attorneys that it was said 'a clerk in *thesi*, is an attorney in *hypothesi*'.[102] Nor was it entirely unknown for a clerk to achieve admission to an inn of court and even be called to the bar through his own abilities and his master's goodwill. Most, however, must have made clerkship a lifelong career. In 1630 the Gloucestershire barrister Jasper Selwyn wrote a letter on behalf of Hugh Price, who had apparently begun as a clerk with Selwyn, then transferred to Selwyn's cousin Thomas Stephens until Stephens's death in 1613, when he was taken into the service of Sir Henry Yelverton, for whom he was still working seventeen years later.[103]

The filing of briefs, miscellaneous case papers, and other records generated by his master's practice seems not to have formed part of a clerk's routine duties. Or so the state of the surviving evidence suggests. With the exception of fee books, invariably compiled by barristers themselves, correspondence and other material which helps to illuminate the patterns of legal practice in our period is largely to be found, not as we might expect among collections of lawyers' papers, but rather in those of their landed family clients. It is always dangerous to argue from the absence of evidence, which may merely reflect what descendants considered worthy of preserving, rather than what those from whom they inherited a collection of documents actually did or thought. Nevertheless, this customary caveat loses much of its force in the present instance; whereas clients had every reason to ensure that deeds and other 'evidences' used in the preparation of cases were returned to their safe keeping for future reference, a barrister had little conceivable motive to retain letters and documents bearing on particular suits.[104] Apart from the occasional self-memorandum, these were unlikely to be of much interest or value once his own role in the proceedings had ended, especially in comparison to the handwritten reports of arguments by

---

[102] Stephens, *Essayes*, 334; Brooks, thesis, 96–7; G. Townesend, *A Preparative to Pleading* (1675), 14; *MTAdmR*, i. 82 (Henry Clarke); L. Hutchinson, *Memoirs of the Life of Colonel John Hutchinson*, ed. C. H. Firth (1885), i. 189–90.

[103] Whitelocke, *Lib. Fam.*, 90; *The Autobiography of Sir John Bramston of Skreens*, ed. Lord Braybrooke (CS, 1845), 17; MT MSS, unclassified, 'Articles exhibited on behalf of the gentlemen ...' (1617); STAC 8/163/26; *Calendar of Salusbury Correspondence, 1553–c.1700*, ed. W. J. Smith (Cardiff, 1954), 71.

[104] Cf. the instructions of Edward Combe, for 'great care to be had over my clients' books and writings, they both carefully to be kept and with as good care delivered to the owners and beware lest the contrary part use the right owners' names'. (PCC 42 Stafford.) See also HL RO, Main Papers, 8 Feb. 1641, petition of Henry Goldingham.

counsel and judges at hearings in the central courts and learning exercises at the inns of court, which survive in vast quantities from this era. It was only an abnormally energetic (and obsessive) individual like Henry Sherfield who religiously annotated, dated, and filed away what must have been very close to every note and scrap of paper which came into his hands throughout the course of his career, as well as keeping draft holograph copies of much outgoing correspondence.[105]

Finally, unlike the country solicitors of slightly later date, whose offices are now proverbial treasure houses of former clients' papers, barristers had no single fixed place of work. Discontinuity, both spatial and temporal, was the keynote of their busy lives. 'I go out of Preston upon Saturday next by eight of the clock and had been gone before but for that business and I shall not return until October. ...' 'By your letters you require alteration of my former days appointed for you which I cannot do. ... Because Monday the 6 day Dasset court is appointed ... and Tuesday the 7 is a day for travel between and Wednesday the 8 is for Fynne [?Finham] and Thursday the 9 for Stowe. So that Friday the 10 and Saturday 11 are at your disposing and then Monday following towards London'; 'Wind and tide have fallen out both against me. ... The term comes on the close of the next week, if I find I cannot master such a time betwixt this and that, I will perhaps find thee Friday morning next.'[106] The centralized structure of the legal system and the inexorable rhythms of its annual calendar imposed a peregrinatory existence upon almost every practising barrister, no matter how far he lived from London and largely irrespective of the size of his practice.

The logistical difficulties of conveying personnel, papers, and money to and from London and the provinces every term were obviously greater for those based furthest from the capital. Coaches, while increasingly used by older and wealthier counsellors, were nevertheless an expensive luxury, requiring two to four horses as well as a coachman. Most barristers still rode on horseback to the

[105] With the exception of the Sherfield archive, the earliest surviving collections of barrister's case-papers known to me both date from after 1640: Essex RO, D/DB/B1 (Sir John Archer's commonplace book, 1648–1655), and the William Salt Lib. Stafford, SMS 28 (William Booth's 'Client Cases 1662 ... 1663').

[106] Lancs. RO, DDke 9/10/16; Huntington Library, Stowe MS 2368; Additional 46500, fol. 11. Cf. HMC, *De L'Isle and Dudley*, vi. 220; Additional 36927, fol. 47; *Leics. Arch. Soc. Trans.*, v (1882), 124.

term and assizes, and a 'good lusty nag' was a prime necessity, particularly for those travelling from the remoter parts of the kingdom.[107] Northcountrymen found it a matter of satisfaction to take 'six days' easy journey' to London, even in summer, while those who had merely travelled from the Midlands would still need an overnight stop, perhaps at Uxbridge or St Albans, on their way.[108] Apart from the notorious discomforts experienced by anyone venturing on to the roads of early modern England, especially in 'the extremity of winter', when the 'shortness of the days and the filthiness of the ways' combined to deter Canterbury lawyers from making the twenty-mile journey to the New Romney quarter sessions, barristers returning from term or riding the circuits presented highwaymen and thieves with a tempting target:

> There needs no cunning settor to betray,
> To his companions, when, nor yet which way,
> You are to ride, nor need the thieves be told,
> What store of coin you carry; they all hold,
> You to be rich, and certain prize.[109]

The Northern circuit was particularly dangerous, so much so that its judges rode from Newcastle to Carlisle under armed guard. When Cuthbert Pepper was recommended for the place of queen's attorney in the North in 1597, relative youth and physical fitness were seen as not the least of his qualifications, since 'it is sometimes requisite for the attorney to accompany some of this council to the furthest northern parts, which journeys require able and strong bodies'.[110]

It has been aptly observed that 'the old books of practice do not conceive of a term as being an even flow of time ... but rather as being a series of procedural crises called return days, which normally occur at intervals of about a week'. Nor were these peaks of activity distributed through terms of equal length; whereas Hilary term was 'very short, less business done in it of any term in the year', Michaelmas, the 'father of the terms', ran more than twice as long as the rest, its early start in October clashing inconveniently with

[107] *Radcliffe Correspondence*, ed. Whitaker, 118.
[108] Ibid., 123: Northants RO, Thornton 2251. In December 1622 Rebecca Sherfield wrote from Salisbury to her husband in London that 'I wish the ways may be so that you come [home] in two days'. (Hants RO, 44M69/xxxi/24.)
[109] Kent AO, NR/AZ 46; J. Clavell, *A Recantation of an Ill-led Life* (1628), sig. A7ᵛ.
[110] Cockburn, *History of English Assizes*, 46; HMC, *Salisbury*, vii. 506.

quarter sessions until it was shortened by statute in 1641.[111] All the terms, but especially Trinity and Michaelmas, were liable to be disrupted by outbreaks of epidemic illness, when the sittings of the courts were curtailed, cancelled, or moved out of London.

While we can hardly assemble a detailed picture of the 'typical' barrister's term-time working day, it is clear that many rose early and retired late. Morning prayer at the Temple Church and the chapels of Gray's Inn and Lincoln's Inn commenced at six o'clock, leaving time for a hurried breakfast before the lawyers left by water or the Strand for Westminster Hall, where the courts sat from eight until at least eleven; readings in the halls of the inns of court also began at eight o'clock during learning vacations.[112] After midday dinner, barristers were free to spend the afternoon and evening in chambers, interviewing clients and studying papers. Protracted evening working sessions were not unknown when papers had to be prepared for presentation in court next day; Roger Hill, a bencher of the Inner Temple, wrote to his wife in February 1649, 'Tis late, I am confident thou hast had two hours sleep already.' In 1605 Francis Moore, Lord Keeper Ellesmere's favourite, was said to have visited his patron at midnight, 'having some occasion of business . . . [and] going then homeward from York House to the Middle Temple at two'.[113] The lawcourts kept a six-day week, but while observance of the Sabbath as a day of rest from worldly activities undoubtedly became more rigorous during the half-century before the Civil War, by no means all barristers refrained from 'studying the case, reading of evidences and the like' on the Lord's Day, or were persuaded by the example of the pious judge Sir Augustine Nicolls, whose 'forbearance to travel' on Sundays was said to have 'wrought a reformation on *some* of his own order'.[114]

A preacher at Thetford assizes in 1619 characterized the lawyer's life as 'painful', 'riding from term to term, from court to court, a work to make a man sweat'. The hint of a sneer in that last word is repeated in Archbishop Laud's advice to the young Bulstrode

---

[111] Cheney, *Handbook of Dates*, 67–8; Knowler, i. 372; Middleton, *Michaelmas Term*, 'Inductio'.

[112] *Inns of Court*, 205; *ITR*, ii. xc; *DLLA*, 129; E. P. Cheyney, 'The Court of Star Chamber', *AHR*, xviii (1913), 728; Knowler, ii. 351.

[113] Additional 46500, fol. 43ᵛ; *Knyvett Letters*, ed. Schofield, 25; Goodman, *Court of James I*, i. 105.

[114] N. Bownde, *The Doctrine of the Sabbath* (1595), 78; *Inns of Court*, 210 (my emphasis).

Whitelocke, that he should continue at the bar despite his father's death, 'yet you need not to sweat so much as others at it'.[115] Nevertheless, barristers in general do not seem to have been discontented with their working lot, despite its attendant discomforts and rigours. Those who were most physically or psychologically unsuited to the 'great labours' and 'troublesome practices of the law' presumably dropped out at a relatively early stage. Of the remainder, a number drew comfort and strength from that sense of calling which encouraged men 'to undertake the profession of the law or some other honest profession to the glory of God and good of his country and not live idly or vainly'.[116] This last quotation, taken from the will of Chief Baron Sir John Walter (d. 1630), expresses a typical expectation that one or more sons will follow in their barrister-father's vocational footsteps. A numerically limited but still significant element of hereditary succession at the bar doubtless reinforced the sense of corporate pride and solidarity fostered by the common life of inns of court, Westminster Hall, and assize circuits.[117]

These various incentives and palliatives were obviously reinforced by a further underlying, if not overwhelming, inducement: the actual or anticipated material rewards of a successful legal career. Yet, as we have already seen, the business of the bar was by no means evenly distributed among its many members. Some implications of that inequality are explored in the following chapter.

---

[115] S. Garey, *Jentaculum Judicum: A Manuall for Magistrates or a Lanterne for Lawyers* (1623), 8; Additional 53726, fol. 74ᵛ.

[116] *The Diary of William Lawrence Covering Periods between 1662 and 1681*, ed. G. E. Aylmer (Beaminster, 1961), xiv; Ellesmere 1401; PCC 93 Scroope.

[117] Cf. PCC 131 Goare, 126 Cope, 82 Kidd, 47 Rivers, 47 Harvey, 35 Dale, and 6 Lee; also below, pp. 319–22.

CHAPTER THREE

DEMAND AND SUPPLY

'Touching oppression, it cometh by unnecessary swarms of lawyers
... if all run to one profession because there is most gains in it, it is no
marvel that other sciences decay and that which entertaineth all may
in the end itself surfeit of success.'

'The humble petition of Maurice Gruffyn, Bachelor of Laws,
to ... Sir Thomas Egerton ... and Sir John Popham',
Ellesmere 2029 (c.1603)

VIRTUALLY every major political, economic, and social development in Tudor and early Stuart England helped make more work for
common lawyers in general, and barristers in particular. Lawyers
played an essential role in the consolidation of centralized monarchical rule, advising both governments and their subjects, whose lives
were increasingly regulated by judicial tribunals, old and new, and
by an ever-expanding body of statutory legislation. The decline of
the Church's independent jurisdiction; the incorporation of Wales,
the North, and Ireland within the ambit of royal justice; the
suppression of casual disorder and 'lawlessness'—all benefited the
legal profession. Demographic growth, inflation, the enclosure
movement, a buoyant land market, commercial and industrial
expansion and diversification, the growth of London, and the
national integration of a capitalist market economy—each of these
interrelated trends brought more grist to the lawyers' mills. Finally,
the internal strains and tensions associated with transition from
'status to contract', from a lineage to a civil society, 'whereby
traditional dependencies and allegiances, conceived in personal and
family terms, gave way to a more complicated pattern of greater and
lesser "interests", related to each other within the pattern of law,
now the dominant bond between them'—all these found outlet in
the courts, resort to which became a form of conspicuous consumption, in itself symptomatic of the great social transformation.[1] But

---

[1] M. James, *Family, Lineage and Civil Society* (Oxford, 1974), 183; for the causes
underlying the growth in lawyers' business, see Clark, *Provincial Society*, 279–84, and
Brooks, thesis, ch. 2.

how widely were the benefits of these developments shared within the legal profession?

i. *Local and occasional courts*

The courts of Westminster Hall, 'that great metropolis of practice', together with the assize circuits, offered barristers their largest and most lucrative sphere of employment. Yet besides 'the great courts of Westminster', there were also what Sir Thomas Widdrington characterized as 'some less rivulets of justice for smaller matters'.[2] These local and regional jurisdictions in which early modern barristers could and did practise included the councils in the North and in Wales, various palatine courts, county quarter sessions, a multiplicity of municipal courts, and a plethora of occasional or special jurisdictions.

While a good deal has been written about the administration of some of these bodies, hardly any attention has been given to the lawyers who appeared before them.[3] So generalization about the extent to which they provided work for members of the upper branch is difficult, especially as their organization and procedures varied quite widely. It is almost anyone's guess how much civil litigation occurred outside the central courts, but the total numbers of suits and parties involved must have far exceeded those passing through Westminster Hall each year. On the other hand, a great deal of this litigation concerned disputes over amounts too small to justify the expense of retaining counsel, rather than, or besides, an attorney (if indeed the services of a pleader were required at all), despite the fact that barristers' fees in local courts were generally lower than at Westminster Hall. A further consideration might be that a successful career at the Westminster bar was the conventional (if not quite the sole) route to promotion to serjeant at law, Crown law officer, or judge. It is clear, nevertheless, that many barristers, and not merely those who lacked the abilities, ambition, or connections to reach the highest rank of their profession, found at least occasional work in these courts, while for others they were the major venue of professional employment.

---

[2] Ellesmere 7659; T. Widdrington, *Analecta Eboracensia*, ed. C. Caine (1897), 78.

[3] The sole substantial modern treatments of any of these jurisdictions apart from the councils in Wales and the North during our period are by W. J. Jones: 'The Exchequer of Chester', in *Tudor Men and Institutions*, ed. Slavin, 123–70, and 'Palatine Performance in the Seventeenth Century', in *The English Commonwealth 1547–1640*, eds. P. Clark, A. Smith, and N. Tyacke (Leicester, 1979), 189–204.

Probably the two busiest, and certainly the most extensive, regional jurisdictions were those attached to the provincial councils seated at Ludlow and York, which exercised judicial authority as an arm of government in traditionally turbulent frontier areas, geographically remote from the capital. According to a former Barnard's Inn student and sheriff of Cardigan, writing in 1603, the Council in the Marches was 'as greatly frequented with suits as any one court at Westminster whatsoever ...'. Between 1574 and 1601 the right of practising as an advocate at Ludlow was limited to less than a dozen specially appointed 'counsellors at the bar'.[4] These places were claimed in 1594 to change hands for £50–60 apiece; when compared with the sums paid for many offices in the London legal bureaucracy, or the £500 regularly required from newly appointed serjeants at law, this hardly suggests that they offered their holders a particularly lucrative monopoly. Most civil suits heard at Ludlow seem to have been of small value and settled without a barrister's intervention; so considering that 'counsellors at the bar' were not supposed to charge clients more than five shillings per term, as against fees of ten shillings, a pound, and more commonly paid to barristers in Westminster Hall for each single service, £50–60 was perhaps a fair market price.[5]

Of twelve counsel known to have been practising at Ludlow in or before 1594 (most of whom hailed from the border counties or Wales itself), only one subsequently achieved any substantial preferment.[6] He was Edward Littleton, who counted a chief justice and the author of a great legal classic among his ancestors, besides being the son-in-law of a Welsh judge; yet Littleton spent more than thirty years practising at the Council bar before he himself became a Welsh

---

[4] G. Owen, *The Description of Pembrokeshire*, pt. III, 'The Dialogue of the Government of Wales', ed. H. Owen (Cymmrodorion Rec. Ser., 1906), 23; Williams, *Council in the Marches*, 173–4. The 1601 instructions permitted more than eight counsel, 'provided always ... that no man is admitted to practise as a counsellor at the bar there, unless he be an utter barrister in court [*sic*] and of good fame and reputation'. (Ellesmere 1757, cl. 28.)

[5] Williams, *Council in the Marches*, 172–3, 336; Lansdowne 60, fol. 109ᵛ; Lansdowne 76, fols. 141ᵛ–142. R. H. Clive, *Documents connected with the History of Ludlow* (Ludlow, 1841), 344–5.

[6] Among these, Richard Babnett, Humphrey Bowen, and one 'Mr Jones' cannot be identified. The others were Richard Broughton (IT, Salop), Brian Crowther (IT, Salop), Richard Davis (IT, Herefs.), Richard Prince (IT, Salop); Richard Smith (MT, Herefs.), Edward Littleton (IT, Salop), and Edward Morgan (IT, Flints.). John Lewis and Thomas Morgan were also Inner Templars, but their counties of origin are unknown. (*ITAdmR*; Lansdowne 76, fol. 141.)

judge, a member of the Council, and a knight in 1621, one year
before his death.[7] Two other barristers pleading before the Council
in 1621 had also been there since at least 1594; indeed, Brian
Crowther, another Inner Templar Salopian like Littleton, claimed to
have practised at Ludlow for no less than thirty-seven years. While
Crowther and his fellow veteran Richard Smith, a Middle Templar
also from Shropshire, both served occasionally as recorders or
judges for the Ludlow gaol delivery, neither attained any significant
fortune or promotion from their long careers at the Council's bar.[8]

So the Ludlow bar was something of a professional backwater, a
world small enough for the advent of a new face to attract
comment.[9] Counsel who practised there might also pick up addi-
tional business on one of the four circuits of the court of Great
Sessions, a common-law jurisdiction covering the twelve counties of
Wales, and theoretically held twice each year, in spring and summer.
Some English barristers also attended the Great Sessions, joining
Welsh lawyers practising on their home ground. However, Lent
term of the Council at Ludlow tended to overlap with the spring
Great Sessions, and in 1640 Charles Jones, MP for Beaumaris in the
Short Parliament and a bencher of Lincoln's Inn, complained that
'the judges in Wales keep their sessions when it is term time in
Westminster'. It would have been more difficult to combine practice
before the Council at Ludlow with pleading in Westminster Hall,
since the Council's Hilary, Trinity, and Michaelmas sittings clashed
directly with the corresponding common-law terms. The common
lawyers appointed as judicial members of the Council served only
three months of each year at Ludlow, spending the rest of their time
in private practice at Westminster Hall and on the English assize
circuits. But there is no evidence that this option was feasible for
members of the Ludlow bar, who almost certainly found it impossible to maintain a practice before the Council if they were not in
constant attendance during its sittings.[10] Some hint of their pro-

---

[7] W. R. Williams, *The History of the Great Sessions in Wales, 1542–1830, together with the Lives of the Welsh Judges* (1899), 93.

[8] CUL MS Dd. 3. 64, fol. 34; *Trans. Salop Arch. Soc.*, 2nd ser. xi (1899), 307, 319.

[9] Salop RO, 212/Box 364, Edward Martin to the earl of Bridgewater, 23 Nov. 1640: 'Another young practiser appeared at the bar in this court the last week; one Mr Owen, an Anglesey man of Lincoln's Inn.'

[10] W. Ll. Williams, *The Making of Modern Wales* (1919), 162; Hall, 'Assize Book', 229–36; Owen, 'Dialogue of the Government of Wales' (1906), 23–4; C. A. Skeel, *The Council in the Marches of Wales* (1904), 152, gives slightly different dates, based on the surviving entry books for 1632–42; Whitelocke, *Lib. Fam.*, 88; HMC, *Thirteenth Rep.*,

fessional isolation is given by the claim of Timothy Turner, king's
solicitor in Wales from 1627 to 1637, then chief justice of the
Carmarthen circuit, when compounding as a royalist delinquent in
1646, that his practice had been 'only in Wales and the Marches,
where there is neither common law nor civil law'.[11]

Despite the disappearance of all judicial records generated by the
Council of the North, it seems clear that, in the words of the
Council's historian, 'something like a separate Northern bar' had
emerged at York by the end of the sixteenth century. In 1564 the
Council had been empowered to 'appoint such attorneys and
pleading counsellors to serve the court as they shall think fit', and
scattered references from the later sixteenth and early seventeenth
centuries indicate that the York pleaders constituted a distinct,
close-knit, regional coterie, from whose number were recruited at
least four 'counsellors of fee', common lawyers who served as the
Council's judges, and also the king's attorney in the North.[12] In 1598
Serjeant Hele 'marvelled that such persons should come to be of her
Majesty's Council in the North parts which were never thought meet
to be of counsel with subjects in Westminster Hall', to which
Archbishop Hutton and the Council could only lamely reply 'that
there be five grave men learned in the laws of that council whereof
some do always attend and most of them readers in [the inns of]
court'. Cecil had previously received the archbishop's nomination of
three candidates for the post of queen's attorney in the North from
'lawyers at the bar here'; another, whom Hutton did not name, was
probably William Hilliard, a barrister of the Inner Temple and
recorder of York from 1582 to 1608, who in 1590 was described as
'altogether commorant at York'. The younger John Lowther, whose
father became a counsellor of fee in 1627, was himself called to the
bar in 1630; according to his own account, he 'presently after began

iv. 250. Fees payable to counsel at the Great Sessions were similar to those fixed by
the Council in the Marches. (CUL MS Dd. 12. 27, fols. 72ᵛ, 74, 76ᵛ, 79ᵛ, 81ᵛ, 83ᵛ, 97ᵛ; I
am grateful to Dr Baker for this reference.) 'The Diary of Henry Townshend', ed.
J. W. W. Bund (*Worcs. Hist. Soc.*, 1920), i. 11; W. Ll. Williams, 'The King's Court of
Great Sessions in Wales', *Y Cymmrodor*, xxvi (1916), 9–10, 40–1; Ellesmere 7659;
HMC, *Salisbury*, xiii. 457.

[11] *CCC*, 1461; cf. Sampson Eure's request to exchange his post of king's attorney in
Wales for that of king's serjeant at law, 'to the end your petitioner may by his practice
in your courts of Westminster be the better enabled to serve your Majesty'. (SP 16/
257/51.)

[12] Reid, *Council in the North*, 253; F. W. Brooks, *The Council of the North* (Hist.
Assoc., 1966), 18; Cottonian, Titus F.III, fol. 167ᵛ; HMC, *Salisbury*, v. 505.

to practise the law at York before my father, and then began my estate first to increase'. When Sir Thomas Wentworth recommended his brother William, yet another Inner Temple barrister, for the place of fee'd councillor in 1637, he noted that William 'hath been long a practiser in that court . . . well understanding the course of these proceedings'. A final piece of evidence pointing to the special interest of some north-country barristers in practice before the Council is a petition against its abolition presented to the Long Parliament from Yorkshire, which bears the signatures of a number of northern lawyers who seem not to have been regular pleaders in Westminster Hall.[13]

Besides the two regional councils (and their Irish counterpart, the Court of Castle Chamber at Dublin), barristers also found employment in a variety of lesser courts, whose overlapping jurisdictions criss-crossed the countryside of Tudor and Stuart England. Great cities like Bristol, Norwich, and London supported a whole complex of law courts, each with its own staff, including in the case of London four 'common pleaders', who monopolized practice at the bar in the Court of the Hustings and the lord mayor's court, as did the four *consiliarios eruditos in lege* appointed to plead at the bar of the Marshalsea, or Palace Court, which Charles I established in 1631 to hear personal actions arising within twelve miles of Whitehall.[14] At York, where there were two main groups of courts, presided over by the lord mayor and sheriffs respectively, cases between private citizens were sometimes pleaded by learned counsel before the

---

[13] Lansdowne 86, fols. 34ᵛ–35; HMC, *Salisbury*, vii. 506; B. M. Wilson, 'The Corporation of York 1580–1660', University of York M.Phil. thesis, 1967, 30; *ITR*, i. 259, 298, 308, 370, 379, 381, 383; HMC, *Salisbury*, xv. 393–4; *Lowther Family Estate Books 1617–1675*, ed. C. B. Phillips (Surtees Soc., cxci, 1979), 52; Knowler, ii. 48; HMC, *House of Lords XI (NS), Addenda 1514–1714*, 256. Among the signatories to this undated document, identifiable barristers include Sir William Belt, recorder of York (GI), John Legard (GI), Cuthbert Morley (GI), Thomas Hesketh (GI), Henry Jenkins (LI), William Lister (GI), none of whom appears as a Westminster pleader in Easter term 1638 (see below, sect. ii of this chapter).

[14] Cf. J. G. Crawford, 'The Origins of The Court of Castle Chamber: A Star Chamber Jurisdiction in Ireland', *AJLH*, xxiv (1980), 40, 45; H. Kearney, *Strafford in Ireland, 1633–41* (Manchester, 1959), 69–74. D. H. Sacks, 'Trade, Society and Politics in Bristol c.1500–c.1640', Harvard University Ph.D. thesis, 1977, 157–63; J. T. Evans, *Seventeenth-Century Norwich* (Oxford, 1979), 58–9; *Minutes of the Norwich Court of Mayoralty, 1630–1631*, ed. W. L. Sachse (Norfolk Rec. Soc., 1942), 98, 157–71; F. F. Foster, *The Politics of Stability* (1977), 15–16; *Second Report of the Commissioners Appointed to Inquire into the Municipal Corporations of England and Wales*, HC Sessional Papers (1837), xxv. 89–90; D. G. Greene, 'The Court of the Marshalsea in Late Tudor and Early Stuart England', *AJLH*, xx (1976), 267–81; PRO PALA 9/6/1.

mayor, aldermen, and common councillors. By contrast, no evidence survives of any such opportunities for barristers at Hastings, the small port-town on the Sussex coast, where suits for debt and legal proceedings were recorded in the same large 'court book' used to keep minutes of assemblies of the mayor and jurats. In general, urban jurisdictions were more often the hunting grounds of attorneys than barristers but the presence of the latter should not be ignored, and may have indeed become more apparent during our period.[15]

The same holds true for county quarter sessions, before which barristers frequently appeared in pauper settlement cases and other more or less parochial disputes, although sessions practice had not yet become a recognized 'course by which an unconnected man may be pretty sure to gain business'.[16] There is no evidence that early modern barristers usually had any dealings with the petty litigation of the county and hundred courts, but they did argue cases before stannary and forest courts (although not, it would seem, commissions of sewers), besides pleading in the palatine jurisdictions at Chester, Lancaster, Durham, and possibly the Isle of Ely.[17] During the 1630s there appeared at the bar of the grandiloquently titled Court of Chancery of the Lord Warden of the Cinque Ports, held before the warden's learned steward in St James's Church, Dover, no less than nine counsellors (including one of the learned steward's sons), mostly local men who were also active at one or more bars in Westminster Hall. Finally, counsel acted as advocates for and against petitions and private bills before both houses of parliament,

---

[15] D. M. Palliser, *Tudor York* (Oxford, 1979), 78–9; York AO, House Book B 36, fols. 60, 331; Hastings Museum and Art Gallery, Hastings Corporation MS C/A a. 1 (Court Book 1595–1621). See also below, ch. 8, sect. ii.

[16] *Warwick County Records Volume I: Quarter Sessions Order Book,... 1625, to ... 1637*, ed. S. C. Ratcliff and H. C. Johnson (Warwick, 1935), 44, 50, 54, 65, 102, 131, 165, 244; *Quarter Sessions Order Book, 1642–1649*, ed. B. C. Redwood (Sussex Rec. Soc., 1954), 54; S. A. Burns, 'The Staffordshire Quarter Sessions Rolls, 1598–1602', *Staffs. Rec. Soc.* (1936), iv. 15; *Memoirs of the Life of Sir Samuel Romilly* (1850), i. 92–3; W. Ballantine, *Some Experiences of A Barrister's Life* (1887), 41–2; Duman, *English and Colonial Bars in the Nineteenth Century*, 84–5.

[17] For forest courts, see W. Jones, *Les Reportes de divers Special Cases* (1675), 285–7, 289–92, 294–5. For stannaries, see *All the Statutes of the Stannary* (1562), sig. Cii^v; *Laws of the Stannaries of Cornwall* (Penzance, 1974; first publ. ?1753), 25, 77. I am grateful to Mr A. E. B. Owen for confirming the apparent absence of barristers from sewers' courts, except as commissioners. PRO Palatinate of Lancaster 11/4 (unpaginated, 17 Apr. 1615, 9 Apr. 1616); ibid., 11/10, fols. 148–52; PRO Chester 14/14, fols. 251^v, 258^v, 260^v; PRO Durham 4/1, pp. 421, 457–8, 469, 475, 483. J. Bentham, *The History and Antiquities of ... Ely* (Norwich, 1812–17), i. App. 25; ii. 37.

in full session and committee, as also on occasion before the Privy Council when it took on a judicial role to hear disputes between party and party.[18]

ii. Central courts

Although it is impossible to tell how much work was available for how many barristers in courts of lesser or local jurisdiction outside Westminster Hall, some indication of the distribution of advocacy at the Westminster bar during our period can be gained from the surviving English-bill court entry books. These volumes served as working records of the progress of each judicial matter in train before Chancery and other superior courts whose procedure was modelled on that of Chancery's equity side—that is to say, the courts of Star Chamber, Requests, Wards, the equity side of the Exchequer, and the Duchy Chamber of Lancaster. From a mass of miscellaneous information in the successive entries for each day of hearing, it is possible to extract the names of barristers pleading before the court, who are most usually mentioned as having moved a motion in a particular suit on which the court proceeded to rule. Most regrettably, the entry books for Star Chamber have disappeared, while a still more serious deficiency is that no directly comparable data can be gleaned from the Latin plea rolls and other surviving official records of the ancient common-law courts of Exchequer and King's Bench. Nevertheless, the information provided by the entry books does give us a good idea both of the minimum size of the practising bar and the way in which work was distributed among its members.

The entry books present certain problems of interpretation, but these are by no means insuperable. Since counsellors are usually mentioned by surname alone, it is sometimes difficult to know whether one and the same lawyer is being referred to on several different occasions, rather than two or more persons with a common surname or close variant, especially since no consistency of spelling can be expected at this time. For example, a 'Mr Smith' is named ten times in the Court of Wards Entry Book of Orders for Easter term

---

[18] Chicago, MS f-286, Cinque Ports Court of Chancery, 'Booke of Causes 1632–48'. The steward was Lancelot Lovelace (for whom see below, Appendix E). F. Clifford, *A History of Private Bill Legislation* (1885–7), ii. 852–9; *LJ*, ii. 207, 212, 237, 523. Northants RO, F(M)C 412, gives a glimpse of the embryonic parliamentary bar in the 1660s. (I am grateful to Mr J. P. Ferris for this reference.) E. R. Turner, *The Privy Council of England 1603–1784* (Baltimore, 1927), i. 114–15, 181–2.

1616 and once in the Exchequer's equivalent volume. There is no way of telling whether all these citations refer to one barrister or rather to two or more of at least six possible candidates. A little biographical detective work may sometimes reduce the field, but it is not possible to eliminate all doubtful cases. So a working convention has been adopted, whereby when a name which appears more than once cannot be firmly identified with a particular individual, it is nevertheless assumed that all references were to a single person, so long as the records of no more than one court yield that same surname. However, where such a name appears in the entry books of two or more courts, as in the case of Mr Smith, it is equally arbitrarily assumed that at least two different lawyers were active— in the case of Smith, one person who appeared on ten occasions in the Court of Wards and another who appeared once in the Exchequer.

Another difficulty is that the entry books do not provide an absolutely comprehensive record of pleaders. In Easter terms 1616 and 1638 only just over half the case entries overall mention *any* counsellor, while the proportion falls to as low as one in five for Duchy Chamber in 1616. But closer inspection reveals that the shortfall is not so serious as these figures might suggest, being largely attributable to entries concerned with routine procedural matters, such as the appearance of defendants and the publication of depositions, where any necessary motions were made by attorneys or solicitors, without the intervention of learned counsel.[19] Indeed, in only 136 (6 per cent) of a total of 2,256 Chancery case entries for Easter term 1638 is no lawyer's name given where it is indicated that counsel represented a litigant, while in Wards for Easter term 1616 the proportion of cases in which counsellors are not named drops to a mere half of one per cent (3 out of 583). Even in Duchy Chamber for 1616, where well over half the entries lack counsellors' names, sufficient appear to identify at least the leading barristers. The only other apparent cause for anxiety is that few entries mention the names of counsel for both defendants and plaintiffs in a particular suit; this is probably due not to clerical omissions (since the names of two or more counsellors retained by a client are frequently pro-

---

[19] E.g. C33/174, fols. 311ᵛ, 396; cf. Jones, *Chancery*, 288. A similar practice of allotting certain fixed times to attorneys' motions also prevailed in the Council at Ludlow, and may well have been common to all English-bill courts. (Williams, *Council in the Marches*, 73–4, 172–3.) A few orders naming counsel merely record their assignment to clients pleading *in forma pauperis*.

vided), but to the fact that the overwhelming majority of recorded orders stemmed from uncontested motions.

As the entry books are bulky folio volumes, in some cases running to several hundred pages per term, it was quite impracticable to survey their contents for our entire period. The only feasible method of sampling was by terms, which in English-bill courts generally corresponded to the terms of the older common-law courts; variations in the number of sitting-days presumably reflect differing amounts of business to be transacted, with Chancery and Requests sitting over the longest period and Duchy Chamber the shortest. To provide both a basis for comparison and some chronological perspective, the Easter terms of 1616 and 1638 have been selected for analysis. No special significance attaches to the choice of Easter term, other than that it was much shorter (and the records therefore more manageable) than Michaelmas, besides being held at a time when counsellors were less likely to be dissuaded from travelling up to London by bad weather or the threat of plague than in the winter (Hilary) or summer (Trinity) terms.[20]

The results of this investigation are set out in Table 3.1. In every court, at both dates, a small group of leading advocates clearly handled a quite disproportionate share of the available business, while the majority of counsellors appeared four times or less in the course of a single term. What is more, most of the eminently successful practitioners can be positively identified as clients or kinsmen of either the judges before whom they practised or of influential figures in the legal bureaucracy attached to that particular court. The outstanding example is Francis Moore, who amassed more appearances than any other barrister, moving no less than 269 times before Lord Chancellor Ellesmere during Easter term 1616. Moore's favoured status in Ellesmere's Chancery can have been no novelty. As long ago as 1603 he had been associated to the bench of the Middle Temple at Ellesmere's urging, while his reader's speech four years later publicly acknowledged dependence upon 'that great, grave and wise senator ... who next under the sceptre serves the magistracy of the kingdom and who of his honourable bounty took me into his favour, calling me to his feet in public and to his elbow in

---

[20] In 1635, Hilary term was said to have 'less business than any other' so far as the Court of Wards was concerned, although in the common-law courts Hilary and Trinity terms tended to be specially busy because they immediately preceded the assizes. (Knowler, i. 372; Style, *Practical Register*, 356.)

Table 3.1. Counsel appearing in English-bill Courts, Easter Terms 1616 and 1638

1616[1]

Chancery

Counsel		Appearances	Total	
Number	Per cent	Number	Number	Per cent
2	1.0	100+	385	17.8
20	10.4	25–99	954	44.1
54	27.0	5–24	600	27.7
65	33.7	2–4	177	8.2
52	26.9	1	49	2.2
193	100.0		2,165	100.0

Range: 1–269; 3,454 cases entered (1,853 with counsel named)

Wards

Counsel		Appearances	Total	
Number	Per cent	Number	Number	Per cent
2	2.4	50+	173	31.1
9	10.6	10–49	206	37.1
11	12.9	5–9	66	11.9
29	34.1	2–4	77	13.8
34	40.0	1	34	6.1
85	100.0		556	100.0

Range: 1–88; 583 cases entered (352 with counsel named)

1638[2]

Chancery

Counsel		Appearances	Total	
Number	Per cent	Number	Number	Per cent
–	–	100+	–	–
12	4.7	25–99	463	33.1
57	22.1	5–24	589	42.1
84	32.5	2–4	243	17.3
105	40.7	1	105	7.5
258	100.0		1,400	100.0

Range: 1–71; 2,256 cases entered (1,176 with counsel named)

Wards

Counsel		Appearances	Total	
Number	Per cent	Number	Number	Per cent
2	2.7	50+	106	27.2
7	9.5	10–49	159	40.9
5	6.8	5–9	32	8.2
21	28.3	2–4	53	13.6
39	52.7	1	39	10.1
74	100.0		389	100.0

Range: 1–55; 862 cases entered (361 with counsel named)

[Table 3.1—cont. overleaf]

Table 3.1 (cont.):

Requests

Number	Per cent	Number	Number	Per cent
1	1.9	10+	23	23.0
2	3.7	5-9	11	11.0
12	22.2	2-4	27	27.0
39	72.2	1	39	39.0
54	100.0		100	100.0

Range: 1–23; 183 cases entered (93 with counsel named)

Number	Per cent	Number	Number	Per cent
3	2.7	10+	96	31.6
7	6.2	5-9	43	14.1
41	36.6	2-4	104	34.2
61	54.5	1	61	20.1
112	100.0		304	100.0

Range: 1–43; 641 cases entered (271 with counsel named)

Exchequer

Number	Per cent	Number	Number	Per cent
4	6.7	10+	65	36.3
6	10.2	5-9	34	19.0
17	28.8	2-4	48	26.8
32	54.3	1	32	17.9
59	100.0		179	100.0

Range: 1–20; 327 cases entered (134 with counsel named)

Number	Per cent	Number	Number	Per cent
8	10.1	10+	192	54.4
6	7.6	5-9	47	13.3
27	34.2	2-4	76	21.5
38	48.1	1	38	10.8
79	100.0		353	100.0

Range: 1–72; 476 cases entered (278 with counsel named)

Duchy Chamber

Number	1616 Number	1616 Per cent	1638 Number	1638 Per cent
10+	—	—	—	—
5–9	4	26.7	31	69.5
2–4	2	13.3	5	10.9
1	9	60.0	9	19.6
	15	100.0	45	100.0

Range: 1–9; 222 cases entered (46 with counsel named)

Number	Number	Per cent	Number	Per cent
10+	3	15.0	36	45.0
5–9	3	15.0	20	25.0
2–4	5	25.0	15	18.8
1	9	45.0	9	11.2
	20	100.0	80	100.0

Range: 1–15; 176 cases entered (78 with counsel named)

Sitting Dates

17 April–1 June
16 April–30 May
17 April–15 May
17 April–13 May
1 May–22 May
17 April–13 May
17 April–8 May

11 April–26 May
11 April–2 June
11 April–23 May
6 April–7 May
13 April–8 May
11 April–7 May
23 April–4 May

[1] *Sources for 1616:*
C 33/129 (A Book), fols. 629–891v
C 33/130 (B Book), fols. 544–781v
REQ 1/28, pp. 335–415
E 124/22, fols. 190–246v
E 124/23, fols. 80–200
WARD 9/535, pp. 1–201
DL 5/27, pp. 551–606

[2] *Sources for 1638:*
C 33/173 (A Book), fols. 492–666v
C 33/174 (B Book), fols. 396–530
REQ 1/79 pp. 1–365
E 125/22, fols. 343–427
E 125/23, fols. 1–119
WARD 9/552, pp. 1–209
DL 5/32, fols. 461v–490

(See also Appendix C below for counsel in Exchequer and King's Bench, 1638.)

private'. According to James Whitelocke, who had good reason to dislike both favourite and patron, it was only the aged chancellor's impotence before Buckingham's rising star which prevented him from securing a Welsh judgeship for Moore shortly before his own death in 1617.[21] Moore's closest rival in Easter term 1616 was Anthony Benn, also of the Middle Temple; while Benn was perhaps more closely linked to Buckingham than Ellesmere, his kinship by marriage to one of the Chancery's Six Clerks must also have assisted the growth of his practice in that court.[22]

Several other Chancery leaders in 1616 are readily identifiable as Ellesmere's men. They include Serjeant Thomas Chamberlain, steward of Ellesmere's midlands estates, who was shortly to be made chief justice of Chester through the chancellor's influence, and Thomas Saunderson of Lincoln's Inn, who took for his second wife a daughter of Sir Julius Caesar, master of the Rolls and one of Ellesmere's allies in the bitterly fought struggle with Sir Edward Coke which was to climax with the chief justice's suspension from office in June 1616.[23] It is indeed striking that among the eighteen men who moved twenty-five or more Chancery motions in 1616, only one member of Coke's house, the Inner Temple, can be positively identified. He was John Walter, attorney-general to Prince Charles, who was joined with the King's counsel 'learned-in-the-law' in the spring of 1616 to rule against Coke's assertion that Chancery had no right to hear appeals from King's Bench. As a Welsh judge, Walter's father had been Ellesmere's colleague on the Council in the Marches, and John himself was nominated by the chancellor as arbitrator in a dispute involving Ellesmere's lands in 1613.[24]

The significance of Sir James Ley's patronage for Henry Sherfield's career in the Court of Wards was discussed in the previous chapter. Yet Sherfield seems to have enjoyed nothing like the pre-

---

[21] CUL MS Hh. 3. 2, fol. 4ᵛ, printed in G. Jones, *History of the Law of Charity 1532–1827* (Cambridge, 1969), 244–5; J. H. Baker, 'The Common Lawyers and the Chancery: 1616', *Irish Jurist*, NS iv (1969), 380 n.; *MTR*, ii. 441–2; Whitelocke, *Lib. Fam.*, 54. Moore may have been distantly related to Ellesmere's second wife. (Cf O. Manning and W. Bray, *History and Antiquities of the County of Surrey* (1804–14), i. 626.)

[22] HMC, *Hastings*, iv. 16–17. Benn married the niece of George Evelyn, a Six Clerk from 1606 to 1635. (Appendix E below; *The Diary of John Evelyn*, ed. E. S. de Beer (Oxford, 1955), i. 136–41; Whitelocke, *Lib. Fam.*, 54.)

[23] Ellesmere 178, 233, 2185–6; *The Egerton Papers*, ed. J. P. Collier (CS, 1840), 453–4; *HS*, lii. 854.

[24] *DNB*, s.v. Walter, John; Ellesmere 233.

eminence in Wards which Moore exercised in Chancery. His nearest competitor in Easter term 1616, with eighty-four motions to Sherfield's eighty-eight, was Nicholas Cholmley, a Londoner and Inner Templar, whose success probably reflects the influence of the former clerk of Wards, John Hare (d. 1613), a close kinsman (possibly an uncle) and fellow member of the Inner Temple (where the clerk's offices were located), whose brother, Nicholas Hare, stood surety to Cholmley when the latter entered the house in 1584.[25]

While the overall pattern of practice in Chancery and Wards for Easter term 1638 still resembled a pyramid, the apex was not quite so far removed from the base, and the leading practitioners are less readily identifiable as dependants of the judges before whom they pleaded or the officials who were strategically placed to direct clients to particular counsellors. In Chancery five of the eight leading practitioners were Lincoln's Inn men, but Lord Keeper Sir Thomas Coventry was himself an Inner Templar; if indeed he showed any partiality to Serjeant John Glanville, who heads the list with fifty-nine motions, on the grounds that both were sons of former justices of Common Pleas, the consequent advantage gained by Glanville was far less spectacular than the benefits of Ellesmere's favouritism in 1616. Coventry's only other personal connection with the Chancery leaders of 1638 appears to be that his will names Sir Thomas Bedingfield, the sixth-busiest pleader, with thirty-one motions to his credit, as one of the trustees for his widow's estate.[26]

The attorney of Wards in 1638 was Sir Rowland Wandesford, an elderly bencher of Lincoln's Inn, who had been among the court's leaders in 1616 and a follower of Sir Thomas Wentworth in the 1620s, but who had received no significant preferment until he was suddenly knighted and raised to the attorneyship in 1637, where he remained until the court's abolition by the Long Parliament.[27] The Wards leader in 1638 was a Mr Morgan, presumably the same barrister described in 1632 as favourite of the then attorney Sir Walter Pye, and hence most likely William Morgan of Brecon and the Middle Temple, who acted as surety for several students

[25] Above, pp. 30–4. *ITAdmR*, 205; Bell, *Court of Wards*, 26–7, 172; *H. of P.*, ii. 251–3.
[26] For a posthumous accusation that Coventry took bribes from litigants, as well as presents from favourites, see above, p. 29. *DNB*, s.v. Coventry, Thomas Lord; Glanville, Sir John. PCC 1 Coventry.
[27] CUL MS Add. 6863, fols. 88ᵛ–89; *Wentworth Papers 1597–1628*, ed. J. P. Cooper (CS, 1973), 201.

admitted to the house by Pye's favour in 1618 and 1621.[28] There is no apparent link between Morgan and Wandesford, nor between Wandesford and Edward Bysshe, the second-ranking counsel with fifty-one motions, other than that both men sat on the bench of Lincoln's Inn and possibly shared a mildly puritanical religious outlook.[29] Wandesford's influence was perhaps less significant than that of the court's senior officials, Sir Miles Fleetwood, Sir Benjamin Rudyerd, and Richard Chamberlain. But despite a political affiliation at least between Fleetwood and Robert Reynolds, the third most-practised counsellor (both sat for the double-member Wiltshire borough of Hindon in the Long Parliament), no patronage nexus comparable to that operated by Ley and Hare under James I is discernible in 1638.[30]

In the Court of Requests, on the other hand, the role of judicial favouritism was plainly no less significant in the Caroline than the Jacobean period. The leading counsellor in 1616, with twenty-three recorded motions to his nearest rival's six, was Ralph Wilbraham of Lincoln's Inn, whose elder brother Sir Roger sat as one of the masters of Requests from 1600 until his death in July 1616. In 1638 the pre-eminent practiser, in a by now far busier court, was Robert Barnard of the Middle Temple, recorder of Huntingdon and steward to Viscount Mandeville, whose father, Sir Henry Montagu, first earl of Manchester and lord privy seal, personally presided over the court's sittings during the 1630s, and whose uncle, Sir Sidney Montagu, served as a master of Requests from 1616 to 1640.[31]

The equity side of the Exchequer seems also to have enjoyed a substantial upturn in its popularity with litigants by Easter term 1638, when the court's undisputed leader was William Lenthall,

---

[28] Smith, ed., *Calendar of Salusbury Correspondence*, 79–80; *MTR*, ii. 630, 663, 668; Keeler, 279–81.

[29] Ibid., 124. Bysshe was fined for serving flesh during his Lent reading in 1632. (*LIBB*, ii. 303.) Wandesford played a significant part in rebuilding LI chapel, and served as its dean from 1638 to 1650; his daughter married the puritan peer Philip, Lord Wharton, who in 1652 presented LI with a silver plate in memory of 'my deceased father in law'. (Ibid., 199, 204, 349, 389, 394; G. F. Jones, *Saw-Pit Wharton*, Sydney, 1967, 17.)

[30] Keeler, 178–9, 322; J. K. Gruenfelder, *Influence in Early Stuart Elections 1604–1640* (Columbus, Ohio, 1981), 194, suggests that Cottington, master of the Wards, was responsible for both Hindon returns in 1640.

[31] *The Journal of Sir Roger Wilbraham*, ed. H. S. Scott, *Camden Miscellany*, x (1902), v–viii; *HS*, lix. 260; Leadam, ed., *Requests*, xlvi. 1; Hunts. RO, M28/1/33–4. Manchester named Barnard ('my loving and trusty friend') as joint executor of his will. (PCC 47 Rivers.)

future Speaker of the Long Parliament, who moved three times as often as any other counsellor. While Lenthall seems not to have had any close personal ties with Chief Baron Sir Humphrey Davenport, the establishment of his Exchequer practice after his call to the bar of Lincoln's Inn in 1616 must have owed a good deal to the favour of his uncle, Chief Baron Sir Lawrence Tanfield, who presided over the court from 1607 until his death in 1625.[32] Lenthall had no real counterpart in 1616, when the distribution of motions was more evenly shared among a smaller group of leaders, notably Edmond Prideaux, James Weston, and Sir John Jackson. Jackson may or may not have been still experiencing the benefit of his marriage to the eldest daughter of Sir John Savile, a fellow Yorkshireman who served as one of the puisne barons of Exchequer from 1598 to 1607; perhaps more significant is the fact that Prideaux, Weston, and Jackson, like Tanfield, all hailed from the Inner Temple, as did the members of the Fanshawe family, who successively held the court's key administrative office of king's remembrancer in the early seventeenth century.[33]

Finally we come to the Court of Duchy Chamber, presided over by the chancellor of the Duchy of Lancaster, which held plea of lands parcel of the Duchy, whether located within or outside the county palatine. Very much a regional court, its bar was monopolized by counsellors from Gray's Inn, where the court's administrative offices were established, and where the counties of Lancashire and Yorkshire were particularly strongly represented. The most prominent pleaders were generally men who themselves held Duchy office, such as the leader in 1616, Thomas Ireland of Bewsey, Lancashire, king's counsel in the Duchy throughout James I's reign; Sir Thomas Tildesley of Wardley, Lancashire, who was appointed serjeant at law and king's attorney in the Duchy in 1604 and vice-chancellor two years later; and Alexander Rigby of Burgh, Lancashire, who first served with, then succeeded his father as clerk of the Crown at Lancaster from 1604 until his death c.1650.[34]

---

[32] *DNB*, s.v. Tanfield, Sir Lawrence. Tanfield appointed 'my nephew William Lenthall of Lincoln's Inn' as overseer of his will, made 21 Mar. 1625. (PCC 45 Clarke.)

[33] *The Visitation of the County of Yorke begun . . .* 1665, ed. R. Davies (Surtees Soc., 1859), 5. Weston, the nephew of an Elizabethan judge, became a baron of the Exchequer in 1631. (Foss, vi. 373.) For the Fanshawes, see Bryson, *Equity Side of the Exchequer*, 67–70.

[34] Somerville, *Office Holders*, 50, 54, 104. However, it is difficult to distinguish Rigby from his namesake, also a GI barrister, clerk of the peace for Lancs. 1608–27

iii. Pleaders and Signers

There seems no reason to doubt that the highly uneven distribution of practice revealed by Table 3.1 was typical of the other central courts (and the assizes) for which no evidence directly comparable to the entry books has survived. If so, only a small fraction of the bar's total membership could have earned a living from the ten or twenty shilling fees commonly paid for the services of advocates in Westminster Hall and on the assize circuits. For most barristers attempting to establish a practice, the importance of finding and exploiting alternative sources of professional earnings must therefore have been very great indeed.[35]

One obvious possibility was practice in the numerous local and subordinate jurisdictions discussed in the first section of this chapter. Yet apart from the bars of the two regional councils, together with the special cases of the four common pleaders in the City and the four counsellors attached to the Court of the Marshalsea, it seems unlikely that the opportunities for advocacy in these lesser courts could have provided many men with anything other than a small and supplementary source of income. At the same time, the pickings they offered were by no means to be sneezed at, especially by those at the outset of their careers, and may well have become steadily more attractive as the numbers of counsel seeking work continued to expand throughout our period.

The second main professional alternative to advocacy in Westminster Hall and the assizes was general out-of-court work, obviously so miscellaneous and heterogeneous in character as to have left little more than random traces on the historical record. The only potentially quantifiable information is provided by barrister's signatures to pleadings exhibited before the English-bill courts. There are formidable difficulties in retrieving this data for systematic analysis, but T. G. Barnes has recovered the names of some 1,250

and MP for Wigan in the Long Parliament. (*DNB*, s.v. Rigby, Alexander; Keeler, 325; *The Lancashire Lieutenancy under the Tudors and Stuarts*, ed. J. Harland (Chetham Soc., 1859), 275 n.

[35] For fees, see below, ch. 5, sect. iii. Professor Cockburn has claimed that early seventeenth-century barristers 'regarded circuit work as their principal means of support'. (*History of English Assizes*, 143.) However, apart from Christopher Brooke's statement late in February 1602 that 'I am held from the sitting at York ... where ... my profitablest practice lies', which might equally well refer to the Council of the North as to the assizes at York, I know of no evidence to support this assertion. (R. Davies, 'Communication', Yorkshire Philosophical Society, *Annual Report* (1872), 3.)

barristers who signed Star Chamber pleadings during the twenty-two years of James I's reign. In Easter term 1616, ninety-five bills and informations were exhibited in Star Chamber, signed by a total of seventy-four different counsellors; Francis Bacon signed nine times as attorney-general, and fifty-one barristers signed once only. About a third of these Star Chamber signers do not appear as pleaders in any English-bill court during this same term.[36] A few may have pleaded without their names being recorded in the entry books. On the other hand some 10 per cent of those mentioned as pleaders in other English-bill courts during Easter term 1616 seem not to have signed a single bill or answer in Star Chamber over the whole of James I's reign. While most Star Chamber non-signers were not professionally eminent, they do include one moderately well-practised Chancery advocate, Thomas Parmenter, who had twenty motions to his credit in Easter term 1616, as well as William Dyos, remembrancer of London; Deane Tindall, son of a master in Chancery; and Thomas Woodward, who became a bencher of Lincoln's Inn in 1620.[37]

So while advocacy and the signing of pleadings were not mutually exclusive activities, it cannot be assumed that a barrister who signed pleadings in one court was generally active as an advocate in other jurisdictions, or vice versa: some degree of jurisdictional specialization evidently characterized all types of practice at the bar, not just advocacy alone. Unfortunately the loss of the Star Chamber entry books makes it impossible to determine whether those who signed bills exhibited in that court were also retained as counsel for the parties concerned when their suits came to hearing. This line of investigation is theoretically feasible for the other English-bill courts, where entry books and files of original pleadings have both survived, although the task is complicated by gaps in the pleadings and inadequate indexes.[38] However, a small sample of pleadings has

---

[36] Signers of Star Chamber bills not represented in the entry books for Easter term 1616 were Barkesdale, J. (LI), Barnewell, J. (GI), Bramston, J. (MT), Chetwinde, J. (GI), Clopton, W. (GI), Cooke, T. (GI), Courtman, J. (LI), Darrell, W. (GI), Faldoe, R. (GI), Ferrour, J. (GI), Flud or Lloyd, E. (IT?), Ford(e) or Foulz, T. (MT?), Hyde, N. (MT), Maynard, W. (LI), Meade, J. (LI), Merefield, J. (IT), Parker, R. (MT), Pyndar, M. (GI), Risden, T. (IT), Stoforde, G. (IT), Trist, T. (MI), Tynte, E. (MT), Walsh, H. (MT), and Wildegose, A. (LI).

[37] I gratefully acknowledge Professor Barnes's help with this paragraph. For Dyos and Tindall, see below, Appendix D; for Woodward, see Appendix E.

[38] Cf. M. Dowling, 'The Equity Side of Chancery 1558–1714', *Rev. of English Studies*, viii (1932), 185–200; R. W. Coldham, 'Genealogical Research in Chancery Records', *Genealogist's Magazine*, xix (1979), 345–7.

been examined for cases on which motions were made by named counsel in Chancery during Easter term 1615 (the year prior to that used as the basis for the statistics in Table 3.1 above).

It was necessary to search over two hundred and twenty case entries to locate forty-seven for which some pleadings survive. Of these only twenty permit comparison of the barrister signing with the barrister appearing for a particular party, where the pleadings are dated no more than two years before the beginning of Easter term 1615. (This last condition serves to reduce the likelihood that the lawyer who had signed a pleading was unavailable to represent the party concerned, because of death or promotion to the judicial bench, perhaps, by the time the suit eventually came into court.) The pleadings in these twenty cases bear the signatures of thirty-three individual practitioners, a few of whom signed more than once. In only six instances did the same lawyer both sign a litigant's pleading and subsequently appear for that party in court (Table 3.2). Indeed nearly half of those who signed do not figure at all in the Chancery entry book record for Easter term 1615. The signers fall into three broad categories: leading or very well-practised Chancery advocates, such as Thomas Chamberlain, Thomas Crew, Francis Moore, John Walter, and possibly Christopher Brooke; generally active and/or senior lawyers, including Anthony Dyot and George Croke of the Inner Temple, a trio of serjeants (Thomas Athow, Charles Chibborne, and Francis Harvey), Attorney-General Bacon, Robert Callis, and William Holt of Gray's Inn; finally, a large mixed bag of relatively unpractised men, both old and young, as well as several enigmatic signatories who cannot be traced in the records of any inn of court and were quite possibly not barristers at all. This third group of twenty includes five men who eventually reached the bench of their inn, one future all-but serjeant (Timothy Leving), who died just after receiving his writ of election in 1636, and another who later served as a master of Chancery (William Hakewill). But the majority achieved not even a modest standing in their profession, although only five of the fifteen whose careers can be traced were of less than ten years' standing at the bar when they signed the pleadings.

Together with the individual case-studies presented in Chapter Two above, the evidence just surveyed encourages some tentative generalizations about the distribution of practice at the early modern bar. To begin with, advocacy was evidently a highly specialized and stratified activity. Among the hundreds who pleaded

Table 3.2. Chancery Counsel, Signers and Pleaders, Easter Term 1615[1]

Suit	Counsel for plaintiff(s)		Counsel for defendant(s)	
	Signed pleadings	Appeared at bar	Signed pleadings	Appeared at bar
Saunders v. Woodward	Sjt. Chamberlain, Sjt. Harvey	Sjt. Harvey	C. Brooke, G. Croke, W. Hakewill, H. Johnson, F. Foe (?)	Martin, Ware
Huntingdon v. Harpur	Bacon, Att.-Gen. et al. W. Jones	Sjt. Chamberlain	—	—
Owen v. Harris	—	Thomas	—	—
Vernon v. Cock	—	—	Sjt. Chibborne	T. Saunderson
Elston v. dean and canons of Westminster	—	—	J. Whitmore, Sjt. F. Moore	Sjt. F. Moore
Cole v. Cole	T. Risden	Sjt. J. Moore	W. Darrell	Sjt. Montagu
Sheldon v. Dormer	Sjt. Chamberlain	Sjt. Chamberlain	T. Tesdale, T. Jones	Sjt. F. Moore
Sutton v. Hudson	—	T. Crew, A. Benn, T. Saunderson[2]	—	—
Michell v. Dalby	T. Henshawe	T. Saunderson	—	—
Peplowe v. Rowley	F. Clyve	—	—	—
Lascelles v. Ogle	A. Dyot	A. Dyot	W. Davye, W. Maye	Sjt. Chamberlain
Upton v. Reade	—	Sjt. G. Wilde	—	—
Halton v. Dean	R. Callis	Sjt. Athow	—	—
Brampton v. Reade	Sjt. Athow	—	N. Holbourn	Sjt. Chamberlain
Golding v. Francis	—	T. Coventry	—	—
Jarret v. Hicks	R. Daston Parsons	Hale	—	—
Lavelis v. Short	—	Michell	H. Berkeley, S. Peck	Stapleton
Strelley v. Beaumont	J. Walter, W. Holt	—	R. Swayne	Sjt. Montagu
Sheldon v. Daston	—	—	—	—
Hollins v. Powre	Sjt. Chamberlain	Sjt. Chamberlain	—	—

[1] *Sources:* C33/128, fols. 861–937; C2/Jac. I, various.
[2] Assigned *in forma pauperis*.

at the various bars of Westminster Hall, and probably in the provinces as well, a small minority of counsellors handled most of the available business. Second, while each court was dominated by one or two leaders, who rarely ventured outside this jurisdiction, the bulk of the remaining work was shared among a 'sub-bar', consisting both of slightly less eminent specialists and of lawyers with substantial practices extending over several courts. So, for example, in Easter term 1616 the ten leading Chancery advocates included three men (Anthony Benn, Thomas Saunderson, and Francis Williamson) who seem not to have appeared in any other court during that term, along with two more, Richard Dover and John Towneley, both from Gray's Inn, who signed enough Star Chamber pleadings to be classified as members of that court's sub-bar, but were not otherwise active (although Towneley moved once in Requests).[39] Among the remaining five, John Walter, Sir Henry Yelverton (respectively attorney-general to the Prince of Wales and solicitor-general) and Phillip Gerrard each appeared several times as advocates in other English-bill courts, while Walter signed three and Yelverton one Star Chamber bill during Easter term 1616. Serjeants Francis Moore and Sir Randle Crew, the first and third busiest Chancery advocates, also kept up a presence in Common Pleas; but whereas Crew appeared as well in Duchy Chamber, Wards, and Exchequer, Moore's name is not found in the entry books of any other English-bill court for this term. Here Moore was atypical, for the serjeants at law stand out as the most prominent group of generally practised counsel. Only four of the seventeen serjeants do not figure in more than one English-bill court (quite apart from their role in Common Pleas and presumably, if to a lesser extent, King's Bench) during Easter term 1616 (as compared with just over one-third of the total body of barristers listed). Nevertheless, it appears that even these relatively generalist pleaders normally concentrated their appearances in one, or at most two, jurisdictions. Thus Sir Laurence Hyde, the third-ranking Wards counsellor in 1616, appeared also in Chancery on twenty-three occasions, but only once each in Duchy Chamber and Requests. Third, and finally, a clear majority of barristers listed in the entry books moved a mere handful of motions each term, and appeared in no more than one central court; just eight of the fifty-two pleaders recorded as having moved

---

[39] Again, I thank Professor Barnes for amplifying his comments in *LRH*, 26.

once only in Chancery during Easter term 1616 show up in any other English-bill court during that same term.

How far was the division between in-court pleading and out-of-court counselling one of personnel as well as function? There was clearly no watertight division between 'movers' and 'signers'. Some very well-practised advocates—for example, Chamberlain and Moore in Chancery—were also prominent as signatories to pleadings in Chancery (and Star Chamber, in Moore's case), although of course one cannot determine whether they were personally responsible for drafting all the documents which bear their signatures. On the other hand, a small sample of Chancery pleadings indicates that the majority of those who signed were not prominent as advocates in that court; indeed, almost half do not appear at all in the relevant entry books.

Contemporaries certainly regarded advocacy as more demanding than chamber work or general counselling. There are several recorded instances of barristers, and even benchers, conducting the overall management of their clients' suits (in a fashion which would later come to be regarded as appropriate to an attorney rather than a learned counsellor), but retaining and instructing specialist advocates to plead the case when it came to hearing.[40] We may also recall that drawing up Chancery bills and answers was seen as the way 'most of the young lawyers nowadays . . . begin their practice'. But the 'orator at the bar hath much the start of a chamber man', in the words of a biographer of Lord Coventry, successively solicitor-general and attorney-general to James I, then lord keeper from 1625 to 1640, explaining how his subject 'first began to grow into the name of an active and pregnant man'.[41] It was precisely the dominance of the bar by such 'great practisers' which drew protests from those less successful, among them the radical Independent pamphleteer John Cooke of Gray's Inn, who later served as solicitor-general at the trial of Charles I and in 1646 depicted his colleagues as 'stirring up and down in our gowns, making men believe that we are full of employment; and so we are indeed in a

---

[40] Lancs. RO, DDke 9/9/38; HMC, *Fifth Rep.*, 418b; HMC, *Buccleuch and Queensberry*, iii. 308, 310–11, 316; HMC, *Longleat*, iv. 137. Barristers occasionally prepared briefs for other counsel to argue. (Cf. Berks. RO, D/ELI C1/48.)

[41] See above, p. 16; IT MS Petyt 538. 17, fol. 361ᵛ; cf. D'Ewes's characterization of Nicholas Hyde as being 'of mean esteem, having a small estate and practising chiefly in his chamber'. (*The Autobiography and Correspondence of Sir Simonds D'Ewes, Bart.*, ed. J. O. Halliwell (1845), ii. 48.)

perpetual motion, measuring the length of the Hall, but not a motion perhaps from the first day of the term to the last'. Cooke maintained that

> if the termers, and such counsel as draw bills and answers, and advise in the country, might be heard at the bar as often as the cause required, then would not many of the great practisers be retained, until the hearing of the cause, or upon some special difficulty; but now the client is enforced to have one counsel in the country, in the vacation, and another in the term to his double charge, or else may chance to attend all the term before his counsel can be heard.[42]

iv. Too many barristers?

But did the problem merely arise, as Cooke thought, from an inequitable distribution of work at the bar? Or was there rather a more fundamental crisis of professional overcrowding, with too many barristers chasing too little work? The answers to these questions are crucial to our understanding of the general condition of the legal profession in the early seventeenth century. It has been claimed that a surplus of trained manpower across all the learned professions of early Stuart England produced a generation of 'alienated intellectuals', whose frustrated career expectations led them to challenge the established order in both Church and State, with momentous consequences for the whole course of English history. Yet a more recent view denies that 'supply ever outran demand' as far as the upper branch of the legal profession was concerned; rather, the booming opportunities for lawyers during the century before the Civil War more than kept pace with the numerical growth of the bar, besides supporting a large underworld of 'cowboy' practitioners, whose disreputable activities largely explain the widespread dissatisfaction with the legal system during our period.[43]

'Overcrowding' is a loose and relative concept, especially in relation to independent practitioners serving a mass of individual clients, rather than, say, clergymen or bureaucrats, whose careers depend upon the availability of benefices or offices. Nevertheless, it might be agreed that an occupation is fairly described as overcrowded when demand for the services it provides and the size of its

---

[42] J. Cooke, *The Vindication of the Professors and Profession of the Law* (1646), 40; *idem, Unum Necessarium* (1648), 67.

[43] M. H. Curtis, 'The Alienated Intellectuals of Early Stuart England', in *Crisis in Europe 1560–1660*, ed. T. Aston (1965), 295–316; Clark, *Provincial Society*, 279–84.

effective membership are so finely balanced that any growth in the latter will diminish the per capita income of the entire work-force. Regrettably, if hardly surprisingly, the surviving evidence is far too scattered to permit statistical analysis of trends in average earnings among early modern barristers. We are therefore forced to rely upon indirect means of gauging the demand-supply balance at the bar during our period.

Here care must be taken to distinguish the effects of short-term fluctuations in the demand for lawyers' services from long-term changes in the structure of legal practice, or overcrowding as such. Because the supply of lawyers was relatively inelastic, owing to the long period of preparation required before men were admitted to plead in the courts, even acute short-term crises of unemployment or under-employment for barristers (such as occurred in the late 1540s, for example, or again a century later during the Civil War) do not necessarily indicate that the profession was overcrowded, in the sense that the supply of services provided by its members exceeded the average or 'normal' level of demand. In other words, we should try to avoid confusing temporary dislocations on the demand side with deep-rooted or 'structural' overcrowding, although the distinction is perhaps ultimately one of degree rather than kind.[44] Second, while overcrowding might exacerbate inequities in the distribution of work and fees among members of the practising bar, the mere existence of such imbalances obviously does not in itself constitute evidence of overcrowding. Even if the favour of judges and court officers had not enabled those whom Cooke called 'great monopolists, impropriators of practice' to enjoy the lion's share of business at the bar in the late sixteenth and early seventeenth centuries, the personal qualities which made for success as a pleader could hardly have been evenly distributed throughout the profession. This was acknowledged by the attorneys and clients who brought their briefs to the busiest barristers: 'if any be well followed with clients, he shall have many more for that only reason', an informed contemporary observed. In condemning what they took to be the evil effects of judicial and bureaucratic favouritism, John Cooke and others who shared his views were actually indicting a competitive, individualistic mode of practice at the bar.[45]

[44] Cf. W. M. Kotschnig, *Unemployment in the Learned Professions* (Oxford, 1937), 165, and ch. 5, *passim*.
[45] Cooke, *Vindication*, 41; SP 14/99/177, fol. 5ᵛ.

Such calls to redress the inequitable distribution of legal practice may sometimes have embodied an element of self-interest. Yet they also reflected a traditional concern which subordinated economic imperatives to broader moral and social considerations. The principle that the welfare of both consumer and producer necessitated curbing the potential for a few to make disproportionate gains, in order to safeguard the livelihood of all engaged in a particular calling, was still occasionally brought forward during our period to defend the restrictive practices of craft guilds and trading companies. But its adherents were fighting a losing battle against a new economic and social order.[46]

The medieval legal profession had been in effect a guild, whose journeyman members practised their trade within the narrow compass of the ancient common-law courts, under the oversight of a body of masters, the judges and serjeants at law. The dominance of the 'order of the coif' depended upon a congruence of rank, seniority, academic learning, courtroom skills, and earning power. Promotion to this fraternity by royal writ was not only a mark of honour, but also gave the recipient access to the lucrative business of the realm's busiest jurisdiction, the Court of Common Pleas; according to Fortescue, there was no 'advocate in the whole world who enriches himself by reason of his office as much as the serjeant'.[47] Even if some serjeants enjoyed larger Common Pleas practices than others, the range could not have been very wide, since the number of competitors was small and readily regulated, while their fees were fixed by custom. Moreover, economic inequalities may well have been substantially offset by the highest status accorded every member of the order and the sense of mutual interdependence engendered by their corporate life both in and out of court.

We still know very little about the organization of medieval legal practice outside Common Pleas. But it seems likely that one implicit function of the learning exercise system at the inns of court, with its elaborate hierarchy of double and single readers, inner and outer barristers, was to control the numbers of 'apprentices' practising in the lesser common-law courts, as well as to ensure that men of greater seniority enjoyed the competitive advantage of pre-audience

[46] Cf. R. H. Tawney, *Religion and the Rise of Capitalism* (1927), 26–8; E. Lipson, *The Economic History of England* (2nd edn, 1934), ii. 224, 237–8.

[47] *DLLA*, 124–5. Cf. Baker, 'Legal Profession', 18–19; Ives, *Common Lawyers*, 64–6, 323–8: the 1523 subsidy assessment, which rated serjeants on lands, fees, or goods, seems not to have distinguished legal from other sources of income.

over their juniors. (Thus, according to Robert Brerewood, writing in the 1630s, 'a reader was wont to have that respect, to be heard in the King's Bench and other courts of justice, before others'.)[48]

During the sixteenth century the rising demand for legal services in the various jurisdictions, old and new, which were beginning to challenge the hegemony of the 'palladium of the coif', created unprecedented professional opportunities for the apprentices of the inns of court, including some who had barely begun to argue moots *'ouster le barre'*. Despite attempts from the 1530s onwards to prevent such *imperitii* from appearing as advocates in Westminster Hall, the minimum standing required of an utter-barrister before he could plead in open court progressively declined. In 1614 the judges sought for the last time, with no more success than before, to impose a fixed annual quota on calls to the bar. Henceforth entry to the upper branch would be regulated by market forces alone, just as counsellors were now free to charge whatever fees their clients were prepared to pay.[49]

The rise of the barristers paralleled the decline of the serjeants at law. The serjeants' former pre-eminence in terms of status and wealth was increasingly relinquished to the Crown's law officers and other counsellors whose high professional standing simply reflected their functional ability as advocates, whether based on innate talent, family connections, or a combination of both. So it is hardly surprising that while the bar continued to be widely regarded as a high road to fame and fortune, from the 1580s complaints are heard that a few counsellors 'carry multitudes before them', linked with proposals intended to ensure 'though that some of them should not grow so exceedingly rich, yet a far greater number should be employed in mediocrity of good fortune, who deserve as well as those that carry away the vanity of the people by their pertinacity of wit and boldness of tongue'.[50]

---

[48] MT MS Brerewood, 29; the author continues, 'But I have heard some of them complain, that of late years they have lost much of that respect, by reason of the favours and kindred of judges.'

[49] *LJ*, i. 151–2; cf. G. R. Elton, *Reform and Renewal* (Cambridge, 1973), 156. The 1546 proclamation providing that none but readers might plead at Westminster was perhaps similarly motivated. (*Tudor Royal Proclamations*, ed. P. L. Hughes and J. F. Larkin (New Haven, 1964–9), i. 371–2, 408–9.) Cf. also the attempted closing of the Star Chamber bar to non-readers, above, p. 13. For fees, see below, ch. 5, sect. iv.

[50] Lansdowne 44, fol. 2; cf. T. Wilson, 'The State of England Anno Dom. 1600', ed. F. J. Fisher, *Camden Miscellany*, xvi (1936), 24–5; Anon., *A Memorable Speech in the House of Commons, 1611* (1612?), 13.

These comments might seem to be clear evidence of the bar having reached saturation point by the late sixteenth century, especially when taken in conjunction with widespread accusations that an excess of lawyers was the prime cause behind what contemporaries saw as an excessive growth of litigation. Yet the claim that there were simply too many lawyers was hardly novel. While often a blanket charge, it seems in our period to have been more usually directed against the proliferation of attorneys, solicitors, and miscellaneous pettifoggers, rather than at the socially better-accepted upper branch.[51] Nor was the undoubted fact of 'practice being drawn into a few hands of those which are most renowned, [while] all the rest live by pettifogging' an unambiguous symptom of overcrowding, rather than the inevitable corollary of unrestricted individual competition.[52] As we shall see shortly, the gap between the most and the least successful competitors at the bar very likely widened during the early seventeenth century, but it still remains to be shown that a state of overcrowding, strictly defined, existed before the end of our period.

In point of fact the bar-call statistics tend to support an opposite conclusion. Since contemporaries were little better informed than we are about changes in the average income of barristers, the real market situation cannot have been much clearer to them than it is to us. They did possess, however, the undeniable advantage of personally experiencing conditions which the historian can know only at second hand. So it is reasonable to suppose that the rate at which new entrants were recruited reflects not just the perceived prospects of individuals aspiring to a career at the bar, but also the actual balance between demand for, and supply of, those services which barristers performed. In other words, as and when the bar reached saturation point, with too little work available to satisfy all those able and willing to undertake it, the numbers called should have tended to decline accordingly.

Of course recruitment to the bar can at best be only a rough-and-ready yardstick. Career choices involve discrimination among the attractions of a changing menu of possibilities. In this process, narrow economic criteria may be outweighed by other factors, such

[51] Ellesmere 2029, fol. 11; Brooks, thesis, 61–2, 75–80; E. W. Ives, 'The Reputation of the Common Lawyers in English Society, 1450–1550', Univ. of Birmingham Hist. J., vii (1959–60), 142–3, 146–7.
[52] Wilson, 'State of England', 24–5.

as family tradition, the status of different occupations, and the nature of the work involved; potential entrants may be reckless, ill informed, or both. Nor is there any sure way of knowing how many of the men called to the bar during our period actually pursued their profession or for how long. Among the sample of 115 barristers chosen for close investigation in this study, at least eight (over six per cent) seem never to have practised at all or soon abandoned the bar, while a further seven died within five years of their call. In the former group were the noted antiquary William Burton, who explains in the preface to his *Description of Leicestershire* (1622) that, 'through the weak constitution of my body, not being able to follow that practice which my calling did require [I] have now retired my self to a private country life'; Thomas Croke, eldest son and heir of the judge Sir George Croke, who was called in 1635, but seems to have abandoned practice, if indeed he ever started by the time his father made a will in 1641, whereby he inherited the family estates, but not his father's legal library; Sir John Bourchier, a younger son who came unexpectedly into a substantial inheritance when his elder brother died three years after he himself was called to the bar; John Ayshcombe, who inherited two Berkshire manors a decade after his call; Henry Ley, who succeeded to the earldom of Marlborough in 1629, having been given the honorific rank of associate bencher only four years after his call at Lincoln's Inn in 1616; Lawrence Hyde, called in 1637, who described himself as a merchant eight years later; and, finally, two barrister knights from Gray's Inn, Sir John Honeywood and Sir Henry Palmer of Kent.[53] While these and others

---

[53] Burton, *Description*, 'To the Reader', sig. ¶2ᵛ; A. Croke, *The Genealogical History of the Croke Family* (1823), i. 604; *DNB*, s.v. Croke, Sir George. *VCH, Yorks. (NR)*, ii. 162–3; cf. Leeds District Archives, TN PO8/III/9. C. G. Durston, 'Berkshire and its County Gentry 1625–1649', University of Reading Ph.D. thesis, 1977, ii. 1–3, finds no 'evidence that [Ayshcombe] augmented [his] estate revenue with money from other sources'. In 1630 Marlborough's chamber was impounded because of his absence from the house. (*LIBB*, ii. 188, 217, 295, 299.) *The House of Commons 1660–1690*, ed. B. D. Henning (1983), ii. 630–1. Honeywood, who was called in 1614, appears on Barnes's list of counsel signing Jacobean Star Chamber pleadings, but probably gave up practice on inheriting his father's estates in 1622. (E. Hasted, *A History or Topographical Survey of . . . Kent* (1797–1801), viii. 38.) Palmer, eldest son of an impoverished Kentish knight and office-holder, was called to the bar in 1638 at Sir John Finch's request, and himself knighted in 1642. (*GIPB*, i. 329; *HS*, xlii. 107; *Oxinden Letters, 1607–1642*, ed. Gardiner, 289–90.) For other non-practising barristers, see Clendinnen, 17; H. A. Wyndham, *A Family History* (1939), 148; R. Gough, *The History of Myddle*, ed. D. Hey (Harmondsworth, 1981), 38; *DNB*, s.v. Grimston, Harbottle.

like them may occasionally have advised friends, conciliated quarrelsome neighbours, or drafted a legal instrument, their life-style, income, and status appear to have derived primarily from their landed estates, and they provided no serious competition to their nominal professional colleagues.

Nevertheless, when all possible qualifications are taken into account, the bar-call statistics plainly indicate that throughout our period, and well into the later seventeenth century, the upper branch of the legal profession both was, and was seen to be, undermanned rather than overcrowded. The recorded decennial totals of calls to the bar at the four inns of court rose progressively between the 1580s and the 1660s. True, the rate of increase was not uniform; there was little growth between the first and second decades of our period, and actually a slight decline in the 1620s, followed by a recovery which only just surpassed the level achieved in the 1610s. But the overall tendency continued upwards, and although it peaked in the 1660s, not until the last decade of the seventeenth century did the numbers called finally drop below the level reached during the years of Charles I's personal rule.[54] So John Cooke's pessimistic prophecy that 'the excessive gains of some lawyers, and others gaining nothing in comparison, if not timely remedied will be the destruction of our profession' remained unfulfilled. Contrary to his prediction, men did not 'give over studying the law when they see the practice is engrossed, for no wise man will venture his money at a lottery'. As Adam Smith would point out over a century later, while a career in the law was indeed a lottery, this hardly discouraged all those 'generous and liberal spirits' who possessed 'the natural confidence which every man has, more or less, not only in his own abilities, but in his own good fortune'.[55]

Yet if the continued flow of new recruits suggests that the early seventeenth-century bar may not have been overcrowded in a strict sense, there seems equally little doubt that the tide was turning against aspiring barristers during the pre-Civil War decades. On the demand side, the land market, a key generator and indicator of legal activity, apparently peaked in the 1610s and declined steadily

[54] See Table 1.1 above. Decennial totals of bar calls 1640–99 kindly supplied by Mr R. Pearce, formerly of St John's College, Cambridge, are as follows: 1640–9, 523; 1650–9, 561; 1660–9, 714; 1670–9, 646; 1680–9, 624; 1690–9, 475. Cf. G. Holmes, *Augustan England: Professions State and Society 1680–1730* (1983), 288–9.

[55] Cooke, *Vindication*, 42; A. Smith, *The Wealth of Nations*, ed. E. Cannan (1904), i. 107–8.

thereafter. By reducing disposable incomes, the economic downturn whose onset roughly coincided with the outbreak of the Thirty Years War in 1618 must have tended to check consumer propensity to go to law; hard times may have created more work for some lawyers, but also presumably exacerbated the difficulties of young men trying to establish themselves in practice. Certainly the volume of litigation handled by Common Pleas and King's Bench grew at a markedly slower rate between 1606 and 1640 than between 1580 and 1606. Business in Star Chamber and, especially, Chancery (where it was claimed, perhaps with pardonable exaggeration, 'the causes are many more than in any court of justice') seems actually to have declined during the 1620s and 30s. Nor were these losses more than partially offset by the gains of rival jurisdictions, such as the Court of Requests.[56]

Although the figures in Table 3.1 above suggest that of the English-bill courts with surviving entry books, only Chancery and Duchy Chamber experienced a net shrinkage in business between 1616 and 1638, the recorded drop in Chancery entries still exceeds the gains of Exchequer, Requests, and Wards put together. Equally important, Table 3.1 also indicates massive increases in the numbers of counsel appearing before every court (except Wards) at the later date. The scale of this expansion is fully revealed when the names of all pleaders mentioned in the entry books are consolidated according to the procedures outlined above, producing a total of 296 individual practitioners for Easter term 1616, and no fewer than 389 for Easter term 1638. Of course these figures ignore counsel pleading before Star Chamber, the three common-law courts of Westminster Hall, and the assizes. Nor is there any systematic means of remedying the omission. Reports of cases taken by barristers and students at the time of hearing provide nothing like a comprehensive coverage, and while many have been published, more remain widely scattered in manuscript form; worst of all, the names of the lawyers whose arguments they report are as often as not omitted. Where counsel are named, they almost invariably turn out to be men who already figure in the entry books; for example, a search of published

---

[56] L. Stone, *The Crisis of the Aristocracy 1558–1641* (Oxford, 1965), 36–7; Barnes, 'Star Chamber Litigants', 28; Additional 41613, fol. 87; Brooks, 'Litigants and Attorneys', 43; Table 3.1 above; *Requests*, ed. Leadam, xlvi. 1; *HEL*, i. 415; R. Coke, *Detection of Church and State* (1694), i. 388. Cf. S. F. Black, 'The Judges of Westminster Hall, 1640–1660', Oxford University B.Litt. thesis, 1970, 83, for continued decline of Chancery business to 1640.

law reports covering Easter term 1616 yielded the names of a mere
two counsellors not previously identified.[57] Assize cases were rarely
reported during this period, and the surviving Western circuit order
books (admittedly by no means a complete record of business,
especially on the *nisi prius* side) show among thirteen counsel named
as movers during the Lent and Summer circuits of 1638 only two
who do not figure in the English-bill entry books for Easter term of
that year.[58]

While we do not know what relation counsel named in the entry
books bore to the entire practising bar, it seems likely that most
barristers who practised in the ancient common-law courts or on the
assize circuits also appeared at least once a term before Chancery or
one of the other English-bill courts whose records survive. Yet the
critical question is not how many more barristers might be identified
if only there were full records for all the central and superior courts,
but whether the relative proportions of practitioners in English-bill
courts and elsewhere were the same in 1638 as they had been twenty-
two years earlier. There is nothing to suggest that this was not the
case, nor that any significant change in the proportion of barristers
who occupied themselves with advocacy, as distinct from out-of-
court work, occurred during our period. Thus, even though the
entry books can provide only conservative minima for the total size
of the practising bar, we have every reason to accept the broad
picture they present, of more barristers competing for less work.

The reality of this underlying trend is confirmed by some suggestive fragments of literary evidence. While there was nothing new
about laymen criticizing the excessive numbers of lawyers, in 1614
the common-law judges justified the imposition of a quota of eight
bar calls per year at each inn of court on the avowed grounds that
'an overgreat multitude in any one vocation or profession doth but
bring the same into contempt; and . . . and excessive numbers of
lawyers may have a further inconvenience, in respect of the multiply-
ing of needless suits'. Like all similar previous measures, this

---

[57] The law reports searched were those incorporated in *English Reports, 1220–1865*
(Edinburgh, 1900–32), and in *English Legal Manuscripts*, ed. J. H. Baker (microfiche,
Zug, Switzerland, 1975–). The two barristers not previously identified were Serjeant
Sir Robert Hitcham (GI) and Thomas Malet (MT); H. Rolle, *Les Reportes . . .* (1675),
367, 381. But see also Appendix C below, for counsel named in Exchequer and King's
Bench order and rule books.

[58] *Western Circuit Assize Orders*, ed. Cockburn, 133–62; the two additional
barristers were John Merefield (IT) and John Polwhele (LI).

restriction proved quite unenforceable; its futility was silently acknowledged when the crucial clause was omitted from the 1630 judges' orders, which otherwise virtually duplicate those of 1614. Nevertheless, senior members of the profession remained uneasily aware of what Lord Chief Justice Richardson termed in 1627 the 'disreputation' of his calling, 'which of latter time it hath fallen into by the multitude. . . . multitude of any place or profession is a great cause to disesteem'. It was one of 'the iniquities of the times', complained a Middle Temple reader the following year, that 'the honour and profit of this profession is much diminished'.[59]

Thomas Powell's optimistic claim in 1631 that the days were past when younger barristers needed to be a judge's favourite, kinsman, or relative by marriage was contradicted within twelve months by an anonymous barrister's *Conscionable Complaint*, which includes a five-page appendix of 'Objections against favourites at the bar of justice'.[60] Divisions between the minority of favourites and their less fortunate colleagues may well have been sharpened by the political and religious tensions of Charles I's reign. Junior barristers were also peculiarly vulnerable to competition from a much-expanded lower branch of attorneys and solicitors. In 1615 the Gray's Inn barrister Robert Blundell exhibited a Star Chamber bill against a Lancashire attorney who had pleaded causes 'as if he had been a counsellor at law' before the Preston quarter sessions and assizes. Similar intra-professional tensions doubtless underlay the order of the Hampshire JPs in 1633 excluding attorneys from their quarter sessions, on the grounds that 'counsellors at law who usually here attend . . . are but seldom employed by reason that attorneys and others under the degree of barristers are suffered to make motions and to plead in causes . . . to the distress of the said counsellors'.[61]

The gloom was not utterly unrelieved, since a few new opportunities for barristers were still being created. In 1585 Serjeant Thomas Walmsley had pulled every possible string to avoid being exiled as chief justice to 'the wild bogs of Ireland'; but with peace and a policy

---

[59] *OJ*, 317, 320–1; CUL MS Add. fol. 37–37ᵛ (although Richardson's comments were directed particularly at the serjeants, they obviously had more general implications); Hargrave 402, fol. 66.

[60] T. Powell, *Tom of All Trades* (1631), 26–7; *The Iust Lawyer*, 16–20.

[61] STAC 8/69/22; Hants RO, quarter sessions order book (1628–47), fol. 50. (I owe this reference to Dr Brooks.) Cf. the 1616 London order that all pleadings in the City's lawcourts be perused by learned counsel. (London Corp. RO, Rep. 32, p. 314.) A similar requirement was introduced at Oxford in 1607. (*Oxford Council Acts 1583–1626*, ed. H. E. Salter (Oxford, 1928), 179.)

of active discrimination against native Catholic lawyers, increasing numbers of English barristers flocked across the Irish Sea, most to take up judicial or administrative office, a few to practise at the Irish bar.[62] Common lawyers also benefited from England's colonial and maritime expansion further afield; besides fees and retainers from the trading companies, there were new offices at home and abroad, like the East Indies judgeship which an Inner Templar thought it worth seeking in 1625.[63] Nevertheless, the general outlook confronting entrants to the upper branch during the twenty years before the summoning of the Long Parliament was probably bleaker than at any time since the beginning of Elizabeth's reign, and the situation appears to have worsened in the later 1630s. Towards the end of Michaelmas term 1639, one disappointed barrister complained: 'This hath been so bad a term for practice as the like hath not been known these many years. Which maketh all, both practisers and officers in all courts, very much to complain of it. But there is no remedy, it must be endured and we must pray to God for better times.' Ironically enough, the crisis was soon to be at least temporarily relieved by the outbreak of civil war, which would leave Westminster Hall deserted, 'the bars that had wont to swell with a fivefold row of lifted gowns ... now so empty that boys may peep over them'.[64]

---

[62] Batho, ed., *Shrewsbury and Talbot Papers*, ii. 133–4; HMC, *Salisbury*, xviii. 5–6; cf. Lansdowne 46, fols. 57–8. D. Creegan, 'Irish Recusant Lawyers in the Reign of James I', *Irish Jurist*, NS v (1970), 306–20; T. C. Barnard, *Cromwellian Ireland* (Oxford, 1975), ch. ix, sects. i, iv. Nat. Lib. of Ireland, King's Inn Dublin, Black Book 1607–1730, fols. 11ᵛ–20; *ITAdmR*, 260; *ITR*, ii. 35; J. I. Okonkwo, 'William Lathum, author of the "Phyla Lachrymarum"', *N & Q*, ccxviii (1973), 376–7.

[63] See below, p. 174. *Calendar of State Papers, Colonial Series, East Indies, China and Persia 1625–9*, ed. W. N. Salisbury (1884), 31–2.

[64] E. Bulstrode to E. Heath, IT, 20 Nov. 1639. (Heath Papers, Rare Book Room, Lib. of Univ. of Illinois at Urbana-Champaign.) Cf. HMC, *Rutland*, i. 521. [John Taylor], *St. Hillaries Teares, Shed upon All Professions* (1642), 3.

CHAPTER FOUR

GROUP PORTRAIT

A mere kickshaw, and an ass laden with
Gold; and to be short, a Lawyer'.
George Ruggle, *Ignoramus* (1630; tr. R. Codrington, 1662),
sig. D2

WE now turn from the work done by barristers to the men themselves. This chapter is essentially an exercise in collective biography, and as such follows well-trodden historiographical paths, although the findings frequently contradict received opinion. After examining the social, geographical, and educational composition of the early modern bar, we shall glance briefly at the collective marital histories of the two sample groups of lawyers whose lives provide the basic subject matter of this inquiry, in the hope of casting further light on that important but neglected figure, the barrister's wife.

i. *Method and sources*

While historians of early modern England are by no means short of primary source material, the abundance of surviving evidence about particular persons tends to be a direct function of their social rank. Yet in approaching the richly varied assortment of men who constituted the late Elizabethan and early Stuart bar, it is important to take into account the more obscure majority, rather than generalizing about the whole group on the basis of a few prominent, but perhaps quite atypical, individuals.

Well over two thousand barristers were called between 1590 and 1639, far too large a number for a single researcher to study in any detail. While some limited biographical information about a good many of them might doubtless be gathered from standard printed sources, the results would almost certainly prove too scattered and superficial to justify the time and effort required. A better strategy is to select a cross-section for more intensive investigation, along the

lines developed by J. E. Neale and his students in their mass-
biographical studies of Elizabethan parliaments.[1]

The sample of barristers whose social characteristics are analysed
in this chapter and used as a reference point, or yardstick, elsewhere
in the book comprises 115 individuals, 5 per cent of the 2,293 men
known to have been called to the bar during the half-century before
the Long Parliament. The sample is stratified by inn of court, with
the aim of ensuring that the distinctive regional (and any other
possibly significant) characteristics of the four houses are adequately
represented. To select the sample, each barrister called during our
period was given a serial number. A table of random numbers was
then used to choose sufficient barristers from each inn to make up
the quota, or subtotal, allocated to that house. The size of these
quotas was calculated as 5 per cent of all calls made at that inn over
the relevant period; thus from Gray's Inn, for example, where 590
men were called to the bar between 1590 and 1639, 5 per cent of the
total equals 29.5, so (rounding up to the next whole number) 30
barristers were selected. The same routine was followed with the
numbered nominal lists of barristers from the other three inns to
produce the final aggregate sample, whose members are listed in
Appendix D below.[2]

These procedures should ensure that the sample of barristers
accurately reflects the characteristics of the entire population from
which it was chosen, provided the sample itself is sufficiently large.
Five per cent is not an unusually small sampling fraction, but in any
case a sample's reliability is primarily a function of absolute size
rather than its proportion of the group sampled. On the other hand,
since the accuracy of samples increases only with the square root of
their size, doubling the present sample would produce a gain in
reliability of less than half; in any case this particular sample is
comfortably above the minimum ceiling of 100 units often adopted

[1] For discussions of mass-biographical analysis, its benefits and pitfalls, see
Aylmer, *King's Servants*, 253–8; *idem, The State's Servants, the Civil Service of the
English Republic 1649–1660* (1973), 168–74. Cf. L. Stone, *The Past and the Present*
(1981), 3–73.

[2] In the case of GI, however, two separate passes were made, the first to select 24
barristers on the assumption that a total of only 472 men were called between 1590
and 1639. When a further 118 barristers were subsequently identified, men whose calls
had been made during a reading and were never entered in the Pension Order Book, it
was necessary to select a further 6 barristers for the GI quota, increasing the size of
the entire sample group from 109 to 115.

as a statistical rule of thumb.[3] Finally, the proportional distribution
of call dates by decade within the sample group is reassuringly close
to that among the entire population of barristers from which the
sample was taken, varying at most by just over 3 per cent for the
decade 1600–1609.[4] This result could not have been predicted in
advance, since the sampling procedures made no attempt to take call
dates into account; we can therefore have considerable confidence in
generalizing about the pre-Civil War bar as a whole, or at least those
who joined its ranks between 1590 and 1639, on the basis of results
derived from the barristers' sample.

Since that group includes men whose calls were distributed over
an entire half-century, their life-spans necessarily embrace a considerably longer period. Far from representing a single generation,
the sample barristers are best thought of as forming a series of
staggered age-cohorts, whose birth dates range as far back as the
penultimate year of Henry VIII's reign, and a few of whose members
were still alive to see the Glorious Revolution in 1688. Most were
men of no great note, in their own lifetime or afterwards, even if a
handful achieved high professional office (notably the judges Sir
John Archer, Sir Edward Henden, and Sir William Wilde), or
played a role on the national political stage, like the Long Parliament MPs Sir John Bourchier, Thomas Gell, and Sir Thomas
Widdrington. Rather more enjoyed some local or regional influence,
as landowners, JPs, recorders, or town clerks. Against these worthies
must be set a sprinkling of utter nonentities, about whom virtually
nothing is known beyond their dates of admission to an inn of court
and call to the bar. Nevertheless, it has been possible to reconstruct
for the majority of the sample at least a skeleton life history,
including details of parentage, residence, education, marriage, and
professional career, plus some indication of economic status, while
occasional biographical or autobiographical fragments sometimes
permit us a tantalizing glimpse of the personality behind the bare
formal record.

Even if its members were palpable flesh and blood, the barristers'
sample itself is plainly an artificial construction. The other group to

[3] Cf. R. Floud, *An Introduction to Quantitative Methods for Historians* (1973), 166,
175; R. Langley, *Practical Statistics* (1970), 45–6.
[4] Distribution of calls by decade for the sample group was as follows: 1590–99, 21;
1600–09, 17; 1610–19, 28; 1620–29, 20; 1630–39, 29. See Table 1.1 above for the
distribution of total calls by decade.

be examined side by side with the barristers is not such a microcosm, but more or less a natural population universe. Its membership includes all those elected as benchers or readers to the governing body of their inn of court between 1590 and 1639, with the significant exceptions of men who held important offices in one of the central law courts and others who appear to have been promoted for some reason apart from their seniority and standing as practising barristers. While election to the bench of an inn seems to have been largely determined by seniority at the bar, and some eligible barristers chose to decline the honour, those who reached this rank could fairly claim to have ascended at least the upper slopes, if not quite the commanding peak of their profession.[5] Since the 385 benchers in this group were an élite, it is hardly surprising that their lives are on the whole better documented than those of the 115 lawyers chosen at random to form the barristers' sample.

The overwhelming theoretical argument in favour of sampling is that it should permit a more balanced and comprehensive portrayal of the bar as a whole than if attention were to be focused exclusively on those common lawyers whose careers are relatively well known. Yet precisely because less information has survived about the least successful members of the profession, the answers to many important questions will inevitably have to be qualified by a varying, and sometimes sizeable, proportion of unknowns. Even when biographical information has survived and been located, it is often too complex, inconclusive, or insufficiently detailed to be easily categorized for statistical analysis.

These difficulties are mentioned by way of cautioning the reader about the limitations of the findings set out in the next two chapters, and indeed wherever the bar and bench groups are referred to elsewhere below. While some blurring of detail is part of the price which must be paid for systematic analysis of any large body of information, the more serious problem in the present case is that caused by missing evidence. The law of diminishing marginal returns sets in very quickly to limit the yield on individual biographical research, but even the application of limitless time and skill would probably not have added much significant additional information to

---

[5] See Appendix F below for office-holders and others excluded from the bench sample, most of whom were associate, rather than full, benchers, and had not been called, or were only associated, to the bar. Although John Hare and Robert Henley are both rather marginal cases (Hare is included in the bar sample), neither seems to have practised as counsel after acquiring his office.

the dossiers summarized at the end of the book. Of course, this is not at all to deny or excuse the gaps and errors which still remain, especially those arising from the author's lack of familiarity with regional sources and the histories of particular families.

Having proclaimed these caveats, it may be added that a combination of sampling and mass-biographical (or prosopographical) analysis offers the only feasible means of obtaining anything remotely approaching a realistic group portrait of the bar in the late sixteenth and early seventeenth centuries, and hence of discovering what sorts and conditions of men were then entering the upper branch of the legal profession, how their careers proceeded, and something of the ways in which they both impinged upon and reflected the great ideological and political divisions of the time. No other technique holds out the prospect of yielding comparable results, even if these must often be expressed in tentative, and usually quantitative, form.

ii. *Parentage*

The early modern bar is generally thought to have been recruited mainly from the younger sons of the landed gentry, even though some contemporaries were at pains to distinguish the 'many worthy gentlemen that are professors of the law' from an alleged 'base-born brood, that creeping into the inns of court, and having scraped together a few fragments ... of the law, because they would not mend shoes, foot stockings, drive the cart and do as their fathers before them ... neither care what laws they pervert, nor what clients they consume'.[6] Historians have taken little notice of such views, perhaps because they seem so blatantly prejudiced, especially when the only published analysis of the social origins of early modern barristers concludes that nearly four out of five men called to the bar at the Middle Temple in the early seventeenth century came from the upper ranks of the landed classes.[7]

This finding was reached by aggregating the status descriptions of entrants and their fathers which appear in the Middle Temple's records. But, given the polite fiction that the four 'Honourable Societies' accepted only gentlemen's sons as members, it is hardly surprising that their admissions registers list no sons of yeomen or

[6] B. Rich, *Roome for a Gentleman* (1609), 25–6; idem, *Allarme to England* (1578), sig. Gii[v]; cf. J. Ferne, *The Blazon of Gentrie* (1586), 95; Wrightson, *English Society*, 29; Ives, *Common Lawyers*, 374; G. Sawer, *Law in Society* (Oxford, 1965), 122.

[7] B. Levack, *The Civil Lawyers in England 1603–41* (Oxford, 1973), 9–11.

other plebeians, apart from the occasional citizen, merchant or official. In 1604 James I issued his 'express commandment that none be from henceforth admitted into . . . any inn of court, that is not a gentleman by descent'. But neither then nor subsequently did the societies introduce any checks or sanctions to enforce this remarkable edict.[8] Incoming students from socially obscure or humble backgrounds continued to be simply upgraded to gentlemen or left without status designation for the purposes of the formal entry of their admission. Only by penetrating the formulaic smokescreen of the admissions registers can we hope to obtain a more accurate picture of the social quality of either the inns' total membership or the minority who were called to the bar during our period.

Of course this is much easier said than done. But a search through standard genealogical and local historical sources can pay significant dividends in individual cases, indicating that a lawyer described on entering his inn as the son of a 'gent', or merely styled by name alone (sometimes with the addition *gen.(erosus)*), actually hailed from a mercantile, professional, or yeoman family. Information of this kind is not always readily available, while its interpretation often presents considerable difficulties, arising from the ambiguities and inconsistencies of the status hierarchy itself.[9] Nevertheless, such an inquiry undertaken for our two groups of barristers and benchers casts grave doubt on the conventional view of the early modern bar as dominated by the landed élite.

Table 4.1 summarizes these findings. Those lawyers described in the admissions registers as *gen.*, or as the sons of gentlemen, esquires, knights, or peers, but whose fathers can be identified from other sources as lawyers or merchants by occupation, or as of sub-gentry landed status, have been placed under the appropriate heading. Since there are still many instances where no evidence of an individual's rank has been found apart from that provided by the registers, the totals presented in the top half of the table (categories I–V) must certainly be regarded as upper-limit figures, and those for the remaining (non-gentry) classifications as conservative minima.

It will be readily apparent that sons of the upper gentry and nobility (categories I–III) are substantially under-represented in both groups, by comparison with those from backgrounds which

---

[8] Cf. *Inns of Court*, 26–7.

[9] On these problems, see Aylmer, *King's Servants*, 261–2, and J. S. Morrill, 'The Northern Gentry and the Great Rebellion', *Northern History*, xv (1979), 69–74.

Table 4.1. Social Origins of Bar and Bench Samples

		Barristers		Benchers	
		Number	Per cent	Number	Per cent
I	Peer's son	0	0.0	2	0.5
II	Knight's son	7	6.1	15	3.9
III	Esquire's son	16	13.9	39	10.2
IV	Gentleman's son	28	24.3	76	19.7
V	*Generosus*	18	15.7	64	16.6
VI	Lawyer's or Office-holder's son[1]	23	19.9	64	16.6
VII	Clergyman's son	4	3.5	6	1.6
VIII	Merchant's son[2]	8	7.0	46	11.9
IX	Yeoman's or Husbandman's son	3	2.6	16	4.2
X	Unstated or unknown	8	7.0	57	14.8
		115	100	385	100

[1] Includes sons of civil and common lawyers, holders of central and provincial legal office.
[2] Includes sons of merchants, aldermen, citizens, clothiers, tanners.

may be broadly classified as professional, bourgeois, and plebeian (categories VI–IX). Of course, some of the latter came from families with quite substantial holdings of wealth and landed property, and indeed were recognized as armigerous, at least by the College of Arms. This was not the case with many in categories IV–V, 'gents' and gentlemen's sons, who comprise a group of roughly comparable size to that of categories VI–IX, and with them account for over four-fifths of the known cases in both samples. For instance, the barrister Maurice Abbott, eldest son and heir of a director of the East India Company and lord mayor of London, is ranked according to our working rules as the son of a merchant (category VIII), although his father held a knighthood; but Abbott must certainly have occupied a higher social stratum than William Dyos, another member of the barristers' sample, who appears in category V, having been described on his admission to Lincoln's Inn in 1594 as 'of London and Staple Inn, *gen.*; sometime a butler of this inn'.[10]

The problem with categories IV–V and category X (men listed in the admissions books by name alone, without indication of rank or title, who cannot be more specifically identified from other sources) is that they include an unknown, but possibly large, proportion of

[10] *DNB*, s.v. Abbott, Sir Maurice; *ITAdmR*, 403. *LIAdmR*, i. 117; *Analytical Index to ... the Remembrancia ... A.D. 1579–1664*, ed. W. H. and H. C. Overall (1878), xi.

lawyers who were in fact of plebeian, bourgeois, or professional parentage. This difficulty is graphically brought out in the course of a splenetic attack by the Kentish puritan diarist Thomas Scott on the presumption of what he called 'our hireling, mercenary barristers' in arrogating to themselves the title of esquire. To exemplify what he took to be the manifest absurdity of such claims, Scott indignantly cited the case of one William Brodnax of Godmersham, who was admitted to the Middle Temple in 1594, called to the bar in 1602, and died five years later, being commemorated by a memorial inscription in his parish church which, like the Middle Temple register, describes his father Thomas as a 'Gent'. Yet, 'so long as this Thomas Brodnax lived, he did write himself Thomas Brodnax yeoman, but since his death, belike, he must be imprinted Gent'.[11]

As this example demonstrates, an individual's status, especially at the crucial but blurred dividing line which separated gentlemen from the 'base multitude', lay to a considerable extent in the eye of the beholder and could change over time. Nevertheless, in cases such as that of John Cremer of Setchey, Norfolk, who appears as son and heir of a George Cremer, 'gent.', in the register of Gray's Inn, but whose father is styled 'yeoman' in a property deed antedating his son's admission by eleven years, it seems reasonable to assign the individual concerned to the lower category.[12] Unfortunately, if inevitably, it is precisely for the most obscure barristers and benchers that such supplementary evidence of social rank is most scarce, men like 'Nicholas Nott of Maidstone, Kent' who seems to be known to history only from his appearances in the Gray's Inn records on the occasions of his admission to the house in 1594 and his call to the bar in 1608, besides the entry of his matriculation as a pensioner of Queens' College, Cambridge, in 1589. Nott's matriculation rank may create a presumption, albeit rebuttable, of his gentle status; if so, we should have to reclassify John Hanmer of Oswestry, Shropshire, who is described equally laconically at his admission to the same inn in 1587, but as a plebeian on his enrolment at Trinity College, Oxford, two years before.[13] While neither Hanmer nor Nott appear in the heraldic visitations of their respective counties, it

---

[11] T. Scott, 'A Discourse of Polletique and Civil Honor', in Scull, *Dorothea Scott*, 172–3; *MTAdmR*, i. 67. On Scott, see P. Clark, 'Thomas Scott and the Growth of Urban Opposition to the Early Stuart Regime', *Hist. J.*, xxi (1978), 1–26.

[12] *GIAdmR*, 162; Norfolk RO, NRS 20759 41 D 6; R. W. Ketton-Cremer, *Felbrigg* (1962), 226.

[13] *GIAdmR*, 71, 84; *GIBP*, i, 183; *Al. Cant.*, iii. 270; *Al. Ox.*, ii. 644.

would be dangerous to make too much of this fact by itself, since many lesser or parochial gentry simply did not bother to appear before the expensive inquisitions conducted by the Heralds. Nor can inclusion of an individual or his family in a visitation pedigree *after* admission to an inn or call to the bar be taken as conclusive proof of prior gentility. Thus the pedigree of Robert Cuffe, who was merely styled 'of Somerset' (i.e. without any status designation) when he entered Lincoln's Inn in 1584, is included in the county visitation of 1623; but a monumental inscription to Cuffe's father in the parish church of Creech St Michael, while bearing a coat of arms, remains significantly unadorned by any title of degree.[14] At all events it is plain that while a few barrister 'gents' or sons of gentlemen in categories IV and V, such as Thomas Gallop of Netherbury, Dorset, or Francis Keat, of East Locking, Berkshire, were genuine representatives of the lesser, parochial, landed gentry, the backgrounds of the majority were quite obscure, and their claims to gentility in any formal sense must often have been highly dubious.

Although there is no hope of winkling out all the lawyers who were not in fact of gentle birth or breeding from the three large groups of 'gentleman's son', 'generosus', and 'unknown', we can at least distinguish those whose urban origins suggest that their fathers were probably not from the landed gentry. About a quarter of the members of both groups are described at their admission as resident in cities and towns throughout the kingdom. The majority of this urban contingent were lawyers' or merchants' sons, and have already been so classified in Table 4.1. But a substantial residue (some 14 per cent of the entire bar sample and 9 per cent of the benchers) appear in the admissions registers as sons of gentlemen, 'gentlemen' or without any status designation (see Table 4.2). To these urban 'pseudo-gentry' may be added a further six sons of esquires from the benchers, making a total for that group of forty individuals, or 11 per cent overall. When all these men, together with those in categories V–IX (professional, bourgeois, and yeoman) are subtracted, the maximum *possible* total of lawyers from landed élite backgrounds in both groups falls to just over half (55 per cent of the benchers, 53 per cent of the barristers). Even these figures are almost certainly inflated, and might be reduced still further if only it were possible to identify all the sons of artisans, tradesmen, peasants,

---

[14] *LIAdmR*, i. 99; *HS*, xi. 30; Francis Bacon described Robert's brother Henry, who was secretary to Essex, as 'a base fellow by birth'. (Bacon, *Works*, ix. 260.)

Table 4.2. Gentry and Unknowns: Geographical Origins

	Gentleman's son (IV)		Gen. (V)		Unknown or Unstated (X)		Total	
	Rural	Urban	Rural	Urban	Rural	Urban	Rural	Urban
Bar sample	21	7	12	6	5	3	38	16
Bench sample	63	13	54	13	49	8	166	34

and professional men who undoubtedly still remain hidden within categories IV, V, and X.

While the representation of the landed élite in both samples seems remarkably similar, their overall social composition shows some interesting differences. By and large the benchers appear to have been a slightly less select group than the barristers, with a marginally smaller representation of the upper gentry (categories I–III) and larger percentages of merchants' and yeomen's sons. The offspring of clerics, lawyers, and office-holders are slightly better represented among the barristers than the benchers, but this apparent difference probably reflects the much higher proportion of unknowns in the bench sample, which in turn is largely a consequence of the different age composition of the two samples. Since call to the bench normally followed well over ten years after call to the bar, the bench sample includes a proportionately larger cohort of men born in and around the mid-sixteenth century, whose family origins are relatively more difficult to trace, due to the greater deficiencies of the inns' records and other biographical sources as one goes further back into the sixteenth century. At the same time there can be little doubt that the overwhelming majority of the unknowns in both groups were of relatively humble parentage, on or below what Aylmer neatly terms 'the Gentleman / Mr borderline', which again serves to emphasize the marginally lower social origins of the benchers.[15]

The ratios of elder to younger sons among the two groups tend to support this general impression (see Table 4.3). Nearly 8 per cent more barristers than benchers can be identified as first-born, only, or elder surviving sons, who would usually expect to inherit the lion's share of their father's estates and hence have far less cause than their younger brothers to depend on the bar for a livelihood. However, both groups show an inverse correlation between social rank and

[15] Aylmer, *State's Servants*, 178–80.

Table 4.3. Birth Order

	First and only sons		Younger sons		Unknown	
	Number	Per cent	Number	Per cent	Number	Per cent
Bar sample	52	45.2	40	34.8	23	20.0
Bench sample	145	37.7	163	42.3	77	20.0

birth order. As might be expected, the upper gentry (categories I–III) tended to put their younger sons to the bar; among 'mere' gentry lawyers (categories IV and V) the ratio of first to younger sons was more evenly balanced, while elder sons actually predominated among men from legal and official (but not mercantile) backgrounds. Of course these findings would be more compelling if the rather large cohorts of unknown cases could somehow or other be reduced. Since most are either 'gents' (category V) or men whose parents' social status is equally obscure, they may include a somewhat higher ratio of elder sons than both groups taken as a whole, although probably not enough to upset their relative positions as far as the distribution of first to younger sons is concerned.

Among both barristers and benchers the proportion of younger sons is somewhat higher than among the Caroline and Interregnum office-holders studied by Aylmer, if much the same as Birken found in his work on London physicians of the early seventeenth century. A more significant contrast is with the early Stuart civil lawyers, whom Levack found to include less than one in ten elder sons of landed gentry families; taking sons of the gentry (defined as categories I–V in Table 4.1, excluding urban residents), the gap between barristers and benchers narrows somewhat, but both groups still show first sons of gentry families in proportions comfortably above those reported by Levack (20 per cent of barristers, 16 per cent of benchers).[16]

Thus, neither in terms of familial origins nor birth order within the family do our two sample groups support the orthodox view of the early modern bar as dominated by younger sons of the landed élite. The barristers appear to have been a slightly more select body, with a higher proportion of elder sons, than the benchers; this

[16] Ibid., 176; W. J. Birken, 'The Fellows of the Royal College of Physicians of London, 1603–1643', University of North Carolina at Chapel Hill Ph.D. thesis, 1977, 299; Levack, *Civil Lawyers*, 12.

finding may well reflect the greater likelihood of younger sons from humbler backgrounds showing high levels of commitment and motivation, a point to which we shall return in a later chapter. Meanwhile, how do these findings relate to what is known about the social composition of the legal profession's upper branch before and after our period?

Ives has recently revised his earlier view, based on the study of some 180 pleaders, serjeants, and judges from the late fifteenth and early sixteenth centuries, that while 'some were of very insignificant birth', most 'came from the middle and upper ranks of the gentry'. Baker has also emphasized the relatively lowly backgrounds of many late Yorkist and early Tudor common lawyers.[17] These conclusions must be taken very seriously, but they are based on a more restricted body of sources and a more senior group of lawyers than those just set out above. Moreover, even if Fortescue's claim in the late fifteenth century that virtually all common lawyers were nobly descended must be discounted as an extravagant boast, it still seems, on the basis of Ives's latest figures, that well over half the serjeants called between 1463 and 1521 were indisputably drawn from landed-gentry stock. This looks like a rather higher proportion than that among the 114 benchers of our group who went on to become serjeants, only just over half of whom could possibly have sprung from the gentry, while no less than 48 per cent were plainly of mercantile, professional, or yeomanry backgrounds. Given the apparent devaluation of status labels over the early modern period as a whole, these figures do imply some broadening in the social catchment area from which common lawyers were recruited between the late fifteenth and early seventeenth centuries.[18]

Looking beyond the end of our period, Holmes has cautioned against the assumption that the 'surging growth' of the legal profession under the later Stuarts entailed 'a corresponding broadening of its social base', pointing out that the landed gentry remained 'an indispensable source of supply' for the Augustan bar and bench. This caveat likewise cannot be ignored, even if its force is somewhat blunted by the accompanying observation of an increased

---

[17] Ives, *Common Lawyers*, 32, 374; *idem*, 'Some Aspects of the Legal Profession in the Late Fifteenth and Early Sixteenth Centuries', *BIHR*, xxxi (1958), 100; Baker, 'Legal Profession', 34.

[18] R. Grassby, 'Social Mobility and Business Enterprise in Seventeenth-Century England', in *Puritans and Revolutionaries*, ed. D. Pennington and K. Thomas (Oxford, 1978), 356 n.

flow to the bar of men from well-to-do business or professional backgrounds during the century from 1640 onwards, as well as by Duman's finding that among Middle Temple barristers representation of the landed gentry dropped from just under a third to as little as a tenth between 1715 and 1774.[19]

So while we must be careful not to obscure the element of continuity (at no point from the later Middle Ages on was the common law the exclusive preserve of the landed élite), nor to reduce the subtle processes of social change to a deceptively neat statistical formulation, there does appear to be evidence of a long-term tendency towards increased recruitment from non-gentry sources, and to that extent, some broadening of the bar's social composition over the early modern period as a whole. Of course it still remained a calling drawn from a relatively narrow segment of English society. Nevertheless, the absence of any formal educational prerequisites for admission to the inns of court probably helped keep the bar in England distinctly more open in social terms than its counterparts in Scotland or Continental Europe, where the requirement of a university degree in civil law for would-be advocates seems to have worked in the opposite direction.[20]

iii. Geographical origins and mobility

The early modern English bar was largely recruited from the more populous and prosperous parts of the kingdom. This is hardly surprising, since we would expect lawyers to be drawn predominantly from those areas which contained the most potential clients for their services, especially given the importance of local connections in establishing and maintaining a practice at the bar.

At the same time the geographical origins of Elizabethan and early Stuart barristers were considerably more diverse than those of their late medieval predecessors, whom Ives found to have originated overwhelmingly from southern England and a small area around York. By contrast, our groups of barristers and benchers include representatives of all but one English and most Welsh counties, together with a scattering of Irishmen. The largest contingents came from London and its environs, East Anglia, and the

---

[19] Holmes, *Augustan England*, 142–5; Duman, 'Georgian Era', 90–5.

[20] Cf. A. Murdoch, 'The Advocates, the Law and the Nation in Early Modern Scotland', in *Lawyers*, 150–2; L. Berlanstein, 'Lawyers in Pre-Revolutionary France', in *Lawyers*, 164, 168–9; R. L. Kagan, 'Lawyers and Litigation in Castile, 1500–1750', in *Lawyers*, 189, 196–7.

clothing counties of the West Country, with Kent, Essex, and Devon particularly well represented. But Yorkshiremen were also prominent, and well over a third of both barristers and benchers hailed from the six northern counties, the midlands, Wales, and the Marches (see Table 4.4).[21]

So while its regional composition continued to reflect the demographic and economic ascendancy of south and east over west and north, the early modern bar was nationally recruited rather than drawn overwhelmingly from the southern half of England. There was little appreciable difference in regional make-up between the

Table 4.4. *Comparative Regional Origins*[1]

	Bar		Bench		Inns of Court[2]	Office-holders[3]	Civilians[4]
	Number	Per cent	Number	Per cent			
North	12	10.3	33	8.3	9.2	4.4	7.2
Midlands	18	15.4	72	18.1	12.7	17.6	11.2
East	25	21.4	84	21.1	21.2	18.0	24.6
South and South-east	16	13.7	56	14.0	17.1	16.6	12.3
South-west	22	18.8	79	19.8	16.0	9.8	13.9
Wales and West	14	12.0	49	12.3	11.5	9.3	17.9
London	8	6.8	24	6.0	8.8	16.1	10.6[5]
Ireland	2	1.7	2	0.5	3.8	0.5	0.6
Foreign and other	—	—	—	—	0.1	7.8	1.7
Totals	117	100.1	399	100.1	100	100	100
Unknown	1	—	4	—	—	—	—

[1] Regions as Aylmer, *State's Servants*, 183. See also Appendix G below.
[2] Source: *Inns of Court*, 32–3.
[3] Source: Aylmer, *State's Servants*, 186.
[4] Source: Levack, *Civil Lawyers*, 37–8.
[5] As no separate total for London is given, the figure for Middlesex was used.
[6] As multiple origins are included, these totals exceed the size of the two sample groups. Because of rounding errors, percentage totals are sometimes 0.1 above or below 100 in this and subsequent tables.

[21] E. W. Ives, 'Some Aspects of the Legal Profession in the Late Fifteenth and Early Sixteenth Centuries', University of London Ph.D. thesis, 1955, 120–1, 124–38. See Appendix G below. On the regional distribution of population and wealth in early modern England, see R. M. Smith, 'Population and its Geography in England 1500–1730', in *An Historical Geography of England and Wales*, ed. R. A. Dodgshon and R. A. Butlin (1978), 199–237, at 227–32; J. Sheail, 'The distribution of taxable population and wealth in England during the early sixteenth century', *Trans. Inst. of Brit. Geographers*, lv (1972), 111–26.

two groups, while they in turn closely resemble in this respect the entrants admitted to the inns of court between 1590 and 1639. That mixed bag of would-be lawyers and gentlemen students actually contained proportionately somewhat fewer men from the midlands and the south-west, with correspondingly more south-easterners. Other contemporary occupational and status groups, including civil lawyers, public administrators, and physicians, display much the same overall pattern.

The relatively strong showing of the north, the midlands, and Wales among our barristers and benchers may reflect the decline of the palatine jurisdictions (which had provided the gentry of Cheshire, Durham, and Lancashire with career alternatives to the common law during the late fifteenth and early sixteenth centuries) and the rise at Ludlow and York of conciliar courts offering a new source of employment to common lawyers. Contemporary and later observers also thought that the Tudor peace encouraged the resolution of disputes by litigation rather than violence, especially in remoter regions of the land. Another important factor was probably the more rapid growth of population in these less densely settled zones during the sixteenth century. This demographic trend was closely associated with the enclosure movement, that cluster of pressures upon customary farming arrangements whose manifestations were particularly evident in the midlands, where they provided a good deal of additional work for lawyers.[22]

Of course the disruptive effects of rapid socio-economic change during the sixteenth and early seventeenth centuries were evident all over the country. In Norfolk, for example, disputes over the use of common or waste lands for pasture were a major source of litigation during our period:

> Through commoning in moor or heath or shack
> More suits arise in Norfolk in a year
> Then matters all in shires which such do lack
> Do mount unto, as by Records appear:
> Not only Lords and Tenants be a jar,
> But commoners among themselves do war,
> And by the suits which thence do spring and grow,

---

[22] Ives, thesis, 129. Stone, *Crisis of the Aristocracy*, 240–2; on the difficulty of testing such plausible assertions, cf. H. A. Lloyd, 'Wales and Star Chamber: A Rejoinder', *Welsh Hist. Rev.*, v (1971), 257–60. Smith, 'Population and Geography', 227–8; *The Agrarian History of England and Wales, Vol. iv*, ed. J. Thirsk (1967), 9–10, 202–5.

Through skaith, surcharge, wrong, commoning or fee,
The rich as poor the commons overthrow,
And gainful but to lawyers only be.[23]

Norfolk was notorious both for the litigiousness of its inhabitants and as the most fruitful nursery of lawyers in all England—hence the adage 'Norfolk wiles many a man beguiles'.[24] The county certainly produced more than its fair share of the most eminent lawyers of the age, including two lord chancellors (Nicholas and Francis Bacon) and three chief justices (Edward Coke, Henry Hobart and Thomas Richardson). Yet in purely quantitative terms Norfolk was by no means the most favoured county of origin for the lawyers in our groups, ranking only fifth (with Northamptonshire and Yorkshire) among the benchers and sharing sixth place for the barristers. However, Norfolk appears to have been favoured with more Common Pleas attorneys in the late fifteenth and mid-sixteenth centuries than any other county (excluding London); it was perhaps their presence which gave rise to the county's reputation as a prime seed-bed of both lawyers and litigation.[25]

We shall probably never be able to chart the geographical distribution of litigiousness during the early modern period with any precision, due to the difficulty of measuring the business transacted by a myriad local and customary courts. What little quantitative evidence is available does in fact bear out Norfolk's reputation as a peculiarly litigious county—for example, its inhabitants appear to have been responsible for no less than 13 per cent of all suits laid in the Court of Common Pleas in 1560.[26] On the other hand, contemporaries also regarded the people of Cornwall, Cumberland, North Wiltshire, and Wales as notably litigious, although none of these regions seems to have been particularly well-populated with lawyers, either in reputation or reality.[27] Thomas Fuller, no stranger to the world of law, said of the men of Devon: 'They in this county seem innated with a genius to study law; none in England (Northfolk [*sic*]

---

[23] *Norfolk Archaeology*, v (1859), 165–6.
[24] A. H. Smith, *County and Court. Government and Politics in Norfolk, 1558–1603* (Oxford, 1974), 1; T. Fuller, *The History of the Worthies of England*, ed. P. A. Nuttall (1840), ii. 446–7.
[25] Cf. J. H. Baker, 'The Attorneys and Officers of the Common Law in 1480', *JLH*, i (1980), 186.
[26] Ibid.; cf. Brooks, 'Litigants and Attorneys', 54.
[27] See following note; *VCH, Cumberland*, ii. 286; J. Aubrey, *The Natural History of Wiltshire*, ed. J. Britton (1847), 11; Williams, *Council in the Marches*, 63–4.

alone excepted) affording so many.' While this observation is entirely corroborated by the present study, Fuller goes on to assert that most of the Devonshire lawyers found their clients outside the county. No doubt he had their Cornish neighbours particularly in mind, for Cornishmen were traditionally depicted as 'very litigious, much inclined to law quarrels for small causes'. Yet, as Richard Carew noted in his *Survey of Cornwall* (1602),

Whether it be occasioned through the country's poverty, or by reason of the far distance thereof from the supremer courts, or for that the multiplicity of petty ones near at hand ... do enable the attorneys and such like of small reading to serve the people's turn and so curtail the better-studied counsellors' profiting ... certain it is that few men of law have, either in our time or in that of our forefathers, grown here to any supereminent height of learning, livelihood or authority.

It is difficult to avoid concluding that the relationship between densities of lawyers and propensities for lawsuits was somewhat more complicated than Neale's pithy adage 'litigation bred lawyers, and lawyers litigation', might suggest.[28]

Complexity is compounded by the fact that barristers were a particularly restless segment of what historians now generally characterize as a highly mobile society. So besides the origins of our lawyers we must also take into account their migrations and eventual destinations. It is obviously desirable to distinguish short-term movements which did not involve a permanent change of abode—such as a barrister's seasonal journeyings between home, London, and assize circuit—from migration as such. In most instances an individual's geographical origins (or at least his father's place of residence) are readily established from the record of his admission to an inn of court; other sources can usually supply this information when the admission record is silent and sometimes supplement it by indicating that his family lived in two or more different places. Since there is no similarly convenient listing of destinations, evidence must be sought in wills, inquisitions *post mortem*, parish registers, memorial inscriptions and miscellaneous

[28] Fuller, *Worthies of England*, i. 413; J. Norden, *Speculi Britanniae Pars. A Topographicall & Historicall Description of Cornwall*, ed. F. Graham (1728; 1966), 27; R. Morton Nance, 'Andrew Boorde on Cornwall *circa* 1540', *J. of the Royal Institute of Cornwall*, xxii (1928), 367–8; R. Carew, *The Survey of Cornwall*, ed. F. E. Halliday (1953), 131; J. E. Neale, *The Elizabethan House of Commons* (1949), 24.

biographical sources. Not surprisingly, therefore, rather more destinations than origins remain unknown.

A more fundamental difficulty is that a man's recorded final destination was not necessarily where he lived all or most of his previous life (although in the absence of other evidence it must usually be treated as such). Obviously the judge Sir Richard Hutton should not be classified as a resident of Middlesex simply because he happened to die in London and be buried in the parish church of St Dunstan's-in-the West, when his main estates were at Goldsborough in the West Riding of Yorkshire, from whence his will is dated. That fact makes it possible to ignore the landed property in Lancashire and Westmorland which the will also mentions and classify Hutton as a migrant who moved from Cumberland, his county of origin, to Yorkshire.[29] But what of Hutton's fellow countryman, Chief Justice Sir John Bankes, who bought Corfe Castle, Dorset, in 1631, yet retained his family house at Keswick until at least three years before his death, and also referred in his will to 'my house in Holborn wherein I lately dwelt', as well as to parcels of real estate in Cumberland, Westmorland, Dorset, and the suburbs of London? Bankes has in fact been categorized, albeit with some misgivings, as a migrant from Cumberland to Dorset, with Middlesex as a second destination, on the grounds that there is no evidence of his having occupied his Keswick property after the purchase of Corfe Castle, when in any case his official duties as attorney-general would presumably have prevented his getting away from London for extended periods.[30]

Bankes and Hutton were both distinguished judges, and at least the broad outlines of their careers are well known. Most members of our sample groups were considerably less prominent, and it is correspondingly more difficult to trace and interpret their geographical movements. Only the lucky survival of a personal account book informs us that Paul Croke lived in Hackney, Middlesex, and Little Burstead, Essex, after having been brought up in Buckinghamshire and before purchasing the large Rutland estate where he ended his days; the same source also indicates that Croke rented various houses and lodgings in Chancery Lane, Fleet Street, and Paternoster Row, besides his Inner Temple chamber; held substantial lands in Berkshire; and, during vacations when he was not on

[29] PCC 66 Harvey; *DNB*, s.v. Hutton, Sir Richard.
[30] Ibid. s.v. Bankes, Sir John; PCC 113 Twisse; *VCH, Middx.*, iii. 43.

circuit, customarily paid protracted visits to relatives in Berkshire, Essex, and Suffolk.[31] By contrast, no conclusive evidence has yet come to light which might determine whether the Edward Hanbury of Brentford, Middlesex, whose will was proved on 26 April 1647, is the same individual as the Edward Hanbury of Beanhall and Feckenham, Worcestershire, who was admitted to the Middle Temple in 1604, called to the bar in 1614, but is not mentioned in the inn's records after 1628, when he had already given up his chamber in the house.[32] Finally, some members of both groups who appear to have remained in the same region or neighbourhood throughout their lives did, nevertheless, move house across a parish boundary or from one hamlet to another; thus, Thomas St George was admitted to Gray's Inn as the son of John, of the village of Hatley St George, Cambridgeshire, in 1627, but in his will made ten years later spoke of 'my house at Tadwell' (sc. Tadlow), a village some two or three miles distant.[33] It may seem absurd to dignify this trivial relocation as a case of migration, but then it is not at all self-evident at what distance from first origin the line could or should be drawn.

Bearing all these potential pitfalls in mind, it is apparent from Table 4.5 that the benchers were collectively almost twice as transient as the barristers; only 25 per cent of the former, as against 46 per cent of the latter, recorded the same origin and destination. Moreover, the relative stability of the barristers was almost certainly even more pronounced than these figures indicate, since at least some of the nineteen barristers whose final destination is unknown should presumably be included in the category of non-movers.

This finding is, if not predictable, at least quite plausible. On reflection, it might well be expected that a close association should exist between horizontal (geographical) and vertical (career) mobility: the higher a lawyer rose in his profession, the easier and perhaps more desirable he would find it to slacken—if not entirely cast off—kinship and neighbourhood ties no longer needed to support his practice. Of course this presupposes that most moves were made over some substantial distance. In fact, those of about

[31] Croke, 'Diurnall', fols. 64, 93, 102, 113, 130, 216, and *passim*. See also *VCH, Berks.*, iv. 287; Ellesmere 2475.

[32] *MTAdmR*, i. 81; *MTR*, ii. 582, 738; PCC 66 Fines. The suggestion that the Worcs. and Middx. Hanburys are identical is made by A. Locke, *The Hanbury Family* (1916), ii. 444.

[33] *GIAdmR*, 180; PCC 153 Goare. The heraldic visitation of 1619 shows the family as of Hatley St George. (*HS*, xli. 91.)

Table 4.5. Migration and Urbanization[1]

	Bar		Bench	
	Number	Per cent	Number	Per cent
Moved from original place of residence	43	37.4	258	67.0
Stayed at original place of residence	53	46.0	98	25.5
Unknown, whether moved or stayed	19	16.5	29	7.5
Totals	115	100.0	385	100.0
Urban origin	30	26.1	96	24.9
Urban destination	34	29.6	141	36.6
Moved from town to country	6	5.2	30	7.8
Moved from country to town	20	17.4	89	23.1
Moved across county border	22	19.1	109	28.3

[1] Due to the presence of unknowns in both sample groups, the figures in the lower half of the table do not balance.

two-thirds of the barristers and half the benchers necessitated crossing at least one county boundary—an admittedly imperfect (albeit convenient) index of distance travelled. More telling is the impact of their moves on the regional distribution of the two groups. A comparison of recorded origins and destinations reveals a marked shift away from the outlying and generally poorer counties of the north, the midlands, Wales and the south-west towards London and south-eastern England (see Table 4.6). Again, the magnetic pull of the metropolitan centre seems to have been felt slightly more strongly by the benchers than the barristers in our sample groups.

The movement was almost entirely one-way. A few Londoners retired to country estates, but nearly always in the home counties. The only peripheral zone to experience a net inflow of lawyers was Ireland, where the immigrants joined the judicial and bureaucratic establishments which burgeoned after the collapse of armed resistance to English rule at the beginning of James I's reign. Here, as elsewhere, hopes of economic and social betterment must have been the prime incentive for migration, even though in only a few instances is it possible to link a man's move to the acquisition of office, or a marriage connection, or both. Usually we can do no more than speculate about the reasons why a particular individual did or did not migrate. Of course some migration was neither voluntary

Table 4.6. Regional Destinations[1]

	Bar		Bench	
	Number	Per cent	Number	Per cent
North	9	8.0	24	6.0
Midlands	16	14.3	66	16.5
East	22	19.6	79	19.75
South and South-east	21	18.8	84	21.0
South-west	17	15.2	64	16.0
Wales and West	10	8.9	36	9.0
London	13	11.6	37	9.25
Ireland	3	2.7	9	2.25
Foreign	1	0.9	1	0.25
Totals	112	100.0	428	100.0
Unknown	19	—	28	—

[1] Regions as in Aylmer, *State's Servants*, 183.

nor associated with personal advancement. The move of David Waterhouse, an Inner Temple bencher, from Shibden, near Halifax, in Yorkshire to London around 1609 appears to be a classic case of betterment migration—until we discover that Waterhouse's London destination was the Fleet Prison, where he was to remain incarcerated as a bankrupt debtor until his death some thirty years later![34]

A further caveat to be borne in mind when considering the impact of migration is that early modern England was a relatively compact and homogeneous society, at least by comparison with the leading states of continental Europe. So, despite relatively poor communications and transport facilities, even long-distance migrants might find it possible to maintain substantial ties with their home town or village. Christopher Brooke of Lincoln's Inn, another Yorkshire lawyer who transferred to London during James I's reign, still retained possession of his family house and other property in the city of York, besides serving as one of the borough's MPs and as fee'd counsel to the corporation until he died in 1628. It was almost certainly London's cultural and intellectual attractions which induced Brooke, John Donne's lifelong friend and himself a poet, to leave the security of York, where his father had been a prosperous

[34] For Waterhouse, see Appendix E. I am grateful to Dr Aylmer for generously sharing his work on Waterhouse with me.

merchant and alderman, for permanent residence in the capital. John Selden, another of Brooke's famous associates, was doubtless similarly motivated, more especially since there was little in his humble Sussex background to outweigh all that London could offer in terms of scholarly patronage and stimulus.[35]

The gravitational pull of London was just the most important instance of a general phenomenon. We have already noticed that about a quarter of both barristers and benchers came from cities and towns throughout the kingdom. In addition a further quarter of the benchers and a fifth of the barristers are positively known to have settled in towns.[36] These are minimum figures which would undoubtedly rise if our evidence were more complete, especially for the nineteen barristers whose final destinations remain obscure. Yet even the totals already to hand are hardly trivial: fully half the benchers and well over a third of the barristers from our two groups had lived in towns at some point in their lives, quite apart from their exposure to metropolitan mores at the inns of court as students and practising counsellors. It must also be remembered that a substantial proportion of those lawyers classified as rural by origin or destination actually resided on the outskirts of towns, or held urban office as recorders, stewards, town clerks, or fee'd counsel. Of course none of this necessarily meant that they were 'bourgeois' in life-style or class identity. However, urban association on such a scale makes it all the more difficult to consider the early modern barrister as a mere appendage of the landed gentry.[37]

Historians have yet to agree upon conventions for defining and measuring population mobility and turnover in past societies. So it is very difficult to say whether early modern barristers were more or less transient than their contemporaries. Judging by the only roughly comparable published data, they may have been slightly less stable than public administrators, both royal and republican, if markedly more so than civil lawyers, nearly 60 per cent of whom

[35] For Brooke and Selden, see Appendix E; Brooke did, however, resign the office of deputy recorder in 1616, largely because of his residence in London. (*VCH, York*, 196.)

[36] I have classified as urban for this purpose, besides such major centres as London, Bristol, Colchester, Gloucester, and Newcastle, a number of smaller county and market towns, including Hereford, Kingston-on-Thames, Marlborough, Woodstock, Newcastle-under-Lyme, Gainsborough, Wells, Beverley, Maidstone, and Yeovil.

[37] For lawyers and urban office-holding, see below, ch. 8, sect. ii; cf., for a slightly earlier period, G. D. Ramsay, 'A saint in the City: Thomas More at Mercer's Hall, London', *EHR*, xcvii (1982), 269–88.

settled outside their county of origin.[38] Yet these crude comparisons are not very revealing in themselves. In the absence of any general laws of migration and its consequences, everything depends upon the details of who moved, where, why, and when.[39]

Thus it has been compellingly argued that the high incidence of geographical mobility among the civilians tended to isolate them from provincial landed society, strengthening their identification with and dependence on the national institutions which they served as royal or ecclesiastical bureaucrats. Common lawyers, by contrast, were both much more numerous, and served a far broader clientele than the tiny band of civilians. No sectional interest could reasonably hope to capture the whole profession, which attracted men from a very wide range of geographical and social backgrounds, offering opportunities no less to townsmen than country dwellers, merchants' as well as landholders' sons, northerners and southerners, cockneys and Welshmen.

Short-term geographical mobility was for most barristers simply a vocational necessity, the inevitable consequence of their role as intermediaries between a judicial system centralized in London and its largely provincial clientele. No other contemporary learned profession required so much travelling of its practitioners or better equipped them to act as brokers between city, court, and country. Migration, on the other hand, was a common, but not universal, experience for barristers. The crucial importance of local connections in building and keeping a practice at the bar doubtless constituted the major deterrent to permanent, long-distance changes of residence. When barristers did migrate, the inducement seems most often to have been the lure of office and reward, an heiress, or both. This close association between horizontal mobility and economic, professional, or social promotion must often have eased the personal dislocation resulting from such moves, especially when the migrant's destination was urban rather than rural. Nevertheless, some long-distance migrants were not readily assimilated into their new environments. Rice or Richard Gwynn, a native of Anglesey, had begun to buy property at Fakenham, about 23 miles north of

[38] Cf. Aylmer, *State's Servants*, 185–6; Levack, *Civil Lawyers*, 37–9.
[39] Ibid., 34–5, 42–3. Cf. W. R. Prest, 'Stability and Change in Old and New England: Clayworth and Dedham', *J. of Interdisciplinary Hist.*, vi (1976), 359–74, and M. A. Vinovskis, 'Recent Trends in American Historical Demography: Some Methodological and Conceptual Considerations', *Annual Rev. of Sociology*, vi (1978), 603–23.

Norwich, shortly after his call to the bar of the Inner Temple in 1591, and took up permanent residence there on being elected recorder of Norwich in 1613. Nearly two decades later Serjeant Gwynn bequeathed £10 to the poor of Fakenham, with the rider that he might have given more 'but that I found them unruly and evil disposed people not regarding me or anything I did or could do for them'. Behind this outburst (which perhaps tells us more about Gwynn than the inhabitants of Fakenham), it is tempting to discern not merely peasant xenophobia or a chance clash of personalities, but also hostility evoked by an immigrant lawyer-landlord who showed less respect for manorial customs and tenants' rights than his predecessors had done.[40]

The surviving evidence is far too fragmentary to uphold such an interpretation. But whatever the actual circumstances underlying Gwynn's case, when proverbial wisdom had it that 'a good lawyer is an evil neighbour', it would be surprising if migrating barristers did not often encounter contempt, fear, jealousy, and resentment. Those who moved to more socially fluid counties, where many gentry were themselves relatively recent arrivals, presumably faced fewer difficulties in assimilation than if they had gone to more isolated parts, where their arrival might be taken as a direct threat to established local hierarchies and values.[41] But irrespective of destination, the mobility (both geographical and social) of members of the bar must have tended to reinforce their image as a slightly marginal class of men; how was it, asked a hostile author in 1653, that lawyers could acquire so much wealth, and 'so quickly come [to] . . . build so many houses in all parts of the kingdom, upon the heads of our foolish gentry and yeomanry, so that . . . in Northamptonshire, the heart of the land, their families make the gentry?'[42]

[40] Smith, *County and Court*, 55; PCC 51 Scrope. Despite (or because of) their litigiousness, the Norfolk peasantry had no love for lawyers. (Cf. S. T. Bindoff, *Ket's Rebellion 1549* (1949), 15–16; J. Cornwall, *Revolt of the Peasantry 1549* (1977), 17, 23, 137, 141.)

[41] J. Ray, *A Collection of English Proverbs . . .* (1670), 15; however, the proverb was originally French, and may not have been current in England during our period: see B. Whitelocke, *Memorials of the English Affairs* (1853), ii. 455. B. G. Blackwood, *The Lancashire Gentry and the Great Rebellion 1640–1660* (Manchester, 1978), 21–3; C. Holmes, 'The County Community in Stuart Historiography', *JBS*, xix (1980), 55–6. For the archetypal backwoodsman's response to the disruptive incursions of lawyers, see W. H. Long, *The Oglander Memoirs* (1888), 2. The Isle of Wight's traditional freedom from lawyers and other 'vermin' is mentioned by T. Scot, *The Second Part of Philomythie, or Philomythologie* (1625), sig. A3.

[42] Anon., *Lex Exlex . . .* (1652), 26–7.

iv. Education

Medieval and early modern educational institutions were typically much smaller and more loosely organized than their counterparts today.[43] Before the nineteenth century the inns of court, like the universities, prescribed no minimum academic qualifications or age limits for the admission of students. The only explicit restrictions on membership of the inns were based rather on ethnic, moral, religious, or social grounds, and none of these seem to have been enforced with much consistency or rigour. So in practice it was largely for the individual student, or his parents, to determine when the time was right for him to come up to London and begin preparing for the bar.[44]

Assuming fluency in English (except perhaps for a few native-born Irish or Welsh entrants), would-be common lawyers needed also some competence in French and Latin. True, the corrupt and formulaic Latin used in indictments, writs, and other legal instruments was a far cry from the classical tongue which provided the main vehicle of instruction in grammar schools and universities. Indeed the 'false and rude' Latin of the inns of court continued to be a standing, if somewhat tired, literary jibe for several centuries after Elyot, Morison, and other early Tudor humanists had first attacked the barbarous latinity of the common lawyers.[45] Nevertheless an Elizabethan bencher of the Middle Temple believed that the reason his father became a merchant rather than a lawyer was 'some lack of the Latin tongue', and command of Latin does seem to have been regarded by barristers as a mark of competence as well as social standing. John Smyth of Nibley, steward to the Berkeleys of Gloucester, disparaged his unlearned predecessor who 'understood not a line of Latin; who used to keep his courts with a white feather in his cap. . . . A man fitter for fairs and markets of cattle . . . than to

---

[43] E. J. Power, 'Persistent myths in the history of education', *Hist. of Education Q.*, ii (1962), 140–51; F. M. Powicke, 'Some Problems in the History of the Medieval University', in *idem, Ways of Medieval Life and Thought: Essays and Addresses* (1950), 182–3.

[44] Cf. *Inns of Court*, 9, 24–7, 42–4, 175, 182, 185–6.

[45] T. Elyot, *The Boke named the Gouernour*, ed. H. H. Croft (1880), i. 162; *The Reports of Sir John Spelman, Vol. II*, ed. J. H. Baker (SS, 1978), introduction, 29–32; T. Starkey, *A Dialogue Between Reginald Pole and Thomas Lupset*, ed. K. M. Burton (1948), 117, 129, 174; Additional 22603, fols. 11–11ᵛ; Additional 34218, fols. 152–3; Anon., *The Stage-Players Complaint* (1641), 5; J. Swift, 'The Answer', in *The Works of Jonathan Swift*, ed. W. Scott (Edinburgh, 1824), xiv. 221.

grapple with [a] watchful adversary in the combats of Littleton'.[46] Yet it is doubtful whether barristers needed more than a rudimentary knowledge of Latin. There would have been little call for Latin composition in routine practice at the bar; when Attorney-General Noy told young Bulstrode Whitelocke, 'I have forgot my Latin and I know you write Latin well and therefore I would have your advice in this patent', he was not necessarily engaging in uncharacteristic flattery. While barristers sometimes interlarded their prose with classical quotations, relatively few chose to write extended passages or entire compositions in Latin.[47]

The authentic and entirely distinctive working language of the bar was law-French. A character in Middleton's *A Chaste Maid in Cheapside* struggling with the Latin tags in his scholar son's letter from Cambridge, and advised to seek a translation from his wife's cousin at the inns of court, knowledgeably responds, 'Fie, they are all for French, they speak no Latin'.[48] In point of fact, by our period law-French seems to have been used mainly as a kind of technical shorthand for case notes and other memoranda. The dialect was not much *spoken* outside the learning exercises of the inns, where the more junior participants recited pleadings verbatim in law-French, a practice almost entirely superseded in the lawcourts by the exchange of written pleadings.[49] This compound of French, English, and Latin had moved a long way towards grammatical simplicity from its medieval Norman-French origins. Although defended by some lawyers as a professional instrument of unsurpassed precision and dexterity, it was more often condemned by laymen for its barbarous inelegance, obfuscatory qualities, and demeaning associations with the Norman Yoke. Yet champions and detractors alike agreed that law-French was unlikely to present significant difficulties to anyone acquainted with the rudiments of French or Latin; contemporary

---

[46] P. A. Bowyer, 'Notes concerning the Bowyer family', *Sussex Arch. Coll.*, lxiv (1923), 106; Smyth, *Lives of the Berkeleys*, ii. 310–11. Cf. Dodderidge, *The English Lawyer*, 39–51.

[47] Additional 53726, fol. 48. See below, pp. 205–6.

[48] T. Middleton, *A Chaste Maid in Cheapside* (1630), in *Works*, ed. A. H. Bullen (1885–6), v. 10. For the fourteenth-century chief justice who wrote his own will in French rather than Latin, '*quia lingua Gallica amicis meis et mihi plus est cognata et magis communis et nota quam lingua Latina*', cf. *Archaeologia*, xi (1794), 54–5.

[49] All previous accounts are superseded by J. H. Baker, *Manual of law-French* (Avebury, 1979), 9–14.

estimates of the time required to master the jargon ranged from no more than ten to a mere two days.[50]

In effect, therefore, some slight knowledge of Latin was probably the sole functional academic requirement of any significance for would-be law students, whose actual educational attainments and backgrounds varied enormously. Most would probably have attended grammar school (either a private or public foundation), although a few received part or all of their schooling from private tutors. Gervase Holles went at the age of six to the Free School of Grimsby, after a few years moved into the house of his master William Taylor, and finally spent three years with his uncle the earl of Clare, who 'even read logic and philosophy to me himself', before entering the Middle Temple at the relatively advanced age of twenty-two.[51] A still more heterogeneous intellectual formation was that of Robert Ashley, who also began grammar school (at Newport, on the Isle of Wight) when aged six, then moved successively to schools at Wimborne Minster, Corfe Castle, Dorset, and an establishment in Southampton run by the emigré Fleming divine, and translator of the Authorised Version of the Bible, Dr Hadrian Saravia, who taught him French and Latin; at the age of twelve Ashley moved again to Dr Adam Hill's school in Salisbury, finally returning home to be taught by a tutor before matriculating from Hart Hall, Oxford, in 1580, at the age of fifteen.[52] Ashley was admitted to the Middle Temple only after spending no less than nine years at Oxford, so it is perhaps small wonder that he was much better known in later life as a bibliophile and translator than as a barrister. By contrast, Robert Heath, the future chief justice, had an entirely straightforward and probably rather more typical education; brought up at home until the age of seven 'and there entered into the knowledge of the Latin tongue', he was then sent to the grammar school at Tunbridge Wells, from whence he was admitted to St John's, Cambridge, at the age of

---

[50] Ibid., 14. K. Lambley, *The Teaching and Cultivation of the French Language in England during Tudor and Stuart Times* (Manchester, 1920), 209, notes that many teachers of French lived close to the inns of court, in the ward of Farringdon-Without.

[51] *Memorials of the Holles Family 1493–1656*, ed. A. C. Wood (CS, 1937), 227–8.

[52] Sloane 2131, fols. 16–20, summarized in *Register of Members of St Mary Magdalen College, Oxford*, ed. W. D. Macray (1901), NS iii. 92–4; R. Ashley, *Of Honour*, ed. V. B. Heltzel (San Marino, Calif., 1947), 2–3.

fourteen, to Clifford's Inn at the age of seventeen, and to the Inner Temple one year later.[53]

Assuming that Ashley and Heath had already received an adequate grounding in the classics by the time they went up to university, we may wonder why they were not sent directly to London to embark upon their legal training at the inns of court or chancery. This would certainly have been the more usual course until around the mid-sixteenth century. Fortescue, writing about 1470, depicts the inns of court and chancery as a self-contained academy or university of the common law, a distinct educational alternative to Oxford and Cambridge, with the inns of chancery serving as preparatory schools or junior colleges to the inns of court. Over the next half-century or so, a trickle of university men made their way to the inns of court, and occasionally pursued distinguished legal careers, but as late as 1531 Sir Thomas Elyot specifically attacked parents who sent boys of fourteen or fifteen straight from school to learn the law, rather than first giving them a broadening exposure to the liberal arts at university, including some training in logic and rhetoric.[54]

As we now know, these and similar humanist arguments in favour of a non-specialist academic education for the sons of the landed gentry and aristocracy fell upon exceedingly receptive ears. By the end of the sixteenth century, both the universities and the inns of court had experienced an unprecedented expansion in enrolments, due largely to an influx of 'non-vocational' students,[55] while a steadily growing proportion of entrants to the inns appear as well in the matriculation registers or college records of the universities.[56]

[53] *Memoirs of Chief Justice Heath*, ed. E. P. Shirley (Philobiblion Soc., *Miscellany*, i, 1854), 18–19; *DNB*, s.v. Heath, Sir Robert.

[54] *DLLA*, 117–21; Elyot, *Gouernour*, i. 136–7; Baker, ed. *Spelman's Reports*, Vol. II, introduction, 125–7.

[55] L. Stone, 'The Educational Revolution in England, 1560–1640', *P & P*, xxviii (1964), 41–80; *Inns of Court*, 21–5. But cf. E. Russell, 'The influx of commoners into the University of Oxford before 1581: an optical illusion?', *EHR*, xcii (1977), 721–45.

[56] Cf. L. A. Knafla, 'The Matriculation Revolution and Education at the Inns of Court in Renaissance England', in *Tudor Men and Institutions*, ed. Slavin, 241–3, 261. Knafla's data relate to an Old Style year beginning 25 March, not 1 January, which explains the discrepancies between his figures and those provided by *Inns of Court*, 243–4. The numbers of students who attended university before or after their admission to the inns are also understated, due to neglect of sources other than *Al. Cant.* and *Al. Ox.* In an unpublished paper, Gary Lynch has shown that at least one out of three entrants to the MT between 1585 and 1589 were Oxford-educated although Knafla suggests that both universities together contributed in 1581 only 38

The average age of students matriculating at university or coming into commons at the inns also seems to have increased, although the evidence on this point is not entirely conclusive.[57] Ironically enough, the only English educational institutions not sharing in this era of massive growth were the inns of chancery, where admissions seem actually to have declined, precisely because their previous function of preparing young men for the inns of court through a grounding in the technicalities of original writs had been largely taken over by more generalized academic studies at Oxford and Cambridge.[58]

These developments largely explain why well over half the lawyers in both our sample groups had attended one or other university (see Table 4.7). By this criterion, Elizabeth and early Stuart barristers were remarkably well educated, more so indeed than any comparable contemporary body of laymen, except of course the advocates and physicians for whom university degrees were a professional prerequisite. Most of our common lawyers left university without bothering to take a degree, like the majority of students who were not destined for the Church, medicine, or the civil law. Even so, a surprisingly large number of the university men were graduates— more than a quarter of the barristers and over a third of the benchers, among whom we find no less than 17 MAs, besides a single BCL (Sir James Whitelocke), and even one head of house (Sir Euble Thelwall, principal of Jesus College, Oxford, from 1620 to 1630).

Those who were not university men had been educated at home, school, an inn of chancery, or a combination of these, sometimes supplemented by service as an apprentice or clerk to a practising lawyer; thus the regicide barrister John Bradshaw, who seems not to have attended university, was articled to an attorney at Congleton, Cheshire, after attending the Middleton Free School and before

---

per cent, and in 1601 48.5 per cent of MT entrants; by the late 1630s no less than 39 per cent of MT entrants had Oxford connections. (I am grateful to Mr Lynch for discussing these results with me.)

[57] L. Stone, 'The Age of Admission to College in Seventeenth-Century England', *Hist. of Education*, ix (1980), 97–9, and references cited therein. M. Hastings, *The Court of Common Pleas in Fifteenth-century England* (Ithaca, 1947), 65; Elyot, *Gouernour*, i. 136; Baker, 'Legal Profession', 33, and n. 79; *Inns of Court*, 9. Baker found that the average age at admission of 39 landholder's heirs who joined the inns between 1470 and 1530 was 20–21 years, but general conclusions can hardly be drawn from such a narrow sample. The mean age at admission of 68 barristers from our sample whose exact or approximate birth dates are known was 19.5 years, and the median just under 19 years.

[58] *Inns of Court*, 129.

Table 4.7. Higher Education

	Bar sample		Bench sample			King's servants 1625–40[1] (per cent)	MPs, 1640[2] (per cent)
	Number	Per cent	Number	Per cent			
Oxford University	37	32.2 ⎫	127	33.0 ⎫		⎫	50.7
Cambridge University	26	22.6 ⎬ 54.8	95	24.7 ⎬ 59.2		40.2 ⎬	
Either or both	—	— ⎭	6	1.5 ⎭		⎭	
Neither	52	45.2	157		40.8		
Inn of Chancery	27	23.5	149	38.7			
Degrees held:							
BA	15		53				
MA	2		17				
BCL	—		1				

[1] Aylmer, *King's Servants*, 273.
[2] D. Brunton and D. H. Pennington, *Members of the Long Parliament* (1954), 7.

entering Gray's Inn at the age of eighteen in 1620.[59] As late as 1631
Thomas Powell (no university man himself) urged that those
intended for the bar should first be placed in an inn of chancery and
'entered as clerks in the office of some prothonotary of the common
pleas to add the skill of the practick to their speculation'.

One who
followed this highly traditional course was Edmund Randolph, who
had served for some thirteen years in the office of Zachary Scott,
second prothonotary of Common Pleas, when he was admitted in
1593 from Furnival's to Lincoln's Inn, his master's own house,
where he was called to the bar seven years later.[60] Unfortunately,
there is no way of telling how many took a similar route to the bar
during our period. But it seems reasonable to suspect that those who
did were rather constrained by economic circumstances than persuaded by broadly educational considerations, let alone fashion,
both of which now pointed firmly towards a university education.
Whatever the practical benefits of a working acquaintance with plea
rolls and writs, late Tudor and early Stuart law students were more
frequently urged to acquire a knowledge of logic and rhetoric at
Oxford or Cambridge, the better to cope with the confused particu-
larity of the common law when they reached the inns of court.[61] Of
course a sojourn at university might also inculcate the sort of
intellectual prejudices summed up in Erasmus's characterization of
the English lawyer's calling as being as 'far removed as can be from
true learning'—which was perhaps one reason why parents sometimes brought their sons home from university to read the law under
supervision for a year or so before going up to London.[62]

[59] R. Head, *Congleton Past and Present* (Congleton, 1887), 79; *DNB*, s.v. Brad-
shaw, John; 'A letter from John Bradshawe of Gray's Inn', *Chetham Miscellanies*,
(Chetham Soc., 1856).
[60] Powell, *Tom of all Trades*, 25; STAC 8/9/4(112); *LIAdmR*, i. 115; *LIBB*, ii. 68;
J. H. Baker, 'Sir Thomas Robinson (1618–83), Chief Prothonotary of the Common
Pleas', *Bodl. Lib. Rec.*, x (1978), 40; *idem, Spelman's Reports*, Vol. II, introduction,
129–30. Cf. William Salusbury's advice that his son Owen should read writs in Mr
John Jones's chamber every morning to learn 'our country business'. (Smith, ed.,
Calendar of Salusbury Correspondence, 152.)
[61] R. J. Schoeck, 'Rhetoric and Law in Sixteenth-Century England', *Studies in
Philology*, i (1953), 110–27. Cf. A. Fraunce, *The Lawiers Logike* (1588), sigs. ¶ᵛ–¶¶3;
Dodderidge, *The English Lawyer*, 27–39; W. Fulbecke, *A Direction, or Preparative to
the Study of the Law* (1600), sigs. B4–5, fols. 81ᵛ–83ᵛ; Bodl. MS Rawlinson C 207, fols.
246–246ᵛ.
[62] R. W. Chambers, *Thomas More* (1938), 85. Cf. J. W. Clay and J. Lister,
'Autobiography of Sir John Savile of Methley, Knight . . . 1546–1607', *Yorks. Arch.
J.*, xv (1900), 423; *Memorials of Father Augustine Baker, O.S.B.*, ed. J. McCann and
H. Connelly (Cath. Rec. Soc., 1933), 45–6; *The Responsa Scholarum of the English
College, Rome, Part One: 1598–1621*, ed. A. Kenny (Cath. Rec. Soc., 1962), 124.

Since the inns of court possessed nothing remotely resembling a collegiate tutorial system, each student or inner-barrister was left to confront this 'most harsh study' by himself, with whatever informal assistance and oversight might be obtained from kinsmen, chamber-fellows, or other senior members. While students usually read on their own, they could and did discuss their reading with each other, as well as attending and participating in various aural 'learning exercises'. The testimony of individual students and the abundance of manuscript notes and reports of case arguments, moots, and readings make it clear that many still took the learning exercises very seriously and gained substantial benefit from them.[63]

Quite apart from their considerable heuristic value, however, during the second half of the sixteenth century, as the degree of utter-barrister was increasingly recognized as the basic qualification for audience in the higher courts, the performance of a minimum quota of learning exercises came to be required of all students seeking call to the bar. Participation alone seems to have sufficed; there were no sanctions to enforce minimum standards of performance, except perhaps for the scorn which an ill-prepared mootman might evoke from his audience. In other words, the learning exercises could function effectively as teaching devices, but not as assessment or examining procedures. Indeed, no specific levels of academic attainment or legal knowledge were prescribed for would-be barristers until long after our period. The criteria were either merely quantitative—so many years' membership, so many moots argued—or else extremely vague—'of good conversation and diligence in observing exercises of learning', 'fittest for their learning and honest conversation, and well given'. It was left to those who actually exercised the power of calling to the bar to determine whether particular candidates satisfied these latter requirements. Their decisions were inevitably influenced by favouritism and patronage, despite standing orders against calls 'by letters or for any reward' and the occasional postponement or rejection of calls ostensibly for this reason. While the more blatant abuses were associated with reader's calls at the Lent and Summer learning vacations, personal and non-academic factors continued to play a significant role, even after the last vestiges of the individual reader's

---

[63] *Inns of Court*, 124–31; cf. D'Ewes, *Autobiography*, i. 149–285; Northants RO, IC 25 (Thomas to John Isham, 1602).

rights to call to the bar had been finally expropriated by the governing bodies of the four inns.[64]

So Francis Lenton's portrait of the young inns of court gentleman who 'achieves much experience before he arrives at the bar, and then (if ever) begins to study, when (for his time) he should begin to plead' cannot be dismissed as mere satirical exaggeration.[65] Collectively, barristers were less often accused of incompetence than attorneys and solicitors, whose calling, conventionally regarded as mechanical and plebeian, could hardly avoid such sneers. But besides individual disappointed clients blaming the defeat of their suits on the ignorance of their counsel—complaints which in the nature of things cannot easily be verified—there are also occasional disparaging references of a more general nature, as, for example, to students 'called to the bar for favour, or money, and of desert in learning seldom'.[66] Given the manifest inadequacies of the inns' educational provisions, it is perhaps surprising that such charges were not more frequent. On the other hand, a barrister's professional success probably depended as much on access to patronage and native wit as on formal legal learning, which in any case could just as well be acquired after, as before, call to the bar, by reading, observation, and experience.

To sum up, the academic formation of common lawyers in the late sixteenth and early seventeenth centuries was far less regulated, systematic, and uniform than it is today, and indeed a good deal more diverse than it had been only a century before. For this change the humanists' emphasis on liberal education rather than vocational training was largely responsible; the results are amply apparent in the cultural and intellectual vitality displayed by the profession during the half-century or so before the Long Parliament.[67]

v. Marriage

A well-connected wife could materially advance her barrister-husband's career, besides increasing his assets with her dowry and

[64] *Inns of Court*, 131–5; W. C. Richardson, *History of the Inns of Court* (Baton Rouge, La., n.d. [?1978]), 169–74. For pre-call lobbying of benchers, see *The Diary of Sir Simonds D'Ewes (1622–1624)*, ed. E. Bourcier (Paris, 1974), 134, 143.

[65] F. Lenton, *Characterisimi: or, Lenton's Leasures* (1631), 29.

[66] *Inns of Court*, 57–8, 58 n., 150; *Lawyers*, 74, n. 30.; Additional 41613 ('The Course of the Lawes of England and the abuse of the ministers thereof, laid open') ([n.d., but *c.*1603–6; cf. fol. 119]), fol. 84; Anon., *Enchiridion Legum* (1673), 123; see also below, pp. 287, 294–5.

[67] Cf. Baker, ed. *Spelman's Reports*, Vol. II, introduction, ch. 4; also below, ch. 6.

overseeing them in his absence at the terms and assizes. So it comes as no surprise that the overwhelming majority of lawyers in both our sample groups (two-thirds of the barristers, virtually nine out of ten benchers) are known to have married at least once, while nearly one in five benchers married twice (see Table 4.8). Sir Thomas Ireland certainly had four wives, and the parliamentarian Welsh judge William Powell may even have married five times, although poor documentation and the special difficulties of Welsh genealogy combine to make this record slightly less convincing than one might wish.[68] Only three barristers and no more than twelve benchers are positively known to have remained bachelors all their lives. Comparable data for other population groups are not readily available, but the benchers' marriage rate was certainly higher than those of both the Elizabethan and early Stuart peerage and the villagers of seventeenth-century Shepshed, Leicestershire.[69]

The benchers' comparatively greater readiness to marry was partly a function of age; few men reached the bench of their inn

Table 4.8. Marriage

	Bar		Bench	
	Number	Per cent	Number	Per cent
Married once	67	58.3	267	69.4
Married twice	13	11.3	62	16.1
Married three or more times	2	1.7	16	4.2
Never married	3	2.6	12	3.1
Unknown if married or not	30	26.0	28	7.3
Total	115	99.9	385	100.1

[68] For Ireland and Powell, see Appendix E below. Cf. V. Larminie, 'Marriage and the Family: the example of the 17th century Newdigates', *Midland Hist.*, ix (1984), 7–8.

[69] T. H. Hollingsworth, 'The Demography of the British Peerage', supplement to *Population Studies*, xvii (1964), 19–21; D. Levine, *Family Formation in an Age of Nascent Capitalism* (New York, 1977), 75. E. A. Wrigley and R. S. Schofield, *The Population History of England 1541–1871* (1981), 257, note the lack of 'direct and general evidence about the detailed incidence of marriage in England before the census of 1851'; the proportion of people never married between 1596 and 1641 is estimated at between 8.4 and 24.1 per cent (Table 7.28), but these figures refer only to the cohort aged between 40 and 44 years. F. D. McKinnon's undocumented claim that the majority of eighteenth-century barristers and benchers remained bachelors must be regarded with some scepticism. (*Johnson's England* (Oxford, 1933), ii. 288.)

before the middle years of life, so the members of the benchers'
sample had been at risk, as the demographers say, rather longer than
the barristers, of whom a small but significant cohort died in their
twenties and early thirties. Another reason why the barristers appear
to have been less prone to marry than the benchers is sheer lack of
evidence—in this as in most other respects, their personal life
histories are generally more poorly documented than the average
bencher's. But since marriage was to a considerable extent both
cause and effect of professional success, the apparent difference in
marriage rates between barristers and benchers was probably real
enough. A lawyer who had no inherited estate of any consequence
would usually have needed to establish at least a minimal practice at
the bar before he was in any position to take a wife—unless, of
course, his own father could be persuaded to support the couple, as
William Gerrard's father contracted to do when his son married the
daughter of a London merchant only a year after being called to the
bar at Gray's Inn.[70] The overriding importance of financial considerations is presumably the main reason why marriages before call
were rare, although not unknown; William Becke's unsuccessful
courtship of Elizabeth Lynn of Ely in 1590, five years before he
became a barrister of the Middle Temple, seems to have foundered
precisely on Becke's failure to convince the girl and her parents that
his estate was as large and unencumbered as he made it out to be.[71]

It may also be significant that no bachelor from either sample
group rose to the judicial bench of Westminster Hall, while only one
(Sir Robert Hitcham of Gray's Inn) was created serjeant at law. This
is not to say that those who never married were an entirely
undistinguished body of men. On the contrary, they included the
eminent antiquaries John Selden and Francis Tate (who became a
Welsh judge); Selden's friend the poet and wit Richard Martin (who
paid £1,500 for the recordership of London in 1618); Sir Euble
Thelwall, master in Chancery and principal of Jesus College,
Oxford; Sir Edward Moseley, attorney-general of the Duchy of
Lancaster; and the notorious miser money-lender Hugh Audley.[72]

[70] Greater London. RO, Acc. 276/315.
[71] CUL MS EDR H 2/1. Cf. the intense discussion of Oliver St John's financial
status and prospects as a match for Joanna Altham, his future wife. (*Barrington
Family Letters 1628–1632*, ed. A. Searle (CS, 1983), 119–20, 123, 131, 136.)
[72] *DNB*, except Moseley, for whom see Somerville, *Office Holders*, 21; in 1617 it
was reported that Moseley was about to marry the widow of Sir William Bowyer.
(*The Letters of John Chamberlain*, ed. N. E. McClure (Philadelphia, 1939), ii. 122,
136.)

Most of these men did not make their names primarily as common lawyers, however, even if their failure to marry should obviously not be ascribed simply to failure in their chosen vocation. Without pressing the point further, many individual exemplars can be cited in support of the proposition that an opportune marriage often materially assisted a career at the bar.

Family alliances within the legal profession were particularly valuable. Their role in securing judicial favour, and hence attracting clients, was discussed in Chapter Two above. While marriage to a judge's daughter, niece, or granddaughter may not have been an infallible guarantee of success, it was far from a hindrance. Among the fourteen benchers who established such connections, two (Sir Henry Hobart and Sir Edward Littleton) achieved chief-justiceships, while Sir Heneage Finch, who married a granddaughter of Sir Robert Bell, chief baron of the Exchequer, would certainly have risen well beyond the rank of serjeant and the recordership of London had he not died in 1631 at the relatively early age of fifty-one.[73] On a rather humbler plane, the barrister John Keeling owed his appointment as one of the four common pleaders of London in part at least to the personal solicitation of Sir John Croke, a puisne justice of King's Bench and his wife's grandfather.[74] Even where a lawyer father-in-law or more distant relative was not able to exercise judicial patronage, he might still be able to provide invaluable advice and professional contacts, such as John Wild and Sir Humphrey Winch doubtless received *en route* to the Westminster Hall bench from their respective fathers-in-law, Serjeant Sir Thomas Harris and Solicitor-General Sir Richard Onslow.[75] The inns of court had always constituted a lively marriage market, so it is not surprising to find a good deal of intermarriage among their professional membership. Typically, young barristers married daughters of senior colleagues, as with the three Middle Templars Robert Breton, Henry Martin, and Arthur Turner, whose brides were respectively the daughters of the benchers Sir Francis Harvey, John Jermyn, and William Gibbes.[76] Apart from the professional advantage such

[73] *DNB.*

[74] London Corp. RO, Remembrancia VIII, fol. 2–2ᵛ; Appendix F, note 2. Bulstrode Whitelocke noted in 1629 that after Harbottle Grimston had married the daughter of Sir John's younger brother, Sir George Croke, who was also a judge, he 'took to the profession of the law and prospered'. (Additional 53726, fol. 83ᵛ.)

[75] *DNB*, s.v. Wild, John; Winch, Sir Humphrey.

[76] A. F. Pollard, 'The Reformation Parliament as a Matrimonial Agency and its

matches might bring, a wealthy lawyer's heiress was no mean prize in purely financial terms. Thus, Sir Robert Heath married his barrister son Edward to Lucy Croke, only daughter and heiress of a rich colleague on the Inner Temple bench, whose landed estate of over £1,000 a year was settled in trust for Lucy after her father's death.[77]

Extra-professional marriage connections could also be of considerable benefit, monetary and otherwise. The particularly fortunate marital ventures of George Radcliffe of Gray's Inn combined the best of both worlds, his first wife being a daughter of John Finch, then bencher of Gray's Inn, subsequently chief justice and lord keeper to Charles I, his second a cousin of Thomas Wentworth, earl of Strafford, who became Radcliffe's chief patron and employer. Sir Edward Coke was married twice outside the profession, first to the Norfolk heiress Bridget Paston, who reputedly brought him 'extraordinary wealth', and then to Lady Elizabeth Hatton, granddaughter of William Cecil, Lord Burghley, a match also highly successful from a financial point of view, if less so in other respects.[78] Had he himself been free to remarry, Coke might not have forced his daughter Frances to marry Buckingham's brother, in an effort to regain favour at court after his dismissal from judicial office in 1616. In 1621 Chief Justice Ley, then aged over seventy, wed a seventeen-year-old niece of Buckingham's 'to be of the kindred', while a few years later Sir Thomas Richardson's elevation to the chief-justiceship of Common Pleas was said to reward his marriage to Lady Elizabeth Ashburnham, Buckingham's maternal second cousin twice removed.[79] The biographers of Hugh Hughes, 'the real founder of the fortunes of Plas Coch', suggest that this enterprising and successful Welsh barrister owed much to his auspicious marriage to Elizabeth Montagu of Brigstock, Northamptonshire.[80] Such unions were inevitably an object of keen interest to curious or envious colleagues. In 1602 the barrister John Manningham noted in his diary that 'Mrs Mary Andrews, daughter and heir to Mr

---

National Effects', *History*, xxi (1936), 223. (I am grateful to Mr K. Thomas for this reference.) *Vis. Northants*, ed. Metcalfe, 70; *HS*, xx. 46; *Al. Cant.*, iv. 273.

[77] Kopperman, thesis, 83–8; Additional 37343, fol. 146.

[78] *DNB*, s.v. Coke, Sir Edward; Radcliffe, Sir George.

[79] Chamberlain, *Letters*, ii. 381; *Diary of Walter Yonge, Esq.*, ed. G. Roberts (CS, 1848), 40–1.

[80] T. Richards and E. G. Jones, 'The Catalogue of the Plas Coch Manuscripts', NLW typescript, 1937, (i)–(ii).

Andrews of Sandy [Bedfordshire] was married to one Mr Main of Gray's Inn; had £1,000 present, and if Andrews have issue, to have another. Main had but £150 per annum.' At his death in 1624 James Main had been twelve years a bencher of Gray's Inn, possessed substantial landed property in Buckinghamshire, Hertfordshire, and Kent, and could afford to leave all five of his daughters marriage portions as large as those which their mother had brought him twenty-two years before.[81]

Barristers also competed with peers and gentry for the daughters and widows of wealthy citizens and merchants, as their predecessors had done since at least the fourteenth century.[82] Two judges renowned for their piety, Sir George Croke and Henry Rolle, both wed daughters of Sir Thomas Bennet, a one-time lord mayor and sheriff of London (Croke, Rolle's senior by a full generation, married for the first time in his early fifties); another judge, Sir John Dodderidge, who was born in Devon but lived most of his life just outside London at Egham, Surrey, was fortunate enough to take for his first wife the daughter of a mayor of Exeter and for his third the widow of a London goldsmith.[83] Apart from the likely value of the dowry, the peculiar advantage of such a match for a barrister in the early and middling stages of his career was as a possible avenue to lucrative urban office. Nicholas Ducke, the eldest son of a well-to-do Exeter citizen, would doubtless have stood a fair chance of becoming recorder of the city even if he had not married the daughter of a mayor and alderman; but Giles Tucker, who came from a Wiltshire yeoman family, must certainly have owed a good deal to the influence of his father-in-law Thomas Eyre, alderman and mayor of Salisbury, when he was elected recorder there in 1600. An even richer prize was obtained by Thomas Coventry the younger, whose marriage to a relative of the town clerk of London helped secure him a judge's place in the City's sheriff's court, which led eventually to his election as recorder of London in 1616.[84]

The surviving, albeit incomplete, evidence suggests that barristers

---

[81] *The Diary of John Manningham of the Middle Temple, 1602–1603*, ed. R. P. Sorlien (Providence, R.I., 1976), 86; *VCH, Herts.*, ii. 222–3, 379; *HS*, xxii. 75; Herts. RO, 89/HW/43.

[82] Cf. S. Thrupp, *The Merchant Class of Medieval London* (Ann Arbor, 1962), 263.

[83] *DNB*, s.v. Croke, Sir George; Dodderidge, Sir John; and Rolle, Henry.

[84] *HS*, vi. 98; [Exeter RO], *Assizes and Quarter Sessions in Exeter* (Exeter, n.d.), 5; R. C. Hoare, *The History of Modern Wiltshire*, vi: *Old and New Sarum* (1843), 306; *HS*, cv. 196; HLS MS 106, fol. 1ᵛ.

intermarried with three main social strata: the landed gentry, the merchant classes broadly defined, and the learned professions. The upper and lower limits are fairly clear. Although a handful of peers married the daughters of lawyers, the reverse connection was most unusual; when Lady Elizabeth Hatton, daughter of the earl of Exeter, married Sir Edward Coke, a man already notorious for the rapidity of his rise to office and wealth, surprise was expressed that the titled widow should have descended to such a person. Only three examples of such *mésalliances* are to be found among the benchers of our sample group (the other two being the marriage of Lady Elizabeth Berkeley, Lord Hunsdon's daughter, to Sir Thomas Chamberlain of Gray's Inn, who was said to have paid £5,000 for his bride, and that of Dionysia, daughter of Sir James Ley, earl of Marlborough but formerly a bencher of Lincoln's Inn, to John Harington, a younger colleague of the same house).[85] Conversely, there is only a single clear instance of a lawyer from our sample groups marrying into the yeomanry, and only one apparent case of a barrister taking an attorney's daughter to wife.[86] (Further research might reveal, however, that some of the many wives whose family origins are at present unknown came from such backgrounds.)

Most doubtless aspired to better their lot by marrying as well as they possibly could. In general, barristers were acceptable marriage partners for the daughters of both the urban and rural magisterial classes of early modern England (the peerage excepted), although sometimes only after considerable anguish and cold-blooded financial calculation on the part of the prospective parents-in-law. In a highly competitive market counsellors enjoyed the special advantage of access to information about potential wives gained in the course of their work. They also showed themselves able and willing to venture abroad if necessary in order to secure a good match; of the fifty-two barristers in our sample group whose wives' regional origins are known only nineteen came from their husband's own county.

---

[85] Chamberlain, *Letters*, i. 54; *DNB*, s.v. Chamberlain, Sir Thomas, Ley, Sir James. However, Sir John Bramston and Sir John Denham both married the daughters of Irish peers, while Sir Thomas Widdrington's wife, Frances, was the daughter of Ferdinando, Baron Fairfax of Cameron in the Scots peerage.

[86] Erasmus Earle's wife, born Frances Fountain, came from a yeomanry family in his home village of Salle, Norfolk. (F. Blomefield and C. Parkin, *Topographical History of . . . Norfolk* (1805–10), vi. 245–7.) Rowland Ward married the daughter of James Harbourne, of Middlesex, who may have been a King's Bench attorney. (*HS*, xii. 275, and Dr C. W. Brooks, personal communication.)

In emphasizing the material benefits lawyers sought, and frequently found, in marriage, it would be wrong to leave the impression that all barristers approached marriage with hard heads and cold hearts, or that those who did invariably achieved the material ends they sought. Among Henry Sherfield's papers is the copy of a letter written to his brother Richard in 1614 explaining his reluctance to remarry (following the death of his first wife) only in order to pay off his debts. Sherfield protested that 'I cannot term the selling of my body to be any other than a most base, vile and abominable thing and no other thing should I do by such a marriage as I am harkened to by your self and others'. When he did eventually remarry three years later, Sherfield gained 'a virtuous and religious wife', but no commensurate financial benefit, since the profits of the lands which his new bride brought him were more than absorbed by the demands of the children from her former marriage, who indeed bore some responsibility for the financial catastrophe which eventually overwhelmed their stepfather.[87]

Nor were the hazards of matrimony merely financial, as other barristers discovered to their cost. Sir Edward Coke and his elderly antagonist Lord Keeper Ellesmere both endured notoriously unhappy marriages. So also, we may infer, did two of Ellesmere's protégés, Sir Thomas Chamberlain, 'a man of good disposition but unfortunate in his marriage' and Sir John Davies, whose clairvoyant wife Eleanor went into full mourning in 1625 immediately upon predicting his death within three years (it actually occurred in 1626), thereafter maintaining the reputation summed up in the anagram of her name ('Never so mad a Ladie') with a stream of apocalyptic prophecies published at frequent intervals down to the time of her own death nearly thirty years later. The 'distraction of mind' from which Bulstrode Whitelocke's first wife suffered was less spectacular, but no less serious, since it led to her death 'in greatest extremity and raging'.[88]

Whitelocke recalled that before her final illness his wife, 'not being well contented with her living in the country, especially in my absence at London for the terms, and at the assizes . . . was desirous to have a house in London, to be near her friends and to have more

---

[87] Hants RO, 44M69, Box S13, unsorted papers, endorsed 'A lre. drawen after my bro Rich. S. jarrings wth me at my retorne from Mich term 1614. but never sent'.

[88] Ellesmere 214; CUL MS Add. 6863, fol. 25; B. J. Harris, 'Davies, Lady Eleanor', in *Radicals*, i. 216–17; Spalding, *Improbable Puritan*, 54.

of my company'.[89] These were not unusual attitudes, although a few women may have positively welcomed the various opportunities created by their husband's periodic absences on legal business. The satirist Henry Fitzgeffrey claimed that lawyers should be afraid to marry,

> That from their wives must all the term time tarry.
> O Sir! if termly absence breeds the fear,
> How many frights each lawyer in a year?[90]

A barrister's frequent absences from home might well tend to exacerbate anxieties about his wife's fidelity; while cuckoldry was a wellnigh universal contemporary obsession, it still seems remarkable that the Middle Templar John Davies should have felt impelled to write no fewer than ten sonnets ridiculing Sir Edward Coke on the basis of a widely reported rumour that Coke's wife was pregnant by another man when they married. Barristers probably did not need reminding that 'a mere common lawyer['s] . . . terms are his wife's vacations'.[91]

It may be that even the limited degree of autonomy fostered by their husband's absences from home tended to breed a certain independence of spirit among barristers' wives, whether expressed in their supposed penchant for 'excess of apparel', which James I criticized, or—on a more individual note—in the 'great boldness and audacity' with which Serjeant Thomas Athow's redoubtable wife Ann was evidently accustomed to greet strangers.[92] Thomas Thornton's eulogy of his wife Bess, written in 1604 just after her death in childbed, portrays a woman of considerable strength of character and all-round competence, a companion and partner, rather than the mere compliant subordinate depicted by some contemporary theologians and modern historians:

She was a great reader of Scripture . . . charitable to the poor, most loving and dutiful to her husband, and careful and provident for her children and household . . . of stature low and slender, of complexion fair and well-favoured, of words only few, in judgement and resolution more excellent

---

[89] Additional 53726, fol. 89.

[90] Fitzgeffrey, *Satyres*, epigram 40; cf. J. Day, *Law-tricks* (1608), sig. D4.

[91] *The Miscellaneous Works in Prose and Verse of Sir Thomas Overbury*, ed. E. F. Rimbault (1856), 86; *The Poems of Sir John Davies*, ed. R. Kreuger (Oxford, 1975), 171–6.

[92] Folger MS M. b. 42, fol. 45; Haward, *Reports*, 57; '*Merry Passages*', ed. Lippincott, 138.

than others of her sex. She only governed the house and servants and received and paid all charges, her husband meddling with no charge at home; she was not contentious but of a mild disposition and would avoid strife; and yet in a right cause she was stout and of great carriage.[93]

Yet when all possible benefits of temporary partial independence were taken into account and weighed against the disadvantages of loneliness and separation, most barrister's wives would probably have wished that their husbands could spend more time at home. We can hardly generalize from the case of Serjeant John Hele, who reportedly 'went no oftener than once by the year to pay his wife her duty', nor even the outspokenness of Mistress Ann Kytchin, the wife of an eminent Elizabethan bencher of Gray's Inn, who 'would often blame herself for marrying so rashly, and would wish that all women would take heed of her for marrying with a lawyer, and would say that she had been better to have married to a thresher, for such when he had had his hire would come home at night and be merry with her'.[94]

Nevertheless, a good many wives must have shared or at least sympathized with these sentiments. Anne Radcliffe's husband wrote to her from Gray's Inn just after the dissolution of the 1624 parliament with the news that 'many good laws were made but Michaelmas term is not altered, which bill might have had your voice, I dare say'. Even before his marriage, the future serjeant at law Erasmus Earle was both sending his future wife assurances of undying affection and at the same time protesting the impossibility of getting away from London to visit her, since 'I cannot so suddenly lay apart my business'. Three months later, having managed a brief trip to Norfolk for the wedding, Earle justified his hasty return to London in a letter to the forsaken bride:

I no sooner give audience unto affection but it persuades me that thy company is to be valued before all gain, all preferment; on the other side reason . . . adviseth me to be careful in a good manner for future times. . . . I am no less loving than heretofore, but more careful for thee, for I protest unto thee, that the end of all my labours, next after the glory of God, is especially intended for thy good.

[93] Northants RO, Thornton 2251. For evidence that Bess was not invariably a model of wifely deference, cf. Huntington Library, MS Stowe 3966, Thomas Thornton to Sir Peter Temple, 20 Feb. 1598.

[94] Guildhall Library, MS 9585 (Liber Depositionum 1581–93, 2 Feb. 1582). (I am grateful to Dr V. Brodsky-Elliott for this reference.)

Romantic conceits are indeed ousted by gainful prudence from Earle's subsequent marital correspondence, which largely consists of detailed admonitions and instructions for the management of his children, house, lands, and servants.[95]

Frances Earle's reaction to her husband's rapid transformation from lover to bread-winner is, unfortunately, not recorded. Yet many barrister's wives probably had similar experiences, just as they also helped facilitate their husband's careers by taking on heavy responsibilities as overseers of estate and household. As we know regrettably little about these women as individuals, the long run of letters written by Rebecca Sherfield to her barrister husband in London has particular value. Since it was the second marriage for both partners, their relationship might easily have been based less on emotional affection than mutual convenience. Yet Rebecca's correspondence conveys an entirely different impression. These reports to 'my best and best beloved friend' on the state of his crops, farms, tenants, kin, neighbours, and acquaintances are pervaded by a constant theme—the pain of separation. Her heartfelt wish 'that your occasions were not such, but that I might have more [of] your company' was, as she recognized, doomed to disappointment, since 'every year brings more occasions of business'. Yet Rebecca still found it hard to cope with Henry's inevitable absences.

Thus she writes of 'the unpleasingness of the remembrance of the beginning of the term', sends her love in anticipation of his imminent return from 'this ungodly term', and claims that 'thinking of the end of the term doth much prevail against my sad discontentedness'. Occasionally, but clearly far too seldom, Rebecca was able to accompany her spouse to London, where he rented a house for them both in Mincing Lane. After one such excursion early in 1624, when Henry was serving as MP for Salisbury, his wife expressed her determination 'if the parliament should hold long when it doth begin next', to

quite turn Londoner, for it will not be in my power to have any more patience for longer time than the terms to be absent from you. There will be by the time this come to you a third part almost of this term past; I wish with

[95] *Radcliffe Correspondence*, ed. Whitaker, 124. Hereford Public Lib. Boycott MSS, Erasmus Earle letter-book, fols. 45–8. Cf. the account of Earle as 'a very covetous man' in North, *Lives*, i. 53. For a much more sensitive concern about the effects of husbandly absences, see Roger Hill's letters to his wife Abigail in the 1640s. (Additional 46500, fols. 7, 11, 19, 21, 30, 31–2^v, 36, 37.)

my heart it were come to the last day. . . . I may wish it for many reasons, but this one is noted by others, that I enjoy much better health when you are at home than when you are absent. I could wish if it might be that our living might be more together, but God's will be done.[96]

It would be somewhat surprising if such conjugal devotion were entirely typical, especially given the various strains arising from the peripatetic life of the bar. Nevertheless, few lawyers' wives are likely to have been much amused by a contemporary jesting claim, that they had 'the sweetest lives of any women, because their husbands return always *crura thymo plenae*'—like bees to the hive, their pockets laden with money.[97]

[96] Hants RO, 44M69/xxxi/16, 19, 24, 28, 31.
[97] '*Merry Passages*', ed. Lippincott, 66; cf. Virgil, *Georgics*, IV. 180–1.

CHAPTER FIVE

ADVANCEMENT

'... the common lawyers (suppose in the beginning they are but husbandmen's sons), come in time to be chief fathers of the land ...'.

Thomas Nash, *Pierce Penilesse his Supplication to the Divell* (1592), sig. D3

'If I were to soar up to the skies (I mean after worldly preferment), the law is the only way ...'.

Robert Wynn to Lady Wynn, 19 November 1611 (NLW, Wynn of Gwydir papers, 552)

TO an age obsessed with the mutability of the human condition, Elizabethan and early Stuart common lawyers generally appeared as rising men. Most later historians have accepted this judgement at face value, without asking how many lawyers actually rose, or how far they ascended. Indeed the work of a near contemporary, Edward Waterhouse (1619–70), still remains the only attempt at a systematic treatment of these matters. Discussing 'the rise and decay of men and families', Waterhouse asserted that of all 'arts, callings or ways of life', the 'rises of persons are not so great, nor so general, as [in] those of law and trade'.

Waterhouse went on to point out that lawyers (by which term he clearly intended barristers, not attorneys, solicitors, or civilians) were 'the most knowing men in business of any profession. . . . They know the nature of estates and the condition of their owners and can thereby pleasure themselves more and surer than other men can'. They also 'monopolise great, rich, noble, trusty places', 'drive a trade of gain with no money stock, nor hazard their gain by no credit, nor exhaust themselves by no charge upon their chambers'. In sum, being 'knowingly bred, well descended, richly fortuned, amply allied, assiduously versed, or bred under such as are these or the most of them', it was hardly surprising that barristers came 'to purchase the best seats, the noblest royalties, the best to be improved lands in the nation, and to match their children with least portions and to most advantage of any men'.[1]

Common lawyers generally agreed that their profession was a particularly fertile source of honour and riches: 'The posterity of lawyers hath more flourished than that either of the clergy or citizens', noted a young law student in 1602. In the contemporaneous preface to the second volume of his law reports, Sir Edward Coke named more than two hundred families who had been raised to nobility, or at least gentility, by a lawyer forbear, concluding with the Psalmist that 'the just shall flourish like the palm tree; and spread abroad as the cedars of Libanus'. Coke's proposal that the worldly gains accumulated by members of his order should be regarded as virtue's fitting reward neatly countered the more prevalent view that lawyers raised themselves at the expense of their unfortunate clients.[2]

An updated and more ambitious version of Coke's list was published in three successive editions by one Henry Philipps during the mid-1680s. Philipps's *The Grandeur of the Law* purported to demonstrate how more than five hundred and fifty 'illustrious families . . . have been raised to honour and wealth by the profession of the law'. Not surprisingly, the compiler showed little caution in asserting genealogical links between gentry families of his own time and their purported lawyer progenitors, besides listing families whose claims to rank among the landed gentry were somewhat dubious. Still more suspect is his working assumption that the legal earnings of a putative lawyer ancestor, rather than any other possible source, are sufficient to explain the founding of a given family's fortunes. Hence Philipps's bland assertion that the house of Cecil had been raised by 'an eminent lawyer of the society of Gray's Inn . . . created Baron of Burleigh in the reign of Queen Elizabeth' — to which the antiquary Anthony Wood justly responded (by way of marginal annotation), 'Twas not his law that promoted him, but politics, industry, favour, etc.'.[3]

---

[1] E. Waterhouse, *The Gentleman's Monitor* (1665), 199–203; *idem, A Discourse and Defence of Arms and Armoury* (1660), 138. Cf. L. Stone, *Social Change and Revolution in England 1540–1640* (1965). 133. *Inns of Court*, 21–3.

[2] Manningham, *Diary*, 78; Prest, 'Fees and Earnings', 165. Cf. James Ley's claim in 1602 that 'no noble family or knight or gentleman's house of any great antiquity but was either founded or augmented by a professor of the common law'. (CUL MS Dd. 11.87, fol. 170: my translation.)

[3] H. P[hilipps], *The Grandeur of the Law: Or, An exact Collection of the Nobility*

Ironically, these exaggerated claims for the law as a socio-economic escalator appeared at a time when the long-term balance of demand and supply seems to have been swinging hard against entrants to the bar, while a number of alternative callings—the Church, the Army, government office, and trade—were offering young men increasingly attractive prospects.[4] In any case, a listing of the most successful lawyers inevitably raises questions about the rest. Marked differences in wealth between senior members of the four inns of court were evident well over a century before Philipps's compilation was published. For example, a survey of benchers and leading utter-barristers in the late 1570s classified six out of twenty lawyers at Gray's Inn, the largest house, as 'poor' or 'smally practised', although another eleven were noted to be 'wealthy', and three more 'of good living'. Unfortunately we have no indication of the criteria on which these judgements were based, nor of how well informed were those who made them. In the early seventeenth century it is also possible to find instances of poverty-stricken barristers supported by pensions from their inn or even their former clients.[5] Such cases have naturally attracted less notice than the spectacular success stories of men like Lord Chancellor Ellesmere, Chief Justice Sir Henry Hobart, or Chief Justice Sir Edward Coke, whose massive land purchases and huge annual incomes placed them amongst the richest individuals of their day. But at either extreme, of wealth or poverty, the extent to which particular examples may be regarded as representative remains quite uncertain.

This chapter seeks to throw light on these questions. It begins by discussing how and why men came to take up law, then outlines the bar's *cursus honorum*, or career structure. We next examine the means by which early modern common lawyers rose and fell, and conclude with an attempt to determine the overall direction and impact of such mechanisms on men entering the profession during the half-century before the Civil War.

and Gentry of this Kingdom, whose Honors and Estates have by some of their Ancestors
been acquired or considerably augmented by the Practice of the Law, or Offices and
Dignities relating thereunto (1684; further editions 1685 and 1686). For Wood's
marginal annotations, see his copy, now at Bodl. Wood 251 (4). Cf. Additional 28205,
fols. 69–96ᵛ.

[4] Prest, 'English Bar', 77–9.
[5] SP 12/111/27, printed in *ITR*, i. 470–3; *GIPB*, i. 228; *LIBB*, ii. 358; C. M. Clode,
The Early History of the Guild of Merchant Taylors (1888), ii. 235; IT MS Misc. 30,
letter 53; *ITR*, ii. 21, 24, 129.

i. Becoming a barrister

One of a father's most onerous responsibilities was to find 'some suitable course of living' for his offspring. The preachers and writers who offered parents guidance in the discharge of this duty generally agreed that individual abilities and inclinations should be carefully observed and respected: 'If thou hast children, bring them up in all noble qualities, to make them worthy instruments either for Church or commonwealth', counselled John Norden, 'but constrain none of them to apply himself to anything against nature, and win them rather by love and gentleness, than harsh severity'.[6] How far such sensible advice was actually heeded is another question. Many biographical sources give the impression of total filial subordination to parental authority, in that children are described as being simply 'put', or sent, to school, university, inns of court, foreign travel, apprenticeship, and so forth.[7]

On the other hand a glance through the wills of lawyers who left specific instructions and financial provision for the upbringing of their sons reveals a wide range of paternal attitudes. At one extreme there is the uncompromising bluntness of William Booth: 'I desire that my eldest son William may study the common law.' By contrast, John Marston, the playwright's father, expressed a kind of philosophical resignation: 'I have taken great pains with delight and hope that my son would have profited in the study of the law, but man purposeth and God disposeth, His will be done . . .'. Edward Rolt charged his executors with schooling his four younger sons, prescribing only that 'such of them as shall be thought most fit' should go to the inns of court, the others being kept at university, bound apprentice in London, or placed as clerks in a prothonotary's office. Henry Martin left his law books to 'such of my sons as God shall please to call to the study of law', while John Keeling merely begged his wife 'to educate my sons in all plenty, learning and virtue, and to

---

[6] L. Stone, *The Family, Sex and Marriage in England 1500–1800* (1977), 179–80, 447; C. H. and K. George, *The Protestant Mind of the English Reformation* (Princeton, N.J., 1961), 293–4; Elyot, *Gouernour*, i. 138–40; H. Peacham, *The Compleat Gentleman* (1622), ed. G. S. Gordon (Oxford, 1906), 34; J. Norden, *The Fathers Legacie* (1625), sig. A5.

[7] Cf. *The Nicholas Papers*, ed. G. F. Warner (CS, 1886), xii–xiii; F. Bamford, *A Royalist's Notebook* (1936), 177; J. Aubrey, *Brief Lives*, ed. A. Clark (Oxford, 1898), i. 33–9; Lowther, 'Autobiography', 210; *The Vindication of Richard Atkyns Esquire* (1669), 3; L. Hutchinson, *Memoirs of the Life of Colonel Hutchinson*, ed. J. Sutherland (1973), 22, 24, 26; Clay and Lister, 'Autobiography of Sir John Savile', 422–3; *Memorials of Father Augustine Baker*, 64–5.

get them honest callings wherein they may serve the common-wealth'.[8]

Sons brought up by a widowed mother may well have had considerable freedom to control their own destinies. But even during their own lifetimes, fathers could not entirely ignore the views of wives and relatives; informing his son's tutor of the boy's imminent departure for the inns of court from Cambridge in 1648, a gentleman lamented, 'my judgement is against so frequent change . . . yet blame not my assent: his mother's friends have a powerful influence; I cannot gainsay what he desires, if seconded by them'. Youths who openly defied paternal plans faced the ultimate sanction of disinheritance. For younger brothers with only a small portion to lose, this risk may sometimes have seemed preferable to a lifelong occupation which was positively disliked; others, reluctant to engage in open confrontation, might appear to accept parental directives while actually pursuing their own inclinations.[9] Nevertheless, defiance or subterfuge was not the typical response. Most sons seem to have accepted their father's rights and qualifications to make decisions in this area, especially when these were exercised with the tact displayed by Sir Daniel Fleming, father of fifteen children, who assured his son George in 1689 that 'You do well to let me know your inclinations, and I shall comply with them so far as I can'. A still more liberal attitude had been shown in 1611 by Sir John Wynn of Gwydir, whose son Robert, 'persuaded in his own conscience that he would never be a lawyer', was allowed 'liberty to take his desired course of life and vocation'; as the boy's tutor pointed out in commending Sir John's decision, 'now he must be more careful of himself and apply his study well, or else bear the blame himself'.[10]

A career at the bar offered two major attractions: money and status. Of course the prospects of substantial monetary and social

[8] PCC 6 Lee, 82 Kidd, 105 Cope, 8 Fenner, 95 Fairfax. Cf. Lincs. RO, LCC Wills 1629/415 (Anthony Holland): 'If my eldest son John Holland will study and practise the laws of England, then I do give him all my law books.'

[9] H. Cary, *Memorials of the Great Civil War in England* (1842), i. 384–5; Whitelocke, *Lib. Fam.*, 13–14; Holles, *Memorials*, 83; 'A Copy of an Original Manuscript of Sir Francis Barnham', ed. T. B. Lennard, *The Ancestor*, ix (1904), 194; *Life of Radcliffe*, ed. Whitaker, 65; G. Burnet, *The Life and Death of Sir Mathew Hale, Kt.* (1682), 5–7. HMC, *Seventh Rep.*, 663; Lenton, *Characterismi*, sig. F4; *idem, The Young Gallant's Whirligigg* (1629), 3–5; T. Lodge, *An Alarum against Usurers* (1584), fol. 4–4ᵛ.

[10] Rydall Hall, Cumbria, Transcripts of Sir Daniel Fleming's Correspondence, M3576, 3631. (I owe this reference to Dr Hainsworth.) NLW MS Wynn of Gwydir, 573.

rewards had to be weighed up against the expense of qualifying for and establishing a barrister's practice. The basic educational requirements must usually have implied at least grammar school attendance or private tuition; then there were the costs of admission to an inn of court, of residence, of commons in hall for at least two and possibly more than seven years before call, of paper, books, levies and gratuities to servants, fees and presents given on call to the bar, even the bar gown itself.

It is impossible to set a firm figure on these costs, which varied somewhat from one inn of court to another, as well as being affected by personal circumstances and tastes. Nevertheless, provided a man could maintain himself as a student at his inn (for around £40 a year in the early seventeenth century), there were no major financial barriers preventing his call to the bar, since it was not until the early eighteenth century that substantial fees began to be charged for the privilege of call, due largely to the compounding of fines previously payable for the non-performance of learning exercises.[11]

Some charges, such as commons and chamber rent, continued after call, together with the additional burdens of riding an assize circuit and maintaining a standard of dress and equipage likely to impress attorneys and potential clients. Yet even though the lack of scholarships for poor mens' sons obliged students at the inns of court to live 'of their own private maintenance' (as the antiquary John Stow put it), we have already seen that it was not just the rich or well-born who thought the potential gains well worth the cost. Of course some must have been deterred; Richard Boyle, first earl of Cork, in his autobiographical memoir, claimed that he had been in the 1580s, as 'the second son of a younger brother . . . a student in the Middle Temple, London, finding my means insufficient to support me to study the laws'. Yet it is difficult to know whether this reported experience was at all representative, especially since no trace of a Richard Boyle appears in the late sixteenth-century records of the Middle Temple.[12]

---

[11] *Inns of Court*, 27–9; cf. Holmes, *Augustan England*, 145–6. Newly called barristers were required to enter bonds of up to £50 as security for their future payment of commons, fines, etc., while at LI a fee of £5 was payable to avoid the obligation to serve as steward of a reader's dinner. (*LIBB*, ii. 80, 126, 144; GI MS order book, fols. 274ᵛ, 306; *ITR*, ii. 15; *MTR*, ii. 561–2.)

[12] J. Stow, *A Survey of London*, ed. C. L. Kingsford (Oxford, 1908), i. 77; above, pp. 88–95; *The Works of the Honourable Robert Boyle*, ed. T. Birch (1744), i. 2. Cf. Sheffield Public Lib., Talbot letters 2/119, Francis Markham to Shrewsbury, 23 Feb. 1594.

The non-economic disincentives are rather better documented. 'A learned man in the laws of this realm is long in making, the student thereof, having *sedentariam vitam* is not commonly long lived, the study abstruse and difficult, the occasion sudden, the practice dangerous,' averred Sir Edward Coke. Learning the law was notoriously 'so hard, so unsavoury, so rude and so barbarous'—so hard indeed, John Barkesdale claimed at his Lincoln's Inn reading in 1628 that 'it requires a very strong and healthy body to endure it'. The rigours of legal practice could also severely strain a barrister's physical and psychological resources. In addition, some potential entrants to the profession may have been deterred by misgivings about the lawyer's ethical standing as a hired mouthpiece, prepared to take on any case for a fee. Yet similar objections could be levelled at most comparable vocations; the clergy, for example, were habitually accused of hypocrisy and simony, while as Stone has observed, the anal preoccupations of contemporary medicine did little to enhance the public image of its practitioners. And even if a law student required 'lead in his seat . . . an iron head and a golden purse', he could still look forward to achieving a level of worldly rewards which very few clergymen, merchants, or physicians might realistically hope to attain.[13]

While a fortunate minority of pluralists, rectors, and unbeneficed lecturers may have kept pace with, or even profited from, the effects of inflation, clerical incomes generally seem to have fallen, both absolutely and in relation to other occupational groups, during the century before 1640. Nor did the special influence and privileged standing of the clergy in both local and national life ever fully recover from the effects of the Reformation, despite improvements in their formal academic qualifications and all Archbishop Laud's efforts to turn back the clock. Apart from a few London-based physicians, mostly foreigners with court connections, the majority of even the most respectable medical practitioners achieved only modest prosperity, and certainly nothing like the power and prestige enjoyed by the legal profession's élite. Much the same held true for the civilians, whose public image was also damaged by their identification with a foreign and popish legal code. The other two avenues

---

[13] E. Coke, *A Booke of Entries* (1614), ep. ded.; Fraunce, *Lawiers Logike*, sigs. [¶2ᵛ–¶3ᵛ]; LI MS Maynard 57 (i), fol. 1ᵛ; Burnet, *Life of Hale*, 3; Benn, 'Essays', fols. 29ᵛ–31ᵛ; Stone, *Crisis of the Aristocracy*, 40–1; A. Thylesius, *Cassius of Parma his Orpheus*, tr. R. Rawlins (1587), ep. ded.

frequently followed by young men from broadly similar educational
and social backgrounds to those who became barristers during our
period were apprenticeship to a merchant and the profession of
arms. Although possibly less demanding in terms of capital resources and educational requirements, both trade and war were less
prestigious and in various ways more hazardous occupations than
the bar; they therefore tended to be largely the resort of younger
sons, unless family connections or traditions dictated otherwise.[14]

Whether or not these general considerations influenced most men
in their choice of a calling, the manner in which such choices were
made was clearly far from uniform. Although individual autonomy
was often restricted by paternal plans and family pressures, it would
be quite wrong to suppose that most barristers were blindly following a course of life determined for them by their parents. Students at
the inns of court were certainly prone to agonize over their aptitude
for a lawyer's life, and sought advice from various sources about
their likely prospects.[15] Yet such crucial life decisions are rarely
based on entirely adequate information or strictly logical reasoning.
As John Barkesdale observed:

Men do in their youth when their judgement is weakest choose the course of
life that they mean to live in longest. . . . Youth is not able rightly to counsel
itself what course of life is fittest to take or what kind of study to undergo,
and yet in youth a man must choose his course of life lest he lose his time of
learning; when I had spent five years at the University and was then to
choose course for spending the rest of my days, I fell upon the study of the
law.

Still more mysterious was the process by which, according to John
Aubrey, Sir John Brograve (1553–1613) became a common lawyer:

Mr Brograve of Hamel near Puckridge in Herts. when he was a young man,
riding in a lane in that country, had a blow given him on his cheek or head.
He looked back and saw that nobody was near behind him. Anon he had
another blow. I have forgot if a third. He turned back and fell to the study of
the law; and afterwards was a judge.[16]

---

[14] O'Day, *English Clergy*, 203–5, 235–8; I. Green, 'Career Prospects and Clerical
Conformity in the Early Stuart Church', *P & P*, 90 (1981), 71–93; Birken, 'College of
Physicians', 204; Levack 'English civilians', 119–21; Grassby, 'Social Mobility and
Business Enterprise', 355–81.
[15] Cf. Harleian 1026, fols. 116ʳ, 118; Bodl. MS Ashmole 180, fol. 122, cited by K.
Thomas, *Religion and the Decline of Magic* (1971), 314; *The Papers of Nathaniel
Bacon of Stiffkey, Vol. 1*, ed. A. H. Smith (Norfolk Rec. Soc., 1979), 121.
[16] LI MS Maynard 57 (1), fol. 1ᵛ; *Aubrey's Brief Lives*, ed. O. L. Dick (1972), 58.

ii. Preferment

The early modern bar resembled the Church rather than the medical profession, in the considerable extent to which the careers of its members depended upon the acquisition of honours and offices. The higher ranks within the inns of court constituted the lower rungs of the bar's promotions hierarchy. Having reached the bench of his inn, a lawyer might aspire to a serjeantship or judgeship in Westminster Hall, but was more likely to obtain one of the many judicial, quasi-judicial, or administrative positions in the central and local courts which did not involve membership in the order of the coif. Barristers also gained a variety of miscellaneous appointments and dignities, such as knighthoods and places on commissions of the peace, which were often awarded in recognition of professional services or standing.

The highest prize within the legal profession itself was a judge's place in one of the superior courts of Westminster Hall, but a barrister's chances of reaching this lofty pinnacle were slim. Throughout our period the central judiciary remained a very small body, generally comprising eight common-law judges and four barons of the Exchequer, plus the lord chancellor or lord keeper and possibly the master of the Rolls, neither of whom was invariably a common lawyer. Between James I's accession in 1603 and the outbreak of the Civil War in 1642, fifty-two men were elevated to the judicial bench. Over the same four decades an average of some forty-seven individuals were called to the bar each year. Some further indication of the heavy odds against finishing one's career as a judge is that only 4 of the 115 barristers in our sample (John Archer, Edward Henden, Thomas Widdrington, and William Wilde) reached the bench of Westminster Hall (and Widdrington's appointment as chief baron of the Exchequer in 1658 was cut short by the restoration two years later).[17]

The serjeants at law had traditionally taken place next after the judges, whom they addressed familiarly as 'Brother', and with whom they lodged during term time at the two Serjeants' Inns in Fleet Street and Chancery Lane. By the late sixteenth century, however, the judiciary was no longer selected exclusively from the serjeants' ranks, even if those promoted to the bench were usually made serjeants pro forma on the way, while from 1623 onwards the king's

[17] H. H. Cooper, 'Promotion and Politics among the Common Law Judges of the Reigns of James I and Charles I', University of Liverpool MA thesis, 1964, 21.

attorney-general and solicitor-general took formal precedence over all but the two most senior serjeants in every court other than Common Pleas, where the serjeants still maintained their ancient monopoly.[18]

The dwindling share of business handled by Common Pleas was one main reason for the declining fortunes of the order of the coif. Another was the ballooning numbers of serjeants under the early Stuarts; between 1590 and 1603 Queen Elizabeth had summoned only thirteen lawyers to the coif, whereas her successor created fourteen serjeants in the first year of his reign and a massive total of fifty-seven before his death. Charles I kept up his father's rate, and for similar reasons—unwillingness or inability to resist the importunities of those seeking the promotion and offering substantial cash payments (at least £500) in return. So from 1603 onwards it was easier to become a serjeant than a judge, and no fewer than six members of our barristers' sample, besides the four judges, achieved what was now becoming a somewhat diminished dignity.[19]

While it was only a formal necessity to be called to the degree of serjeant before taking a judge's place in Westminster Hall, all but one of the serjeants and judges created during the half-century before the Civil War had been promoted to the bench of their inn of court.[20] This was still the crucial promotion step for the upper branch of the legal profession, as it seems to have been since at least the late fifteenth century. During our period, however, call to the bench was more than twice as difficult to come by as during the first half of the sixteenth century; some two-fifths of the utter-barristers called by Lincoln's Inn between 1518 and 1550 became benchers, whereas only just over one-sixth of our sample of barristers called between 1590 and 1639 rose to the governing body of their inn of court. Moreover, the difficulty seems to have increased steadily throughout our period, even though the numbers called to the bench grew from fifty-eight in the decade 1590-9 to ninety-four in the decade 1610-19, dropping back to seventy-eight in the 1630s (see Table 5.1). This is shown by the rising number of years barristers

[18] W. J. Jones, *Politics and the Bench* (1971), 42–3; *Lawyers*, 20, 72; Baker, *English Legal History*, 142.

[19] These statistics were derived (with the compiler's kind permission) from the typescript of Baker's *Serjeants*. For an instance of 'bon et sufficient apprentices de ley' refusing the promotion, cf. CUL MS Add. 6863, fol. 2ᵛ.

[20] The exception was Sir John Davies, created serjeant at law in 1606 while serving as attorney-general in Ireland.

Table 5.1. Benchers Called[1]

	GI	IT	LI	MT	Total
1590–99	17	14	12	15	58
1600–09	15	16	22	15	68
1610–19	26	19	29	20	94
1620–29	25	22	19	21	87
1630–39	20	18	24	16	78
Totals	103	89	106	87	385

[1] Including 34 associates to the bench (of whom 13 became full benchers before 1640 and are counted only as such), while excluding 43 office-holding and other non-practising barristers, for whom see Appendix F.

had to wait before promotion to the bench of their inn; whereas it took from sixteen to eighteen years after entry to the house for barristers of Lincoln's Inn and the Middle Temple to reach the bench in the first half of the sixteenth century, the interval had risen to an average of over twenty-three years at all four inns by the last decade of the sixteenth century, and continued rising to reach twenty-six and a half years during the 1630s.[21]

These figures may be slightly misleading, in that not all those called to the bar sought, or were available to accept, promotion to the bench. Some practised law little, if at all, or withdrew from practice after a few years, while others died too young to have achieved the age and standing usually required for elevation to the governing body of their inn. In our sample, these two categories of non-practising and short-lived barristers (somewhat arbitrarily defined as those who died within fifteen years of call to the bar) constituted at least a quarter of the whole group. Nor can it be assumed that every man who remained theoretically available to accept the promotion would in fact have done so had it been offered to him; at the Middle Temple and Gray's Inn the rank of 'ancient' provided for those who had declined an invitation to the bench of their house. Yet despite these various qualifications, it remains clear by the early seventeenth century a barrister's chances of joining the bench of his inn, presuming that he lived and practised long enough

[21] *Lawyers*, 30; E. W. Ives, 'Promotion in the legal profession of Yorkist and early Tudor England', *LQR*, lxxv (1959), 350–1. Table 5.1 supersedes the figures in *Inns of Court*, 60.

to be eligible for the honour, were not much better than about one in five.

While few strictly professional privileges still attached to the rank of bencher (or reader), this promotion was crucial to a lawyer's prospects of advancement outside his inn. The relationship was not exactly one of cause and effect, but in the same way that judges were made serjeants as a formality on their way to the judicial bench, so appointments to some high offices and honours more or less automatically resulted in the recipient receiving an invitation to join the governing body of his inn.[22] Partly for this reason, and partly because the benchers constituted a self-perpetuating cohort of the ablest and most experienced barristers, it is hardly surprising that they held most of the more desirable preferments open to common lawyers. Their dominance in the holding of office is clearly seen when the twenty-one members of our barristers' sample who became benchers are compared with the majority who did not receive this promotion. Among the barrister-benchers were four Westminster Hall judges, three Welsh judges (Edward Bulstrode, John Clarke, and William Powell), a long-serving clerk of Wards (John Hare), a still longer-serving master in Chancery (Sir Robert Rich), a common serjeant of London (Ralph Latham), and seven recorders (John Baber of Wells, George Browne of Taunton, Thomas Lake of Maidstone, Timothy Leving of Derby, Evan Seys of Gloucester, John Strode of Bridport, and Nicholas Willimot of Nottingham).

Among the ninety-four barristers who remained below the bench, two-thirds seem never to have acquired an office of any kind. The remainder held mainly local and relatively lowly positions, such as escheator, feodary, and manorial steward.[23] On a slightly more elevated plane were three town clerks (James Dyer of Bristol, Richard Langley of London, and Thomas Rich of Ipswich), four recorders (Robert Bysse of Dublin, Thomas Gell of Derby, James Kyrton of Wells, and James Metcalfe of Richmond), a clerk of the Crown in the county palatine of Lancaster (Alexander Rigby), two common pleaders of London (John Keeling and Stephen Phesant), the attorney-general of the commissary court of Connaught, Ireland, from 1647 (Christopher Elliott), and one of the 'Commissioners of Justice' imposed by the Rump Parliament upon the defeated Scots in 1652 (George Smith).

---

[22] Ibid., 63–9.
[23] For escheators and feodaries, see Bell, *Courts of Wards*, 38–45; for manorial stewards, see Brooks, thesis, 145–8, 185–90.

So offices of profit were not confined to benchers; nor did all offices necessarily guarantee their holder a place on the bench of his inn. Although Welsh judges could usually expect this promotion, Irish judges did not; such minor revenue-gathering posts as escheator and feodary also lacked sufficient cachet for the purpose.[24] Like the office of town clerk, these latter were as often held by attorneys as barristers, and offered no particularly dazzling financial prospects. Indeed, none of the offices held by the ninety-four non-bencher members of the barristers' sample are likely to have been very lucrative, with the possible exception of the various posts in the Irish legal bureaucracy enjoyed by Robert Bysse, initially in reversion from his father.[25] And the overriding general point is that, even taking all 115 members of the barristers' sample together, more than half appear to have received absolutely no further preferment, whether within or outside their inn, following their initial call to the bar.

What factors influenced a barrister's chances of obtaining office or preferment? How important was individual ability or merit, as opposed to the notorious three Ps which Aylmer identified in his study of Charles I's central administration: patrimony, patronage, and purchase? Aylmer singled out lawyers as much the largest group to attain office because of their professional qualifications, possibly unaided by other (to our eyes more dubious) influences.[26] At the inns of court, election to the bench largely depended upon either seniority or office holding. Extreme poverty, religious heterodoxy, or unsociability may have been negative qualifications, but the surviving evidence is thin and largely uninformative on this point. Only two instances emerge from the late sixteenth and early seventeenth centuries of men qualified by seniority being refused promotion to the bench of their inn; perhaps others kept a discreet silence. But quite apart from the calling ex officio of office-holders or men who had been knighted, patronage and patrimony could, and did, come into play to single out particular individuals for accelerated promo-

---

[24] Neither Sir Richard Bolton nor his son Edward, who in 1639 succeeded his father as chief baron of the Exchequer in Ireland, were called to the LI bench, while Sir Gerard Lowther, justice of the Common Bench in Ireland 1610–24, was similarly treated at the IT. (F. E. Ball, *The Judges in Ireland 1221–1921* (1927), i. 323–4, 330–2, 338.) Cf. the case of Sir Marmaduke Lloyd. (Williams, *Welsh Judges*, 133.)

[25] See Brooks, thesis, 199–204; for Bysse's offices, see *Calendar of the Patent and Close Rolls of Chancery in Ireland of the Reign of Charles I*, ed. J. Morrin (Dublin, 1863), 318; Bodl. MS Carte 62, fol. 370; J. L. Hughes, *Patentee Officers in Ireland 1173–1826* (Dublin, 1960), 21.

[26] Aylmer, *King's Servants*, 89, 93–4.

tion to the bench, while on one or two rare occasions an element of purchase may also have been involved (as, for example, when William Ravenscroft paid £30 to the fund for the construction of the new Lincoln's Inn chapel on his elevation from associate to full bencher in 1621).[27]

Elsewhere clientage, nepotism, and venality were standard operating parameters, whether or not some minimal legal competence was thought necessary for a particular appointment. True, many barristers who rose to high office had established successful practices at the bar before their elevation. But because judicial and official favour were crucially important for success as an advocate, it is difficult to be sure that such individuals owed their achievements to innate ability rather than patronage. Of course some patrons particularly sought out and encouraged young men of talent, as, for example, William Noy supported Mathew Hale in his early days at Lincoln's Inn, and Edward Littleton helped young Bulstrode Whitelocke on the Western circuit.[28] Nevertheless, the fact remains that in early modern England connections and cash served where today elaborate bureaucratic devices are supposed to ensure that the best qualified candidate gets the job. So we should not automatically suppose, even in the absence of contrary evidence, that professional talent was the sole or paramount consideration in the appointment of barristers to offices during our period, especially since we usually lack any independent yardstick by which to measure that elusive quality.[29]

Yet it would be equally mistaken to rush to the opposite conclusion, and assume that all placemen gained preferment *merely* by means of favour or money, entirely without regard to personal abilities or qualifications. The real position lay somewhere between these two extremes. Although too much of our knowledge depends upon second-hand gossip and rumour, a rough distinction may be drawn between the operation of clientage or patronage broadly defined, which probably figured to some extent in most appoint-

[27] The two refused promotion to the bench were Robert Ashley and Christopher Mollineux. (Cf. *Inns of Court*, 62, 63–8, and for Mollineux, London Corp. RO, Rem. II, fols. 47–8.)

[28] Burnet, *Life of Hale*, 19–20; Additional 53726, fol. 82ᵛ. Efforts were also made occasionally to ensure that candidates for office had the support of the benchers of their inn; cf. A. Collins, *Letters and Memorials of State* (1746), i. 313–15; HMC, *Salisbury*, xii. 646–7; SP 29/13/90(1).

[29] Cf. J. Hurstfield, *Freedom, Corruption and Government in Elizabethan England* (1973), 137–62; Aylmer, *King's Servants*, ch. 4, *passim*.

ments and was by and large not condemned by contemporary opinion, and cash transactions, which were both generally less frequent and more widely disapproved of, especially where judicial office was involved. It is surprisingly difficult to find convincing evidence that judges' places in Westminster Hall were up for sale at any time during our period, including the notoriously corrupt years of Buckingham's ascendancy. Mere accusations of venality, especially by those with personal or political axes to grind, can hardly be taken at full face value, and most of the evidence is of this nature.[30] In the 1626 impeachment proceedings against Buckingham, the only allegations advanced about the favourite's role in the sale of 'places of judicature' concerned Montagu's lord-treasurership and Cranfield's promotion as master of Wards, two offices which were primarily of an administrative, rather than judicial, nature. In view of Walter Yonge's claim that Montagu paid £15,000 for the chief-justiceship of King's Bench in 1616, it seems particularly significant that this charge was not brought up a decade later.[31]

There can be little doubt that judgeships in Wales, and also perhaps in Ireland, were in effect purchased on occasion; the same appears to hold true for masterships in Chancery and Requests, while the office of master of the Rolls (not formally regarded as judicial, although increasingly assuming at least a quasi-judicial character) was regularly auctioned off to the highest bidder (not necessarily a common lawyer).[32] It should also be noted that both

[30] Cf. HMC, *De L'Isle and Dudley*, vi. 224; references cited by Jones, *Politics and the Bench*, 38, and Veall, *Law Reform*, 41–2. For a more careful discussion, see Cooper, thesis, ch. 5.

[31] J. Rushworth, *Historical Collections of Private Passages of State* (1682–1701), i. 334–5, 338, 387; Yonge, *Diary*, 29; although admitted to the MT in 1600 (*MTAdmR*, i. 77), there is no indication that Yonge was called to the bar, *pace DNB*. Yonge's second-hand comments from Devon on London events must be treated cautiously; e.g. his reference in 1626 to a 'John' Richardson giving £17,000 for the chief-justiceship of Common Pleas. (*Diary*, 97–8.) In 1627 Sir Richard Hutton was uncertain whether to believe that George Vernon had, as 'generalment reported', paid £1,000 or £1,500 for his promotion as baron of the Exchequer. (CUL MS Add. 6863, fol. 41.)

[32] Bulstrode Whitelocke attributed his failure to secure a Welsh judgeship for his uncle Edward Bulstrode in 1638 to 'money being that which carried it'. (Additional 37343, fol. 162.) Sir Thomas Milward was said to have paid nothing for the chief-justiceship of Chester the following year, although another had offered £5,000 for the place. (SP16/415/61, but cf. G. P. Higgins, 'The Government of Early Stuart Cheshire', *Northern Hist.*, xii (1976), 43; Aylmer, *King's Servants*, 43; Ball, *Judges in Ireland*, i. 247; *CSPIre.*, *1615–25*, 546). For the master of the Rolls, cf. references cited in n. 30 above, and Chamberlain, *Letters*, i. 111, 117; Bodl. MS North c4, fol. 11.

Bacon and Coke, who should have had a fair idea about what was going on, explicitly condemned the sale of judicial office, while bills against the practice were introduced into each of Charles I's early parliaments. On the other hand, one MP asserted in 1628 that the judges of the central courts did not in fact buy their places, although they were to blame for buying the prior degree of serjeant![33]

While appointments to many non-judicial offices were accompanied by cash payments, this is not to say that such posts were simply up for purchase by the highest bidder. In the last year of Elizabeth's reign it was cynically alleged that '*argent* makes serjeant', and more recently Baker has stated that under the early Stuarts 'coifs were sold for bribes'.[34] Yet sums of £500–600 regularly paid by newly called serjeants were perhaps not so much bribes as payments in the nature of a levy or tax, publicly acknowledged licensing fees rather than secretly given corrupt inducements. Furthermore, what seems to have been the standard procedure of forwarding an agreed list of potential serjeants to the Crown by the common-law judges, through the lord chancellor or lord keeper, must have provided some measure of control over the quality of candidates.[35]

Although it was alleged that the sum of £10,000 had been offered by Sir James Ley for the attorney-generalship in 1616, and £4,000 was certainly paid to James I by Sir Henry Yelverton *after* he had obtained the post, Cooper concluded that during the period 1603–40, 'payment for the office was a relatively slight factor in its acquisition'. The same appears to hold true for the significantly less prestigious and profitable post of solicitor-general.[36] Again, while recorderships were commonly the subject of interventions on behalf

[33] Bacon, *Works*, xiii.18–19, 35–6, 327; *The Fortescue Papers*, ed. S. R. Gardiner (CS, 1871), 42, 200–1; HMC, *Lonsdale*, 58–9; *CD 1621*, v. 95; *CJ*, i. 810, 820, 878, 920; *CD 1628*, iii. 54. For claims by John Cooke and John Lilburne that Charles I's judges bought their places, cf. *State Trials*, ed. T. B. Howell (1816–28), iv. 1022; *The Leveller Tracts 1647–1653*, ed. W. Haller and G. Davies (New York, 1944), 438.

[34] Manningham, *Diary*, 173; Baker, *English Legal History*, 136, and *Serjeants*, 110–11. The practice of payments evidently began before 1600; cf. Wilbraham, *Journal*, 10.

[35] Cooper, thesis, 121–4; Bramston, *Autobiography*, 5–6; Whitelocke, *Lib. Fam.*, 44, 108; CUL MS Add. 6863, fol. 2ᵛ; *CSPD 1640*, 308. A copy of a list of potential serjeants, forwarded from the judges in 1637, is among the Bramston papers at Essex RO, D/DEb 17; cf. CUL MS Add. 6863, fol. 39. For evidence of similar procedures prior to judicial appointments, cf. Ellesmere 2935; Additional 12504, fol. 123.

[36] Cooper, thesis, 127–8. Christopher Fulwood offered 'a considerable sum' to Lord Holland for help in forwarding his suit for the place of either queen's or prince's attorney in 1634. (HMC, *Cowper*, ii. 62; cf. Additional 37343, fols. 132, 152ᵛ).

of their clients by aristocratic or courtly patrons, they seem rarely if ever to have been available to the highest bidder, despite the disgruntled comment made after Sir Anthony Benn became recorder of London in 1617, that '*Regina Pecunia*' governed all such transactions. On the other hand, most administrative positions and clerkships attached to both the central and provincial courts were treated as lucrative sinecures and openly traded as such.[37]

Much depended upon the nature and value of the position in question, as well as who controlled appointments to it. An especially profitable office which nevertheless required some specialized legal skills, such as the attorneyship of the Wards, might attract very sizeable offers. In 1608 Henry Yelverton was said by a professed confidant and well-wisher to desire this place even above that of attorney-general and hence to be prepared to pay Robert Cecil (who had it in his gift), no less than '£1,000, for a stock to be employed upon your hospital at Waltham or any other wise ... thankfully, secretly and willingly'. As it happened, Yelverton did not secure the post and it is unknown how much was paid by James Ley, who did.[38] Cecil's cupidity is beyond reasonable doubt, but Sir Thomas Wentworth was, at least ostensibly, devoted to the elevated ideal of advancing merit in his royal master's service. Nevertheless, Wentworth still surprised Secretary Coke and Lord Keeper Coventry in 1637 by his proposal to appoint to a vacant judge's seat in Ireland 'one Mr Fletcher, sometime of the Temple, a grave man, learned in his profession ... being one no further known to me than as I have observed him sometimes when he hath been counsel against me'. This sounds like a splendid instance of an appointment based on merit alone, even if the merit was as discerned by a single autocratic patron and the transaction actually fell through because Fletcher proved to be over seventy years of age at the time. Yet, to complete the story, it should be noted that the vacancy Wentworth sought to

---

[37] For recorderships, see below, ch. 8, sect. ii. HMC, *Hastings*, iv. 16. For other offices, see Aylmer, *King's Servants*, ch. 4, *passim*; H. R. Trevor-Roper, *The Gentry 1540–1640* (1953), 28–9; T. Birch, *The Court and Times of Charles I*, ed. R. F. Williams (1848), ii. 16; *Trevelyan Papers, Pt. iii*, ed. W. C. and C. E. Trevelyan (CS, 1872), 52; CUL MS Add. 6863, fol. 90ᵛ.

[38] BL, Dept. of MSS, Film M 485 (82), p. 529 (calendared HMC, *Salisbury*, xxi. 373); Richard Hutton noted that Rowland Wandesford's appointment as attorney of Wards in 1637 was made 'without his suit or solicitation but on account of his worthiness by the sole and principal desire of Lord Cottington Master of the Wards'. (CUL MS Add. 6863, fols. 88ᵛ–9.)

fill had arisen because his own brother was unwilling to take a job which Charles I had granted his lord deputy to dispose of as he saw fit.[39]

So there was no single pathway to preferment for early modern barristers—rather a series of winding stairs. Well-placed patrons and extensive family connections were probably the job-seeking lawyer's best assets, if perhaps not absolutely indispensable. Cash, whether in the form of a bribe or a straightforward purchase price, did not inevitably change hands, especially where judicial office was concerned. Having said this, the next question would seem to be whether any general characteristics distinguished those who succeeded in gaining office of some kind from those who did not. Partial and tentative answers have already been suggested in the previous chapter, the two sample groups whose social characteristics were analysed there representing, on the one hand, a cross-section of all barristers called over the half-century before the Long Parliament, and on the other, the more eminent and successful benchers from whose number serjeants, judges, and most other holders of high offices were chosen. However, a sharper picture can be obtained by comparing the barristers from our sample of 115 who obtained preferment with those who were less fortunate.

Fifty-two members of the barristers' sample are known to have held office of one sort or another, ranging from county escheatorships to judges' seats in the three main common-law courts of Westminster Hall. The most striking difference between these officeholders and the remainder of the sample was simply one of age or longevity. While the distribution of birth dates appears remarkably similar in both groups (a mean of about 1589 for the office-bearers and 1591 for the rest), the officers seem to have lived on the average eleven years longer (their mean date of death being around 1650, as against 1639 for the non-preferred majority). Thus the typical placeholder lived to reach the age of sixty-two years, but the life-span of his less fortunate colleague extended only to his early fifties. Seven office-holders died before they had practised at the bar for more than fifteen years, less than half the equivalent figure for the non-officers. Whether or not office-holding encouraged longevity, there can be little doubt that the reverse relationship held, as we might expect in a society where age and authority tended to go together.[40]

---

[39] Knowler, ii. 44, 46, 51, 93–4; Ball, *Judges in Ireland*, i. 308–11.

[40] Cf. K. Thomas, 'Age and authority in early modern England', *Proc. Brit. Acad.*, lxii (1976), 205–14.

Some other less dramatic demographic differences also emerge. Among the office-holders, the proportion of first and only sons (40 per cent) was markedly less than it was for non-officers, among whom they comprise the largest single group (49 per cent); presumably the career incentives for men who had no prospects of receiving more than a token inheritance were a good deal stronger than for those favoured by primogeniture. There is no difference between the mobility rates of office- and non-office-holders, doubtless because of the significant representation of local office, both urban and rural, for which local men must have had some competitive advantage. At the same time, more than a quarter of the office-holders, but only an eighth of the non-office-holders, recorded urban destinations.

University attendance was significantly higher among the non-office-holders, almost two-thirds of whom had been to Oxford or Cambridge, as against well under half the placemen, which reverses the situation found when the entire bar and bench samples were compared in this respect. While more office-holders than non-office-holders in the barristers' sample attended an inn of chancery, the proportion was considerably smaller than that among the benchers' sample as a whole. These features probably reflect differences in the overall age structure of the bar as against the bench sample, and changes in educational patterns during the course of the late sixteenth and early seventeenth centuries. However, they may also indicate a competitive advantage which accrued to those who started their careers at a slightly earlier age by coming straight to the law, rather than spending time at university first.

Although the social origins of the two groups seem broadly similar, it is noticeable that both upper and 'mere' gentry were less well represented among the officers than the rest, whereas sons of merchants and professional men, including lawyers, were proportionately more prominent in the office-holding category. This finding supports the common-sense assumption that while the bar was not a caste, family connections or limited prospects of inheriting a substantial estate, or both, functioned as important aids to perferment.

Those who gained office certainly found the law more profitable than those who did not. How they accumulated their wealth, how much, and to what effect are the matters to which we now turn.

iii. Economic analysis

In order to test contemporary views about the lucrativeness of a
career at the bar, we need to conduct an economic analysis of a
cross-section of early modern barristers. Of course this is much
easier said than done. There are no convenient contemporary
indices—national economic surveys, tax-lists, or the like—which
supply a comprehensive and reliable picture of the comparative
financial status of all or most individual lawyers. Surviving collections of estate and personal accounts, rentals, surveys, and so forth
extensive enough to permit detailed reconstruction of a family's
income and wealth over any length of time are few and far between
outside the titular peerage and upper gentry. So analysis must
depend on piecing together miscellaneous bits of information drawn
from a wide variety of sources, with results which can be at best
suggestive rather than conclusive.

Sufficient evidence exists to permit at least an informed guess
about the wealth of just over half the members of the barristers'
sample. Given unlimited amounts of time and energy, it might have
been possible to accumulate more information on some individuals.
But the quantity and quality of the data would never be sufficient to
support a comprehensive statistical breakdown of incomes and
wealth at the early modern bar, or to allow adequately for regional
and chronological variations within a group of 115 men drawn from
all over England, Wales, and Ireland, and including individuals born
before the mid-sixteenth century as well as several who lived on past
the Glorious Revolution.

These various difficulties mean that there is little point in using
any but the crudest classifications of economic standing, within
which lawyers can be sorted according to a broad range of variables,
including personal income, capital assets, land transactions, the size
of daughters' marriage portions, bequests of cash and personal
property, and so on. This strategy may also help to avoid raising
expectations of objectivity and precision which the state of the
evidence hardly warrants; even so, it should still be emphasized that
the process of categorizing individuals necessarily depends as much
upon subjective judgement as the mechanical application of quantitative criteria.

At least 8 of the 115 barristers in our 5 per cent random sample of
men called to the bar between 1590 and 1639 appear never to have

practised law at all, or to have abandoned their profession shortly after call to the bar.[41] There is obviously no case for including these non-practisers in our analysis. But what about men who died soon after call, and hence had little or no opportunity to demonstrate that they could make a profitable career at the bar? Twelve members of our sample group lived only a decade or less after call, but then early death was a risk facing the entrants to any occupation. Nevertheless, it is worth bearing this group in mind during the following discussion; most of its members cannot be classified in terms of their wealth, but those who can were, unsurprisingly, not well off, with the notable exception of William Beriffe junior, whose quite substantial assets were clearly inherited from his barrister-father namesake, since he himself died less than twelve months after call to the bar of Gray's Inn in 1631.[42]

Eight of the 107 practising barristers in our sample group must be classified as more or less poor, if not actually destitute. Maurice Abbott and George Quarles both appear to have been in severe financial difficulties by the end of their lives, although the precise extent of the estates which their heirs managed to salvage is unknown.[43] William Dyos, at one time remembrancer of London, spent his latter days as a prisoner for debt in the Compter, while it was reported of his colleague Richard Langley, the City's town clerk, that although he 'bore a high sail, yet he died a poor man and in debt' in 1612.[44] None of the other four attained even these modest degrees of eminence or notoriety; they include Giles Phelpes, a barrister of the Middle Temple, whose sole landed assets seem to have consisted of small parcels amounting to some fourteen acres (valued at twenty shillings per annum) in and around the Somerset market town of Yeovil; Henry Pindar of Gray's Inn, presumably related to a family of Chancery office-holders, who died only three

---

[41] See above, pp. 77–8.

[42] For Beriffe, see P. Morant, *The History and Antiquities of the County of Essex*, ed. G. H. Martin (1978), i. 383, 450, and PCC 26 Audley.

[43] Abbott seems to have been outlawed in 1642, following the bankruptcy of his brother and business partner Edward; although assessed at £1,000 by the Committee for the Advancement of Money in 1645, the assessment was deferred while his lands remained subject to a writ of extent. (*CSPD 1638–9*, 153; SP 16/493/50, 19/76/633; HMC, *Cowper*, ii. 279; *CCAM*, 559. Derbs. RO, Gell 30/15 (a); HL RO, Main Papers, 10 June 1641). For Quarles, see Northants RO, YZ 8378, 8379; PCC 144 Ent; *East Anglian*, iii. 186.

[44] London Corp. RO, Rep. 41, fol. 110v; ibid., 54, fol. 332. *Memorials of the Goldsmiths Company*, ed. W. S. Prideaux (n.d.), i. 142–4. SP 14/113/87 (i); Chamberlain, *Letters*, i. 440.

years after call, leaving his father all his 'goods, chattels, debts and ready money'; Thomas St George, a younger son from a decayed Cambridgeshire gentry family, who just before his death in 1637 estimated his total estate as worth some £1,800 (which would have converted to about £90 per annum rental income), but was able to leave only one third of his possessions to his eldest son and heir (the rest going to pay his debts and his wife's dower); and Richard Sandell, who lived out his life in the isolated Norfolk village of Saham Tooney, where his personal estate was valued by inventory taken just after his death in 1627 at some £33, including livestock (four cows, one gelding, two calves, and two pigs), clothing and books (total value £5), but little furniture or plate (apart from six pewter spoons).[45]

It is anyone's guess how many more might be added to this group of eight at the bottom end of the economic scale if the evidence were fuller. But the very absence of information about the economic standing of nearly two-fifths of the practising barristers in our sample is itself strongly suggestive of their limited means, even if some undoubtedly would have slipped into our next and largest category. The broad, and in some respects conservative, guide-lines by which thirty-nine barristers (a third of the practisers) were grouped together as of middling or modest wealth include notional annual incomes of more than £100, a history of land purchases, and the ability to provide their daughters with dowries of up to £500 value.

To start from the lower end of the range, William Becke claimed in 1590, five years before he was called to the bar at the Middle Temple, that his estate was worth 100 marks (£66. 13s. 4d.) annually, and would increase to more than £100 per annum after his mother's death. However, these estimates were doubted by his prospective parents-in-law; we also know that Becke sold a manor in 1602, and bequeathed property to pay off his debts at his death in 1614. While it is just possible that Becke may have made a large fortune at the bar, his self-composed epitaph in St Edward's Church, Cambridge, which embroiders a conceit based on Christ's advice to 'forsake all other and follow me', suggests a life distinguished rather by spiritual than worldly gains.[46]

[45] C 142/630/2. PCC 95 Soame. PCC 153 Goare; *HS*, xli. 91; C 142/545/64. Norfolk RO, INV 33/218.
[46] CUL MS EDR H2/1, copy of undated letter, W. Becke to E. Lynne, marked

A less well-documented case is that of Anthony Dering, the fourth or fifth son of a Kentish knight and brother of a Long Parliament MP, who died unmarried in London in the year of Charles II's restoration, leaving only a farm of 38 acres, besides money, unspecified quantities of plate and jewellery, furniture, and household stuff. The fact that Dering's will was proved in the archdeaconry court of London suggests that his estate cannot have been sufficiently large to justify or require probate through the prerogative court of Canterbury. It is also interesting that Dering instructed his executor to spend no more than £5 on his funeral, to do without a memorial sermon, and—perhaps a revealing inconsistency—to display no more than twelve heraldic escutcheons on his cortège.[47]

Despite the lack of further evidence, it seems reasonable to place Dering, like Becke, just slightly above what for our purposes is the poverty line, even though neither seems to have possessed resources comparable to those of more prosperous members of the same middling group, such as Thomas Gell and John Richardson. Gell, also a younger son who never married, and characterized by one of his political opponents in Derbyshire during the Civil War as 'of mean estate' (as well as exhibiting 'want of learning, law and honesty'), held minor local office under the duchy of Lancaster from 1633–1642, was elected recorder of Derby the following year, and served as recruiter MP for the city in the Long Parliament from 1645 to 1648. In addition to whatever he may have made from the law, Gell appears to have built up a money-lending business (his clients including a fellow Inner Temple barrister already mentioned, Maurice Abbott); however, Underdown believes that Gell's total annual income did not exceed £500.[48] John Richardson's father was also a lawyer, holding the office of solicitor-general to two successive bishops of Durham, and outliving his son (who died in 1623 after only twelve years practice at the bar) by some eighteen years. Since father and son shared the same Christian name, it is difficult to distinguish their professional careers, but our sample barrister was probably escheator for the county of Durham two years after call to the bar, and may have been seeking further preferment from the earl

H2/6/1; also letter of T. Pagytt to Sir John Brograve, 25 Sept. [1590?]; *VCH, Hunts.*, iii. 94; PCC 11 Rudd.

[47] *Al. Cant.*, ii. 36; *HS*, xlii. 140; Guildhall Library, MS 9052/13.

[48] *DNB*, s.v. Gell, Sir John; Derbs. RO, Saunders 1232 M/09a and Gell D258, Box 30/11; D. Underdown, *Pride's Purge* (Oxford, 1971), 374, 392; PCC 301 Wooton; J. T. Brighton, *Royalists and Roundheads in Derbyshire* (Derby, 1981), 28–9.

of Shrewsbury around the same time. The surviving probate documents suggest that John Richardson junior enjoyed a comfortable and far from straitened existence; his personal estate was inventoried at £446 value, and included some substantial items of furniture (a 'great table in the parlour', a pair of 'great andirons', a long hall table with two drawers), besides 'his picture with sarcenet curtains', a bass viol, and a gilt cup valued at £5. Richardson's civilized lifestyle was supported by rents from a farm in Weardale, as well as leases to the annual value of at least £45.[49]

At the upper end of this middling group were some quite well-to-do lawyers, including the royalist Robert Anderson, second son of Sir Richard Anderson of Pendley, Hertfordshire, by Margaret, eldest daughter of Baron Spencer of Wormleighton, Northamptonshire, who was reputed 'to have by him the most money of any person in the kingdom'; Anderson's assessment by the Committee for the Advancement of Money in 1648 suggests an annual income of at least £400, while in 1667 he was taxed in Chichester for thirteen hearths, one of the highest assessments in the town, besides owning the nearby manor of Felpham.[50] Walter Moyle, of Kent and the Middle Temple, in 1597, two years before his death, and a year before final confirmation of his call to the bar, acquired five manors and other lands in Kent, the property of an outlawed traitor; from these lands, leased in fee farm at an annual rent of £40, Moyle proposed that his executors should raise sufficient funds to cover personal bequests totalling £562, with the residue to his wife.[51] A fellow Kentish man, Richard Pickes of Crayford and Lincoln's Inn, left three daughters portions of £400 each at his death in 1632, while bequeathing to his son and heir Edward a 'mansion house', lands, and tenements in Ulcombe, Tenterden, Rolvenden, Crayford, Bexley, Dartford, Tonbridge, and Westfield, with the proviso that if necessary lands should be sold for payment of the portions and his own debts.[52]

[49] R. Surtees, *The History and Antiquities of . . . Durham* (1816–40), iv. (2), 151; Univ. of Durham, Dept. of Palaeography, Probates 1624 (Marjorie Richardson), 1638 (John Richardson, declaration of account and inventory); P. H. Horton, 'The Administrative, Social, and Economic Structure of the Durham Bishopric Estates, 1500–1640', University of Durham M. Litt. thesis, 1975, 369.

[50] *HS*, xxii. 109; M. E. Finch, *The Wealth of Five Northamptonshire Families 1540–1660* (Northants Rec. Soc., 1956), 38; *CCAM*, 983; *CCC*, 1493; *Sussex Arch. Coll.*, xxiv. 83, xxxix. 61.

[51] *CSPD 1595–7*, 498; *Arch. Cant.*, xlix. 162; *MTR*, i. 356, 364, 385–6; PCC 58 Wallopp.

[52] PCC 106 Audley; Hasted, *Kent*, ii. 276.

Nearly at the opposite end of the country, Alexander Rigby of Burgh, Lancashire, succeeded his father and grandfather in the office of clerk of the Crown in the county palatine of Lancaster; Rigby's landed income was assessed at over £200, and his personal estate valued at no less than £2,000 in 1648.[53] Two final examples of the more well-to-do are Nicholas Cholmley and John Hare, who were kinsmen and workmates, as well as colleagues on the bench of the Inner Temple, since Hare was clerk of the Court of Wards from 1590 until his death in 1613, while (as we have already seen) Cholmley became one of the leading counsel at the Wards bar during a career which stretched over half a century. Unfortunately there is little specific surviving evidence about the size of Cholmley's estate; his will, however, mentions personal bequests to the value of £160, plus unspecified quantities of plate, money, goods, bonds, and personal belongings, while the fact that his resources were not insubstantial is suggested by his ability to loan parliament the sum of £1,900 shortly before his death in 1644.[54] Hare, who died long before Cholmley, was said to have left his son Nicholas 'but £300 a year and his office'; the value of the latter must have been considerable, however, since it enabled Hare, a younger son, to acquire (partly on his own and partly in conjunction with his brother Hugh) the Hertfordshire manor of Totteridge, plus at least a further seven manors in Norfolk, Suffolk, and Cambridgeshire.[55]

Finally, we come to the economic élite of the barristers' sample, which comprised eighteen indisputably rich men, distinguished by such characteristics as annual incomes of £1,000 upwards, large-scale holdings or purchases of land, and the provision of marriage portions of more than £500 for their daughters. Among them was Francis Bradshaw of Derbyshire, an elder son whose father's marriage to a wealthy local heiress had enabled him to build up an estate of nearly 3,000 acres plus some valuable lead mines, to which his son added after his call to the bar at the Inner Temple in 1603. Bradshaw married twice, on both occasions daughters of respected

[53] Alexander Rigby is helpfully distinguished from two contemporary namesakes, including another GI barrister (for whom see *DNB* and Keeler, 323) in *Chetham Soc.*, l.275 n.; see also xxxi. 107–8, and lxii. 108, 126; *Lancs. and Ches. Rec. Soc.*, xii. 167, 211, 218–23; Somerville, *Office Holders*, 104.

[54] *HS*, xliii. 127, and lv. 1333–5; *ITAdmR*, 205. SP 16/538/84; *CCAM*, 527; *CJ*, iii. 181, 536; PCC 16 Rivers. Although a younger son, Cholmley was assessed on lands nominally worth £3 p.a. (a relatively high figure) in 1594, only a year after his call to the bar. (*Surrey Arch. Soc.*, xix. 49.)

[55] *H. of P.*, ii. 251; Chamberlain, *Letters*, i. 457; Norfolk RO, Hare 5614, 224 x 3; Ellesmere 2475; Greater London RO, Acc 349/150.

knightly families, rebuilt Eyam Hall, his principal residence, served as sheriff of the county in 1630, and died five years later, leaving a personal estate valued at over £4,000, including £2,328 worth of debts due upon specialities or bonds.[56]

John Carill of the Inner Temple, who had distinguished legal ancestors on both sides of his family, moved from Kingston-on-Thames to Ely when he inherited the manor of Chatteris towards the end of his life. He left his younger daughter Prudence a marriage portion of £1,000 in 1669, when he also held the manor of Heslington, near York; 750 acres of fenland in the process of reclamation; and various other unspecified freehold lands.[57] Sir John Cremer of Setchey, Norfolk, although apparently bankrupt in 1633, recovered his fortunes sufficiently to become sheriff of the county in 1659–60, was knighted in 1660, and set aside annuities of £340 per annum from a portion of his property when making his will six years later, in addition to providing for the renovation of Setchey parish church.[58] While Cremer was made an ancient of Gray's Inn in 1645, it is worth observing that, like Bradshaw and Carill, he otherwise gained no significant professional preferment in the course of his career. Indeed, we cannot be altogether certain that either Bradshaw or Carill ever actually practised law, even if Bradshaw at least was chosen and evidently served as steward of the reader's dinner at the Inner Temple in 1618, fifteen years after his call.

A striking contrast is provided by a trio of eminently successful and distinguished lawyers: Sir Edward Henden, Sir John Strode, and Sir William Wilde. Their family backgrounds were very different. Henden's father, the most obscure of the three, was probably a clothier of Biddenden, Kent, while Strode was the second son of a landed gentleman from Parnham, Dorset, and Wilde the son and heir of a London vintner. Strode entered the Middle Temple in 1583, and was called to the bar in 1590, having already obtained 'good advancement' through his marriage to the daughter of a local squire. While his subsequent rise was not spectacular, he evidently gained the name of 'an honest, trusty, learned, religious gentleman', not-

---

[56] *Derbs. Arch. and Nat. Hist. Soc. J.*, xxv. 37–43; J. R. Dias, 'Politics and Administration in . . . Nottingham and Derbyshire, 1590–1640', University of Oxford D. Phil. thesis, 1973, 90.

[57] *HS*, xliii. 89; *VCH, Cambs.*, iv. 105; PCC 16 Penn. For a namesake of Tangley, Surrey, and GI, cf. *HS*, lx. 37, and Cockburn, *History of English Assizes*, 318.

[58] Norfolk RO, King's Lynn Borough Archives, Recorder's Notebook, fols. 39–40; Ketton-Cremer, *Felbrigg*, 226; PCC 390 Berkeley; PCC 68 Coke.

withstanding a bitter and prolonged dispute with his niece and her husband, who accused Strode of fraudulently exploiting his professional connections in order to retain the family estates at his elder brother's death in 1616. By this date Strode was a bencher of the Middle Temple and had begun buying land on a large scale, spending at least £11,000 between 1606 and 1637, besides some £1,142 for the construction of his manor-house at Chantmarle. Strode's standing in his county was strengthened by a second marriage to the heiress of a Somerset magnate, Sir John Wyndham of Wyndham Orchard, his election as MP and recorder of Bridport in 1614, and his appointment to the county commission of the peace in 1625, where he served until his death at the outset of the Civil War.[59]

While Edward Henden and William Wilde both pursued more distinguished public careers than Strode, our knowledge of them as individuals unfortunately does not extend very far beyond a chronicle of their public offices and actions. It is not clear whether Henden ever married, and although Wilde certainly had three wives, the identity of the first is unknown. Henden seems to have lived out his life in Biddenden, Kent, where he was born, while Wilde bought a manor at Ash, in the same county, and moved there from London on becoming a judge. His judicial career was considerably longer than that of Henden, who, although created serjeant in 1616 under slightly dubious circumstances, was not made a puisne baron of the Exchequer until 1639, four years before his death. Thus Henden's assessment by the parliamentary Committee for the Advancement of Money towards the end of 1643 must largely reflect his earnings at the bar of the Court of Common Pleas and elsewhere, rather than his gains as a judge. His assessment was as high as £2,000, which supposedly represented one-twentieth of the capital value of his estate, or roughly what it might be expected to yield in annual rental income, confirming that at least some serjeants were still doing very nicely.[60]

William Wilde had been a barrister only three years when the

[59] J. Hutchins, *History and Antiquities of the County of Dorset* (1861–70), ii.130–2; STAC 8/204/14; Dorset RO, MW M4; A. Oswald, *Country Houses of Dorset* (1935), 42; A. R. Bayley, *The Great Civil War in Dorset 1642–1660* (Taunton, 1910), 37–9; C. Aspinall-Oglander, *Nunwell Symphony* (1945), 152–3. (I am exceedingly grateful for Mr J. P. Ferris's help with Strode and other Dorset barristers.)
[60] Foss, vi. 327–8; Hasted, *Kent*, iv. 311, 356; *CCAM*, 301; HMC, *Salisbury*, xxii. 14; Kent AO, PRC 31/131; Baker, *Serjeants*, 110, 328–9.

Long Parliament met in November 1640; his assessment in 1643 was a mere £50, and two years later he claimed that his full 'twentieth' should not have been half that sum once his debts were deducted and if no account were taken of lands which he would inherit after his father's death. Wilde's property holdings at this stage were obviously meagre, while he claimed that the exigentership of Common Pleas (an office he may have held since 1631, two years after his admission to the Inner Temple) had not brought in more than £15 over the previous eighteen months. The next few years of Wilde's life are obscure, but hints of his growing practice are provided by the acquisition of an additional chamber in Figtree Court in 1649, his election as bencher in 1652, and possibly his second marriage that same year. In November 1659 Wilde was chosen recorder of London; his services in this strategic office over the next few crucial months, as MP in the Convention Parliament which summoned Charles II back to England (Wilde himself being one of the party which carried the message to The Hague), and as commissioner for the trial of the regicides, were rewarded with a knighthood, to which a baronetcy was added before the year was out. Sir William Wilde was created serjeant and king's serjeant at law in 1661, raised to the bench of the Court of Common Pleas in 1668 and translated to King's Bench in 1673, where he remained until six months before his death in late 1679. His will reveals that besides Goldston manor at Ash, Wilde possessed other lands at Dunmow, houses at Lewisham and in Lincoln's Inn Fields, chambers both at Serjeant's Inn and the Temple, numerous leases, mortgages to the value of £1,500, and a loan of £1,000 to the City, much plate, furniture, and jewellery, including a 'diamond ring with a Latin posey, and an ebony cabinet'. We do not know how large an inheritance Wilde received at his father's death in 1650, nor the size of the settlements made on his three wives; all doubtless contributed to his accumulated wealth, but probably to a lesser extent than the fruits of judicial and other office, given that Wilde's basic salary as a judge was £1,000, which, with fees and perquisites, would have amounted to an official income of perhaps twice that amount.[61]

To sum up, if our sample can indeed be taken as properly representative of all barristers called during the half-century before the Civil War, it is clear that the personal economic circumstances of

[61] *HC 1660–90*, iii. 720–1; Foss, vii. 193–5; *DNB* s.v. Wilde, W.; E 215/658/1; *CCAM*, 181; HMC, *Finch*, ii. 53; PCC 169 King; Hasted, *Kent*, ix. 196.

the early modern bar were far from uniform. While perhaps one-sixth of its members may have died rich men, the remainder ranged through moderate and modest degrees of wealth down to what can hardly be called anything but poverty. This is not a particularly shattering revelation; much the same could be said of most other contemporary occupational and social groups, including peers, the landed gentry, clergy, merchants, and yeomen. At the same time, diversity is itself a relative matter; as compared with the vast majority of the population, barristers were clearly among the haves rather than the have-nots. Moreover, in emphasizing the gap which separated the poorest from the richest practitioners, it should not be forgotten that most barristers about whose economic standing any information survives may be classed as more or less well-to-do. On the other hand, the largest single subset in our group (nearly 40 per cent of the practisers) consists of men whose wealth is unknown, but was probably quite insubstantial.

Predictably, perhaps, barristers who were promoted to the bench of their inn seem to have comprised a somewhat more economically homogeneous and prosperous élite. True, when the bench sample is divided into the same categories by which the bar sample was analysed, the percentage breakdown appears quite similar for the two groups; but when the broad middling category is further subdivided, the barristers clump predominantly into the lower, the benchers into the upper division; similarly, those benchers classified as rich include a number of fabulously wealthy men, like Hugh Audley, Sir Edward Coke, Sir Henry Hobart, Sir Roger Wilbraham, and Sir Henry Yelverton, whose assets and earnings were hardly equalled by any of the barristers in our sample.[62] Yet the bench also had its quota of bankrupts and paupers.[63] How did such large disparities of wealth arise?

iv. *Mechanisms of mobility*

A lawyer's wealth—or lack of it—was obviously not just the product of his legal earnings. The financial significance of marriage and

---

[62] *DNB*; Veall, *Law Reform*, 48 n.; Jones, *Politics and the Bench*, 37; Wilbraham, *Journal*, viii–ix. A comparably successful careerist from our sample group was Sir John Archer, for whom see *DNB* and *Essex Rev.*, xxxi. 160–73, 179–94.

[63] Benchers who may be classified as poor or in financial difficulties include Jeremy Bettenham (*GIPB*, i. 88); Richard Daston, who died 'indebted to sundry persons in great sums' (PCC 48 Skynner); Richard Digges, serjeant at law (CUL MS Add. 6863, fol.68); Sir Henry Finch (*Radicals*, i. 281–2); Gabriel Ludlow (*CSPD 1639–40*, 521,

office-holding have already been mentioned; moreover, a barrister's economic status could also be powerfully affected by the size of his inheritance, as well as by the profits and losses of farming, money lending, and other miscellaneous enterprises.

Demographic factors inevitably exerted a considerable influence. Whether a man was a younger or elder son, how long he lived and worked, whether he married, how many sons and daughters (especially the latter, with their need for marriage portions) his wife or wives produced—all these could significantly affect his financial status. After election as Speaker of the House of Commons in 1597, Serjeant Christopher Yelverton claimed that:

> My estate is nothing correspondent to the maintenance of this dignity, for my father dying left me a younger brother and nothing unto me but my bare annuity, then growing to man's estate and some practice of the law, I took a wife by whom I have had many children, the keeping of us all being a great impoverishing of my estate and the daily living of us all nothing but my daily industry.

Nevertheless, Yelverton seems to have accumulated substantial wealth by 1613, when he died 'of very age' as a puisne justice of King's Bench. Indeed, his distinguished career exemplifies the stimulus provided by the working of primogeniture in Elizabethan and Stuart England.[64] Of course, elder brothers might be disinherited (like the 'unkind and undutiful' John Keyt of Woodstock, whose civil-lawyer father cut him off with a £20 annuity); alternatively, their inheritances could turn out to consist of little more than debts (as was the unfortunate experience of James Metcalfe, son and heir of a declining North Riding gentry family). But first or only sons who did inherit a large estate often abandoned legal practice altogether—many presumably regarding the bar as little more than a stopgap until they came into their own. On the other hand, younger sons who unexpectedly acquired family lands through the death or disinheritance of elder brothers seem more usually to have persisted with their vocation. In either case, the possession of a substantial alternative source of income, status, and responsibility doubtless

and HL RO, Main Papers, 16 Mar. 1641); Adam Sare (PCC 30 Byrde); Henry Sherfield (*Radicals*, iii. 166); Robert Shute (*DNB*); Richard Swayne (PCC 17 Goare), and David Waterhouse (above, p. 103).

[64] A. F. Pollard and M. Blatcher, 'Hayward Townshend's Journals', *BIHR*, xii (1934-5), 7; cf. H. J. Habakkuk, in Finch, *Five Northants Families*, xviii-xix.

tended to induce a more relaxed attitude to the competitive pressures of practice at the bar. This may help explain why Francis Yarborough never rose beyond the bench of Lincoln's Inn, despite having married a niece of Chief Justice Wray and enjoying the support of Sir Thomas Egerton, who, recommending Yarborough for a vacancy on the Council of the North in 1592, wrote that 'he hath not given himself much to the troublesome practices of the law, being otherwise of good hability and livelihood'.[65]

Naturally enough, a great deal depended upon individual personalities. In 1632 Benedict Llanden, a bencher of the Middle Temple, prefaced his will with a disclaimer to the effect that his estate could not be expected to amount to much:

I being a younger brother and had nothing from my father ... but only a bare yearly allowance ... which only continued until I had been an utter-barrister two years, which profession although it hath been in a reasonable manner from time to time gainful unto me, yet in regard of the considerable charge of housekeeping and breeding my children in a chargeable fashion and of the great charge which my reading did occasion I have not much enriched myself thereby.

Although few details of his financial affairs survive, Llanden did not die rich; he may only have left his two sons a lump sum of £750 each, while his wife received a payment in lieu of her jointure which would not have yielded as much as £100 a year.[66]

By contrast, Thomas Tempest of Lincoln's Inn and Northumberland, in his reader's speech eight years later, made a point of dwelling on his success in overcoming the comparative disadvantages of belonging to

one of the lowest branches of my poor stock and family; being descended of younger brothers for many generations, and that of a far and remote country where those of reasonable regard there have but small revenues, which affords not so plentiful allowance to younger brothers.
Yet by God's providence and my parents' care I was designed to this profession, wherein by God's blessing I have attained a means of subsistence in the world.

[65] Oxfordshire RO, WI 39/3/12. W. C. and G. Metcalfe, *Records of the Family of Metcalfe* (1891), 137–222; J. T. Cliffe, *The Yorkshire Gentry from the Reformation to the Civil War* (1969), 137, 154. Cf. Gough, *Myddle*, 38. All but one of the non-practising barristers in our sample were first or only sons. Ellesmere 1401.
[66] PCC 34 Audley; *HS*, li. 602.

Tempest proceeded to give the reader's customary eulogy of the common law an interestingly meritocratic twist, remarking that if they lacked legal knowledge, 'those who may seem to have been born superior in degree or estate, must seek help and and be informed and governed of others, whom they might formerly think their inferiors'. So if men of 'the greatest birth or fortune' neglected to take full advantage of their opportunities to learn the law when at the inns of court, preferring 'idleness or any other vanities or pleasures', they would be forced in later life to 'use other men's eyes to look into their own estates, and sometimes are at great cost, for a little of their company whom they esteemed so cheap before'. On the other hand, Tempest concluded, 'those who diligently apply their studies here (though some of small estates or beginnings) are by God's blessing instruments of much good unto others; and oftentimes also advance their own fortunes and families'.[67]

Discretion and modesty doubtless restrained Tempest from enumerating real-life exemplars, of whom there would have been no shortage among his auditory and acquaintance. He might have cited the case of Sir John Lowther (1582–1637), an elder son but a fellow Northcountryman (albeit from the other side of the Pennines), of undeniably gentle if somewhat straitened origins, whose memoirs tell us that while still a student at the Inner Temple his father was constrained to marry him off, 'being indebted and not able to maintain me'. Once married, Lowther nevertheless determined 'to return to my book and make it a profession to preserve our estate, which was then too like to fall to decay, we being too many to have gentlemanly maintenance out of that small living'. Accordingly, he left his new bride with her mother, 'at no charge to me for her diet nor mine when I came, by means whereof my estate at Meaburn being but then of the yearly revenue of £72 did maintain us'. By 1627, ten years after Lowther had entered into his diminished inheritance, he estimated that he had 'bettered my estate in purchases and in stock yet remaining . . . near £20,000'; a decade later he calculated that he would be able to leave his children lands worth

[67] Additional 27380, fols. 5–5ᵛ. However, Tempest's success in establishing an Exchequer practice, to which he also referred on this occasion, doubtless owed something to the assistance of William Lenthall, to whom Tempest was distantly related, perhaps through his first wife (Bodl. MS Tanner 66, fol. 166). Cf. Bulstrode Whitelocke's account of why he persisted at the bar after his father's death. (Additional 53726, fol. 81.)

more than £2,350 yearly, plus capital in the form of marriage portions and stock to the value of at least £3,000.[68] This was no small achievement, but how was it done? Lowther's earnings from legal practice were not primarily responsible for his spectacular economic ascent. Just before he took up a position as counsellor-in-attendance (or judge) at the Council of the North in 1627, Lowther noted, 'Truth is, my fees at law never amounted to £150 per annum', while in 1636 he mentioned '£300 per annum that I have at York and in fees elsewhere by my own daily pains'. The answer probably lies in a combination of thrift, astute management and exploitation of resources (especially the coal-mines on the family estate at Whitehaven, which became the basis of a flourishing trade across the Irish Sea), and relentless litigation to gain clear title to lands originally held by his grandfather.[69]

Evidently a man of quite exceptional abilities and energy, Lowther might well have accumulated on a comparable scale whatever his profession, or indeed without any profession at all. Yet his legal training and qualifications plainly conferred some considerable advantages, as, for example, in helping him to outface the intimidating Lord William Howard, 'Belted Will', who dominated Cumberland and Westmorland 'by his hard dealing and many suits', as also in gaining the powerful office of steward of the barony of Kendal, and not least (as he tells us) 'in the government of my own estate and the understanding thereof'.[70]

Few barristers were more successful than Sir John Lowther in augmenting their original inheritance. Nevertheless most of those in the two sample groups studied who can be classified as rich appear to have accumulated their own wealth, rather than merely inheriting a fortune. Two further examplars, both barrister-sons of barrister-fathers, help make the point. Stephen Phesant (1617–60) inherited a large estate in Huntingdonshire from his father, whose career had culminated in a puisne judgeship of Common Pleas; but Stephen was able to add at least three more manors to these lands, presumably from the fruits of the office of common pleader of London, in which he succeeded his father after the latter's election as recorder of the

---

[68] *Lowther Family Estate Books*, ed. C. B. Phillips (Surtees Soc., 1979), xiv–xvi, 27, 40–1, 58–9, 210–12, 230.
[69] Ibid., xiv, 27, 40.
[70] Ibid., 212, 214–31.

City in 1643.[71] Another prosperous legal dynasty represented among our barristers' sample was that of the Seys, of Lincoln's Inn and Glamorganshire, whose rise to prominence in the late sixteenth and early seventeenth centuries has been characterized as 'a remarkable example of the success which could be achieved as the result of following a legal career'. Roger Seys of Boverton, founder of the family's fortunes, reached the bench of Lincoln's Inn in 1573, and became attorney-general for Wales in 1591, with the support of the earl of Pembroke and Sir Robert Sidney. His son Richard, called to the bar in 1594, served the Herberts as steward, and acquired the office of attorney-general of Glamorgan. Finally Richard's second son Evan (c.1604–82) succeeded to the same office in 1635, and then to his father's lands four years later (his elder brother having been previously disinherited). Evan was promoted serjeant at law during the Interregnum, and confirmed in that degree at the restoration of Charles II, when he also became recorder of Gloucester; he had cemented his connections with the city through his marriage in 1638 to the daughter of Robert Bridges of nearby Woodchester, who brought him a marriage portion of no less than £2,500 (which by the terms of the settlement was to be used for buying more land). While it is not possible to determine exactly how far Evan Seys improved his already quite substantial inheritance, there is every reason to think that his office and estates were at least as profitable to him as they had been to his father.[72]

But how far did the wealth of Seys and comparably prosperous colleagues derive from legal practice? The case of Sir John Lowther indicates that the fee income of even an eminently successful common lawyer might be surprisingly small, as compared to the rental roll of even a moderately well-to-do country squire. Contemporary critics certainly tended to exaggerate both the size of fees which barristers charged their clients and the total incomes typically earned at the bar. An anonymous complainant asserted in 1631 that 'the noble or royal [6s. 8d.] (which within memory was an unusual reward for a counsellor) is now risen to four pound, five pound, twenty nobles or ten pound with some'. Yet scrutiny of fee books

---

[71] *HS*, xvii. 158; PCC 176 Fairfax, 293 Nabbs; A. Woolrych, *Commonwealth to Protectorate* (Oxford, 1982), 424–5; London Corp. RO, Rep.57, ii. fol. 242ᵛ.

[72] M. Robbins, 'The Agricultural, Social and Cultural Interests of the Gentry of South-East Glamorgan, 1540–1640', University of Wales, Cardiff, Ph.D. thesis, 1974, 192–7; G. T. Clark, *Limbus Patrum Morganniae et Glamorganniae* (1886), 219–20; Glamorgan RO, Fonmon D/D F1281 and F E/28, 34.

kept by barristers and accounts of fees actually paid to counsel in the
late sixteenth and early seventeenth centuries indicates that very few
practitioners ever took single fees of this size. The most common
amounts demanded and received by barristers, benchers, and serjeants were ten or twenty shillings, although slightly larger sums
might be paid for drafting an original bill or providing a written
opinion.[73]

While the critic just quoted seems to have exaggerated the
prevailing level of barristers' charges, his claims accord with other
evidence pointing to the concurrent inflation and destabilization of
counsellors' fees during the course of the sixteenth century. An
undated draft among the papers of Sir Henry Spelman, who was one
of the commissioners appointed by the Crown in 1623 to regulate
legal and other fees, asserts as a matter of common knowledge that
'in former times' the charges levied by 'counsellors and practisers . . .
were much more regular and moderate than they now are . . .'.[74] It
may indeed be that the combined impact of inflation, currency
manipulations, a boom in litigation, the declining practice of paying
counsel fixed annual retainers, the proliferation of new forms of
action and procedural devices, together with structural changes in
the profession which accompanied the rise of the barristers, introduced a new flexibility to lawyers' fees, which had previously been
determined largely by collective tradition. In reaction to the rise of a
free market element, and despite obvious difficulties of application
and enforcement, the imposition of standard scales of barristers' fees
was canvassed in bills read before the parliaments of 1571, 1604, and
1621, as well as by numerous individual proponents of law reform
throughout the late sixteenth and seventeenth centuries.[75] Such fixed
scales actually applied in two provincial prerogative courts, the
councils in the North and in the Marches, and may also have
survived in Common Pleas, which was probably less affected by
competitive pressures than other jurisdictions.[76]

[73] *LRH*, 165–84.
[74] Additional 34601, fol. 75ᵛ.
[75] *LRH*, 166 n. 1; see also Lansdowne 44, fols. 25–26ᵛ, 30–33; Lansdowne 487, fols. 203ᵛ–205; Additional 34324, fol. 52; HMC, *House of Lords ii, 1689–90* (*Twelfth Rep., App. 6*), 315; HMC, *House of Lords iii, 1690* (*Thirteenth Rep., App. 5*), 23–4; E. Gee, *The Jesuit's Memorial* (1690), 243; Durham Univ. Dept. of Palaeography, York Book, fol. 102.
[76] Reid, *Council in the North*, 265–6, 268; Williams, *Council in the Marches*, 336; T. Rymer, *Foedera, Conventiones, Literae, . . .* (1739–45), viii, pt. III, 275, cl. 53; Additional 34601, fol. 125; Bodl. MS Rawlinson D 1123, fol. 2.

Elsewhere, by the end of the sixteenth century, barristers were in effect free to charge what the market would bear. The ten or twenty shillings usually paid for a single motion at the bar was substantially more than the mark (3*s*. 4*d*.) which seems to have been the serjeant's standard fee around the middle of the fifteenth century, although it must be remembered that the general price level rose by about 700 per cent over the next two hundred years.[77] Nor can there be any doubt that some leading barristers usually, and many others sometimes, charged much more than the most common fees, depending on the status of both lawyer and client, as well as the nature and difficulty of the task performed. In the mid-1620s Sir John Bridgeman received the staggering sum of £40 for his written opinion on twenty-six questions of law submitted by a consortium of Welsh manorial proprietors; this is by far the highest single fee noted to date over our period as a whole, as well as the only one known to have reached double figures.[78]

While the prime concern of clients was with the size, and perhaps the number, of fees they had to pay counsel, lawyers were presumably more interested in the sum total of their professional earnings. Fortunately for historians who share that interest, sufficient account books recording fees received by barristers survive from the late sixteenth and early seventeenth centuries to give a reasonably clear indication of the range of incomes at the bar earned by practitioners at different stages of their careers. These fee-books are particularly valuable as a corrective to contemporary literary evidence, such as the Elizabethan clergyman William Harrison's suggestion in his *Description of England* that serjeants at law earned a minimum of £1,200 annually, or the assertion of his near contemporary, the civil lawyer Thomas Wilson, that common-law judges and most serjeants enjoyed five-figure annual incomes. Rather closer to the mark was one Anthony Atkinson, who claimed in 1603 that some common lawyers 'in the space of one year can gain three, four or five hundred pounds', although it is still very doubtful whether most barristers earned as much as even the minimum figure suggested by Atkinson.[79]

---

[77] *LRH*, 167, 171, 178.

[78] Ibid. 168; NLW, Wynnstay MSS, Manorial Miscellanea 10, printed in *Bull. of the Board of Celtic Studs.*, ix, pt. iv (1939), 350.

[79] *LRH*, 171–2, 178; Anthony Atkinson was dismissed from the post of searcher at the port of Hull *c*.1602; his 'Discovery of Frauds and Abuses about the revenues of

John Hoskyns, the future serjeant and Welsh judge who was called to the bar in 1600, told his wife eleven years later that he hoped 'my practice ... will be in London better than £200 a year'. This giddy prospect was communicated in the middle of Michaelmas term, when Hoskyns had already gained the princely sum of £23, and had hopes of making it up to £30 by Christmas. Hoskyns did tend to give a rather pessimistic view of his financial situation in correspondence with his wife, perhaps for fear of encouraging her to domestic extravagance; nor does he specify the possible gains which might be expected from his circuit practice. Nevertheless, his somewhat surprising testimony is not at all contradicted by the evidence of the fee books summarized in Figure 5.1.[80]

While the identity of the first of the six lawyers who compiled this material is unknown, the others were all men of some standing in their profession: benchers and recorders (Sherfield and Thornton), a serjeant (Arthur Turner), a judge (Sir James Whitelocke), and his son Bulstrode Whitelocke, who served as one of the commissioners for the Great Seal during the Civil War and Commonwealth. Yet it appears that even the highly successful Whitelocke senior never earned more than about £600 per annum during his two decades at the bar, while his average annual fee income throughout that period was only just £400. Henry Sherfield, the next most successful—over the short term at least—was also a leading counsel in the Court of Wards. Sherfield evidently faltered after an auspicious start, although a gap in the record between 1613 and 1620 makes it impossible to tell whether the sharp decline from his peak earnings of £547 for 1620–1 was part of a continuing downward slide which began in the previous decade. Sherfield's last decade's fee income fluctuated widely, from a peak of over £500 to a trough of under £200, but averaged well under £400 per annum.

Serjeant Turner's earnings look even less impressive, although they must have been somewhat reduced by the disruptions of the Civil War and its aftermath. Yet Turner was evidently a good deal more successful from a financial point of view than Thomas Thornton (whose best recorded gains for any one year were only just over £250), let alone the anonymous practitioner from the middle

the Crown 1603' (BL MS Royal 17. c. iv) is a petition signed 'your Majesty's poor oppressed prisoner Anthonie Atkinson'.

[80] Osborn, *Life of Hoskyns*, 68.

years of James I's reign, whose average earnings were only just over
the £100 mark. Finally, the decline in Bulstrode Whitelocke's
earnings immediately after his father's death in 1632 reflects the
crucial importance of judicial connections or favour for young men
starting out at the bar.[81]

In addition to the evidence set out in Figure 5.1, there is also
some other more fragmentary and impressionistic material. In 1605
William Saxey, having then served ten years as a judge in Ireland,
claimed that his gains as a counsellor before leaving England had
been as much as £500 yearly. This was also the annual sum paid to
Sir George Radcliffe from 1635 onwards, to compensate him for loss
of income from private practice while he was in the Crown's service,
and the amount gathered by practice at the bar, on which Mathew
Hale, in 1660, while a bencher of Lincoln's Inn, claimed that he had
to support a large family. While Saxey's claim is almost certainly
inflated, the figures for Radcliffe and Hale (especially the latter) may
not be too far off the mark. In the early 1620s Sir John Lowther
estimated that his practice at the bar was worth only between £50
and £150 per annum; by contrast, Sir Francis Bacon boasted in 1608
that his annual income from private practice alone was £1,200, and
from his office of solicitor-general another £1,000, while in 1660
William Lenthall was said to have lost more than £2,000 a year when
he gave up private practice to become Speaker of the Long Parliament.[82]

Given what we already know about the grossly unequal distribution of work at the bar, such huge gains are not inherently
impossible, even though the evidence of the fee books must be
regarded as more reliable than isolated individual statements of
earnings. On the other hand, in some cases the fee books may
slightly understate professional incomes; for example, neither Sherfield nor Thornton list their stipends as recorders, while payments in
kind, such as presents of venison, or the silver gilt bowl which Sir

[81] Cf. Whitelocke's own jaundiced comments in Additional 53726, fols. 71–2, 80–2,
83ᵛ, 107ᵛ.
[82] HMC, *Salisbury*, xvii. 635; Cliffe, *Yorkshire Gentry*, 87–8; *A Collection of Tracts
Relative to the Laws of England*, ed. F. Hargrave (1787), I. x; Lowther, 'Autobiography', 9, 17, 23, 27; Bacon, *Works*, xi. 48, 86; J. N., 'An Account of the Gains of the
late Speaker William Lenthall', in *Collection of Scarce and Valuable Tracts . . .
selected from . . . libraries particularly that of the late Lord Somers* (1748–51), pt. III, ii,
253. Cf. the claim that Sir Thomas Widdrington's pre-Civil War practice was worth
more than £1,500 p.a. (W. Lilly, *An Astrological Prediction of the Occurrences in
England, part of the years 1648, 1649, 1650* (1648), 64.)

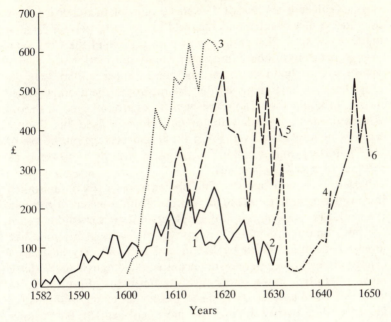

Fig. 5.1. Barrister's Fees (to nearest £)

1. Anonymous. *Source:* Additional 25231, fols. 3–14.
2. Thomas Thornton (1553–1632, called to bar 1584, associated to bench 1620). *Source:* Northants RO, Th. 2251.
3. James Whitelocke (1570–1632, called to bar 1600, bench 1619, serjeant 1620). *Source:* BL MS Additional 53725, fols. 31–130.
4. Bulstrode Whitelocke (1605–75, called to bar 1626). *Source:* Additional 37343, 53726.
5. Henry Sherfield (c.1574–1634, called to bar 1606, bench 1620). *Source:* Hants RO, 44M69/xxv/i–iv.
6. Arthur Turner (?1589–1651, called to bar 1613, bench 1624, serjeant 1637). *Source:* HLS, MS Turner 137.

Christopher Hatton presented to John Croke 'as a fee for his counsel in law' were also generally excluded.[83] Yet these omissions hardly invalidate the general picture of unexpectedly modest earnings for even the most successful barristers, and quite minimal incomes for their less successful and younger colleagues. Of course these are relative matters. The median fee income of a Sir James Whitelocke or a Henry Sherfield compares very favourably with the £50–150 which might have been earned yearly by a provincial merchant in the

[83] Croke, *Genealogical History*, i. 457, ii. 828. Annuities paid in the form of retainers are also likely to be listed with other fixed-income items, such as rents, rather

early seventeenth century, or the £20–60 value of an archdeaconry in the diocese of Coventry and Lichfield at the same period; for that matter, among the Lancashire gentry on the eve of the Civil War, over 40 per cent of those families for whom information is available appear to have had incomes of less than £100 per annum.[84] On the other hand, Aylmer suggests that by the 1630s the average yearly income of knights was £800, and of esquires around £500. It should also be borne in mind that an annual income of £500 was about a tenth of the estimated average for the titular peerage on the eve of the Civil War, while a handful of the most wealthy nobles enjoyed incomes of over £10,000 a year.[85]

Nevertheless, early modern Englishmen were clearly not mistaken in considering practice at the bar a most effective means of rising in the world. For a start, even if the majority of barristers did not earn the huge amounts commonly supposed, a few certainly did. The levels of income claimed by Bacon and Lenthall may have been exaggerated, but they were by no means wholly impossible. We have already seen that in the course of Easter term 1616 Francis Moore was retained in at least 269 Chancery cases; assuming that most of his fees were twenty-shillings or more, as befitted the leading favourite in one of the busiest central courts, and that he took no less in each of the other three terms, it is not difficult to understand how his annual income from litigation alone could easily have exceeded £1,000. Indeed, since Moore was not an office-holder (other than as counsel and under-steward to the University of Oxford), and appears to have made a not particularly profitable marriage, it is difficult to explain his impressive achievements as land-purchaser and house-builder except on the assumption that they were financed chiefly and directly from legal earnings.[86]

than with fees. Although retainers were no longer the chief form of support for most barristers, if indeed they ever had been (cf. R. Palmer, 'The Origins of the Legal Profession in England', *Irish Jurist*, NS xi (1976), 132–3), they were still granted by peers, wealthy gentry, and corporations into the eighteenth century, see, e.g., *Arch. Cant.*, x. 199–200; *CSPD 1603–10*, 633; Chicago, MS Bacon 4446; Ellesmere 499–506; Blomefield and Parkin, *Norfolk*, vi. 245–7; *Chetham Soc.*, xiii. 118; HMC, *Wells*, ii. 461; *Gentleman's Magazine* (July 1853), 38.

[84] Cf. W. B. Stephens, *Exeter in the Seventeenth Century* (Exeter, 1958), 41, 43; W. T. MacCaffrey, *Exeter 1540–1640* (Cambridge, Mass., 1958), 263–5; O'Day, *English Clergy*, 147; Blackwood, *Lancashire Gentry*, 12. Cf. Wrightson, *English Society*, 25–6, 32–3.

[85] Aylmer, *King's Servants*, 331; Stone, *Crisis of the Aristocracy*, 139–40, 762.

[86] Cf. pp. 58–62 above; *DNB*, s.v. Moore, Sir Francis; Berks. RO, D/EW E 17; *VCH, Berks.*, iii. 127, iv. 27, 119, 176; Durston, thesis, ii. 111–15.

In the second place, as has already been emphasized, legal earnings were not necessarily a barrister's sole resource. In 1624, when John Lowther had been practising at the bar for fifteen years, his fees amounted to less than £80, but his landed income had grown to £935.[87] The extent to which Lowther's legal practice was overshadowed by the proceeds of a carefully managed estate and various business ventures may have been exceptional, but if so, his case was merely an extreme instance of a general phenomenon. For many barristers, especially elder sons who had inherited large estates and the more successful élite who used any surplus of income over expenditure to purchase land, the main economic function of legal practice was to supplement their landed earnings and provide the means of acquiring more land. This helps to explain the claim of Lowther's Gray's Inn colleague Alexander Rigby in 1646, that 'my profession [was] formerly as profitable to me annually as my estate'—rather than the reverse, as we might expect.[88]

The ratio of legal earnings to other income obviously varied according to the personal circumstances of each individual, and also rose and fell over the course of a working life at the bar. Non-fee income was presumably most important at either end of a barrister's career, during the early stages of building a practice and after profits invested in land or other income-bearing assets had begun to yield a significant return. The uniquely long and detailed series of personal financial data preserved in the two surviving account books of Thomas Thornton show that only towards the end of his first decade at the bar did fees constitute as much as half of the total amounts received from his own and his wife's lands. By 1603, when he had been in practice nearly twenty years, Thornton's fees had risen just slightly above his landed income, and although both tended to fluctuate sharply from year to year, this trend continued until almost the end of James I's reign. By then, interest received on monies loaned out was assuming substantial proportions; in 1618, for example, when Thornton earned his highest recorded amount in fees (some £252), his lands brought in a further £127, and the profits from 'use' another £108. While the records become more difficult to interpret over the last seven years of Thornton's life, it would appear

---

[87] Lowther, 'Autobiography', 17–18.
[88] Blackwood, *Lancashire Gentry*, 16; cf. Herefs. RO, F76/IV/10, cl. 9, Sampson Eure's claim that 'his practice . . . was his chief support'. The significance of landed income for early modern common lawyers is noted by Keeler, 24–5.

that during this period his earnings at the bar fell a good deal below his other receipts.

Thornton's account books provide a uniquely comprehensive and detailed financial record, but there is no lack of additional evidence to show that many barristers drew incomes from sources other than legal practice. Land was both the chief means of extra-legal income, and notoriously the favoured investment for surplus legal earnings:

> We see those changes daily: the fair lands
> That were the client's, are the lawyer's now.[89]

Jonson's audience would certainly have been aware of cases where barristers were accused of having fraudulently acquired property by betraying a client's trust, or otherwise 'abusing the simplicity of some ignorant persons', as Serjeant Thomas Harris had done, according to the plaintiffs in a Chancery suit over a Herefordshire manor late in Elizabeth's reign. Such charges must often have been coloured by personal or social animus, even when they were not merely convenient pegs on which to hang litigation; nevertheless it would be straining credulity to suggest that no barristers ever exploited the tempting opportunities for illicit gain which their professional expertise and standing obviously afforded them.[90]

All lawyers enjoyed special advantages in dealings on the land market, whether they were purchasers on the enormous scale of Lord Keepers Bacon, Puckering, and Egerton, or more modest buyers like Serjeant John Stone, whose properties in the home counties were acquired, as he put it, 'by quillets and small purchases at different times'.[91] In the absence of estate agents or newspaper advertisements to put potential buyers in touch with vendors, land for sale generally became known only by direct word of mouth or through third

---

[89] B. Jonson, *The Diuell is an Asse* (1631), II. iv. 33–4; cf. the claim that common lawyers 'undo the country people and buy up all the lands that are to be sold . (Wilson, 'State of England', 24–5.)

[90] Ellesmere 6804. Cf. STAC 8/9/4 (112), 16/11, 42/16, 106/8, 158/3, 177/6, 187/24, 221/10, 241/24, 263/05; E 149/28/2; *CSPD 1598–1601*, 266–7; *Wilts. N & Q*, viii. 237–9; K. H. D. Haley, *The First Earl of Shaftesbury* (Oxford, 1968), 17–19; Ellesmere 5964; UCNW MS Plas Coch II, 3017; HMC, *Sixth Rep.*, 143b, 182a.

[91] A. Simpson, *The Wealth of the Gentry 1540–1640* (Cambridge, 1961), ch. 2; L. Knafla, *Law and Politics in Jacobean England* (Cambridge, 1977), 10–11, 23–4; E. Hopkins, 'The Bridgewater Estates in North Shropshire in the First Half of the Seventeenth Century', University of London MA thesis, 1956, 5, 22–3, 31–3; Ellesmere 732; PCC 172 Coventry; *VCH, Herts.*, iii. 267, 311, 314, iv. 13.

parties, particularly lawyers and scriveners.[92] Besides serving as manorial stewards and drafting conveyances for their clients, barristers were naturally called on to provide expert advice on particular land transactions. In one such instance Lord Chandos expressed himself (perhaps naïvely) 'glad to be directed' by Thomas Chamberlain of Gray's Inn, 'who I know is better acquainted with the value of the land than myself', while Christopher Fulwood of the same house not only gave Sir John Coke the chance to acquire at a bargain price five acres of land brought him for conveyancing by another client, but also offered to rent them out on Coke's behalf at £3 a year above their nominal value. In short, barristers were generally familiar with the market, well placed to hear of land coming up for sale, and likely to have ready access to sources of capital from which land purchases could be financed.[93]

Lastly, and perhaps most important of all, lawyers plainly had more chance and skill than most laymen to turn the complexities of the law of real property to their own advantage, whether in challenging or defending a title. Sir Robert Hitcham's purchase of the manor of Framlingham, Suffolk, for £14,000 evidently 'met with many difficulties', so much so that, according to Fuller, 'had he not been of a sharp wit, strong brains, powerful friends, plentiful purse and indefatigable diligence, he had never cleared the title'.[94] While many landowners were constantly involved in lawsuits of one kind or another, lawyers 'could with more ease and less charge maintain unjust suits', to use the words of a Star Chamber bill which accused the Inner Templar Thomas Best of defrauding his partners in a Welsh mining venture, and bringing seven different actions against them in the names of other persons. Even without resort to chicanery, barristers obviously enjoyed the benefits of free legal advice and inside familiarity with the workings of the legal system.

[92] I owe this point to G. H. Glanville's 'Aspects of the History of the County of Surrey, 1580–1620', University of London Ph.D. thesis, 1972, 235–53.

[93] Ellesmere 146; HMC, *Cowper*, ii. 27. Cf. Bodl. MS Tanner 283, fol. 73, and 284, fol. 8; Hants RO, Kingsmill 1356. For lawyers as purchasers of monastic lands and royalist estates, see H. A. L. Fisher, *The Political History of England ... 1485–1547* (1924), App. II, 499; G. W. Woodward, *Dissolution of the Monasteries* (1966), 131; K. S. Wyndham, 'In pursuit of Crown Land: the Initial Recipients of Somerset Property in the Mid-Tudor Period', *Som. Arch. and Nat. Hist. Proc.*, cxxiii (1979), 68; H. E. Chesney, 'The Transference of Lands in England, 1640–1660', *TRHS*, 4th ser. xv (1932), 185. Cf., however, I. Gentles, 'The Sales of Biship's Lands in the English Revolution, 1646–1660', *EHR*, xcv (1980), 573.

[94] Fuller, *Worthies of England*, iii. 189.

But given what Chief Baron of the Exchequer Sir Lawrence Tanfield was able to get away with in his own court (where he sat in judgement on a *quo warranto* action brought against the burgesses of Burford, Oxfordshire, which resulted in all their privileges being transferred to Tanfield as lord of the manor of Burford), one would hesitate to assert that underhand practices were exceptional.[95]

Barristers also enjoyed a significant competitive edge as land-owners, at a time when estate management was as much a matter of keeping manorial courts and manipulating tenancies as of direct agricultural production.[96] While the evidence is incomplete, it does suggest that successful lawyers were usually no less successful landlords, well able to appreciate and apply to the management of their own properties the prudent counsel given Sir Henry Sidney by his steward Roger Seys of Lincoln's Inn: 'Where is disorder, there is confusion'. Simpson's study of the administration of Lord Keeper Nicholas Bacon's Norfolk estates depicts a careful and conservative proprietor, while Roger Seys also sought to avoid overburdening the tenants on his own 'expertly-managed' lands. Another paternalistic Welsh proprietor, John Puleston of Emral, Flintshire, made it a condition of his tenants' leases that each should keep a Bible in his house, rather than, as previously, a hawk or a hound; the economic impact of this innovation is unfortunately not recorded.[97]

The leading ranks of the late Tudor and early Stuart bar also included a number of aggressive 'improving' landlords intent on increasing the productivity of their estates. The attempted enclos-ures of common fields by Lord Keeper Ellesmere at Welcombe, Warwickshire, were blocked by Sir Edward Coke on circuit as an assize judge; five hundred tenants of Richard Kingsmill, surveyor of the Court of Wards, petitioned the Privy Council in 1591 against his disregard of manorial custom and wholesale conversion of arable land to pasture; Sir Robert Heath's ruthless enclosing and fen-draining activities provoked at least one full-scale riot from 'the unruly people' near Soham, Cambridgeshire, in the 1630s, while Chief Justice Sir Thomas Richardson sought to forestall a similar

---

[95] STAC 8/177/6; M. S. Gretton, *Burford Past and Present* (1945), 78–80.
[96] R. H. Tawney, 'The Rise of the Gentry, 1558–1640', in *Essays in Economic History*, ed. E. M. Carus-Wilson (1954–62), i. 184–5.
[97] Collins, *Letters and Memorials*, i. 313; Simpson, *Wealth of Gentry*, 78–83; Robbins, thesis, 193–8; *DWB*, s.v. Puleston, John; cf. Sir Henry Hobart's concern lest his lessee might sublet at rack-rents to 'base beggarly fellows ... that will spoil the grounds'. (Bodl. MS Tanner 215, fol. 191.)

reaction by bequeathing the sum of £20 to the poor of East Carleton, Norfolk, on condition that his heirs were unmolested in their enjoyment of 'that part of the waste which I caused to be enclosed there'.[98] These and other instances stand as footnotes to Tawney's memorable characterization of the economic progress of the bar: 'Their profession had taught them what, properly handled, land could be made to yield; naturally, they used their knowledge.'[99]

Lawyers who attended the Westminster terms and followed an assize circuit were necessarily absentee landowners for at least a third of each year, and more if they held very extensive estates or lived far from London. Such absences cannot have facilitated good management, but it is difficult to show that they caused actual financial loss in particular cases. Most counsellors who owned property in the country were farmers as well as *rentiers*; while the actual working of their lands was usually delegated to a bailiff or steward, the master could nevertheless maintain some contact with farming activities by correspondence during his temporary absences.[100] Surviving accounts and inventories suggest that most barrister-farmers were producing for the market rather than for status or subsistence purposes, and that their resources were exploited in a thoroughly business-like fashion, whether to raise cash crops—including cattle, wool, wheat, rye, barley, saffron, and rabbits—or to yield minerals and timber.[101]

---

[98] Ellesmere 239–40; *VCH, War.*, iii. 267; *APC 1590–1*, 160–1; Univ. of Illinois at Urbana-Champaign, Heath Papers, I. Barrow to R. Heath, 27 June 1633, and J. Symes to R. Heath, 15 Apr. 1638; PCC 35 Sadler. For other enclosing lawyers, see Norfolk RO, NRS 12058, 27 A 6 and 15943, 31 F 5 and 15945, 31 F 5 (Henry Hobart); *Lancs. and Ches. Rec. Soc.*, iii. 30 (Edward Walmseley); *VCH, Hants*, iii. 419 (William Brooke); PCC 47 Rivers (Henry Montagu); *VCH, Oxon.*, xi. 224, 229, 234–5 (Lawrence Tanfield); Bodl. MS d.d. Risley A. vii 1/5 (Thomas Chamberlain).

[99] Tawney, 'Rise of the Gentry', 188. Cf. E. Hughes, 'The Professions in the Eighteenth Century', *Durham Univ. J.*, xliv (1951–2), 49: 'Legal fortunes were not made on modest half-guinea "opinions" . . . but from deals in real estate.'

[100] While Peter Mutton of Flints was 'remaining in Lincoln's Inn', he 'entreated . . . his uncle and his mother, being then a widow, to set and let such lands as [he] then had, and to make the best of it'. (Clwyd RO, Gwysaney 694.) Cf. the correspondence of Erasmus Earle (Hereford Public Lib. MSS Boycott 48–55), and Henry Sherfield (Hants RO, 44M69/xxi, xlviii, liii).

[101] Sherfield records receipts from the sale of produce in his memoranda books. (Cf. Hants RO, 44M69/xxv and Northants RO, Thornton 2251; see also John Smyth of Nibley's accounts, Bodl. MS Eng. Misc. e.6, fol. 131.) Relevant inventories include Lancs. RO, Inv. (Roger Downes, 1638; Sir Thomas Ireland, 1625; Hugh Rigby, 1642); UCNW, MS Plas Coch 184; NLW MS 1593 E, pp. 167–76. *The Reliquary*, NS iv (1890), 98–102.

Since many lawyers relied on farming profits for a substantial proportion of their annual income, it is hardly surprising that counsellors took a keen personal interest in agricultural matters. So we find Sir William Methwold of Lincoln's Inn writing to his Norfolk neighbour Bassingbourne Gawdy about arrangements for the temporary accommodation of a flock of lambs, and Sir Cuthbert Pepper, surveyor of the Court of Wards, specifying in his will precisely which stock should go to his wife on his death—namely, all the milking cows, the eight best oxen, all her own sheep, forty of his best ewes, and three mares. Nor was their interest confined to immediate practicalities: Serjeant Sir Sampson Eure compiled for Richard Prythergh, his colleague on the Council in the Marches, a series of 'Notes and Observations touching the time and exact practice of Limeing', which describes the method and advantages of this soil-improvement technique in some detail, and includes two paragraphs on the virtues of compost.[102]

Besides drawing rents from tenants and farming their own lands, barristers engaged in a variety of other more or less profitable economic activities. Elize Hele, Robert Sheffield, and Serjeant Rowland Ward all owned corn mills, while Sir Edward Moseley leased two mills in Leeds from the Crown, paying the very substantial entry fine of £66 13s. 4d. for the privilege. Others involved in food-processing and allied industries were Richard Swayne, who owned a butcher's shambles in his native town of Blandford; Thomas Lambert, the proprietor of a beerhouse in Colchester; James Dyer, town clerk of Bristol, who had an interest in a soap-boiling business there, and Toby Wood of London, who owned a bakery in Redcross Street and 'a brewhouse called the Three Kings'.[103] Whether these establishments were directly operated by their owners or merely rented out to tenants is unknown. Serjeant Richard Amherst appears to have leased his furnace in the Kentish weald to an ironmaster. Although Thomas Aynscombe of the Inner Temple and Mayfield, Sussex, hailed from a family of ironmasters, there is no sign that he ever actively engaged in that kind of work himself, nor that John

---

[102] HMC, *Gawdy*, 58; Borthwick, Reg. 31, fols. 72–72ᵛ; cf. similar arrangements by Sir Thomas Coventry (PCC 13 Huddlestone). NLW, 5977D; for Sir Robert Brerewood's profitable use of advanced farming techniques, see SP 23/197, fol. 93, quoted by M. D. G. Wanklyn, 'Landed Society and Allegiance in Cheshire and Shropshire in the First Civil War', University of Manchester Ph.D. thesis, 1976, 333–4.

[103] C142/270/132 and 664/ 33; PCC 17 Goare, 2 Pile, 512 Alchin, 69 Wood; Leeds District Archives, TN LA 1/8; *VCH, War.*, v. 12–13.

Harington of Lincoln's Inn retained the two stamping mills and a 'boring house' in Cornwall which he inherited from his father in 1612 while he was still a student under the bar. On the other hand, the Derbyshire barristers Edward Manlove and Christopher Fulwood took an active interest in lead mining in their county, as did the outsider Sir Robert Heath, in characteristically disruptive fashion.[104]

A venture on a much larger scale was the Mines Royal, one of the earliest English joint-stock companies, which had been first incorporated in 1568, with the barrister Robert Wethereld of Lincoln's Inn among its six assistant governors, or directors. The Lincoln's Inn connection continued into the following century; when the company was reconstituted in 1605, its twenty-one shareholders included Arnold Oldisworth and Roger Owen, both members, and later associate benchers, of the house, although the former was a legal bureaucrat, and the latter, although called to the bar, seems not to have practised as a counsellor.[105] The twin company of Mineral and Battery Works also had strong inns-of-court ties. During the 1620s its governing body met on occasion in the Lincoln's Inn chamber of George Mynne, Oldisworth's successor as clerk of the Hanaper in Chancery; among those attending were the barristers Challenor Chute and Edward Palmer of the Middle Temple and Euseby Wright of Lincoln's Inn.[106] Mynne, an extraordinarily versatile projector, was also involved during the 1620s in a partnership for growing madder and oil-seed with Henry Sherfield of Lincoln's Inn and his stepson, George Bedford; although Mynne backed out in 1625 after failing to obtain a patent for the sole cultivation and sale of madder in England, Sherfield continued to invest in Bedford's supposed expert knowledge of the dyestuff for at least another five years.[107] The satire on projects and projectors

[104] PCC 61 Audley, 35 Dale, 51 Alchin; C142/394/80; B. Irving, *Mayfield, the story of a Wealden Village* (1903), 158-9. Dias, thesis, 90-1, 432; [E. Manlove], *The Liberties and Customes of the Lead Mines ...* (1653); Brighton, *Royalists and Roundheads in Derbs.*, 22; J. W. Gough, *The Rise of the Entrepreneur* (1969), 141-3. Cf. STAC 8/177/6 for Thomas Best's involvement with mining.

[105] M. B. Donald, *Elizabethan Copper* (1935), 34-5, 43-4, 59, 93-4; *H. of P.*, iii. 151, 162-3; see Sheffield Univ. Lib., MS Hartlib 62/4/2, for the association of Welsh barristers with the Mines Royal in Cardiganshire, c.1640.

[106] BL MS Loan 16, part 2, fols. 1, 2, 4ᵛ, 90; PCC 35 Brent.

[107] J. Thirsk, *Economic Policy and Projects* (Oxford, 1978), 171; Hants RO, 44M69/xxxiii, and Box S14 (unsorted papers: Mynne to Sherfield, 16 Sept. 1623); *Select Charters of Trading Companies, A.D. 1530-1707*, ed. C. T. Carr (SS, 1913), lxxix; J. H.

which preceded the great masque mounted by the four inns of court in 1634 may indicate some sensitivity about the legal profession's association with the dubious schemes of would-be patentees; a pamphlet published in 1641 claimed that lawyers were 'exceeding forward' in floating projects, 'drawing the conveyances, and assignments of the shares, half parts and deputations of shires'. Of course, by no means all companies and projects in which barristers participated brought lucrative rewards. Bulstrode Whitelocke wisely advised his children 'not to adventure any of your stock in ways wherein you are not experienced', having burnt his own fingers before the Civil War 'in the way of merchandise' with some traders of Poole and Southampton, as well as in abortive schemes for draining Yorkshire fenland and dredging the River Avon, these last in partnership with his Middle Temple colleague William Saye.[108]

The historian of the Newfoundland Company reminds us that 'lawyers had from the time of the elder Richard Hakluyt been intimately connected with England's overseas expansion'. The particular prominence of Middle Templars in overseas colonizing and trading ventures under Elizabeth and the early Stuarts probably reflects the large cohorts of men recruited to that house from the maritime counties of the south and south west. However, barristers of all four inns were closely associated with the East India and Virginia companies, besides playing a significant role in establishing the Ulster plantations of the early seventeenth century, and in the later, more ideologically inspired Massachusetts Bay and Providence Island ventures.[109] Closer to home, the first meeting of the

Bettey, 'The Cultivation of Woad in the Salisbury area during the Late Sixteenth and Seventeenth Centuries', *Textile Hist.* ix (1978), 112–17. For Sir Robert Heath's madder interests, see Bodl. MS Bankes 9/15.

[108] T. Brugis, *The Discovery of a Projector* (1641), 14–15. Additional 37343, fols. 145ᵛ, 196ᵛ. For lawyer involvement in fen drainage projects, cf. L. E. Harris, *Vermuyden and the Fens* (1953), 27, 43, 64, 91, 94; K. Lindley, *Fenland Riots and the English Revolution* (1982), index, s.v. Heath, Edward and Robert; Quarles, George.

[109] G. T. Cell, 'The Newfoundland Company: A Study of Subscribers to a Colonising Venture', *William and Mary Quarterly*, 3rd ser. xxii (1965), 618; *Inns of Court*, 37, 207–8. T. K. Rabb, *Enterprise and Empire* (Cambridge, Mass., 1967), 102 n.; *The English New England Voyages 1602–1608*, ed. D. B. and A. M. Quinn (Hakluyt Soc., 1983), 28, 76; S. M. Kingsbury, *The Records of the Virginia Company of London* (Washington, D.C., 1906), i. 394, 607, 611, ii. 272. G. Hill, *An Historical Account of the Plantation in Ulster* (Belfast, 1877), 90, 122, and index, s.v. Davies, John; Ley, James; Winch, Humphrey. T. W. Moody, *The Londonderry Plantation 1609–1641* (Belfast, 1939), 81; A. P. Newton, *The Colonising Activities of the English Puritans* (New Haven, 1914), 59, 61–2, 70. At least nine members of our barristers'

New River Company, set up to supply London with fresh water, was held in 1619 at the Serjeants' Inn chambers of Chief Justice Sir Henry Montagu; the company's twenty-nine initial members included Montagu's former colleagues on the Middle Temple bench, the brothers Sir Laurence and Sir Nicholas Hyde. Many of the chartered companies operating abroad and at home in which lawyers participated, alongside merchants, courtiers, peers, and country gentlemen, may not have been much more profitable than the New River venture, at least in the early days; nonetheless, some did bring in handsome returns, while all generated large amounts of work for lawyers, both during the initial stage of incorporation and in the subsequent incessant litigation which companies and patentees usually carried on against interlopers and rivals.[110]

Money-lending was another profitable sideline for many barristers. Small cash loans were constantly exchanged at virtually every social level in Tudor and Stuart England, due to the absence of banks and other institutional providers of short-term credit. But in addition to the wellnigh universal practice of helping out colleagues, kinsmen, and neighbours with small sums to tide them over limited periods, some barristers also engaged in large-scale and, as we might say, professional money-lending. Between 1600 and 1608 Henry Denne of Lincoln's Inn lent at least £2,600 to the earl of Hertford; just before his death in 1638 Sir Edward Clarke, master in Chancery and bencher of Lincoln's Inn, had more than £4,000 out at use, including £2,000 to Sir Henry Sambourne and £1,100 to a cousin, John Gregory, both loans secured by mortgage; Robert Mason had £1,560 out to the earl of Southampton, Sir Henry Hobart £2,000 to the earl of Arundel, and Serjeant John Hele, that 'most griping and excessive usurer', claimed to have loaned Lord Cobham over £4,600 before the latter's attainder for treason in 1603 (slightly more than

sample were investors in colonizing and trading companies, while Richard Langley served as secretary of the Spanish Company, and William Dyos as a director of the Irish Company. (P. Croft, *The Spanish Company* (London Rec. Soc., 1973), i; Moody, loc. cit.)

[110] J. W. Gough, *Sir Hugh Myddleton* (Oxford, 1964), 65, 71–2, 79; Kingsbury, *Virginia Company*, i. 71, 259, 262, 394, ii. 150–1, 155; *Calendar of State Papers, Colonial Series, East Indies, China and Japan, 1513–1616*, ed. W. N. Sainsbury (1867), 106; ibid., *1622–4*, 121–3; ibid., *1625–9*, 280, 349; J. Latimer, *The History of the Society of Merchant Venturers of the City of Bristol* (1903), 139; *Extracts from the Records of the Merchant Adventurers of Newcastle-Upon-Tyne*, ed. F. W. Dendy (Surtees Soc., 1899), xii–xiv, 55, 63, 84; Anon., *A Short and True Relation of the Soap Business* (1641), quoted by W. H. Price, *English Patents of Monopoly* (Cambridge, Mass., 1906), 125.

he had lost when the earl of Essex was attainted two years before).[111]

The peers' legal privilege of immunity from arrest meant that large loans to noblemen were inevitably somewhat speculative in character unless secured by mortgage, although barristers could doubtless be persuaded to take the risk of accommodating a titled client with whom they had had (or hoped to have) a long and profitable association. At the same time many barristers clearly regarded money-lending as a regular source of income, not just an occasional gamble; Thomas Thornton, for instance, consistently recorded earnings from 'use' in his annual accounts, alongside his legal fees and farming income. The amounts ranged between £5 and £235 per annum, frequently exceeding his profits from either the law or his lands. Thomas Gell of the Inner Temple seems to have kept his loans to a maximum of £500–600, even if he sometimes lent to aristocratic clients as well as to fellow barristers.[112]

Neither Thornton nor Gell operated on the same scale as the notorious financier Hugh Audley, whose fabulous wealth and miserly habits were commemorated in a sensationalist character sketch published immediately after his death. Yet it is worth emphasizing that Audley, a nephew of John Hare, clerk of Wards, began his career as a barrister of the Inner Temple, was made an associate bencher on becoming co-chief clerk of Wards in 1638, and thereafter kept up an active association with the house.[113] Barristers were ideally placed to profit from clients needing to borrow money if they were in a position to supply the cash themselves. If not, they might be asked to act as surety for loans raised elsewhere, a request which could be difficult to refuse, despite the considerable risks which acceptance often entailed, as demonstrated by the unfortunate experiences of a number of lawyers, driven close to insolvency

[111] HMC, *Bath*, iv. 347; PCC 28 Harvey, 13 Pile; Norfolk RO, NRS 15928, 31 F 4, fol. 5; Stone, *Crisis of the Aristocracy*, 533–4; Ellesmere 2702, 2707–8. For other lawyer money-lenders, see *The Reliquary*, NS iv (1890), 102 (Francis Bradshaw); Kent AO, U 24832/Z1 (Henry Hall); PCC 66 Audley (Francis Mingay); Bacon, *Works*, vii. 248, 300, 323 (Nicholas Trotte); HMC, *De L'Isle and Dudley*, vi. 71 (Sir Ralph Whitfield); Clark, *Provincial Society*, 286; J. E. Kew, 'Mortgages in Mid-Tudor Devonshire', *Trans. Devonshire Assocn.*, xcix (1967), 176–7.

[112] Cf. Stone, *Crisis of the Aristocracy*, 534. Northants RO, Thornton 2251, *passim*. Derbs. RO, Gell 30/11 (a–d, l, o–r, t), 30/14 (a–c), 30/15 (a).

[113] *DNB*, s.v. Audley, Hugh; PCC 66 Cappell; Anon., *The Way to be Rich, According to the Practice of the Great Audley Who began with two hundred Pound, in the Year 1605, and dyed worth four hundred thousand Pound . . .* (1662); *ITR*, ii. 247, 295, 306, 315; PCC 134 Laud, provisions for IT servants and repair of Temple Church.

through the default of principals for whom they had gone surety.[114]

Finally, an important ancillary source of income was provided by offices of many different kinds, proceeds, and perquisites. Official salaries are certainly no guide to actual values; for example, the annual stipends of municipal recorderships rarely exceeded £5, but in addition, recorders usually received a cut of all fees paid in the town courts, besides valuable patronage rights, gratuities in cash or kind, and opportunities to lease town lands at concessional rates.[115] Like most other holders of local offices, including escheators, feodaries, and manorial stewards (but probably not town clerks), recorders were also able to maintain a private practice at the bar. Crown law officers and Welsh judges could also remain in practice on their own account, but not those who held judicial office in the central courts. Hence Westminster Hall judges might conceivably find themselves worse off than before their promotion to the bench, as appears to have been the case with at least two early seventeenth-century puisne justices of King's Bench, Sir John Croke and Sir James Whitelocke.[116]

Barristers frequently held administrative positions and sinecures attached to the Westminster courts, even though call to the bar was neither a necessary, nor a specific, qualification for such posts. It is not always clear whether counsellors who obtained offices of this type were obliged or chose to give up active practice of their profession. A practising barrister might also draw profits from an office held in another's name, as Sir Henry Finch apparently sought to do when his two barrister sons John and Nathaniel acquired shares in the office of *Custos Brevium* of King's Bench.[117] On the other hand, it is uncertain whether the £600 per annum which Sir Robert Heath and Robert Shute received for 'executing' Sir John Roper's office of chief clerk in King's Bench was in the nature of a salary for work done, or was merely used to pay for some deputy to

---

[114] Cf. Sir Randle Crew's collection of cautionary Scriptural aphorisms, Ches. RO, DCR 26/15/3. For individual barristers who suffered financially through suretyship, see C2/Jac. I/F10/2; Clode, *Merchant Taylors*, ii. 235; *Fortescue Papers*, ed. Gardiner, 171; PCC 145 Fairfax; *Reports of Cases decided by Francis Bacon . . . in the High Court of Chancery (1617–1621)* (1932), 139.

[115] See below, pp. 242–3.

[116] Ellesmere 7466; Croke, *Genealogical History*, iii. 480; Additional 53726, fol. 11.

[117] C2/Jac. I/FI/23. As chief justice of Common Pleas, Sir Henry Hobart had in his gift the office of clerk of Warrants and Estreats, which he granted to his son Miles, a LI barrister, on condition that all fees belonging to the office should be paid directly to himself. (Norfolk RO, NRS 11078, 25 E 3. In an obituary note, his judicial colleague Sir Richard Hutton noted that Hobart had 'raised large sums of money by offices'. (CUL MS Add. 6863, fol. 26.)

carry out the actual duties of the position while Heath and Shute pocketed the difference. At all events, there can be no doubt that most barristers who sought and obtained offices of this kind prospered as a result.[118]

v. Conclusions

So even if large fee incomes (of, say, £500 and upwards) were confined to a few leading practitioners, quite modest earnings at the bar could and did help some counsellors rise in the world, especially when combined with the various ancillary sources of wealth available in principle to all barristers. The remaining questions are obvious enough: how many rose, and how far did they ascend?

Given the perennial problem of inadequate evidence, plus some fairly intractable difficulties of definition and measurement, only partial and tentative answers can be offered. Contemporaries were by no means agreed on the relative importance of a man's birth, education, occupation, 'port', or life-style, and wealth for his social standing, although historians have noticed a tendency throughout the early modern period for emphasis to shift from birth to the other criteria. Nor were the social gradations themselves uniform or clearly marked, despite the best efforts of the College of Arms.[119] So the sorting of individuals into social categories inevitably places considerable reliance on the historian's subjective judgement.

In the sample of 115 barristers selected for intensive study, 16 individuals may be identified with some confidence as having risen to a socio-economic position appreciably higher than that of their fathers; another 10 seem to have remained on much the same level as their parents, while 2 certainly, and 4 possibly, appear to have fallen in the world. Unfortunately, by far the largest group comprises those whose own circumstances, or those of their parents, are now too obscure to permit any firm judgement on the matter—which is not to imply that the information available about the others is anything like as full as might be wished. However, this large group of unknowns probably contained few upwardly mobile barristers, if only because we might reasonably expect the worldly careers of the

---

[118] Whitelocke, *Lib. Fam.*, 46; Chamberlain, *Letters*, ii. 180–1; S. R. Gardiner, *History of England . . . 1603–1642* (1883–4), iii. 31–3; *CSPD 1611–18*, 380, 407, 433; Kopperman, thesis, 41–3.

[119] Cf. Morrill, 'Northern Gentry and the Great Rebellion', 69–70; also Wanklyn's perceptive discussion in his thesis, ch. 2.

successful to be better documented than those of their less fortunate contemporaries. The number of 'risers' would be substantially increased if titles of degree alone were used as sufficient indicators of social status, since every barrister whose father was known as a mere 'gent.' (or less) automatically gained at least nominal promotion by virtue of the courtesy title 'esquire' which went with his call to the bar. What, if anything, this formality meant in practice it is hard to say. That newly called barristers lacking any other claim to the title would normally have been accepted as the equals of men well established by inheritance among the landed gentry proper seems unlikely. On the other hand, the vehemence with which it was occasionally denied that barristers had any legitimate claim to the title suggests that its use was not yet a mere formality. There is a similar problem with grants of heraldic arms, but since these were made individually to men usually well into middle age, the case for taking them into account is a good deal stronger.

Among the sixteen risers it is somewhat surprising to discover only three (Sir Edward Henden, John Keeling, and Sir William Wilde) whose ascent into the ranks of the landed gentry can be indisputably associated with successful careers as practising barristers.[120] Two more (Sir John Cremer and John Hare) also joined the ranks of the gentry; but although the former's ascent from the Norfolk yeomanry to a Restoration knighthood was probably the highest social leap achieved by any barrister in the sample, it is not absolutely certain that Cremer ever practised at the bar, while John Hare, the younger son of a London citizen, accumulated his extensive home counties estates from the profits of his office in the Court of Wards.[121] Most of the other risers came from gentry stock to begin with, although Stephen Phesant belonged to a well-established legal dynasty (both his father and grandfather had been benchers of Gray's Inn), and Timothy Leving's father was probably on the most marginal fringes of the Warwickshire parochial gentry.

Of the rest, John Archer, Francis Bradshaw, Thomas Gallop, Robert Rich, John Strode, Thomas Widdrington and Nicholas Willimot all shared fairly similar minor gentry antecedents and accumulated substantial landed estates, plus knighthoods in the cases of all but Bradshaw and Gallop. Finally, there are two

---

[120] For Henden and Wilde, see above, pp. 153–4; for Keeling, see Appendix F, n. c, and references therein.

[121] See above, pp. 151–2.

barristers, Robert Maltiward and Montague Watts, whose main
claims to be classified as upwardly mobile are that they were
recipients of grants of arms; another grantee, Richard Langley,
might also have been included on this ground had he not died in
poverty shortly after the death of his patron Robert Cecil in 1612.[122]

Assuming that our sampling techniques are reasonably reliable,
these results suggest that about one in seven of all barristers called
during the fifty years before the Long Parliament were to some
extent upwardly mobile, while something like sixty of these men rose
into the ranks of the landed gentry as a direct result of their careers
at the bar. It has been estimated that in the early 1630s the upper
gentry (peers, baronets, knights, and esquires) numbered between
some nine and eleven thousand individuals all told.[123] So the
contribution of the bar to upwards socio-economic mobility, either
into or within the ranks of the pre-Civil War gentry, was plainly not
spectacular in statistical terms, especially since the upwards movement was spread over more than half a century. It should be added
immediately, however, that our findings were deliberately con-
structed on a conservative basis, and it may be that a few more risers
are hidden among the large category of unknowns. On the other
hand, it is equally possible that this picture accurately reflects the
impact of a deepening employment crisis at the bar in the early
decades of the seventeenth century, together with the disruptive
impact of the revolutionary decades on the legal system as a whole.

A systematic national index of mobility both between and within
the constituent strata of early modern English society has yet to be
compiled. However, during the last thirty years or so, a considerable
body of research has illuminated the recruitment and fortunes of the
landed classes over a broad geographical cross-section of England,
between the reformation of Henry VIII and the restoration of
Charles II. These detailed local studies amply vindicate the general
proposition that the law frequently served as a powerful economic
and social escalator, whether in early Tudor Yorkshire, Elizabethan
Sussex, or later Stuart Warwickshire.[124] Yet local historians' assess-

---

[122] For biographical details, see Appendix D and references cited there.

[123] Aylmer, *King's Servants*, 331.

[124] Cf. R. B. Smith, *Land and Politics in the England of Henry VIII* (Oxford, 1970),
89; J. E. Mousley, 'The Fortunes of Some Gentry Families of Elizabethan Sussex',
Eco. Hist. Rev., 2nd ser. xi (1958–9), 477; P. Styles, 'The Social Structure of Kineton
Hundred in the Reign of Charles II', *Birmingham Arch. Soc. Trans.*, lxxviii (1962),
113–17; T. G. Barnes, *Somerset 1625–1640* (Cambridge, Mass., 1961), 19–20.

ments of the extent to which the gentry were being replenished and refreshed by *arriviste* counsellors-at-law vary markedly. In their work on Devon and Northamptonshire, Hoskins and Finch both emphasized the importance of 'lawyers and judges who built up fortunes and raised an obscure family to eminence and landed wealth', while Cliffe and Glanville have pointed to the prominence of lawyers among purchasers of land in pre-Civil War Surrey and Yorkshire.[125] But Ferris noted that in Caroline Dorset lawyers' purchases were 'less impressive' than those of businessmen, and according to Everitt 'careful marriages . . . [were] a more important factor than either trade or the law in the rise of most of the Kentish county families of 1640', less than one in twenty of which had ascended by the law 'to any considerable extent'. Of thirty families who augmented the Berkshire landed élite between 1500 and 1640, only one, we are told, owed its promotion to the law. At the other end of the country, in Cumberland and Westmorland, among sixty-three newly arrived gentry families in 1642, Phillips found that no more than two derived their status from the profits of office or legal practice. Finally, in his exemplary study of *The Lancashire Gentry and the Great Rebellion*, Blackwood notes that most of the families rising within that county's landed ruling class during the early seventeenth century were 'mere' gentry, dependent entirely upon agriculture and rents. Lawyers, merchants, and office-holders together accounted for only 19 of 48 rising gentry families; it also seems likely that most of those 289 families who rose into the gentry over the same period did so 'on the profits of yeoman farming' rather than by trade, office, or the professions.[126]

So the efficacy of the law as an agent of social change varied according to regional as well as individual circumstances. But if we should not exaggerate the impact of upwardly mobile barristers on the social fabric of early modern England as a whole, let alone imply that a career at the bar was an infallible means of personal advancement, there should equally be no doubt that a significant

[125] W. G. Hoskins, *Devon* (1954), 79; *idem* and H. P. Finberg, *Devonshire Studies* (1952), 87 n., 141, 358–9; Finch, *Five Northants Families*, 50–1, 135–7, 168; Cliffe, *Yorkshire Gentry*, 94; Glanville, thesis, 354.

[126] J. P. Ferris, 'The Gentry of Dorset on the Eve of the Civil War', *Genealogist's Magazine*, xv (1965), 110; A. Everitt, *The Community of Kent and the Great Rebellion 1640–60* (Leicester, 1966), 38, 40 (but cf. C. W. Chalklin, *Seventeenth-Century Kent* (1965), 200, and Clark *Provincial Society*, 284–5). Durston, thesis, i. 55; Phillips, thesis, 39; Blackwood, *Lancashire Gentry*, 16–17. See also *A Survey of Stafford-shire . . . by Sampson Erdeswicke*, ed. T. Harwood (1844), lviii.

minority of barristers did reap very handsome returns from their professional labours, or that the bar served as a major channel of mobility within this still largely rural, non-industrialized society. The rewards offered to practising barristers in early modern England were also almost certainly larger than those available to their counterparts elsewhere in Europe. The uniquely centralized common-law system meant that all practising barristers had access to the benefits, fees, and preferments offered by a national market, whereas continental lawyers were typically organized in smaller regional units incorporating fewer potential clients and more restricted promotion opportunities. The English profession was better integrated vertically as well as horizontally; in civil-law jurisdictions judges generally formed a distinct cadre of royal servants, whereas the common-law judiciary was appointed directly from the ranks of practising barristers. Finally, thanks to the relative underdevelopment of a state bureaucracy or hereditary office-holding class in Renaissance England, common lawyers faced considerably less competition for a share of the private and public surplus than their counterparts across the Channel; the size and power of the state apparatus in continental Europe meant that there the real prizes for trained jurists were to be found in royal service rather than private practice.[127]

In 1653 the merchant and reformist pamphleteer Henry Robinson claimed that 'this one tribe' (of lawyers) 'is thought to make a shift to gain or reap one fifth part of all the gains and increase of the whole nation'. While doubtless exaggerated, Robinson's estimate may not have been entirely outside the right order of magnitude; indeed, it received some independent support from the calculations published by his contemporary William Cole in 1659.[128] These figures related to the legal profession as a whole, although it was success at the bar which offered the largest and most glittering prizes. What such success meant is still apparent today in some of the great houses built by men who had scaled the heights of their profession, such as Sir Edward Phelipps's Montacute and Sir Henry

---

[127] Berlanstein, 'Lawyers in Pre-Revolutionary France', 165, 170–1; R. L. Kagan, *Lawsuits and Litigants in Castile, 1500–1790* (Chapel Hill, 1981), 63–6; Aylmer, *King's Servants*, 439–44, 452–3.

[128] H. Robinson, *Certain Proposals in Order to a New Modelling of the Lawes and Law-Proceedings* (1653), 2; W. Cole, *A Rod for the Lawyers* (1659), 8; Aylmer, *King's Servants*, 328–9.

Hobart's Blickling; many more have long since disappeared, like Sir Francis Moore's Fawley Court, Sir John Popham's Wellington and Sir Francis Bacon's Verulam House at Gorhambury. Yet, as we shall now see, it was not only in brick and stone that early modern barristers left a mark on their world, and ours.

CHAPTER SIX

LAWYERS AND LETTERS

'He imagines that ... his profession only is learning ...'.

'A mere Common Lawyer', in *The Miscellaneous Works* ...
of Sir Thomas Overbury, ed. E. F. Rimbault (1856), 84

'But there have been lawyers that were orators, philosophers, historians: there have been Bacons and Clarendons, my lord.'

Henry St John, Viscount Bolingbroke, 'On the Study and
Use of History', in *Works*, ed. D. Mallett (1754), ii. 353

LAW and letters (including some of the newer social sciences as well
as the traditional *literae humaniores*) today inhabit largely separate
worlds. Legal practice and the writing of novels, plays, poetry,
history, philosophy, or sociology are in effect mutually exclusive
vocations; that an occasional individual of exceptional talent man-
ages to combine them (but without achieving the very highest rank
in either sphere) merely goes to prove the point. If most modern
intellectuals are legally illiterate, the workaday world of the practising lawyer is to a considerable extent culturally and intellectually
isolated.

While the first quotation at the head of this chapter may suggest
that nothing has changed since the early seventeenth century, the
second reminds us that individual common lawyers did make
significant contributions to the flowering of Renaissance humanism
in England. This chapter examines the nature of their involvement,
and seeks to explain not only why barristers were prominent in the
cultural and intellectual life of Elizabethan and early Stuart England, but also why that fact seems to have failed to register on their
public image, then or later.

i. Interpretations

In February 1588 the gentlemen of Gray's Inn presented 'certain
devices and shows' before Queen Elizabeth and her court at Greenwich. Their main offering was a laboured melodrama entitled *The*

Misfortunes of Arthur (Uther Pendragon's Sonne) reduced into Tragicall Notes, written jointly by seven barristers and one student member of the house. It has been plausibly suggested that *The Misfortunes of Arthur* presented oblique references to the political uncertainties facing England on the eve of the Spanish Armada and guarded advice about how they should be tackled.[1] If so, the distinctly separate prologue by Nicholas Trotte, which is set firmly in the present rather than in a misty Arthurian past, may have been intended to establish the lawyer's qualifications for the role of royal counsellor. At the same time it conveniently outlines two divergent contemporary assessments of the cultural standing of the common law and its practitioners.

The prologue, or 'introduction', begins with the entrance of three Muses 'apparelled accordingly, bringing five gentlemen students with them ... as captives'. One of their number steps forward to explain that she and her sisters have long sought to exact 'the service by choice wits to Muses due' from these followers of Astraea, imperial virgin and goddess of justice (with whom Queen Elizabeth was frequently identified).[2] Unfortunately, the 'flowering wits' attached to Astraea's train

> ... she schooleth to forget and scorn,
> The noble skills of language and of arts,
> The wisdom, which discourse of stories teach,
> The ornaments which various knowledge yields;
> But poesie she hath in most disdain. ...

In place of these 'noble skills', Astraea offers her followers nothing better than

> ... some old reports of altered laws
> Clamours of courts and cavils upon words,
> Grounds without ground, supported by conceit,
> And reasons of more subtlety than sense

—all this in 'a tongue that barbarism itself doth use'.

The Muse's declamation is answered at length by one of the captives, who, predictably, takes issue with all her claims. Astraea's followers (he maintains) have resisted the Muses' blandishments in

[1] *Certain Devices and Shewes presented to her Maiestie* (1587); M. Axton, *The Queen's Two Bodies* (1977), 76–9.
[2] *Certain Devices* [t.p.ᵛ]. F. Yates, *Astraea: The Imperial Theme in the Sixteenth Century* (1975), ch. 1.

the past and will continue to do so, for 'all the vaunted store of Muses' gifts' impresses them far less than Astraea's 'sound perfections':

> They with attentive minds and serious wits,
> Revolve records of deep judicial acts,
> They weigh with steady and indifferent hands,
> Each word of law, each circumstance of right
> . . . .
> One doubt in moots by argument increased
> Clears many doubts . . .
> The language she first chose, and still retains,
> Exhibits naked truth in aptest terms,
> Our industry maintaineth unimpeached,
> Prerogatives of prince, respect to peers,
> The commons' liberty, and each man's right
> . . . .
> Yet never did we banish nor reject
> Those ornaments of knowledge nor of tongues.
> That slander envious ignorance did raise.
> With Muses still we intercourse allow
> T'enrich our state with all their foreign freight
> But never homage nor acknowledgement
> Such as of subjects allegiance doth require.[3]

The critique of law and lawyers which called forth this response from Astraea's men recalls the polemical rhetoric of Italian Renaissance humanists. In the fourteenth century Petrarch complained of wasting seven years in legal studies, his father having burnt his copies of Cicero and the Latin poets 'as impediments to that study which was supposed to be the source of fat earnings'. According to the Florentine chancellor Leonardo Bruni a hundred years later, the ancients had fully recognized the narrow tedium of the law, calling it the 'yawning science'. True, humanist authors were not invariably hostile to legal studies; the educational writer P. P. Vergerius, Bruni's near contemporary, expressed high regard for law as a branch of moral philosophy, although he maintained that 'law as practised becomes a mere trade'.[4] But of course by law these

[3] *Certain Devices*, sigs. [A–Bᵛ].

[4] M. Bishop, *Petrarch and his World* (1964), 26–7; *Renaissance and Reformation 1300–1648*, ed. G. R. Elton (New York, 1968), 47; W. H. Woodward, *Vittorino Da Feltre and other Humanist Educators* (Cambridge, 1921), 108; cf. D. R. Kelley, *Foundations of Modern Historical Scholarship* (New York, 1970), 39–41; B. L. Ullman, *The Humanism of Coluccio Salutati* (Padua, 1963), 31–2; Ovid, *Amores*, I. xv.

scholars meant civil law, the *Corpus Iuris*; the representative humanist verdict on English common law is that of Erasmus, who
maintained that no discipline could be further removed from true
learning (*a veris literis alienissima*), a view seemingly endorsed on at
least one occasion by his English common-lawyer friend Sir Thomas
More.[5] The twin themes of the common law's barbarous aridity and
the common lawyers' plodding dullness continued to be elaborated
throughout the sixteenth and early seventeenth centuries, achieving
their literary apotheosis in George Ruggle's Latin comedy *Ignoramus*, first staged at Cambridge University before James I in 1615.[6]
Ruggle's portrait of an opinionated, puritanical, and unlearned
common lawyer (perhaps inspired by the town's recorder, Francis
Bracken of Gray's Inn) pleased the king so much that he returned
for a second command performance, while John Chamberlain noted
that the play

> so nettled the lawyers that they are almost out of all patience, and the Lord
> Chief Justice [Coke] both openly at the King's Bench and divers other places
> hath galled and glanced at scholars with much bitterness and there be divers
> inns of court men have made rhymes and ballads against them. . . .[7]

Some faint echoes of *Ignoramus* linger on in the writings of
modern historians. Maitland's influential 1901 Rede lecture, 'English Law and the Renaissance', attributed the survival of the
common law in the face of humanist criticism and a threatened

---

[5] *Opus Epistolarum Des. Erasmi Roterdami*, ed. P. S. and H. M. Allen (1906), iv. 17,
quoted by R. W. Chambers, *Thomas More* (1935), 85; J. H. Hexter, *More's Utopia:
The biography of an idea* (New York, 1952), 109.

[6] E.g. B. Jonson, 'The Poetaster', in *Works*, ed. C. H. Herford and P. and E. M.
Simpson (Oxford, 1925–52), iv. 212–13; B. Googe, *Eglogs, Epytaphes and Sonettes*,
ed. E. Arber (1871), 12; *The Collected Poems of Joseph Hall*, ed. A. Davenport
(Liverpool, 1949), 26; J. Day, *Law-tricks, or who would have thought it* (1608), sigs.
[A4ᵛ]–B; J. Donne, *The Satires, Epigrams and Verse Letters*, ed. W. Milgate (Oxford,
1967), 7–10; J. Hayward, *Of Supremacie in Affairs of Religion* (1624), 87; IT MS Petyt
538. 38, fol. 101; R. Montagu, *Diatribae upon the First Part of the late History of
Tithes* (1621), 121–9; Additional 22603, fol. 11ᵛ; *Elizabeth of England: Certain
Observations Concerning the Life and Reign of Queen Elizabeth by John Clapham*, ed.
E. P. and C. Read (Philadelphia, 1951), 61; *Archaeologia*, xv (1806), 52; HMC, *Var.
Coll.*, ii. 203; *The Miscellaneous Writings of John Evelyn*, ed. W. Upcott (1825), 166–7;
Inns of Court, 141–2.

[7] J. L. Van Gundy, *Ignoramus . . . An Examination of its Sources and Literary
Influence* (Lancaster, Pa., 1906), 7, 12, 66. Chamberlain, *Letters*, i. 597–8. Cf. J. B.
Leishman, *The Three Parnassus Plays* (1949), 61–6, 287–9, 294–9, 314–15, 318–22,
329–31. Lawyers' responses to *Ignoramus*, besides those cited by Van Gundy and in
Inns of Court, 209, include Additional 34218, fols. 152–4; Fitzgeffrey, *Satyres*, sig. C4;
Folger MS V.b.303, fols. 301–3.

reception of civil law under Henry VIII to the 'toughness' of a code which had developed its own idiosyncratic language and logic in the non-academic setting of the inns of court. According to Maitland, the isolation of common lawyers from the scholarship of the universities bred a fiercely independent cast of mind, which enabled both the lawyers and the code they professed to overcome the threat of incorporation within an alien universalist tradition. This parochial chauvinism also brought forth one of the pivotal figures of English legal history, 'that wonderful Edward Coke', who was largely responsible for adapting the medieval legal heritage to meet the needs of a post-medieval society.[8]

Coke is also central to Pocock's account of the influence of the 'common-law mind' upon seventeenth-century English historical and political thought. According to Pocock, the idealization of common law as immemorial custom achieved its classical statement in Coke's writings, which 'may be taken as a safe guide to the thought of his profession'—insular, ahistorical, empiricist, proto-Burkean. Kelley's recent elaboration of Pocock's thesis detects a linkage between the geographical and intellectual narrowness of English historical scholarship from the seventeenth century onwards, and the introverted guild-mentality of the early modern common lawyers, whose tendency, it is claimed, was 'to deny the relevance either of a comparative approach or the utility of contact with other disciplines'.[9]

There is plainly an element of paradox in arguing for the influence of an ahistorical and antitheoretical outlook on the development of historical writing and political thought. More to the point, even if early modern common lawyers did enjoy a degree of academic and cultural autonomy denied to their Continental counterparts, it does not follow that English barristers were effectively isolated from the major intellectual currents of their age, *pace* Pocock, Kelley, and, to a lesser extent, Maitland. To use the terms of the prologue to *The Misfortunes of Arthur*, historians may too readily have accepted the

---

[8] F. W. Maitland, *English Law and the Renaissance* (Cambridge, 1901), *passim*; cf. *Year Books of Edward II, Vol. I*, ed. *idem* (SS, 1903), lxxx–lxxxi. The continuing discussion of Maitland's thesis is conveniently summarized in D. Jenkins, 'English Law and the Renaissance. Eighty Years On: in Defence of Maitland', *J. of Legal Hist.* ii (1981), 107–42; see also G. R. Elton, *F. W. Maitland* (1985), 79–88.

[9] J. G. A. Pocock, *The Ancient Constitution and the Feudal Law* (Cambridge, 1957), ch. 2; D. R. Kelley, 'History, English Law and the Renaissance', *P & P*, 65 (1974), 24–51.

Muses' assertions, and have paid insufficient attention to the demurrers of the common lawyers, both as to the nature of their legal
learning and the extent to which it prevented them from acquiring
other 'ornaments of knowledge'.

ii. Contributions

Largely as a result of John Baker's massive researches, the later
sixteenth and seventeenth centuries now appear to have been a
somewhat less crucial era in the historical development of the
common law than the first fifty years of the sixteenth century. Yet
even if Slade's case, the Statute of Monopolies, and the exploitation
of procedure by bill of Middlesex in the Court of King's Bench
should properly be regarded as no more than 'finishing touches . . .
to the new jurisprudence', it is still worth remembering that this later
period also saw the first real flowering of a printed legal literature in
England.[10] Among its choicer blooms were the earliest law reports in
recognizably modern form, gathered by Edmund Plowden and
Edward Coke; the first comprehensive collections of parliamentary
statutes, compiled by Ferdinando Poulton; the first legal mono-
graphs, detailed and to some extent systematic treatises on particular branches of law, a genre inaugurated by Staunford's *Les Plees del
Coron* (1557), and rapidly expanded by diverse contributions from
authors such as Coke, Crompton, Dalton, Kytchin, Lambard,
Manwood, Powell, and West; the pioneering handbooks or guides
to method for law students by Dodderidge, Fraunce, and Fulbecke;
and the first post-medieval attempts to provide a comprehensive
overview of the whole body of the law, in the work of Henry Finch
and, again, Edward Coke.[11]

This spate of publications was part of what Maitland characterized as 'a little Renaissance of our own; or a Gothic revival if you
please'. Besides augmenting the technical literature of the common
law, printing helped make that law more accessible to readers

---

[10] Baker, ed., *Spelman's Reports*, Vol. II, ch. 1 and *passim*; *idem*, 'The Dark Age of
English Legal History, 1500–1700', in *Legal History Studies 1972*, ed. D. Jenkins
(Cardiff, 1975), 14.

[11] E. G. Henderson, 'Legal Literature and the Impact of Printing on the English
Legal Profession', *Law Lib. J.*, lxviii (1975), 288–93; Baker, *English Legal History*,
156–7, 163–5; H. S. Bennett, *English Books and Readers 1603 to 1640* (Cambridge,
1970), 120–1, 125; A. W. B. Simpson, 'The Rise and Fall of the Legal Treatise: Legal
Principles and the Forms of Legal Literature', *Univ. of Chicago Law Rev.*, xlviii
(1981), 632–68.

outside the inns of court and chancery. As more law books were printed, the contents of some at least became less arcane, and their readership less narrow. Unlike the technical texts—yearbooks, abridgements, reports, registers of writs (some of which, like the abridged statutes, clearly did reach a non-professional audience), the treatises and student books were almost all published in English, rather than law-French. So too were Coke's *Institutes* and Finch's *Law*.[12] Moreover, numerous works, including Dalton and Lambard on the duties and powers of JPs, sheriffs, constables, and other officers, set out explicitly to meet lay needs. The anonymous compiler of *The Lawes Resolutions of Womens Rights* (1632) explained that the four hundred-odd pages of this book were 'chiefly addressed' to women, with 'things behoveful for them to know . . . laid plain together, and in some orderly connection'.[13]

This last phrase is particularly significant. While printing, the substitution of English for law-French, and the compilation of law manuals designed specifically for lay use may all have helped erode the esoteric character of legal knowledge during our period, serious efforts were also under way to clarify and systematize the law's substantive contents. In the words of the first scholar to give this important movement the close attention it deserves, the aim was 'to make the law more coherent, more systematic, more teachable'.[14] The motivation was twofold. First, it reflected a practical concern with reducing the delays and inequities of legal process, which were often held to derive in part from the law's complexity, inconsistency, and uncertainty. Second, this reformist urge was reinforced by the influence of humanism, which rejected the subtleties of scholastic

---

[12] Maitland, *Law and the Renaissance*, 29, 91–2. Cf. Essex RO, D/AMW/1/66 (will of John Perry, yeoman of Sheering, 1625, bequeathing 'all my statute books & other my law books'); H. Finch, *Law* (1627), sigs. A3ᵛ–A4; E. M. Eisenstein, *The Printing Press as an Agent of Change* (Cambridge, 1979), i. 362.

[13] Page 403. Cf. F. Poulton, *De Pace Regis et Regni* (1609), sig. Aiii; T. Wentworth, *The Office and Duty of Executors* (1676; first published 1641), sigs. A2, [A4ᵛ]. John Trussell's 1637 treatise on forest law (Bodl. MS Eng. hist. d. 242), which sought to aid those whose ignorance exposed them to fines for encroachment on royal forests (fols. 71–2), remained unpublished despite a fulsome dedication to the judges Sir John Finch and Sir Thomas Trevor; the possibility that it was censored cannot be dismissed.

[14] T. K. Shaller, 'English Law and the Renaissance: The Common Law and Humanism in the Sixteenth Century', Harvard University Ph.D. thesis, 1979, 10. (I am grateful to Dr. Shaller for permission to consult his valuable study, on which the following two paragraphs draw heavily.) See also W. R. Prest, 'The Dialectical Origins of Finch's *Law*', *Cambridge Law J.*, xxxvi (1977), 326–52.

logic and sought to reorganize all the arts and sciences according to certain rules of 'method', so as to facilitate their mastery by laymen and students.

In the course of the sixteenth century, French and Italian legal scholars, most notably Claudius Cantiuncula, François le Douaren, François Connan, and Hughes Doneau, produced numerous abridgements and treatises inspired by these concerns. Over the same period English common lawyers were increasingly exposed to the intellectual stimulus which nourished this philosophical or pedagogical legal humanism on the Continent, as the universities of Oxford and Cambridge gradually superseded the inns of chancery as preparatory schools for the inns of court.[15] It is therefore hardly surprising that common lawyers adopted similar dialectical and rhetorical techniques in the hope of achieving the ends pursued by their European humanist counterparts, with whose works English lawyers were not at all unfamiliar. Both those who unashamedly borrowed from the methodizing jurisprudence of the civil law and those who sought to devise a more rational order for the common law without explicit reference to the *Corpus Iuris* had necessarily acquired more than a passing acquaintance with Roman law. Indeed, there is much evidence to suggest that early modern common lawyers were far less hostile towards, or ignorant about, the civil law than has hitherto been generally supposed.[16]

Some further indications that the early modern common law was no wholly insular and narrowly vocational anti-discipline is provided by the oratorical and rhetorical abilities which barristers frequently demonstrated. Speeches at learning exercises of the inns of court, charges delivered to juries, and other public addresses (such as the speeches commonly made by borough recorders at the swearing-in of a new mayor) were often elaborate compositions, replete with classical allusions and quotations. Thus Adam Winthrop noted approvingly that the young law student William Clopton of Gray's Inn 'gave the charge very oratory-like' when keeping his father's manorial court at Sampford in 1608, while in sentencing a

---

[15] See above, pp. 111–12.
[16] H. S. Pawlisch, 'Sir John Davies, The Ancient Constitution and Civil Law', *Hist. J.*, xxiii (1980), 689–702. See also Northants RO, Thornton 2251 (30 Sept. 1585, Thomas Thornton's purchase of Justinian's *Institutes*); J. H. Baker, '*The Newe Littleton*', *Cambridge Law J.*, xxxiii (1974), 148–51. Burnet, *Life of Hale*, 13; J. E. Stephens, *Aubrey on Education* (1972), 126; LI MS Hale 125 (J. Briscoe, '*Axiomata sive regula juris*').

man convicted of chopping down a tree near Donnington Castle
known as 'Chaucer's oak', Aubrey tells us that 'Judge Richardson
harangued against him long, and like an orator, had topics from the
Druids, etc.'[17]

This brings us conveniently to the other side of the Muses' case,
the claim that the common law was incompatible with the artistic
and literary pursuits for which those ladies were primarily responsible. The notion of an inherent conflict between law and all other
arts and letters had deep roots in European culture, and was further
reinforced by contemporary English circumstances. The complex
and disorderly bulk of the common law made it a notoriously
demanding and difficult study. According to Francis Osborne, in his
Advice to a Son (1656), it was 'esteemed by all a full employment for
a whole man'; any 'considerable digression' might lead clients to
suppose that a common lawyer was neglecting the duties of his
calling, just as 'the several books incomparable Bacon was known to
read, besides those relating to law' were used (Osborne claimed) to
argue against his fitness for high legal office.[18]

Whatever the truth of this last assertion, authors from the inns of
court and chancery did sometimes make a point of emphasizing that
they had completed their books before starting legal studies, while
others evidently felt it necessary to provide specific justification for
venturing beyond the bounds of their calling. When he published a
poetical tribute to Queen Elizabeth from Barnard's Inn in 1575,
Edward Hake defended himself against critics who 'will reckon it a
matter more than ordinary that I should after this sort so transcend
the limits of my vocation'. Hake accordingly argued that every
occupation had a vested interest in praising virtue, that lawyers were
especially concerned for good government, and that in any case the
members of all professions ('yea to the lawyer himself') should be
permitted on occasion to 'intermingle with the painful travails of the
mind the pleasure of some exercise more plausible and mild'.[19]
Traditional prejudices against venturing outside one's occupational

[17] *Inns of Court*, 121–2. Models of juristic oratory were provided by the lord
keepers' Star Chamber charges and the speeches made to newly called serjeants at
law. (Cf. Haward, *Reports*, 19, 56, 101, 186, 326, 367; Wilbraham, *Journal*, 17, 35–6,
48; *Winthrop Papers*, ed. G. Robinson *et al.* (Boston, 1929), i. 97; Aubrey, *Brief Lives*,
i. 170; Baker, *Serjeants*, 324–5, 326–7, 328, 333–4, 350, 351–3, 353–5, 361–2.
[18] *The Works of Francis Osborne* (1682), 74–5; cf. Roger North's comment that 'the
study of the law ... is thought ordinarily to devour the whole studious time of a
young gentleman'. (*Lives*, i. 18–19.) See also Dodderidge, *The English Lawyer*, 29.
[19] E. Hake, *A Commemoration of the ... Raigne of our ... Soveragne Lady*

specialization might be buttressed by religious scruple; it has been noted that 'constancy in or restriction to a particular calling' was even more emphatically urged by Protestant divines than diligence in the works of that calling. This helps explain why when Robert Ashley of the Middle Temple published his translation of a Spanish romance in 1627, he emphasized that the basis of his linguistic skills had been acquired at university, and only in the 'ebbs and tides' of legal practice had he 'stolen and snatched at vacant times some opportunities ... to get some knowledge of foreign countries and vulgar languages'.[20]

Yet in Ashley's case, as in so many others, these constraints hardly prevented him from engaging in a wide variety of extra-curricular activities. At the same time, the existence of such prohibitions makes the scale and significance of the early modern common lawyers' contribution to the artistic and literary culture of their age all the more remarkable. The leading role of the inns of court as centres of creative writing, patronage, and scholarship under the Tudors and (to a somewhat lesser extent) the early Stuarts has long been recognized. Simply by concentrating large numbers of students in an exceptionally lively metropolitan environment, virtually free of academic or any other supervision, the inns could have hardly failed to play an important part in the English Renaissance.[21] But it was not only those whose ambitions and talents ranged beyond the law who benefited from this situation; the leading inns of court poets of the 1590s included, besides a future Anglican clergyman (John Donne) and physician (Thomas Campion), a later all-but-lord chief justice (John Davies), a Welsh judge and serjeant at law (John Hoskyns), a recorder of London (Richard Martin), and a bencher of Lincoln's Inn (Christopher Brooke). Brooke, Hoskyns, and Martin were among the group of wits associated with the Mitre tavern, to whom the travelling littérateur Thomas Coryate addressed his greetings from India in 1615; other common lawyers similarly favoured were Sir Edward Phelipps, then master of the Rolls, and William Hakewill, the antiquary, MP, and law-reformer. Brooke, Hoskyns, and Martin were also members of the circle which dined

Elizabeth (1575), sigs. Aiiii–Aiiii^v; cf. J. Barston, *The Safeguard of Societie* (1576), sigs. Aiii^v–Aiiii^v; W. Fulbecke, *An Historical Collection* (1601), sig. A.

[20] George, *Protestant Mind*, 134; cf. R. Brathwait, *The Gentleman* (1630), 123; A. A. Abenzusian, *Almansor. . . . His Life and Death* (1627), sig. [C4].

[21] Cf. G. M. Young, 'Shakespeare and the Termers', *Proc. Brit. Acad.*, xxxiii (1947), 81–99; *Inns of Court*, 153–68, and references cited therein.

and drank with Ben Jonson at the Mermaid; Jonson was a friend of John Selden, 'that treasury of all kinds of learning', and wrote a prefatory verse epistle to Selden's *Titles of Honour* (1614). Among other lawyers praised in Jonson's poems were Edward Coke, Thomas Egerton, and Antony Benn (Richard Martin's colleague on the Middle Temple bench and predecessor as recorder of London). Whether from tact or ignorance, Jonson does not refer to Benn's literary pretensions, as manifested by a number of overwritten and perhaps deservedly unpublished essays on miscellaneous topics.[22] Obviously, not all the lawyers' extra-vocational accomplishments could have been of the first order of excellence. On the other hand, without those 'behemoths of learning, Sir Thomas More, Sir Francis Bacon and Mr. Selden, all lawyers by profession', the cultural and intellectual contours of early modern England—even Europe as a whole—would conceivably have looked rather different.[23]

Despite some exceptionally important individual contributions, it was not primarily as dramatists, poets, or writers of fiction that common lawyers made their collective mark on the literary culture of the English Renaissance. The only plays known to have been written by Tudor and early Stuart barristers were all occasional pieces—John Roo's interlude performed at Gray's Inn in 1526; George Gascoigne's adaptation of Ariosto's *Supposes*, also staged at Gray's Inn, in 1566; Sackville and Norton's *Tragedy of Gorboduc*, played in the Inner Temple hall five years earlier; and *The Misfortunes of Arthur* presented at Greenwich in 1588. Modern critical opinion tends to discount the significance of these works as influences on the mainstream development of English drama, though *Supposes* and *Gorboduc* are traditionally regarded as the first English prose comedy and the first English tragedy in blank verse, respectively.[24] Nor were the lawyer poets undeniably of the first rank; Anthony Wood's claim that John Hoskyns was 'the most

[22] Ibid., 153–6; E. Guilpin, *Skialetheia*, ed. D. A. Carroll (Chapel Hill, 1974), 7; R. F. Hardin, *Michael Drayton and the Passing of Elizabethan England* (Lawrence, Ka., 1973), 163–4; M. Prestwich, *Cranfield* (Oxford, 1966), 93–100; T. Coryate, *For the English wits . . . Greetings . . .* (1616), 2–9, 44–7; B. Jonson, *Poems*, ed. I. Donaldson (1975), 152, 179–81, 206–7.

[23] Waterhouse, *Discourse*, 137.

[24] Cf. R. M. Fisher, 'Simon Fishe, Cardinal Wolsey and John Roo's Play at Gray's Inn, Christmas 1526', *Archiv für Reformationsgeschichte*, lxix (1978), 297–9; Axton, *Queen's Two Bodies*, ch. 4; P. J. Finkelpearl, *John Marston of the Middle Temple* (Cambridge, Mass., 1969), 23–4. I am grateful for Mr F. J. Mares's comments on these points.

ingenious and admired poet of his time' must be regarded with some scepticism when so little of Hoskyns's verse has survived, especially by comparison with his near contemporaries Donne and Jonson.[25] Even More's *Utopia* is no exception to the general rule, although its central core of moral and social criticism is presented as a fantastical humanistic *jeu d'esprit*.[26] The main contribution of the barristers, both qualitatively and quantitatively, was rather as scholars, collectors, and purveyors of useful information, especially in the fields of antiquarian and historical studies.

A close association between the practice of the law and the study of the past went back at least to the thirteenth century in Italy, where notaries and lawyers were responsible for slightly more than one-third of the total number of historical works produced before 1415. It was from quattrocento Pavia that Lorenzo Valla launched his famous attack on the dominant Bartolist school of lawyers and their ahistorical approach to the *Corpus Iuris Civilis*. Valla's disciples and successors in sixteenth-century France went on to establish a tradition of etymological legal-historical scholarship, which from its initial focus on the history of law developed into a sophisticated treatment of French medieval antiquities and civilization.[27]

Lacking the institutional and intellectual framework provided by the law faculties of Continental universities, the English common lawyers spread their historical energies more widely. Thomas More's *History of King Richard III* and Francis Bacon's *History of Henry VII* were both fairly conventional examples of humanistic political biography, works less of scholarship than of literary elegance and moral-cum-political instruction. But Bacon also visualized a new kind of history which would embrace all aspects of human exper-

---

[25] A. Wood, *Athenae Oxonienses* . . . , ed. P. Bliss (1813–20), ii. 626; cf., however, Aubrey's story that Hoskyns's 'book of poems . . . bigger than Dr Donne's poems' was lost by his son (*Brief Lives*, i. 418).

[26] My interpretation essentially follows that of Hexter, *More's Utopia*; but cf. C. S. Lewis, *English Literature in the Sixteenth Century Excluding Drama* (Oxford, 1954), 169, and W. S. Allen, 'The Tone of More's Farewell to *Utopia*: A Reply to J. H. Hexter', *Moreana*, li (1976), 108–18. Dr Paul Salzman informs me that *The Golden Aphroditis* (1577) by John Grange ('student in the Common Law of England') is the only work of narrative fiction written by a common lawyer from this period.

[27] Cf. E. Cochrane, 'The Profession of the Historian in the Italian Renaissance', *J. Soc. Hist.*, xv (1981), 51–72; W. J. Bouwsma, 'Lawyers and Early Modern Culture', *AHR*, lxxviii (1973), 325; M. Gilmore, *Humanists and Jurists* (Cambridge, Mass., 1963), 63–4; G. Huppert, *The Idea of Perfect History* (Urbana, Ill., 1970); J. H. Franklin, *Jean Bodin and the Sixteenth-Century Revolution in the Methodology of Law and History* (New York, 1963); Kelley, *Foundations*.

ience, and provide a basic data source for the scientific study of man and his world.[28] Selden, whom Bacon at one time planned to appoint his literary executor, went some way towards realizing his patron's lofty ambitions, harnessing his own prodigious polyglot learning to a series of published historical analyses of contemporary beliefs and institutions, English, European, and Oriental. This much is clear, even if the full sweep of Selden's achievement has yet to be evaluated by a scholar who can bring something approaching an equal measure of erudition to the task.[29] Selden's earlier work, including his *Titles of Honour* (1614) and *Brief Discourse Touching the Office of Lord Chancellor* (1617), also built on a more parochial scholarly tradition, one particularly associated with the Elizabethan Society of Antiquaries, England's first learned society.

Although James Ley of Lincoln's Inn was the only practising common lawyer among the four young men who founded this discussion group in the late 1580s, barristers and legal office-holders soon came to dominate its ranks, to such an extent that the procedures adopted at meetings of the Society were reminiscent of those used in case-argument exercises at the inns of court. The absence of any substantial representation of the other learned professions, especially the Church, doubtless made it easier for common lawyers to take the leading role in the Society's affairs. While the papers (or indeed opinions) delivered and discussed at meetings covered many topics, most sought to establish the historical origins of particular English institutions, including the common law and the inns of court themselves.[30] Far from uncritically endorsing nationalistic myths of the law's immemorial antiquity, both lawyer and non-lawyer members showed on occasion a keenly questioning attitude to their sources. Here is young William Hakewill of Lincoln's Inn on Chief Justice Fortescue's claim that the laws of the ancient Britons were essentially unchanged by successive foreign invasions:

[28] F. S. Fussner, *The Historical Revolution* (1962), 230, and ch. 10; *idem, Tudor History and Historians* (New York, 1970), 255–7; Bacon, *Works*, iii. 329–43.

[29] D. S. Berkowitz's 'Young Mr. Selden', Harvard University Ph.D. thesis, 1946, concentrates on Selden's political activities, but see R. Tuck, *Natural Rights* (Cambridge, 1979), ch. 4; *Ioannis Seldeni Ad Fletam Dissertatio*, ed. D. Ogg (Cambridge, 1925), xix–lxvi; and P. Christianson, 'Young John Selden and the Ancient Constitution, *c.*1610–18', *Proc. Amer. Philosophical Soc.*, 128 (1984), 271–315.

[30] J. Evans, *A History of the Society of Antiquaries* (Oxford, 1956), 12; R. Schoeck, 'The Elizabethan Society of Antiquaries and Men of Law', *N & Q*, NS i (1954), 417–21; M. McKisack, *Medieval History in the Tudor Age* (Oxford, 1971), ch. 7.

For which opinion of his, because I see no other proof, than *ipse dixit*, though indeed the authority of the writer be great, and the opinion such, as for the honour of our laws I could willingly embrace; yet there being (as I conceive it) many and those sound reasons, which prove the contrary, I may justly suppose, that the great affection which he bore to the profession which had brought him to so high a place in the commonwealth, might move him in honour thereof to say more than his best learning could otherwise enable him to maintain.[31]

The antiquaries ceased meeting around 1607 for reasons which are now obscure, but probably included both internal political dissension and pressure from above to curb discussion of such sensitive questions as the antiquity and authority of parliament.[32] No doubt these would have been matters of particular interest to lawyer-members who also sat in the Commons, such as Hakewill, Ley, John Davies, and James Whitelocke. During its two decades of existence, the Society had not only provided these men with an opportunity to meet like-minded enthusiasts, but, more specifically, had acted as a bridge between an older generation of scholars (represented pre-eminently by William Camden and John Dodderidge) and a new wave who were to make a name for themselves as legal antiquarians in the parliaments of the early Stuarts.[33]

Another historiographical genre to which common lawyers contributed during the late sixteenth and early seventeenth centuries was the topographical survey, and local, usually county, history. Pioneered by William Lambard of Lincoln's Inn, with his *Perambulation of Kent* (1574), a work based on information gathered for what Lambard had originally intended as a national historical gazeteer, the vogue continued throughout the seventeenth century and beyond. Among its exponents were William Burton, whose 'concise yet satisfactory account of the subject' in his *Description of Leicestershire* (1622, revised edition 1633) provided the model for James Wright's *History of Rutland* (1684); Gilbert Bowne or Bohun, whose collections were incorporated into his son-in-law Robert Thoroton's *Antiquities of Nottinghamshire* (1677); Henry Chauncy

---

[31] *A Collection of Curious Discourses*, ed. T. Hearne (Oxford, 1720), 2–3.

[32] See especially K. Sharpe, *Sir Robert Cotton 1586–1631* (Oxford, 1979), 28–32, and ch. 1, *passim*.

[33] Cf. R. B. Wernham, 'The Public Records in the Sixteenth and Seventeenth Centuries', in *English Historical Scholarship in the Sixteenth and Seventeenth Centuries*, ed. L. Fox (1956), 24–5; P. Styles, 'Politics and Historical Research in the Sixteenth and Seventeenth Centuries', in ibid., 49–72.

of Hertfordshire, Anthony Ettricke of Dorset, and two early urban historians, Nathaniel Bacon and Thomas Widdrington, chroniclers of the town of Ipswich and the city of York respectively. It is also worth noting that the barrister Samuel Roper of Lincoln's Inn was responsible for first interesting William Dugdale in antiquarian research and then introducing him to his future collaborators Roger Dodsworth and Sir Christopher Hatton, while Aubrey tells us that 'Mr William Yorke (counsellor-at-law and a lover of this kind of learning)' persuaded a meeting of Wiltshire gentry in 1659 to undertake a co-operative venture for their county 'in imitation of Mr Dugdale's Illustration of Warwicks', and that 'he himself would undertake the middle division'.[34]

Besides institutional, legal, and local history, a number of barristers (including Hayward Townshend, Simonds D'Ewes, William Prynne and John Rushworth) were active in documenting current or recent parliamentary and political events.[35] Thomas May and Bulstrode Whitelocke wrote two of the earliest participant accounts of the causes and course of the English Revolution, while from the opposite political camp, Whitelocke's former Middle Temple chamber-mate Edward Hyde produced the crowning achievement of English Renaissance historiography in his *History of the Rebellion*. A brief account of two lesser works from the same canon may round off this catalogue of barrister-historians and their writings. The poet Richard Martin's brother William, also a Middle Templar and the recorder of Exeter, published in 1615 his *Historie, and Lives, of The Kings of England*, specifically aimed at providing 'the gallant gentry' with a handy and methodical conspectus of their nation's history. In

[34] Besides the works cited in the text, see J. Dodderidge, *The History of the Ancient and Moderne Estate of the Principality of Wales* (1630); *Lives of the Berkeleys*, ed. MacLean; H. Chauncy, *The Historical Antiquities of Hertfordshire* (1700); J. Sydenham, *The History of the Town and County of Poole* (1839), 241; N. Bacon, *The Annalls of Ipswche* (1654), ed. W. H. Richardson (Ipswich, 1884); Widdrington, *Analecta Eboracensia; DNB*, s.v. Roper, Samuel; *Aubrey's Brief Lives*, ed. O. L. Dick (1972), 36. William Pole (1561–1635), whose collections on Devonshire were printed in 1791, was the son of an IT bencher, but not himself a lawyer; cf. *Collection Towards a Description of the County of Devon By Sir William Pole* (1791), xi. For a perceptive account of Lambard and lawyer-historians generally, see R. W. Southern, 'Aspects of the European Tradition of Historical Writing: 4. The Sense of the Past', *TRHS*, 5th ser. xxiii (1973), 256–63.
[35] H. Townshend, *Historical Collections, or An Exact Account of the Last Four Parliaments of Elizabeth* (1680); S. D'Ewes, *The Journals of All the Parliaments During the Reign of Queen Elizabeth* (1682); W. Prynne, *Canterburies Doome...* (1646); Rushworth, *Historical Collections*.

no way purporting to be a work of original research, Martin's compilation was rather a textbook on public policy, its lessons neatly summarized in lists and marginal notes for the reader's convenience. Some of these were sufficiently pointed for the author to be summoned before the Privy Council in 1615, and forced to make 'humble submission and hearty repentance and acknowledgement of his fault'. Martin's comments on the need for princes as well as subjects to bow before God's will (with special reference to Edward III's defeat by the Scots) and his criticism of Henry VIII's cruelty and avarice may well have been less offensive to James I (on whose initiative the Council apparently acted) than his disparaging references to 'the Scottish nation', especially in his account of Anglo-Scots hostilities during the 1540s.[36]

An equally strong didactic purpose, albeit aimed at a different audience, lay behind *Britannica, sive de Regibus Veteris Britanniae* (Frankfurt, 1609), by the Inner Temple barrister John Ross. Both the place of publication and the elegant Latin of this little book suggest that it may have been intended as much for a Continental as an English audience. The text comprises verse summaries of the fabulous narrative of Geoffrey of Monmouth, followed by a prose defence of the Galfridian version of Britain's origins, beginning with the supposed settlement by Brutus, great-grandson of Aeneas. This apologia is essentially a rhetorical, rather than a scholarly, exercise, for Ross surveys the century-long debate over Geoffrey's veracity without introducing any new evidence. He argues that while the case against Geoffrey remains (as he attempts to demonstrate) unproven, and numerous respectable scholars, including foreigners as well as Englishmen, still uphold Geoffrey's version of things, the only rational course is to follow suit, especially bearing in mind the venerability of the narratives and their status as a kind of national monument to Britain's glorious past.[37] There can be no denying the overall superficiality of this approach, especially when compared to the high standards of contemporary Continental scholarship. Yet it is perhaps a little harsh to judge Ross's slim work by such elevated criteria, given its overtly literary and polemical character, or to

---

[36] Martin's *Historie* was nevertheless reprinted in both 1628 (with additional marginal glosses) and 1638. *APC 1615–16*, 100. Cf. F. J. Levy, *Tudor Historical Thought* (San Marino, Calif., 1967), 272–3.

[37] This paragraph depends heavily on R. Hardin, 'Humanism and History at the Inns of Court: John Ross of the Inner Temple', *Res Publica Literarum* (1978), 101–12. Ross is also briefly noticed by T. D. Kendrick, *British Antiquity* (1950), 100.

represent him as typical of common-lawyer historians. Indeed the
fact that he presented Geoffrey's stories in versified form suggests
that Ross might well have agreed with his Inner Temple colleague
John Selden, who, in the preface to *Analecton Anglo-Britannicon*
(written the same year that Ross's *Britannica* was published),
remarked, with reference to Geoffrey of Monmouth, that in historical matters it is necessary to 'excuse the artists and poets'.[38]

Early modern barrister-authors clustered most thickly in antiquarian and historical studies.[39] Otherwise their surviving writings
cover an extremely wide spectrum, including translations (most
notably by Robert Ashley, John Briscoe, John Sparrow, and William Style), essays and treatises in moral philosophy (by Francis
Bacon, Anthony Benn, and Robert Mason), many different kinds of
religious works (which will be discussed in the following chapter),
and even a self-help medical tract, Walter Rumsey's *Organon
Salutatis* (1657).[40] A similar breadth of interest and learning is
revealed by the wills and inventories of barrister-bibliophiles and
scholars. Thanks to the survival of detailed catalogues, we know
how far the libraries of Robert Ashley, Edward Coke, Edward
Parker, and John Selden extended beyond the confines of the
common law, although unfortunately there is no surviving list of the
books appraised at £200 value in the inventory of Roger Downes's
estate.[41] Lawyers' wills sometimes provide for the dispersal of
libraries, with the law books typically going to a son or nephew,
perhaps the first to take up and practise the law, but English books,
especially devotional works, to the widow or daughter(s), and the
remaining works to friends or professional colleagues. Thus the
bencher Robert Tanfield bequeathed all his English divinity books
to two daughters; his French, Italian, and Spanish books to his
neighbour Zouch Tate (nephew of Tanfield's uncle and former

[38] Quoted in ibid., 109.
[39] Other lawyer-historians besides those already mentioned were Serjeant Sir
Aegremont Thynne, friend and colleague of John Davies, who 'had a good library
and was skilful in antiquities' (CUL MS Add. 6863, fol. 88ᵛ); the Welshman John
Lewis, whose *The History of Great Britain* remained unpublished until 1729 (cf. BL
MSS Royal 18a, xxxvii; Additional 6921 and 15043; and Harleian 4872); John Smyth
of Nibley, and John Ferne (for whom, see *DNB*).
[40] John Briscoe's works, now collected in the LI Hale MSS, include 'The Mirrour
of Justice Sett forth by Plato ... faithfully translated out of the original Greeke' (LI
MS Hale 130); for Benn, see above, n. 22; otherwise *DNB*.
[41] *Inns of Court*, 165; Lancs. RO, Inv. Roger Downes 1638 and DDB 85/6a;
Borthwick, Reg. 48, fol. 653.

Middle Temple colleague Francis Tate, founding secretary of the Society of Antiquaries, who had earlier bequeathed all *his* books 'to my nephew Robert Tanfield'); the law books in his Middle Temple study to his cousin, neighbour, and Middle Temple colleague Richard Lane; his law books at home in Northamptonshire to another neighbouring barrister, Joseph Brian of Gray's Inn; and the remainder of his library to two sons-in-law. Sir Edward Clarke of Lincoln's Inn gave his law-French and Latin books to his son, and his 'English books, divine, moral, history or other' to his wife. While Henry Bourchier of the Inner Temple, another early member of the Society of Antiquaries, bequeathed all his goods and chattels to his wife Anne, he reserved to his patron, Robert Devereux, earl of Essex, 'all my books of histories, Latin, French, Italian and Spanish and such other of antiquities as he shall please to accept of'.[42] Paul Croke of the Inner Temple left his barrister son-in-law Edward Heath all his non-legal books in languages other than English; these amounted to about a hundred and fifty titles in French, Latin, Greek, and Hebrew, with particular emphasis on the Greek and Roman poets, biblical texts, commentaries, and concordances, and works by modern Continental authors such as Bodin, Rabelais, J. C. Scaliger, and Lorenzo Valla. Croke's surviving accounts, although by no means complete, show that he also purchased professional, literary, and English-language books in considerable numbers and varieties. During the 1620s, for example, Croke acquired Selden's editions of Fortescue and Hengham, Michael Dalton's handbooks for JPs and sheriffs, William Turner's famous *Herbal*, Gervase Markham's *Farewell to Husbandrie*, Hill's *Arte of Gardening*, and many religious works.[43]

The German lawyer Paul Hentzner, who visited London in 1598, noted that at the inns of court, 'numbers of the young nobility, gentry and others are educated, chiefly in the studies of philosophy, theology and medicine—for very few apply themselves to that of law'.[44] Hentzner was quite right to suppose that law was not the only subject read at the inns of court. Yet his account may suggest that the extra-curricular interests of the inns' membership were mainly literary or scholarly in nature, whereas lawyers, would-be lawyers,

[42] PCC 46 Welden; 28, 55 Harvey; 74 Lewyn.
[43] PCC 113 St John; Egerton 2893, fols. 28–28ᵛ; Croke, 'Diurnall', fols. 45ᵛ, 46, 48ᵛ, 53, 58ᵛ.
[44] W. B. Rye, *England as seen by Foreigners* (1865), 283.

and gentlemen students at the inns had ample opportunity to follow more broadly artistic or scientific pursuits. While the figure of the virtuoso is generally associated with Restoration England, men like John Selden and his younger protégé Mathew Hale displayed no less catholicity of interests and talents than, say, Francis North, Lord Guilford, who became a barrister in 1661. Anatomy, astronomy, geography, mathematics, and physics were all becoming increasingly fashionable during our period, and London offered better facilities than anywhere in the country for pursuing them.[45] This may not have been so true of dancing or music, but the masques and revels of the inns of court did provide some specific encouragement and reinforcement for members whose interests ran in those directions.[46] Finally, although common lawyers were not conspicuously innovative or numerous as connoisseurs and patrons of the visual arts, a number of barristers, including three leading members of the Society of Antiquaries, Christopher Brooke, William Hakewill, and Sir James Ley, bequeathed works of art in their wills. While most of these were probably family portraits, Brooke specifically mentions a Virgin and Child with St Joseph and a 'picture of Apollo and the Muses being an original of an Italian master's hand'. In architecture, legal taste was often downright conservative, as instanced by the old-fashioned façade of Sir Henry Hobart's Blickling and Inigo Jones's neo-Gothic chapel for Lincoln's Inn.[47]

iii. Qualifications

It is much easier to demonstrate that philistinism was not a defining characteristic of the early modern bar than to say to what extent common lawyers of broad intellectual and literary interests were characteristic of their profession as a whole. Our sample group of 115 barristers includes seven published authors, which at first sight may seem a remarkably creditable total, especially since it excludes

---

[45] Cf. Burnet, *Life of Hale*, 15–16; B. Shapiro, 'Law and Science in Seventeenth-Century England', *Stanford Law Rev.*, 21 (1969), 736–40; *Inns of Court*, 159–67; cf. J. Boehme, *Mysterium Magnum*, tr. J. Sparrow (1654), sig. [A3ᵛ]; R. Mason, *Reasons Academie* (1605), 49. Cf. also M. Hunter, *Science and Society in Restoration England* (Cambridge, 1981), 127.

[46] Cf. A. Brissenden, *Shakespeare and the Dance* (1981), 6–7, 10. R. W. Wienpahl, *Music at the Inns of Court* (Ann Arbor, 1979), chs. 5–10, brings together some of the evidence. Serjeant John Maynard is said by Aubrey to have been one of William Davenant's backers in his establishment of 'an opera *stilo recitativo*' during the Interregnum. (*Brief Lives*, i. 208.)

[47] PCC 122 Barrington, 27 Ridley; Fuller, *Worthies of England*, i. 273.

those with works remaining in manuscript, such as John Hare's compilation of Court of Wards decrees, now surviving in at least six copies, or Sir John Strode's voluminous memoirs, which were, however, intended solely for domestic consumption.[48] Yet on closer inspection the achievement appears somewhat less impressive. William Wilde's loyal speech to Charles II as recorder of London in 1660, and Thomas Gell's co-authored apologia for his conduct during the Civil War are mere political ephemera. Edward Bulstrode's *Golden-Chain* (1657), a compendium of biblical extracts arranged under subject headings, the spiritual equivalent of the typical legal commonplace-book, with appended notes from a sermon by the Jacobean master of the Temple Church, was hardly a considered work of great originality or deep learning, although Bulstrode also published three substantial volumes of *Reports* (1657–9). Rather more significant as extra-vocational achievements were Thomas Widdrington's annals of York, although these remained unpublished until late last century, and William Burton's *Description of Leicestershire* (1622). Yet if Burton's scholarly ability and achievements are beyond question (albeit slightly overlooked today), his status as a common lawyer was merely formal; by the time he was called to the bar in 1603, nearly two decades before his *magnum opus* was published, he had contracted the disease which would prevent him from ever practising law.[49] This leaves us with a slim treatise on conveyancing, of which Edward Henden was purportedly one of the compilers, and—at the opposite extreme— the enormous output of William Hughes, ancient of Gray's Inn, who published some fifteen volumes of abridgements, practice books, law reports, and treatises between 1641 and 1663. Apart from *The Parson's Law*, which went into four editions before 1700, and *Anglo-Judaeus* (1656), a tract arguing on historical grounds against readmission of the Jews to England, the titles which appeared under Hughes's name were all abridgements, compilations, and translations of the work of others. Unfortunately, hardly anything more is

---

[48] For Hare's 'briefe Collection', see Bell, *Court of Wards*, 90 and n.; 'Sir John Strode's Book' is held by the Isle of Wight RO; I have used a nineteenth-century transcript, Dorset RO, MW M4.

[49] Cf. *The Speech spoken by Sir William Wylde, Knight and Baronet* (1661); *The General Accounts of Sir John Gell & His Brother Thomas Gell* (1645). An associate of Michael Drayton, Burton also wrote verse and was a translator; see his *The Most Delectable and pleasant Historye of Clitiphon and Leucippe . . . by Achilles Statius*, ed. S. Gaselee and H. F. B. Brett-Smith (1923).

known about Hughes than what little his own publications tell us, but their sheer bulk and overwhelmingly bread-and-butter character suggest that he may well have been working as a professional legal author and editor in the latter years of his life. While the organization of legal publishing in this period is a largely unexplored topic, practitioner's books of the kind in which Hughes specialized could evidently yield lucrative returns, especially when the compiler controlled their production himself, as Hughes in fact often appears to have done.[50]

If, as our sample suggests, practising lawyers in general were likely to be neither prolific authors nor distinguished scholars, were they any more notable as collectors and hence, presumably, readers, of non-legal literature? The wills and inventories of seventeen barristers from our sample group contain references to the possession of books, but in no more than four instances is it perfectly plain that at least some of the works referred to were anything other than law texts.[51] Of course, argument from the absence of evidence is hardly conclusive, especially since only about half the sample can be definitely linked with surviving probate documents. Nevertheless, even granting that some barristers whose wills or inventories make no specific mention of libraries must in fact have possessed some books, it seems unlikely that many of these unnoticed collections can have been particularly substantial.

In two of the three surviving inventories which list books among

---

[50] E. Henden, W. Noy, R. Mason, and A. Fleetwood, *The Perfect Conveyancer; or Severall Select and Choice Presidents* (1650, 1655, 1663). Hughes's published works consist of *The Parsons Law* (1641, 1663, 1673); A. Horne, *The Booke called the Mirrour of Justices . . . with the book called the Diversity of Courts . . . translated out of the old French . . . by W. H.* (1646, 1768, 1840); *Reports of certain Cases* (1652, 1653); *The Commentaries upon original writs* (1655); *Anglo-Judaeus or the History of the Jews* (1656); *Nomotomia, in two parts* (1657); *An Exact Abridgement of Public Acts* (1657); [W. Leonard], *Reports and Cases of Law . . .* (1658); *The Declarations and other Pleadings contained in the eleven parts of the Reports of Sir E. Coke, rendered into English by W. H.* (1659); *The Grand Abridgement of the Law Continued* (1660–3); *Gregories Moot-book . . . Much inlarged* (1663); *An exact abridgement of all the Statutes* (1663); *An Exact Abridgement of the Cases reported by Sr. F. More* (1665); *An Abridgement of the . . . Reports of . . . Sir G. Croke* (1665); *Hughes's Quaeries* (1675); *A Discourse of Pluralities* (1680). Hughes probably died in 1663; a second edition of his *Parson's Law* published that year includes a signed preface dated from GI, Dec. 1662, whereas a 'third edition', also of 1663, has a different preface written in the third person. W. A. Jackson, ed., *Records of the Court of the Stationers' Company 1602 to 1640* (1957), ix. 82.

[51] Book-owning barristers included Archer, Beriffe jun., Browne, Carill, Dering, Girling, Holland, Locke, Maltiward, Metcalfe, Parker, Richardson, Whitfield, and Wilde (see Appendix D for sources).

the deceased lawyer's possessions, the valuations given were very low—a mere £3 in the case of John Richardson of Durham, who died in 1623. This possibly amounted (allowing for inflation) to something like the sixty-four volumes valued at £5 owned by James Metcalfe of Richmond, Yorkshire, when he died in 1671, many of which would have been law books, tools of trade. The literary tastes of Adam Winthrop as revealed by his records of books lent were perhaps not entirely atypical of the country-based barrister with a small London practice; modern religious and theological works predominated, although Winthrop also owned copies of Lambard's *Kent* and the works of Petrarch.[52]

On one occasion in the 1590s, when Serjeant John Hele pleaded that a certain bargain had been made bona fide, opposing counsel responded by asking the court for a writ of *quo warranto*, questioning by what right Hele spoke Latin, *'qui n'ad este edoct in ascun liberal science'*. Hele does not seem to have attended university; no more had his fellow Westcountryman and near contemporary Sir John Strode, who, while specifically counselling his son 'in thy youth' to 'get learning', evidently considered that fulfilment of this precept required only 'to understand well the Latin tongue. But Hebrew and Greek, the French and Italian tongues, respect them not, leave them to others, whose study and travail require them to be conversant with strange tongues.' Unsurprisingly, Strode equally opposed 'travel into foreign parts', believing that those who left home, friends, neighbours, and parents for journeys abroad must be either criminals or madmen.[53] Such parochialism may not seem so remarkable in a backwoods Dorset barrister-squire. On the other hand, it is slightly sobering to come across a passage in a posthumous elegy to Lord Chancellor Coventry which states that although 'learned in the sciences and most profound in his profession', this eminent common lawyer 'rather leaned to his native strength than depended on any artificial reliance', that is to say, upon 'erudition and acquisitions of art'.[54] Even Coventry's mentor Sir Edward Coke, the supposed high priest of common-law

[52] Leeds Archives Dept., Richmond Archdeaconry Court, J. Metcalfe, 25 Feb. 1671/2; Univ. of Durham, Dept. of Palaeography, Probate 1638 (Richardson); *Winthrop Papers*, ed. Robinson, i. 41, 71–2, 82, 139–40.
[53] Folger MS M.b.42, p. 70 (journal of Sir Roger Wilbraham); Dorset RO, MW M4, fol. 83.
[54] Norfolk RO, MS NRS Hare 156, 228 x 4, unfoliated; but cf. IT MS Petyt, 538 17 fols. 361–9, which stresses Coventry's command of French and 'remembrances of his rhetoric & logic'.

obscurantism, had maintained that knowledge of the art of logic was 'necessary to a complete lawyer'. The frequent reiteration of these and similar sentiments in favour of a liberal education for lawyers from the early sixteenth century onwards suggests that the case won by no means universal acceptance, even if by the 1630s few men called to the bar had not put in at least a year or so at university.[55]

The modern editor of John Davies's poetry has noted that after 1603, when the poet was appointed solicitor-general in Ireland, 'the records of his life multiply by the same ratio as the quantity and quality of his verse diminishes'.[56] It can hardly be doubted that the busy routine of legal practice often inhibited scholarship or writing which had no immediate vocational relevance, especially for the more successful and conscientious practitioners. Many of those who did manage to put their pens to work on something other than briefs and Chancery bills seem to have held a distinctly ambivalent attitude towards the common law, like another Middle Temple poet, Serjeant Hoskyns, whom Aubrey describes as 'a great master of the Latin and Greek languages; a great divine. He understood the law well, but worst at that'.[57] Of the three lawyer 'behemoths of learning' in early modern England identified by Edward Waterhouse, Thomas More evidently shared with Erasmus a humanist contempt for the barbarism of the common law, and exiled all lawyers from his Isle of Utopia; Francis Bacon believed 'the ordinary practice of the law' was 'no good account of the poor talent which God hath given me', and consistently sought to distance himself from what he felt to be the characteristic narrowness of lawyers, who 'as it were talk in bonds'; while John Selden, although in some ways more closely identified personally with the common law, pursued a life effectively devoted to politics and scholarship, supported not by his earnings at the bar (which, as he cheerfully admitted, were negligible), but from the generosity of aristocratic patrons.[58] Again, many of the active lawyer members of the Society of Antiquaries and the later Mitre

[55] E. Coke, *The First Part of the Institutes of the Laws of England* (1628), sig. A5. For Coke as a poet, see his Latin verses printed in Smyth, *Lives of the Berkeleys*, ii. 401, and cf. W. Leighton, *The Teares or Lamentations of a Sorrowful Soule* (1613), sigs. *4–*4ᵛ. *Inns of Court*, 145–9; above, pp. 111–13.

[56] *Davies, Poems*, ed. Kreuger, vi, xliv; cf. H. Pawlisch, *Sir John Davies and the Conquest of Ireland* (Cambridge, 1985), 17, 23–4.

[57] *Brief Lives*, i. 418.

[58] See above, p. 194; Hexter, *More's Utopia*, 109; Bacon, *Works*, iii. 475, iv. 292, viii. 314, 358; J. L. Marwil, *The Trials of Counsel* (Detroit, 1976), 77, 87, 143; Aubrey, *Brief Lives*, ii. 220, 224.

and Mermaid circles were relatively young men still establishing themselves in the world; indeed, most of the creative non-legal work of early modern common lawyers seems to have been produced either before they reached the age of thirty or after they had given up legal practice altogether.

It is difficult to avoid concluding that the vast majority of early modern barristers probably had little claim to be considered authors, bibliophiles, connoisseurs, scholars, virtuosi, or wits. Even the small minority who constituted an exception to this rule evidently found the law a demanding and not wholly satisfying taskmistress, one whom in William Burton's words, 'is jealous and will admit of no partner'. Nevertheless, in England, as on the Continent, lawyers do seem to have been responsible to a large, and probably disproportionate, extent for the Renaissance flowering of arts and letters. Their prominence in this 'formation of modern culture' (as Bouwsma calls it) clearly sprang from various converging circumstances.[59] By ability, training, and calling, lawyers were literate, articulate, wordy, as well as worldly, men; their work brought them into contact with a large cross-section of humanity, and to London's uniquely rich cultural milieu, where the inns of court occupied a strategically favoured position; the unrivalled opportunities for personal advancement open to a successful common lawyer during our period ensured that the profession skimmed off an excessive share of available talent from each successive generation of young men. Lawyers were particularly attracted to historical studies. Apart from whatever special vocational aptitudes for evaluating evidence and constructing coherent narrative they may have possessed, practising barristers were above all led to applied historical research by their professional preoccupation with establishing family lines and tracing the descent of landed property. So in sixteenth- and seventeenth-century England, as in late medieval and Renaissance Italy, the relationship between the law and at least some branches of letters was as much complementary as antagonistic. Assertions to the contrary usually expressed resentment at the lawyers' manifest power and wealth, plus the fact that by drawing on a common educational background lawyers could occasionally emulate the men of letters at their own game.[60]

[59] Bouwsma, 'Lawyers', 309; *Inns of Court*, 167–8.
[60] Cf. H. Wieruszowski, 'Arezzo as a Centre of Learning and Letters in the Thirteenth Century', *Traditio*, ix (1953), 321–91, esp. 324, 341–2, 366, 382–3 (I owe this reference to Jonathan Rée); Gilmore, *Humanists and Jurists*, 62–4. See also Montagu, *Diatribae*, 21, 121–3.

In conclusion, the significant difference between English common lawyers and Continental civil lawyers was not that ignorance of, or indifference to, the civil law deprived the former of broadening comparative insights, but simply that the common law itself lacked an institutional base in the universities of Oxford and Cambridge. Barristers were not automatically university alumni, let alone graduates, and the code which they practised derived no authority from an academic tradition tracing its direct lineage back to classical Rome. In this formal and technical sense, common lawyers were indeed unlearned men, at a time when polite—that is, classical—learning was increasingly becoming a mark of social status. Hence the sensitivity of barristers to jibes at their barbarous and plodding dullness, and counter-claims that the inns of court constituted the equivalent of a university, or that the quality of argument in Westminster Hall was just as high as in 'any of these doctors' acts in their schools'.[61]

An alternative response, available to barristers with some cultural or intellectual interests outside the law, was to seek to distance themselves from their colleagues by the public cultivation of such extra-legal accomplishments and activities. If, as casual inspection suggests, the quality and quantity of the common lawyers' contribution to learning and the arts declined progressively from *c*.1660, part of the explanation may lie in a continued expansion of the legal profession's autonomy and self-confidence, which significantly lessened the need for barristers to seek status and respect outside, and apart from, their calling.

[61] Harleian 980, fol. 81; *Inns of Court*, 115 n.

CHAPTER SEVEN

RELIGION

'Religion is a term he'll think upon
I' th' country, when all other Terms are done.'

> T. Jordan, *Pictures of Passions, Fancies & Affections*
> [n.d. (1641)], sig. [D6ᵛ]

'His law was not contrary to the Gospel.'

> Memorial Inscription for Walter Darrell (*c.*1564–1628),
> St Nicholas Church, Abingdon

i. *Perspectives and problems*

BOTH Thomas More and William Prynne would surely hold high
places on any ecumenical list of religious martyrs in post-Reformation England. But the willingness of Catholic saint and puritan
confessor to go to scaffold and pillory, respectively, for their faith
tells us nothing about the strength and direction of religious
commitment among the mass of common lawyers. How far, if at all,
did early modern barristers share a common religious outlook? Is it
possible to generalize about the religious attitude of the legal
profession, or the involvement of lawyers in religious conflicts
during the late sixteenth and early seventeenth centuries?

The pre-Civil War bar was plainly not monolithic, from a
religious viewpoint. Many historians have noted links between
common lawyers and radical protestants, including their shared hostility towards ecclesiastical courts, the powerful influence exercised
by a succession of eminent puritan preachers at the inns of court,
and the prominence of barristers in groups of godly activists like the
Feoffees for Impropriations and the Providence Island Company.[1]
However, attention has also been drawn to the continued presence
of popish recusants and Catholic sympathizers at the inns of court
and within the ranks of practising lawyers,[2] and, by other historians,

---

[1] *Inns of Court*, 204–19, and references cited therein.
[2] *Inns of Court*, ch. 8, and references cited therein; for corrections, elaborations,
and modifications, see G. Parminter, 'Elizabethan Popish Recusancy in the Inns of
Court', *BIHR*, Special Supplement 11 (1976), and R. M. Fisher, 'Privy Council

to the pervasiveness of anticlerical, Erastian, and perhaps ultimately secularist attitudes among members of the bar during our period.[3] Since individual exemplars and contemporary comment can be cited to back up each of these perspectives, the problem is less one of choosing between conflicting interpretations than of finding how they might best be reconciled. First, however, we must try to see the extent to which such prominent individual counsellors as the Catholic Edmund Plowden, the puritan Nicholas Fuller, and the Erastian John Selden were representative of their colleagues.

Although religion was far from being a purely personal or private affair in early modern England, the personal religious beliefs of the vast majority of early modern Englishmen remain a matter for speculation. Indeed the difficulty of discovering anything about the spiritual outlook of most individual lay people explains why historians of religion are usually forced to concentrate upon the clergy, the professed and professionally religious, while virtually ignoring their congregations.[4] Even where we are fortunate enough to find some trace of an individual's religious convictions or denominational adherence, clear statements of belief are less common than tantalizing clues and hints. Then there are problems of definition arising from the complex and evanescent nature of the liturgical, organizational, and theological differences characterizing the various denominations and sects found within and outside the Church of England during our period. When contemporaries could hardly agree on the distinguishing characteristics of a puritan or papist, later historians may well quail at the task of identification.

Yet these difficulties are not wholly intractable. Since all barristers were literate, and most owned some property, evidence about their religious attitudes, particularly in their wills, is more likely to have survived than for the majority of the early modern population. Wills, like funeral sermons and memorial inscriptions, may give a misleadingly heightened impression of piety, besides freezing the testator's outlook at one point in time, usually during his middle years or old age, although religious attitudes were obviously not always static over a whole lifetime. Nevertheless, because wills

Coercion and Religious Conformity at the Inns of Court, 1569–84', *Recusant Hist.*, xv (1981), 305–24.

[3] *Inns of Court*, 217–19; Bouwsma, 'Lawyers and Culture', 321–2; Clark, *Provincial Society*, 292, 461, n. 78.

[4] Cf. P. Collinson, *English Puritanism* (Hist. Assoc., 1983), 25–6.

frequently include specific bequests of religious significance as well as a personal avowal of faith, they provide the single most useful source of information for the present purpose.

Correspondence, diaries, journals, and autobiographical material can also be helpful, as well as a wide range of other evidence about a man's associations and behaviour which may convey some indication of his religious outlook. Thus, in the absence of information to the contrary, it seems reasonable to assume that lawyers who accepted administrative or judicial office under the Long Parliament and Protectorate between 1642 and 1659 were, in some sense, puritans, even if it is not possible to classify them more exactly as presbyterians, independents, sectaries, or pious Low-Churchmen. This points to the kind of working rules which constraints of evidence force us to adopt if the investigation is to proceed at all. Applied to the surviving source material, fragmentary and exiguous as much of it is, such rules permit at least an educated guess, and at best a firm identification of the religious outlook of slightly over a quarter of our 115 barristers and just under a third of our 385 benchers.

The large remaining balance of men whose religion cannot be so categorized poses an obvious problem which will be discussed further below. In the meantime, however, it may be noted that such a shortfall is not inconsistent with those reported by students of other comparable groups from this period. Thus of 774 pre-Civil War Lancashire gentry families investigated by Blackwood, only 335 can be confidently described as either Catholic or puritan; while among a sample of 200 Caroline office-holders alive in 1642 whom Aylmer examined, a mere 23 are of known religious leanings or affiliations.[5]

ii. *Catholics and puritans*

Two main impressions emerge from the admittedly incomplete evidence for both sample groups: on the one hand, the relative scarcity of Catholics and High-Churchmen; on the other, the overwhelming preponderance of puritans (broadly defined), among those whose religious preferences can be classified. Despite the reputation of the inns of court as hotbeds of popery, acquired during

---

[5] Blackwood, *Lancashire Gentry*, 27; Aylmer, *King's Servants*, 404. Cf. Keeler, 12–13.

Elizabeth's reign and lingering on until the Civil War, it is difficult to identify more than a handful of possible papist barristers or benchers during our period. Of the sample barristers, Alexander Rigby, Thomas St George, and perhaps John Hanmer came from recusant families, but there is no evidence that they themselves failed to conform to the Established Church (indeed, Rigby appears to have taken the presbyterian Solemn League and Covenant in 1646, if only for reasons of family or self-preservation).[6] Among the benchers, Francis Poulton, Thomas Valence, and Edward Walmsley of Lincoln's Inn; Robert Blundell, Roger Downes, and Sir Richard Osbaldeston of Gray's Inn (all, like Walmsley, Lancashire men), and Sir Richard Weston, an Inner Templar before he became one of the puisne barons of the Exchequer in 1634, had more or less close associations with Catholicism by birth, upbringing, marriage, or other ties, although none of them seems to have been actually convicted of recusancy.[7]

Of course, the widespread practice of occasional conformity and the inconsistent enforcement of anti-Catholic measures meant that there was 'no sharp dividing line between recusant and church papist'. So it is perhaps not entirely surprising that such an evidently notorious papist as John Lancaster gained promotion to the bench of Gray's Inn as late as 1589 (with Lord Chancellor Hatton's support), or that Andrew Brown, expelled from Lincoln's Inn in 1626 for having 'declined from the true christian religion . . . unto the popish and Romish religion', should nevertheless have been practising as a counsellor at the bar of the Court of Requests twelve years later.[8] A still more intriguing case is that of Sir Francis Moore, the great favourite and leader in Chancery under Lord Keeper

[6] Lancs. and Ches. Rec. Soc., *Miscellanies*, i (1885), 134–8, 244; *East Anglian*, 3rd ser. ix (1901–2), 31; *CSPD 1581–90*, 326.

[7] G. Lipscomb, *The History and Antiquities of the County of Buckingham* (1831–47), ii. 58; *DNB*, s.v. Pulton, Ferdinando. *Responsa Scholarum*, ed. Kenny, 126; PCC 83 Woodhall. C. Haigh, *Reformation and Resistance in Tudor Lancashire* (Cambridge, 1974), 284–5; *VCH, Lancs.*, vi. 35 n., 77 n. T. E. Gibson, *Lydiate Hall and its Associations* (1876), 110–20; H. Foley, *Records of the English Province of the Society of Jesus* (1877–84), i. 246, vi. 397. W. Longford, 'Some Notes on the Family of Osbaldeston', *Trans. Hist. Soc. of Lancs. and Ches.*, lxxxvii (1936), 82–3; *CCC*, 323. H. V. Hart-Davis, *History of Wardley Hall* (1908), 58, but cf. *VCH, Lancs.*, viii. 92 n. *CCAM*, 1408. The widow of another judge, Sir Thomas Foster (d. 1612), was presented as a recusant in the 1620s. (*Hertfordshire County Records: Calendar to the Sessions Books . . . 1619 to 1657*, ed. W. Le Hardy (Hertford, 1928), 8, 17, 20.)

[8] Haigh, *Reformation and Resistance*, 277; *Inns of Court*, 178, 183, 185 (Browne in fact came from Newbury, Berks., not Ireland); REQ, 1/79, pp. 216, 281.

Ellesmere. Moore had close connections with the Catholic Percy family, earls of Northumberland, and although in the 1601 parliament he appeared publicly to support stronger measures against recusants, he married a woman who was accused of popery, permitted his daughter to marry into the Catholic Blount family of Oxfordshire, and appointed as overseer of his own will another well-known midlands recusant, 'my ancient true and good friend' Sir Francis Englefield. Ellesmere himself was a lapsed Catholic and no friend to puritans; despite the lack of direct evidence that his patronage of Moore was seen as a form of covert support for popery, it would be surprising if at least some contemporaries failed to make the connection.[9]

Of course 'papist', like 'puritan', was a pejorative term. Simonds D'Ewes's characterization of the anti-Sabbatarian Lincoln's Inn barrister and MP Thomas Sheppard as a 'base Jesuited papist' tells us as much about D'Ewes's as Sheppard's religion, while in the absence of independent corroboration, the hostile claim that the Middle Temple bencher and Long Parliament royalist MP Richard Seaborne was a 'papist' must also be treated with considerable caution. From a strongly puritan viewpoint, fine distinctions between crypto-Catholicism, Arminianism, and mere hostility towards godly zeal would presumably have had little meaning. Full-blown doctrinal Arminianism is not explicitly represented in either of our sample groups (and indeed Tyacke has identified only one common-lawyer Arminian before the Civil War—Richard Dyot of the Inner Temple).[10] Although the evidence is by no means conclusive, a few barristers and benchers did display attitudes which *may* indicate religious sympathies compatible with at least some aspects of the Arminian platform; thus Henry Ley's will in 1636 left £10 to purchase a silver flagon 'for the service of the Lord's Supper' in his parish church at Westbury, Wiltshire, while twelve years later, Francis Keat of the Middle Temple bequeathed the sum of forty shillings 'for the reparation or rather beautifying' of the church at East Locking, Berkshire. Another member of the bar sample who

[9] *H. of P.*, ii. 72–3; Durston, thesis, ii. 111–15; *CCC*, iv. 298; PCC 98 Dale. For the later recusancy of the Moore family, see *Trans. Newbury District Field Club*, ii. 162.
[10] *Inns of Court*, 184; *Diary of Simonds D'Ewes*, ed. Bourcier, 142; *CCAM*, 722; cf. Anthony Weldon's characterization of William Noy as 'a great papist if not an atheist'. (A. Weldon, *The Court and Character of King James* (1651), 95.) N. R. N. Tyacke, 'Arminianism in England, in Religion and Politics, 1604 to 1640', University of Oxford D. Phil. thesis, 1968, 173.

appears to have been no friend of the puritan cause was William Hughes, whose treatise *The Parson's Law*, although not published until 1641, was evidently considered unobjectionable by Archbishop Laud.[11]

Among the benchers, Sergeant Robert Hitcham named Mathew Wren, the Arminian bishop of Norwich, as overseer of his will, which left £20 per annum for prayers to be said daily in Hitcham's parish church at Framlingham, Suffolk, while Sir Richard Shelton, Charles I's solicitor-general, defended the arch-Arminian Richard Montagu in the parliament of 1629, although not on doctrinal grounds. Others might best be characterized as determinedly non- or anti-puritan, like the MPs Richard Martin and Robert Mason, for example. The miser money-lender Hugh Audley, in a will made in 1662, left £400 for distribution among forty maidservants 'such as are known to be protestants and live under the episcopal government and are not reputed to be of the presbyterian religion, Quakers, or any other of the new upstart religions', while Nicholas Franklin a few years earlier bequeathed £100 to relieve sequestered Anglican clergy, and sought burial 'according to the liturgy heretofore used and established in the Church of England in the time of Edward VI and Queen Elizabeth and continued by her Christian and pious successors of happy memory'.[12]

Yet even taken together, those who might be designated Catholics, High-Churchmen, or anti-puritans are overwhelmingly outnumbered in both our sample groups by committed radical or reformist protestants of one kind or another (see Table 7.1). Given that they were probably both more numerous and more vocal than their opponents and rivals in virtually all geographical regions and social strata, the predominance of the godly brethren is not entirely unexpected, although its scale is surprising. Among the twenty-six barristers so classified, Edward Bulstrode and Sir John Strode left ample evidence of pious zeal in their published and unpublished religious writings, as did (among others) Anthony Holland, John Keeling, Henry Martin, and Edward Parker in their wills. William Crashawe, the puritan preacher and scholar who lectured during the

[11] PCC 70 Lee, 125 Pembroke. Hughes, *Parson's Law*, 2nd edn. (1663), sigs. A2ᵛ–A3; *CSPD 1660–1*, 537–40.

[12] PCC 33 Goare; *Commons Debates for 1629*, ed. W. Notestein and F. H. Relf (Minneapolis, 1921), 123; PCC 134 Laud, and cf. Aylmer, *King's Servants*, 383–4; PCC 455 Ruthven.

Table 7.1. Religious Affiliations

	Barristers		Benchers	
	Number	Per cent	Number	Per cent
Puritan	26	22.6	105	27.3
High Church or Anti-puritan	3	2.6	17	4.4
Papist	3	2.6	7	1.8
Unknown	83	72.2	256	66.5
Total	115	100.0	385	100.0

first decade of the seventeenth century at the Temple Church, testified to the 'many moral and religious virtues' of 'that worthy, virtuous and religious' Inner Templar John Hare, whose colleague Andrew Newport described himself in his own epitaph as 'a true professor of the doctrine according to the best reformed churches . . . ever hating the Church of Rome'.[13] The recorded actions and associations of other barristers are strongly suggestive of puritan leanings; besides the ten appointed to office by parliamentary or republican regimes between 1642 and 1659, they include George Browne, recorder and MP for the notoriously zealous Somerset town of Taunton during the 1620s; Thomas Gell, recorder and recruiter MP for Derby in the 1640s; Deane Tindall, brother-in-law to John Winthrop, the first governor of the Massachusetts Bay Colony; and Robert Cuffe, who, as JP for Somerset, signed a famous petition against church ales from that county in 1633.[14]

As this slightly miscellaneous catalogue indicates, puritans and puritanism are more easily recognized than defined. Zealous piety of a broadly Calvinist orientation, confidence in personal election to the company of God's saints, ties of association—by education, friendship, or patronage—with godly ministers, preachers, and

[13] E. Bulstrode, *A Golden-Chain* (1657); Dorset RO, MW M4 (and see below, n. 15); Lincs. RO, LCC 1629/415; PCC 95 Fairfax, 8 Fenner; Borthwick, Reg. 48, fol. 653; St Bernard of Clairvaux, *The Complaint or Dialogue betwixt the Soule and the Bodie of a Damned Man*, tr. W. Crashawe (1616), sigs. A3ᵛ–A4; *H. of P.*, ii. 131.

[14] The ten appointed to office between 1642 and 1659 were Archer, Clarke, Gallop, Honeywood, Phesant, Powell, Seys, Smith, Widdrington, and Willimot, for whom see Appendix D. Barnes, *Somerset*, 358; *CD 1628*, iv. 382; R. Clark, 'Anglicanism, Recusancy and Dissent in Derbyshire 1603–1730', University of Oxford D. Phil. thesis, 1977, 144 (but cf. Underdown, *Pride's Purge*, 374); *Winthrop Papers*, ed. Robinson, i. 349, 366, 410; *CSPD 1633–4*, 350.

laymen, vehement anti-Catholic views, and overall support for further ecclesiastical reform in a protestant direction are some of the signs which help identify the godly. It would be misleading, as well as impracticable, to distinguish statistically between different expressions of the puritan impulse over the long period covered by this survey, or to draw a hard and fast line between 'puritans' and 'anglicans'—if, indeed, that convenient distinction has any basis in contemporary fact, at least before the Civil War. The end result may be criticized as an omnium gatherum, erring on the generously inclusive side. But since puritanism was never a strict analytical category, there is a good deal to be said for working procedures which acknowledge the diversity of those gathered under that banner: zealous visionaries like Sir Henry Finch or Samuel Gott, hard-working politico-social engineers like Henry Sherfield or Christopher Sherland, and numerous orthodox Elizabethan Calvinists 'of singular piety towards God', such as the antiquary William Lambard. It is very likely that most of these men would have joined with the Middle Temple bencher William Gibbes in protesting their abhorrence of 'the vulgar imputation of puritanism'.[15]

But what of the majority in both sample groups, those about whose religious attitudes there is insufficient evidence for even an informed guess? In a few cases we have some testimony to an individual's piety or spiritual concerns, although too brief, formal, or vague in nature for identification with any specific ecclesiastical tendency.[16] Presumably all were members of the Church of England by virtue of their baptism and confirmation; all were obliged by the Act of Uniformity and other penal statutes to attend weekly church services, and by the regulations of their inn to receive Holy Communion at least once a term in the Temple Church or the chapel of their house, although we know that both requirements were some-

[15] R. Rokeby, 'Oeconomica Rokebiourum', in T. D. Whitaker, *A History of Richmondshire* (1823), i. 175; PCC 11 Weldon. Cf. P. Collinson, *The Religion of Protestants* (Oxford, 1982), 81–3; the classical 'church puritan' or 'Calvinist episcopalian' position is exemplified by Sir John Strode, sufficiently conformist to have his chapel at Chantmarle consecrated by 'my good Lord Bishop of Salisbury', the Calvinist John Davenant, but also the sponsor of a bill against breaches of the Third Commandment in the parliament of 1621 (*Wilts. N & Q*, vi. 214; *CD 1621*, ii. 162; Mr J. P. Ferris, personal communication).

[16] Cf. the wills of John Clough, 1623 (Borthwick, Reg. 37, fol. 387), Roger Dale, 1622 (PCC 3 Byrde), and Sir Thomas Ellis, 1625 (PCC 106 Skynner); however, Dale's personal ties with George Croke, Elize ('Pious Uses') Hele, and Thomas Crew suggest puritan sympathies.

times circumvented. Yet each might have been a covert unbeliever or atheist; apathetic or indifferent towards the claims of institutionalized Christianity, while still a conforming 'orthodox' member of the Church; or sympathetic towards popery or puritanism without having left any clear evidence of the fact. Even if, as common sense suggests, most probably fell into the second and third categories we are still unable to determine whether contemporaries were justified in suggesting that common lawyers showed a particular inclination towards irreligion or secularist indifference (as compared with either the bulk of the population or the landed, literate classes).

iii. Interpretations

So each of the three perspectives on the religion of early modern barristers outlined at the start of this chapter is compatible with the evidence just surveyed. Assuming that our two sample groups provide a reasonably representative cross-section of the whole bar during the half century before 1640, we can say that zealous protestants, or puritans, constituted the largest single identifiable bloc; thus George Ruggle had good reason to specify 'great Puritania' as the birthplace of his archetypal common lawyer, Ignoramus.[17] Yet a handful of papists, Catholic sympathizers, High-Churchmen, and anti-puritans could also be found at the bar throughout our period, while a clear majority of common lawyers cannot now—and perhaps could not then—be associated with any specific religious alignment or commitment.

Given the economic, geographical, and social heterogeneity of the bar in the late sixteenth and early seventeenth centuries, the diversity of its members' religious affiliations is hardly surprising. The formal constraints on their beliefs and practices were minimal and inconsistently enforced, while the pluralistic structure of legal practice meant that barristers were not universally obliged to adopt the religious outlook of a single major client or employer.[18] In short, the bar was sufficiently large, unregulated, autonomous, and amorphous to

[17] Ruggle, *Ignoramus* (1662), sig. Hᵛ.
[18] From 1563 on utter-barristers were required to take the oath of supremacy, while after 1609, all entrants to the inns of court supposedly took the oath of allegiance; attendance at prayers and annual receipt of Communion were prescribed by judges' orders and the inns themselves; see *Inns of Court*, 180–1, and ch. 8, *passim*. Cf. Levack, *Civil Lawyers*, 160, 168, 176, 186.

accommodate a wide range of religious attitudes among its members.

But were the mass of barristers in fact much interested in religious matters? One might well ask the same question about the bulk of their contemporaries; and indeed, as noted above, the proportion of our sample groups for whose religion no evidence has survived is not notably larger than that among members of the Long Parliament, Charles I's civil servants, or the gentry of early seventeenth-century Lancashire. Yet this does not quite settle the matter, for a large body of contemporary opinion depicts common lawyers as wholly given up to secular materialism, so preoccupied with their pursuit of Mammon as to have no time left for God. Indeed, some common lawyers themselves endorsed the charge that 'a jurisprudent (or man of the law) . . . commonly is little or nothing acquainted with . . . the rules and practices of real virtue and religion'. In the early eighteenth century, one of Mathew Hale's works was published with a preface recounting that its author had 'demonstrated by a living argument, how practicable it was to be both an able lawyer and a good Christian': 'Never was the old monkish maxim, *Bonus Jurista malus Christa*, more thoroughly confuted than by his example.'[19]

This adage, or slogan, seems actually to have originated in Reformation Germany, possibly with Martin Luther himself, as a Latin version of a vernacular saying, also perhaps of no great antiquity.[20] In England, as throughout Western Europe, clerical resentment at the rising wealth and influence of the legal profession evoked broadly similar sentiments, if no exactly equivalent phrase. How far such claims were justified is very difficult to say. While some common lawyers may indeed have been distracted from religious duties by the pressures of work, others found spiritual fulfilment in the conscientious discharge of their worldly vocation. Indeed, Edward Bulstrode asserted that 'when religion is not suitable with the lawful vocation of any man . . . that religion is false: For true

[19] M. Hildesley, *Religio Jurisprudentis* (1685), sig. A5; M. Hale, *Historia Placitorum Coronae*, ed. S. Emlyn (1736), vi. Cf. *Inns of Court*, 217–18; J. Harington, *Epigrams* . . . (1615), sig. D2ᵛ; *Diary of the Rev. John Ward, A.M.*, ed. C. Severn (1839), 133.
[20] C. Kenny, 'Bonus Jurista Malus Christa', *Law Quarterly Rev.* xix (1903), 326–34; M. Luther, *Tischreden oder Colloquia* (1566), quoted by F. F. Lipperheide, *Spruchwörterbuch* (Berlin, 1907), 438; cf. H. Grisar, *Luther*, tr. E. M. Lamond (1917), 360–2. (I gratefully acknowledge the help of Professor R. Helmholz and Mr John Simmons with this topic.)

Godliness is so far from prejudicing any employment, that it adorns and beautifies it, all persons becoming more acceptable in their vocation, joining it with true devotion.'[21] The latent secularizing thrust of this argument can hardly be ignored. Nevertheless, many of the most successful, and presumably busiest, practitioners from our period have left concrete evidence of their personal religious zeal. The erudite Sir Henry Finch, king's serjeant under James I, although best known as the author of a standard legal treatise, also published no less than five religious tracts of a markedly presbyterian inclination during his long and distinguished career at the bar. The last of these, *The Worlds Great Restauration. Or the Calling of the Iewes* (1621), earned both the author and his friend William Gouge, the puritan minister of Blackfriars parish, London, who was probably responsible for organizing its publication, a period of imprisonment, after the king took offence at the prospect foreshadowed there of the converted Jews regaining Zion and exercising 'chief sway and prospect of sovereignty' over the rest of the world.[22] Sir Henry Yelverton, Finch's near contemporary at Gray's Inn and, like Finch, a graduate of Christ's College, Cambridge (that famous puritan forcing-house), had a still more successful career in conventional terms, serving as solicitor-general under James I and puisne justice of Common Pleas from 1625 until his death in 1630. Yelverton was a well-known patron of puritan ministers, some of whom publicly acknowledged his generosity in their published sermons, and was largely responsible for the appointment of Richard Sibbes as lecturer at Gray's Inn in 1617, after the High Commission had deprived him of the Trinity Church lectureship at Cambridge; further witness to his appetite for godly preaching is a bulky volume of Edward Philips's sermons 'taken by the pen of H. Yelverton of Gray's Inn', which was published in 1605. The text of 462 pages includes 31 sermons, prefaced by two lengthy dedicatory epistles, in which Yelverton justifies his labour as providing 'physic' for sick souls 'in these desperate diseased times'.[23] His example was

[21] Bulstrode, *Golden-Chain*, sig. A3.
[22] W. R. Prest, 'The Published Writings of Sir Henry Finch', *N & Q* NS xxiv (1977), 501–3; *idem*, 'The Art of Law and the Law of God: Sir Henry Finch (1558–1625)', in *Puritans and Revolutionaries*, ed. Pennington and Thomas, 94–117.
[23] Cf. P. Baynes, *A Commentarie upon the first Chapter of the Epistle to the Ephesians* (1618); W. Crashawe, *The Parable of Poyson* (1618); T. Gataker, *Abraham's decease* (1627); S. Hieron, *All the Sermons* (1620). *DNB*, s.v. Yelverton, Sir Henry; [E. Philips], *Certain Godly and Learned Sermons . . . as they were delivered . . .*

followed by a younger Northamptonshire common lawyer and kinsman, Edward Bagshaw, who in 1632 published a volume of posthumous sermons by Robert Bolton, the puritan minister who owed his benefice at Broughton to the patronage of Sir Augustine Nicolls, serjeant at law and later justice of Common Pleas. Nicolls's own religious preferences are sufficiently indicated by a passage in his funeral sermon (which Bolton preached) reporting with approval the departed judge's remark that 'what you call puritanical sermons, they come nearest to my conscience and do me the most good'.[24]

Besides published editions of sermons and devotional works, such as George Strode's *Anatomie of Mortalitie* (1618), Chief Justice Sir Henry Montagu's neo-Stoic *Contemplatio Mortis et Immortalitas* (1639), William Austin's *Devotionis Augustinianae Flamma, or Certayne Devout, Godly, and Learned Meditations* (1635), and Nathaniel Bacon's *Relation of the Fearful Estate of Francis Spira* (1638 and many later editions), a large number of religious writings by barristers from our period survive in manuscript. Among them may be mentioned Michael Dalton's fiercely anti-Catholic 'Breviary of the State of the Roman Church and Empire', Serjeant Sir John Glanville's verse paraphrases of the psalms, the autobiographical 'Psalme of Thanksgiving, yea of Prayer and Prayses ... by Sir John Strode, kt., after his many Visions & Victoryes ...', Thomas Saunderson's 'manuscripts and translations ... of Solomon's Proverbs and Ecclesiastes ... finished after many years labour ...', and a 'certain Concordance that would be the best help for explaining scripture that ever was known', compiled by the Middle Temple barrister Jephson Jewell, a work of which John Pym informed Samuel Hartlib in the mid-1630s.[25] Other literary manifestations of the religious fervour of individual barristers include 'The Foundation of the faith of Sir Edward Coke all written with his own hand ...', the diaries or journals of John Harington and Thomas Thornton, the letters of spiritual advice written by Paul Croke to his

in Saint Saviours in Southwark (1605), sig. A4. The radical clergyman Andrew Willet bracketed Finch, Yelverton, and Nicholas Fuller as '*piisimi viri et causarum optimi patroni*' in his list of eminent Christ's alumni prefaced to *An Harmonie ...* (1614).

[24] *DNB*, s.v. Bolton, Robert and Nicolls, Sir Augustine; [R. Bolton], *Mr Bolton's Last and Learned Work of the Foure last Things ...* (1632), 168.

[25] CUL MS Add. 6325 (also Sloane 4359 and Yale University, Beinecke Library, MS Osborne b 277); Egerton 2590; Dorset RO, MW M4; PCC 128 Cambell. Sheffield University Library, MS Hartlib 29/2/1, fol. 33ᵛ. (I am indebted to Christopher Hill for drawing my attention to this important source.)

daughter Lucy, Sir Robert Heath to his son, and Roger Hill to his wife, and the single item now surviving from the correspondence of Sir Sidney Montagu (Sir Henry's younger brother) and Dr Samuel Ward, master of Sidney Sussex College, Cambridge, involving the former's efforts to 'attain to the true meaning' of a scriptural passage about the conversion of the Jews.[26]

A more than merely formal religious commitment is also argued by the chapels which the judges Sir James Altham, Sir John Bridgeman, Sir George Croke, and Sir James Whitelocke established in their houses, as well as by the collections of divinity books in the libraries of Sir Francis Aungier, Sir Samuel Browne, Sir Edward Coke, Sir John Dodderidge, Richard Hadsor, William Littleton, Richard Prythergh, Sir Euble Thelwall, and John Selden.[27] The same may be said of the gifts for ecclesiastical purposes which are commonly found in lawyers' wills from our period; these typically include provisions for the repair and adornment of churches, doles to the poor, more or less elaborate schemes for setting the poor to work, the provision of sermons (funeral and otherwise), and marks of friendship and respect to individual ministers, such as those whom Sir Roger Wilbraham termed 'instructors of my soul: Mr Dr Westfield, and the preachers of Gray's Inn, Nantwich and Hadley, and the incumbents of my churches on my manors of Plumpton, Newbottle and Radbourne'.[28]

As the slightly proprietorial tone of this last clause may suggest,

[26] Additional 22591, fol. 289; *The Diary of John Harington, M.P., 1646–53*, ed. M. F. Stieg (Som. Rec. Soc., 1977); Northants RO, Thornton 2251; P. Croke to L. Croke, 9 Nov. 1630; R. Heath to E. Heath, 22 June 1627, uncatalogued letters of P. Croke and R. Heath, Rare Book Room, Lib. of Univ. of Illinois at Urbana-Champaign. Additional 46500, fols. 1–48; Bodl. MS Tanner 74, fol. 15.

[27] For chapels, see PCC 26 Weldon; S. Rudder, *A New History of Gloucestershire* (Cirencester, 1779), 609; R. Atkyns, *The Ancient and Present State of Glostershire* (1768), 417; *VCH, Oxon.*, iv. 58; Whitelocke, *Lib. Fam.*, 110–11; see also Sir John Strode's account of the building and consecration of his chapel at Chantmarle, Dorset RO, MW M4, fols. 22–4. For divinity books see PCC 15 Russell; PCC 1668, fol. 61; W. O. Hassall, *A Catalogue of the Library of Sir Edward Coke* (New Haven, 1950); *Inns of Court*, 165; PCC 96 Barrington, 22 Sadler, 231 and 247 Brent, 105 Scroope; Lancs. RO, DDB 85/6a.

[28] PCC 109 Cope. Other wills demonstrating close ties between clergymen and common lawyers include those of Sir Francis Ashley (PCC 44 Pile), who records his gratitude to John White of Holy Trinity Church, Dorchester, for 'sincere affection' and 'spiritual comfort'; Sir Robert Hyde, who in 1664 left £20 for restoring Salisbury Cathedral and £50 for restoring St Paul's Cathedral (PCC 49 Hyde); Richard Reynell (PCC 48 St John); and Richard Swayne (PCC 17 Goare). See also Matthews, *William Sheppard*, 18–19.

personal friendship with, or deference to, individual clergymen in their spiritual capacity hardly inhibited common lawyers from vigorously asserting the subordination of the Church to the lay magistracy and the common law. The diary of John Harington, bencher of Lincoln's Inn from 1633 until his death in 1654 and recruiter MP for Somerset in the Long Parliament, shows this devout and learned counsellor maintaining the closest scholarly and spiritual rapport with James Ussher, the Low-Church archbishop of Armagh who served as preacher at Lincoln's Inn from 1647; yet at the same time Harington also took the view that 'Parliament is to follow the advice of the synod [or Westminster Assembly of Divines, of which Ussher was a member] no further than [it] see[s] good cause to do', while upholding the lay judge's right 'to punish evil doers of every sort' (hence denying the church courts' jurisdiction over delinquent clergymen or sexual offences). Harington was also a close associate of John Selden, the archetypal lawyer Erastian and a fellow MP, with whom he frequently exchanged books; on Tuesday 8 January 1653 Harington noted returning to Selden his 'Arabic *confessio pap:*', borrowing an Arab and Latin psalter, and their 'Discourse of counting our selves the greatest sinner knowing nothing but Christ'.[29] Years before, Selden's *Historie of Tithes* (1618) notoriously 'drew a great deal of envy upon him from the clergy'. But the Inner Temple reading on the statute of tithes (2 Edw. VI, c. 13) delivered in 1631 by Selden's fellow-bencher and later Long Parliament colleague John Wild, commended the book as an 'exquisite work', which demonstrated how under popery 'the Church gained upon the laity'. Tithes might be considered due by divine right, Wild playfully added, in the sense that they were required by the 'laws of Holy Church which are ingrossed and incorporated into the body of the realm'; in other words, in so far as they were sanctioned by the common law.[30]

Nor was this the first time that such sentiments had been voiced at learning exercises in the Inner Temple hall. A decade before the

[29] Harington, *Diary*, 28, 36, 79. Four barristers and six of the benchers in our sample groups had clergymen fathers. John Lany of GI (*c.*1549–1633) was the father of Bishop Benjamin Lany (1591–1675), as well as John Lany jun., also a GI bencher, while his colleague John Whistler (*c.*1580–1646) had two clergymen brothers. (Keeler, 387; Appendix E below.)

[30] Aubrey, *Brief Lives*, ii. 220; cf. Montagu, *Diatribae*, 1–135; R. Tillesley, *Animadversion upon M. Selden's History of Tithes* (1619), sig. 4ᵛ. CUL MS Dd. 5.8, fols. viii–ix. Christianson, 'Selden', 299–307.

appearance of Selden's *Historie*, when the dispute between Arch-bishop Bancroft and Chief Justice Coke over the prohibitions addressed by Common Pleas and King's Bench to the ecclesiastical courts was well under way, Rice Gwynn chose the same Edwardian statute of tithes for his reading before an audience of practitioners and students which may well have included both Coke and Selden. In his prefatory speech Gwynn flatly asserted that 'the canon law was never the law of this land, and that the common law excels and overbears' the ecclesiastical law, which originated when the king, whom the common law 'hath always ... recognised to be the superior and chief over all estates and in all causes both ecclesiastical and temporal', created archbishops and bishops to exercise his spiritual jurisdiction. Hence, Gwynn concluded, 'all advancement, power, authority and jurisdiction that [the clergy] have within this realm was at the first given or granted unto them by the king or by parliament'. Of course there was nothing original in Gwynn's views, which look back at least to Christopher St German and the Henrician Reformation and forwards to the eve of the Long Parliament, when Edward Bagshaw argued in his Middle Temple reading (before being silenced by Archbishop Laud) that the clergy might have kept many of the privileges which they lost at the Reformation 'had they not most unthankfully and unnaturally gone about quite to suppress the common law of the land, which first gave them these favours, and instead thereof to advance and set up the civil and canon laws'.[31]

We do not know how many of Bagshaw's colleagues would similarly have denied the Church any authority beyond what the common law allowed it. But arguments to the opposite effect, or defences of the clergy's secular rights and standing, were certainly no part of most common lawyers' rhetorical stock-in-trade. Although Sir William Ellis of Gray's Inn and Euseby Andrew of Lincoln's Inn both deprecated the impropriation of church lands by the laity, Ellis at least seems to have been primarily concerned at the consequent disadvantages for tenants and the royal exchequer (if indeed he was in earnest and not joking on this, as on other

---

[31] Additional 11405, fols. 5–5ᵛ; another version is in Additional 28607, fols. 3–16ᵛ; cf. the strongly anticlerical reading of Thomas Trist in 1620 (Additional 25233, fols. 1–56ᵛ.) For Bagshaw, see *Inns of Court*, 211, 214–15; for the anticlericalism of early Tudor common lawyers, C. Haigh, 'Anticlericalism and the English Reformation', *History*, xviii (1983), 398–9.

occasions). And Sir John Strode, who portentously advised his son to 'reverence the priests', rather spoilt the effect by adding 'yea although some of them be heady, high-minded, covetous, unpatient, vicious and the like'.[32]

Nevertheless, lawyers rarely ventured a direct attack on the intellectual, moral, and spiritual failings of the clergy. Apart from the odd jibe at clerical greed or stupidity,[33] barristers showed considerable restraint in the face of the twice-yearly barrage of assize sermons which regularly castigated the corruption, avarice, and injustice of their profession.[34] The occasional exasperated response to these and other clerical provocations contrasts quite sharply with the intensity and volume of caveat, criticism, and exhortation levelled at common lawyers by clergymen of all ranks and doctrinal persuasions.

Some part of this chorus reflected widespread public dissatisfac-

[32] Bodl. MS Bodley 307, fols. 156–66ᵛ; Staffs. RO, D661/11/1/7, fol. 60. Andrew must not be confused with his puritan near-namesake, Sir Euseby Andrews of Charwelton; cf. W. J. Sheils, *The Puritans in the Diocese of Peterborough 1558–1610* (Northants Rec. Soc., 1979), 112, 117, and M. Toynbee, 'The Andrew Family of Daventry', *Northants Past and Present*, iii (1962), 95–105. William Ellis was accused by Robert Callis, in a Star Chamber case over the disputed recordership of Lincoln, of countenancing known papists; but other evidence suggests that his religious sympathies were firmly protestant (STAC 8/98/9; PCC 81 Goare; *Wentworth Papers*, ed. Cooper, 277). Dorset RO, MW M4, fol. 81; a prime example of the 'heady and high-minded' clergyman was Paul Micklethwaite, master of the Temple 1626–38, for whom see *Inns of Court*, 199–201. Although Hughes claimed that his *Parson's Law* was drawn up at the 'earnest request of some eminent men of the clergy' and endorsed by Archbishop Laud (Hughes, *Parson's Law*, sig. A2ᵛ), it is essentially a technical manual, comparable to Book 4 of Henry Finch's *Nomotechnia* (1613), or Sir John Dodderidge's *A Compleat Parson* (1630). Cf. Prest, 'Dialectical Origins of Finch's Law', 344–5.
[33] Staffs. RO, D661/11/1/7, fols. 1, 17; '*Merry Passages*', ed. Lippincott, 25; R. Callis, *The Case and Argument against Sir Ignoramus* (1648); Lowther, 'Autobiography', 213. However, cf. the Laudian clergyman Robert Chestlin's claim 'that not a lawyer in a parish, but commonly was the parson's busy enemy'. (*Persecutio Undecima* (1648), 12–13; I am indebted to Mr J. Hogg for this reference.) In the 1628 parliament, lawyer-MPs generally supported a bill against scandalous ministers, although Sir Edward Littleton and Christopher Sherland expressed reservations. (*CD 1628*, iii. 430–2.)
[34] Cf. Cockburn, *History of English Assizes*, 65–6, 231; M. F. Wadmore, 'A Launceston Assize Sermon of 1635', *J. of the Royal Institute of Cornwall*, xxi (1925), 414–16. Relevant examples of assize sermons (besides those cited by Cockburn) include A. Cade, *A Sermon of the Nature of Conscience* (1621), 8, 14–17; Garey, *Jentaculum Judicum*, 41–3, 49–54, 60, 62–4; W. Hayes, *The Paragon of Persia* (Oxford, 1624), 17; Reeve, *Moses Old Square*, sig. K2, 75, 79–80, 84–6, 88–99; T. Scot, *The high-waies of God and the King* (1632), 4; J. Squire, *A Sermon Preached at Hartford Assises* (1617), 13–14, 16.

tion with the workings of the legal system, as well as more specifically religious scruples about the place of litigation in a Christian community. But jealousy of the common lawyers' rising eminence and power since the Reformation was also an important element. Thus Bishop Latimer labelled the common-law judges as 'upskips'; Archbishop Whitgift complained that 'the temporal lawyer (whose learning is no learning anywhere but at home) being born to nothing doth by his travail and labour (in that barbarous knowledge) purchase to himself and his forever £1000 a year', whereas 'the poor divine, labouring all his life in true learning', gained a mere pittance; and Bishop Goodman claimed that by their conspiracy to nullify both ecclesiastical and manorial jurisdictions, the common lawyers had become 'more absolute governors than any legal prince in Christendom'.[35]

Some churchmen also resented the role of the inns of court and the legal profession generally in fostering the spread of puritanism. Responding to the presbyterian leader Thomas Cartwright's suggestion that some of those studying at the inns might become preachers if the ministry were thoroughly reformed, Whitgift commented:

What store of fit preachers those inns would yield, if your church were framed, I know not, but I think that some of them would not refuse the spoil of this. I doubt not but that there are many in the inns of court well affected in religion: God continue them ... that they be not seduced by overmuch credulity in themselves and pretensed zeal in others.

Dean Richard Cosin claimed (with good cause) that the puritans' technical objections to the exercise of ecclesiastical jurisdiction 'were put into their heads by some lawyers', while William Wilkes, chaplain to James I, urged 'gentlemen apprentices at the law' to 'go with the current and stream of the law', so that the king 'shall not have cause so much as to hear complaint of your any further connivance to enormities, or indulgence to factions, or supportance of dissentious partialities'. In 1638 Archbishop Laud lamented his inability to suppress Brownists and separatists, without 'some

[35] *Sermons by Hugh Latimer, sometime Bishop of Worcester, Martyr, 1555*, ed. G. E. Corrie (Parker Soc., 1844), 127; IT MS Petyt 538.38, fol. 101; Goodman, *Court of James I*, i. 293–6. R. G. Usher, *The Reconstruction of the English Church* (1910), ii. 219. Cf. the numerous qualifications attached to going to law by William Perkins, *The Whole Treatise of the cases of conscience* (1636), 289–91; for discussion of this and similar works, see R. L. Greaves, *Society and Religion in Elizabethan England* (Minneapolis, 1982), 651–7.

temporal assistance from the judges'; five years earlier, in response
to Wentworth's congratulations at his translation to the see of
Canterbury, Laud had cautioned his friend against unrealistic
expectations:

For, as for the Church, it is so bound up in the forms of the common law,
that it is not possible for me, or for any man, to do that good which he
would . . . they which have gotten so much power in, and over the Church,
will not let go their hold; they have, indeed, fangs with a witness.[36]

Laud's vision of the church autonomous was hardly compatible with
the common-law's continued jurisdiction over disputes about
advowsons, benefices, and tithes, the basic structural elements of
ecclesiastical life, while the remarkable imagery of trussed victim
and ravening lawyer sufficiently conveys the intensity of feeling
which underlay what might be termed clerical antilegalism. It is not
hard to understand how churchmen who held such views would tend
to discount the possibility that the average common lawyer could
possess any strong or authentic faith.

Yet, as we have already seen, there was no shortage of protestant
zeal among the ranks of the late Elizabethan and early Stuart bar.
Common lawyers had their own reasons, part principled, part self-
interested, to join with puritans in seeking to circumscribe, or even
abolish, the independent jurisdiction of the church courts. A long
and living tradition of mutual jealousy and mistrust between the two
oldest learned professions must have predisposed many lawyers to
applaud proposals for reducing the authority of the episcopate and
expanding lay participation in church government. Successful barristers may also have been attracted by the puritan emphasis on hard
work in one's earthly calling and that sense of England's national
mission which could help transform the common law's insularity
into a positive virtue. Of course, puritanism appealed to a wide
cross-section of the laity, and in the absence of comparative studies
the possibility remains that common lawyers were no more susceptible to its peculiar charms than any other occupational group among
the governing classes. But one can hardly fail to be impressed by the

---

[36] *The Works of John Whitgift, D.D.*, ed. J. Ayre (Parker Soc., 1851–3), i. 312–14;
R. Cosin, *An Apologie of and for Sundrie Proceedings by Jurisdiction Ecclesiasticall*
(1591), sigs. A2ᵛ, [A4]; W. Wilkes, *Obedience or Ecclesiasticall Union* (1605), 47–8; *The
Works of . . . William Laud*, ed. W. Scott and J. Bliss (Oxford, 1847–60), v. 336–7, 355;
Knowler, i. 110–11. For an instance of Laud's own reliance upon the technical
expertise of common lawyers in 'church business', see *CSPD 1634–5*, 214.

number and power of the various ideological and material forces at work to bring lawyers and puritans together.[37] In the long run, to be sure, the strongest influence on a lawyer's religion was almost certainly the beliefs of his clients and patrons. To say this is emphatically not to claim that counsellors merely adopted puritanical attitudes in the hope of gaining business from the pious. True, a reputation for godliness probably did a lawyer's practice no harm; Hugh Audley, according to his posthumous biographer,

> took care to accompany himself with some grave and reverend divine to his dying day; from whom if he gained not piety he gained the reputation of it. You should have in his chamber upon the table a large Bible and Bishop Andrewes's sermons, and if you surprised him not you might find him busy with one of these books; but if you came suddenly he was in his closet.[38]

Yet to assert that the religious outlook of barristers was likely to reflect and be reinforced by the attitudes of those whose affairs they handled, is not to accuse barristers *en masse* of apathy or hypocrisy in religious matters. 'Papist and puritan lawyers', according to Clarendon, 'got more money than their neighbours, for the opinions they had, not which they delivered'. It would surely be surprising if fervent believers did not prefer to employ like-minded co-religionists as legal advisers, all other things being equal; puritan laymen obviously had a much wider choice than papists, which doubtless explains why the latter were often obliged to retain protestant lawyers when seeking to minimize the impact of the penal statutes on their estates and life-styles.[39]

---

[37] Cf. C. Hill, *Society and Puritanism in Pre-Revolutionary England* (1964), chs. 8–9; *Inns of Court*, 209–11. Although unconvincingly presented in J. D. Eusden's *Puritans, Lawyers and Politics in Early Seventeenth-Century England* (New Haven, 1958), the notion of an 'ideological parallelism' linking common lawyers and puritans, especially in their literalism and particularistic attitude towards authority, cannot be entirely discounted; cf. R. Pound, 'Puritanism and the Common Law', *American Law Rev.*, lv (1911), 811–29; D. Little, *Religion, Order and Law* (New York, 1969); P. Lake, 'Laurence Chaderton and the Cambridge Moderate Puritan Tradition 1570–1604', Cambridge University Ph.D. thesis, 1978, 107; R. Ashton, *The English Civil War* (1978), 125. The assistance given non-conforming ministers by sympathetic barristers early in James I's reign is highlighted in SP 14/10A/81, which I. W. Gowers has transcribed and discussed in 'Puritanism in the County of Devon between 1570 and 1641', University of Exeter MA thesis, 1970, 51, 281–9; see also Usher, *Reconstruction*, i. 406–7, 410–11.

[38] Anon., *The Way to be Rich*, 10.

[39] E. Hyde, earl of Clarendon, *The History of the Rebellion and Civil Wars in England*, ed. W. D. Macray (Oxford, 1888), i. 406. Cf. *Memoir of Rokeby*, 3–4; J. C.

The role of an ideologically committed advocate was not always comfortable or easy. In 1632, when Peter Smart sought to pursue his campaign against Archdeacon John Cosin and other high-flying clergy of Durham Cathedral by legal action from prison, his wife told him: 'there is not one man that will show himself in all this country for you', apart from Smart's former pupil Edward Wright of Gray's Inn and Thomas Tempest of Lincoln's Inn, 'an honest gentleman', whose 'abundant religiousness' was later noted by his equally pious fellow-bencher John Harington.[40] Nicholas Fuller of Gray's Inn, who was notorious for vigorously supporting the puritan cause in parliament, as well as in the law courts, during the 1590s and 1600s, doubtless attracted some clients on that basis alone. But it would be quite absurd to suggest that Fuller consciously chose his religion because it might bring him work, especially given the substantial penalties (imprisonment and a stalled career) which he eventually paid for his puritan advocacy.[41]

So the strength of puritanism at the bar in the late sixteenth and early seventeenth centuries may best be regarded as a particular instance of the gradual dissemination of zealous protestantism throughout early modern England, a process facilitated in the case of lawyers, as, no doubt, other occupations by certain specific vocational factors. From our vantage-point, and indeed that of many contemporaries, legal anticlericalism and the lawyer-puritan nexus may well seem distinctly individualistic and secularizing in tendency, not least because they denied any special place or privilege to the Church and the clergy: all men stood equal before the common law, as they were also supposed to do in the sight of the Lord. Yet in seeking to understand the forces which moulded the religious outlook of the legal profession, as well as its long-term implications, we need not deny or denigrate the authenticity, depth, and variety of religious commitment found among at least some early modern barristers. If Audley's Bible was indeed displayed mainly for public relations purposes, we have the word of the Catholic priest Augustine Baker, a practising barrister before his

H. Aveling, *The Handle and The Axe* (1976), 147–8; Clark, thesis, 176–7; Clark, *Provincial Society*, 292; A. Fletcher, *A County Community in Peace and War: Sussex 1600–1660* (1975), 101.

[40] [C. Hunter], *An Illustration of Mr. Daniel Neal's History of the Puritans, In the Article of Peter Smart A.M.* (Durham, 1736), 63–4; Harington, *Diary*, 7, 39, 71, 79; cf. HL RO, Main Papers, 22 Mar. 1641, deposition of E. Wright.

[41] *Radicals*, i. 306–7, and references cited therein.

conversion to Rome, that the Bible, Foxe's *Martyrs*, and 'other books of protestant piety' which his Inner Temple contemporary, the future judge George Croke, kept in his ante-room were placed there for the edification of his clients, Croke having 'more piety, religiosity and zeal of justice' than 'ordinary lawyers'.[42]

The difficulty of discovering anything much about the religion of most 'ordinary lawyers' has been sufficiently insisted upon. Croke was an exceptionally godly lawyer, perhaps, but the faith of those barristers who did take religion seriously, tended, like his, to be evangelical rather than quietistic. Lawyers were particularly active patrons and promoters of sermons and preaching ministers. In 1602 John Manningham, a student soon to be called to the bar of the Middle Temple, began his journal with the following scoffing definition: 'A puritan is a curious corrector of things indifferent.' Yet, despite his consistent hostility to what he saw as the hypocrisy of the self-professed godly, Manningham was an inveterate frequenter of sermons preached by ministers of all ecclesiastical persuasions, from the High-Church Lancelot Andrewes to the populist Stephen Egerton.[43] Other common lawyers were somewhat more single-minded, like Edmond Prideaux of the Inner Temple, the father of a famous Long Parliament lawyer and MP, whose 'public esteem of the word and its true professors' was praised in 1621 by his kinsman Dr John Prideaux, the Calvinist theologian and Regius Professor of Divinity at Oxford. The prolific puritan divine Richard Bernard commended those 'reverend and religious judges' Sir John Denham and Sir John Walter for their 'holy attention to the word' and 'worthy respect unto God's ministers' on the Western assize circuit in the 1620s, while Richard Sibbes, lecturer at Gray's Inn from 1617 until his death in 1635, eulogized his friend and co-religionist Sir Thomas Crew as 'a marvellous great encourager of honest, laborious, religious ministers'.[44] At his death in 1646, William Eyre, a bencher of Lincoln's Inn and member for Downton

---

[42] Baker, *Memorials*, 69; there seems no reason to doubt the contemporary biographer's identification with Sir George Croke, d. 1642, rather than his elder brother Sir John, d. 1620, although the latter was also an Inner Templar who became a judge.

[43] Manningham, *Diary*, 29, 44, 77, 114, 124, 163.

[44] J. Prideaux, *Christs Counsell for Ending Law Cases in Eight Sermons* (1621), sig. A2ᵛ; R. Bernard, *A Guide to Grand Iury Men* (1629), sigs. A3–A4ᵛ; R. Sibbes, *The Brides Longing for her Bridegroomes Second Comming* (1638), 123; cf. R. Harris, *Sixe Sermons of Conscience* (1630), ep. ded; R. Webb, *Two Sermons of Christian Love and Life* (1631), ep. ded.

in the Short Parliament, left the large sum of £100 to support the Salisbury town lecture; Thomas Stephens of the Middle Temple (whose son Edward married one of Thomas Crew's daughters) bequeathed property worth £10 per annum for the maintenance of a 'godly learned preacher' in his parish of Stroud, Gloucestershire, in 1613, at roughly the same time that Toby Wood of Lincoln's Inn provided for 'some learned and religious divine' to preach in his parish church of St Botolph's-without-Aldgate, London.[45]

Collectively, common lawyers may have been no more committed in their appreciation and furtherance of godly preaching than, say, merchants or country gentlemen. What made the religious zeal of even a minority of barristers particularly significant was their unique opportunities to put the faith they possessed to work. Both locally and nationally, by virtue of their calling, barristers had access to positions of great potential influence on the lives and opinions of their fellow men and women. Their activities as JPs, MPs, and recorders of urban boroughs will be discussed further below. Here we need only note the leading role of a number of barristers, including Christopher Brooke, Thomas Crew, Nicholas Fuller, William Martin, John Strode, and William Wiseman, as proponents in the late Elizabethan and early Stuart House of Commons of legislation designed to alleviate crime, drunkenness, poverty, and unemployment by regulating and reforming individual conduct, whether 'in the interests of morality or of the social, economic and political welfare of the state'.[46] Yet it was when confronting these problems face to face, as justices and magistrates in towns and villages all over England, that barristers probably made their greatest impact.

The presbyterian leader and minister Thomas Cartwright hailed the appointment of Serjeant John Puckering to the recordership of Warwick in 1590 as 'a singular mean[s] of doing much good towards the town'. What Cartwright had in mind is suggested by the dedication of a volume of sermons to Sir James Altham, baron of the Exchequer and one of the 'worthy justices and magistrates of the town of Watford', by the eminently godly minister Thomas Taylor,

---

[45] PCC 192 Twisse, 109 Capell, 69 Wood. For William Towse as friend and patron of Thomas Barnes, cf. W. A. Hunt, *The Puritan Movement* (Cambridge, Mass., 1983), 177–8.

[46] J. Kent, 'Attitudes of Members of the House of Commons to the Regulation of "Personal Conduct" in late Elizabethan and Early Stuart England', *BIHR*, xlvi (1973), 42–3, 46, 62. For Wiseman, cf. *H. of P.*, iii. 642; for Martin, above, pp. 198–9.

who praised Altham's 'zeal against vice and vicious persons', together with his 'care of promoting the pure worship of God'. As steward of the borough of Reading, Sir Edward Clarke was instrumental in establishing a weekly town lecture in 1628, when he also attempted to have the House of Commons's Petition for Religion written into the corporation minutes. In 1621, as recorder of Boston, Anthony Irby was responsible for blocking a Privy Council investigation into the iconoclastic disfiguring of the town mace by zealots who removed its silver crosses, while in 1634 the bishop of Lincoln's chancellor complained to Archbishop Laud that the recorder of Bedford, Richard Taylor, had 'questioned at a sessions one of my apparitors for troubling, as he said, these godly men, and there delivered publicly that if men were thus troubled for going to hear a sermon when their minister at home did not preach, it would breed a scab in the kingdom'.[47]

Apart from such occasional initiatives, recorders had a regular channel for impressing their view of the world on at least the more respectable townsfolk, in the jury charges they customarily delivered at sessions of the peace and their speeches at the installation of civic officers; JPs enjoyed similar opportunities, since their lay colleagues often and perhaps usually allowed barrister justices to give the charge.[48] The speeches made on these occasions read like secular sermons, on account of both their elaborate rhetorical structure, complete with classical and scriptural allusions, and also their blurring of distinctions between crime and sin, nature and grace, Church and State. In addressing the Grand Inquest of the borough of King's Lynn on 15 August 1632, the recorder, Francis Parlett of Lincoln's Inn, began with the proposition that 'the sins we have are the causes of the laws we have. Sin is a transgression of the law of God and whoever is a transgressor of the laws of God is also a

[47] *VCH, War.*, viii. 493. (I owe this reference to Dr Brooks.) T. Taylor, *Iaphets First Publique Perswasion* (Cambridge, 1612), sigs. A, A2; *Reading Records: Diary of the Corporation*, ed. J. M. Guilding (1892–6), ii. 117, 250, 256; (I am grateful to Mrs M. Connelly, née Jobling, for her help with Clarke and other godly Berkshire lawyers); G. B. Blenkin, 'Boston, England and John Cotton in 1621', *New England Historical Genealogical Register*, xxviii (1874), 126–8, cited by C. Holmes, *Seventeenth-century Lincolnshire* (Lincoln, 1980), 49–50; *CSPD 1634–5*, 149.

[48] Responding to requests that he should deliver the charge at the Oxfordshire quarter sessions *c*.1633, Bulstrode Whitelocke 'told them I was not of that standing in my profession as to take upon me to give a charge in the country. . . . It was replied to me that I was not in commission of the peace as a lawyer ... yet being of the profession of the law, that did enable me to perform the office.' (Additional 37343, fol. 13ᵛ; cf. Goodman, *Court of James I*, i. 294.)

transgressor of the laws of man.' Parlett went on to outline the main
categories of offenders with whom the jury should concern themselves: first, 'those that break the peace of the church' (including
both popish recusants and separatists, as well as profane persons,
witches, wizards, fortune-tellers, conjurers, and cunning men and
women), then 'those that through other sins break the peace of the
commonwealth ... according to the several qualities of the several
sins which reign in the several peace-breakers, which sins I shall
divide into three as the most principal—(1) sin of wrath and blood,
(2) sin of covetousness, (3) sin of idleness'. So, although no friend to
'schismatical aberrations' or frequenters of 'unlawful conventicles',
Parlett was at one with his famous puritan colleague Henry Sherfield of Salisbury in visualizing his duty (like that of all magistrates)
as being equally 'to advance the glory of God and good of our
common weal', since 'the peace of the Church and the peace of the
burgh are so involved and woven together'.[49]

While lawyers of every religious colouring would probably have
accepted this truism of contemporary discourse without demur,
some took it particularly to heart. They were encouraged to do so by
the preaching of (among others) John Preston at Lincoln's Inn and
Richard Sibbes at Gray's Inn, both of whom laid heavy emphasis on
the duty of all men in places of authority to advance the cause of
God's true religion, jointly with the godly ministry.[50] In 1632,
preaching a funeral sermon for a former member of his Gray's Inn
congregation, the anti-Arminian MP and Feoffee for Impropriations Christopher Sherland, 'this holy and blessed man', Sibbes
claimed that the departed saint 'had a desire while he lived to take all
opportunities to do good.... After God had wrought upon his
heart, he had a public heart to do good.' Sibbes made special
reference to Sherland as 'a faithful, prudent governor', who was 'so
careful of the town [Northampton] where he was recorder, that he
provided for them after his death, and gave them a large legacy, 200
marks, to set the poor on work'.[51] Recalling the unusual piety

[49] Norfolk RO, King's Lynn Borough Archives, Recorder's Notebook, fols. 2–5ᵛ,
8–9, 13ᵛ–15ᵛ, 45ᵛ–6, 129–30ᵛ, 140ᵛ; Hants RO, 44M69, Box S14 unsorted papers,
charge to grand jury, n.d. Cf. Collinson, *Religion of Protestants*, ch. 4.

[50] Cf. C. Hill, 'The Political Sermons of John Preston', in *idem, Puritanism and
Revolution* (1962), 247–8, 258–74; J. C. Harris, 'Richard Sibbes: A Moderate in Early
Seventeenth-Century Puritanism', University of Melbourne MA thesis, 1979, 140,
146–7, chs. 7–9, *passim.*

[51] R. Sibbes, 'Christ is Best: Or a Sweet Passage to Glory', in *idem, The Saints
Cordialls* (1637), 206–8.

displayed by the rising barrister George Croke of the Inner Temple in the 1590s, it does not seem entirely fanciful to suggest that a similar principled concern to do good in the world lay behind the judgement against the Crown in the ship-money case, delivered with such momentous consequences by the same man, now puisne justice of King's Bench.[52] Even if most common lawyers were indifferent or hostile to the claims of religion (and that case is still not proven), the faith of those who did profess the Gospel as well as the law might move mountains.

[52] Cf. C. Russell, 'Justice Croke and the Hampdens', *N & Q*, ccxiii (1968), 367.

CHAPTER EIGHT

GOVERNMENT AND POLITICS

'To be a lawyer ... was indeed to be a governor of one's country. Thus, the recorders and town-clerks governed corporations; the country-lawyer is in commission of the peace, and gives the charge at the quarter-sessions, and rules all there.'

> Godfrey Goodman, bishop of Gloucester, *The Court of King James I*, i. 294

'In time of popery, the church did swell ... then the law crept up, and at last grew to be so numerous and to such a vast body, as it swelled to be too big for the kingdom, and hath been no small means to foment and continue this late and unfortunate rebellion.'

> William Cavendish, duke of Newcastle, to Charles II, in S. A. Strong, *Catalogue of Letters and Other Historical Documents ... at Welbeck* (1903), App. I, 192

'"O but", says one, "all the great lawyers followed the king!" Not so neither, I am sure the politick lawyer stayed behind: ambition and avarice make many a man argue against their own liberties.'

> J. Cooke, *Redintegratio Amoris* (1647), 12

SINCE lawyers were widely blamed as promoters of discord between neighbours, it was not such a large step to the duke of Newcastle's claim that their excessive numbers had helped precipitate a national collapse of social harmony and order in the form of civil war. This diagnosis was indeed foreshadowed as early as 1616, when an anonymous author warned James I that unless he took steps to 'sift and cleanse' the ranks of the common lawyers, 'they will turn your people's love to hatred, their faith to faction and their loyalty to disobedience'.[1]

Historians in more recent times have also identified practitioners of the common law as leaders of opposition to the early Stuarts, both within and outside parliament. But the graphic suggestion that the 'common law forged the axe which beheaded Charles I' does

---

[1] Ellesmere 34/C/2, pp. 179-80; cf. B. Rich, *Opinion Deified* (1613), 31. *Lawyers*, 132, 194-5. Cf. *The Life of William Cavendish, Duke of Newcastle, by Margaret Cavendish*, ed. C. H. Firth (1907), 125.

present certain difficulties.[2] Even Gardiner, whose work might seem to support this general interpretation, emphasized the rallying to Charles I's government of the 'principal lawyers of the day', following the dissolution of the 1629 parliament.[3] Since Gardiner wrote, the complex and ambivalent forces acting upon early Stuart common lawyers have been more closely examined, while some historians have recently questioned the extent and significance of political divisions within England before 1640 and their connection with the outbreak of hostilities in 1642. So it is hardly surprising that a recent survey of the political role of common lawyers under James and Charles I should cautiously conclude that in politics, as much else, 'diversity was an important feature of the early modern legal profession'.[4]

Yet it is still not entirely clear that the concept of an alliance between common lawyers and parliamentary opponents of the would-be absolutism of the early Stuarts must be abandoned as mere Whig myth. Even the arch-revisionist Conrad Russell admits the 'exceptional dominance' of common lawyers in the 1628 parliament, while maintaining (reasonably enough) that outside the House, lawyers were by no means united behind Sir Edward Coke's view of the law's supreme role in the constitution.[5] No doubt the early seventeenth-century legal profession was internally divided in this as in other respects. Yet on balance its members may still have played a more significant role as critics and opponents than as supporters of James I, Charles I, and their governments. Before attempting to determine whether this was in fact the case, however, it will be helpful to take a general view of the involvement of early modern common lawyers in administration and politics.

i. Roles and functions: local government

Lawyers have played an active part in public life throughout the Western world since the Middle Ages. The growth of centralized

[2] C. H. McIlwain, 'The English Common Law, Barrier against Absolutism', *AHR*, xli (1943), 23–31; C. Ogilvie, *The King's Government and the Common Law 1471–1641* (Oxford, 1958), chs. 17–19. The phrase quoted is from A. K. Kiralfy, *Potter's Historical Introduction to English Law and its Institutions* (1958), 43. (I owe this reference to Professor Levack.)
[3] Gardiner, *History*, vii. 220–4; Aylmer, *King's Servants*, 56–7; Prestwich, *Cranfield*, 93–102, 140–1; Clark, *Provincial Society*, 290–4.
[4] Brooks, 'Common Lawyers in England', 59–60.
[5] C. Russell, *Parliaments and English Politics 1621–1629* (Oxford, 1979), 349–63.

states depended upon a pool of literate and worldly men, able to help rulers formulate policy and to oversee its implementation. While churchmen at first monopolized these roles, princes jealous of their sovereignty turned increasingly to men of the long robe as councillors, secretaries, and bureaucrats of all kinds. According to Weber, everywhere in Western Europe, 'political management in the direction of the evolving rational state has been borne by trained jurists'.[6]

The usual title for members of the bar during our period was 'counsellor', the same term used for the advisers of monarchs and magnates. This may not have been entirely accidental, given the intensive involvement of early modern common lawyers in all facets of public life. The theoretical correlate of that social fact appears plainly in the opening sentence of an essay written by Sir Anthony Benn, recorder of London from 1616 until his death two years later: 'The end that every good lawyer ought to propose to himself in the course of his calling is not so much to gain, nor yet to direct a client in his course and process of a suit, as to be able to govern and assist his country with profitable and good counsel.' This was hardly a novel idea. Sir Thomas Elyot's enormously influential *Boke named the Gouvernour* (1531) had advocated training well-born youths in law and the liberal arts to produce a generation of statesmen rivalling the best the ancient world had known. The notion of an intimate link between legal knowledge and government was sufficiently well established by 1559 for an anonymous author to argue that 'none except he be immediately descended from a nobleman or gentleman' should be permitted to study the laws, since 'they are the entries to rule and government'. In 1596 the benchers of Gray's Inn justified their refusal to elect a senior barrister to their number on the grounds that 'he is not fit . . . to be employed at such services of the commonwealth as are expected to be performed by men of such place'.[7]

So the association between government and the legal profession was conceived of in quite practical terms. Lawyers could expect to be

---

[6] Bouwsma, 'Lawyers and Culture', 309–11; M. Weber, 'Politics as a Vocation', in *From Max Weber*, ed. H. H. Gerth and C. W. Mills (New York, 1958), 93. Cf. L. Martines, *Lawyers and Statecraft in Renaissance Florence* (Princeton, 1968), esp. chs. 5–8; G. Dahm, 'On the Reception of Roman and Italian Law in Germany', in *Pre-Reformation Germany*, ed. G. Strauss (1972), 285–313; R. Bonney, *Political Change in France Under Richelieu and Mazarin* (Oxford, 1978), 90.

[7] Benn, 'Essays', fol. 23; HMC, *Hatfield*, i. 163; *GIPB*, i. 123.

involved in government primarily because government was carried on in legal institutions and according to legal forms. From manorial, hundred and county courts, quarter sessions, and assizes, to the Privy Council and the High Court of Parliament, public administration was inextricably caught up in the terminology and procedures of the law. Conversely, what happened in the lawcourts had considerable significance for the public realm, which explains why more than half of Sir Thomas Smith's constitutional handbook *De Republica Anglorum* (1583) is concerned with the detailed workings of the legal system.

Common lawyers played a particularly important role in local government, as county JPs and recorders of urban boroughs. Their professional expertise was recognized as a specific qualification for both offices; from the late fourteenth century all commissions of the peace were required by statute to include at least two 'men of the law' in the quorum, and where royal charters gave towns the right to appoint a recorder, the grant usually prescribed that the office must go to a man 'learned in the laws'. As far as JPs were concerned, the minimum statutory requirement was almost invariably exceeded during our period; indeed, as an Elizabethan observer remarked, 'The policy of this government hath made a special choice of lawyers to be justices of the peace'.[8]

The proportion of lawyers to laymen JPs varied quite markedly in different parts of the country, although tending to rise overall from the mid-sixteenth century onwards. One published survey of commissions from six counties shows that those classified as lawyers (that is, practising barristers and serjeants) increased from about 14 per cent in 1562 to 21 per cent in 1636, although at the latter date the numbers of barrister JPs in each shire surveyed still ranged from two out of thirty-five for Worcestershire to sixteen out of sixty-two for Norfolk. There may have been occasional exceptions to this general growth in legal representation on the bench, especially in remoter counties where resident barristers were few and far between; again, a slight drop in the proportion of lawyers in commission has been detected following the criticisms of their increasing presence voiced

---

[8] E. W. Ives, 'The Law and the Laywers', in *Shakespeare in His Own Age*, ed. A. Nicoll (1964), 73–6. W. Lambard, *Eirenarcha: Or, of the Office of the Justices of Peace* (1581), 46–7; G. Whetstone, *The English Myrror* (1586), 233. Cf. Ellesmere 6091, Edward Hake to Thomas Egerton, n.d. [*c.*1580]: 'I being by degree and calling a counsellor of the law . . . the laws of this realm do thereby enable me . . . for a justice of the peace.'

in the 1621 parliament. But the general trend is unmistakable.[9] The increase resulted primarily from deliberate government policy, helped along by the occasional urgings of assize judges, the growing number of lawyers available (and presumably often pressing) for appointment, and—as Michael Dalton suggested in the preface to his *The Countrey Justice* (1618)—some greater reluctance on the part of 'divers both honourable and worthy persons', who 'for want of knowledge of the many and particular statutes in force . . . do seek to be exempt out of the commission of the peace'.[10]

The key point is not just the rising number of lawyers on each commission (many of whose members were in any case national dignitaries who took little interest in local affairs), but rather the nature of the lawyers' contribution to the routine work of the justices. Here, most available research points in the same direction. According to Quintrell, the Essex bench (whose active membership in the middle of James I's reign included some sixteen counsellors, or about one third of the total) was dominated in the 1630s by William Towse and John Darcy, two serjeants at law who 'by weight of experience as much as by social rank were the natural leaders of the county'. In pre-Civil War Wiltshire, barristers were 'by far the most active' JPs and, as assiduous attenders at quarter sessions, 'increasingly dominated the decisions' of the bench. Their counterparts in Sussex tended to be 'outstandingly industrious' and 'exceptionally diligent', usually chairing quarter sessions. The Somerset bench during the 1620s and 30s was chaired by two barristers holding the office of deputy *Custos Rotulorum*, the outspoken Hugh Pyne and the later Long Parliament MP John Harington; only three quarter sessions between 1625 and 1638 saw no lawyers at all in attendance.[11]

[9] J. H. Gleason, *The Justices of the Peace in England, 1558–1640* (Oxford, 1969), 49–51; some judges and office-holders classified here as 'court' might equally well be grouped with the lawyers. Cf. Dias, thesis, 71–2, 125; H. A. Lloyd, *The Gentry of South-West Wales 1540–1640* (Cardiff, 1968), 144.

[10] Dalton, *Countrey Justice*, sig. [A6ᵛ]. Harleian 286, fol. 197.

[11] B. W. Quintrell, 'The Government of the County of Essex, 1603–1642', University of London Ph.D. thesis, 1965, 44–5; *idem*, 'The Making of Charles I's Book of Orders', *EHR* xcv (1980), 559 n.; A. D. Wall, 'The Wiltshire Commission of the Peace: A Study of Its Social Structure', University of Melbourne MA thesis, 1966, 119–21, 129–34; Fletcher, *Sussex*, 220; Barnes, *Somerset*, 70–1; (John Farwell and Robert Cuffe, who served as chairmen in Harington's occasional absences, were also barristers: see Appendices D and E below); Clark, *Provincial Society*, 279–80; B. J. Richmond, 'The Work of the Justices of the Peace in Hampshire 1603–1640', University of Southampton M.Phil. thesis, 1969, 109.

In poorer and more remote counties, which supported fewer barristers, those who did reach the bench may have exercised slightly less influence than elsewhere. Thus Morrill notes that in Cheshire during the 1620s and 30s no core of 'professional' JPs emerged; indeed, only three justices, none of them barristers, attended sessions more than twice a year on the average after their apppointment. In other parts of the country there may have been some occasional resentment at the heightened involvement of the legal profession in county administration, but what little evidence there is also suggests that most lay justices respected and valued the contribution of their barrister colleagues.[12] Some lawyers tended to restrict their activities to quarter sessions and assizes, leaving routine out-of-sessions work to more leisured neighbours; but of course it was precisely when the bench gathered as a corporate body that questions of general policy were decided and county opinion mobilized. We can hardly doubt that the leadership role of barrister JPs extended to these occasions. It seems to have been a combination of puritan conscience and common-law principles which gradually led a group of Norfolk justices to adopt a constitutionalist opposition stance at their quarter sessions in the later years of Elizabeth's reign. Hugh Pyne chose to launch his attack upon forced loans and the duke of Buckingham at the Ilchester quarter sessions of 1626. It cannot be proven, but it is at least plausible that the lawyer MPs of Somerset and Devon prominent among the signatories to petitions from the justices of those counties protesting against the illegality of the 1614 benevolence were the prime movers in this act of resistance.[13] Of course the qualities which enabled lawyers to take the lead among their colleagues on the bench were not invariably exercised in hostile response to central government policies, although it is difficult to take wholly at face value the fascinating account by Richard Taylor, a bencher of Lincoln's Inn and MP for Bedford in the 1620s, of a meeting between justices from six Bedfordshire hundreds, and 'the

[12] J. S. Morrill, *Cheshire 1630–1660* (1974), 9; cf. Dias, thesis, 92, 125; Barnes, *Somerset*, 46; *CD 1621*, iii. 113, 427; Wall, thesis, 131; Clark, *Provincial Society*, 396; Brooks, 'Common Lawyers in England', 58; Bodl. MS Douce 280, fol. 6ᵛ.

[13] Smith, *County and Court*, 339–40, and pt. III, *passim*; Barnes, *Somerset*, 34; Yonge, *Diary*, 110, 114; Ellesmere 2504–5. Among the 30 Devon JPs signing, the following barristers can be identified: Henry Rolle, William Bastard, Francis Fulforde, Arthur Harris (?), Richard Reynell, James Welshe, and Humphrey Were; among 33 Somerset JPs were the barristers Sir Edward Hext, Thomas Warre, Thomas Southworth, Robert Cuffe, Humphrey Wyndham, James Bisse, and William Swanton.

most able and sufficient gentlemen and householders' in August 1626, at which he claimed to have acted as 'spokesman' in a vain attempt to break the resolution of the subsidy men, 'not to give to his majesty . . . but in a parliamentary way'.[14]

JPs were mainly country residents and rulers. True, county commissions often included one or more borough recorders, while many towns had their own commission of the peace, usually comprising the mayor or other chief elected office-holder, the recorder or chief legal officer, and some, if not all, aldermen. However, the posts available to practising barristers in towns had fees attached, whereas a place on the county bench was honorific as well as honourable, carrying no salary and bestowing only indirect rewards on its holder. Another difference was that appointments of recorders, stewards, fee'd counsel, and town clerks were made by the borough's rulers, not the central government, even if courtiers and the Crown might bring considerable pressure to bear on their decisions. Finally, and again in sharp contrast to the county JP post, offices in towns, once acquired, were often regarded in practice as the incumbent's freehold, to be enjoyed for life and perhaps even passed on (with the town's agreement) to a successor of his own choosing.[15]

It has been estimated that the number of recorderships sanctioned by royal charter jumped from fifteen to over fifty in the course of the sixteenth century, with about the same number of posts being added in the seventeenth century prior to 1660. These figures undoubtedly understate the numbers of urban openings for barristers during our period. Many recorderships were originally instituted without warrant from the Crown, and some continued on that informal basis

---

[14] C. D. Gilmore, 'The Papers of Richard Taylor of Clapham', *Beds. Hist. Rec. Soc.*, xxv (1947), 107–8.

[15] For general discussions of lawyers and urban office-holding, see Ives, thesis, ch. 7; M. V. Jones, 'The Political History of the Parliamentary Boroughs of Kent 1642–1662', University of London Ph.D. thesis, 1967, ch. 7; Clark, *Provincial Society*, 281, 289, 298; Holmes, *Seventeenth-Century Lincolnshire*, 49–50. For county commissions and recorders, see Barnes, *Somerset*, 49. For modes of appointment and tenure of recorders, see W. B. Willcox, *Gloucestershire: A Study in Local Government 1590–1640* (New Haven, 1940), 207; *Durham Civic Memorials*, ed. C. E. Whiting (Surtees Soc., 1952), 4–6; C. Brown, *A History of Newark-on-Trent* (1905–7), 31; SP 14/134/125 (Evesham, 1622); Norfolk RO Norwich City Records 17b, City Revenue and Letters, fols. 2–3; H. Manship, *The History of Great Yarmouth*, ed. C. J. Palmer (Yarmouth, 1854), 372; Lincs. RO, LI/1/4, fol. 81ᵛ, and STAC 8/98/9; Guilding, ed., *Reading Records*, ii. 9–10.

(as, for example, at Ipswich, Leominster, and Sandwich).[16] Some towns retained legal advisers under another title, but they filled the same functions as recorders elsewhere; at East Retford, Lichfield, Lymington, and Stratford-upon-Avon, for instance, the officer in question was known as 'steward', and at Kidderminster as 'under-steward', while at Colchester and Devizes the position of town clerk was equivalent to that of recorder. Charters commonly prescribed that the recorder was to be 'an upright and discreet man learned in the laws of England', or words to that effect. But where the office was essentially honorific, or in practice reserved for a prominent courtier or local magnate, as at Barnstaple, Liskeard, Warwick, and Yarmouth, the relevant administrative and judicial functions would be discharged by a barrister-deputy, and likewise in many towns where the recorder, although a barrister, was not a local resident.[17] In addition, most urban boroughs offered one, two, or more barristers occasional employment and the title of learned, fee'd, or town counsellor, with the payment of a small annual retainer. During the early seventeenth century the place of town clerk, although more typically occupied by an attorney, was also some-times held by a barrister, not only in such major metropolitan centres as London and Bristol, but also at Dover, Plymouth, and Worcester, among others.[18]

The increased opportunities for lawyers to be formally associated with town life during the early modern period were in part simply a consequence of the two hundred or so town charters granted by the Tudors and Stuarts. Indeed, recorderships tended to become some-thing of a civic status symbol, although their importance was far

[16] Ives, thesis, 358–60; G. F. Townsend, *The Town and Borough of Leominster* (Leominster, 1863), 77; R. L. Cross, *Justice in Ipswich 1200–1968* (Ipswich, 1968), 19; W. Boys, *Collections for An History of Sandwich in Kent* (Canterbury, 1792), 423; Kent AO, Sa Ac/7, fol. 24ᵛ.

[17] Cf. J. S. Piercy, *The History of Retford* (Retford, 1828), 43; T. Harwood, *The History and Antiquities of the Church and City of Lichfield* (Gloucester, 1806), 437–9; *VCH, War.*, iii. 249–50; Gribble, *Memorials of Barnstaple*, 297–9; Cornwall RO, B/Liskeard/268–9, 272, 276, 280, 285; E. O. King, *Old Times Revisited in the Borough and Parish of Lymington* (1879), 48; B. H. Cunnington, *Some Annals of the Borough of Devizes . . . 1555–1791* (Devizes, 1925), viii; J. R. Burton, *A History of Kidderminster* (1890), 74; E. Fripp, *Shakespeare, Man and Artist* (1964), ii. 762; P. C. Heap, 'The Politics of Stuart Warwickshire', Yale University Ph.D. thesis, 1975, 90–7, 104–6; Morant, *Essex*, i. 52, 104, App. 5.

[18] Jones, thesis, 333; Bacon, *Annalls of Ipswche*, 408; *The Chamber Order Book of Worcester*, ed. S. Bond (Worcs. Hist. Soc., 1974), 29–31; Sacks, thesis, 82–4; B. R. Masters, 'The Town Clerk', *Guildhall Miscellany*, iii (1969), 62–3, 72–3.

from merely symbolic. The sixteenth-century litigation explosion and the growing complexity of the common law itself had a discernible impact on many towns, as they sought to defend themselves against ancient or upstart economic rivals, to maintain control of local markets and manufacturing activity, and to suppress internal challenges to their increasingly exclusive ruling oligarchies. The determination of the Tudors to extend their authority into every aspect and corner of national life also made it vital for towns to have a man knowledgeable both in the laws and the ways of the great world to give advice at home and represent their interests in London.

If these were among the reasons why towns sought to add barristers to their payrolls in the sixteenth and early seventeenth centuries, it is perhaps less easy to see why lawyers themselves so eagerly sought recorderships and other municipal offices. After all, the annual stipend attached to such positions rarely exceeded £10, and recorders were frequently required to undertake that they would reside within the town boundaries.[19] Yet a vacant recordership regularly attracted a number of hopeful applicants, who busily lobbied the electors, and enlisted influential patrons to commend their suits.[20] Part of the answer is that, as with most contemporary offices, the salary comprised only a fraction of the total income attached to the position. Recorders usually received a fixed percentage of all fees payable by litigants in the town courts at every procedural step and for every necessary document. In addition, the recorder might enjoy rights to nominate the town clerk, the clerk or clerks of the courts, and perhaps even the attorneys who pleaded before them. Other substantial perquisites of office often included

---

[19] Samples of the annual fees paid to recorders are £1. 6s. 8d. (Bedford and Durham, early seventeenth century), £2 (Newark, 1559), £3. 6s. 8d. (Woodstock, 1609), £5. 6s. 8d. (Oxford, 1622), £10 (Kingston-upon-Thames, 1618, Beverley 1609, Exeter 1636–7), and £13. 6s. 8d. (York, late sixteenth and early seventeenth centuries). Whiting, ed., *Durham Memorials*, 5; *The Minute Book of Bedford Corporation, 1647–1664*, ed. G. C. Parsloe (Beds. Hist. Rec. Soc., 1949); G. C. Parsloe, 'The Growth of a Borough Constitution: Newark-upon-Trent, 1549–1688', *TRHS*, 4th ser. xxii (1940), 180; A. Ballard, *Chronicles of the Royal Borough of Woodstock* (1896), 35; Salter, ed., *Oxford Council Acts*, 418; Surrey RO, Kingston Borough Archives, KD5/1/1, fol. 385; *Beverley Borough Records 1575–1821*, ed. J. Dennett (Yorks. Arch. Soc., Rec. Ser., 1933), 101; Devon RO, ECA, Receiver's Accounts, 1636–7; Palliser, *Tudor York*, 74; *VCH, York*, 185.

[20] Cf. *Records of the Borough of Leicester . . . 1603–1688*, ed. H. Stocks and W. H. Stevenson (Cambridge, 1923), 5–6; *A Calendar to the Records of the Borough of Doncaster*, ed. W. J. Le Hardy (Doncaster, 1899–1903), iv. 121; Hants RO, 44M69/xxxii/20(3); Brown, *Newark-on-Trent*, ii. 31; York City AO, House Books B34, fol. 324 and B35, fols. 325ᵛ–326.

preferential leases of town lands and a burgess's seat in parliament, as well as lavish entertainments and occasional presents of cash or consumables (typically wine, sugar-loaves, or local fish and game).[21] Besides these material benefits, a recorder (and to a lesser extent a fee'd counsellor) derived considerable prestige from his office, which served both to advertise and increase his practice. When Henry Sherfield was elected recorder of Salisbury in 1623, five years after becoming recorder of Southampton, his brother Richard wrote to him in terms which leave no doubt as to the perceived significance of this promotion for his future career:

Although you gave me no employment in the action of recordership . . . this night I lay at Salisbury in your house to expect the fortune of the morning. Which proved so happily that about eleven of the clock in this forenoon you are chosen recorder, and not with any hazard in respect of number. It is not ordinary, if we look backwards, that a good prophet should be so esteemed in his own country . . . you know the place and reputation of the place, but surely both are nothing, being compared with the love that hath begot them both. . . . Be you assured that your strength in your country will be noted by the rank of great persons.[22]

An admirable reconstruction of Sherfield's leading role in the efforts of a group of godly citizens to establish an ambitious scheme for the relief and regulation of the Salisbury poor during the 1620s was published some years ago.[23] But how usual was it for recorders and other lawyers holding urban office to be so intimately involved with the affairs of 'their' town? After all, the recorder was very much a part-time official, as has been remarked in the case of Ludlow, where recorders did not even consistently discharge in person their sole formal responsibility of presiding over gaol deliveries. It ap-

---

[21] For fees, see Guilding, ed., *Reading Records*, i. 226; F. Foster, 'Merchants and Bureaucrats in Elizabethan London', *Guildhall Miscellany*, iv (1972), 153 n.; Surrey RO, Kingston Borough Archives, KB 14/1, 'A Table of all such ordinarie fees . . .'. For patronage, see SP 12/150/83; *Calendar of the Chester City Council Minutes 1603–1642*, ed. M. J. Groombridge (Lancs. and Ches. Rec. Soc., 1956), xvii–xviii; J. Scott, *Berwick upon Tweed* (1888), 482; J. K. Hedges, *The History of Wallingford* (1881), ii. 243. For perquisites, see Clark, *Provincial Society*, 286; Lincs. RO, L1/1/4, fols. 4, 12, 13ᵛ; B. B. Woodward, T. C. Wilks, and C. S. Lockhart, *A General History of Hampshire* (1861–9), ii. 111–12n.; *The Municipal Records of the Borough of Dorchester*, ed. C. H. Mayo (Exeter, 1908), 455; Sydenham, *History of Poole*, 254; Suffolk RO (Bury St Edmunds), D6/4/1 (6b), 'A Bill of Charges for . . . Sr Thomas Richardson knight Recorder for the Burghe of Burye St Edmondes . . . 1623'.

[22] Hants RO, 44M69/xxxii/19.

[23] P. Slack, 'Poverty and Politics in Salisbury 1597–1666', in *Crisis and Order in English Towns 1500–1700*, ed. P. Clark and P. Slack (1972), 183–6.

pears that the recorder of Bath's 'only real duty was to attend the court of quarter sessions next after the election of the mayor and administer the oath to him', while another authority tells us that the offices of recorder and town counsel at Ipswich were 'largely honorific and advisory'.[24]

Many town corporations evidently experienced considerable difficulty and frustration from the habitual absence or only intermittent attendance of their recorders. Thus in 1612 the rulers of Lincoln minuted that

> this city hath not had for these many years past any help or advice of George Anton esq., recorder there, either in keeping their sessions of the peace or otherwise in their courts or affairs, though they have had many great occasions to stand in need thereof and to crave the same, and yet have borne with his not using the said place and office, though the fees of the same have been continually paid to him, and thereby have been enforced to be very troublesome to divers others learned in the law to no small charge of this city.

This problem was less severely felt in the very largest centres. London is the chief case in point; the City drew on a national pool of talent to fill its twenty or so specialized legal offices, and population size alone guaranteed an attractively high volume of litigation and fees for its learned counsel. Determined to keep the reins of government firmly in their own hands, London's wealthy, self-confident merchant-rulers confined their salaried legal officers to an essentially apolitical, bureaucratic role. It has been observed that unlike 'modern boards of experts', the City's legal staff did not 'devise plans and recommend them to the politicians for enactment. Initiative and final authority remained with the aldermen'.[25]

The situation was similar in Bristol, Norwich, and York. There, recorders, stewards, and fee'd counsel did not normally sit on the corporation's governing body (although occasionally attending its meetings), and while often recruited from the surrounding hinterland, came sometimes from rather further afield; thus Sir Laurence and Sir Nicholas Hyde, successively recorders of Bristol from 1605 to 1630, lived in south Wiltshire and Hampshire respectively, while

---

[24] P. Williams, 'Government and Politics in Ludlow 1590–1642', *Trans. Salop. Arch. and Nat. Hist. Soc.*, lvi (1960), 283; A. J. King and B. H. Watts, *The Municipal Records of Bath* (1885), 44; M. Reed, 'Ipswich in the Seventeenth Century', Leicester University Ph.D. thesis, 1973, 221.

[25] HMC, *Fourteenth Rep.*, viii. 86, Foster, *Politics of Stability*, 86–7.

their successor Sir John Glanville hailed from Devon. If they did not usually reside in the city, or even spend much time there out of term, that was not necessarily a serious handicap, since their formal judicial responsibilities could always be discharged by a deputy. In any case, the recorders of such large provincial capitals were primarily expected to represent and safeguard their city's interests in London, whether before the lawcourts, at sessions of parliament, or by lobbying influential courtiers, ministers, and law officers.[26]

Smaller, less prosperous, and more isolated communities generally lacked the resources to support a large team of learned counsel, while their rulers also sometimes lacked the self-confidence and civic pride which enabled aldermen in the urban first league to deal with barristers on a nearly equal footing. This perhaps explains why they were more likely to insist that their recorder or steward become a freeman and reside within the town, or at least undertake to be present for quarter sessions and the gaol delivery, stipulations which, besides their obvious functional utility, must have helped induce a greater sense of dependence on the part of the lawyer concerned. Unless it was extremely small and poor, like most of the Welsh and some West Country boroughs and the Cinque Ports, the recorder might be already resident in the town or on its outskirts at the time of his appointment. Some cities and towns, including Chester, Hull, and Worcester, habitually filled the office with native-born sons of civic families. Indeed, the post was occasionally handed down from father to son, as with the Lanys at Ipswich and the Keelings at Hertford.[27]

In such circumstances, recorders and stewards could hardly remain aloof from day-to-day administrative concerns and political

---

[26] Sacks, thesis, 88–9. Serjeant Richard Hutton expressed some reluctance to accept the recordership of York in 1608, considering 'the place of my dwelling, the occasions of my absence out of the country and your continual use of counsel and assistance'; nevertheless, he took the post, receiving two years later an increased stipend to provide a deputy who could attend sittings of the sheriffs' court on a regular basis. (York City AO, House Book B33, fols. 133–4, 216–19ᵛ.) MacCaffrey, *Exeter*, 50–1.

[27] Cf. HMC, *Ninth Rep.*, i, 256, and *Fourteenth Rep.*, viii. 276; *The History and Antiquities of Southampton . . . by John Speed, M.D.*, ed. E. R. Aubrey (Southampton, 1909), 49; *The First Ledger Book of High Wycombe*, ed. R. W. Greaves (Bucks. Rec. Soc., 1958), 167; Manship, *Yarmouth*, 372; Brown, *Newark-on-Trent*, ii. 31; J. Lawson, *A Town Grammar School through Six Centuries* (1963), 156; *Beverley Borough Records*, 101–3; Bond, ed., *Order Book of Worcester*, 29; Bacon, *Annalls of Ipswch*, 341, 524, 531; L. Turnor, *History of the Ancient Town and Borough of Hertford* (Hertford, 1830), 122.

conflicts, especially when their duties included attending meetings of the governing body (as at Leicester, Lincoln, Oxford, and Reading), or nominating aldermen (as at Salisbury), or again, if they simultaneously held other urban offices, like James Franklin at Maidstone and Robert Brerewood at Chester.[28] While recorders might profess concern for 'good success in the government of our mother city' (Thomas Lawton, recorder of Chester, 1605), or that citizens would 'rather continue in the fair way of unity than discontent and distraction' (William Denny, steward of Norwich, 1623), they themselves were often storm-centres in the factional struggles which plagued many early modern towns. For the decade after 1619 there is evidence of serious disputes involving the recorders of Abingdon, Canterbury, Chester, Chichester, Oxford, and Reading, all except the last being the subjects of petitions to, and orders from, the Privy Council.[29]

If these conflicts are evidence of the recorder's absorption in the turbulence of urban life, they also reflect his strategic political importance within the civic community. While the recorder's office was part-time, it was permanent and typically held for life. The power and prestige of the position were visibly attested whenever the recorder, robed in his red gown, gave the charge at quarter sessions, sentenced convicted felons, administered oaths to incoming mayors and officers, acted as the town's orator on royal visits, or merely joined with the mayor, schoolmaster, 'and others intelligent and judicious' in electing a scholarship boy to Oxford. Usually taking precedence next after the mayor on formal municipal occasions, the recorder was indeed the mayor's natural ally and counsellor 'concerning the government of the borough, as well in matters of law and otherwise', to quote the minute of John Moore's appointment as steward of Lymington in 1607.[30]

[28] *Records of Leicester . . . 1603–88*, 254; Lincs. RO, L/1/1/4, fol. 21; Salter, ed., *Oxford Council Acts*, 110; Guilding, ed., *Reading Records*, ii, *passim; VCH, Wilts.*, vi. 105; *Records of Maidstone: Being Selections from Documents in the Possession of the Corporation* (Maidstone, 1926), 101; Groombridge, ed., *Chester City Minutes*, 89.

[29] Chester City RO, ML/2/175; Norfolk RO, Norwich City Records 17b, City Revenue and Letters, fol. 37; *APC 1628–9*, 651, 667; A. C. Baker, *Historic Abingdon* (Abingdon, n.d.), 11–12; *APC 1619–21*, 31, 61, 65; *APC 1627*, 157, 372, 484–5; Fletcher, *Sussex*, 238; D. Hirst, *The Representative of the People?* (Cambridge, 1975), 205; Guilding, ed., *Reading Records*, ii. 106–17, 122–33, 327.

[30] For gown, see York City AO, House Book B36, fol. 62. For royal visits, see *Records of the Borough of Nottingham*, ed. W. H. Stevenson *et al.* (Nottingham, 1882–1956), iv. 411; *The Black Book of Warwick*, ed. T. Kemp (Warwick, 1898), 87–92; *Mr.*

Henry Sherfield received regular bulletins of news and queries from successive mayors of Southampton, who sought his services as arbitrator in an involved dispute with the city's wine merchants, and his advice on handling obstreperous aldermen like Mr Long, who evidently challenged the recorder's authority with the question, 'Must we be ruled all by one man? (meaning yourself)'. When Francis Parlett swore in the new mayor of King's Lynn in 1633, he delivered a lengthy homily on the duties of the mayoral office, especially urging the suppression of schismatical offenders against Church doctrine and discipline, an enterprise in which 'I shall be ready upon just cause of complaint to join with you and assist you'.[31]

Urban office-holding lawyers were likely to bring a broader perspective to bear on the problems of towns than most members of civic governing bodies. Precisely what part they took in drafting and implementing the schemes for discouraging drunkenness, setting the poor to work, and generally establishing 'better government', which were so widely adopted by towns during our period is often difficult to say, but the words and actions of Henry Sherfield at Salisbury, John Bradshaw at Congleton, Francis Harvey at Leicester, Rice Gwynn at Norwich, and Talbot Pepys at Cambridge exemplify concerns and initiatives in these areas undoubtedly shared by many lawyers with urban connections.[32]

The influence which recorders and other lawyers could bring to bear on town affairs obviously depended in part on their experience and standing outside those towns. Unlike his nominal masters, the recorder or steward did not reach his exalted position by slowly ascending a hierarchial ladder of guild and minor civic offices. His election, unlike theirs, was an extraordinary event, not a standard

Charles Dallison, *Recorder of Lincoln, His Speech to the Kings Majesty* (1642); Guilding, ed., *Reading Records*, ii. 38. At York in 1625 it was 'agreed that the wife of him that shall be now chosen recorder of this city shall take her place next unto the Ladys, and before such aldermens' wives as have not been Lord Mayor'. (House Book B34, fol. 324ᵛ.) As recorder of Exeter, Sir John Hele had a yearly allowance of '8 salmons of the river of Exe, which is the like number that is allowed unto the mayor of this city' (Devon RO, ECA, Act Book B 1/5, fol. 259ᵛ). King, *Old Times in Lymington*, 41.

[31] Hants RO, 44M69/xxxv/3, and *passim*; 44M69/xxxvi; Norfolk RO, King's Lynn Borough Archives, Recorder's Notebook, fol. 9. For Sherfield's award in Southampton's dispute with the wine merchants, cf. HMC, *Eleventh Rep.*, iii. 95.

[32] Cf. Slack, 'Poverty and Politics', 183–6; Head, *Congleton*, 79–83; *Records of Leicester ... 1603–88*, 160; Norfolk RO, Norwich City Records 17b, City Revenue and Letters, fol. 36ᵛ; C. H. Cooper, *Annals of Cambridge* (Cambridge, 1842–1908), iii. 218–19. Cf. Williams, 'Government in Ludlow', 285; *Records of Maidstone*, 233.

feature of the municipal calendar. Educational background and
social standing also set him apart to some extent; the recorder of
Winchester dismissed from office in 1657 for defaming the citizenry
as 'a company of beggarly fellows' was exceptionally outspoken, but
may have been voicing sentiments shared by a good many of his
counterparts elsewhere.[33] The recorder's role as chief urban am-
bassador further emphasized his ambivalent status; unlike many
townsfolk, his life and work regularly extended to a wider world
beyond the city walls.

The range of 'external' business referred to recorders for their
advice and assistance was not confined to opinions on doubtful
points of law and suits already in process. Recorders played an
essential part in the complex and protracted negotiations required
for the grant of a new charter, in lobbying for private acts of
parliament, and for the appointment of civic worthies as JPs.[34] They
were also the chief channel of communication between towns and
assize judges; in 1627 the mayor and corporation of Salisbury wrote
to Henry Sherfield entreating his 'direction and advice' to prevent
the removal of the Wiltshire assizes from their city, requesting 'if you
conceive it fittest, to petition unto their lordships, that you give us
your direction herein and the manner thereof, for that we know not
how to give them their styles and titles as you do'.[35]

While the recorder's function as broker or intermediary might
seem to have distanced and separated him from the town which he
represented in the outside world, his effectiveness in this role
depended not merely on the possession of certain personal and
professional skills, but also on an ability to maintan a credible image
of concern for, and identification with, the interests of that town. In
other words, recorders needed both to translate legal complexities
and political subtleties into terms which their citizen clients could

[33] C. Bailey, *Transcripts from the Municipal Archives of Winchester* (Winchester, 1856), 64.
[34] Neither S. Bond and N. Evans, 'The Process of Granting Charters to English Boroughs', *EHR*, xci (1976), 102–20, nor R. Tittler, 'The Incorporation of Boroughs 1540–1558', *History*, lxii (1977), 24–42, make specific reference to recorders in this context, but cf. Norfolk RO, Norwich Chamberlain's Accounts, 1589–90; R. C. Latham, *Bristol Charters 1509–1899* (Bristol Rec. Soc., 1947), 16; Hoare, *Modern Wiltshire*, vi. 312; W. B. Bridges *et al.*, *Some Account of the Barony and Town of Okehampton*, ed. W. H. Wright (Tiverton, 1889), 131; HMC, *Exeter*, 118, 121, 124, 132; *Weymouth and Melcombe Regis Minute Book*, ed. M. Weinstock (Dorset Rec. Soc., 1964), 26; Stevenson, ed., *Notts. Borough Records*, iv. 385.
[35] Hoare, *Old and New Sarum*, 364.

comprehend, and to ensure acceptance of that translation by presenting themselves as fully committed to upholding the town's
honour and well-being.[36]

Thus when in 1633 John Keeling upbraided the mayor and
burgesses of Hertford for failing to back up his efforts to prevent the
assizes being moved away to St Albans, he managed to suggest that
his concern for the town actually exceeded that of its ruling body:

... I expected to have heard from you many days since concerning this
business. ... I conceived that you respected it not in that you never made the
least overture of your desire, howbeit I have not been careless for the town
but have done my best endeavours ... and indeed within these three hours it
was my request before all the judges.

Again, when Timothy Turner addressed the mayor of Shrewsbury in
1639 urging him not to neglect the customary respects to the assize
judges, he began in the second person, but then changed to an
incorporative mode of address half way through his letter:

You know how you were blamed at the last assizes that you had not done
fitting observances to my lords the judges of our circuit in producing to them
our new charter, and presenting them with velvet coats, or to make them
coats; the things to be done are neither chargeable nor troublesome. The
displeasure that may increase by the neglect may be very prejudicial to our
town, and confirm our censure of pride. It is unsafe and indiscreet for us to
contend with judges. I pray you to consult with the company about it, and
resolve on a course to recover that we have lost.[37]

Such protestations of interdependence were doubtless rendered
more plausible by the fact that both Keeling and Turner lived at
least part of the year in the towns they served. Despite a well-
developed sense of social distinctions displayed by the profession at
large, however, recorders seem rarely to have adopted an arrogant
or blustering tone in their dealings with townsmen. On the contrary,
as is suggested by the presents of sugar-loaves, cash, and local
delicacies sent up by towns to furnish their recorders' readings at the
inns of court, and the charitable benefactions to towns which

[36] For some useful insights and parallels, see A. P. Cohen and J. L. Comaroff, 'The
Management of Meaning: On the Phenomenology of Political Transactions', in
*Transaction and Meaning: Directions in the Anthropology of Exchange and Symbolic
Behaviour*, ed. B. Kapferer (Philadelphia, 1976), 87–107.
[37] Herts. RO, Hertford Corporation Records, vol. 33, p. 19; HMC, *Fifteenth Rep.*,
x. 64. Cf. Chester City RO, ML/2/175.

recorders included in their wills, the relationship was often both close and cordial.[38]

It would be difficult to exaggerate the potential influence of common-lawyer office holders on the external relations of the towns with which they were associated. Even their insistence that town courts should adhere to 'the order of the common law' could have large implications for townsmens' relations with the Crown.[39] Recorders were likely to be at the forefront of resistance to invasions of municipal liberties and privileges, whether by the neighbouring cathedral, the JPs of the surrounding county, or the state itself.[40] It is hardly surprising that governments, both royal and parliamentary, sought to channel and constrain towns in appointing and dismissing the incumbents of such a crucial office, 'the only eyes of light and direction to cities and corporations', according to James I's Privy Councillors.[41] Elections to the recordership of London, a particularly important post, attracted royal intervention throughout the early seventeenth century. Sir James Whitelocke, an unsuccessful candidate, left a remarkably frank and graphic account of how, by the 'high hand' of the king himself, 'I was barred from that . . . which by the liberty of a subject was lawful for me to ask . . . and this as a revenge for doing my duty in parliament' (a reference to his outspokenness in 1610 and 1614). So the recorder of London inevitably came to be regarded as a court puppet, which helped ensure the rejection of Sir Thomas Gardiner, the Crown's favoured candidate for the speakership of the House of Commons, by the electors of London in the autumn of 1640.[42]

[38] Cf. Mayo, ed., *Records of Dorchester*, 455; Kingston-upon-Hull RO, Bench Book 4, fol. 305ᵛ; J. C. Cox, *The Records of the Borough of Northampton . . . 1550–1835* (1898), 105; Oxon. RO, Oxford Corporation MSS, Audit Book 1592–1682, fols. 211, 226, 253; Hants RO, 44M69/li/1. For benefactions, see e.g., PCC 44 Pile (Sir Francis Ashley), 49 St John (George Beare), 161 Gray (Ambrose Manaton), 10 Audley (Christopher Sherland), 46 Weldon (Francis Tate).
[39] Hardy, ed., *Records of Doncaster*, ii. 219–20; Additional 33512, fol. 45 (Nathaniel Finch to mayor of Sandwich, 28 May 1640).
[40] Cf. Weinstock, ed., *Weymouth and Melcombe Regis Minute Book*, 26; G. C. Moore Smith, *Club Law* (Cambridge, 1907), xxiv; Additional 19399, fol. 24 (Erasmus Earle to mayor of Norwich, 22 June 1647); Norfolk RO, Norwich City Records 17b, City Revenue and Letters, fols. 132–5; York City AO, House Book B36, fols. 41, 43; P. Slack, 'Religious Protest and Urban Authority: the Case of Henry Sherfield, Iconoclast', in *Studies in Church History*, ed. D. Baker (Cambridge, 1972), 297–8; J. S. Morrill, *The Revolt of the Provinces* (1976), 95.
[41] *APC 1599–1600*, 75; *APC 1619–21*, 31; Jones, thesis, 139–40; B. Poole, *Coventry: Its History and Antiquities* (1870), 369.
[42] V. Pearl, *London and the Outbreak of the Puritan Revolution* (1961), 66;

Similar pressures were felt even in provincial centres during the 1630s. According to Henry Sherfield's own account of a meeting in February 1633 with his colleague and old acquaintance William Noy (who, as attorney-general, had just presented the prosecution case at Sherfield's Star Chamber trial), he was 'moved and counselled' by Noy 'to resign my recordership, saying it would be well taken'. Sherfield suspected, and Noy did not deny, that 'it had pleased the king's majesty to express himself to him touching me', but refused to give up his place except at specific royal command. This the king was evidently reluctant to give (despite other tokens of his close interest and partisanship in the case), so Sherfield remained in office until his death a year later. The recordership of Salisbury then passed briefly to Edward Herbert, a rising Welsh lawyer lacking any local connections, except with the earl of Pembroke, high steward to the town. Herbert was succeeded in 1635 by Robert Hyde, whose father, also a successful barrister, kept a house in the cathedral close, and whose own High-Church sympathies were well known.

In both parliamentary elections of 1640, Hyde managed to stave off a strong campaign against him, led by the party of puritan oligarchs who had worked so harmoniously with Henry Sherfield. Hyde was accused of favouring the interests of the cathedral clergy against the town, as well as enthusiastically supporting the collection of ship-money. At the poll one hostile alderman was alleged to have said 'in very uncivil manner':

That it was no news to have the recorder of a town rejected, for the recorder of London was refused, and so was the recorder of Exeter, and divers others, and he knew no cause why their recorder should not be refused likewise . . . because that recorders were rising men and must serve the times.[43]

Only by successfully identifying himself with the interests of the town he served could a recorder hope to avoid imputations of the self-seeking ambition which proverbially characterized his profession. But where he did manage to present himself successfully as

Wh.telocke, *Lib. Fam.*, 63–9. Leics. RO, DG 7, Box 4966, Law 3 (Sir Heneage Finch's notes and speeches as recorder of London, 1621–7), which amply document Finch's lack of identification or involvement with civic interests). Gruenfelder, *Early Stuart Elections*, 197–8; Clarendon, *History*, i. 220–1.

[43] Hants RO, 44M69/xxv/6 (see also below, Appendix H); A. H. Dodd, 'Wales's Parliamentary Apprenticeship (1536–1625)', *Trans. Cymmrodorion Soc.* (1942), 70; G. A. Harrison, 'Royalist Organisation in Wiltshire 1642–1646', University of London Ph.D. thesis, 1963, 47; Hirst, *Representative of the People?*, 206–7; P. Slack, 'An Election to the Short Parliament', *BIHR*, xlvi (1973), 108–14.

benevolent patron or committed partner, the potential influence of a barrister holding urban office was very large indeed.

ii. *Roles and functions: central government*

During our period common lawyers were on the whole somewhat less prominent in central than in local government; an ambitious young Oxford student noted in the 1580s that they 'know how to use the forum, but not the court . . . involve themselves in services to the citizens, but not in offices of the palace'.[44] Some of the chief ministers to Elizabeth, James I, and Charles I could claim a brief exposure to the common law as students at the inns of court; but after Nicholas Bacon and William Cecil, no one who had actually practised at the bar reached a position comparable to that achieved by Thomas Cromwell under Henry VIII, or Dudley and Empson in the last years of Henry VII. Those few common lawyers who managed to gain some influence on the Privy Council or at court, notably Sir Thomas Egerton, Sir Henry Montagu, Sir James Ley, and William Noy, were more highly regarded as legal functionaries than as courtiers or statesmen; Sir Francis Bacon, the only possible exception to this generalization, was obsessed through his political career with demonstrating that his abilities far exceeded those of a mere lawyer.[45]

Bacon and any colleagues who nursed similar ambitions had to contend with the notorious antipathy of James I and Charles I for common lawyers. Not surprisingly, the monarchs' views were shared by their chief advisers. According to the royalist duke of Newcastle, Charles I was advised by Wentworth to 'have no lawyer of your privy council, for they did but distract state affairs'. Newcastle also told the young Charles II that Chief Justice Popham had been placed on Elizabeth's council at Robert Cecil's instigation, in the hope that he might act as a counterweight to Lord Keeper Egerton, who continually delayed government business with legal quibbles; but after a few years Popham and Egerton sank their personal differences and concerted their objections, so 'they were worse [off] than ever'. However apocryphal, these stories fit well with both Wentworth's professed aim to set his royal master's 'power and greatness . . . above the expositions of Sir Edward Coke and his year

---

[44] V. F. Stern, *Gabriel Harvey* (Oxford, 1979), 164.
[45] Cf. Ives, *Common Lawyers*, 420–1; Marwil, *Trials of Counsel*, 77, 134, and *passim*. Cf. Jones, '"The Great Gamaliel of the Law"', 217; Quintrell, 'Charles I's Book of Orders', 561.

books' and the ponderous unreality of Ellesmere's prescriptions for curing the nation's ills, now buried among his voluminous papers in the Huntington Library.[46]

When Bacon and his protégé Sir Anthony Benn promulgated the notion that common lawyers could and should be the prince's trusted servants, occasionally bending the strict letter of the law to meet pressing exigencies of state, they were plainly seeking to counter the prejudice that lawyers were at best technicians, incapable of seeing the political wood for the legal trees, besides the damaging suspicion that the expertise they possessed was as likely to be used in their own interests as those of their royal master. Hence Bacon's celebrated vision of the judges as lions under the throne, powerful instruments of executive authority, which was expressed with startling clarity in February 1640 by yet another of his former protégés, Lord Keeper Finch, when he informed the assize judges about to depart on their circuits: 'My Lords, it is your part to break the insolency of the vulgar before it approacheth too nigh the royal throne.'[47]

The one organ of central government in which common lawyers did play a prominent, and even crucial, role was parliament. Sitting next door to Westminster Hall, with committees frequently meeting at the inns of court, both Houses entrusted the formal conduct of their affairs to lawyers—the Chancellor and Speaker who chaired proceedings, the clerks who organized and recorded each day's business, the judges, serjeants, and masters in Chancery who acted as advisers and assistants to the Lords and as messengers between the two Houses. Throughout our period common lawyers comprised the largest identifiable status or occupational group in the Commons, next to the landed gentry, many of whom were themselves

[46] S. A. Strong, *Catalogue of Letters at Welbeck* (1903), App. I, 218–19; C. V. Wedgwood, *Thomas Wentworth* (1961), 40–2; Knowler, i. 201, 223; Knafla, *Law and Politics in Jacobean England*, esp. chs. 4–5, 11–13; W. J. Jones, 'Ellesmere and Politics, 1603–1617', in *Early Stuart Studies*, ed. H. S. Reinmuth (Minneapolis, 1970), 11–63.

[47] Bacon, *Works*, vi. 509–10, xiii. 206; Benn, 'Essays', fol. 23ᵛ: '... albeit it be the safest course ever to stand with the law and to hold the same firm and regular yet as occasion serveth the law must grow, must give place to the benefit of the common-weale ... the prince, the counsellor of a state, the judge or subordinate magistrate, for them it is more fit, more noble and free to moderate, dispense or to urge as occasions serve and not to be holden up to the dead letter of the law'. Leics. RO, DG 7, Box 4974, Lit. I, 'Sir John Finch ... his Speech to all the Judges of Engl: in the Starrechamber ... 13 February 1639'. On the assize judges as agents of royal policy, cf. Cockburn, *History of English Assizes*, pt. III.

members of an inn of court.[48] True, the majority of lawyer-MPs were not especially active, and left no significant or lasting imprint on proceedings, even if the taciturnity of Richard Trefusis of Lincoln's Inn, who sat for the Cornish borough of Camelford in the parliaments of 1584, 1586, and 1589 'without—as far as is known—contributing to the business of any of them', seems to have been exceptional.[49] The important point is that some barrister-MPs were always particularly busy and effective debaters and committee-men, not least on such crucial issues as monopolies in 1601, union with Scotland in 1607, and the legality of extra-parliamentary impositions in 1610. John Hoskyns of the Middle Temple and Thomas Wentworth of Lincoln's Inn were committed to the Tower for their part in the events which provoked James I to dissolve the Addled Parliament, while throughout the 1620s William Hakewill, John Glanville, Edward Littleton, William Noy, John Selden, Christopher Sherland, Henry Sherfield, and, above all, Sir Edward Coke made vital contributions to the deliberations of the Commons on a wide range of matters, most notably the impeachment of Buckingham and the Petition of Right. Only a few of these men were still alive and eligible for election as MPs by 1640, but the Long Parliament nevertheless included some outstanding barrister-politicians, among them John Pym's political heir Oliver St John and Edward Hyde, the *de facto* leader of the emergent royalist minority.[50]

Despite complaints about the Commons 'swarming with mercenary lawyers', the numerical prominence of counsellors-at-law in the parliaments of Elizabeth, James I, and Charles I was no novelty. In Henry VI's first parliament, we are told, 'men of the law constituted ... between a quarter and a fifth of the Commons', and lawyers have continued to gain election as MPs, if not always in such large proportions, down to the present day. Nor is it difficult to understand why: law and government were (and are) closely related in form and substance. The diaries and letters of early modern common lawyers shows that they talked politics a good deal; their travels between home, term, and circuit gave them access to much news,

---

[48] Jones, *Politics and the Bench*, 45–8; Clendinnen, 201–3.

[49] *H. of P.*, iii. 524; cf. Brooks, 'Common Lawyers in England', in *Lawyers*, 59.

[50] J. E. Neale, *Elizabeth I and her Parliaments 1584–1601* (1957), 376–83; Clendinnen, ch. 7; T. L. Moir, *The Addled Parliament* (Oxford, 1958), 146–7; S. White, *Sir Edward Coke and 'The Grievances of the Commonwealth', 1621–1628* (Chapel Hill, 1979), *passim*; Russell, *Parliaments and Politics*, 349–50; E. W. Ives, 'Social Change and the Law', in *The English Revolution 1600–1660*, ed. *idem* (1968), 121–6.

domestic and foreign, while involvement in local affairs provided experience in making and implementing policy, not to mention electioneering. Barristers who were recorders of parliamentary boroughs could usually expect election as a perquisite of office; others might look to an aristocratic patron or exploit their connections at court. However obtained, a seat in the Commons offered considerable career benefits, including local prestige and the chance of finding additional patronage or promotion by making a name in London. Nor need election as an MP unduly disrupt a barrister's practice in Westminster Hall or at the assizes. Many lawyer-MPs continued to plead at the bar even while the Commons was actually sitting, and went off on circuit without licence from the House; on 5 February 1606 the serjeant-at-arms with his mace had to be sent down the steps from St Stephen's chapel into Westminster Hall 'to require the lawyers . . . [who were] members of the House to come up and give their attendance', and the following year letters were sent to five MPs who had departed on the Western circuit, ordering their immediate return to assist in debating the proposed Anglo-Scots union. One reason 'all the lawyers of the house' were so frequently added to the membership of Commons' committees was to ensure that at least some attended.[51]

Lawyers would doubtless be expected to possess skills in marshalling and presenting arguments. But besides whatever rhetorical abilities they might have, barrister-MPs also enjoyed the huge advantage of a working knowledge of the common law, at a time when much political debate was actually conducted in the form of legal case-argument. They were thus able to speak with special authority about such central issues as impositions, forced loans, elections, parliamentary privilege, or indeed any topic on which they could bring to bear the 'cases, antiquities, records, statutes, precedents and stories' with which, it was claimed in 1626, 'the lawyers are fit ever in parliament to second any complaint against both Church, and King'.[52]

[51] SP 14/7/82, fol. 265ᵛ, quoted by Clendinnen, 197–8; J. S. Roskell, *The Commons in the Parliament of 1422* (Manchester, 1954), 65–6. D. Podmore, 'Lawyers in Politics', *Brit. J. Law and Society*, iv (1977), 155–85. For electioneering, see Som. RO, DD/PH216, fols. 207–8; F. Jessup, 'The Kentish Election of March 1640', *Arch. Cant.*, lxxxvi (1971), 4. R. E. Ruigh, *The Parliament of 1624* (Cambridge, Mass., 1971), 92–4, 109, 110, 396; E. and A. G. Porritt, *The Unreformed House of Commons* (Cambridge, 1903–9), i. 492–3.

[52] Anon., 'To his Sacred Majestie', in *Cabala: sive Scrinia Sacra. Mysteries of State & Government* (1654), 226.

This is not to say that barrister-MPs all spoke with one voice, even on measures which might seem directly to affect their collective professional self-interest. Nor did they ever entirely succeed in overcoming the disdain and suspicion of at least some of their lay colleagues, who occasionally echoed popular hostility towards the legal profession, complaining about the avarice and inflated numbers of counsellors and attorneys, and demanding measures to regulate lawyers' fees. A member's avowal in 1625 that he was 'neither courtier nor lawyer but a plain country gentleman' suggests no warmth of feeling for the profession.[53] When Sir Edwin Sandys declared in 1604 that the cunning of the lawyers had caused matters to be carried 'clean contrary to the meaning of the house' in the last three parliaments, the Speaker (Edward Phelipps of the Middle Temple) 'offering to free the lawyers from this tax, was interrupted and not suffered to speak'. In James I's last parliament Sir John Eliot commented that he could not accept something to be true simply because a lawyer said it, or 'believe that law which is not reason'.[54] But of course all these incidents were backhanded acknowledgements of the political centrality of legal issues, and the absence of any comparable body of specialist expertise in early Stuart parliaments.

iii. Values and Alignments

But did common lawyers make use of their considerable potential to influence the course of events in any one direction? Because the lines of political division in pre-Civil War England were far from clearly defined, the notion of 'a struggle between royal prerogative and common law, between king and parliament' is somewhat over-simplified as it stands; political alignments during the half-century before the Civil War were nothing like so clear-cut, mutually exclusive, or consistently principled as that.[55] Nor did the legal

---

[53] For an instance of common-lawyer-MPs closing ranks, see the defence of Richard Martin in 1614, as reported in *CJ*, i. 488; cf. the attack on John Baber in 1628, in *CD 1628*, ii. 374–5, 377–9, 383–93; iv. 19–20. *Proceedings in Parliament, 1610*, ed. E. R. Foster (New Haven, 1966), i. 155, 163; White, *Coke*, ch. 3, *passim*, and references cited at n. 12; P. Zagorin, *The Court and the Country* (1969), 35.

[54] *CJ*, i. 979; H. Hulme, *The Life of Sir John Eliot, 1592–1632* (1957), 58; cf. Eliot's motion in 1624 that the subcommittee for grievances should contain 'no lawyers, nor dependants'. (Harleian 6383, fol. 102ᵛ; I am indebted to Dr P. M. Crawford for this reference.)

[55] M. H. Maguire, 'Attack of the Common Lawyers upon the oath ex officio as administered in the Ecclesiastical Courts in England', in *Essays in Honor of C. H.*

profession at large present a united front, either before or after 1642, while the bar, for its part, included some of the Crown's most valued servants, as well as bitter critics of government policies and personnel. Indeed, these roles were by no means mutually exclusive, as the careers of Coke, Littleton, Noy, and others amply testify. So we should hardly expect early modern barristers to exhibit a uniform politico-religious outlook, a single 'common-law mind'. Pocock, who first coined that evocative phrase to characterize a school of historiography centered around Coke's glorification of the antiquity of England's constitution and law, also took pains to point out that 'there was a common-law case for the Crown as well as against it'.[56] Hence the stormy passages between Sir Edward Coke and James I which used to occupy so much space in textbooks when the history of seventeenth-century England was still 'written with primary reference to the conflicts fought out in parliament and the courts of common law', are nowadays either passed over in silence by historians or discounted as reflecting no more than the narrow self-interest of common-law judges and practitioners.[57]

Yet, however salutary in principle, revisionism has its own perils. By determinedly eschewing the risks of hindsight and playing down all evidence of political conflict or division in pre-Civil War England, we are liable to end up with a minimalist caricature no less distorted in its own way than the highly coloured piece of Whiggish expressionism it seeks to replace. While members of the early seventeenth-century bar plainly did not espouse a single politico-religious outlook, let alone a common commitment to 'oppose' the government, most were influenced by a corporate ethos which at the very least sat uneasily with the political values generally favoured at Court.

The large volume of hostile comment and criticism directed at common lawyers in post-Reformation England seems to have bred in its recipients both a certain defensiveness and a boastful, or even defiant, pride. Besides being widely acknowledged as the most

McIlwain, ed. C. Wittke (Cambridge, Mass., 1936), 198. Cf. G. P. Gooch, *Political Thought in England from Bacon to Halifax* (1927), 58.

[56] Pocock, *Ancient Constitution*, 31, 55.

[57] D. L. Keir, *Constitutional History of Modern Britain since 1485* (1938), 162. Cf. B. Coward, *The Stuart Age* (1980), index, s.v. Coke, Sir Edward; J. P. Kenyon, *Stuart England* (Harmondsworth, 1978), 83–4; K. Sharpe, 'Parliamentary History 1603–1629: In or Out of Perspective?', in *Faction and Parliament*, ed. *idem* (Oxford, 1978), 31; *Before the Civil War*, ed. H. Tomlinson (1983), *passim*.

learned common lawyer of the day, Sir Edward Coke was one of the
leading contemporary defenders of his order and what we would
term its place in society. Like a surprising number of his colleagues,
Coke seems to have found his work and occupational identity
intensely satisfying, in both psychological and material terms. Even
their grumblings about the rigours of the lawyer's life have a ring of
masochistic boastfulness, just as legal writers plainly relish recounting the wearisome pains of studying the common law. The assurance
that such virtuous efforts would eventually bring rich rewards was
the theme of the Inner Temple's 'ancient song usually sung when the
judges walk around the hall on the Grand Days':

> By learning men advanced be
> To places of high dignity,
> When pains and toils are overpast,
> Thence come the joys which ages last.
> . . . . . .
> The flowers of youth do fade full soon,
> and pass by changes of the moon;
> But younger years in study spent,
> To elder years new joys present.[58]

The conviviality of Grand Days and reader's feasts, the ordered
round of learning exercises, commons in hall, prayers and sermons
in chapel or Temple Church, journeys to and from term and assize
circuits, the shared possession of esoteric knowledge, kinship and
marriage ties—all tended to encourage *esprit de corps* among
practising common lawyers. This sense of occupational solidarity
underlies their continual assertion of the common law's supremacy
over all other codes, especially canon and civil law. These claims
embroider and restate themes which received their classical formulation in Sir John Fortescue's *De Laudibus Legum Anglie*, first
published *c.*1545, and Christopher St German's *Doctor and Student*
(*c.*1530).

Among the battery of arguments customarily marshalled, appeals
to prescription or the common law's immemorial antiquity were by
no means the most prominent. The central assertions seem rather to
have been classically Aristotelian and scholastic; human law is
generally presented as an emanation of reason and divine law, while

---

[58] J. H. Baker, 'The Old Songs of the Inns of Court', *LQR*, xc (1974), 188; Lowther,
'Autobiography', 213, quoted as epigraph to ch. 2 above.

the common law is said to represent the quintessence of right reason and God's law embodied in Scripture.[59] Such claims might be combined to produce an omnibus boast 'Of the Antiquitie, Ampleness and Excellencie of the Common Laws of England', as in Sir Roger Owen's tract of that title from the middle years of James I's reign:

Of positive laws, the common law is most ancient; of discursive reason, the purest and nearest resembling the eternal policy of God in governing the commonwealth of the Jews ... Whatsoever is not disagreeing from the law of God and is consonant to the law of nature and nations, allowed by the custom of our country, is the undoubted common law of this realm, which acknowledgeth no other author but God and Nature.[60]

An even more comprehensive case was put forward in the mid-1620s by an anonymous author who presented five reasons for the common law's superiority over all other codes. Thus 'our laws greatly enrich a kingdom', and better guarantee private property, 'peace and quiet ... so that every man may sit under his own vine'. The common law also advanced the royal prerogative, while both prince and people disliked the civil law. Finally, 'the laws of our land maintain and advance God's true religion and worship, which the other laws do not'.[61]

Similar defences and vindications of the common law frequently featured in the introductory speeches at the twice-yearly readings of the inns of court. The attitudes they exhibit undoubtedly permeated the upper branch of the legal profession; how characteristic and commonplace they were is suggested by the civilian Thomas Wilson in his *Discourse uppon Usury* (1572), where a common lawyer is

[59] Cf. P. Vinogradoff, 'Reason and Conscience in Sixteenth-Century Jurisprudence', *LQR*, xxiv (1908), 373–84. (I have benefited from Dr C. W. Brooks's unpublished paper 'Law, politics and the ancient constitution in Elizabethan England', delivered at the second Australian Law and History Conference, May 1983.)

[60] LI MS Misc. 207, fols. 1–2; for other versions and texts, see E. A. Strathmann, 'Ralegh's *Discourse of Tenures* and Sir Roger Owen', *HLQ*, xx (1956–7), 219–32. Owen was a non-practising barrister and bencher of LI. (Cf. *H. of P.*, iii. 162–3, and Appendix F below.)

[61] Ellesmere 1182a, fols. 75–6. Cf. M. Judson, *The Crisis of the Constitution* (New Brunswick, 1949), 335–9; although there is little technical argument, the author does cite Bracton and Staunford's *Les Plees del Coron* (1557); his central thesis, that the 'laws of England' were 'first framed ... after the pure and undefiled laws of God and are at this day more agreeable to the law of God, than the civil or canon laws, or any other laws in this world', echoes the earliest surviving version of Henry Finch's 'Nomotechnia'. (Cf. *Puritans and Revolutionaries*, ed. Pennington and Thomas, 98; also G. Saltern, *Of the Antient Lawes of great Britaine* (1605), sig. F2ᵛ, and *passim*.)

made to boast that, 'If time and leisure might serve, I could bring you infinite reasons to prove that our law is the best, the worthiest and the most ancient law in the world'.[62] Whether founded upon consonance with divine law or the law of nature and right reason or the ancient constitution, such claims for the common law were difficult to reconcile with the elevated view of the Crown's prerogatives as dependent upon no earthly source of authority, which James I, his son, and some of their clerical and courtier supporters seem to have held.[63]

So the notorious animosity towards common lawyers expressed in the public utterances of the early Stuarts was based on something more than mere royal whim. James I himself indicated as much in 1616 when he complained that 'the popular sort of lawyers have been the men that most affrontedly in all parliaments have trodden upon [my] prerogative'.[64] James's occasional disingenuous efforts to deny 'the imputation which some had cast upon him, that he favoured more the civil law than the common law' can hardly have carried much conviction, especially after his blatantly partisan patronage of *Ignoramus* in 1615, let alone the extraordinary passage in his proclamation issued before the 1621 parliament, which warned against returning any 'curious and wrangling lawyers, who may seek reputation by stirring needless questions'.[65] (The 'scornful indignation' and attendant sarcastic snubs with which the king reacted to the arguments of counsel appearing before the Privy Council in 1612 to debate the precedence of baronets, however, may

---

[62] Cf. Hargrave 206, fols. 3–3ᵛ (Edward Bagshaw, 1640); *Le Reading del Mon Seigneur Coke, sur Lestatute de 27 E I* (1662), 1–4; Longleat House MS 196 (Thomas Coventry, 1594); CUL MS Dd. 11.87, fol. 170 (James Ley, 1602), and above, pp. 222–3. T. Wilson, *A Discourse Upon Usury*, ed. R. H. Tawney (1925), 213.

[63] Cf. Russell, *Parliaments and Politics*, 362–3. Despite some hedging in 1610, James I always insisted that his 'absolute' prerogative lay outside the constraints of the common law, and emphasized his personal competence 'to supply the law, where the law wants'; cf. *The Workes of the Most High and Mightie Prince, James* (1616), 494, 512, 519; J. P. Kenyon, *The Stuart Constitution 1603–1688* (Cambridge, 1966), 7–8, 12–14; *Constitutional Documents of the Reign of James I 1603–1625*, ed. J. R. Tanner (Cambridge, 1961), 19; R. Eccleshall, *Order and Reason in Politics* (Hull, 1978) ch. 3.

[64] *APC 1615–16*, 602.

[65] *Memorials of Affairs of State . . . from the Original Papers of . . . Ralph Winwood, Kt.*, ed. E. Sawyer (1725), iii. 136; 'The Hastings Journal of the Parliament of 1621', ed. Lady de Villiers, *Camden Miscellany*, xx, (1953), 129. Tanner, ed., *Constitutional Documents*, 17–18; *Stuart Royal Proclamations*, ed. J. F. Larkin and P. L. Hughes (1973–), i. 493–4; Marwil, *Trials of Counsel*, 19, 203.

merely reflect James's habitual treatment of any subjects who had the misfortune to keep their sovereign from the hunting-field.)[66]

In this, as much else, Charles I was more discreet or inhibited than his father, but nevertheless made it known that he held the common-lawyer-MPs largely responsible for the difficulties he faced with his earlier parliaments, and was rumoured to have contemplated proclaiming the total exclusion of common lawyers from the Lower House in 1628.[67] A little later the king personally supervised arrangements for the Star Chamber prosecution of Henry Sherfield, who had knocked out a stained glass window from his Salisbury parish church on the grounds that it encouraged idolatry. Sherfield was told by his Lincoln's Inn colleague and former parliamentary associate William Noy that

the king had written his particular letters to every one of his counsel learned who did then plead against me to encourage them to be well prepared and to maintain the cause against me ... [and] his Majesty had by word of mouth charged and enjoined him not to desert him nor his cause for my sake or for any old familiar acquaintance that had been betwixt us.[68]

The correspondence of Archbishop Laud and Sir Thomas Wentworth shows that they fully shared their royal master's concern to ensure that the common lawyers were, as the former put it, 'contained within their ancient and sober bounds'. Although—or because—he had spent some time at the Inner Temple in his youth, Wentworth was particularly caustic about the incompatibility of the jurists' pretensions with the proper prerogatives of the Crown. After complaining to Cottington that the dignity of the Council at York had been slighted by Sir George Vernon, sitting as an assize judge on the Northern circuit, whom he sought to have formally rebuked by the Privy Council, Wentworth went on:

I confess I disdain to see the gownmen in this sort hang their noses over the flowers of the Crown, blow and snuffle upon them, till they take both scent

---

[66] Additional 47182, fols. 32–32ᵛ; for other instances of James on common lawyers, see Tanner, ed., *Constitutional Documents*, 288, and Jones, *Politics and the Bench*, 155–6.

[67] Ibid., 48, 169; Gardiner, *History*, vi. 226. Charles's personal antipathy towards lawyers is recorded in *The History of the Troubles and Tryal of ... William Laud*, ed. H. Wharton (1695), 9.

[68] Hants RO, 44M69/xxv/6 (reproduced below, Appendix H). Noy's acquaintance with 'my very good friend Mr Henry Sherfield' went back to 1611 at least. (Wilts. RO, MS 479/1; I am grateful to Mrs A. Wall for this reference.) For Charles's involvement with the details of Sherfield's submission after sentence, cf. HMC, *Cowper*, ii. 2–3.

and beauty off them; or to have them put such a prejudice upon all other
sorts of men, as if none were able or worthy to be entrusted with honour and
administration of justice but themselves.

Five months later, in March 1634, the Lord Deputy sought and
received authority to sit at Dublin as a judge in civil suits between
party and party, a power withdrawn from his predecessors on the
recommendation of a commission of common lawyers sent to
Ireland in 1621. Three years later, he reported with satisfaction that
the Irish judges were 'never in so much power and estimation . . . yet
contained in that due subordination to the Crown as is fit . . .
without squinting aside upon the vulgar and vain opinions of the
populace'.[69]

One of the charges brought against Wentworth in the early
months of the Long Parliament was that he had sought to subject
the common law to the arbitrary jurisdiction exercised by the
Council of the North at York and the Court of Castle Chamber at
Dublin. But Wentworth's preference for these English-bill courts
was by no means unprecedented. For many years before the
dismissal of Chief Justice Coke in 1616, the judges of the common-
law courts of Westminster Hall had waged a series of running battles
with various rival jurisdictions, notably the Church courts, the
provincial councils, the Court of Requests, the Court of Admiralty,
and Chancery.[70] Historians once regarded these contests as part of
an epic constitutional conflict leading up to the outbreak of the Civil
War. More recently it has been argued that jurisdictional disputes
were endemic to the early modern legal system and did not necessarily possess any constitutional significance. All the royal courts
competed vigorously for business; Chancery, the prime target of
Coke's writs of prohibition, was itself accustomed to issue prohibitions to lesser courts which had supposedly trespassed upon its
jurisdiction. Legal-historian revisionists, speaking with the authority
of those who have studied the records at first hand, depict the so-
called prerogative, or conciliar, courts as constituent units of a
national legal system, rather than newly arisen institutions challenging the interests of the ancient common-law courts. After all,
barristers pleaded in Chancery, Requests, Wards, and the provincial

[69] Knowler, i. 129–30, 155, 201, 223; ii. 18.
[70] J. Rushworth, *The Tryal of Thomas Earl of Strafford* (1680), 161–4. There is no
adequate account of these conflicts, but see Knafla, *Law and Politics in Jacobean
England*, chs. 6–7, and Ogilvie, *King's Government and Common Law*, ch. 16.

councils just as they did in Common Pleas or King's Bench; in the former, as the latter, judges and clerical personnel included a large proportion of trained common lawyers, while the law they administered was plainly the common law of England, not the civil law of Rome. So, it is claimed, disputes between King's Bench or Common Pleas and Chancery, for example, should be understood as primarily motivated by personality clashes or short-term economic considerations—competition for litigants' fees in other words—rather than by any fundamental issues of principle.[71]

Although many of these points are entirely unexceptionable, the revisionists fail to explain why contemporaries attached such significance to the quarrels of the courts, nor why the Crown consistently supported the English-bill courts against Coke and the common-law judges. In an understandable eagerness to correct the superficialities and exaggerations of the traditional interpretation, there has been some tendency to overlook the real differences which distinguished English-bill courts from their common-law rivals, particularly the fact that the former were much more closely identified with, and controlled by, the executive than the ancient common-law courts. This fact itself is hardly surprising, given that Common Pleas, King's Bench, and Exchequer had existed as judicial institutions for some four centuries by the time James I came to the throne, whereas most of the English-bill or conciliar courts had emerged by direct royal action only within the previous hundred years or so. Places on the common-law judicial bench were filled exclusively from the upper ranks of the practising bar and, at least in the later years of Elizabeth's reign, after consultation with the two chief justices. The judges of the conciliar courts, by contrast, were often Privy Councillors and other high officers of state, as most obviously in the case of the lord chancellor or keeper, who presided over both Chancery and Star Chamber, and whose disjunction from the common-law judges and serjeants at law was symbolically underlined by his residence at his own establishment, not one of the two serjeants' inns. All the chancellors appointed by the early Stuarts were common lawyers, with the notable exception of Bishop John Williams, who succeeded Bacon in 1621; it was plausibly rumoured in 1640 that Lord Keeper

---

[71] Cf. Jones, *Chancery*, pt. III, esp. 491–3; T. G. Barnes, 'Due Process and Slow Process in the late Elizabethan-early Stuart Star Chamber', *AJLH*, vi (1962), 224–5; *idem*, 'Mr Hudson's Star Chamber', in *Tudor Rule and Revolution*, ed. D. J. Guth and J. W. McKenna (Cambridge, 1982), 306–8.

Coventry would similarly be replaced by a clergyman, but someone evidently thought better of it. (Professional reaction to Williams's appointment is not well documented; one pamphleteer thought that the common lawyers were more concerned by James's failure to support his son-in-law Frederick in the Palatinate, and the circumstances of Bacon's dismissal perhaps help to explain their silence.) Career common lawyers were often appointed to English-bill courts to provide technical expertise and administrative continuity. Yet, even where their role was in fact judicial, as with the attorney of Wards and the learned counsellors of fee at Ludlow and York, they took precedence after the court's titular lay head (the master of Wards or lord president respectively), and their places were in effect bought and sold through courtier brokers, unlike the Westminster Hall judgeships.[72]

The conditions under which barristers practised before the conciliar courts varied widely, but were generally more restrictive than in the three common-law courts and on the assize circuits. As noted earlier, during the late sixteenth century attempts were made to limit Star Chamber practice to readers of the four inns of court, while the right of practice as an advocate before the Council in the Marches was confined to a small group of 'counsellors at the bar'; both there and at York, barristers were under close supervision, with fees fixed by the lords-president of the councils. No such formal or practical restrictions applied in Chancery or the other central English-bill courts, with the exception of the Earl Marshal's Court and the body variously known as the Verge, Palace, or Marshalsea Court, both of which were claimed by an Interregnum pamphleteer to have operated in a 'monopolising manner', giving audience only to counsel who had purchased their places.[73] A less direct, but possibly no less effective, means of controlling barristers pleading in these courts was through their relations with the judges before whom they appeared. It will be recalled that in Chancery, Requests, and Duchy Chamber, possibly Wards as well, suits were heard by a single judge. However, four men sat on each of the common-law judicial benches after 1604, which must have tended to reduce the power of any one judge to affect the fortunes of individual barristers. While much remains unclear about the implications of judicial favouritism in the early

---

[72] Knowler, ii. 4; G. W. Thomas, 'James I, Equity and Lord Keeper John Williams', *EHR*, xci (1976), 506–28.
[73] See above, pp. 13, 51; W. Leach, ·*Bills Proposed* ... (1651), 25, 27.

modern legal system, the apparent ability of Lord Ellesmere, for example, to discourage members of Sir Edward Coke's inn of court from appearing before him in Chancery is at least suggestive of the power wielded by the judges, often not trained as common lawyers, who presided in the English-bill courts.[74]

So, by supporting the provincial councils and Chancery in their disputes with the common-law judges, the Crown and Privy Council were not merely championing 'prerogative' against 'law', as Dudley Carleton put it, perhaps naïvely, in 1605, but also seeking to maintain and expand jurisdictions which accorded barristers (and judges) a lower status and less autonomy than they enjoyed in the central common-law courts. James I spelt out his personal preferences very plainly when he told a group of common-law judges in February 1608 that 'the distribution of justice after the French manner was better for the people and fitter for his greatness ... this course to draw all things to Westminster was to make him king as it were of the Isle of France and not other provinces'.[75] (In France, as in Scotland, Spain, and other predominantly civil-law jurisdictions, the conditions under which advocates practised, including the fees they charged, were closely regulated by the state, while the judiciary was a distinct order of office-holders under the Crown, not recruited as in the English common-law courts exclusively from the senior ranks of the practising bar. Continental advocates were specifically admitted to practice in particular courts after examination by the judges, unless, as with the advocates before the king's council in France, admission depended upon purchase of a place. According to one observer at the beginning of James I's reign, the Councils at Ludlow and York were indeed 'fashioned according to the form of parliaments in France'.)[76]

We do not know precisely how far the distinction between

---

[74] See above, pp. 28, 62. For complaints about the dominance of practice before the Council in the North by favourites, see Additional 41613, fols. 116^v–117^v.

[75] *Memorials of Winwood*, ed. Sawyer, ii. 44; Bacon, *Works*, xi. 89. For a revealing example of the deference shown by a judge in the Council in the Marches to the lord president, cf. Ellesmere 7412.

[76] N. Wilson, 'The Scottish Bar: the Evolution of the Faculty of Advocates in its Historical Social Setting', *Louisiana Law Rev.*, xxviii (1968), 240, 242; J. H. Shennan, *The Parlement of Paris* (1968), 46–7; Berlanstein, 'Lawyers in Pre-Revolutionary France', 169–71; R. Mousnier, *The Institutions of France under the Absolute Monarchy*, tr. B. Pearce (1979), 442–3; Kagan, *Lawsuits and Litigants*, 66–7; *idem*, 'A Golden Age of Litigation: Castile, 1500–1700', in *Disputes and Settlements*, ed. J. Bossy (Cambridge, 1983), 164 n; B. Barnes, *Foure Bookes of Offices* (1606), 136.

common-law and English-bill courts was reflected in the internal politics of the bar. Some coolness between Westminster Hall practitioners and the provincial councils is apparent in the late sixteenth century, while it may be that the 'Mr Hitchcock' who in 1584 disparaged Chancery, Wards, and Requests as 'but paper courts' was a Lincoln's Inn student, Thomas Hitchcock, who subsequently represented the merchants against the Crown in Bate's case.[77] Practice at the bar was sufficiently specialized by jurisdiction for a lawyer to be identified as a Chancery or King's Bench man, especially when jurisdictional rivalries were rampant, but the extent to which barristers generally felt threatened by the Crown's expressed preference for English-bill over common-law courts is uncertain. One who plainly did was Timothy Turner, a Gray's Inn barrister of five years' standing when he recorded James I's Star Chamber speech of 20 June 1616 (which sought to end the controversy between Chancery and King's Bench with a decisive pronouncement in favour of the former). On this occasion Turner noted his private fears that the common law was about to be 'enthral[led]' by 'the irregular power of the Chancery', the subjects' liberties 'taken away and no law practised on them but prerogative'. So 'the government . . . will lie in the hands of a small number of favourites who will flatter the king to obtain their private ends'. While the only remedy for this 'breeding mischief' was a parliament, 'some say no parliament will be held again in England, *et tunc valeat antiqua libertas Anglie*'.[78]

Whether or not Turner's radical pessimism was justified by the Crown's stance in the prohibitions controversy, as well as the general discountenancing of common lawyers and official patronage of civilians (whose recovery from their early seventeenth-century crisis 'came about almost completely as a result of royal action', according to Levack), he was certainly not alone in his fears. A few years earlier James Whitelocke, seeking to reverse the earl of Northampton's disapproval of his appearance as a pleader before

[77] See above, p. 53; Bell, *Court of Wards*, 135.
[78] Additional 35957, fol. 55ᵛ, quoted by J. H. Baker, 'Common Lawyers and Chancery', 384–5 (I have generally followed Dr Baker's translation of the law-French text); cf. Francis Ashley's allusion in his 1616 reading on Magna Carta to 'restrain[ing] the swelling and exorbitant power of ecclesiastical or any other jurisdiction which by way of encroachment seeks to impeach the vigour of our municipal laws'. (Harleian 4841, fol. 4.) For a more cynical view, however, see *Letters of John Holles 1587–1637*, ed. P. R. Seddon (Thoroton Soc. Rec. Ser., 1975), 117.

the Privy Council (on the purported grounds that cases of honour were 'designed to the determination of the civil law'), told Sir Robert Cotton that 'the use of your country's law ... as you know, is now sought to be more straitened and confined, than it hath been this many hundred years', and asked that he and his fellow 'professors ... may be heard for themselves, before they be disinherited of their practice'. It was, of course, the Earl Marshal's court which claimed jurisdiction over cases of honour; Whitelocke was imprisoned in 1613 for attacking its authority, and 'the opinions and reasons of the common lawyers in opposition to the power and jurisdiction of the Marshal court' did not finally triumph until it was abolished by the Long Parliament, following a petition from the gentlemen of Gray's Inn.[79] After Bishop Williams's appointment as lord keeper in 1621, when James I made the celebrated remark (reported in the diary of a Middle Temple law student) that his common lawyers were all knaves, and Williams asserted that he himself 'ever was of opinion that the king was above his laws', the Devonshire diarist Walter Yonge recorded a rumour that 'civilians shall practise in all courts of equity, viz. the Chancery and others'. This did not come to pass, although Charles I reversed the replacement of civilians by common lawyers as masters in the courts of Chancery and Requests. Nevertheless, some common lawyers clearly continued to regard themselves as members of an embattled order.[80]

Their disquiet could have sprung from various sources, including the dismissal of Chief Justice Sir Randle Crew in 1626 for his unwillingness to endorse the legality of the forced loan, the extension of martial law over much of southern England in 1627–8, and perhaps a fear that these recent events had revealed the common law's inability to 'erect a secure bulwark for protection of liberty and property'.[81] Among more parochial concerns were the effects of overcrowding at the bar and the wholesale auctioning-off of legal

---

[79] Levack, 'English Civilians', in *Lawyers*, 122; Bodl. MS Smith 71, fols. 59–60; cf. Cottonian Vesp. CXIV, fols. 232–3; Additional 47182, fols. 20–1. Jones, *Politics and the Bench*, 146–7; *The Journal of Sir Simonds D'Ewes*, ed. W. Notestein (New Haven, 1923), 54, 375–6, 540; G. D. Squibb, *The High Court of Chivalry* (Oxford, 1959), 48–62.

[80] D'Ewes, *Autobiography*, i. 188; *Fortescue Papers*, ed. Gardiner, 167; Yonge, *Diary*, 47; Levack, 'English Civilians', 122.

[81] Jones, *Politics and the Bench*, ch. 3; Russell, *Parliaments and Politics*, 349–50. Crew later claimed that the lack of attention paid to his dismissal by the 1628 parliament reflected his own efforts to suppress the issue. (Cf. G. Ormerod, *History of ... Chester* (1875–82), iii. 167.)

office under Buckingham, a practice which continued after the favourite's death. The diary of Sir Richard Hutton, who served as justice of Common Pleas from 1617 until his death in 1639, records strong disapproval of laymen profiteering in this fashion, as when Thomas Cory gained the chief prothonotary's place in his own court on the payment of £9,500 to agents of the marquis of Hamilton, to whom the king had evidently granted the right of presentation with the acquiesence of Attorney-General Heath and Chief Justice Finch, although 'from time without memory', according to Hutton, the presentation had been a prerogative of the chief justice.[82] It would also be surprising if persistent royal intervention in the administration of justice, including the establishment in 1631 of a standing Privy Council commission to 'hear and examine all questions, controversies and debates . . . about the jurisdiction of any of our . . . courts ecclesiastical or civil', did not arouse at least some disquiet within the profession.[83] But we can only speculate about the impact of these issues on the bar at large.

After the fiasco of 1626, when both judges and serjeants at law refused to pronounce forced loans legal, Charles I largely succeeded in taming his judiciary, although it took another sacking (that of Chief Baron Sir John Walter in 1630) to complete the process. Indeed, something of a *rapprochement* developed between some prominent barristers and the royal government in the aftermath of the 1629 parliament. In Gardiner's view, the acceptance of Crown office by erstwhile 'opposition' MPs like Edward Littleton and William Noy sprang not solely from self-interested careerism, but also reflected the merits of the Crown's claims to be defending the constitution, and distrust of the House of Commons's attempts to review judicial decisions upholding the validity of impositions. Yet, while direct evidence about the political attitudes of the bar as a whole is as meagre for the 1630s as for preceding decades, the markedly ambiguous message of the combined inns of court masque in 1634, and the patchy response to the Crown's appeal for funds to fight the first Bishops' War, suggest that reconciliation was by no means complete.[84]

---

[82] CUL MS Add. 6863, fols. 26, 90ᵛ.

[83] Cf. J. P. Dawson, 'The Privy Council and Private Law in the Tudor and Stuart Periods', *Michigan Law Rev.*, xlviii (1949–50), 393–428, 627–56. Ellesmere 7928 is a copy of the original commission dated 6 May 1631.

[84] Cf. *Inns of Court*, 230–2; S. Orgel and R. Strong, *Inigo Jones: The Theatre of the Stuart Court* (1973), 63–6. See also above, pp. 173–4, 235; in 1641 the barrister

Of course, none of this is to claim the common lawyers (whether individually or *en masse*) as self-conscious 'opponents' of the early Stuart governments. While lawyers of all people were sufficiently aware of the legal penalties for criticizing, let alone 'opposing' kingly rule, we need not suppose that their protestations of personal loyalty to the monarch and monarchy were anything but authentic and sincere. At the same time it is easy to understand why the regime tended to regard common lawyers in general as argumentative trouble-makers. In the debates on the proposed Anglo-Scots union in 1607, the Great Contract and impositions in 1610, impositions again in 1614, the impeachment of Buckingham in 1626 and the Petition of Right in 1628, common-lawyer-MPs like Hakewill, Hoskyns, Whitelocke, Coke, Glanville, Selden, Sherland, Littleton, Noy, and others used their rhetorical skills and technical expertise to considerable effect, almost always in directions contrary to the Crown's expressed preferences and interests. Barristers were disproportionately prominent among the MPs imprisoned after the sessions of 1610, 1614, and 1621. Outside parliament, Nicholas Fuller of Gray's Inn, Henry Sherfield and William Prynne of Lincoln's Inn, and Edward Bagshaw of the Middle Temple all suffered publicly as martyrs for godly reformation, a cause to which so many of their colleagues were also committed. We have also seen that, as local governors, lawyers played a crucial role in concerting resistance to administrative innovation and extra-parliamentary taxation. Barristers were haled before the Privy Council in 1596 for counselling resistance to conscription for military service overseas, and in 1613 (more obscurely) for maintaining the illegality of imprisonment 'for matters of suggestion to his highness until the first suggestion be proved true'. At his Star Chamber prosecution for circulating a 'scandalous letter' against the benevolence raised after the Addled Parliament, Lord St John claimed he had been misled 'by a lawyer who sat near his elbow, who affirmed unto him that compulsory courses were intended'.[85]

Edward Hyde referred to the early 1630s as a time when 'there was no more hope of parliaments and when the common law was declining in its power and honour'. (*Journal of D'Ewes*, ed. Notestein, 376.) SP 16/538/84 shows a distinct lack of enthusiasm for the Scottish campaign in March 1639, signalled by contributions of a mere £6. 13s. 4d. from Serjeant Callis and £10 from Serjeant Ward (as compared with sums of £50 paid by Sir Robert Heath and Sir Ralph Whitfield). Equally derisory amounts (of £3. 6s. 8d.) were offered by Nicholas Cholmley and Thomas Gates among the IT benchers. (Cf. *CSPD Add. 1625–49*, 604–5.)

[85] *APC 1595–6*, 459–60; *APC 1596–7*, 3–4; *APC 1613–14*, 6–7, 265; Ellesmere 2745.

The diary of Simonds D'Ewes as a young law student and barrister shows that the inns of court buzzed with political gossip and rumour, much of it startlingly hostile to Buckingham and the court, during the early 1620s. The administration, like later historians, presumably heard only a fraction of this, such as another 'scandalous' letter 'concerning a very great person' found in a drinking pot at the Middle Temple in 1626, or the libel issuing from Gray's Inn which urged 'all English freeholders' to resist the forced loan on the grounds of its illegality and purpose 'to suppress parliament', or the Lincoln's Inn bencher Hugh Pyne's public outburst from the chair at Somerset quarter sessions in 1628 that the king was 'as fit to rule as his shepherd, being an innocent', or Oliver St John's circulation of the notorious 'Leicester' letter, purporting to advise the Crown of extra-parliamentary sources of revenue, the following year.[86]

It is difficult to match these instances of dissent with expressions of unqualified support for the policies and principles being urged upon the early Stuarts in the 1620s and 30s by their more extreme advisers. A number of barristers and judges, including some quondam critics of government ministers and measures, are on record as advocates of an extremely liberal construction of royal prerogative powers. But all those who so argued—including Sir Francis Ashley, Sir Francis Bacon, Sir Anthony Benn, Sir Robert Berkeley, Sir Robert Heath, Sir John Hele, Sir Henry Hobart, Sir Henry Montagu and Sir Henry Yelverton—seem to have been either in possession or anticipation of office under the Crown at the time. Of course this is not to say that we should accept John Cooke's claim that 'avarice and ambition' were their main motivation, or Sir Roger Twysden's conviction that 'the air of a court' would always seduce some lawyers to betray their calling and 'by steps to win upon the people's liberty'.[87]

If more charitably inclined, we might well suppose that the

Cf. SP 16/40/58, Hugh Pyne's attack on levies for muster masters in his quarter sessions charge at Ilchester in the spring of 1626; I am grateful to Mr Ferris for this reference.

[86] *Diary of Simonds D'Ewes*, ed. Bourcier, 64, 72, 87, and *passim*; HMC, *Fifteenth Rep.*, ii. 289; SP 16/54/82; Yonge, *Diary*, 110; SP 16/151/81; *APC 1629–30*, 170, 174. Other instances from the late 1630s include SP 16/420/135; Bodl. MS Bankes 19/7; *LIBB*, ii. 458–63.

[87] J. Cooke, *Redintegratio Amoris* (1647), 12; Kent AO, U48Z3, 261; cf. F. W. Jessup, *Sir Roger Twysden 1597–1672* (1965), 191.

elevated and mystical conceptions of the kingly office which gained wide currency in the late sixteenth and early seventeenth centuries also influenced some lawyers to highlight the wide discretionary authority which the common law gave to English monarchs. Sir Henry Finch, for example, adopted in his *Law or a Discourse thereof* (1627) some extravagantly divine-right phraseology to portray the king (in words echoing James I himself) as 'head of the commonwealth, immediate under God, and therefore carrying God's stamp and mark among men, and being, as one may say, a God upon earth, as God is a king in heaven, hath a shadow of the excellencies that are in God . . . all by similitude from the divine perfection'. Finch then went on to enumerate various specific prerogatives of the Crown, but concluded with a crucial rider stating that 'the king's prerogative stretcheth not to the doing of any wrong; for it groweth wholly from the reason of the common law . . . the *primum mobile*'.[88]

So Finch's concession to the fashionable ideology of divine right absolutism may have been little more than cosmetic in nature. On the other hand, Sir Anthony Benn went much further in arguing that the dictates of reason must prevail over the letter of the common law: 'Let us not impound all reason into book law and law authorities . . . but if law be universal reason let us examine it by that reason which is every man's reason.' This passage comes from a tract written at the height of the conflict between Chancery and King's Bench. Benn, a leading Chancery pleader, asserted that equity as dispensed by the lord chancellor was no less part of the law of England, the *lex terrae*, than the common law, and so must be equally upheld 'by the countenance and protection it receives from the king, but for which the law were as useless as a sun dial where the sun shines not. God before all, after the king and his justice.'[89]

The Baconian influence, both in style and substance, is unmistakable. Yet even among those common lawyers who supported and assisted the claims of James I and Charles I to raise extra-parliamentary revenues by exploiting their prerogative powers, remarkably few were prepared to subordinate the common law to the dictates of either lay reason or the Crown's necessities. At about the same time as Benn's pro-Chancery tract was written, his Middle Temple contemporary William Martin, recorder of Exeter, published the

---

[88] Eccleshall, *Order and Reason in Politics*, 80–96; Finch, *Law*, 77–85.
[89] Stowe 177, fols. 192, 198; see also above, p. 253 n.47.

first edition of an extremely popular survey of English history, which incorporates a far more characteristic perception of the relationship between kings, their servants, and the common law. Martin presents the common law as the subject's ancient inheritance, which the Conqueror had overlaid with 'sundry new courts for the administration of his new laws', which Henry I had promised to restore, which Henry II had 'refined and reformed', and which had been 'ratified and confirmed' by Magna Carta. Martin also claimed that Wolsey as chancellor had

erected sundry courts of equity (which might more truly be termed courts of iniquity) . . . by means whereof the seats of justice, belonging to the common laws, were little frequented for a while . . . until the people, perceiving . . . that the sentences and judgements of those courts were not final but controllable . . . forsook them and commended their controversies to the censure of the common laws.[90]

We do not know precisely which 'passages so unaptly inserted' in his book impelled James I to have Martin summoned before the Privy Council in 1615, but it is difficult to believe that his readers were not intended to draw a direct parallel between the activities of Ellesmere and Wolsey in advancing English-bill courts at the expense of the common law. While Martin and his professional colleagues did not necessarily oppose Chancery as such, their strong sense of occupational identity and mutual perception of the common law as having been frequently subverted, then painfully restored, over the course of its long history helps explain why a third Middle Templar, Sir James Whitelocke, could describe Ellesmere as 'the greatest enemy to the common law that ever did bear office of state in this kingdom'. This judgement from a protégé of Coke closely echoes Coke's own claim that victory for Ellesmere's Chancery would mean 'the common law of England will be overthrown'. In short, the long drawn-out jurisdictional dispute which culminated with James I's famous 1616 Star Chamber speech upholding Lord Chancellor Ellesmere, and the subsequent dismissal of Chief Justice Coke, was evidently seen at the time by common lawyers and others as involving rather more than a mere clash of personalities and narrow vested interests.[91]

[90] Martin, *Historie*, 18, 34, 63, 366–7.
[91] Whitelocke, *Lib. Fam.*, 53; *APC 1615–16*, 100; Ellesmere 5973. Cf. Hutton's description of Ellesmere as having opposed the jurisdiction of the common law and 'in many things laboured to derogate from the common law and the judges'. (CUL MS Add. 6862, fol. 127.)

So it is not at all far-fetched to postulate a sense of distance, perhaps even alienation, between a good many practising barristers and the early Stuart regime. As noted above, few common lawyers played a significant role in central administration during our period, at least as compared to their early Tudor predecessors. Nor can much significance be attached in this context to the fact that the governments of James and Charles relied upon legal advice and decisions in the common-law courts to uphold some of their most unpopular policies, notably the levying of impositions and ship-money. During and after the Civil War, royalist commentators presented this apparent concern for legality as evidence that the monarchy was the true guardian of the ancient constitution against parliamentary lawlessness: thus Charles I's secretary, Philip Warwick, claimed that no prince had even been 'more willing that the benches in Westminster Hall should determine of his prerogatives'.[92] Yet the extent to which this policy was a matter of choice rather than necessity remains debatable; the legality of benevolences, free quarter, and the imposition of martial law in peacetime were never tested in the courts, and it has been argued persuasively that with regard to ship-money it was Lord Saye and Sele who 'outmanoeuvred the government and finally forced a legal confrontation that Charles could neither control nor afford'.[93] In any case, the fact that the early Stuarts could always find some barristers willing to advise, represent, or accept judicial office under them probably tells us more about the inducements and sanctions at the Crown's disposal than the state of feeling in the legal profession at large. A better guide to that may well be the continued willingness of barristers to defend the regime's proclaimed opponents, especially between 1629 and 1640 when (as the Grand Remonstrance later put it) 'lawyers [were] checked for being faithful to their clients'.[94] Some further indication of the political sympathies of barristers before 1640 may also be gained by reading back from their alignments during the Civil War.

The fact that when war came the lawyer-members of the Long Parliament apparently divided between king and parliament in

[92] P. Warwick, *Memoires of the Reigne of King Charles I* (1701), 76; cf. D. Jenkins, *Works* (1648), sig. B2.
[93] N. P. Bard, 'The Ship Money Case and William Fiennes, Viscount Saye and Sele', *BIHR*, l (1977), 184.
[94] *The Constitutional Documents of the Puritan Revolution 1625–1660*, ed. S. R. Gardiner (Oxford, 1927), 213. Concrete evidence of such intimidation is rare, but cf. Knowler, ii. 74, 85; D'Ewes, *Autobiography*, ii. 196; Rushworth, *Historical Collections*, ii. 611.

much the same proportions as the entire House has been taken to indicate that the bar lacked any distinct political identity, let alone marked radical propensities. This view would seem to be borne out by the transformation in 1641 of a number of erstwhile reforming barrister-MPs, such as Sir John Glanville, Sir Robert Holborne, and especially Edward Hyde, into the leadership of the king's party in the Commons. Thus (it is argued) the heirs of Coke's defence of the ancient constitution in 1628 were actually the proponents of Charles I's brand of mixed-monarchical constitutionalism in 1641–2.[95]

There are, however, two difficulties with this broad line of interpretation. First, as Tuck has shown, there was a good case in law for parliament's militia ordinance, possibly better than the one against it; the king and his followers by no means monopolized all the good arguments in 1641–2 (nor indeed the best lawyers, given the adherence of William Hakewill, John Selden, and Oliver St John, among others, to the parliamentary cause).[96] Second, the assumption that the Long Parliament, in whole or part, can be taken as representative of the political nation at large is obviously dubious. At all events, as Tables 8.1 and 8.2 show, the political preferences of members of our sample groups of barristers and benchers ran far more strongly against the Crown than did those of the Long Parliament's lawyer-MPs.[97]

Within the barristers' sample, parliamentarians (thirty-four) easily outnumbered royalists (fifteen) among lawyers who were still alive in 1642 and whose political loyalties thereafter are known. The parliamentarian predominance is less marked among the bench sample, which, however, includes thirteen Westminster Hall judges

---

[95] Ashton, *English Civil War*, 106; Brooks, 'Common Lawyers in England', 60; B. S. Manning 'The Nobles, the People and the Constitution', *P & P*, 9 (1956), 54.

[96] R. Tuck, '"The Ancient Law of Freedom": John Selden and the Civil War', in *Reactions to the English Civil War*, ed. J. Morrill (1982), 137–61.

[97] D. Brunton and D. H. Pennington, *Members of the Long Parliament* (1954), 5–6, 187; cf. Keeler, 12, 21–2. Brunton and Pennington identify 75 barristers among the 552 individuals they classify as original members, 33 royalists and 42 parliamentarians. Keeler refers to 74 'professionally trained' lawyers, who 'divided almost evenly by the time war came'; if so, lawyers were more inclined to royalism than the 547 original members, whom she identifies as split between 226 royalists and 316 parliamentarians. I can identify only 70 barristers in the original House, two of whom, Charles Pym and Thomas Earle, were not called until 1644 and 1647 respectively, while others (e.g. D'Ewes and Rudyerd) did not practise. I also exclude Ralph Assheton, whom Keeler mistakenly describes as a GI barrister and bencher, the politician Nathaniel Fiennes, and the office-holder William Pennyman, as well as Anthony Barker, recorder of Wallingford, who was excluded in February 1641. The allegiances of these 70 MPs were as follows: royalist 33, parliamentarian 36, and neutral/unknown 1.

Table 8.1. Civil War Alignments of Bar Sample

	Definite or very likely	Likely or possible	Trimmer	Total
Parliamentarian	28	3	3	34
Royalist	9	4	2	15
Neutral				2
Unknown				11

and two lord keepers, whose allegiances (after some initial hedging) lay overwhelmingly with the royalist camp, while omitting another twenty-one barristers promoted to the bench of their inn between January 1640 and August 1642, whose sympathies were overwhelmingly parliamentarian.[98] When the judges are excluded, and the benchers called between 1640 and 1642 are added to our totals, the resulting breakdown accords more closely with that of the barristers' sample, with eighty-two identifiable parliamentarians, thirty-eight royalists, two neutrals, and twenty-two men whose Civil War allegiance remains obscure. By comparison, Brunton and Pennington classified parliamentarians and royalists among Long Parliament MPs as 55 and 43 per cent respectively of the membership of the Lower House.

These figures inevitably mask certain problems of categorization and evidence, not least by blurring different degrees of commitment

Table 8.2. Civil War Alignments of Bench Sample

	Definite or very likely	Likely or possible	Trimmer	Total	Plus calls 1640–2	Less judges	Net totals
Parliamentarian	66	1	5	72	+ 14	− 4	82
Royalist	38	3	3	44	+ 5	− 11	38
Neutral				2	0	0	2
Unknown				20	+ 2	0	22

[98] The 21 benchers called after December 1639 and before August 1642, with their Civil War allegiances and inns, are as follows: parliamentarians: Bacon, N. (GI); Browne, S. (LI); Glynne, J. (LI); Lade, R. (GI); Parker, J. (GI); Pepys, R. (MT); Prideaux, E. (IT); St John, O. (LI); Thorpe, F. (GI); White, J. (MT); Williams, T. (LI); Wyott, P. (IT); possible/probable parliamentarians: Hussey, W. (MT); Weld, T. (LI); royalists: Bagshaw, E. (MT); Littleton, T. (IT); Norborne, W. (IT); Seaborne, R. (MT); possible/probable royalists: Holloway, C. (IT); neutral/unknown/died pre-August 1642: Newton, J. (LI); Thornes, R. (GI).

by individuals on both sides. A minority of partisan activists like
Richard Goddard, who raised a troop of horse for the king in his
native Hampshire, or Thomas Gell, who served as lieutenant-
colonel in Derbyshire under the command of his better-known elder
brother Sir John, are lumped in with men whose allegiances were
constrained, lukewarm, or ambivalent, like Chief Justice Sir John
Bramston, whose decision not to obey his royal master's summons
to Oxford must have been powerfully affected by the £10,000 bail
and extensive Essex estates which he would have forfeited had he left
London.[99] This difficulty is inherent in the methodology. However,
both main categories of royalists and parliamentarians have been
subdivided in order to distinguish those whose political allegiances
are reasonably well established from those for whom the evidence
is insufficient to permit more than an educated guess, as well as the
trimmers whose loyalties fluctuated during the course of the war.
Where no other evidence has been discovered, lawyers who appear
to have resided or practised in London between August 1642 and
December 1645 are classified as parliamentarians, while anyone
whose estates were sequestered or who paid a fine for delinquency
has been regarded as a royalist. Some men in both sample groups
have been left unclassified for sheer lack of evidence. A number of
these may have been more-or-less principled neuters, but the majority were almost certainly too old or too infirm to take an active part
in the conflict.[100]

The preponderance of parliamentarians among both the senior
ranks and a random sample of the bar as a whole suggests that the
bulk of common lawyers must have been very seriously disaffected
from court and government before 1640, if only because the rallying
of erstwhile critics and opponents to the royal cause after 1640 was
generally more frequent than movement in the opposite direction.
Moreover, support for Charles's regime once war began appears to
have been confined to a small segment of the profession. The
judiciary were largely loyal, despite some last-minute wavering, as
also the Crown law officers, such as Sir Peter Ball, solicitor-general
to the Queen, and Sir Richard Lane, attorney-general to the Prince

[99] J. Waylen, 'The Wilts. Compounders', *WAM*, xxiv (1853), 78; Underdown,
Pride's Purge, 374, 392; *DNB*, s.v. Bramston, Sir John; Aylmer, *King's Servants*, 386.
[100] Benchers apparently alive in mid-1642 who died before January 1644 were
Cressy; Sir Henry Montagu, earl of Manchester; Rigby; Saunderson; Talbot; and
Trotman; see below, Appendix E. Eight of the eleven barristers whose Civil War
allegiance is unknown may possibly have died before August 1642.

of Wales. Yet the government clearly failed to command anything like the undivided allegiance of the serjeants at law; among twenty-one men in the bench sample who held the rank of serjeant at the outbreak of hostilities in 1642, no fewer than thirteen sided with parliament. Francis Bacon's advice to James I, 'not to call serjeants before parliament, but to keep the lawyers in awe' was obviously based upon a realistic assessment of the independence of the order of the coif.[101]

Royalist lawyers, both barristers and benchers, came in largest numbers from the midlands and the south-west, whereas East Anglia and the south-eastern counties, including London, were most favoured by the parliamentarians (see Table 8.3). Lawyers from the north, Wales, and the March counties leaned heavily, although not overwhelmingly, towards the Crown. This pattern broadly reflects the national distribution of loyalties and armed forces when the Civil War began. Charles I's failure to move the lawcourts to Oxford cannot have helped his cause among practising barristers, especially those with chambers at an inn of court, let alone a house or lodgings in London. Yet most barristers held less property in London than the provinces, and while a few more might have sided with the

Table 8.3. Regional Distribution of Royalists and Parliamentarians[1]

	Royalists		Parliamentarians	
	Bar	Bench	Bar	Bench
North	2	5	3	3
Midlands	4	10	4	11
East	—	3	8	21
South and South-east	3	8	7	21
South-west	4	13	4	6
Wales and West	1	7	4	5
London	1	1	5	11
Totals	15	47	35	78

[1] Regions as in Table 4.4; benchers are those in the sample, including judges but not men called after 1639; multiple residences, except London lodgings, included where known.

[101] Cf. T. P. Woods, *Prelude to Civil War 1642* (Wilton, 1980), 114–16. The parliamentarian serjeants were Atkyns; Ayloffe; Clarke, J.; Cresheld; Finch, N.; Godbold; Greene; Jermyn; Phesant; Rolle; Turner; Whitfield; and Wild. The royalists were Bowne, Brerewood, Eure, Glanville, Hyde, Milward, and Wightwick, while Ward was neutral. (See below, Appendix E.) Bacon, *Works*, xi. 40.

Crown if the courts had been situated in an area under royalist control when war broke out, the allegiances of the majority were probably not so much affected by this particular geographical factor as by the location of their estate or place of residence outside London. In any case, the occasional London-based royalist, like Francis Walstead of Fetter Lane, deputy of the secondary's office in the City, and the rather more numerous cadres of Welsh parliamentarians, sound a warning against excessive geographical determinism.[102]

Another main difference between the bencher parliamentarians and royalists is that the latter were considerably more likely to hold a legal office of profit under the Crown. Only about a quarter of the royalist benchers were *not* office-holders, whereas a mere one in seven of the parliamentarians appear ever to have held any office from the Crown, and of these ten individuals, two (William Hakewill and Richard Shelton) had lost their places a good many years before war broke out. As might also be expected, committed puritans were somewhat more commonly found on the parliamentarian than the royalist side: there is, however, no apparent significant difference in age between the two groups.

Among the barristers, by contrast, parliamentarians were slightly more likely than royalists to have begun their professional careers before 1630. They included only two holders of royal office (Sir Robert Rich, a master in Chancery, and Evan Seys, attorney-general in South Wales). On the royalist side, however, were Sir Edward Henden, baron of the Exchequer; Alexander Rigby, clerk of the Crown in the county palatine of Lancaster; as also Richard Weston, the son of another baron of the Exchequer and himself joint holder of a Chancery sinecure; besides the sons of Sir Nicholas Hyde, the former chief justice, and Sir Henry Palmer, controller of the Navy to Charles I. The parliamentarian barristers included two men (Maurice Abbott and Sir John Cremer) whose severe financial difficulties before and perhaps during the war are not known to have been paralleled among the royalists. Finally, three of the parliamentarians (Edward Bulstrode, John Clarke and William Powell) were in their early to mid-fifties at the outbreak of hostilities. Although all three had reached the bench of their inn, their careers seem

[102] Cf. *Inns of Court*, 236–7. Walstead, however, was also a Staffs. landowner (*CCC*, 544). PCC 452 Ruthven; T. C. Dale, *Inhabitants of London in 1638* (1931), 232; London Corp. RO, Rem. VIII, fol. 47.

otherwise to have been stalled until they received significant promotion under the Long Parliament after the Civil War.[103]

Of course the alignment of the bar in 1642 and after cannot be analysed satisfactorily in terms of 'ins' and 'outs' alone. While there undoubtedly were disappointed and frustrated older men among the barristers who opted for parliament (Bulstrode, for one, had been an unsuccessful candidate for office several times during the 1630s), they also included such able and ambitious younger lawyers as Stephen Phesant, Evan Seys, George Smith, William Wilde, and Nicholas Willimot, none of whom had been at the bar for as long as ten years when the Long Parliament met.[104] Nor should we suppose that it was merely failure to win preferment which turned counsellors against the regime; on the contrary, the nature of a man's political and religious opinions might sufficiently explain both his inability to gain office and the side he took once hostilities broke out.

Broad generalizations about political attitudes in pre-Civil War England can hardly be anything other than impressionistic and inferential. Nevertheless, the corporate ethos and interests of the bar, the hostility towards lawyers expressed at the highest levels of government before 1640, legal anticlericalism, and the strongly parliamentarian bias apparent in both our sample groups do all tend to bear out the traditional view of common lawyers as prominent opponents of the early Stuarts. Of course, there are exceptions and qualifications. Unlike the advocates and judges of the Paris *Parlement* during the Fronde, for example, the bar was not a corporate entity self-consciously playing an active political role. Nor were political divisions within the pre-Civil War bar any more clear-cut than elsewhere in pre-Civil War England. While the conflict between Coke and Ellesmere during the second decade of the seventeenth century may have temporarily polarized barristers into opposing factions, much of the heat seems to have gone out of the Chancery v. common law confrontation after Ellesmere's death in 1617. The main political legacy of this clash was probably to reinforce doubts about the monarchy's attitude towards the common law, outside, as well as within, the legal profession. Tension between Westminster Hall lawyers and the provincial councils continued throughout our period, but if practitioners in the latter did tend to support the

---

[103] See below, Appendix D; for Abbott's and Cremer's financial problems, see above, pp. 147, 152.

[104] For Bulstrode's disappointments, see Additional 37343, fols. 146ᵛ, 162.

Crown in the 1640s, such a tendency could well be accounted for by geographical rather than specifically vocational factors.[105] Nor were all those whose practices lay chiefly in English-bill courts bound together by any sense of sectional solidarity; indeed Henry Sherfield, a leader in the English-bill Court of Wards, used his 1624 Lincoln's Inn reading to attack the 'upstart' fiction of the double use, or 'trust and confidence', developed by Chancery, claiming it would prove 'no doubt as perilous to the common laws' as the use had been, and urging that 'it were most happy to this state if uses and trusts of that kind were extirpated totally . . . a most pernicious thing to receive in the bosom of the law, any fraud whatsoever'. Sherfield evidently perceived no conflict between this elevated conception of the common law and his practice in an English-bill 'prerogative' court; his attitude rather suggests that the common lawyers' prime concern was to incorporate these institutions within the common-law paradigm.[106]

Finally, perhaps the most difficult problem for our understanding of the politics of early seventeenth-century common lawyers is to know what weight should be attached to the acceptance of office under the Crown by erstwhile champions of the subjects' liberties. Russell suggests that the main lawyer-proponents of the Petition of Right cannot have been 'profoundly alienated from the regime', since they subsequently accepted official preferment. However, by no means did all the important lawyer-MPs of the 1620s later take office under the Crown; besides their leader, Sir Edward Coke, whose age alone may have rendered him ineligible for office, John Glanville, William Hakewill, Christopher Sherland, and Henry Sherfield all remained conspicuously unpromoted after 1628.[107] Conversely, of the three most prominent opposition-MPs of the 1620s who did later serve Charles I, William Noy is described by his latest biographer as 'simply an employee', who in 1634 personally

---

[105] In September 1641 Serjeant Timothy Littleton (a future royalist) wrote to the Shropshire JPs asking them to raise the sum of £25 'to be employed for the passing of the act for the exempting of the four shires' from the jurisdiction of the Council in the Marches. (Ellesmere 7542.)

[106] Hargrave 402, fol. 34ᵛ. A similar high moral concept of the law is shown by John Briscoe of LI in the 'Argumentum Lectori' prefaced to his translation of Plato's Dialogues. (LI MS Hale 130, unfoliated.)

[107] Russell, *Parliaments and Politics*, 349–50. Russell mistakenly claims William Hakewill as solicitor-general to Charles I's queen, rather than his father's; it should also be noted that Robert Mason waited until seven years after the Petition of Right debates before accepting royal preferment. (See below, Appendix E.)

supported an attack upon projectors 'which blatantly ridiculed official policies', while the ultimate loyalties of both Sir John Bankes and Sir Edward Littleton remained uncertain until just before the outbreak of hostilities in 1642.[108] Lawyers who advanced their careers by accepting offices in the Crown's gift may or may not have retained some sense of distance from the regime, but in any case most did not thereby identify themselves whole-heartedly with all policies promulgated in the king's name. Neither government nor opposition was a clearly defined, homogeneous, or mutually exclusive entity before 1640.

No doubt the sweets of office tended to condition the behaviour of those who enjoyed them, as they usually do, but their influence depended to some extent on the individual concerned. Sir James Whitelocke became a justice of King's Bench in 1624, after playing a prominent opposition role in the parliaments of 1610 and 1614. Yet as a judge, Whitelocke did not passively acquiesce in Charles I's efforts to raise extra-parliamentary revenue, and indeed resisted administration attempts to secure judicial legitimation for the 1626 forced loan. His acceptance of a seat on the bench does not thereby indicate that Whitelocke may be dismissed as a mere ambitious time-server, any more than his earlier mistrust of Ellesmere's campaign against the common law can be ascribed to mere personal animus compounded by resentment at his inability to gain a larger Chancery practice (as James I, for instance, professed to believe that greed for fees was the sole motive underlying the campaign against Chancery waged by Coke and his fellow common-law judges).[109]

Timothy Turner, another lawyer whose privately expressed hostility to Ellesmere's policies was noted above, appears twenty years later as solicitor-general in Wales, reporting to Ellesmere's son, the first earl of Bridgewater and lord president of the Council in the Marches, on a clash with Sir John Corbet at Shropshire quarter sessions, after the latter had invoked the Petition of Right in protest against a levy to pay the county muster-master. Yet Turner also expressed considerable dissatisfaction to Bridgewater about abuses in the administration of justice by the Council, and although sequestered in 1646, his commitment to the king's cause in the Civil War may have been largely a function of geography, as was later

---

[108] Jones, '"The Great Gamaliel of the Law"', 216–17; A. Fletcher, *The Outbreak of the English Civil War* (1981), 278–9; Clarendon, *History of the Rebellion*, ii. 106–8.
[109] Cf. Spalding, *Improbable Puritan*, 73.

claimed on his behalf by William Bradshaw, a Gray's Inn colleague and president of the High Court of Justice which tried Charles I.[110] John Cooke, another prominent Gray's Inn regicide, appears to have spent some time in Ireland during the 1630s as a member of Strafford's entourage, and actually addressed a letter of advice and encouragement to the former lord deputy while the latter was imprisoned in the Tower awaiting his trial for high treason. Such (to our eyes) extraordinary inconsistencies of behaviour and outlook reflect a world of highly personalized administration and government, as well as the absence of party political organization and, in a sense, of politics as an autonomous and legitimate public activity. Even so, it may be that common lawyers were particularly prone to compromise and to being compromised; as Cooke himself recalled in 1648, 'the temptation was very great to be for the king's side in all arguments; besides, parliaments have been discontinued and shortened'.[111]

[110] Ellesmere 7389, 7399, 7644, 7650, 7693, 7527; *CCAM*, 732–3; *CCC*, 1461. See also *Trans. Salop Arch. Soc.*, ii (1878), 398–9; HMC, *Thirteenth Rep.*, i. 35.

[111] *Radicals*, i. 166–7; 'Papers Relating to Thomas Wentworth', ed. C. H. Firth, *Camden Miscellany*, ix (1895), 14–20; Cooke, *Redintegratio Amoris*, 8.

CHAPTER NINE

LAW, LAWYERS, AND LITIGANTS

'Now I cannot tell what I should call the study of law, whether I should term it to be a profession, a science, or an art; a trade, I cannot call it, yet there be some that do think it to be a craft. . . . But I think it may rather be called an occupation.'

> Barnabe Rich, *My Ladies Looking Glasse* (1616), 67

i. Images

BEN Jonson's 'An Epigram to the Counsellor that Pleaded and Carried the Cause' pays tribute to a barrister (most probably Sir Anthony Benn of the Middle Temple) whose personal and professional virtues were found by the poet's own experience to contradict

> . . . the names so rife,
> Of hirelings, wranglers, stitchers-to of strife,
> Hook-handed harpies, gowned vultures, put
> Upon the reverend pleaders. . . .

Jonson also eulogized other lawyers, included several among his literary intimates, and characterized the inns of court as 'the noblest nurseries of humanity, and liberty, in the kingdom'. Yet, on occasion he, too, was quite capable of endorsing the contemporary stereotype of the avaricious and deceitful lawyer:

> That, with most quick agility, could turn,
> And re-turn, make knots, and undo them;
> Give forkèd counsel; take provoking gold
> On either hand . . . .[1]

The origins of this unflattering portrait—or caricature—stretch far back in the history of western culture, as Thomas Draxe demonstrated in his *Bibliotheca Scholastica* (1616), which lists the biblical and classical antecedents of such adages as 'A lawyer's purse in the

---

[1] Jonson, *Poems*, 23, 30, 152–5, 179–81, 206–7; *idem, Works*, iii. 421, iv. 212–13, v. 34; Prestwich, *Cranfield*, 97–9. I am indebted to Professor Donaldson for his helpful comments and suggestions on these points.

mouth of hell', and 'If hell were not full, the lawyer could not be saved'. Christ's denunciation of the scribes and Pharisees ('Woe unto ye lawyers! for ye have taken away the key of knowledge', in Luke 11.52) and Cicero's complaint that the ingenuity of the jurisconsults had corrupted and perverted the law's original purity were echoed by medieval satirists and moralists. In the twelfth century Peter Cantor wrote a chapter 'Contra advocatos', while his near contemporary Peter of Blois complained that 'the once venerable name and glorious profession of advocate is now debased by notorious venality'.[2] A clerical and literary anti-lawyer tradition, to which Gower, Langland, Wyclif, Petrarch, Erasmus, Luther, and Latimer all made notable contributions, was matched, if not exceeded by a parallel stream of popular hostility. Besides surfacing occasionally in complaints and demands by insurgent peasants for the reform or abolition of the legal profession, its main form of expression was in such everyday sources of collective opinion as jokes and proverbs.[3] Thus we hear of the judge who referred a matter to two lawyers for arbitration, whereupon 'the poor petitioner desired that he would be pleased to refer it to two honest men', and of how a priest who should have read, 'The devil was a lyer from the beginning', instead informed his appreciative congregation that 'The devil was a lawyer from the beginning'. (Satan's close identification with the legal profession remained a commonplace throughout the later medieval and early modern periods.) When a disputed election resulted in the return of a civilian and a common lawyer, both claiming to be knight of the shire for Cardiganshire in 1601, another MP commented that it hardly mattered which took the position, the hangman or the thief.

[2] E. F. G. Tucker, *Intruder into Eden: Representations of the Common Lawyer in English Literature 1350-1760* (Columbia, S.C., 1984), ch. 1. T. Draxe, *Bibliotheca Scholastica Instructissima* (1616), 112. Cicero, *Pro Murena*, 27–8; cf. *idem, De Legibus*, ii. 19. A. Murray, *Reason and Society in the Middle Ages* (Oxford, 1978), 222–3; J. A. Yunck, 'The Venal Tongue: Lawyers and Medieval Satirists', *American Bar Assoc. J.*, xlvi (1960), 267–70; *idem, The Lineage of Lady Meed* (Notre Dame, Ind., 1963), 143–59; L. Thorndike, '*Liber de Similitudinis et Exemplis*', *Speculum*, xxxii (1957), 791; J. Mann, *Chaucer and Medieval Estates Satire* (Cambridge, 1973), 86–91; G. R. Owst, *Literature and Pulpit in Medieval England* (Oxford, 1961), 317–18, 338–9.
[3] See references cited in n. 2 above, plus Bishop, *Petrarch and His World*, 38; P. Burke, *Popular Culture in Early Modern Europe* (1979), 159–60; D. Erasmus, *The Praise of Folly*, tr. C. H. Miller (1979), 52, 85; *Select English Works of John Wyclif*, ed. T. Arnold (Oxford, 1869–71), iii. 153–4; Ives, *Common Lawyers*, 285–6, 308; *idem*, 'Reputation of Common Lawyers', 130–61; R. Hilton, *Bond Men Made Free* (1973), 114–15, 226–7; B. Capp, *Astrology and The Popular Press* (1979), 106–9.

Epitaphs, both fictitious and real, embroidered the same general theme:

> See how God works his wonders now and then,
> Here lies a lawyer and an honest man.

This couplet survives in at least three versions, one attributed to Ben Jonson. James Motte was buried in the parish church of Mattishall, Norfolk, in 1618 with the following memorial inscription:

> He did profess the law, yet he embraced peace
> Abhorred bribes and therefore now his soul doth live at ease.

Motte's name does not appear in the records of any inn of court, so he was presumably an attorney or a solicitor. Yet the epitaph of Sir Augustine Nicolls, puisne justice of King's Bench from 1612 until his death in 1616, suggests that freedom from corruption might be regarded as a notable virtue even among the most eminent jurists:

> He whom no bribes could blind, nor terror turn,
> Nor favour fawn, no course compel from right.[4]

So contempt for, and dislike of, lawyers evidently transcended time, place, and class. But if, as the literary evidence suggests, legal practitioners had long been more or less unpopular, how much significance can be attached to particular instances of that low repute? There is abundant evidence of hostility towards common lawyers, both attorneys and counsellors, during the half-century before the Civil War, culminating in a wholesale assault on the profession during the revolutionary decades of the mid-seventeenth century. But was the corrupt and venal lawyer pilloried in pamphlets, sermons, and plays any more than a convenient literary fiction, or for that matter, a stereotyped class enemy? Is it indeed possible that most complaints levelled against the legal profession during our period were mere conventional rhetoric, which no one took very seriously?

It would certainly be difficult to prove that lawyers were more

---

[4] Staffs. RO, D 661/11/1/7, fol. 26; '*Merry Passages*', ed. Lippincott, 27; Tucker, '"Ignoramus"', 313–30 (cf. IT MS Petyt 538. 151, fol. 83ᵛ, and G. F[idge], *The Great Eater of Grayes-Inne* (1652), 4); Dodd, 'Wales's Parliamentary Apprenticeship', 17; J. Le Neve, *Monumenta Anglicana* (1717–19), i. 66; J. M. Ewbank, *Antiquary on Horseback* (Kendal, 1963), 6; J. Aubrey, *The Natural History ... of Surrey* (Dorking, 1975), v. 414; I. C., *Alcilia, Philopharthens loving Folly* (1613), sig. M4ᵛ; Gad Benarod, *The Wandering Jew Telling Fortunes to English-men* (1640), 24–5; Stephens, *Characters*, 155.

unpopular in early modern England than they had been during the Middle Ages. Perhaps even more than other literary forms, satire involves an element of repetition, extending to metaphor and figures of speech; for example, the conceit of Aeneas Sylvius the humanist Pope Pius II (d. 1471), that suitors were as birds hunted by lawyer-fowlers, was still in use among English writers of the early seventeenth century.[5] On the other hand, anti-lawyer sentiment was not simply a continuum, unchanged in content and form, from the twelfth century, or even biblical times, onwards; and critics of the profession in the late sixteenth and early seventeenth centuries were not merely retailing traditional motifs. While there were, regrettably, no opinion polls to tell us whether the popularity rating of lawyers during our period was higher or lower than at other times and places, both the vehemence and volume of recorded anti-lawyer comment do appear to increase steadily from the late sixteenth century onwards. Of course, this may be an illusion, arising from greater familiarity with the post-1590 sources than the earlier ones, which could also explain why post-medieval moralists and satirists seem to concentrate more attention on the legal profession than did earlier commentators, who were seemingly no more anxious to denounce lawyers than sinners of any other calling.

Yet both these developments are precisely what might be expected at a time when the numbers, influence, and wealth of common lawyers and the volume of litigation were all growing very rapidly. The expanding body of anti-lawyer material may also reflect the impact of population growth and the printing press; the printed word was doubtless a more effective means of disseminating such attitudes than sermons or manuscripts. Moreover, while the scale and intensity of complaints against common lawyers seem to increase markedly during our period, their substance also shows some changes. True, many of the criticisms were entirely traditional. Thus lawyers were said to be arrogant in dealings with clients, and neglectful of the poorer sort, mischievous exploiters and fomentors of neighbours' quarrels who encouraged people to go to court and then deliberately delayed their suits for gain. They were also widely

---

[5] Cf. Stern, *Gabriel Harvey*, 164, and CUL MS Dd. 3. 88, (10), fols. 48–50. Another persistent motif is that of the laws as cobwebs which 'catch flies but let hornets go free'. (M. P. Tilley, *A Dictionary of the Proverbs in England in the Sixteenth and Seventeenth Centuries* (Ann Arbor, 1950), 371.)

accused of charging exorbitant fees. While all these complaints might equally be found in medieval sources, a number of new indictments, reflecting changes in the structure of the profession, begin to appear in the late sixteenth century. There is a growing tendency to distinguish between the shortcomings of counsellors on the one hand and attorneys and solicitors on the other; among the former, the favourites and leading counsel are particularly singled out, for accepting fees on both sides, failing to represent litigants after having been retained, and taking up too large a share of the available work at the bar, to the detriment of both clients (who feel constrained to retain them, if they can afford the ruinous fees) and the remaining barristers (who have insufficient work to live on). Another novel criticism is that too many counsellors are simply incompetent and ignorant.[6]

Thus, hostility towards common lawyers seems to have burgeoned precisely as the profession grew in size and social prominence during the sixteenth century, while the specific complaints mirror recent changes in its organization and structure, as well as much older jealousies and topoi. In other words, the unpopularity of lawyers was not just a literary convention, but rather reflects the central relevance of the legal system and its practitioners to the everyday life of early modern England. Whereas today most of us have little direct contact with the law, and so scant reason to single out lawyers as scapegoats for society's ills and failings, it has been plausibly suggested that in sixteenth- and seventeenth-century Europe, lawyers, like other professional men and merchants—the middle classes, in short—served as social lightning-conductors, diverting popular hostility away from the landed ruling élite.[7] Hard evidence about the attitudes of peasants and artisans towards lawyers and other professional men before the Civil War is not easily come by; but, given the strength of anti-lawyer sentiment among the radical sectaries of the 1640s and 50s, it seems entirely possible that the Dorchester craftsman who was said to have complained in 1631 that lawyers and clergymen 'had gotten all the riches of the land into their hands

[6] W. Harrison, *The Description of England*, ed. G. Edelen (Ithaca, 1968), 174; Lansdowne 44, fol. 2; *The Iust Lawyer* 16–21; Knafla, *Law and Politics in Jacobean England*, 111–13; Powell, *Attourney's Academy*, 229; Ives, 'Reputation of Common Lawyers', 131–5; H. Rolle, *Abridgment des Plusiers Cases* (1668), 54–5.
[7] Burke, *Popular Culture*, 159.

and were grown so proud that they will not vouchsafe to speak to a poor man' was voicing a widely held resentment.[8]

Nor was such hostility confined to the poorer elements of the population. It took a particularly virulent form among the clergy, who could neither forget nor forgive their displacement from positions of worldly power and influence by common lawyers since the Reformation. Even the saintly Hugh Latimer, beseeching Edward VI to adjudicate poor men's suits in person, could not resist a sneer at those parvenus, the common-law judges: 'Now a man can scarce know them fron an ancient knight of the country.'[9] In the 1630s Bishop Goodman chronicled at length the ways and means by which lawyers had become, as he claimed, 'more absolute governors than any legal prince in Christendom', an ascent which he epitomized in the striking observation that, 'as it is for matter of profit and honour, so for pleasure and sport, I dare boldly say that there is not a mean lawyer but spendeth as much venison in his house as he doth that hath an ordinary park'—a matter on which that epicurean bishop was well qualified to speak with authority.[10]

While the civilian Thomas Wilson's complaint that common lawyers were buying up all the lands was a pardonable exaggeration, the attempts of *arriviste* lawyers—and their wives—with newly acquired estates to establish themselves in county society often irritated older established residents. Sir John Oglander, surveying the landed families of the Isle of Wight early in James I's reign, recalled that the father of Lord Chief Justice Sir Thomas Fleming, who now held Heasley Manor and the abbey of Quarr, 'was a merchant in Newport and the most miserable of men', underlining the point with a doggerel verse about 'the drunken Flemings'. 'Many a counsellor', sniffed Thomas Scott, 'thrusts himself and his wife, before good esquires, and them whose fathers kept better men to wait at their tables'; 'a rich lawyer's wife', claimed the author of a late sixteenth-century tract, 'will make no ceremony to sit down . . . and take place before any poor gentlewoman'.[11] Presumably it was

---

[8] Mayo, ed., *Records of Dorchester*, 616. Cf. R. Greene, *A Quip for an upstart Courtier* (1592), sig. E ('The lawyer was never friend to cloth breeches'); SP 14/19/47; Veall, *Law Reform*, ch. 9.

[9] Latimer, *Sermons*, ed. Corrie, i. 127. Cf. above, pp. 224–5.

[10] Goodman, *Court of James I*, i. 294–6.

[11] Wilson, 'State of England', 25; *A Royalist's Notebook*, ed. F. Bamford (1936), 163–4; Scull, *Dorothea Scott*, 174; *The English Courtier and the Country-gentleman*, ed. W. C. Hazlitt (Roxburghe Library, 1868), 44.

in reaction to such usurpations that the Elizabethan antiquary Robert Reyce relegated the arms of the lawyers to the belfry of his parish church when he beautified it with stained glass depicting the heraldic bearings of the neighbouring gentry community.[12]

Many of the lawyer's unprepossessing personal characteristics as depicted by contemporary writers similarly reflect envy and resentment of a body of men who have risen too far, too fast. As in the Middle Ages, avarice or covetousness remained the main charge: 'For indeed he is all for money', wrote Thomas Overbury of the 'mere common lawyer', a theme later brilliantly developed by Samuel Butler, who portrays the lawyer as 'a retailer of justice, that uses false lights, false weights and false measures'. 'Covetous lawyers', 'land monsters . . . whose vulture avarice, devours men living', were proverbially both ambitious and arrogant:

> A lawyer is ambitious and his head
> Cannot be praised nor raised too high,

according to a character in *Eastward Hoe*.[13] Taken up with money-making, lawyers were graceless boors, unacquainted with the liberal arts, ill at ease in polite society, fit only to clamour at the bar and overbear poor clients. By discontinuing his career at the bar, the priggish Simonds D'Ewes hoped 'to prepare my way to a better life . . . avoiding those two dangerous rocks of avarice and ambition'.[14]

While the lawyers' aggressive new wealth disrupted the established hierarchical ordering of society, the works of their calling seemed to threaten the peace, and perhaps the very existence, of the commonwealth. Law might be widely regarded as the divinely ordained cement which bound human societies together, but it was also held that 'policies, states or common-weals are most corrupt wherein there be many laws established'. Plato, Cicero, and the New Testament were all invoked to demonstrate that lawyers and law-

---

[12] Suffolk RO (Bury St Edmunds), GC 17/774, Blois's Church Notes, p. 293, quoted by D. N. J. MacCulloch, 'Power, Privilege and the County Community: County Politics in Elizabethan Suffolk', University of Cambridge Ph.D. thesis, 1977, 286.

[13] G. Chapman, B. Jonson, and J. Marston, *Eastward Hoe* (1605), III. ii. 255–6. Overbury, *Works*, 84; S. Butler, *Characters*, ed. C. W. Daves (1970), 111; S. Rowlands, *Looke to it; for Ile Stabbe ye* (1604), sig. Bᵛ; Day, *Law-Tricks*, sig. Bᵛ; W. Jackson, *The Celestiall Husbandrie* (1616), 22.

[14] Ruggle, *Ignoramus*, sig. H; Hall, *Poems*, ed. Davenport, 25–6; J. Marston, *The Scourge of Villanie* (1599), 69; N. Breton, *The Uncasing of Machivils Instructions* (1613), sigs. A4, B3; T. Middleton, *Father Hubbert's Tales* (1604), in *Works*, viii. 67–8; H. Browne, *A Map of the Microcosme* (1642), 129–37; D'Ewes, *Autobiography*, i. 307.

suits constituted, at best, a necessary evil, while excessive numbers of lawyers

> which are bred
> (Like horse-flies) from a state distempered
> Are signs of ill-disposed bodies, sure
> And long's that state not likely to endure.[15]

Before the Civil War only a few radical separatists would have denied the legitimacy of any resort to the secular legal system. Nevertheless it is striking how even a conservative Calvinist like William Perkins hedges about with qualifications his grudging approval of true Christians going to law, which may be done only 'against great injuries', and after having explored all other possible solutions, dispassionately, and with great reluctance. If litigation was such a desperate remedy, the status of those who administered it inevitably came into question.[16]

Critics of the legal profession often insisted that the lawyer's vocation was in itself honourable and virtuous—hence 'a dangerous madness to envy generally against lawyers'—but the very frequency of such protestations points to the popularity of the opposite view. Above all, a multitude of lawyers was felt to be not merely a symptom, but a prime cause, of social divisiveness and excessive litigation:

> Woe to the weal where many lawyers be,
> For there is sure much store of malady.[17]

The conflicts which led to litigation were said to be provoked, or at least encouraged, by lawyers, who should rather have been seeking to conciliate disputes and settle quarrels. Hence 'the lawyer is the only man', according to Bishop Earle, whom a 'Grave divine' would hinder: 'He is [re]spited for taking up quarrels'. Once in court, their barbarous jargon, technical quibbling, and unnecessary delays confused all issues of right and wrong, dragging suits out over a period of terms, if not years, leaving the final outcome dependent not on the

---

[15] Barnes, *Foure Bookes of Offices*, 138; R. Burton, *The Anatomy of Melancholy*, ed. A. R. Shilleto (1893), i. 92–5; R. Brathwait, *Times Curtaine Drawne* (1621), sig. F4 ('of Hospitality'). Cf. Brooks, 'Litigants and Attorneys', 55–7.

[16] Perkins, *Cases of Conscience*, 289–90. Cf. Prideaux, *Christ's Counsel*, 11; T. Scott, *The Proiector* (1623), 22; Greaves, *Society and Religion*, 650–61.

[17] *The Poems of Robert Herrick*, ed. L. C. Martin (1965), 244; Whetstone, *English Myrror*, 233; Hall, *Poems*, ed. Davenport, 26.

merits of each party's case, but on the size of his purse and his counsellor's influence with the presiding judge.[18] Thus corruption, mystification, and trickery triumphed over justice, with the lawyer's full connivance—or at least that of all except 'the worthy professors of the law, who make not private wealth but the good and peace of the commonwealth, the end of their study and practices'.[19]

For, as we saw at the outset of this chapter, the contemporary image of the legal profession was not wholly one-sided. The obverse of the corrupt and unscrupulous lawyer was the 'worthy advocate', or 'honest lawyer', whose virtues mirrored his reprobate opposite's shortcomings. We meet them side by side in character books and in poetic tributes to individual counsellors, which use the conventional attributes of the bad lawyer as a foil to highlight the merits of their subject.[20] It was also common form for critics of the profession to accompany their attacks with a general disclaimer to the effect that they honoured the lawyer's calling, and were concerned only to denounce those who disgraced it. These might, nevertheless, constitute the majority of practitioners, as an Elizabethan author maintained:

> I mean the false and subtle ones
> I speak not of the true,
> Nor such as are affected well
> (as many there are such
> Although the false in number do
> exceed them very much.)

But were the 'worthy professors' indeed a distinct and hapless minority, 'clientless and few, friendless and poor'?[21]

---

[18] Earle, *Microcosmographie*, sigs. B7–B7ᵛ; Rich, *Allarme to England*, sigs. ciii–ciiiᵛ; T. Churchyard, *The Honor of the Lawe* (1596), *passim*; R. Brathwait, *The Good Wife* (1618), sig. G4ᵛ; Burton, *Anatomy of Melancholy*, i. 66–7, 92–5; Hayes, *Paragon of Persia*, 16–17; N. Rogers, *The True Convert* (1632), 64; Garey, *Jentaculum Judicum*, 49–54; T. Jordan, *Pictures of Passions, Fancies, & Affections* (n.d. [1641]), sigs. [D6–7].

[19] Scot, *Second Part of Philomythie*, sig. A3.

[20] Cf. A. Garden, *Characters and Essayes* (Aberdeen, 1625), 27–9; T. Fuller, *The Holy State and the Profane State* (1642), 51–3; H. C., *The Character of an Honest Lawyer* (1676), in *Somers Tracts* (1748), pt. I, iv. 305–8; Stephens, *Characters*, 192–8; R. Brathwait, *A Strappado for the Divell* (1615), 60–2; *idem, Times Curtaine Drawne*, sig. H3; R. H[ayman], *Quodlibets* (1628), 15; Herrick, *Poems*, 201.

[21] Hake, *Newes out of Powles Churchyarde*, sig. [B7ᵛ]. Cf. Burton, *Anatomy of Melancholy*, i. 92; Ruggle, *Ignoramus*, sigs. Hᵛ–H2; J. Heath, *The House of Correction* (1619), sig. C4ᵛ; Jonson, *Works*, vi. 544; J. Downame, *Foure Treatises* (1609), 217.

ii. Realities

It has been maintained that the poor public image of the Yorkist and early Tudor legal profession derived largely from a combination of jealousy, misinformation, and distrust. Generalized 'condemnation of the lawyers seems usually to have been the result of ignorance', while the validity of specific accusations usually cannot be assessed for want of evidence. A few lawyers may have delayed justice or shown partiality for or against particular litigants, but 'allegations of widespread corruption do not seem warranted'.[22] Can these conclusions be extended to our later period?

The standards by which the conduct of early modern lawyers is judged must plainly be those of their time, not ours. Of course these were not entirely fixed and uniform. Clerical critics, for instance, tended to condemn outright all lawyers who defended 'bad' causes, whereas barristers took a more instrumental view of their role, arguing that a lawyer must not prejudge the outcome of a trial, and therefore could legitimately offer his services to any client, so long as he avoided 'injury to the right cause or any man's person'. (How exactly this rather vague rider might be implemented in practice was not specified.)[23] Nevertheless, broad agreement existed that lawyers should not encourage frivolous, malicious, or hopeless suits, take on more causes than they could handle, fail to plead after having been retained, slander witnesses or the opposing litigants, seek to corrupt judge or jury, use delaying tactics, or, in general 'hurt any just trial'.[24]

Even if we can settle on the criteria, their application inevitably poses major difficulties. The incidence of improper conduct among legal practitioners anywhere, at any time, necessarily resists precise measurement. Delinquent lawyers are unlikely to volunteer much information about their own misdeeds, while unsupported allegations of corruption, incompetence, or negligence, especially from disappointed clients, can hardly be taken at face value. However, let

---

[22] Ives, 'Reputation of Common Lawyers', 133, 150, 155; cf. *idem, Common Lawyers*, 309–21.

[23] Scot, *Vox Dei*, 42–7; E. Gee, *Two Sermons* (1620), 24; J. Squire, *A Sermon Preached At Hartford Assizes* (1618), 16; Folger MS X.d. 122, 3 (one of a series of notes on the ethics of legal practice by William Lambard); J. Davies, *Le Primer Report des Cases in les Courts del Roy* (Dublin, 1615), sigs. *6ᵛ–*7ᵛ; Benn, 'Essays', fols. 29ᵛ–31ᵛ.

[24] Cf. sources cited in n. 23 above; Lansdowne 211, fols. 109ᵛ–112; CUL MS Add. 6863, fols. 7ᵛ–8ᵛ; Haward, *Reports*, 128; *Somers Tracts*, vi. 232–3.

us begin by looking at some specific charges levelled against particular barristers in the late sixteenth and early seventeenth centuries. This may at least help to place the generalized literature of complaint in context, as well as illustrate the problems of interpretation posed by the detailed evidence.

To begin with, it must be said that complaints setting out detailed allegations of malpractice against named barristers are not exactly widespread, as Ives also found for the earlier period which he studied. Of course, the reasons for this may well include diffidence, mystification, resignation, a shortage of remedies, and fear of retaliation on the part of injured laymen, rather than, or as well as, widespread public satisfaction with the ethics and efficiency of the upper branch. The largest body of evidence comprises bills or petitions from Star Chamber and other conciliar courts, in which counsellors were typically accused of cheating clients out of their property by providing fraudulently misleading professional advice.[25] In most cases only the plaintiff's original petition survives, but where we also have the defendant barrister's answer, it predictably claims that his possession of the disputed lands or goods was the result of an entirely legitimate transaction.[26] Other allegations against barristers, which did not involve claims of a breach of trust, included browbeating litigants or witnesses in legal proceedings before another court, signing slanderous bills, and prosecuting malicious suits.[27] Although the outcome of these cases is generally unknown, it can be presumed that most were unsuccessful, since those accused seem rarely to have suffered any noticeable interruption of their careers; however, the penalties imposed in the few more-or-less fully reported Star Chamber cases involving accusations of malpractice against barristers did not invariably include disbarring from practice. In the 1590s counsel who signed bills held to be slanderous or of no substance (in a case where the plaintiff's suit was dismissed with costs to the defendant) were debarred, as was a barrister held to have suborned witnesses. But a colleague whom the court 'condemned for a cunning and subtle practice' by manipulating the words of a dying man in order to construct a seemingly valid will got off scot-free.[28]

---

[25] E.g. STAC 8/42/16, 106/8, 158/3, 177/6, 221/10; *Exchequer Proceedings Concerning Wales, in tempore James I*, ed. T. I. Jones (Cardiff, 1955), 165, 209–10; HL RO, Main Papers, 1 May 1628, petition of Nicholas Hoaker; Ellesmere 5964, 6084.

[26] E.g. STAC 8/6/11, 116/14, 241/24, 263/5; *APC 1618–19*, 256–7.

[27] STAC 8/134/3, 177/6, 187/24; Monro, *Acta Cancellariæ*, 72.

[28] Haward, *Reports*, 55, 82, 90, 160, 195–9.

Needless to say, it cannot be assumed that conviction and sentencing necessarily imply guilt, or vice versa. In 1604 Sir John Hele, the king's senior serjeant at law, was prosecuted in Star Chamber and fined £1,000 for allegedly seeking to deprive the Crown of lands formerly held by the attainted traitor Lord Cobham, Hele's erstwhile client and debtor. Part of the case against the serjeant was that he had misled Cobham about the true nature of a defeasance or quitclaim, drawn up 'cautelously and craftily' for Cobham's signature. When sentence was given, the majority of the common-law judges, Sir Robert Cecil, and a number of other lay lords 'acquitted the serjeant of all note and blemish of infamy', but Lord Chancellor Ellesmere found him 'guilty in all of corruption and ambition, craft and covetous practices', proposing a fine of £2,000 and suspension from office. In fact, Ellesmere had been gunning for Hele since at least November 1600, when the latter called in a debt of £400 in retaliation for Ellesmere's refusal to support his efforts to acquire the office of master of the Rolls. Ellesmere's dossier on the serjeant includes claims that two hundred persons could bear witness 'that he ordinarily taketh fees on both parts', as well as six detailed instances of such practices. Of course, the chancellor's prejudice does not necessarily invalidate such evidence, if indeed it ever really existed; but unless, and until, some other source corroborating these accusations can be located, it might be prudent to suspend judgement on the charge that Hele was 'a notorious and common ambidexter'.[29]

Allegations of this kind could lead barristers to bring actions for defamation. The commonest slanders alleged incompetence or double dealing, sometimes in picturesque language: 'He is a paltry lawyer and hath as much law as a jack-an-ape.' 'He is a dunce and will get little by the law.' 'Thou art no lawyer, thou canst not make a lease, thou hast that degree without desert, they are fools that come to thee for law.' 'Thou art a daffa-down-dilly' [ambidexter]. 'He will deceive you, he was of counsel with me and revealed the secrets of my case.' 'Thou art no barrister, thou art a barretor. . . . Thou study law? Thou hast as much wit as a daw.' But although truth was an

---

[29] STAC 8/9/4; Haward, *Reports*, 171–6; J. S. Cockburn, 'The Spoils of law: the trial of Sir John Hele, 1604', in *Tudor Rule and Revolution*, ed. Guth and McKenna, 309–44. There seems, however, to have been more substance to the charges of corruption which were used as a pretext for suspending Lord Chief Baron Manwood in 1591 (Clark, *English Provincial Society*, 291).

absolute defence in such actions, the reported cases rather turn on the question of whether the words objected to could be construed in a milder and hence non-actionable sense.[30]

While charges culled from the records of litigation tend to be constrained and distorted by the demands of legal formalism, complaints against individual barristers from other quarters are much rarer, and no easier to interpret. Nicholas Assheton grumbled that the delay of a suit in the Court of Wards was due to the 'slowness' of his counsel Henry Sherfield; but next term, when the case came to hearing, Sherfield secured a favourable outcome, so for all we know the hold-up may have been both unavoidable and in Assheton's best interests. On the other hand, the dean of Winchester, who expressed dismay at the lack of prior instruction displayed by counsel on both sides at the hearing of a suit before the Privy Council in the 1630s, was evidently not alone in his disquiet, since he recorded that 'his Majesty said he never saw so much good counsel come so ill-prepared'. Another suitor's tale of woe, which also carries the ring of conviction, recounts how during the Interregnum,

Serjeant Conyers took a fee of me to move in Chancery and kept it four several days . . . yet this serjeant just as he came to the bar gave me my fee and ran into the court and told me that the attorney-general was against me and he durst not, nor would meddle in the cause; so I was forced to move the commissioners myself.

Again, a barrister-diarist noted with disgust in 1602 how 'this day Serjeant Harris was retained for the plaintiff and he argued for the defendant; so negligent that he knows not for whom he speaks'. At the same time none of these personal accounts impute dishonesty, as distinct from negligence, to members of the bar, and the allegations against Serjeant Conyers are accompanied by explicit commendations of 'some I have had trial of . . . Serjeant Twisden, William Wilde, Shelton and a few others', as 'mild to their clients and honest . . . and had great care'.[31]

In short, while specific accusations against named individual barristers may give us a clearer idea of the varieties of improper

---

[30] *English Reports*, lxxii. 846, lxxvii. 1480–1, lxxvii. 590, lxxii. 670; Rolle, *Abridgement*, 54–7; Coke, *Reports*, ed. Wilson, xii. 71; J. March, *Actions for Slander* (1655), 84–5. Cf. Harleian 4552, fol. 131ᵛ.

[31] *The Journal of Nicholas Assheton of Downham*, ed. F. R. Raines (Chetham Soc., 1848), 115–16, 125–6; cf. Bell, *Court of Wards*, 102; *The Diary of John Young S.T.P.*, ed. F. R. Goodman (1928), 133–4; Scull, *Dorothea Scott*, 45; Manningham, *Diary*, 76.

conduct in which early modern lawyers engaged, their interpretation is fraught with difficulty. Charges made in the course of legal proceedings are likely to have been substantially influenced, and perhaps distorted, by the requirements of legal process. Hence, the prevalence or absence of certain kinds of allegations is no necessary indication of the actual frequency of particular varieties of misconduct. While generalized complaints by preachers and others often alleged that barristers encouraged clients to embark upon unnecessary or unwinnable suits, the lack of specific charges to this effect against individual barristers during our period indicates not the rarity of such practices, but that they were both hard to prove and not formally illegal.

In any case, even if it could be assumed that most or all of the recorded complaints against particular barristers were in fact true and fully justified, it might still be argued that such delinquents constituted only a tiny and quite unrepresentative minority of the entire working bar. The problem is not whether some or any early modern barristers were careless, lazy, stupid, or venal, because it must be presumed that every occupational group, then as now, had its quota of fools and knaves. The real question is how far barristers' shortcomings can be ascribed to the inherent conditions of legal practice in the early modern period, rather than to the moral failings of individual lawyers. The mushroom growth of the bar and the inadequacies of legal education at the inns of court lend plausibility to accusations that individual barristers were incompetent, even if we cannot tell whether any specific charge to this effect was no more than a mischievous or malicious slander; again, the strong pressure of demand from clients for the services of favourites and other leading counsel illuminates complaints that barristers were ill prepared or even absent when suits came to hearing. In the same way, consideration of the general nature and functions of litigation in early modern England may clarify the prevalence of the most serious charges, of corrupt and dishonest behaviour, levelled against barristers during our period.

Private law and litigation now play such a relatively insignificant part in the life of most modern western societies that a major effort of imagination is required to grasp their central prominence in early modern times. The late sixteenth and early seventeenth centuries constituted possibly the most litigious era in English history, as well as a time when legal forms and institutions impinged upon almost every aspect of daily life. The explosion of litigation which so alarmed contemporaries was facilitated by the low initial cost of going to law, and the fact that attorneys commonly allowed their clients to sue on credit.[32] If litigation was a favourite indoor sport of the period, as some historians have suggested, the players were not drawn solely from the landed élite, but also included peasants, artisans, craftsmen, and merchants. True, no substantial landowner could expect to avoid being drawn into court by disputes about titles, wardships, inheritances, marriage settlements, and the like. Going to law may also have involved an element of conspicuous consumption—besides providing a convenient pretext for frequent visits to London. 'Suits in law are grown so common,' as the fifth earl of Huntingdon informed his son, 'he that hath not some is out of fashion.' In 1632 Nathaniel Walworth invited his friend Peter Seddon to 'come up to London and cast away a little money of that you have hoarded up, by being so long at rest from suits and law businesses'. Sir Thomas Pelham of Halland in Laughton was one of the landed gentry of early Stuart Sussex for whom (their historian tells us) 'litigation was a major pastime'. In the 1620s and 30s Sir Thomas regularly spent more than £100 a year on legal expenses, a substantial sum which was nevertheless dwarfed by the £800-odd which Sir Ralph Assheton of Walley, Lancashire, laid out for his lawsuits in 1628. As the poet Samuel Butler later pointed out, those who could not resist the peculiar charms of Westminster Hall were bound to pay a high price for their self-indulgence:

> Others believe no voice t'an Organ;
> So sweet as Lawyers in his Bar-gown
> Until, with subtle Cobweb-Cheats,
> Th'are catch'd in knotted Law, like Nets:
> . . . . . .
> And while their Purses can dispute,
> There's no end of th' immortal Suit.[33]

For most litigants of all classes, going to law, far from being a game, was, rather, a deadly serious enterprise, hazardous of out-

---

[32] Brooks, thesis, 40–1.
[33] Stone, *Crisis of the Aristocracy*, 242; HMC, *Hastings*, iv. 335; B. G. Blackwood, 'The Lancashire Gentry, 1625–1660: A Social and Economic Study', University of Oxford D.Phil. thesis, 1973, 61–2; *The Correspondence of Nathan Walworth and Peter Seddon of Outwood*, ed. J. S. Fletcher (Chetham Soc., 1880), 17; Fletcher, *Sussex*, 54–7; S. Butler, *Hudibras*, ed. J. Wilders (Oxford, 1967), II. iii. 15–22.

come and proverbially expensive in 'both charge and travail'. The third earl of Huntingdon may have spent the staggering sum of £10,000 in legal costs for a suit over the manor of Canford and its mines between 1581 and 1586; expenses associated with litigation were certainly a major factor in the economic decline of many noble and gentry families, the Hastings among them, during our period.[34] Nor were these burdens shouldered by the laity alone; in the late sixteenth century the 'aggressively litigious' Bishop Overton of Coventry and Lichfield estimated that he had laid out some £740 (almost a whole year's revenue) in bringing suits at common law to resume lands and rents of his diocese, while the fellows of Lincoln College, Oxford, spent £33 on law charges in 1595 and over £50 the following year, amounts which the college's historian considers 'extremely heavy ... not to say ruinous' in relation to their average annual income.[35] Urban boroughs, guilds, and trading companies were other corporate bodies particularly prone to involvement in substantial legal transactions and expenses. When Christopher Brooking made a 'voyage' up to London from deepest Devonshire in 1601 to defend the interests of the citizens of Totnes, he claimed more than £65 spent on a suit over one of the town's charities. In 1617, not an exceptionally litigious year, the London Vintners' Company paid in fees to lawyers and other legal charges some £150, well over 10 per cent of their total annual expenditure. In 1641 it was claimed that the Soap Boilers' Company set up in the 1630s had spent no less than £6,000 in lawsuits to defend their monopoly.[36] The Virginia Company appointed a solicitor in 1622 at a salary of £30 per annum 'for following of suits of law whereof many are like to arise'. In 1629 the East India Company's solicitor reported that since coming on the payroll two years before, he had been engaged in following twenty-six separate lawsuits, 'besides other employments

[34] C. Cross, *The Puritan Earl* (1966), 90–3; Cliffe, *Yorkshire Gentry*, 135–8; Finch, *Five Northants Families*, 81–2; Chalklin, *Seventeenth-Century Kent*, 202; Stone, *Crisis of the Aristocracy*, 240–2, 485.

[35] R. O'Day, 'Cumulative debt: the bishops of Coventry and Lichfield and their economic problems', *Midland Hist.*, iii (1975), 84–5; V. H. H. Green, *The Commonwealth of Lincoln College, 1427–1977* (Oxford, 1979), 211–13. Cf. F. Heal, *Of Prelates and Princes* (Cambridge, 1980), 265, 297–8.

[36] Devon RO, Totnes Borough Archives, 1579 A/10/17; Clode, *Merchant Taylors*, i. 343; A. Crawford, *A History of the Vintners' Company* (1977), 94; E. B. Jupp, *An Historical Account of the Worshipful Company of Carpenters ...* (1848), 274–5; *Warden's Accounts of the Worshipful Company of Founders ... 1497–1681*, ed. G. C. Parsloe (1964), 256–99; J. Youings, *Tuckers Hall, Exeter* (Exeter, 1968), 51; Anon., *Soap-Business*, 26.

which have in effect taken up his whole time'. This was perhaps not
an excessively heavy work-load by contemporary standards; the
courtier and projector Sir Arthur Ingram, who evidently regarded
litigation as a normal extension of his somewhat disreputable
business dealings, was at one point in his career conducting simultaneously no fewer than twenty-one lawsuits in five Westminster
courts.[37]

Yet if civil litigation in early modern England was anything but a
light-hearted pastime, it would be equally misleading to depict the
lawcourts as the domain of economic man (and woman) seeking
merely an expeditious resolution of material disputes. Contemporary notions of law emphasized its absolute and transcendent qualities as the earthly reflection of God's will. So far from being
regarded merely as a problem-solving instrument, an established set
of principles which prescribed rights and duties, the law was
expected to mete out strict justice in final and infallible pronouncements on the conflicting claims of plaintiff and defendant. High
expectations of the law as ultimate oracular arbiter may well have
encouraged resort to litigation, and must certainly have raised the
emotional investment of litigants in the outcome of their cases.

The law was also seen as a means of maintaining social harmony;
according to Sir Henry Finch's definition, 'Law is an art of well-
ordering a civil society', binding the community of the realm
together by the proper apportionment of individual rights and
obligations.[38] In practice, however, going to law often proved a
costly, protracted, and uncertain means of achieving this end, while
legal process was easily exploited to prosecute malicious suits and
pursue private vendettas. The lowly 'barrator', who 'vexes his
neighbours with frivolous and malicious suits', 'of very contentious
and malicious humour', 'troubling his neighbours and others with
unjust suits and vexations' joined hands with the over-mighty
subject in exploiting the law for private ends—men like Lord
William Howard, 'Belted Will', of Naworth Castle, Cumberland,
who was described as 'most powerful in the country by his hard
dealing and many suits . . . half of which would make a mean man a

---

[37] Kingsbury, *Virginia Company*, ii. 150–1, 155; *Cal. State Papers Col., 1625–9*,
674; A. F. Upton, *Sir Arthur Ingram c.1565–1642* (1961), 204–7.
[38] Brooks, 'Litigants and Attorneys', 56–7. Cf. W. Lambard, *Archeion* (1635), sigs.
*1–*8; R. Tisdale, *The Lawyers Philosophy* (1622); Pulton, *De Pace Regis*, sigs. [Aiv–
Aivᵛ]; L. Lloyd, *A Briefe Conference of Divers Lawes* (1602), ch. 1; R. Bolton, *A
Justice of Peace for Ireland* (1638), 1.

common barrator`.[39] As in sixteenth-century Castile, where litigation 'closely resembled feuding, except that ... contestants armed themselves not with arquebuses and rapiers but with a brace of lawyers and a torrent of legal briefs', going to law in early modern England was often rather a means of continuing and expanding conflicts than bringing them to an end. The martial metaphors in which John Smyth of Nibley chronicled the 'combats of Littleton' engaged upon by the house of Berkeley during the sixteenth century were thus entirely appropriate to his subject.[40]

Each move in a protracted legal battle (and some were exceedingly drawn out—Edmund Plowden noted that a number of cases he reported were argued over eight, ten, or twelve terms, while wealthy litigants in Chancery could easily keep a suit going for decades) was likely to attract the attention of an appreciative and well-informed audience.[41] Sir Richard Cholmley gained 'much honour and applause' in his native Yorkshire for foiling Sir Thomas Hoby's 'several suits' (stemming from a quarrel on the bench at quarter sessions). During a tithe dispute at Chipping Campden, Gloucestershire, copies of an injunction handed down by the Council in the Marches were 'thrown about the town as thick as play bills in London' by one faction, while their opponents were accordingly entreated, 'what you may do by law that you would do for the plaguing of that vicar and his damned crew and that you would have them all come up to London'. After the successful conclusion of a Star Chamber suit in 1630, a Lancashire lawyer told his brother that he had cause to thank God for delivering him from wicked men: 'although He hath suffered your adversary to insult you yet it was before the victory and I hope their lungs will not hereafter be so lavish nor their boasts so great'.[42]

[39] HL RO, Main Papers, 24 June 1641, petition of inhabitants of Grafton Regis, Northants; *APC, 1590–1*, 197–8; *APC, 1591–2*, 266; MacCulloch, thesis, 81; Lowther, 'Autobiography', 214–28; *Yorks. Arch. Soc., Rec. Ser.*, iii (1888), 41, 79.

[40] Kagan, *Lawsuits and Litigants*, 161; Smyth, *Lives of the Berkeleys*, ii. 311 n. Cf. the interesting qualifications advanced by J. A. Sharpe, in Bossy, ed., *Disputes and Settlements*, 167–88.

[41] E. Plowden, *Les comentaries, ou les reportes . . . de dyvers cases* (1571), sig. [¶iiii]. For other examples of protracted suits, cf. H. Berry, 'Sir John Denham at Law', *Modern Philology*, lxxi (1974), 267–76; Beds. RO, OR 1086–1283, 1941–62; Hoare, *Modern Wiltshire*, iii: *Warminster Hundred*, 37.

[42] *The Memoirs of Sir Hugh Cholmley* (1787), 21; C. Whitfield, 'Lionel Cranfield and the Rectory of Campden', *Trans. Bristol and Gloucs. Arch. Soc.*, lxxxvi (1962), 104; Lancs. RO, DD Ke 9/9 (38).

So litigants plainly risked reputation and status, as well as time and money, when they went to court. No wonder the perils of litigation were so widely canvassed, or that it was generally agreed, on prudential as well as moral grounds, that men should seek by all means to avoid suits whenever they could. Newly called serjeants at law were admonished 'first advise your client to attempt all the means possible to procure his right and to seek it by mediation and treaty; let suit be the last remedy'.[43] In the early seventeenth century the Welsh lawyer Thomas Powell and John Daccombe, a master in Chancery, both supported proposals for arbitration services designed to settle poor men's disputes out of court; the townspeople of Basingstoke formally appointed their recorder Robert Mason to the role of community mediator in 1625, while the Middle Temple barrister Charles Cocks left £40 per annum by his will in 1637 to establish a panel of barristers who would act as informal arbiters and conciliators in petty causes, 'having observed that multiplicity of suits in the law tend not only to the disquiet of the commonwealth but the decay of many families'.[44]

Many of those who nevertheless found themselves embroiled in litigation heartily regretted the experience, like the dowager countess of Pembroke who complained in 1654 to her man of business about the 'slow progress of her law suits . . . and the burthensome charge and grievousness thereof'. The letter-writer John Chamberlain, a man of the world if ever there was one, wrote in disgust to Sir Dudley Carleton in mid-June 1624:

The term is come to an end but my suit in Chancery is not ended though I have done my uttermost both by myself and by friends. The fair shows and proceedings in the beginning promised a more speedy success; but as I ever had (though but in speculation) no great good opinion of the law so now by practice and experience of these dilatory courses, I am the more confirmed to think it one of the greatest grievances of our commonwealth.

A year later a Norfolk gentleman, Thomas Knyvett, complained indignantly to his wife when he heard that his Chancery cause would

---

[43] CUL MS Add. 6863, fol. 5; cf. Berks. RO, D/ELI c 1/7.
[44] CUL MS Dd. 3. 88 (10), p. 52; BL MS Royal 18 A, xxxvi; F. J. Baigent and J. E. Millard, *A History of the Ancient Town and Manor of Basingstoke* (Basingstoke, 1889), 453; MT MS unclassified, Indenture tripartite 1637; *MTR*, iii. 1160, 1190–5; *Master Worsley's Book*, ed. A. R. Ingpen (1910), 199–200.

not be heard before the end of term that it was the 'most unconscionable dealing that men should be forced to attend a whole term and disburse his (*sic*) money for nothing'. But at least Knyvett had not actually lost his case, unlike a neighbour, Sir Francis Lee, who threw 'a great feast for his counsel' the night before his hearing, where the case was debated, with Sir Randle Crew acting as judge, 'and there it went clearly of Sir Francis his side . . . but the next day the case was altered'. The unfortunate Sir Francis was 'not so much dejected, as cast down, and swears he will never go to law again'—a resolution doubtless shared by most unsuccessful litigants. Thus Giles Moore concluded a list of his law costs in 1662 with this rueful observation: 'All which money was foolishly cast away upon lawyers. . . . He who goeth to law when he can possibly avoid it is an absolute fool and one that loveth to be fleeced.'[45]

Given all that might ultimately depend on the outcome of a suit, besides its considerable immediate demands on litigants' time, money, and energy, it is hardly surprising that cases tended to be heard in a tense and highly charged atmosphere. Courtroom drama was an Elizabethan literary invention, and although the trial scene from *The Merchant of Venice* unfortunately provides little guidance with regard to the details of contemporary common-law procedure, it is clear that major courts were crowded, confused, and noisy places. Barristers jostled shoulder to shoulder in Westminster Hall, clamouring for audience, interrupting each other's arguments, and occasionally disputing with the bench, attorneys, or bystanders; even serjeants at law had to be cautioned not to 'speak at once for by that means neither can the judges understand the matter nor yourselves therein get any credit especially by interrupting'.[46] Brawling and railing were part of the lawyer stereotype: according to Ben Jonson, it was necessary only to 'plod enough, talk and make noise enough, be impudent enough' in order to succeed at the bar. One of the most obnoxious characteristics of his professional colleagues, in Sir Anthony Benn's view, was their habit of denigrating and taunting the opposing party and witnesses; among the law-reform measures debated in the 1621 parliament was a bill aimed at curbing

---

[45] Yorks. Arch. Soc. MS DD 121/109; Chamberlain, *Letters*, ii. 564; *Knyvett Letters*, ed. Schofield, 61, 67; *The Journal of Giles Moore*, ed. R. Bird (Sussex Rec. Soc., 1971), 86–8.
[46] CUL MS Add. 6863, fol. 5ᵛ. Cf. F[idge], *Great Eater*, 3; *Table Talk of John Selden*, ed. F. Pollock (1927), 111; Manningham, *Diary*, 100; Herrick, *Poems*, 303; '*Merry Passages*', ed. Lippincott, 32, 195; Donne, *Satires*, ed. Milgate, 135.

'opprobrious speeches' by counsel. Besides verbally harassing the opposition, barristers were also liable to taunt the presiding judge or judges. Indeed, Benn felt it necessary to advise lawyers who lost a case not to 'be so much as heard to let fall any word that may tend to the blemish of the court, as that either the judge denied hearing or understood not the cause or was partial in judgement'.[47]

For their part, judges were accustomed to browbeat counsel from the bench; at the Lincoln assizes in August 1606 Mr Justice Walmsley was said to have so intimidated Sir Richard Ogle's lawyers that neither 'durst speak a word', while John Haward's Star Chamber reports preserve some striking examples of the tirades Lord Keeper Egerton customarily directed against counsel who displeased him, including the puritan Nicholas Fuller ('Fuller of all lawyers the worse') and Thomas Hitchcock of Lincoln's Inn (who was 'sharply rebuked all day by the Lord Keeper with such words as "you must go to school to learn more wit, you are not well advised, you forget your place and to be plain it is a lie"'). Conversely, those pleaders whose words and demeanour gratified the bench could expect fulsome praise, like John Croke, recorder of London, who was 'commended for his discretion, judgement, learning and good and reverent regard to this court'. In his essay 'Of Judicature', Sir Francis Bacon, Ellesmere's successor, approved of 'some commendation and gracing, where causes are well handled and fair pleaded' and a 'civil reprehension of advocates, where there appeareth cunning counsel, gross neglect, slight information, indiscreet pressing or an over-bold defence'. At the same time Bacon warned judges not to have 'noted favourites: which cannot but cause multiplication of fees and suspicion of bye-ways'.[48]

The conventions governing the behaviour of judges, counsel, and litigants in early modern England plainly differed from those which apply in most Western societies today. Proportionately more people were directly involved in legal proceedings conducted at a much higher emotional and psychological temperature than our modern, purpose-built, and publicly deserted courtrooms normally witness, except for the occasional *cause célèbre*. Moreover, it is now usually (and on the whole reasonably) assumed that judges and other legal

[47] Jonson, *Works*, iv. 212–13; Benn, 'Essays', fols. 27ᵛ, 35ᵛ; *CD 1621*, vi. 105, and *CJ*, i. 595. Cf. *The Comedies of George Chapman*, ed. T. M. Parrott (1914), 126–7; STAC 8/134/3; H. Hobart, *Reports in the reign of James I* (1641), 328.

[48] HMC, *Salisbury*, xviii. 220–1; Haward, *Reports*, 43–5, 55, 74, 82, 126, 128–9; Bacon, *Works*, vi. 508; '*Merry Passages*', ed. Lippincott, 134.

functionaries concerned with the hearing of civil actions are neither corrupt nor consciously partial. In Tudor and early Stuart times the opposite assumption seems often, perhaps generally, to have prevailed.

Belief that the favour of judges was both worth winning and capable of being won came naturally to what Weber termed a 'status' society, where all branches of public administration were strongly influenced by clientage, personal loyalties, and deference to rank or degree. Indeed the pre-Civil War English judge had as much in common with Weber's ideal-typical 'master ... moved by personal sympathy and favour, by grace and gratitude' as with the 'personally detached and strictly "objective" *expert*'.[49] At the same time, judges' behaviour both on and off the bench continually reinforced the widespread scepticism about the impartiality and integrity of their order, expressed by, among many others, James I, Sir Walter Ralegh, Thomas Hobbes, Robert Burton, Henry Barrow, John Downame, Robert Herrick, George Whetstone, and Thomas Scott.[50]

Judicial favouritism of individual counsellors may have been neither so firmly institutionalized nor so blatantly corrupt as in sixteenth- and seventeenth-century Scotland, but the practice was widespread, aroused grave (and by no means unjustified) suspicions, and depended entirely upon the sanction of individual judges for its continuance.[51] During our period Chief Baron Sir Lawrence Tanfield, Sir Robert Hitcham as an assize judge, and the Welsh judge Richard Broughton all seem to have presided at the trial of causes to which they were effectively parties.[52] Although common-law judges of Westminster Hall were sworn not to provide counsel to private individuals, this oath was violated during our period by, among

[49] *From Max Weber*, ed. Gerth and Mills, 216.

[50] D'Ewes, *Autobiography*, i. 188; Chamberlain, *Letters*, ii. 383; T. Hobbes, *Leviathan*, ed. M. Oakeshott (Oxford, 1946), 181; Herrick, *Poems*, 123; *The Poems of Sir Walter Ralegh*, ed. A. M. C. Latham (1929), 44; Downame, *Foure Treatises*, 225–8; Burton, *Anatomy of Melancholy*, i. 67; Whetstone, *English Myrror*, 237–8; T. Scott, *Foure Paradoxes* (1602), sig. B3; T. Churchyard, *The Firste parte of Churchyardes chippes* (1591), 14; *Wentworth Papers*, ed. Cooper, 19–20. Cf. *Calendar of State Papers and Manuscripts ... in ... Venice ...*, ed. R. Brown et al. (1864–), xxiv (1636–1639), 165–6.

[51] J. I. Smith, 'The Transition to the Modern Law, 1532–1660', in *An Introduction to Scottish Legal History*, ed. G. C. H. Paton (Stair Soc., 1958), 26; see above pp. 27–30.

[52] R. H. Gretton, *The Burford Records* (Oxford, 1920), 53–9; Haward, *Reports*, 145; *Reports of Cases in Star Chamber and High Commission*, ed. S. R. Gardiner (CS, 1886), 117.

others, the saintly Sir Augustine Nicolls, whom Thomas Fuller noted for his 'exemplary integrity, even to the rejection of gratuities after judgement giving'. No such provision constrained the Welsh judges, most of whom accordingly practised at Westminster Hall, and were sometimes retained there in cases on which they would later sit as judges at the Great Sessions of Wales.[53]

Other dubious practices from which judges benefited and which they made no apparent effort to discontinue or discourage included the presentation of Christmas and New Year's gifts by suitors and counsel, the acceptance of annuities from private individuals, and the provision of lavish hospitality on assize circuits by local gentry, townsfolk, and lawyers.[54] An equally questionable custom was the solicitation of judges by litigants or their patrons, both in person and by letter. To preserve the proprieties, such approaches would of course disavow 'any intention to lose my labour in going about to draw partiality or undue respect from a learned and religious judge' (the earl of Bridgewater to Mr Justice Whitelocke, 1621), purporting to seek only 'what favour you lawfully may for my sake' (the duke of Buckingham to Lord Chancellor Bacon, *c*.1620).[55] Perhaps requests of this nature were so common as to have little effect on the conduct or outcome of trials; indeed, Sir Anthony Benn maintained that suitors would abandon such importunities if they only knew 'how little it prevails and how much it hurts their own cause'. But as long as the practice was not actually proscribed, suitors were hardly to be blamed for thinking that its possible benefits amply justified efforts like those of Sir John Harington of Kelston, who, in August and September 1600, arranged for at least thirteen letters to be written on his behalf in connection with a suit, including three by the queen herself, and another by the master of the Wards Sir Robert Cecil to Thomas Hesketh, attorney of the Wards.[56]

[53] Ellesmere 7539; Baker, *English Legal History*, 143–4; Northants RO, Letters of the Montagu Family 1536–1747, vol. I, fol. 65; Fuller, *Worthies of England*, ii. 512; Bolton, *Foure last Things*, 155.
[54] For gifts see Whitelocke, *Lib. Fam.*, 45, 49, 92–3; E. Cust, *Records of the Cust Family . . .* (1898–1927), ii. 54–6; HMC, *Rutland*, i. 432; Foss, vii. 375; *DNB*, s.v Cowper, Lord William. For annuities see HMC, *Rutland*, iv. 473, 492. For hospitality see Cooper, ed. 'Expenses of the Judges of Assize', 1–53; *The Farington Papers*, ed. S. M. Ffarington (Chetham Soc., 1856), iv–v, 28–55.
[55] Ellesmere 6472; *Fortescue Papers*, ed. Gardiner, 21–2, 88, 148. Cf. HMC, *De L'Isle and Dudley*, vi. 118; A. Day, *The English Secretorie* (1586), 192–3.
[56] Benn, 'Essays', fols. 51ᵛ–52ᵛ; F. J. Poynter, *Memoranda, historical and genealogical, relating to the Parish of Kelston, in the County of Somerset* (1878), pt. iii, 78. For

Approaches in person to judges (or their servants) naturally left less trace on the record. But they may well have occurred as a matter of course, judging from a graphic description of Lord Keeper Ellesmere as

wont every morning during term time, after the dispatching suitors of the better rank, in his great chamber gallery in York House, to come into the chapel to public prayers, wherein the meanest suitors might accompany his lordship; who upon ending of prayers, came through a waiting room down the stair into the hall, and so through it to his coach, that all petitioners might take their opportunities to put up their complaints or deliver their petitions to himself.[57]

The customary lack of physical and psychological distance between judges and litigants was highlighted by an incident in 1616, when Sir John Tindall, one of the masters in Chancery, was accosted on the doorstep of his Lincoln's Inn chamber by a disgruntled suitor, 'who moved Sir John that the matter might be put to compromise', and on receiving what he took to be a refusal, produced a pistol with which he shot and killed the unfortunate Tindall.[58]

It is not difficult to understand how these circumstances and practices combined to encourage both general suspicion and specific charges of judicial corruption. No doubt many such accusations sprang from the bitter frustration of unsuccessful litigants, like the king's printer who in 1630 claimed that a decree made against him in Chancery had been secured by means of a £600 bribe paid to Lord Keeper Coventry's secretary. (Sir Francis Ashley, then one of the king's serjeants at law, was prepared to sign a bill to this effect, although he seems subsequently to have tendered a formal apology.) Given the number of such claims and charges, one can see why 'a judge of clean hands and good integrity' might be positively commended for these virtues.[59]

illuminating comparisons, cf. J. M. Kelly, *Roman Litigation* (Oxford, 1966), ch. 2; K. B. McFarlane, *The Nobility of Later Medieval England* (Oxford, 1973), 114–16.

[57] R. W[illis], *Mount Tabor* (1639), 144. Cf. HMC, *Exeter*, 102–3; HMC, *Salisbury*, xxii. 254; G. Norburie, 'The Abuses and Remedies of Chancerie', in *A Collection of Tracts Relative to the Laws of England*, ed. F. Hargrave (Dublin, 1787), 433; Jonson, *Works*, i. 201.

[58] Anon., *A True Relation of a most desperate Murder . . . (1617)*; *DNB*, s.v. Tindall, Sir John; Yonge, *Diary*, 29. Cf. *Diary of John Rous . . . 1625 to 1642*, ed. M. A. E. Green (CS, 1856), 62 for assaults on the judges Sir Thomas Richardson and Sir Walter Pye in 1631.

[59] H. R. Plomer, 'The King's Printing Works under the Stuarts', *The Library*, NS ii (1901), 353–75; SP 16/169/5, 175/123; Ellesmere 7956; Rushworth, *Historical Collections* I. ii. 30; *Analecta Hibernica*, viii. 135.

Thus, in 1580, Thomas Baker was sentenced to lose his ears for 'slanderous words against the Lord Dyer saying he was the corruptest judge in England'; William Hilliard, vice-president of the Council in the North, was said in 1594 to be 'a bloodsucker' whose favour could be bought 'for a couple of capons or a couple of wethers'; Lord Cavendish called Mr Justice Jones a 'corrupt judge' in Star Chamber in 1624; two separate charges of corruption against Sir Euble Thelwall in his capacity as master of Chancery were the subject of Star Chamber trials during the early years of Charles I's reign, while the barrister John Puleston, himself a future judge, brought a petition against Sir Thomas Milward, chief justice of Chester, to Parliament in 1641, accusing him (rather obscurely) 'for taking of the presents money'.[60]

Predictably, sheer lack of evidence makes it very difficult to take these accusations any further. To borrow Sir Anthony Benn's words once more, 'Men are modest and secret in causes of such nature, they give their bribes as Nero did his offices of justice.' The evidence which has survived is also not always easy to interpret. We know from his book of personal expenses that in December 1611 the Inner Temple bencher Paul Croke presented a sugar-loaf, dried currants, and raisins, presumably for making punch or spiced wine, to his brother Sir John, a puisne justice of King's Bench, together with twelve gallons of muscadine wine (worth just over three shillings per gallon), to Chief Justice Sir Edward Coke, and fourteen gallons of a slightly less expensive sack to Sir Edward Phelipps, master of the Rolls. These latter two gifts, which do not recur in subsequent years, were possibly quite as innocent as the former undoubtedly was; Croke's kinship connections must have been more than sufficient to ensure his favoured status before the court of King's Bench, without any additional *douceurs*. Yet it is interesting to find Coke, with whom Paul Croke does not otherwise seem to have been familiar, as the recipient of such presents, given his firm public stance against judicial corruption, and the handsome testimonial of James Whitelocke following Coke's dismissal from office in 1616:

Never was man so just, so upright, free from corruption, solicitations of great men or friends, as he was. Never put counsellors that practised before him to annual pensions of money or plate to have his favour. In all causes before him the counsellor might assure his client from the danger of bribery,

---

[60] Ellesmere 2740; *English Reports*, lxxii. 667; Knowler, i. 21; Rushworth, *Historical Collections*, I. ii. 12, 31; *Salusbery Correspondence*, 117, 119.

the secret mischiefs growing by wife, children, servants, chamber motions, courtiers great or small.

So consumables of relatively small cash value (like the salmon worth twenty-two shillings Whitelocke himself sent Coke in 1615) were evidently exchanged as marks of affection and respect, courtesies which might strengthen a client–patron relationship but which had no further, sinister connotations.[61]

Yet Whitelocke's eulogy of Coke's high ethical standards casts immediate and serious doubts on the integrity of his fellow judges. This may not have been unintentional, and such an assessment from a practising barrister has to be taken seriously. So too must the anecdotes and gossip retailed by a number of Whitelocke's colleagues. For example, Richard Dyot, recorder of Stafford, notes in his commonplace book that Sir Thomas Tildesley, one of the fee'd counsellors who acted as judges for the Council of the North at York, 'useth to say to one that hath made him good cheer, or sent him a good present, "Indeed you are to blame, God's blessing on your heart",' and also records a story of Edmund Plowden avoiding indictment for recusancy by presenting £100 to the judge before whom he appeared. Again, Roger Wilbraham of Gray's Inn, a master of Requests, noted that 'to tickle a judge in the ear is nothing; but to anoint him in the hand with *ungentum aurum* is cordial to his heart'.[62]

Of course, these professional in-jokes are no more than straws in the wind—hardly conclusive, but nevertheless suggestive. Yet even that most celebrated of all cases of judicial corruption, Sir Francis Bacon's impeachment in 1621 for accepting bribes as lord chancellor, depended upon the evidence of single individuals, each themselves a party to the act, whose motives for testifying against the chancellor were by no means above suspicion. As it happened, Bacon in effect pleaded guilty to all charges, while simultaneously claiming that neither his own nor his servants' acceptance of bribes offered before and after judgement involved any conscious intention of perverting the course of justice. Despite Gardiner's apparent wish

[61] Benn, 'Essays', fol. 53; Croke, 'Diurnall', fol. 5; Whitelocke, *Lib. Fam.*, 50; White, *Sir Edward Coke*, ch. 3. Such gifts had always been excluded from the provisions of statutes regulating judicial behaviour (see S. Shetreet, *Judges on Trial* (Amsterdam, 1976), ch. 1).
[62] Staff. RO, D 661/11/1/7, fols. 16, 25; Folger MS M. b. 42, fol. 25.

to believe 'that his heart was pure while his actions were guilty', this piece of special pleading has generally carried little more weight with historians than it did with contemporaries. But (apart from under-lining the problem of evidence once more), the critical importance of Bacon's case for our purposes is the light it casts upon the mechan-isms of corruption, especially the role of the barrister-favourite as intermediary in transmitting bribes from litigant to judge.

The first two charges laid against Bacon by petitioners to the House of Commons in 1621 both involved Sir George Hastings, a barrister of Gray's Inn and younger brother of the earl of Hun-tingdon, who by his own account passed a total of £500 to Bacon on two separate occasions. Admitted to Gray's Inn in 1611 during Bacon's treasurership, Hastings was almost immediately given chief place on the ancients' table, and was called to the bar only six years later, having been knighted in 1615. Shortly after becoming a barrister, young Sir George was unexpectedly singled out to move the first motion heard by the newly installed lord chancellor. Although this honour was 'performed but poorly', Hastings evi-dently continued on terms of easy intimacy with his patron; when the storm broke in 1621, he was described as one of the chancellor's 'own friends', and Sir Robert Phelipps spoke of him 'struggling with himself betwixt ingratitude and honesty'.[63]

Zaller points out that Bacon's disgrace raised awkward questions about the integrity of the judicial bench as a whole, especially since it was followed almost immediately by the indictment of Sir John Bennet, a judge of the Prerogative Court of Canterbury, whose appalling record of gross and persistent corruption moved one contemporary observer to remark that it 'hath made my lord chancellor an honest man'.[64] Fortunately for the leadership of the Commons Bennet was a civilian, and no further accusations sur-faced. But at least one member of the Lower House could have contradicted from his own experience the optimistic boasts of Sir Edwin Sandys and Sir Robert Phelipps about the freedom of the common-law bench from any taint of corruption. Ironically enough,

[63] Marwil, *Trials of Counsel*, 43–62; Gardiner, *History*, iv. 99–100; *GI AdmR*, 125; *GIPB*, i. 193; *Al. Cant.*, ii. 328; Chamberlain, *Letters*, ii. 73, 354–5; *CD 1621*, ii. 237, v. 44–5.

[64] R. Zaller, *The Parliament of 1621* (Berkeley, 1971), 97–9; on 7 October 1619, Paul Croke recorded in his private code of law-French with Greek letters a payment to Sir John Bennet 'for his favour in the administration of the goods of Susan Milward' (Croke, 'Diurnall', fol. 30ᵛ).

the delinquent in this instance was Bacon's immediate successor on
the Woolsack, Chief Justice Sir James Ley, the later earl of Marlborough characterized by Milton as 'that good Earl . . . unstained with
gold or fee'. But Sir James Whitelocke, Ley's contemporary, claimed
that 'this old dissembler . . . was wont to be called Vulpone'—a
judgement which Henry Sherfield, who sat for Southampton in the
parliament of 1621, might have amply corroborated, if only at the
expense of his own name and reputation. For on the penultimate
page of his first fee book Sherfield had inscribed in law-French an
account of his own role as Ley's acknowledged favourite, in a
straightforward, if rather trivial, episode of corruption a decade
before:

Memorandum that the case between Richard Corbett Esq by information
plaintiff and Sir Robert Needham defendant was decreed in the Court of
Wards at the end of Michaelmas term 8 Jac., 1610. And on this decree Sir
Robert Needham left with me a gilt standing cup worth £10 as I estimated
for Sir Ja. L. This I delivered to him on December 2nd 1610, in his inner
chamber at Lincoln's Inn. But this was after the decree was signed by him
and before the decree was carried to him to enter.

It is not clear when this brief passage was written, but it is followed
immediately by a revealing gloss, this time in English:

For which I humbly ask forgiveness at God's hands, having given me the
grace never to offend in that kind since that evil act I then detesting as
abominable the same with promise to God never to offend again in that
manner which he hath enabled me to do hitherunto viz 3 June 1626
     Sit Deo Laus
and hitherunto viz 1 June 1627 Deo Laus[65]

These unique autobiographical fragments are fascinating, not
merely because they provide irrefutable evidence of the involvement
of counsel in corrupt dealings between litigant and judge. (True, Ley
did not then bear that title, but as Bell says, 'the influence of the
attorney of Wards, as the court's chief legal officer, was paramount'.) They also show that durable and readily negotiable gifts,
even of relatively small cash value (as compared with the amounts

[65] During Michaelmas term 1610 Sherfield received six fees from Sir Robert
Needham in this suit. For John Strode's assessment of Ley as 'a very partial judge',
see Dorset RO, MW M4, fols. 11ᵛ–12. *DNB*, s.v. Ley, Sir James; Hants RO, 44M69/
xxv/1 (my translation). In 1635 Sir Daniel Norton presented plate worth £100 to the
then attorney of Wards, Sir Walter Pye, in an attempt to gain his favour (Haley,
Shaftesbury, 18).

Bacon was supposedly taking in bribes ten years later), and even if made after the donor's suit had been actually decided, were regarded as 'evil' and 'abominable', not just by sermonizing clerics but also by a practising barrister, whose ethical standards in this respect seem little different from our own. How far Sherfield's scruples were shared by his colleagues it is impossible to say, although their surviving public and private pronouncements suggest that on this point his principles were entirely orthodox.[66] But if a man of such intense moral and religious convictions could not resist the inducements or pressures to assist a client in this way, it is hard to believe that his fellows, especially those who also enjoyed the privileged status—and access—of favourites, were less susceptible.

So we must conclude both that judicial corruption was a fact of life in pre-Civil War England, and that barristers played an integral role as go-betweens in the corrupt relationships of judges with litigants. At the same time, Sir Anthony Benn and other lawyers were right to insist that the fault did not lie all on one side: 'Corruption in justice and government ariseth not so much out of the evil disposition of judges and magistrates as out of evil men that pervert and abuse them.'[67] Of course, that formulation is not entirely convincing either. Judges and lawyers were not completely passive instruments of a litigant's desires, but quite capable of actively exploiting their ample opportunities for underhand gain. As long as the stakes invested in litigation and the number of investors remained at the height they reached during our period, some litigants would inevitably seek to use every possible means of gaining advantage over their opponents, and some lawyers would be found to assist them to this end. On the other hand, those whose suits were defeated found a convenient excuse in professional conspiracy, partiality, and venality. There was just enough chance of such claims being well-founded to lend them plausibility, and hence further reinforce the profession's traditionally dubious ethical reputation, although, as the barrister John Smyth of Nibley rightly maintained, the hazards of going to law were not solely attributable to the misconduct of lawyers:

---

[66] For helpful modern discussions of corruption, cf. Aylmer, *King's Servants*, 178–81; J. Hurstfield, 'Political Corruption in Early Modern England: The Historian's Problem', in *idem, Freedom, Corruption and Government in Elizabethan England* (1973), 137–62; L. L. Peck, *Northampton: Policy and Patronage at the Court of James I* (1982), ch. 8; Bell, *Court of Wards*, 98.

[67] Benn, 'Essays', fol. 52.

Clients, witnesses, jurors, counsel and judges are men and no angels ...
neither will be otherwise so long as men are men, neither may a paradise be
expected to be, where any man may innocently fall by the law, as by
ignorance or misprision; by his attorney or counsellor; by practise or
combination of the adversary; by perjury of witnesses; by forging of deeds;
by subornation or corruption of witnesses, jurors or officers of courts; by
affection, inclination or corruption in the judge, and by many other bye and
black ways, whereof many men have made experience.[68]

iii. Ideology

This grim recital doubtless embodies an element of vocational
special pleading. But Smyth's contemporaries did not condemn all
lawyers indiscriminately, nor hold them collectively responsible for
all the law's shortcomings. We have already noted that the stereotype of the bad lawyer had a mirror image, the good lawyer, whose
virtues counterbalanced the former's vices, even if he was generally
agreed to be far outnumbered by his unworthy opposites. Proverbial
wisdom also recognized that the foolish or greedy client was no less
to be condemned than the avaricious and crafty lawyer. Lawyers'
houses were said to be built upon the heads of fools, their gowns
lined with the wilfulness of their clients; in prudence one should not
'go for every quarrel to the lawyer', for 'the law is costly', and 'he
that goes to law holds a wolf by the ears'. In short, 'Fools and
obstinate men make lawyers rich'.[69] Most of these adages were
originally published in the first half of the seventeenth century, when
a few dramatists and poets were also beginning to depict individual
lawyers in a slightly more sympathetic fashion. Besides Ben Jonson's
commendatory verses to Sir Anthony Benn, Sir Edward Coke, and
other legal dignitaries, John Davies of Hereford saluted his 'highly
valued friend Mr William Hackwell, learned in the law', as did
Richard Hayman, one-time governor of the plantation at
Newfoundland, who also published verses addressed to William
Noy and to Nicholas Ducke, recorder of Exeter, while Robert
Herrick praised the integrity of 'his honoured friend, M. John
Weare, Councellor'.[70]

---

[68] Smyth, *Lives of the Berkeleys*, ii. 312.

[69] Tilley, *Dictionary of Proverbs*, 232, 370, 446–7; Draxe, *Bibliotheca Scholastica*,
112; G. Herbert, *Outlandish Proverbs* (1640), sigs. B3ᵛ, D3ᵛ, E; *The Macmillan Book of
Proverbs, Maxims and Phrases*, ed. B. Stevenson (New York, 1948), 1371.

[70] Jonson, *Poems*, 41, 152, 180, 206–7; J. Davies, *The Scourge of Folly* (1611), 97
(cf. ibid., 44–5, 229); H[ayman], *Quodlibets*, 15–16; Herrick, *Poems*, 201–2. Cf.
Donne, *Satires*, ed. Milgate, 55–9.

A few sober, upright counsellors appeared on the early Stuart stage, albeit less conspicuously than the sinister Volpone, the ridiculous Ignoramus, and a host of avaricious pettifoggers. Ariosto, 'the very miracle of a lawyer' in Webster's *The Devil's Law Case* (1623), gives free counsel in 'honest causes', and prefers to settle disputes out of court. In Thomas May's *The Heire* (1633), a 'subtle lawyer' named Matho is entreated to devise some formula for the reprieve of a prisoner condemned to death. On professing his inability to bend the strict letter of the law, Matho's royal master retorts that he would certainly have found a way if the object were merely to oppress the poor; whereupon the lawyer falls to his knees, protesting:

MATHO: ... I cannot do more than your laws will let me,
  Nor falsify my knowledge, nor my conscience.
KING: Then I am miserable; rise, Matho, rise,
  I do not discommend thy honesty.[71]

So early modern common lawyers were not universally regarded with contempt, fear, and loathing. If the legal profession's public image was not in general very favourable, it was not uniformly negative; hostility plainly varied in degree and kind across the occupational and social spectra, as well as being influenced by individual experiences of, and personal relationships with, lawyers. Antagonism was probably strongest among the upper ranks of the landed classes and the clergy, at one extreme, and artisans, craftsmen, and small farmers, at the other end of the scale. But barristers were generally much better regarded, or at least less fiercely and frequently attacked in public, than attorneys and solicitors, presumably because their higher socio-economic standing made them in every sense more respectable opponents. So, as the differentiation of the bar from the lower branch became steadily more pronounced, it might be expected that the image of barristers would show at least a relative improvement.[72]

Another reason why critical attitudes towards the bar may have softened slightly during our period is suggested by Thomas Mun's revolutionary economic treatise *England's Treasure by Forraign Trade*, a work dating from the early 1620s, although not published until 1664. Besides arguing that the balance of trade was the basic

[71] *The Complete Works of John Webster*, ed. F. L. Lucas (1927), ii. 255; T. May, *The Heire* (1633), sigs. G3ᵛ, G4ᵛ.
[72] Tucker, *Intruder into Eden*, 66; cf. *Lawyers*, 79.

determinant of national prosperity, Mun sought to demonstrate that various 'excesses and evils in the commonwealth', customarily condemned by moralists, 'decay not our trade nor our treasure'. In this category he placed usury, 'pomp of buildings, apparel and the like', and 'charges by multitude of suits'. Whether these last 'proceed from the lawyers' covetousness, or the people's perverseness, it is a great question'—but one in which Mun declined to meddle, maintaining that the 'cases, quillets, delays, and charges' of lawyers were 'cankers in the estates of particular men, but not of the commonwealth, as some suppose, for one man's loss becomes another man's gain'.[73]

Here the traditional anti-lawyer critique is simply cut through by ignoring its moral content, and by denying its relevance to a society conceived of as a loose network of economic relationships rather than a holistic organism. Fifty years before, Sir Philip Sidney had explained that although '*Ius* be the daughter of Justice, the chief of virtues', the lawyer merely constrained men to be good: 'Therefore as our wickedness maketh him necessary and necessity maketh him honourable, so is he not in the deepest truth to stand in rank with these who all endeavour to take naughtiness away and plant goodness in the secretest cabinet of our souls.'[74] The contrast with the utilitarian rationalism of Mun's analysis is very striking. Nevertheless, when barristers spoke up in their own defence before the Civil War, they wisely appealed to the traditional scale of values represented by Sidney (without accepting his conclusions), rather than to the bourgeois individualism of Thomas Mun.

Elizabethan and early Stuart common lawyers were able to draw upon a far more sophisticated vocational model than their medieval predecessors. Indeed, the classical statement of late medieval legal mentality, Lord Chancellor Fortescue's treatise in praise of the laws of England, does not seek to justify or eulogize the practice of the common law. Fortescue rather emphasizes the aristocratic character of the inns of court and the close parallel between serjeants at law and university doctors, suggesting that he accepted the characteristic medieval view of the lawyer as a necessary, but hardly desirable or model, member of the commonwealth.[75]

    [73] T. Mun, *England's Treasure by Forraign Trade* (1664; Oxford, 1959), 59–60; cf. G. Hakewill, *An Apologie of the power and providence* . . . (Oxford, 1635), 547–8.
    [74] *The Complete Works of Sir Philip Sidney*, ed. A. Feuillerat (Cambridge, 1923), iii. 13.
    [75] *DLLA*, chs. 49–50; J. Le Goff, 'Licit and Illicit Trades in the Medieval West', in

It was a judge's son, an Oxford BCL and a Middle Templar, who in 1531 provided barristers with the basis of a more positive image and the beginnings of a professional ideology. Sir Thomas Elyot's influential humanist educational tract *The Boke named the Gouernour* depicts the ideal lawyer as a gentleman of independent means, accomplished in the liberal arts, who employs his legal learning for the public good, both by pleading on behalf of fellow citizens in the lawcourts and aiding government with his wise counsel. Therefore, instead of putting their teenage sons ('I dare not say with persuasions of avarice') to learn the common law, parents should bring them up in humane studies until they have reached twenty-one years of age, 'whereby at last we should have in this realm a sufficiency of worshipful lawyers and also a public realm equivalent to the Greeks and Romans'.[76]

In fact, Elyot was proposing that the common lawyers of England should model themselves upon the lawyers of classical Rome: wellborn men whose learning was by no means confined to the law, and whose legal practice was ostensibly undertaken as a public duty, not just a means to personal wealth. While the social implications of this prescription are not explicitly spelt out, they would have been clear enough to contemporaries, especially since the entire treatise is directed towards the nobility and gentry, the natural governing class because, *inter alia*, having 'competent substance', they were 'less desirous of lucre (whereof may be engendered corruption)'. A fellow humanist, Thomas Starkey, made the point explicit when he asserted that many shortcomings of the common law would be remedied if its practitioners did not need to 'look for all their livings to their clients', but were 'gentlemen which have other land, office or fee sufficient to maintain them withal'.[77]

Yet Elyot was not merely urging the transformation of the upper branch of the legal profession into a closed aristocratic caste. The paradoxical effect of his insistence upon learning as 'a universalised ideal attribute of ... noble status', and on the common law as an 'honourable study' was rather to create an opposite possibility; if common lawyers were not in fact gentle by birth, they might nevertheless be ennobled by their virtuous calling. This was in

idem, Time, Work and Culture in the Middle Ages, trans. A. Goldhammer (Chicago, 1982), 61, 63; see also nn. 3–4 above.

[76] Elyot, *Gouernour*, i, 133–62.

[77] Ibid.; Starkey, *Dialogue*, 173. (I have benefited from discussing the Roman lawyer motif with Drs Baker and Brooks.)

accordance with a central humanist tenet, which defined true
nobility as learning applied to the public good, and seems to be the
reasoning behind the famous claims of Sir Thomas Smith and
William Harrison fifty years later, that 'whosoever studieth the laws
of the realm shall . . . be called master . . . and reputed for a
gentleman'.[78] The same doctrine is spelt out at greater length in
Henry Peacham's *The Compleat Gentleman* (1622): since 'the weal
public in every state is preserved *armis et consilio*', those 'advocates
and counsellors' who know and interpret the laws are 'commend-
able', and 'their calling is honourable'. The Heralds translated these
theoretical premises into a form of social reality when they granted
coats of arms to barristers on the basis of their 'good life and civil
conversation, bred in times of peace . . . by the profession of the laws
of the realm'. This is plainly a long way from Fortescue's insistence
that most common lawyers were noblemen's sons, let alone the
assertion made of a fourteenth-century chief justice that he was 'no
gentleman because he is a man of the law'.[79]

The crucial point behind Elyot's conflation of Roman jurist and
English common lawyer was its emphasis upon the lawyer's *non-
professional* role and identity. Lawyers should be, first and foremost, not lawyers but gentlemen versed in the laws who serve the
public good. The obvious logical consequence was that none but
gentlemen should be admitted to the inns of court or to practise law
(a view supported by, among others, Richard Mulcaster, Sir John
Ferne, and James I). This proved impossible to achieve, but the inns
of court continued to be characterized as honourable societies, and
the common law as a 'free and liberal' profession, while those who
did enter the inns and were called to the bar seem increasingly to
have been accorded the status of gentlemen, irrespective of their
actual social origins.[80]

[78] J. P. Cooper, *Land, Men and Beliefs*, ed. G. E. Aylmer and J. S. Morrill (1983),
50, and ch. 3, *passim*; Smith, *De Republica Anglorum*, 40; Harrison, *Description of
England*, 113.
[79] Peacham, *Compleat Gentleman*, 12–13, 20; cf. [H. Braham], *The Institution of a
Gentleman* (1555), sig. Diii; J. Cleland, *The Institution of a Young Nobleman* (Oxford,
1607), ed. M. Molyneux (New York, 1948), 4–5, 95–6, 155–6; *HS*, lxxvi. 65, 123, and
lxxvii. 214. E. L. G. Stones, 'Sir Geoffrey Le Scrope (c.1280 to 1340), Chief Justice of
the King's Bench', *EHR*, lxix (1954), 8.
[80] Cooper, *Land, Men and Beliefs*, 56; R. Mulcaster, *Positions . . . the training up of
children* (1581), 208–9. Cf. L. Humfrey, *The Nobles or of Nobility . . .* (1563), sig. qᵛ;
Lowther, 'Autobiography', 203–4; J. Hacket, *Scrinia Reserata* (1693), i. 72. Baker,
'Counsellors and Barristers', 224–9.

Direct evidence of Elyot's influence on the outlook of common lawyers during our period is lacking, although the Roman lawyer analogy remained current, and indeed was incorporated in the earliest known literary vindication of the legal profession by a practising barrister, Sir John Davies's preface to the volume of Irish law cases which he published in 1615. Here Davies closely echoes Ulpian's *Digest* in expounding the doctrine of the *honorarium* in order to explain why English barristers can neither be sued for negligence nor sue for their fees. This passage is part of an extensive rebuttal of certain 'vulgar imputations cast upon the [common] law and lawyers'. We are informed, for example, that despite its apparent barbarity, law-French is actually an efficient working tool, easily acquired by all who need it; that the common law suffers from far less uncertainty than the civil law; that delays in litigation arise only out of the 'malignant and unquiet disposition of many clients', as well as the press of legal business occasioned by the growth of wealth and commerce. The imputed 'corruptions and prevarications' of lawyers are certainly not responsible, since 'no men of any other calling or profession whatsoever are more careful to preserve their good name and reputation'. Having disposed in this fashion of some stock criticisms of the common law and its practitioners, Davies launches into an extended encomium of his 'profession of the law', which, he claims, ranks 'before all other humane professions and sciences':

For what is the matter and subject of our profession but Justice, the lady and queen of all moral virtues? And what are our professors of the law, but her counsellors, her secretaries, her interpreters, her servants? Again, what is the King himself but the clear fountain of Justice? And what are the professors of the law but conduit pipes deriving and conveying the streams of his justice unto all the subjects of his several kingdoms?

So lawyers uphold justice, serve the state, and much more besides:

Doth not this profession every day comfort such as are grieved, counsel such as are perplexed, relieve such as are circumvented, prevent the ruin of the improvident, save the innocent, support the impotent, take the prey out of the mouth of the oppressor, protect the orphan, the widow and the stranger? Doth she not withal ... many times stretch forth ... in defence of the Church and true religion ... register and keep in memory the best antiquities of our nation ... preserve our ancient customs and forms of government, wherein the wisdom of our ancestors doth shine far above the policy of other kingdoms?[81]

Davies may have envisaged this extravagant literary boosterism reaching an audience which extended well beyond the inns of court. By sharp contrast, Sir Anthony Benn's contemporaneous essay 'Of the lawyers' still remains in manuscript, and seems to have been directed towards at most a limited audience of colleagues. So it is particularly significant that Benn's rambling observations on the ethics and etiquette of legal practice are suffused with the neo-classical ideal of the noble counsellor, as is amply apparent from his opening sentence:

The end that every good lawyer ought to propose to himself in the course of his calling is not so much to gain nor yet to direct a client in his course and process of a suit, as to be able to govern and assist his country with profitable and good counsel. This ought to be his way, though profit be his *viaticum*.

Hence the lawyer should seek to attain 'a virtuous and wise', rather than a 'cunning and curious', knowledge of the law; this will help him to temper its rigours to the urgent necessities and higher interests of the commonwealth, without allowing any 'error in affection' to pervert his judgement. Barristers need not 'refuse lawful gain; God forbid, we should then be singular, let us gain it and enjoy it, in God's name, but as means only to enable us to better serve our king and country and to maintain and increase our state and calling'.[82]

Very conscious, like many colleagues, of his profession's poor public image, Benn drew up an extensive inventory of the underlying causes. Laymen resent making any payment to a lawyer, think legal fees too high, dislike having to pay someone else to fight their courtroom battles ('being few that think but they could as well word it out as their lawyers') and feel 'a kind of envy and disdain to see the prosperity, wealth and flourishing estate of lawyers in the common-wealth'. They also confuse the honest lawyer with 'certain barrators ... vile dishonest people that grow up in our field' and affect 'the fashion of the long robe', who foment trouble between neighbours, and bill clients for counsel's fees which were never paid. The public further fails to understand how 'lawyers, even they that profess

[81] Davies, *Le Primer Report*, sigs. *3–*9.
[82] Benn, 'Essays', fols. 23–4ᵛ.

themselves honest, should say and justify that they may well and lawfully be retained in bad causes'.

Benn attempted to defend and justify his vocation against all these aspersions and (as he conceived them) misapprehensions. But at the same time he urged his colleagues to take care lest by imprudence or greed they discredited their profession, expressing the wish that 'if a lawyer offend wittingly against the honour of his calling, let his calling be but as his setting up on high that he may fall so much the more dangerously and irrevocably'. Counsellors should be honest and virtuous, industrious and studious: 'He that is not going on still improving upon the knowledge of his profession betrays his profession and himself to scorn and contempt'.[83]

How widespread were such concerns and ideals among ordinary members of the bar? We cannot generalize from the quite exceptional cases of Benn and Davies; there is nothing to suggest that most early modern barristers devoted much time to composing extended apologias for their profession or pondering its social persona. Davies's preface never became a general professional manifesto or rallying point, although many barristers must have absorbed the slightly homelier aphorisms which Sir Edward Coke, among others, invoked to uphold the dignity of their calling. Since barristers were frequently accused of profiting from the legal system's manifold imperfections, any assertion of the common law's consonance with 'the very laws of eternal God' presumably tended to support a similar conclusion.[84]

Yet if few barristers felt impelled to speak out publicly in defence of their profession, this did not mean that they lacked a sense of occupational identity and solidarity. John Kytchin's wish to displace 'ignorant persons . . . who do not profess the law' from the stewardships of manorial courts, William Lambard's brief jottings on the duty of advocates to their clients, and Edward Hake's avowal that he had caused no disgrace to his 'degree and profession' of 'counsellor of the law' by a 'base form of living' are three indications to the contrary from the later years of Elizabeth's reign.[85] We might well be

[83] Ibid., fols. 25–32ᵛ.

[84] Saltern, *Antient Lawes*, sig. B2; Bolton, *Iustice for Ireland*, Introduction; LI MS Misc. 366, fols. 326ᵛ–7; Yale University, Beinecke Library, Osborne Tracts, Box 1, nos. 13–15, unbound pages headed 'No free subject . . .'.

[85] J. Kytchin, *Le Court Leet, et Court Baron* (1580), sig. ¶iiiiᵛ; Folger MS X. d. 122(3); Ellesmere 6091; cf. James Ley's encomium of the 'dignity de la ley' and its professors (CUL MS Dd. 11. 87, fol. 170.)

inclined to dismiss as typically self-serving Francis Bacon's avowal, when presenting his *Maxims of the Law* to Queen Elizabeth in 1597, that he believed 'every man [to be] a debtor to his profession, from the which as men do of course seek to receive countenance and profit, so ought they of duty to endeavour themselves ... to be a help and ornament thereunto'.[86] Nevertheless there is reason to believe that many of Bacon's colleagues did indeed feel a sense of commitment to, and identification with, their calling.

True, the bar was then, as it is today, a loose collectivity of individuals competing with each other for business, albeit in a highly protected market. Mr Practise, a counsellor-at-law in Ben Jonson's play *The Magnetick Lady*, is 'a man so dedicate to his profession', that he would scarcely notice 'the thundering bruit of an invasion, / Another '88, threatening his country';[87] but it is to the fruits of his calling that Mr Practise is so attached, not the well-being of his clients and colleagues. We should not exaggerate or sentimentalize the extent of camaraderie and mutual goodwill at the early modern bar: ill feeling and disputes breaking out in exchanges of verbal abuse, and even physical violence, were certainly not uncommon during our period.[88] Even serjeants at law had to be cautioned against seeking 'to entangle one another' in their practices at the bar. As we saw earlier, tensions existed between Westminster Hall practitioners and those based in the provincial conciliar courts, as also, at least during the later years of Ellesmere's chancellorship, between Chancery and King's Bench men.[89]

Nevertheless, barristers did at very least share a basic common interest in preserving, and if possible enhancing, their privileged occupational status, especially an effective monopoly of advocacy in the superior courts and the right to set their own level of fees. As suggested in Chapter Two above, the level of job satisfaction within the profession seems to have been high, despite the arduous nature of barristers' working lives (which, interestingly, did not prevent many counsellors reaching a ripe old age; more than a quarter of our

---

[86] Bacon, *Works*, vii. 319; Marwil, *Trials of Counsel*, 83–5.

[87] Jonson, *Works*, vi. 523–4.

[88] Apart from the famous incident of John Davies's armed assault on Richard Martin at the Middle Temple in 1598 (*MTR*, i. 379–80, and Pawlisch, *Davies*, 18–22), see STAC 8/187/24, 241/10, 242/20; *LIBB*, ii. 331–2, and Appendix E below, s. v. Smith, Sir Roger; *Inns of Court*, 94–100.

[89] Folger MS X. d. 122(2), speech of Sir Christopher Hatton, 16 Oct. 1589; cf. Baker, *Serjeants*, 327; above, pp. 53, 266.

bench sample were over seventy when they died). Besides the shared routine of term and circuit, corporate solidarity may well have been strengthened by defensiveness in the face of the general unpopularity of lawyers, as well as by a consciousness of sharing a lucrative form of esoteric knowledge. Nor should we underestimate the role of the inns of court in fostering an *esprit de corps* and group loyalty, as evidenced by the gifts of plate to the house and money or rings to fellow members and domestic servants which figure frequently in common lawyers' wills.[90] The survival of readings and other relics of the medieval aural learning-exercise system, long after the printed text had become the primary means of instruction in the common law, would hardly have been possible without some sense of obligation on the part of practising lawyers to maintain 'the ancient forms of exercise in our profession' (as one reader put it) and thus repay debts of gratitude for past encouragement and instruction.[91] The bar was not a self-perpetuating caste, but hereditary links did create a dynastic element which grew more pronounced during our period. While sixteen of the 115 lawyers in our bar sample group were themselves the sons of barristers, at least twenty-two had sons (or grandsons in two cases) who followed them to the bar, and a further four indicated similar intentions by bequests of law books or specific instructions to their executors.[92]

Hopes that a son would 'by this profession raise himself to a good fortune' doubtless influenced many fathers, even if few went so far as the Middle Temple bencher Robert Thorpe, who cut off his eldest son and heir with a mere £5, 'to the end that he may apply himself to the study and practice of the law to get his living thereby . . . and not to depend upon my estate any longer'.[93] Not surprisingly, it tended

[90] The mean age at death of the barristers sampled was 58.2 years, but among the benchers 67 years, with unknown cases comprising 50% and 32% of each group respectively; 113 benchers and 15 barristers reached 70 or more years of age. For examples of gifts, see *LIBB*, ii. 300; *ITR*, i. 340; PCC 33 Soame, 101 Wood, 128 Cambell, 47 Rivers, 99 Barrington.

[91] MT Library, Rare Books Room, MS 'Whitelocke's Reading', fol. 3; cf. LI MS 486(5) John Bankes, reading of 1630, on 21 Jac. I, c. 16, unfoliated, reader's speech.

[92] Besides the 16 barrister's sons, another 19 members of the group were nephews, grandsons or 'cousins' of common lawyers, or married into legal families. Those whose sons or grandsons followed them to the bar were Abbott, Baber, Beriffe (sen.), Breton, Bulstrode, Cholmley, Clarke, Gallop, Griffith, Keeling, Lake, Leving, Martin, Parker, Powell, Richardson, Sandford, Talbot, Tindall, Whitfield, Wilde, Willimot; those expressing the hope or wish that sons would take up the law were Browne, Locke, Whitfield, and Widdrington. Note also that at least 14 members of the sample group died without male issue.

[93] PCC 47 Harvey.

to be those who themselves had prospered at the bar who sought to have their sons and nephews follow suit. Yet that mere material considerations alone do not adequately explain the attachment of early modern barristers to their calling is suggested by an extraordinary passage from the will of Edward Skipwith, who seems to have achieved no great professional distinction apart from serving as MP for Grimsby in 1601, and reaching the bench of Lincoln's Inn. Writing in 1620, just before his death, Skipwith was at pains to express his reverent regard for 'the most worthy and famous common law of this realm, whereof I being an unworthy member have desired to honour it in my heart, though in practice of it I have disgraced it'.

This last seems to be a reference to Skipwith's failure to deliver a double reading at Lincoln's Inn, from which onerous task he had been excused a decade before on the grounds of ill health. At all events he went on to seek pardon of 'the worthy society and fellowship of Lincoln's Inn', while protesting that he had at all times in his career acted with integrity, for 'neither in open nor private action of that profession I have by no dishonest or unjust or disgraceful means to my knowledge wronged or stained the profession'.[94]

iv. *Conclusion*

The modern rhetoric of professionalism still lays emphasis upon the deservedly privileged status of those who employ knowledge to serve their clients and society at large, rather than primarily for personal gain. The origins of this notion have never been properly investigated, but the concept of the good lawyer, as first elaborated in the sixteenth and seventeenth centuries, appears to have been among its earliest, and perhaps not least influential, formulations.

The precise nature and significance of that influence must remain conjectural until more is known about this curiously neglected aspect of the history of the professions. Meanwhile, however, it seems clear that common lawyers in general, and the bar in particular, constituted the pre-eminent English profession over a period of some three hundred years, between, roughly, the Henrician reformation and the mid-nineteenth century. The bar became England's 'proto-modern profession' *par excellence* (to adopt Duman's

[94] PCC 19 Soame.

phrase) by establishing its independence from lay control and exploiting a lucrative vocational monopoly.[95] The barrister's autonomy, in relation to clients on the one hand and the state on the other, was not complete during our period (and has arguably always remained relative rather than absolute). But while the continued differentiation of upper and lower branches placed the attorney as buffer between barrister and client more frequently in the later than the earlier seventeenth century, the ideological and institutional components of the bar's favoured position were firmly established by 1640. Similarly, the failure of radical demands for the wholesale abolition of the lawyer's trade during the Interregnum probably helped the profession repel subsequent more moderate attempts at reform; but then bills and proposals to regulate various aspects of legal practice had been advanced frequently since the 1530s, with not much greater result than was achieved by those of the 1640s and 50s. Lastly, while the early Stuarts displayed a discernible bias against common lawyers and in favour of the civilians, they never quite got to the point of seriously threatening the long-standing monopoly of advocacy in the superior courts enjoyed by counsellors from the inns of court.

In summary, both the essential structural forms and the vocational privileges of the modern English bar had clearly crystallized by the eve of the Civil War, although there was further consolidation and extension after 1660. The numerical expansion of the bar, the emergence of the barrister as a professional figure in his own right, and the changing patterns of promotion at the top of the profession challenged the traditional leadership of the serjeants at law. In the lower branch, analogous moves in a recognizably modern direction saw the appearance of the solicitor, whose early history is still quite obscure, and the proliferation of trained attorneys throughout the land. These developments took place against a background of population growth, political centralization, and economic diversification. But above all else, it was probably the continuing decline in authority and prestige of the Church, the first learned profession, which gave common lawyers their great chance, and made the inns of court the most promising gateway to upward mobility in early modern England. Moreover, the outcome of the English Revolution (in both its 1640–59 and 1688–9 manifestations) secured their

[95] D. Duman, 'Pathway to Professionalism; the English Bar in the Eighteenth and Nineteenth Centuries', *J. Soc. Hist.*, xii (1980), 618.

independence, power, and—admittedly still somewhat ambivalent—status.

The rise of the barristers in early modern England presages that 'enormous growth of the organised professions' which Richard Pares saw as 'perhaps the greatest change in the whole of modern history'.[96] It was also a crucial ingredient in the making of a modern state and society. Now that Holmes, Duman, and others have broken the hitherto orthodox historiographical nexus between 'professionalisation' and 'industrialisation', there seems little point in debating whether it was the half-century before 1640 or the half-century after 1680 (as Holmes avers) which saw the more fundamental and far-reaching transformation of the legal profession. How does one in fact determine whether the rise or the triumph of the barristers was the more momentous event?

What must be insisted upon is that in the late sixteenth and early seventeenth centuries barristers occupied strategic positions in a notably turbulent and unstable world, as brokers and mediators between court and client, city and country, citizen and state. Nor were the transactions in which they participated concerned merely with material items; barristers also acted as cultural ambassadors and politico-religious plenipotentiaries, transmitting attitudes, beliefs, ideas, and ideologies from the national to the local level, besides representing villagers and townsmen in their dealings with the wider world.[97]

Possessed with such opportunities for exercising authority and influence, it is hardly surprising that barristers were widely regarded by contemporaries as disruptive agents of change. Their contribution to the reconstruction and extension of the powers of central government, to the development of parliament as an increasingly formidable political institution, to restraining the power of the Church, to assisting the spread of protestantism, and to devising measures of social control to cope with the mass poverty and other symptoms of social dislocation which proliferated in Elizabethan and early Stuart England lend considerable support to this view. So, too, does their prominence in more private capacities, as entre-

---

[96] R. Pares, *George III and the Politicians* (1953), 16–17.

[97] For the concept of the lawyer as broker or intermediary, see Holmes, *Seventeenth Century Lincolnshire*, ch. 3; *Country Towns in Pre-Industrial England*, ed. P. Clark (Leicester, 1981), 23 and my 'Communications and Authority: Town and Country Lawyers in Early Modern England', mimeographed paper, for History section of ANZAAS conference, Melbourne, 1977.

preneurs and enclosers, money-lenders and projectors, purchasers of estates and builders of houses.

Yet barristers were professional intermediaries, to be found on both sides of many fences, assisting Catholic recusants and small tenants, as well as radical protestants and enclosing landlords. We must be careful not to exaggerate the extent to which the early modern legal system in general, and the bar in particular, functioned merely to advance the interests of the rich, well-born, and powerful against the poor and the weak. Even if that was the outcome overall, at least some barristers were sometimes willing to take on cases brought by men of very modest rank against their superiors, and to help politico-religious nonconformists use the law to defend themselves against the might of the state. Civil litigation was not yet gentleman's business alone, and lawyers were not noticeably more popular with the aristocracy and gentry than with the lower classes. Unlike the common lawyers of late medieval England, the early modern bar was no mere dependency of the landed ruling élite; as we have seen, in terms of social origins, urban links, geographical and social mobility, sources of income, life-style, and attitudes to work, its membership indeed displayed some remarkably bourgeois traits, exemplifying that 'permanent, partial interpenetration' of aristocratic land-owners by urban commercial and financial interests peculiarly characteristic of British society from the seventeenth down to the earlier twentieth century.[98]

In fact, the rise of the barristers can hardly be separated, both as cause and effect, from the victory of an economic and social order which was already in the process of creating the world's first industrial nation. Weber's claim that 'England achieved capitalistic supremacy ... not because but rather in spite of its judicial system' gives rather too little credit to the role played by common lawyers in facilitating the advance of English capitalism.[99] Mingling and intermarrying with both rural and urban élites, barristers assisted in the transfer of personnel and values between them, and adapted the

---

[98] P. Anderson, 'Origins of the Present Crisis', *New Left Rev.*, xxii (1964), 30.
[99] *Max Weber on Law in Economy and Society*, ed. E. Shils and M. Rheinstein (New York, 1967), 231. An inconclusive, but important, debate about the economic attitudes of Sir Edward Coke and, by implication, the early modern bar as a whole, is summarized in Little, *Religion, Order and Law*, 243–6. See also P. S. Atiyah, *The Rise and Fall of Freedom of Contract* (Oxford, 1979), and the introduction by G. R. Rubin and D. Sugarman to *Law, Economy and Society* (Abingdon, 1984), 23–42, 91–2, and references cited therein.

common law itself to meet the needs of a more flexible and market-oriented society. The individualistic, even meritocratic, nature of work at the bar, plus the sizeable financial rewards it offered the successful, also helps to explain why, both during our period and beyond, common lawyers generally seem to have favoured freeing economic activity from guild and other regulatory constraints. Nor should it be assumed that the fees paid to lawyers squandered resources which might have been invested more productively elsewhere. On the contrary, it is arguable that the litigation boom of the late sixteenth century may have speeded economic growth, in so far as it popularized an object of consumer spending which required cash payment and hence, very often, market production for its fulfilment, besides incidentally adding a substantial impetus to the growth of London, and helping emancipate agricultural land from the restraints of manorial custom.

Conversely, the extension of a market economy helped to create the heightened demand for legal services which, in turn, led to the barristers' professional emergence during the sixteenth century, to a more competitive mode of legal practice, and to the development of a new institutional structure where barristers, serjeants, and judges were sharply differentiated from the lower branch of attorneys and solicitors. As barristers, like clergymen and physicians, developed a distinctive professional ideology and self-image, which emphasized their separation and elevation above the laity and other practitioners in the same field, they became correspondingly more vulnerable to charges of conspiring to put a Norman yoke on the necks of plain men with their learned mumbo-jumbo. Such complaints had a long ancestry, as we have seen; nor did these particular ones cease altogether, despite the failure of the assaults launched during the Interregnum on the monopolistic privileges and class-biassed practices of the common lawyers. Even today, when law reform has come to be a matter left largely to the lawyers themselves, some faint echoes of those cries is still heard from time to time. Yet it remains to be seen whether we can come any closer to the goal of a humane society in which law rules, and lawyers merely serve.

APPENDIX A

Measuring the Early Modern Bar

Neither the concept of a 'bar' composed of all advocates practising in the superior courts, nor the term itself, were current during our period. Before about the mid-sixteenth century, no single institutional criterion clearly determined an individual's eligibility to plead before the king's judges, while distinguishing those who possess that right from those who actually use it has remained quite difficult down to the present day. Nevertheless it seems worth risking some anachronism to attempt an estimate of the growth in the numbers of common lawyers as a result of the sixteenth-century litigation boom, and a comparison of the *per capita* density of barristers then and now.

A list of 'pleaders or apprentices of the king's courts' compiled for Wolsey in 1518 names 49 individuals, while J. A. Guy has recovered the names of 69 counsellors active in Star Chamber during Wolsey's chancellorship (1515–29). (*Lawyers*, 28; Guy, *Cardinal's Court*, 112.) By 1574 the four inns of court housed at least 176 barristers and benchers, according to a survey of that year now in the PRO: SP 12/95/91, printed in *ITR*, i 468–9. However, other surviving lists for the Inner Temple and Lincoln's Inn from around the same date suggest a total nearly twice as large. (Cf. Lansdowne 106, fols. 90–1, 97.) Another, *c.* 1579, records only 70 'of name for their practise', but includes few barristers, except from GI (*ITR*, i. 470–3).

In 1602 Sir Edward Coke claimed that the four inns of court together had over 320 bencher and barrister members (Coke, *Reports*, ed. Wilson, ii. xx). Contributions to levies at the Middle Temple in 1614 and the Inner Temple in 1616 were paid by more than 130 barristers and benchers of each house; if we assume that at least as many would have been found at Gray's Inn and Lincoln's Inn (the call figures in Table 1.1 above suggest that this is a conservative assumption), and add another, say, 15 serjeants at law, we have a grant total of around 535 barristers, benchers, and serjeants for the middle years of James I's reign. (MT, MS unclassified, box labelled 'Temple Church and Master of the Temple', preacher's rolls 1614; IT MS Accounts Book 1606–48, fol. 117; Baker, *Serjeants*, 327.) However, an unknown, but not insignificant, fraction of these men would have been office-holders and others not practising as pleaders in the central courts; in Easter term 1616 only some 296 individual counsellors appear in the entry books of the London-based English-bill courts, although the figure rose to nearly 400 by Easter term 1638 (see above, pp. 79–80). There is, unfortunately, no sure way of estimating how many more barristers pleaded before all other courts (but see Appendix C below). However, assuming a population of 5.265 million for England and Wales in 1636, and a practising bar of around 450 individuals, the number of barristers per head of population would have been about 1 in 11,700. In 1978 a population of 49.244 million supported a total of 4,263 practising barristers, giving a *per capita* ratio of 1 to 11,522; it should also be noted that the 1978 bar is almost twice the size reported only ten years earlier. (E. A. Wrigley and R. S. Schofield, *The Population History of England 1541–1871* (1981), 208, 566; *Report of the Royal Commission on Legal Services* (1979), Cmnd., 7648, i. 54. These calculations supersede those presented in *Lawyers*, 67 and 82 n.)

APPENDIX B

Favourites and the Hearing of Suits

Favourites may have been attractive to litigants for various reasons, not least the prospect of greater expedition in the progress of their suits. An early Jacobean tract claims that Chancery's Six Clerks, who 'ought to rank their client's causes for hearing according to their dependencies in court, do now sell their hearings at excessive rates'; in the Court of Requests, however, hearings are said to be granted on the mere motion of counsel, suggesting that no docket or order of business at all was kept. (Leadam, ed., *Requests*, xc.) Among the Coventry Papers in the Birmingham Reference Library is a cause list (MS 660743/9) from the Court of Wards, covering a portion of Michaelmas term 1617, which lists motions in serial order set down for hearing between October 10 and November 12 on Mondays and Fridays, these being the days set aside, as the court's historian tells us, 'for the more routine business of motions'. (Bell, *Court of Wards*, 98.) In 1621 it was proposed that at least twenty days' notice be given to defendants in Chancery and Star Chamber before their causes were heard; sixteen days' notice was given to a party in an Exchequer Chamber suit in 1626. (HMC, *Rutland*, iv. 215; Northants RO, Montagu (Buccleuch), vol. 14, p. 311.) However, it seems likely that even in courts where hearings and procedural motions were usually set down to be dealt with in order, the intervention of favourites could upset such arrangements, if only by preventing other counsel from moving until the favourites had exhausted their motions for the day. Cf. the proposals of Interregnum law-reformers for a register of causes and motions in Chancery and other English-bill courts in order to eliminate this abuse by favourites. (T. Faldoe, *Reformation of Proceedings at Law* (1649), 3, 22; Philodemus, *Seasonable Observations*, 17; 'Draught of an Act to Prevent Solicitations of Judges, Bribery, Extortion, Charge of Motions and for Restrictions of Pleaders' (1653), in *Somers Tracts*, vi. 189.)

How suits were ordered for hearing in the common-law courts during our period is not much clearer. However from at least the late seventeenth century, and possibly before, the practice in King's Bench was 'to begin every day with the senior counsel within the bar, and then to call upon the next senior, in order, and so on, as long as it was convenient for the Court to sit; and to proceed again in the same manner upon a next and every subsequent day; although the bar had not been half, or perhaps a quarter gone through, upon any of the former days'. Counsel 'within the bar' included Crown law officers, king's counsel, and possibly, in our period,

Appendix B

favourites (A. Pulling, *The Order of the Coif* (1897), 214–15; *English Reports*, xcvii. 189). A similar seniority system for motions operated in Star Chamber (Haward, *Reports*, 46).

(I am grateful to Professor C. M. Gray for his helpful discussion of these and related points.)

Counsel in Exchequer and King's Bench

Names of barristers and serjeants on whose motions orders or rules were made in the courts of Exchequer and King's Bench are listed in the Exchequer of Pleas order books (E 12) and the King's Bench rule books (KB 21: Crown Side, and KB 125: Pleas Side). It is not clear that all motions recorded in these paper books were actually pleaded in person, rather than presented in written form under counsel's signature, or that all apppearances by counsel were minuted by the courts' clerical staff. A further difficulty is that most of the pre-1640 Pleas Side books are at present deemed too fragile for production. The Crown Side and Exchequer books covering Easter term 1616 (KB 21/5a and E 12/11) list few counsel by name, and the former is markedly more miscellaneous in content and haphazard in arrangement than its later supposed counterparts.

At the moment, therefore, it is not possible to merge data derived from these sources with the English-bill court material summarized in Table 3.1 above. However, preliminary analysis of counsel listed for Easter term 1638 yields the names of at least 42, perhaps 48, barristers who seem not to appear in the corresponding English-bill court entry books; when collated with all other evidence, according to the procedure outlined in ch. 3, sect. ii above, a grand total of some 440 practising counsel results. King's Bench, Pleas Side, evidently provided more work for counsel than any other court in 1638, apart from Chancery; the distribution of motions between counsel there also seems to have been marginally less unequal than in the busier English-bill courts. (I am most grateful to Mr D. Lemmings for alerting me to these sources, and thank Drs J. H. Baker and R. Ball for their helpful comments.)

Easter Term 1638

King's Bench, Pleas Side[1]

| Counsel | | Appearances | Totals | |
Number	Per cent	Number	Number	Per cent
2	1.5	20+	69	13.9
11	8.4	10–19	149	30.0
15	11.5	5–9	89	17.9
46	35.1	2–4	132	26.6
57	43.5	1	57	11.5
131	100.0	(Maximum 47)	496	99.9

Easter Term 1638 (cont.)

King's Bench, Crown Side[2]

Counsel Number	Per cent	Appearances Number	Totals Number	Per cent
1	1.9	20+	20	18.3
—	—	10–19	—	—
3	5.8	5–9	27	24.8
10	19.2	2–4	24	22.0
38	73.1	1	38	34.9
52	100.0	(Maximum 20)	109	100.0

Exchequer of Pleas[3]

Counsel Number	Per cent	Appearances Number	Totals Number	Per cent
—	—	20+	—	—
1	4.3	10–19	11	19.6
2	8.7	5–9	13	23.2
8	34.8	2–4	20	35.7
12	52.2	1	12	21.4
23	100.0	(Maximum 11)	56	99.9

[1] *Source:* KB 125/69.   [2] *Source:* KB 21/12.   [3] *Source:* E 12/13.

Biographical Tabulation of Bar Sample

This appendix provides biographical outlines in tabular form for the 5-per-cent random sample of barristers called between 1590 and 1639 (details of selection procedures in Ch 4. Sect. i above). After each name, the following information appears: inn of court, dates of birth and death if known, regional origins and/or destination, university attendance if known (C = Cambridge, O = Oxford), and abbreviated references. In general no reference is made to printed records of the inns of court, to *Al. Ox., Al. Cant.*, or to the main body of the text above.

Name	Inn	Dates	Locale	Univ.	Sources
Abbott, Maurice	IT	c.1602–c.1645	London	O	*CSPD 1641–3*; *CCAM*
Abnet, William	GI	d. 1628	Staffs.	–	Lichfield Joint RO, Inv. 1628
Adderley, Henry	LI	c.1610–c.1639	London	C	LI MS Red Book, fol. 192
Anderson, Robert	LI	c.1669–c.1672	Herts./Sussex	O	*CCAM*; *Sussex Arch. Coll.*, xxiv, xxxix; CCC
Archer, Sir John	GI	d. 1672	Essex	C	*DNB*; *Essex Rev*, xxxi; papers at Essex RO
Ayshcombe, John	MT	1568–1655	Berks.	O	Durston, thesis, PCC 262 Berkeley
Baber, John	LI	1592–1644	Glos./Som.	O	See Appendix E below
Becke, William	MT	c.1562–1614	Herts./Cambs.	C	PCC 11 Rudd
Beriffe, William (i)	GI	c.1546–1628	Essex	C	Morant, *Essex*, i; PCC 11 Barrington
Beriffe, William (ii)	GI	d. c.1631	Essex	C	STAC 8/202/6; PCC 26 Audley
Best, Thomas	IT	d. 1626?	Herefs./Middx.	O	PCC 91 Hele; *ITR*, ii; *LRH*
Betton, Robert	LI	d. 1646	Salop	O	CCC; PCC 102 Twisse
Bourchier, Sir John	GI	c.1591–1659	Yorks. (NR)	C	Underdown, *Pride's Purge*
Bradshaw, Francis	IT	1576–1635	Derbs.	–	*Derbs. Arch. J.*, xxv; *Reliquary*, NS iv
Bradstock, Henry	MT	c.1591–1635	Dorset	O	Dorset RO, WM/W/B95
Breton, Robert	MT	1592–1641	Northants	O	PCC 62 Evelyn; C142/615/119
Bridges, John	MT	d. 1640	Essex/London?	–	PCC 151 Coventry
Browne, George	MT	c.1583–1631	Dorset/Som.	O	See Appendix E below
Bulstrode, Edward	IT	c.1589–1659	Bucks./War.	O	See Appendix E below
Burton, William	IT	1575–1645	Leics./Staffs.	O	*DNB*; Nichols, *Leics.*, iv.
Bysse, Robert	LI	d. 1642	Ireland	–	Bodl. MS Carte 62; A. Vicars, *Prerogative Wills of Ireland* (1897)
Calmadie, Arthur	MT	1593–1632	Devon	–	*The Visitation of ... Devon*, ed. J. L. Vivian (1895); *HS*, vi
Cari(y)ll, John	IT	c.1604–1669	Surrey/Cambs.	–	PCC 16 Penn; *HS*, xliii
Cholmley, Nicholas	IT	d. 1644	London/Surrey	–	See Appendix E below
Clarke, John	LI	c.1591–1657	War./Oxon/Northants	O	See Appendix E below
Cottle, Richard	MT	1583–1618	Devon	–	W. H. Cottell, *Hist. of the ... Cottle Family* (1871)
Cre(a)mer, Sir John	GI	d. 1668	Norfolk	–	PCC 68 Coke; Ketton-Cremer, *Felbrigg*

Name	Inn	Dates	County		References
Cro(o)ke, Thomas	IT	1613–c.1641	Oxon.	—	Croke, *Genealogical History*
Cruse, Thomas	IT	d. 1642	Devon	—	SP16/32/114; PCC 60 Cambell
Cuffe, Robert	LI	d. c.1639	Som.	—	Gleason, *Justices*
Day, George	LI	d. 1681	Middx.	C?	PCC 105 North; *CCAM*
Dengayne, Henry	LI	*fl.* 1602–38	Norfolk	C	Norf. RO, Rye MS 3, ii. 211, 224
Dering, Anthony	MT	1604–62	Kent/London	—	Guildhall Library MS 9052/13
Dickenson, Leonard	MT	d. 1650	Sussex/London	—	PCC 16 Pembroke
Dyer, James	MT	d. 1653	Som./Glos.	—	Sacks, thesis; PCC 512 Alchin
Dyos, William	LI	*fl.* 1594–1640	London	—	Overall, *Remembrancia.*
Elliott, Christopher	LI	*fl.* 1608–47	Ireland	—	R. Lascelles, *Liber Munerum ... Hiberniae* (1852)
Fair(e)clough, Edward	LI	1576–c. 1652	Herts./London?	C	*HS*, xv.; *Trans. E. Herts. Arch. Soc.*, iv. 66; PCC 156 Bowyer
Farewell, Thomas	MT	d. 1641	Som.	—	*MTR*, ii; Charlton Musgrave parish reg.
Ga(o)llop, Thomas	MT	c.1558–1663	Dorset	O	Hutchins, *Dorset*, ii; Dorset RO; *CCAM; AOI*
Gell, Thomas	IT	1594–1656	Derbs.	—	Keeler; Brighton, *Royalists and Roundheads in Derbs.*
Girling, William	GI	d. 1627	Suffolk	—	PCC 70 Skinner
Griffith, Brochfael	LI	1594–post-1648	Montgoms.	—	*Montgoms. Colls.*, vi, xvi; J. R. S. Philipps, *The Justices of the Peace in Wales ... 1541–1689* (1975); *AOI*
Hanbury, Edward	MT	1583–1646?	Worcs./Middx.	O	Locke, *Hanbury Family*; PCC 66 Fines
Hanmer, John	GI	c.1567–1601	Salop	—	J. Hanmer, *Memorials of ... Hanmer* (1878); C142/298/93
Harby, Clement	LI	d. by 1681	Northants/Ireland	C	*HS*, lxxxvii; LI MS Red Book, fol. 146
Hare, John	IT	1546–1613	London/Norf./Herts.	O	*H. of P.*, and Appendix F below
Hende(o)n, Sir Edward	GI	c.1568–1644	Kent	—	See Appendix E below
Hicks, John	IT	d. 1651	Bucks./Middx.	O	PCC 58 & 194 Bowyer; *CCC; AOI*
Holford, Henry	MT	d. 1649	Essex	C	*MTR; HS*, xiii; Bodl. MS Bankes 18/22
Holland, Anthony	LI	d. 1630	Lincs.	—	Lincs. RO, LCC 1629/415; *HS*, li

Name	Inn	Dates	Locale	Univ.	Sources
Holland, Edward	LI	d. post-1642	Anglesey	–	*Trans. Anglesey Antiq. Soc.*, Supp. (1915); NLW Carreg-lwyd 162
Honeywood, Sir John	GI	c.1583–1652	Kent	C	Everitt, *Community of Kent*; PCC 118 Brent
Hughes, William	GI	c.1588–c.1663	London	O	Greater London RO, Acc 826/1; PCC 219 Brent
Hyde, Laurence	MT	c.1610–1682	Wilts.	–	*Commons 1660–90*, ed. Henning
Keat, Francis	MT	1584–1650	Berks.	–	HS lvi; PCC 125 Pembroke
Keeling, John	IT	1576–1649	Staffs./London	O?	HS, xvii; PCC 95 Fairfax; Appendix F below
Keyt(e), John	GI	*fl.* 1604–34	Oxon.	O	HS, v; Oxon. RO, MS Wills Oxon. 39/3/12
Kyrton, James	MT	d. 1611	Som.	–	*H. of P.*
Lake, Thomas	GI	d. 1667	Kent	–	HS, liv; *MTR*, ii–iii; PCC 88 Carr
Lambert, Thomas	GI	d. 1616	Essex	C	C142/664/33
Langley, Richard	LI	d. 1613	Salop/London	–	Overall, *Remembrancia*
Latham, Ralph	MT	c.1588–c.1641	Essex	O	See Appendix E below
Leving(e), Timothy	IT	c.1574–1636	War./Derbs.	O	See Appendix E below
Ley, Sir Henry	LI	1595–1638	Wilts.	O	G. E. Cokayne, *The Complete Baronetage* (1900), i
Lloyd, Thomas	IT	d. 1631	Denbs.	–	PCC 131 St John; W. M. Myddelton, *Chirke Castle Accounts* (1931); Additional 33373, fol. 101
Locke, Thomas	GI	?1579–1623	Essex	C	See Appendix E below
Lukyn, Thomas	IT	c.1592–post-1634	London	O	A. Tudor-Craig, *The Romance of Melusine* (1932)
Machen, Edward	MT	c.1586–by 1651	Glos.	O	*Trans. Bristol and Glos. Arch. Soc.*, lxiv; PROB 6/36, fol. 86
Maltiward, Robert	GI	d. 1691	Suffolk	C	PCC 216 Vere; HS, lxxvii
Martin, Henry	MT	c.1570–1611	Som.	O	PCC 8 Fenner
Metcalfe, James	LI	c.1604–1671	Yorks. (NR)	C	*VCH*, Yorks. (*NR*), i
Moyle, Walter	MT	d. 1599	Kent	–	PCC 58 Wallopp; *Arch. Cant.*, xlix; W. Berry, *County Genealogies: Kent* (1836)

Name		Dates	County		References
Newport, Andrew	IT	1563–1611	Salop	—	H. of P.
Norden, Richard	IT	c.1610–1641	Wilts.	C	PCC 15 Evelyn; C142/606/48; *HS*, cv
Nott, Nicholas	GI	*fl.* 1594–1608	Kent	C	Hasted, *Kent*, xi; *CCAM*
Palmer, Sir Henry	GI	1611–59	Kent/Middx.	C	Borthwick, Reg. 48, fol. 653; Lancs. RO; *CCAM*
Parker, Edward	GI	1602–67	Yorks. (WR)	C	*Visitation of Yorkshire in 1584–5 and 1612*, ed. J. Foster (1875); *Yorks. Arch. Soc., Rec. Ser.*, lxi C 193/13/3, 4
Pearson, Richard	LI	*fl.* 1598–1653	Yorks. (ER)	C	PCC 293 Nabbs; Woolrych, *Commonwealth to Protectorate*
Phe(a)sant, Stephen	GI	1617–60	Hunts.	C	C142/630/2
Phelpes, Giles	MT	c.1568–1631	Som.	O	Hasted, *Kent*, ii; *Misc. Gen. et Her.*, 2nd ser., v; PCC 106 Audley
Pickes, Richard	LI	1589–1632	Kent	—	PCC 95 Soame
Pindar, Henry	GI	d. c.1620	Hants	C	PCC 144 Coker; Metcalfe, ed., *Wilts. Vis*; *WAM*, xxvi
Po(o)re, Phillip	IT	c.1610–c.1693	Wilts.	O	See Appendix E below
Powell, William	LI	d. c.1654	Glam.	—	*HS*, vi
Preston, Roger	GI	c.1590–post-1632	Devon	O	*East Anglian*, iii, iv; PCC 144 Ent
Quarles, George	GI	1605–89	Northants/London	—	H. of P.
Reynolds, Cuthbert	IT	d. c.1627	Herts.	—	See Appendix E below
Rich, Sir Robert	LI	d. c.1646	Essex/Middx.	—	E. Suffolk RO; Bacon, *Annalls of Ipswche*
Rich, Thomas	LI	d. post-1601	Suffolk	—	Surtees, *Durham*, iv; Univ. of Durham, Probate 1624, 1638
Richardson, John	GI	d. 1623	Durham	—	*Chetham Soc.*, l; *Rec. Soc. Lancs. and Ches., Misc.*, i
Rigby, Alexander	GI	1583–c.1650	Lancs.	—	*HS*, xli; PCC 153 Goare; *VCH, Cambs.* iv, viii
St George, Thomas	GI	d. 1637	Cambs.	—	Blomefield and Parkin, *Norfolk*, ii; W. B. Rye, *Norfolk Families* (1913)
Sandell, Richard	LI	d. 1627	Norfolk	—	
Sandford, William	GI	*fl.* 1618–46	Glos.	O	

Name	Inn	Dates	Locale	Univ.	Sources
Seys, Evan	LI	c.1604–1682	Glam./Glos.	O	Commons 1660–90, ed. Henning
Shaftoe, Christopher	IT	c.1561–1593	Northumb.	O	W. Hutchinson, History of ... Durham (1828) ii; A History of Northumberland (1893–1940), xiii
Smith, George	GI	c.1603–1658	Sussex/Herts./Scotland	O	PCC 15 Pell; AOI; J. Foster, Members of Parliament, Scotland (1882)
Snigge, William	MT	c.1587–1646	Glos./Som.	O	Wilts. N & Q, v; HS, Reg. ser., xxvii
Somerscales, Henry	GI	d. 1609	Lincs./Yorks. (WR)	—	Borthwick, Reg. 31, fols. 193ᵛ–4ᵛ; T. Bagshaw & R. Robinson, History of ... Giggleswick (1932)
Spinke, William	GI	d. 1648	Yorks. (ER)	C	VCH, Yorks. (ER), ii; Gt. Driffield parish reg.
Strode, Sir John	MT	1561–1642	Dorset	—	See Appendix E below
Talbot, Thomas	LI	1585–1642	Norfolk	C	See Appendix E below
Tilston, Henry	IT	c.1589–1613	Cheshire	O	Ormerod, Chester, i; HS, lix
Tindall, Deane	LI	c.1586–1678	Essex	C	AOI
Vaughan, Edward	IT	c.1599–1661	Montgoms.	—	Underdown, Pride's Purge; DWB; NLW MS Wynnstay 87/27
Vic(k)arman, Francis	MT	d. c.1618	Yorks. (ER)	C	Borthwick, Admon., 5 Mar. 1618 (Harthill); Yorks. Arch. Soc., Rec. Ser., liii
Walstead, Francis	MT	d. 1657	Staffs./London	—	HS, xvii; Overall, Remembrancia; PCC 452 Ruthen; CCC
Warren, William	IT	fl. 1600–32	Worcs./War.	O?	Metcalfe, ed., Vis. Northants; Genealogist, NS xxix; LI MS Red Book, fol. 268ᵛ
Watts, Montague	LT	1575–1642	Northants	O	Keeler
Weston, Sir Richard	IT	c.1609–1652	Staffs.	O	See Appendix E below
Whitfield, Sir Ralph	GI	d. 1645	Kent/London	—	See Appendix E below
Widdrington, Sir Thomas	GI	c.1600–1664	Northumb./Yorks.	C	See Appendix E below
Wilde, Sir William	IT	c.1611–1679	London/Kent	—	DNB; Commons 1660–90, ed. Henning
Willimot, Sir Nicholas	GI	c.1612–1682	Derbs.	O	Glover, Derbs., ii; Derby Central

Biographical Notes on Benchers

Brief biographies in standardized form are provided below for the 385-member bench sample; 43 legal office-holders and other non-practising counsel, most of whom were only associated to bar and bench, are treated more summarily in Appendix F. Each entry includes information, where available, about its subject's life-span, parentage, geographical origins, education, appointments and offices, marital history, religious and political affiliations, and wealth.

Abbreviated references are given, mostly to standard sources already cited; in general, however, no reference is made to the published records of the inns, nor to *Al. Ox.* or *Al. Cant.* NB: benchers distinguished with a preceding asterisk are covered by a *DNB* entry; information provided there usually has not been duplicated here, apart from dates of birth and death, and inn of court career.

Additional abbreviations

AB	associated to bench	JK(Q)B	justice of King's (Queen's)
assoc.	associated to bar		Bench
att.	attorney	ktd.	knighted
b	called to bar	KSL	king's serjeant at law
B	called to bench	LCB	lord chief baron
BExch	baron of the Exchequer	LCJ	lord chief justice
bro.	brother (of)	LdCh	lord chancellor
bt.	baronet	LdKpr	lord keeper
C	Cambridge	mar.	married
CB	chief baron	MCh	master in Chancery
CJ	chief justice	MR	master of the Rolls
clk.	clerk	MReq	master of Requests
commr.	commissioner	O	Oxford
cr.	created	parl.	parliament, parliamentarian
ct.	court	rec.	recorder
d.	died, death	s.	son (of), 1 = first, 2 = second,
da.	daughter (of)		etc.
dep.	deputy	sjt.	serjeant
Exch	Exchequer	SL	serjeant at law
illeg.	illegitimate	sol. gen.	solicitor-general
IPM	inquisition *post mortem*	w.	wife
Ire.	Ireland	wid.	widow
j.	judge	y.	younger
JCP	justice of Common Pleas		

ABDY, Edmund (*fl.* 1561–1623), 1 s. Roger, London, and Lydd, Kent, merchant, by Mary, da. George White, Hutton, Essex. Magd. Hall, O, 77; Thavie's Inn; LI 80, b 89, B 04, AB 08. Mar. Judith, da. Sir C. Yelverton, JKB. Assessed @ £20 for privy seal, Poplar, Middx. 13, 'hath been often sent unto'. (*HS*, xliii, lxxiv; Hasted, *Kent*, iii; Ellesmere 2503; Kent AO, NR/CPL16.)

*ALTHAM, Sir James (d. 1617), 2 or 3 s. James, Latton, Essex. Trin., C, 71; GI 75, b 81, B 95, SL 03. Among Walter Travers's auditors at Temple Church, built chapel at Oxhey House, Herts., 12, where library provided for use of preacher. Wealthy; acquired manor of Mark, Walthamstow, 01, Boones Hall and Oxhey 04; other lands worth £364 p.a. bequeathed. Of Oxhey, Herts., at d. (*H. of P.*; Fuller, *Worthies of England*, ii; *VCH, Herts.*, ii.)

AMHERST, Richard (1565–1632), 1 s. Richard, Pembury, Kent, by Margery Rixon or Rixne. St John's, O, 82; Staple Inn; GI 85, b 92, B 12, SL 23, Queen's sjt. by 30. JP; MP 14, 21. Mar (i) Anne, da. William Reynes, Mereworth, Kent; (ii) Margaret, da. Sir Thomas Palmer, Bt., Wingham, Kent. Steward to four successive Sackvilles, earls of Dorset. ?Puritan leanings. Acquired lands from Sackvilles, but owed at least £1,000 at d. (Fletcher, *Sussex*; *Sussex Arch. Coll.*, xix, xx, xxii, xxxvii; HMC, *Hastings*, ii; Additional 33895, fol. 38; PCC 61 Audley.)

ANDREW, Euseby (*c.*1577–1628), 3 s. Thomas, Daventry, Northants, by Jane, da. Nicholas Belson, London. LI 00, b 08, B 23; clk. of Crown, Dublin, 05. JP. Mar. (i) da. John Dudley, Hackney, sjt-at-arms; (ii) Barbara, da. Anthony Powell and wid. Francis Dayrell, Bucks. Reporter. Endorsed Sir Henry Spelman's condemnation of lay impropriations. Assessed @ £20 for privy seal 25, Edmonton, Middx., where d. (*Northants P & P*, iii; Harleian 3209; Bodl. MS Bodley, 307, fols. 156 *et seq.*; PCC 110 Barrington.)

ASHLEY, Sir Francis (1569–1635), 3 s. Anthony, Damerham, Wilts., by Dorothy, da. John Lyte, Lyte's Cary, Som. Magd. Hall, O, 89; MT 90, b 96, B 16, SL and ktd. 17, KSL 25; rec. Dorchester; steward of Marshalsea by 18. JP; MP 14, 21, 25. Mar. Ann, da. Bernard Samways, Toller Fratrum, Dorset, esq. Admirer of Dorchester puritan minister John White. Censured by HL 28 for opposing Petition of Right, accused LdKpr Coventry of corruption 30. Wealthy; estate worth £1,200 p.a. Of Dorchester at d. (Hutchins, *Dorset*, ii; P. M. Crawford, *Denzil Holles*, 1979; Birch, *Court and Times of Charles I*, i; Mr J. P. Ferris, personal communication; PCC 44 Pile.)

ASKE, Richard (d. 1656), 1 s. John, Aughton, Yorks., by Christian, da. Sir Thomas Fairfax, Yorks. IT 07, b 15, B 33, SL and JKB 49; rec. Colchester 38; common pleader London 43; coroner KB 44. Mar. da. Thomas Heber (and wid. Thomas Lister). Counsel at king's trial; wealthy, left cash bequests of £4,050 (at least). ?London at d. (PCC 273 Berkeley; *Chetham Soc.*, xiv; Cliffe, *Yorkshire Gentry*; Foster, ed. *Yorks. Vis.*)

ATHOW(E), Thomas (*c.*1560–1630), 2 s. Christopher, Beachamwell, Norfolk, by Dorothy, da. Thomas Jennyson. Clare, C, 76; Barnard's Inn; GI 80, b 86, B 08, SL 14; rec. King's Lynn. JP. Mar. Ann, da. John Wingfield, East Winch, Norfolk. Dedicatee T. Heywood, *The Fair Maid of The West* (1631). Wealthy, extensive lands and substantial cash bequests. Of Beachamwell and King's Lynn at d. (B. Cozens-Hardy, 'Norfolk Lawyers', *Norfolk Arch.*, xxxiii (1960); Norfolk RO, Hare 3955, 209 x 4 and Rye MS 4, Vol. i, 35; Gleason *Justices*; PCC 95 Scroope.)

*ATKYNS, Edward (1587–1669), 3 s. Richard, Hempsted, Glos., j. N. Wales by Eleanor, da. Thomas Marsh, Waresby, Hunts. Queen's, O, 04; LI 06, b 13, B 30, SL 40; steward of Hertford. JP. Mar. (i) Ursula, da. Sir Thomas Dacres, Cheshunt, Herts.; (ii) Frances, da. John Berry, Lydd, Kent; (iii) 'the wid. Goulstone'. Puritan sympathies; commr. for sequestrations, Herts. Bought four manors for £5,000 + . Of Albury, Herts., at d. (Glos. RO, D2212/2; *Trans. Bristol and Glos. Arch. Soc.*, l; *AOI*, i; Atkyns, *Glos.*)

*AUDLEY, Hugh (d. 1662), 3 s. John, London and Sutton, Kent, mercer, by Maud, da. John Hare, mercer, London. IT 04, b 11, AB 38; co-clk. of Wards 18. Never married. Remained in London at outbreak of Civil War, sequestered by parl. 43, loaned £1,000 to parl. 44. Very wealthy; cash bequests totalled £14,388. Of Malmesbury, Wilts. at d. (*HS*, xcii; Bell, *Court of Wards*; Aylmer, *King's Servants*; Beds. RO, HY 921–2, 924; *CCC*; PCC 134 Laud.)

AUNGIER, Francis Lord (1558–1632), 1 s. Richard, Barton, Cambs., bencher GI, by Rose, da. William Stewart, Ely, Cambs. Trinity, C, 74, GI 77, b 83, B 02, MR (Ire.) and ktd. 09, cr. Baron Longford 21, rec. Guildford. JP; MP 89, 97. Mar. (i) Douglas (?), sister of earl of Kildare, and da. Henry Fitzgerald; (ii) Anne, da. Sir George Barne, lord mayor of London; (iii) Margaret, wid. Sir John Wynn of Gwydir, and da. Sir Thomas Cane, Stanford, Northants. Wealthy; lands in Surrey and Ireland; assessed @ £20 in 94. Dublin at d. (*H. of P.*; PCC 15 Russell.)

AYLOFFE, William (*c.*1570–post-Oct. 1645), s. William, Bretons, Hornchurch, Essex, by Alice, da. John Searle, Herts. LI 85, b 94, B 10, SL 27, KSL 27; rec. Walden 35. JP. Mar. Alice, da. Thomas Holecroft, Battersea, Surrey. Petitioned against, as debtor, 44; defaulted on parliamentary assessment of £400, but exempted as assistant to HL 45. Not to be confused with namesake, son of JQB, cr. bt. 11, d. 27. (J. Peile, *Biographical Register of Christ's College*, 1910–13; *Essex Rev.*, xlv, lix; Morant, *Essex*, i, ii; *HS*, xli; HL RO, Main Papers, 25 Nov. 1644; *CCAM*.)

AYNSCOMBE, Thomas (d. 1620), ?1 s. Thomas, Buxted, Sussex, ironmaster, by Mary Porter of Bagham, Sussex. Magd., C, 85; Clifford's Inn; IT 89, b 98, B 13; clk. of peace for Lewes 99. Mar. Catherine, da. Thomas Eversfield, Hollington, Sussex. Wealthy; cash bequests £2,885+, leases and lands Mayfield, bought manors 98, 15. Of Mayfield at d. (*Sussex Arch. Coll.*, xxi, lv, lxx; PCC 35 Dale; C142/394/80; *Sussex Rec. Soc.*, xix.)

BABER, John (1592–1644), 1 s. John, DD, rector of Tormarton, Glos., by Mary, da. John Woolton, bp. of Exeter. Lincoln, O, 08, BA 11; LI 14, b 21, B 39, disbenched 41; rec. Wells by 29, counsel to cathedral 36. JP; MP 28, Apr. 40. Mar. Elizabeth, da. William Walrond, Isle-Brewers, Som. Client of Sir Edward Rodney. Attacked in HC 28 for billeting troops at Wells; possible debtor for £200 (at least) 37; argued at 40 LI reading that secretaries of state had no place *de iure* in HL. Royalist? (Barnes, *Som.*; Brown, *Som. Wills*, 5th ser.; *The Visitations of . . . Somerset . . . 1551 and 1575*, ed. F. W. Weaver, 1885; *Som. Rec. Soc.*, lxvi; *CD 1628*; HMC, *Wells*, ii; *CSPD 1637–8, 1639–40*.)

BABINGTON, William (1585–1657), 4 s. Humphrey, Rothley Temple, Leics., by Margaret, da. Francis Cave, Baggrave, Leics. Queens', C, 98; IT 04, b 12, B 32; MCh (extraordinary) 55. Bought manor of E. Laughton, Leics., 24, with T. Pilkington. (Nichols, *Leics.*, iii; *HS*, ii; *Records of Leicester . . . 1603–88; List and Index Soc.*, clxi.)

*BACON, Sir Francis (*c.*1587–1657), 1 s. John, King's Lynn, Norfolk, and IT, by Elizabeth, da. Henry Paynell, Belaugh, Norfolk. Peterhouse, C, 02; Barnard's Inn; GI 08, b 16, B 34, SL 40; rec. Norwich. Bought lands in Norfolk. (Not to be confused with namesake, also of GI and Shrubland Hall, Suffolk, for whom see Underdown, *Pride's Purge*, 366. *HS*, lxxxv; Blomefield and Parkin, *Norfolk*, iv, x.)

BALL, Sir Peter (1598–1680), 1 s. Giles, Dowland and Mamhead, Devon, gent., by Ureth, da. Humphrey Coplestone, Instow, Devon. Lyon's Inn; MT 16, b 23, AB 36, B 42; rec. Exeter 32, sol-gen. to queen 36, later att.-gen., ktd. 46, cr. bt. 72. MP 26, 28, Apr. 40. Mar. Anne, da. Sir William Cooke, Highnam, Glos. Antiquary, wrote on law reform. Royalist, fined @ 1/10, or £1,250 in 46. (G.E.C., *Baronetage*; Additional 32096, fols. 177–8; *Trans. Devon Assocn.*, lxvii; J. Prince, *Danmoni Orientales: or the Worthies of Devon*, 1810; *CCAM*.)

*BANKES, Sir John (1589–1644), Queen's, O, 04; GI 07, b 14, B 29; counsel to Camb. Univ. 34. JP; MP 24, 26, 28. Dep.-lieut. Dorset 33. Dedicatee R. Sibbes, *The Soules Conflict* (1633). Wealthy; house at Stanwell, Middx.; substantial land purchases, income at d. £1,263 p.a. (SP 23/197/284; *VCH, Middx.*, iv; papers at Bodl.; PCC 113 Twisse.)

BARKER, Richard (1554–1636), 2 s. James, Haughmond Abbey, Salop, gent, by Dorothy, da. Richard Clive, Styche, Salop. Barnard's Inn; GI 69, b 76, B 94; Council in Marches 01, j. N. Wales 02, rec. Shrewsbury 03, CJ 10; MP 84, 04. Mar. Dorothy, da. William Poyner, Shrewsbury, Salop. Of Shrewsbury and Wroxeter at d. (*H of P*; Clendinnen.)

BARKER, Robert (1563–1618), 2 or 3 s. John, Bildeston, Suffolk, clothier, by Elizabeth, da. Edward Bestney, Soham, Cambs. St John's, C, 77; Clifford's Inn; IT 79, b 87, B 01, SL 03; fee'd counsel Ipswich 10, town clk. Colchester by 05. JP; MP 92, 04, 14. Mar. Margaret, da. Robert Coke, Mileham, Norfolk (sister of Sir Edward Coke, for whom, see below.) Extensive lands Essex, Suffolk, and Kent. (*H of P*; Clendinnen.)

BARKER, Thomas (*c.*1566–1630), 3 s. William, Sonning, Berks., gent., by Anne, da. Sir Lawrence Stoughton, of Stoughton, Surrey. ?Broadgates Hall, O, 81, BA 84; MT 87, b 94, B 15. Mar. da. Valentine Saunders, esq. Awarded 100 marks damages after falsely accused of forgery in 13. Requested burial 'decently and without unnecessary expense and vain ceremony'; MI (Chiswick) describes as 'faithful member of God's church'. Wealthy; purchased land worth £1,400 p.a., left portions of £2,600 to four das. and £1,000 to another; had ready money £1,600. Of Chiswick, Middx. at d. (*VCH, Middx.*, vii; D. Lysons, *The Environs of London*, 1792–6, ii; *English Reports*, lxxii. 927; PCC 36 Scroope.)

BARKESDALE, John (d. 1629), s. of ?John, attorney, *fl.* 97, Newbury, Berks. Corpus Christi, O, 96, BA 99; LI 00, b 08, B 23. Mar. Margaret. At his reading, 28, James Fiennes, s. of Lord Saye and Sele, high steward of Newbury, admitted to LI. Wealth modest only; rated for 29 Newbury subsidy @ £3 in lands; bequests total £460, lands and house in Newbury. (HLS MS 1089; W. Money, *A History of Newbury*, 1972; PCC 81 Ridley.)

BARTLETT (Barthelett), Edward (d. 1605), of London. LI 71, b 80, B 94. Probably follower of earl of Sussex. Censured by judges for curtailed reading, 05. Mar. Cicely. JP. Listed among 'lawyers of practice', 99–00. Assessed @ £20 for privy seal 04, but daughters' portions only £450 × 2. Of Attleburgh, Norfolk, at d. (Smith, *County and Court*; *APC 1599–1600*; Blomefield and Parkin, *Norfolk*, i; PCC 1 Stafford.)

BASTARD, William (*c.*1560–1639), 3 s. John, Gerston and West Arlington, Devon, gent., by Thomasine, da. Geoffrey Gilbert. Lyon's Inn; MT 78, b 85, B 06; rec. Totnes 96, Dartmouth 04. JP; MP 97, 01. Mar. Will requests funeral without 'feasting, banqueting, excessive quaffing and beastly drinking ... or disorder or common dole', sermon by learned minister 'such as shall live orderly submitting himself to the government of the Church'. Well-to-do, lands Cornwall and Devon, cash bequests £2,068 + 100 sheep and farm gear. Certified able to lend king £20 in 11. (*H of P*; *Devon & Cornwall N & Q*, xxvi; PCC 88 Harvey.)

BAWTRY, Leonard (*c.*1561–1626), s. William (?), Boston (?), Lincs. Furnival's Inn; LI 75, b 84, B 02, SL 14. Mar. (i) Agnes Chester; (ii) Mary, wid. Robert Tighe, rector of All Hallows, Barking, London. MP 14. Puritan sympathies? Of Boston, Lincs., at d. (*HS*, l; Holmes, *Seventeenth-Century Lincolnshire*; History of Parliament, 1604–29: draft biography.)

BEARE, George (d. 1662), 1 s. John, Barnstaple, Devon, gent., by Agnes, da.

John Snedel (or Sindall). MT 05, b 13, B 33, SL 60. JP. Mar. (i) Grace, da. Balthazar Boteler, Parkham, Devon; (ii) Mary, da. John Newport, Pickwell, Devon (separated, 1640). Att. in Star Chamber 93? Claims in 62 to be 'a true son of the Church of England'. Active royalist, sequestered. Modest wealth. (*HS*, vi; Viviun, *Devon Vis.*; PCC 151 Laud; Haward, *Reports*; *CCC*; Devon RO, 50/11/24/3.)

BEDINGFIELD, Sir Thomas (1555–1636), 1 s. Thomas, Fleming's Hall, Bedingfield, Suffolk, by Mary, da. William Methwold, Langford, Norfolk. Christ's, C, 71; Furnival's Inn (barrister); LI 75, b 83, AB 03; steward of Duchy of Lancaster, Norfolk, Suffolk, Cambs. JP; MP 86. Mar. Dorothy, da. John Southwell, Barham, Suffolk. Wealthy; bought Darsham Manor 95, held at least 2 other manors and properties in Norfolk and Suffolk; cash bequests £2,219, and rent charges £180 p.a.; assessed @ £20 for Middx. privy seal *c.*1595. Of Darsham, Suffolk, at d. (*H. of P.*; A. Suckling, *The History . . . of Suffolk*, 1846–8, ii; PCC 109 Pile.)

*BEDINGFIELD, Thomas (*c.*1592–1661), 2 s. of the preceding. Caius, C, 09; GI 08, b 16, B 36. MP 21. Mar. Elizabeth, da. Charles Hoskins, Oxted, Surrey, formerly citizen of London. Commr. for assessment, Norfolk and Suffolk, 47. Inherited properties from father and bought Darsham from elder brother. (*HS*, lxxxv; Suckling, *Suffolk*, ii; *AOI*, i.)

BENN, Sir Anthony (*c.*1568–1618), 1 s. Robert, St Nicholas Cole Abbey, London, linen-draper. Broadgates Hall, O, 84, BA 87; MT 83, b 94 (as Bennet), B 12; rec. Kingston-on-Thames 10, rec. London 16, ktd. 17. JP. Mar. Jane, da. John Evelyn, Kingston and Godstone, Surrey, and West Dean and Everleigh, Wilts. Dedicatee E. H[owes], *The Abridgement of the English Chronicles* (1618). Bought manor of Norbiton Hall, Surrey, from father-in-law. Essayist. Bequeathed marriage portion of £2,000 to da. from 'a plain, downright, honest, clear estate, though small', and appointed God as executor—'I leave nothing to the trust of worldly friends'. (*HS*, xliii; *Misc. Gen. & Her.*, 2nd ser., i; *VCH, Surrey*, iv; Aubrey, *Natural History of Surrey*, i; Manning and Bray, *Surrey*, i; HMC, *Hastings*, iv; Whitelocke, *Lib. Fam.*; Beds. RO, L 28/46; CUL MS Dd. 5.14; PCC 97 Meade.)

*BERKELEY, Sir Robert (1584–1656). Queen's, O, 96; MT 01, b 08, B 25, SL 27; rec. Worcester by 21. MP 21, 24. Mar. Elizabeth, da. Thomas Conyers, East Barnet, Herts., and Yorks.; she declared insane 36. Left writings and evidences for benefit of grandson, if a protestant. Inherited two manors, acquired two more, leased house Holborn. Of Spetchley, Worcs., at d. (T. R. Nash, *Collections for the History of Worcestershire*, 1799, ii; Metcalfe, ed. *Wilts. Vis.*; Foster, *Yorks. Vis.*; PCC 324 Berkeley; C142/718/155.)

BETTENHAM, Jeremy (d. 1606), 2 s. Thomas, Cranbrook, Kent, by Joan, da. Seth Bowthe, Bromley, Kent. GI 66, b 69, B 90. Never married.

Allowed by GI Pension 20 marks for expenses at his reading 'in respect he hath been a continual and diligent keeper of learning in the house and . . . no great gainer by the law'. Will mentions no landed property, most bequests to GI colleagues; held some land in manor of Eltham. (*HS*, lxxiv; *GIPB*; Bacon, *Works*, x; PCC 86 Stafforde.)

BEVERCOTES, Samuel (d. 1603), s. Anthony, Ordsall, Notts., by da. Philip Rawson. Trinity, C, 70; Staple Inn; GI 74, b 81, B 99; feodary Notts. by 88, member Council of North 99, rec. Nottingham 00, Newark 02. JP. Mar. Matilda Leigh, of Southwell, Notts. Dependant of and possibly steward to, earls of Rutland. (*HS*, iv; Dias, thesis; HMC, *Salisbury*, xv, *Rutland*, i; Borthwick, Act Book Retford, 1603, fol. 417.)

BING (Byng), Henry (1573–1635), 1 s. Thomas, Grantchester, Cambs., Professor of Civil Law, by Catherine Randall. Clare, C, 93; GI 92, b 99, B 16, SL 23; counsel King's College, C, 1606, steward Camb. Univ. 03, Sudbury 14. MP 14. Mar. Katherine, da. Thomas Clench of Holbrook, Suffolk. Had interest in *Custos Brevium* office, KB. First and second s. both married grand-das. of Sir Edward Coke (see below). Of St Giles-in-the-Fields, Westminster, and Grantchester, Cambs., at d. (Additional 19121, fols. 353–4; C. F. Sperling, *A Short History of . . . Sudbury*, 1896; CUL MS U/Ac. 2(1); C2 Jas. I F5/2; PCC 26 Sadler.)

BLENNERHASSET, Sir John (d. 1624), 4 s. John, steward to duke of Norfolk, by Margaret Etchingham. Furnival's Inn (barrister); LI 83, b 91, B 09; BExch (Ire.) and ktd. 09, CBExch (Ire.) 20. Mar. Ursula, da. Richard Duke, Benhall, Suffolk. Commr. Wexford plantation. Of Dublin at d. (Ball, *Judges in Ireland*; M. A. Hickson, *Selections from Old Kerry Records*, 1872.)

BLUNDELL, Robert (c.1574–1658), 1 s. Robert, Ince Blundell, Lancs., gent., by Marcia, da. Richard Massey, Rishton, Lancs. St John's, C, c.91; GI 93, b 00, B 18; att.-gen. Chester and Flint 23. JP. Dependant of earl of Derby. Mar. (i) Ann Carmaeden; (ii) Anne, da. William Wall or Hall, Crondall, Hants. Strong Catholic connections, lost place as JP in 39 for recusancy. Royalist. Substantially augmented family estates, although sequestrated. Papers at Lancs. RO; Blackwood, *Lancashire Gentry*, and personal communication; Gibson, *Lydiate Hall*; *CCC*; PROB 8/51, fol. 401ᵛ.)

BOOTH, William (c.1568–1637), 1 s. William, Birmingham and Witton, War., and St Clement Danes, London, att., by Dorothy, da. Richard Dilke, Kirkby Mallory, Leics. Magd. Hall, O, 03; MT 05, b 13, B 33. Mar. Alice, da. Richard Fox, Birmingham and Moseley, War. Purchased lands in War. Of Witton at d. (*HS*, cvi; *Dugdale Soc.*, xxx; *VCH, War.*, iv, vii; PCC 6 Lee.)

BOURCHIER, Henry (d. 1598), illeg. s. of Hunt or Huntley, by Anne, Baroness Bourchier. IT 73, b 84, B 96. MP 89, 93, 97. Mar. Anne (Scott?).

Follower and kinsman of Robert Devereux, earl of Essex, 'my very good Lord'. Member, Society of Antiquaries. (*H. of P.*; PCC 74 Lewyn.)

BOURNE, William (d. 1606), of Chesterton, Staffs. New Inn; MT 78, b 85, B 05. Mar. Sara, wid. of London. Cash bequests total £172, copyhold and freehold property to be sold to pay debts. Of East Betchworth, Surrey, at d. (PCC 55 Stafforde.)

BOWNE (Bohun, Boone, Boune), Gilbert (*fl.*1602–1664), 1 s. John, lawyer of Derbs. and Nottingham, follower of earl of Rutland, by Barbara, da. John Leek of Notts. LI 02, b 18, B 36, SL 37; rec. Newark, Nottingham. JP; MP Apr. 1640. Mar. (i) Maria, da. Edward Forset, Bilsby, Lincs.; (ii) Millicent, da. John Waring, esq. Antiquary. Active royalist. Wealth unknown; sold land, but paid second highest assessment for St Mary's church, Nottingham, 37. (Dias, thesis; A. C. Wood, *Notts. in the Civil War*, 1937; *Thoroton Soc. Trans.*, xxxiii; PCC 33 Juxon.)

BRACKE(I)N, Francis (d. 1628), 2 s. Richard, Chesterton, Cambs., gent., by Elizabeth, da. Thomas Wren, Haddenham, Isle of Ely. Queens', C, 61; Staple Inn(?); GI 67, b 77, B 96; dep.-rec. and rec. Cambridge 90; counsel, King's College, Cambridge. JP; MP 14, 24. Recommended by Viscount De L'Isle as CBExch (Ire.) 06. Mar. Barbara, da. Thomas Gooderich. Caricatured in Ruggle's *Ignoramus*. Described in 04 as 'of mean ability and as little in reputation'. (*HS*, xli; HMC, *Salisbury*, xvi, xviii; A. Gibbons, *Ely Episcopal Records*, 1891.)

*BRAMSTON, Sir John (1577–1654). MT 97, b 05, B 23. JP. Substantial Irish property. Paid £8,000 for Essex lands of Thomas Weston, s. Lord Treasurer Portland, 35. (Papers at Essex RO; Knowler, i.)

BRANTINGHAM, Elias (*c.*1555–*c.*1632), of Norwich. Staple Inn; GI 78, b 85, B 05. JP. Mar. Cicely, da. Robert Gibson, East Beckham, Norfolk. Requested night burial. Assessed £10 for 1611 benevolence; left w. all 'temporal estate which I never desired to make great having no children'. Inventory value £282 (including £20 worth of books). (Gleason, *Justices*; W. Mason, *History of Norfolk*, 1884; Norfolk RO, NCC 17 Morse and Norwich City Records 17b, Revenue and Letters, fol. 27, and INV 38, no. 54.)

*BREREWOOD, Sir Robert (*c.*1588–1654), 1 s. MT 07, b 15, B 38; town clk. and clk. of Pentice court, Chester, 18; removed from all Chester offices 46. Sequestered. Will laments 'the great losses I have sustained in these late troublesome years'; charges estate with £1,200 debt, but personal bequests of £1,000. (*APC 1627, 1627–8*; *Lancs. & Ches. Rec. Soc.*, cvi; Chester City RO, AB/2/76; PCC 383 Berkeley.)

BRIAN, Joseph (*c.*1590–*c.*1639), s. John, mayor of Northampton. Magd. Hall, O, 04; GI 07, b 17, B 32. Mar. Eliza Tresham. Puritan father, and devoutly pious will, 'utterly abandoning any mine own merits as rags and rottenness'. GI chamber and books to be sold towards son's education;

portions to 5 das. total £2,100. (PCC 23 Harvey; *Northants Rec. Soc.*, xxx.)

BRICKENDEN, Thomas (*c.*1585–1673), 1 s. Thomas, Cranbrook, Kent, and Inkpen, Berks., gent., by Elizabeth Bennet, Wallingford, Berks. Magd., O, 01; GI 05, b ?, B 29; j. of lord mayor's ct., London, 29, dep.-rec. by 40; John Cooke's 'worthy master, who honoured me with a lodging in his chamber'. Mar. Elizabeth, da. Thomas Colwell of GI and Faversham, Kent. (*HS*, liii; Metcalfe, ed. *Berks. Vis.*; *VCH, Berks.*, iv; Overall, *Remembrancia*; Cooke, *Vindication.*)

BRIDGEMAN, Sir John (1568–1638), 1 s. John, Mitcheldean and Sudeley, Glos., by Anne, da. William Gernon, Herefs. Magd. Hall, O, 82; Clifford's Inn; IT 91, b 00, B 15, SL and ktd. 23, CJ Chester 26; rec. Gloucester, Shrewsbury, Ludlow, and Wenlock, counsel to Gloucester 14. Mar. Francis, da. Henry Daunt, Owlpen, Glos. Author. Dedicated room in Nympsfield manor as chapel; bought land, bequeathed £1,500 as marriage portion to da. (Williams, *Welsh Judges; HS*, xxi; Rudder, *Glos.*; PCC 30 Lee; *Index Lib.*, xiii; Devon RO, 96M/Box 2/8.)

BRISCOE, John (1577–1652), 1 s. Alexander, of Aldenham, Herts., by Margery, da. Thomas Baldwin. Trinity, O, 92; LI 94, b 02, B 20. Mar. Elizabeth, da. Thomas Earlesman, Isle of Wight (or Beckingham Butler?). Author and translator. Adopted Augustine Wingfield, radical puritan MP 53. (*HS*, xx; Herts. RO; R. Clutterbuck, *History ... of Hertford*, (1815–27), ii; HMC, *Fifth Rep*; *LJ*, vi; Woolrych, *Commonwealth to Protectorate*; papers, LI.)

BROMLEY, Sir Edward (1563–1626), 2 s. Sir George, CJ Chester, of Salop, by Joan, da. John Waterton, Worfield, Salop. IT 80, b 90, B 03, SL, BExch and ktd., 10; rec. Wenlock, Bridgnorth, surveyor south parts, Duchy of Lancaster. JP; MP 1586–1604. Mar. Margaret, da. Nicholas Lowe of Enville, Staffs. 'God hath plentifully blessed me with a good estate.' Of Shifnal, Salop, at d. (*H. of P.*; Clendinnen; PCC 128 Hele.)

*BROOKE, Christopher (d. 1628), mother Jane Maltby. LI 87, b 94, B 11; counsel and dep.-rec. York 08–16; member Council of North 26, nominated councillor of fee 28. MP 04–26. Associate of Sir Arthur Ingram and Mitre tavern group. Regretted that 'I have been so ill an husband of mine own fortunes ... that I cannot testify my love to my brothers and sisters by legacies of moment'; held property in York, Essex, Westmorland, and London, the last mainly leases, including house near Covent Garden from Lady Drury, where d. (*VCH, York*; Widdrington, *Analecta Eboracensia*; Prestwich, *Cranfield*; Leeds District Archives, TN/F 17/5; Chicago MSS Bacon 2755–6; PCC 112 Barrington.)

BROOKE, Thomas (*c.*1561–1612), 2 (but only surviving) s. Richard, Whitchurch, Hants, by Elizabeth Twyne. New Coll., O, 81, BA 84; Clement's Inn; IT 85, b 95, B 07. JP; MP 04. Mar. Susan, da. Sir Thomas Foster,

JCP. Bequeathed lands and tenements including parsonage of Whitchurch to eldest s.; IPM shows numerous small parcels in Whitchurch, valued @ £16 p.a. (Clendinnen; Berry, *Hants Genealogies; HS*, lxiv; PCC 107 Fenner; C142/338/52.)

BROOKE (Brocke), William (1566–1611), 1 s. Robert, Chester, gent., by Jane, da. John Cotgrave, Cotton Edmunds, Ches. Brasenose, O, 83; Clifford's Inn; IT 84, b 93, B 05; counsel for Chester 97, alderman 03; rec. Southampton 03. JP; MP 97, 04. Mar. Anne, da. Sir Benjamin Tichbourne, of Tichbourne, Hants. Reporter. Puritan sympathies. Held lands in Hants, Wilts., Surrey, Ches.; bequeathed a gold piece to each of 16 named 'gentlemen of mine own profession'. Of Longwood, Hants, at d. (*H. of P.*; Mr J. P. Ferris, personal communication; Clendinnen; Chester City RO, AB/1/277; PCC 101 Wood.)

BROWNE, George (*c.*1583–1631), 2 s. Sir John, Frampton, Dorset, by Jane Portman, of Orchard Portman, Som. Magd., O, 98, BA (ex Univ. Coll.) 02; MT 02, b 09, B 28; rec. Lyme Regis, Taunton. JP; MP 14, 26, 28. Mar. Christian, da. Christopher Derby, Askerswell, Dorset. Puritan? (Barnes, *Somerset*; Hutchins, *Dorset*; PCC 49 St John; *CD 1628*; Hargrave 402; Mr J. P. Ferris, personal communication.)

*BULSTRODE, Edward (*c.*1589–1659), 2 s. Sir Edward, Upton, Hedgerley, Bucks., by Cicely, da. Sir John Croke, Chilton. St John's, O, 04; IT 06, b 14, B 29; j. N. Wales 49, CJ 53. JP. Mar. Margaret, da. Richard Chamberlain, Astley, War. Sister Elizabeth mar. Sir James Whitelocke (for whom, see below). Contributed £3. 6s. 8d. to king's expenses Mar. 39. (*HS*, viii, lviii; Williams, *Welsh Judges*; *CCC*; Additional 37343; SP 16/538/84.)

BYSSHE, Edward (*c.*1584–1655), 1 s. Thomas, Burstow, Surrey, by Anne, da. John Bisshe, Worth, Sussex. Furnival's Inn; LI 05, b 12, B 30; escheator Surrey 08, feodary 14. JP; MP 24–8. Mar. Mary, da. John Turner, Bletchingley, Surrey. Fined for serving flesh in Lent at LI reading 32. Granted arms 17. Bought several manors in Surrey, built Smallfield Place, Burstow. Aubrey claimed family of local yeomanry origins. (Glanville, thesis; *VCH, Surrey*, iii, iv; *HS*, lxxvi; Manning and Bray, *Surrey*, ii; Keeler.)

*CAESAR, Sir Thomas (1561–1610). IT 82, b 91, AB 07, B 10. (*H. of P.*)

*CALLIS, Robert (d. 1642), s. Robert, Great Hale, Lincs., yeoman. GI 96, b 01, B 22, SL 27; fee'd counsel Lincoln 04, dep.-rec. 12. JP. Mar. Esher (or Hester), da. William Fitzwilliam, Mablethorpe, Lincs. Acquired farm at Dalderby; houses, close, and other freehold lands in Lincoln and suburbs. Portion £1,500 to da.; 10s. to poor in every parish of Lincoln; law books to GI library. (Holmes, *Lincolnshire*; PCC 56 Cambell; STAC 8/98/9, 107/9.)

*CALTHORPE (Calthrop), Sir Henry (1586–1637), 2 or 3 s. Trinity, C, BA

05; MT 07, b 16, AB 35, B 36. Attorney of Wards 36. Author; reporter; antiquary. Wealthy; inherited estates from father, possessed at least 10 manors at d., bequeathed marriage portions of £2,000 to 2 das. (Blomefield and Parkin, *Norfolk*, viii; C. W. C. Calthrop, *Notes on the Families of Calthorpe*, 1933; PCC 131 Goare.)

CASON, Edward (*c.*1563–1624), 1 s. Edward, Hertford, Herts., and New Inn, London, by Elizabeth, da. Thomas Bowle, Herts. Trinity, C, 80; New Inn; MT 82, b 91, B 10; steward Hertford. JP. Mar. (i) Jane, da. Sir Henry Boteler, Herts.; (ii) Susan, da. Sir Robert Oxenbridge, Hants. MI claims '*legum humanarum interpres erat, custos divinarum cultor non minus duram quam duodecim tabularum . . .*'. Bought manor house, Furneaux Pelham, held other manors and lands in Cambs., leases in Lincs., and London. (Clutterbuck, iii; *HS*, xxii; C149/748/4; *VCH, Herts.*, iii, iv; PCC 83 Byrde.)

CA(U)LFIELD, George (d. 1603), s. Alexander, Great Milton, Oxon., gent., bro. First Lord Charlemont. Christ Church, O, 61, BA 66; GI 68, b 81, B 97; freeman and counsel Oxford; j. S. Wales 00. JP; MP 1584–1601. Mar. Mary, da. Richard Taverner, Woodeaton, Oxon. Of Kettle Hall, Oxford, at d. (*H. of P.*; HMC, *Salisbury*, xiv.)

CAVELL, John (d. 1612), 1 s. Humphrey, Croydon, Surrey, and bencher MT. New Inn; MT 71, b 77, B 94; perhaps retained by Henry, ninth earl of Northumberland from c. 95. Mar. Eliza Beswick (or Berwick). (*Arch. Cant.*, xx; Manning and Bray, *Surrey*, ii; *The Household Papers of Henry Percy . . .*, ed. G. R. Batho (*CS*, 1962); *HS*, xlii.)

CHAMBERLAIN(E), Sir Thomas (d. 1625), s. William, Brackley, Ire. GI 78, b 85, B 07, SL 14, rec. Banbury, Ludlow, and j. N. Wales 15, ktd. 16, Council in Marches and CJ Chester 16; JKB 20; steward to Ellesmere; solicitor to Henry, Lord Berkeley. Mar. (i) Elizabeth, da. Sir George Fermor, Northants, wid. Sir William Stafford; (ii) Elizabeth, da. Lord Hunsdon, wid. Sir Thomas Berkeley. William Whately, puritan vicar of Banbury, his 'loving friend'. Wealthy; acquired Barford, Kirtlington, Ilbury manors, Oxon., and other lands in Oxon., Glos., War. £2,000 portion for da. Of Wickham, Oxon., at d. (Williams, *Welsh Judges*; *Lives of the Berkeleys*, ed. MacLean; *VCH, Oxon.*, vi, ix; Oxon. RO, Dash. III–IX; *Banbury Hist. Soc.*, xv; Ellesmere 178, 233, 2185–6; PCC 20 Skynner.)

CHAPMAN, Thomas (*c.*1580–*c.*1663), 1 s. Edward, Foxton, Leics. Lincoln, O, 97; Clement's Inn; IT 01, b 09, B 27, SL 48; rec. Leicester 24. JP. Mar. Alice, da. Sir William Farmer, Leics. Requested burial 'without any pomp or ceremony at all'. Dedicatee T. Gataker, *An Anniversarie Memorial* (1626). Held at least four manors and various lands around Leicester and Foxton. (Leics. RO, Commissary Court Wills, 1663, C 67; Nichols, *Leics.*, i, iii; *VCH, Leics.*, iii, iv.)

CHAWORTH, George (d. 1615), 3 s. George, Linby, Notts., gent., by Mary, da. Sir Henry Sacheverell, Morley, Derbs. Trinity, C, 72; Barnard's Inn; GI 76, b 83, B 01. JP; MP 89; member of Council in North was probably nephew, Sir George. (*H. of P.*; STAC 8/238/24.)

CHIBBO(U)RNE, Sir Charles (d. 1619), s. Christopher, Messing Hall, Essex, gent., by Elizabeth Lawrence, Tilbury, Essex. Furnival's Inn; LI 86, b 94, B 10, SL 14; rec. Maldon; SL to Prince Charles; ktd. 19. MP 14. Mar. (i) Anne, da. Thomas Spilman, Great Chart, Kent; (ii) Winifred, da. Robert Wiseman, Mayland, Essex; (iii) Margaret, da. Sir George Young, York. Dedicatee T. Gataker, *Of . . . Lots* (1619). Daughters' marriage portions £300 × 3 and £400 × 3. Bought lands in Essex. Assessed £20 for privy seal in 14(?), as of St Giles-in-the-Fields, Middx., but described at d. as 'a great Essex lawyer'. (*HS*, xiii; Chamberlain, *Letters*, ii; Ellesmere 2475; Harleian 1692, fols. 21ᵛ *et seq.*; PCC 24 Soame.)

CHOLMLEY, Nicholas (d. 1644), s. John, London and Bletchingley, Surrey, gent., by Isabel, da. John Hare, London and Homersfield, Suffolk. IT 84, b 93, B 07; escheator Essex and Herts. 95; deputy feodary Lincs. 01; fee'd counsel Lincoln 04. Mar. Susan Gawdon. Leading counsel in Ct. of Wards; accused of concealing wardship pre-1605. Contributed £3. 6s. 8d. to king's expenses 39; loaned parliament £1,900, *c*. 43. (*HS*, xliii, lv; *Surrey Arch. Coll.*, xiv, xix; U. Lambert, *Bletchingley*, 1949, ii; *List and Index Soc.*, lxxii; Lincs. RO, L1/1/4, fol. 29ᵛ; SP 16/538/84; HMC, *Salisbury*, xxiii. 221; *CJ*, iii. 181, 536; *CCAM*; PCC 16 Rivers.)

CLARKE, Sir Edward (d. 1639), s. Edward, Oxon. (Dorchester?), and LI. LI 92, b 00, AB 19, B 26; steward Reading 05, MCh (extraordinary) 19, MCh 24, ktd. 25. JP. Pious; helped establish lecture at Reading; dedicatee T. Taylor, *The Parable of the Sower* (1621), and *idem, The Principles of Christian Practice* (1635). Clashed with Reading corporation during 20s, when supported by William Knollys, Lord Wallingford. Subsidy assessment £12 lands in Berks., 28. Money-lender; left wife £130 p.a. Had his bowels interred in St Mary's, Reading, his body at Dorchester, Oxon. (W. A. Shaw, *The Knights of England* (1906); C. Coates, *History of Reading*, 1802; Guilding, ed., *Reading Records*, ii; Berks. RO, D/EX 49; PCC 28 Harvey.)

CLARKE, Henry (*c*.1580–1652), 2 s. Edward, Willoughby, War., esq., and servant to F. Morgan, bencher. MT 04, b 12, B 28, SL 37; rec. Rochester by 14. JP; MP 21, 25, 26. Mar. Grace, da. George Morgan, Rochester and IT. Commissioned as assize judge 47. Income *c*. 40 around £400 p.a. Will mentions manor of Ulcomb, cash bequests £70. Of Rochester, Kent, at d. (*HS*, liv; *MTR*, i; *Leics. Arch. Soc.*, v; F. F. Smith, *Rochester in Parliament 1395–1933*, 1933; Everitt, thesis; PCC 131 Bowyer.)

CLARKE, James (d. by 1621), of Somerset. Trinity, O, BA 91, MA 95; LI 95, b 03, B 20. (Not 1 s. James Clarke of the Mount and Norton Fitzwarren, Som., d. 12, for whom see *H. of P.* Another James Clarke, of Lydeard,

Som., was admitted to Caius, C, 90, aged 15 yrs, BA 94, MA 97, for whom, see J. Venn, *Biographical History of Gonville and Caius College*, 1897–1912, i; LI MS Red Book, fol. 88.)

CLARKE, John (*c*.1591–1657), 1 s. Jerome, Willoughby, War., lawyer, by Margaret Dormer, Barton, Oxon. Magd. Hall, O, 07, BA, Queen's 10; LI 08, b 15, B 33, SL 48; j. W. Wales 47; sheriff Bucks. 48. JP. Mar. Rebecca, da. Rowland Lee, Bucks. and London. Commr. for assessment Northants 47. Assessed @ £500 in 43; acquired manor of Aston Rowant, Oxon., and rebuilt house. Of Guilsborough, Northants at d. (*HS*, lxxxviii; W. Dugdale, *The Antiquities of Warwickshire*, 1730; Williams, *Welsh Judges*; *AOI*, i, ii; *VCH, Oxon.*, viii.)

CLOPTON, William (1584–1640), 1 s. William, Groton, Suffolk, and GI, counsellor, by Margaret, da. Edward Waldegrave, Lawford, Essex. Christ's, C, 05, MA 08; GI 05, b 11, B 28. JP. Mar. Alice, da. Edmund Doyley, Shottisham, Suffolk. Sister Thomasine mar. John Winthrop; defendant in Ct. of Chivalry case 37. Inherited Castlyns manor and adjoining lands, Groton and Essex; provided portions of £200 for 11 children. (Peile, *Biographical Register*; *The Visitation of Suffolk [1561]*, ed. J. J. Howard, 1864–71, i; J. J. Muskett, *Suffolk Manorial Families*, 1900–14, i; *APC 1599–1600*, 31; *HS*, cvi; PCC 148 Coventry.)

CLOUGH, John (d. 1623), y.s. John, Skipton-on-Swale, Yorks. Clifford's Inn; IT 97, b 06, B 22. JP. Mar. Maria Pormeinghurst(?), Sussex. Fervently pious preamble to will. Substantial land purchaser; inherited Carlton Miniott manor from father. Bequeathed £1,900 to 4 younger children, including £80 to da. Left w. her dower, 'protesting that if I were not charged with so many poor infants ... I would show my love to her in such fashion as would content her'. (*VCH, Yorks. (NR)*, ii; Borthwick, Reg. 37, fol. 387; C142/397/74.)

*COKE, Sir Edward (1552–1634), 1 s. Robert, Mileham, Norfolk, bencher LI, by Winifred Knightley, da. of a Norwich att. Trinity, C, 67; Clifford's Inn; IT 72, b 78, B 90. (*Radicals*, i, and sources cited therein; C. Hill, *Intellectual Origins of the English Revolution*, 1965; Little, *Religion, Order and Law*.)

COLLINS, Nicholas (d. 1616), of Braxted, Essex. LI 71, b 79, B 94; fee'd counsel London 94. JP. Married Judith, of Essex. May have owned manor of Enfields, Ongar (Little Laver), 03; bought lands Wickford 08. Subsidy assessment @ £40 in land in 93? (*VCH, Essex*, iv; Essex RO, D/DU 376/7, 8; London Corp. RO, Rep. 23, fol. 283; PCC 126 Cope.)

CONYERS, William (*c*.1586–1659), 1 s. Robert, London, grocer, by Blanche, sister of Dunstan Ducke, Putney, Surrey. St John's, C, 02; MT 05, b 13, B 31, SL 48. JP; MP 14, 21, 24. Mar. Mary, da. Sir Francis Harvey, JKB (for whom, see below). Inherited lands in Essex, Lincs. and Yorks. (manors of Scarborough and Cleyton-in-Skipway) from uncle, d. 19.

Assessed £400 in 44. Of Walthamstow, Essex, at d. (*HS*, xiv; Morant, *Essex*, i; CUL MS Dd. 5. 51, fol. 6; *CCAM*.)

COOPER (Cowper), Ralph (*c*.1573–1656), 2 s. Robert, Slinfold, Sussex, by Alice, da. Thomas Burgh. GI 95, b 01, B 21. JP. Mar. Dorothy, sister of Sir Richard Michelbourne, Horsted Keynes, Sussex. Parliamentarian committee-man, Arundel rape, 43. As heir to elder bro. Edward (d. 23), inherited Strood manor and lands in Surrey. Paid £10 for knighthood composition 30. (*HS*, liii; J. Comber, *Sussex Genealogies*, 1931–3, i; Fletcher, *Sussex*; *Sussex Arch. Coll.*, xx.)

COPLEY, Godfrey (*c*.1589–1648), 1 s. John, Skelbrooke, Yorks., esq., by Jane, da. Ralph Angier. Magd., O, 06, BA 08; LI 07, b 14, B 33; rec. Doncaster and Pontefract. Mar. Thomasine, da. Thomas Ravenscroft, Chipping Barnet, Herts. Royalist, estates sequestered. At d. held lands in Plumtree, Notts., and S. Yorks.; to be sold to pay debts and legacies, including £500 portions to 2 das. Paid £15 knighthood composition in 1628–30. (J. Foster, *Pedigrees, of ... Yorkshire*, 1874, i; A. C. Wood, *Nottinghamshire in the Civil War*, 1937; Borthwick, PC York, November 1648, Doncaster D and annexed executor's accounts; *Yorks. Arch. Soc., Rec. Ser.*, li.)

*COVENTRY, Sir Thomas (1547–1606), b. Bewdley, Worcs., and according to will, brought up in Worcester. IT 68, b?, B 91; member Council in Marches 02. Bought manors of Croome D'Abitot 92 and Ryall, 01. Left marriage portions of £300 to 4 das. Anon. contemporary life of son (see below) claims Coventry's 'acquirings in the progress of his profession (as it seems) were not much'. (Nash, *Collections*, i. 260; Longleat MS 196; PCC 13 Huddlestone; Norfolk RO, NRS Hare 6156.)

*COVENTRY, Thomas Lord (1578–1640). IT 95, b 03, B 14; j. sheriff's ct. London 14; rec. Worcester 24. MP 21. First w., Sarah, grandda. William Seabright, town clk. London 1574–1613. Very wealthy; acquired 14 manors in Worcs. 15–39; left 3 das. portions of £4,000 each, £500 to poor, and £930 to servants. (London Corp. RO, Rep. 31, fol. 394ᵛ; *VCH, Herts., Herts. Families; VCH, Worcs.*, ii–iv; Longleat MS 196; papers at Birmingham Reference Lib.; Sheffield Public Lib., Wentworth-Woodhouse MSS; HMC, *Coventry*; PCC 1 Coventry; papers, at Bodl., BL.)

*CRAWLEY, Sir Francis (1584–1650), s. Thomas, Luton, Beds., husbandman or maltster, by Dorothy, da. John Edgerley, Milton, Oxon. Caius, C, 92; Staple Inn; GI 98, b ?, B 22. JP. Dedicatee, T. Adams, *The Divells Banket* (1614). Inherited Haverings manor, bought Somery's Place, Luton, and various farms from father-in-law. Assessed at £10 in lands 28–9. (*VCH, Beds.*, ii; Beds. RO, Crawley papers and T/53/10, p. 16.)

CRESHELD, Richard (d. 1652), 2 s. Edward, gent., Mattishall Burgh, Norfolk, by Bridget, da. Robert Hurleston, same. LI 08, b 15, B 33, SL 36, JCP 48; rec. Evesham 22. JP; MP 24–40. Mar. Elizabeth, da. Richard

Egiocke, Salford Priors, War. Income perhaps £275 p.a. Cash bequests total £720, including £100 as stock for poor of Evesham; buried St Andrew's, Holborn. (Keeler; Silcock, thesis; PCC 67 Bowyer; Baker, *Serjeants*.)

CRESSY, Hugh (d. *c.*1643?), 1 s. William, Holme, Notts., by da. Thomas Hutchinson, Owthorpe, Notts. Furnival's Inn; LI 90, b 98, B 14; JKB (Ire.) 33. Mar. Margaret D'Oyley, da. London physician. Follower of Strafford. Reporter. In petition to king *c.*33, claimed that he had many children and no hope of making his eldest son 'an heir of any competency'. Son became Benedictine monk. (Ball, *Judges in Ireland; DNB*, s.v. Cressy, Hugh; Additional 35947; Sheffield Public Lib., Wentworth-Woodhouse MSS.)

*CREW(E), Sir Randle (1558–1646). Furnival's Inn; LI 77, b 84, B 00; fee'd counsel Banbury 08; rec. Yarmouth. Dedicatee, T. Gataker, *A Sparke* . . . (1621); provided £20 p.a. plus board for 'an honest and religious minister' to live at Crewe Hall after his death to instruct family in the fear of God. Parliamentarian. Wealthy; held manors in Cheshire and Norfolk, leases Herts., and house in London; provided portion of £3,000 for grandda. (Papers at Cheshire RO; *Rec. Soc. Lancs. and Ches.*, xix; PCC 65 Twisse.)

*CREW(E), Sir Thomas (1564–1634). GI 85, b 90, B 12. Puritan; named in 18 by James I as only man he would not have as rec. of London; Feoffee for Impropriations; funeral sermon preached by Richard Sibbes; friend and legal adviser to William, Viscount Saye and Sele; thanked God 'that I live in this daylight of the Gospel and that I was born of believing parents whose eyes in the dark mist of popish blindness God enlightened . . . to bring me up at learning and to set me at a calling, which under God hath been the means to raise my estate'. Said to have died worth £4,000 p.a. (Cheshire RO, DDX 210, fol. 12ᵛ; *Banbury Hist. Soc.*, xv; Whitelocke, *Lib. Fam.*; Knowler, i. 206; *Cake and Cockhorse*, vii; PCC 45 Seager.)

*CROKE, Sir George (1560–1642). IT 75, b 84, B 97. Call to bar solicited by LdCh Hatton. Pious; established chapel in house at Studley and stipend of £20 p.a. for preacher, plus £10 p.a. for preaching minister at Chilton, Bucks. Wealthy; bought lands Bucks., Oxon.; cash bequests £1,805. (*H. of P.*; Croke, *Genealogical History*; PCC 58 Cambell; IT MS Misc. 30, fol. 19; Additional 28607.)

CROKE, Sir John (1553–1620). BA, O, 71; IT 70, b ?, B 92. Forced to mortgage manor of Easington and owed bro. Sir George (next above) £550 at d. (*H. of P.*; PCC 17 Soame.)

CROKE, Paul Ambrose (d. 1631), 4 s. Sir John, Chilton, Bucks., by Elizabeth, da. Sir Alexander Unton, Bucks. Clement's Inn; IT 82, b 90, B 05. Lived Hackney, Middx.; Little Burstead, Essex; Cottesmore, Rutland. Mar. (i) Frances, da. Oliver Wellesbourne, East Hanney, Berks.; (ii) Susanna, da. Thomas Coe or Choes, Boxford, Suffolk. Pious; requested funeral without superfluous costs, blacks, heralds, alms, etc.; bequeathed £500 for widows and orphans of preaching ministers. Wealthy; acquired manors in Leics., Rutland. (Croke, *Genealogical History*, i; *VCH, Berks.*, iv; *VCH, Rutland.*, ii; papers at University of Illinois, Urbana-Champaign; PCC 113 St John.)

*CROKE, Unton (*c.*1593–1671), 4 s. Sir John (next but one above), by Catherine, da. Sir Michael Blount, Mapledurham, Oxon. Christ Church, O, 10; IT 09, b 17, B 35, SL 55. JP; MP 26, Apr. 40. Mar. Anne, da. Richard Hore, Marston, Oxon. Parl. sympathies(?), although named as commr. to investigate non-attendance in Oxford by Ct. of Wards officers, Feb. 43. (*Oxon. Rec. Soc.*, iv, xxi; Black, *Docquets.*)

CURLE, Edward (d. 1621), 1 s. William, Hatfield, Herts., auditor Ct. of Wards. MT 94, b 02, B 21. Sought reversion of father's place 03. JP. Mar. ?Mary Scrope. Anti-puritan. Held house and lands, Hatfield, manor of Buttermere, and other Wilts. lands. (*VCH, Herts.*, iii; Manningham, *Diary*; Bell, *Court of Wards*; PCC 27 Dale.)

DALE, Roger (d. 1623), 2 s. Robert, Prestbury, Ches., by Katherine Leigh, Ches. Clement's Inn; IT 77, b 84, B 99. Steward, manor of Mortlake 93. JP. Mar. Margaret. Acquired lands in Rutland and Northants. Cash bequests £1,329, including marriage portions of £666 and £500 to das.; w. to bestow £3,000 on land for son. Assessed £8 in 09. Of Tixover, Rutland, at d. (*VCH, Rutland*, ii; *HS*, lix; PCC 3 Byrde; Gleason, *Justices*; Additional 5524, fol. 205ᵛ.)

*DALTON, Michael (d. 1644), 1 s. Thomas, Hildersham, Cambs., by Eleanor Jellebrand. Trinity, C, 80; Furnival's Inn; LI 81, b 89, AB 22; dep.-steward Camb. Univ. 04. JP. Assessed @ £20 in lands 09; £6 in 41. Of West Wratting, Cambs., at d. (CUL MSS EDR H3, West Wratting, 44, and Add. 6325, 6920, EPR WRC 28, fols. 99ᵛ–100, 222–222ᵛ; *AOI*, i. 90, 621, 961; Gleason, *Justices*; *East Anglian*, 3rd ser., ix.)

DALTON, Sir William (*c.*1578–1649), 2 s. Thomas, mayor of Hull, Yorks., by Anne, da. Sir Robert Tyrwhit, Kettleby, Lincs. Caius, C, 85; Furnival's Inn; LI 88, b 97, B 13; rec. Hull 11; king's att. York 11, member Council of North and ktd. 29. Mar. Theophania, da. John Boothe, Killingholme, Lincs. Mother and other kin recusants 04; son John prominent royalist. Assessed @ £26. 13s. 4d. for knighthood fine 28–30; bought manors of Yafforth, East and West Hauxwell, where he died. Buried York Minster. (*Surtees Soc.*, xxxvi; Foster, *Yorks. Pedigrees*, i; *VCH, Yorks. (ER)*, i; *VCH, Yorks. (NR)*, i; Hull RO, BRR 2/5, fol. 10; Borthwick, Testamentary Bond, Feb. 1650.)

DANVERS, Charles, (*c.*1580–1627), 2 s. Henry, Edington, Wilts., esq., by Joan, da. Anselm Lambe, East Coulston, Wilts. MT 97, b 05, B 23. JP; MP 14. Mar. Mary, of Steeple Ashton, Wilts. Kinsman and follower of Henry Danvers, earl of Derby. Afflicted by 'an infirmity of bashfulness' at his reading. Not well-off; provided marriage portions of £100 for 8 das., plus £200 more to Elizabeth and Mary; w. to have his third-share of manor of Potterne to pay debts. Of Baynton at d. (F. N. McNamara, *Memorials of the Danvers Family*, 1895; PCC 74 Skynner; *Index Lib.*, xxiii; D'Ewes, *Diary*.)

DARCY, John, (*c.*1570–1639), s. Brian, St Osyth, Essex, gent. Caius, C, 85; LI 93, b 01, B 18, SL 23. JP. Mar. Dorothy Audley, Berechurch, Essex. Wealthy; assessed @ £20 in 09, owned at least 6 Essex manors, bequeathed £4,140 in cash including £1,000 each to three granddas., plus rent charges of £140 p.a., various lands, leases, inn, houses, and other properties in the Strand, Middx. Declared insane shortly before death. MI St Osyth describes as 'kinsman and friend' to Thomas Darcy, Earl Rivers. (*HS*, xiii; Gleason, *Justices*; PCC 94 Harvey; C142/574/85.)

DARRELL (Dayrell), Walter (*c.*1564–1628), 3 s. Paul, Abingdon and Lillingstone Dayrell, Bucks., by Frances, da. William Sanders, Welford, Northants. St Mary's Hall, O, 79; Staple Inn; GI 91, b 98, B 16; rec. Abingdon 10, steward of ct. of Richard Chetwode, Northants. JP. Assessed @ £4 in 09. Abingdon at d. (Baker, *Abingdon*; *HS*, lviii; Gleason *Justices*; Northants RO, Th. 3086.)

DASTON, Richard (d. 1626), 1 s. George, Wormington, Glos., gent. New Inn; MT 73, b 82, B 98; j. W. Wales 04. Mar. Anne, da. Francis Savage. Bought 2 Glos. manors 00, but will mentions indebtedness 'to sundry persons in great sums', and provides for sale of farm in Dumbleton, Glos. (Williams, *Welsh Judges*; *Trans. Bristol and Glos. Arch. Soc.*, xvii; PCC 48 Skynner.)

*DAVENPORT, Sir Humphrey (1566–1645), 3 or 4 s. Barnard's Inn; GI 85, b 89, B 11; steward of manors of Christ's College, Manchester, 97; counsel to earl of Derby in Ches. and Flints. 19. JP; MP 89. Mar. Mary, da. Francis Sutton, Ches. Opposed High Commission persecution of protestant nonconformists 89, but later religious views unknown; mother seemingly a Catholic. (*H. of P.*; *Chetham Soc.*, 3rd ser., xix.)

DAVIES, John (d. 1631), of London, gen. Clement's Inn; IT 02, b 11, B 28. Mar. Prudence. Of London at d., buried Temple Church. Will mentions ownership of 'house now inhabited by Lord Baltimore', own dwelling, newly-purchased tenements, leases in Bell Alley, Coleman St. Bequests to poor of St Dunstan's in the West, and 'Zealing alias Yealing', i.e., perhaps Yelling, Hunts. (PCC 105 St John.)

DAVIES, Robert, (d. 1617), 1 s. Gilbert, Crediton, Devon, gent., by Margaret Gere of Heavitree, Devon. MT 84, b 94, B 13. JP. Mar. Anne, da. John Northcote, Crediton. (*Trans. Devon Assocn.*, ix; *HS*, vi.)

DAVY, Henry, (*c.*1564–1619), 1 s. Richard, mayor of Norwich, of LI, by Christian, da. Richard Butler, Yarmouth. Caius, C, 80; LI 80, b 89, B 03; fee'd counsel Norwich 98, steward 14. Mar. Susan Hyrne. Modest wealth;

assessed £6. 13s. 4d. for 1612 benevolence; owned houses and land Great
Melton, dwelling-house (on which £300 still owing) in St Mary's parish,
Norwich, orchards in St Julian's; all household stuff and plate to be sold
to pay debts and provide maintenance for sons. (Cozens-Hardy, 'Norfolk
Lawyers'; *HS*, xxxiii; Mason, *History of Norfolk*; PCC 100 Parker.)

DELABERE, Richard (*c.*1559–1636), 2 s. Kennard, Southam, Glos., by
Elizabeth (Eleanor?), da. Sir John Huddleston. St Mary's Hall, O, 75;
Lyon's Inn (barrister); LI 80, b 89, B 03; att.-gen. for W. Wales 95–13. MP
86, 01. Inherited lands from bro. John, barrister MT; bought manor of
Minsterworth *c.*04, Southam (for £3,200) *c.*08. Knighthood fine *c.*28–30,
£25. (*HS*, xxiii; *H. of P.*; Glos. RO, D 1637/L2; *Trans. Bristol and Glos.
Arch. Soc.*, xxviii; C142/781/100.)

*DENHAM, Sir John (1559–1639), 2 s. William, London and Egham,
Surrey, goldsmith, by Joan (Prideaux?). Furnival's Inn; LI 79, b 87, B 03.
Sought burial without pomp, and buried at night. Wealthy; bought and
rebuilt mansion of Imworth, Egham; owned property Essex and Suffolk.
(*Surrey Arch. Coll.*, lxiv; *VCH, Surrey*, iii; Surrey RO, Acc. 922, Add. Box
2; PCC 41 Harvey.)

DENNE, Henry (*c.*1574–1640), 1 s. Thomas, Adisham, Kent, counsellor-at-
law, by Jane, da. John Swift, Sussex. New Inn Hall, O, 94; LI 94, b 02, B
18. Mar. Mary, da. John Hyde, London. Reported after W. Prynne's Star
Chamber conviction 34 presence of MS of parliamentary proceedings 21
and books written by Prynne in LI library, 'whether fit to be retained?'.
Loaned £2,800 to earl of Hertford 00–8; buried at expense of LI 40.
(Additional 5507, p. 245; *LIBB*, ii. 319, 355; HMC, *Longleat*, iv.)

DENNE, Thomas (d. 1656), 1 s. Robert, Kingston, Kent, by Thomasine, da.
Thomas Dane, Herne. Clifford's Inn; IT 99, b 07, B 26; rec. Sandwich 41,
Canterbury 43. JP; MP 24. Puritan. Chairman parl. accounts committee
at Canterbury. Income £678 p.a. *c.*40. Of Upper Hardres at d. (*HS*, xlii;
Hasted, *Kent*, iii; Boys, *Sandwich*, ii, Clark, *Provincial Society*; SP 16/472/
47; Everitt, thesis; *idem, Community of Kent*; PCC 1 Alchin.)

DENNY, Sir William (*c.*1578–1642), s. John, Beccles and Gislingham,
Suffolk, yeoman. Caius, C, 94; Barnard's Inn; GI 98, b ?, B 24; ktd. 27;
fee'd counsel 17, steward 18 and rec. Norwich 29, fee'd counsel Yar-
mouth. JP; MP 21–5. Mar. (i) da. Knevitt(?); (ii) Frances, da. James
Taverner; (iii) Dorothy, da. Reginald Kempe, Kent. Dedicatee, R. Sibbes,
The Soules Conflict (1633). Son created bt. 42, d. 'in extreme indigence'
76. (*Genealogist*, NS, xxxviii; G.E.C., *Baronetage*; Norfolk RO, Norwich
City Records 17b, Revenue and Letters; Manship, *Yarmouth*, ii.)

DEWELL, Henry (*c.*1580–1652), of Heston, Middx. Gloucester Hall, O, 97;
BA Hart Hall 00, GI 02, b 08, B 26. Mar. Julian, eldest da. Beckingham
Boteler, Herts. Sent for as delinquent for non-payment of contribution
43, but paid and discharged; commr. for Middx. assessment 44. Will

mentions customary lands, cottage, and close, Heston and Stanwell. Assessed @ £5 and £2 for lay subsidy 28. (J. E. Cussans, *History of Hertfordshire*, 1870–81, I. ii. 18; E 179/142/300; *CJ*, iii; *AOI*, i; PCC 219 Brent.)

DEWHURST, Robert (*c*.1577–1645), 4 s. Barnard, Cheshunt, Herts., by Anne Warde. Trinity, C, 95; GI 00, b 08, AB 27; *Custos Brevium* KB by 26. Mar. (i) Prudence, da. Sir Thomas Dacres, Cheshunt; (ii) Anne, da. Roger Dye, London, citizen. Endowed school and almshouses, Cheshunt. Requested daytime burial 'without any great solemnity'. Cash bequests total £3,900; assessed £13. 6s. 8d. for forced loan 25; bought Cheshunt Nunnery, inherited Lincs. lands. (*HS*, xxii; *VCH, Herts*, ii; Clutterbuck, ii–iii; W. Berry, *Herts. County Genealogies*, 1842; Cussans, *Herts*., I. i; PCC 85 Rivers; PROB 11/155/126.)

DIGGES, Richard (*c*.1564–1634), 2 s. John, Pirton, Wilts., by Elizabeth Neddall, Yorks. BA, O, 79; New Inn; LI 81, b 89, B 08, SL 23; counsel, rec. Marlborough by 05. MP 1597–1628. Mar. (i) Margaret, da. Richard Gore, Aldrington, Wilts; (ii) Elizabeth, da. Thomas Waldron. Said to have 'become poor through improvidence'. (*H. of P*.; Clendinnen; CUL MS Add. 6863, fol. 68.)

*DODDERIDGE, Sir John (*c*.1555–1628), 1 s. New Inn; MT 77, b 85, B 03; fee'd counsel Plymouth and Barnstaple. JP; MP 89, 04. May not have approved of attempts to free recusants from penal statutes, *pace DNB*. (*H. of P*.; Clendinnen; Yonge, *Diary*.)

DOWNES, Roger (d. 1638), 6 s. Roger, Shrigley, Ches., gent., by Elizabeth, da. Alexander Worsley, Lancs. (or Thomas Stanley, Aldersley). Staple Inn; GI 90, b 98, B 15; vice-chamberlain, county palatine of Ches. 25. MP 01, 21. Mar. (i) Elizabeth, da. Miles Gerard, Ince; (ii) Anne, da. John Calvert, Cockerham; (iii) Mary, wid. of Adam Eccleton. Presented puritan, Robert Shaw, to living 33, but sons Catholics and possibly reconciled himself. Substantial land acquisitions in South Lancs. Account book shows involvement in farming and sale of textiles to London. (*H of P*.; Hart-Davis, *Wardley Hall*; *VCH, Lancs*., iv–v, viii; Lancs. RO, WCW supra, Roger Downes, of Wordly, 1638; Ellesmere 11826.)

*DUCKE, Nicholas (1570–1628), 1 s. Richard, Exeter, citizen, by Joan. New Inn; LI 89, b 98, B 15; fee'd counsel Exeter 17. Mar. Grace, da. Thomas Walker, alderman of Exeter. MP 24, 25. Granted arms 02; freeman of Exeter 09. Reporter. Assessed @ £3 in lands, Exeter, 02. Bought Mount Radford, Exeter, from Sir J. Dodderidge (above) 14. (*HS*, vi, lxxvi; *Devon and Cornwall Rec. Soc*., NS, 2; *Trans. Devon Assocn*., lx, lxii; HMC, *Exeter*; Hargrave 51.)

DYOT, Anthony (*c*.1560–1622), 1 s. John, bailiff of Lichfield, Staffs., civilian, by Margaret, da. Robert Hill, Lichfield. Clement's Inn; IT 76, b 87, B 99; rec. Tamworth 99. Counsel to earl of Shrewsbury. JP; MP 01,

04, 14. Mar. (i) Catherine, da. John Harcourt, Ranton Abbey, Staffs.; (ii) Dorothy. Added commendatory verses to W. Leighton, *The Teares* ... (1613). Put out of commons at IT for permitting flesh to be served during Lent. Inherited Freeford manor; purchased properties in Lichfield, including dwelling-house and messuage 'which he useth for a barn for corn and cattle'. (*H. of P.*; HMC, *Salisbury*, ix; *Staffs. Rec. Soc.*, 3rd ser., xxxvii; *ITR*, i. 72; Staffs. RO, D661/1/115.)

*EARLE, Erasmus (1590–1667), 1 s. Thomas, Sall, Norfolk, yeoman, by Anne, da. John Fountayn, Sall. Peterhouse, C, 09; Furnival's Inn; LI 11, b 18, B 36; rec. Thetford 42; steward of Norwich 44. JP. Grant of arms 35. Political Independent, very moderate towards Quakers. Parliamentarian, after initial reluctance. Began acquiring Norfolk manors in 30s, and continued until d. (Underdown, *Pride's Purge*; Cozens-Hardy 'Norfolk Lawyers'; *Genealogist*, xiv; W. L. Parsons, *Salle*, 1937; Blomefield and Parkin, *Norfolk*, vi, viii; Norfolk RO, NRS 25973F 142 x 1; Hereford City Library, Boycott MSS; PCC 149 Carr.)

ELLIS, Sir George (1567–1626), s. Thomas, Langsett, Yorks. Barnard's Inn; GI 90, b 98, B 18 and ktd; member Council of North 19. JP. Mar. (i) Christian Gilmining; (ii) Margaret, da. Roger Lepton, wid. Thomas Harrison, esq. Will states his conviction of salvation, 'utterly detesting and abhorring all popish superstitions ...'. Held lands and leases Yorks. and houses in Barbican, London, leased @ £39 p.a. Buried St Michael le Belfry, York. (*HS*, xxxviii; Reid, *King's Council in the North*; G. Poulson, *The History ... of Holderness*, 1840, i; Borthwick, Reg. 39, fols. 484^v–5^v; W. S. Ellis, *Notices of the Ellises*, 1857; STAC 8/116/14.)

ELLIS, John (d. 1607), s. William, Bothel, Cumberland, GI 67, b 77, B 91. Mar. Anne, da. Thomas Benton, Warnell, Cumberland. Of York at d. (Foster, *Yorks. Vis.*; *Top. and Gen.*, iii; Haward, *Reports.*)

ELLIS, Sir Thomas (1569–1627), 1 s. Thomas, Witham, Lincs., esq., by Jane, da. John Hutchinson, Owthorpe, Notts. Christ's, C, 86; GI 89, b ?, B 18; escheator Cumberland and Lincs. 00, Westmorland 03; member Council of North, 16; ktd. 17. JP; MP 97. Mar. Jane, da. Gabriel Armstrong, Wishall, Notts. Sought burial without pomp or sermon. Said to have been worth £1,500 p.a.; left portions of £1,000 to 2 das., £200 to 7 sons. (*H. of P.*; G.E.C., *Baronetage.*)

ELLIS, Sir William (1553–1636), 2 s. Lionel, mayor of Lincoln. GI 74, b 81, B 98; freeman of Lincoln 69, reversion of recordership 86, rec. 12; member, Council in North 06. Mar. Anne or Agnes, da. Sir Edmund Thorold, Hough-on-the-Hill, Lincs. JP. Accused of corrupt collusion with attorneys. Clashed with Wentworth 28–9. Puritan? Buried Lincoln Cathedral, as requested, unless d. York, when sought burial in same grave as 'my dear friend Sir Richard Williamson' (for whom, see below). (*HS*, l; Ellis, *Notices of the Ellises*; Reid, *King's Council in the North*; Upton, *Sir*

Arthur Ingram; Wentworth Papers, ed. Cooper; Sheffield Public Lib., Wentworth-Woodhouse MSS; Lincs. RO, Li/1/4, fols. 4, 81ᵛ; PCC 81 Goare; STAC 8/98/9; HMC, *Fourteenth Rep.*, viii; Leeds District Archives, TN/POi/118.)

ELTONHEAD, John (d. 1662), 2 s. William, Eltonhead, Lancs., gent., by Ann, da. James Bowers, Brierley, Yorks. Christ's, C, 02, BA 06; New Inn; MT 08, b 16, B 38; CJ S. Wales 47; SL 48. Member High Ct. of Justice 51. Mar. Elizabeth, da. John Osbaldeston, Lancs. Not wealthy; bequests totalled £30 p.a. + £170; estates inherited from bro. Edward, MCh 47–60, to be sold to pay debts and legacies. Of Plumstead, Kent, at d., buried Temple Church (*Chetham Soc.*, lxxxii; Williams, *Welsh Judges.*)

ESCOURT, Edmund (*c.*1571–1651), s. Thomas, Long Newnton, Wilts., lawyer, by Emme Ascough. Magd. Hall, O, 86; LI 84, b 98, B 15. JP. Mar. Christian. Reporter. Sought 'private and moderate' burial, 'without any vain solemnity'. Cash bequests toteled £2,820. Houses Norton, Bristol, Sherston, Eston, Malmesbury, and London. Owed £1,000 by Sir John Danvers. (*HS*, xxi; *H of P.*; Harleian 4552; Williams, *Welsh Judges*; PCC 184 Grey.)

EURE, Sir Francis (d. 1621), 2 s. William, Lord Eure, Heyford, Oxon., by Lucy, da. Sir Andrew Noel, Dalby, Leics. MA, C, 83; GI 98, b 03, AB 09, B 11; ktd. 04, CJ N. Wales and rec. Bewdley 16. MP 04. Mar. Ellen, da. Sir William Morris, Caernarfonshire. Held Easley manor, Yorks. (NR), and lease of Coundon Grange, Durham. Of Partington, Salop, at d. (*HS*, v; Clendinnen; Williams, *Welsh Judges*; PCC 33 Dale.)

EURE, Sir Sampson (d. 1659), 3 s. of preceding. GI 10, b 17, B 35, SL and KSL 40; king's att. in Wales 22, co-examiner Council in the Marches 25, att.-gen. Denbighs. and Montgoms. 26. JP; MP 21, 40. Unsuccessful candidate for promotion in 30s. Mar. (i) Martha, da. Anthony Cage, Cambs.; (ii) ? (*c.*1635). Requested burial without pomp or show, to be saved by God's mercies and only merits of Jesus Christ. Speaker, Oxford Parl. Bought Gatley Park 33, 'a great purchase' worth at least £300 p.a., and Welsh lands. (Keeler; Herefs. RO, Gatley papers.)

EWENS, Mathew (*c.*1548–98), 3 s. John., gent., Wincanton, Som., by Ankaret, da. Alex Dyer, Wincanton. MT 68, b 75, B 91, SL, BExch, 2nd j. at Lancaster, steward Blandford Forum and Wimborne 94. JP; MP 72, 84, 86. Mar. Frances, da. Sir John Rogers, Bryanston, Dorset. Puritan sympathies; counsel to Henry, 3rd earl of Huntingdon and his bro. Sir Francis Hastings, from whom he bought North Cadbury and other estates. Wealthy; owned at least 7 Som. manors and other lands; personal bequests totalled £560. (*H. of P.*; *Som. Rec. Soc.*, lxix.)

EYRE(S), Robert (*c.*1569–1638), 1 s. Thomas, mayor of Salisbury, by Elizabeth da. John Rogers, Poole, Dorset. Hart Hall, O, 84; LI 88, b 97, B 14; steward of bishopric of Bath and Wells 98. Mar. (i) Anna, da. John

Still, bp. of Bath and Wells; (ii) Alice Tooker, Dorset. Feoffee for
Impropriations. Of Salisbury and Coleman St., London, at d. (Metcalfe,
Wilts. Vis.; P. Hembry, *The Bishops of Bath and Wells*, 1967; *Guildhall
Misc.*, iii. 103.)

EYRE(S), William (*c.*1589–1646), 5 s. Thomas, mayor of Salisbury by
Elizabeth Rogers, Poole, Dorset. Balliol, O, 05; LI 06, b 13, B 30. MP
Apr. 40. Puritan; £100 bequest to Salisbury town lecture. Served on
parliamentary committees Wilts. Bequests totalled over £6,000; held
lands in South Newton, lease of rectory of Amesbury. Named Anthony
Ashley Cooper as executor. (Metcalfe, *Wilts. Vis*; *VCH, Wilts.*, viii; PCC
192 Twisse.)

FALDOE, Robert (*c.*1566–1621), s. Richard, Maulden, Beds., by Amphillis,
da. John Chamberlain, ?Normanton. Pembroke, C, 83; GI 86, b 94, B 21.
Acted as Sir Francis Bacon's dep. in Star Chamber. JP. Mar. (i) Anne, da.
John Palmer, London; (ii) Elizabeth Reeve, Bedford. Bought and sold
Dallow manor, Beds., inherited and sold Maulden lands, bought Brook-
mans and Potterels manors, North Mimms, Herts. Of Bedford at d. (*HS*,
xix; *VCH, Beds.*, ii–iii; Cussans, *Herts.*, iii; *Beds. N & Q*, i.)

FARRER, William (d. 1639), s. Thomas, London, by Alice Rydge, London
IT 06, b 14, B 32. Mar. Sybil. Acquired Biddenham and Newnham
manors, leases in Harrold, Beds. Buried Temple Church. (Beds. RO, TW
collection; *Beds. N & Q*, iii; PROB 6/17/114.)

FAR(E)WELL (Farrell), John (1575–*c.*1642), 1 s. John, Holbrooke, Som.,
attorney, by Ursula, da. John Phelipps, Montacute, Som. IT 95, b 03, B
20; att. of Ulster 09–*c.*17. JP. Mar. Elizabeth Johnson, South Petherton,
Som. Counsel for Winchester Cathedral in dispute with city 37. Accused
of taking forcible possession of Wilts. copyhold 40. (STAC 8/139/10;
Weaver, *Som. Vis.*; Hughes, *Patentee Officers*; *Hants Rec. Soc.*, xii;
Barnes, *Somerset*; HMC, *Fifth Rep.*; Prof. D. Underdown, personal
communication.)

FETTIPLACE, Edward (1585–1650), 2 s. Sir Edward, Swinbrook, Oxon.,
and Childrey, Berks., by Anne, da. Roger Alford, Hitcham, Bucks.
Queen's, O, 01; LI 04, b 11, B 28; att.-gen. N. Wales 13–15. Mar. Anne,
da. Robert Cox, London, cooper. Catholic connections, son and heir
John royalist MP for Berks., but Edward named commr. for assessment
Oxon. 49, and served as treasurer LI 48. (J. R. Dunlop, *The Family of
Fettiplace*, 1918; *HS*, lvi; *AOI*, ii.)

FINCH, Francis (*c.*1586–1657), 6 s. Sir Moyle, Eastwell, Kent, and Eliza-
beth, da. Sir Thomas Heneage, Copt Hall, Essex. Corpus Christi, O, 01;
IT 05, b 14, AB 28. MP 24–8. Mar Anne, da. Michael Barker, Bromley
Middx. Neutral 42. Nuncupative will; owed £150+ to bro. Sir Heneage
(see below) at latter's death. Of Kensington, Middx. at d. (*HS*, xlii;
Everitt, thesis; Gruenfelder, *Early Stuart Elections*; PCC 8 Wooton.)

*FINCH, Sir Heneage (1580–1631). Trinity, C, 92, BA 96; IT 98, b 06, B 21; steward to Duchy of Lancs. in Essex 14; fee'd counsel Maidstone 26, Cinque Ports 30. JP. Pious. Wealthy; left £600 p.a. to wife, £2,000 + £1,500 for 2 das. (*HS*, xlii; Leics. RO, DG7, Law 3; PCC 132 St John.)

*FINCH, Sir Henry (1558–1625), 3 s. GI 77, b ?, B 03, SL 14, KSL 16; freeman and counsel Canterbury 90; high steward Faversham 17. JP; MP 93, 97, 14. Author, presbyterian, Hebraist, law-reformer, Ramist, philosemite. In financial difficulties from early 00s, bankrupt by 19. (*H. of P.*; *Radicals*, i; *Trans. Jewish Hist. Soc.*, xxvi.)

*FINCH, Sir John, Baron Finch of Fordwich (1584–1660), 1 s. of preceding. GI 01, b 11, B 17. Dep.-rec. London 19. Spoke 'very earnestly against the Arminians'; claimed in Long Parl. to have protected Richard Sibbes from Laudian persecution; will shows orthodox predestinarian beliefs. Inherited estate from bro. Nathaniel (see below), acquired Fordwich manor 36 for *c.* £6,750. (London Corp. RO, Rep. 34, fol. 162; J. Nalson, *An Impartial Collection* ..., 1682–3, i. 693; *CD 1628*, vi; Kent AO, PRC 32/53, fol. 186–186ᵛ and U449 T3; Leics. RO, DG 7, Box 4974, Lit. I.)

FINCH, Sir Nathaniel (d. *c.*1649), 2 s. of Sir Henry, above. GI 04, b 11, B 35, SL 37; sjt. to queen; rec. Sandwich 36; KSL and ktd. 40. MP Apr. 40. Dedicatee, J. Ford, *The Lovers Melancholy* (1629). Mar. Elizabeth, da. Sir John Fotherby, Barham, Kent. Acted as assistant to HL until 46 at least, and no evidence of sequestration, *pace* Everitt, *Community of Kent*, 172. Bought Esture manor, Chilham, 42. (Hasted, *Kent*, iii; *CJ*, iii; *LJ*, viii; PCC 92 Fairfax.)

FISH, Sir William (d. 1633?), 1 s. William, Southill, Beds., gent., by Margaret, da. John George, Northill. Christ's, C, 93; GI 95, b 00, B 21; ktd. 17. JP. Mar. Elizabeth, da. Sir Thomas Barnardiston, Witham, Essex. Assessed @ £5 in 09. Owned mills, to be sold for payment of debts and portions for 8 das. Mentioned 68 as among gentlemen who had sold estates and 'quite gone out of Beds.' within past 50 yrs. (*HS*, xix; Beds. RO, AD 997, PE 465; Gleason, *Justices*; PCC 96 Twisse.)

FLEETWOOD, Henry, (*c.*1562–1633), 4 s. Thomas, Vache, Bucks., gent., by Bridget, da. John Spring, Lavenham, Suffolk. GI 80, b 86, B 09. Feodary Bucks. 02–12; rec. Kidwelly 07. MP 89, 01, 04. Mar. Elizabeth, da. Edward Fust, London. Fined £120 for calling unqualified students to bar 09. Land speculator Glos., Bucks., and Herts., 1590s–1600s. Sir Francis Bacon godfather to son. Granted protection from creditors 16. (*H. of P.*; Clendinnen; *Arch. Cambrensis*, 3rd ser., iii; *Trans. Bristol and Glos. Arch. Soc.*, lxxxi; HMC, *Sackville*, i; *CSPD 1611–18*; Bacon, *Works*, xiv; *GIPB*, i.)

FLEETWOOD, Sir Thomas (*c.*1573–after 1619), 3 s. William, Great Missenden, Bucks., SL, by Marian, da. John Barley, Kingsey, Bucks. Magdalen, O, 90; MT 93, b 01, AB and att.-gen. to Henry, Prince of Wales, 04; ktd.

19. Mar. Susanna, da. Sir William Whorwood. (Smyth, *Obituary*; Lipscomb, *Bucks.*, iii; *MT Bench Book*.)

FLETCHER, Thomas (1594–1657), 1 s. Bartholomew, Campsall, Yorks.,
esq., by Jane, da. Thomas Ricard, Hatfield, Yorks. Christ's, C, 09, BA 13;
LI 15, b 22, B 39, SL 54; dep.-rec. Bury, Suffolk, by 42. Mar. Frances, da.
Robert Wood, esq., Tharston, Norfolk. Initial allegiance uncertain;
summoned to HC for non-response to proposition for raising funds Oct.
42, pleaded 'smallness of his fortune and great charge', agreed to give one
horse and released; named as JP from Oxford 43. Of Bury and Croxton,
Norfolk, at d. (*HS*, lxxxvi; Cozens-Hardy 'Norfolk Lawyers'; Blomefield
and Parkin, *Norfolk*, ii; Suffolk RO (Bury), EX Y4/W2/145; *CJ*, ii; Black,
Docquets.)

FLETCHER, William (*c.*1562–by 1647), of Makeney, Duffield, Derbs. Univ.,
O, 81; IT 84, b 93, B 07; rec. Nottingham 02–42; nominated sol.-gen. (Ire.)
03, j. (Ire.) 37. (*Records of Nottingham*, ed. Stevenson, v; Knowler, ii;
HMC, *Rutland*, i and *Salisbury*, xii; Ball, *Judges in Ireland*, i.)

FORD, Thomas (1567–1635), 1 s. John, Ashburton, Devon, esq., by Mary,
da. Hugh Pomeroy, Exeter, O, 88; MT 93, b 00, B 18. JP. Mar. Elizabeth,
da. Peter Coriton, Devon. Requested Christian burial with 'my fourteen
teeth which are in a paper in a little red bag which I usually carry with
me'; bequeathed 20s. each to ministers of Ashburton in lieu of omitted
tithes. Assessed @ £2. 10s. in 22 benevolence. Modest wealth; da. and y.s.
left £150 each and £120 from profits of 2 farms. (*HS*, vi; Devon RO,
Z1/40/8, 46/1/2/4; PCC 78 Pile; *Trans. Devon Assocn.*, ix.)

*FOSTER, Sir Robert (1589–1663), y.s. of the next following. IT 04, b 11, B
29, SL 37; fee'd counsel Kingston-on-Thames 11. JP. Anti-puritan;
royalist. Acquired manor of Fosters, Egham, Surrey, 39, and moved from
Battle, Sussex. Low subsidy rating 27. Bequeathed 2 das. marriage
portions of £1,000 ea. (*HS*, xliii; Aubrey, *Surrey*; Fletcher, *Sussex*; PCC
130 Juxon.)

FOSTER, Sir Thomas (*c.*1569–1612), s. Thomas, Hunsdon, Herts., by
Margaret Browning, Chelmsford, Essex. IT 71, b ?, B 95, SL 03; ktd. 04,
JCP 07; steward Amwell Parva, alias Rusheyne manor, 90; fee'd counsel
London 94. JP. Mar. Susan, da. Thomas Foster, Sussex and London.
Wid. presented as recusant 20–2. Estate of Hedley, Surrey, conveyed to in
93. Assessed @ £10 in 99 lawyers' subsidy. (*HS*, xliii; Herts. RO, 72209;
London Corp. RO, Rep. 23, fol. 283; *Herts. Sessions Books ... 1619 to
1657*, ed. Hardy; *APC 1599–1600*; Manning, *Surrey*, ii.)

FRAN(C)KLIN, James (1578–1641), y. s. Arthur, Wye, Kent, gent., by Alice,
da. Robert Lucas, Woodchurch. St Alban Hall, O, 93, BA (ex Merton)
97; Clifford's Inn; MT 02, b 09, B 27; rec. and town clk. Maidstone 34. JP.
Mar. Elizabeth, da. Henry Smith, Godalming, Surrey. Requested funeral
sermon a year after d. Left w. annuity of £40 p.a. during her widowhood,

otherwise nominal cash bequests, excepting £100 in 'gold that lies in my iron chest'. Of Maidstone at d. (Hasted, *Kent*, iii; C. H. Francklyn, *A Short Genealogical History of Francklyn*, n.d.; Kent AO, Q/JC1; *Records of the Borough of Maidstone*, 1926; PCC 125 Evelyn.)

FRANKLIN, Nicholas (d. 1657), 3 s. George, Bolnhurst, Beds., esq., by Ann Styles, Kent. Christ's, C, 13; LI 15, b 23, B 39. Never married(?) Learned; subscribed £10 to printing multilingual Bible, and left Christ's College library £20, plus books. Protestant conservative; bequeathed £100 to 20 sequestered clergy and £40 for silver communion vessels for LI chapel. Attended LI councils throughout 40s. Occupying house Fetter Lane, London, worth £35 p.a., 38. Of High Holborn, Middx., at d. (Peile, *Biographical Register*; PCC 455 Ruthen; T. C. Dale, *Inhabitants of London in 1638*, 1931; *VCH, Beds.*, ii; *CCC.*)

*FULWOOD, Christopher (1590–1643), mother Anne, da. Thomas Bentley, GI, esq. GI 06, b 16, B 28. Dep.-steward royal manor of Wirksworth Derbs., 34; king's counsel 42. JP. Married, perhaps twice. Sir John Coke of Melbourne a client, kinsman, and patron. Owned extensive lead mines and grazed 400 sheep. (Brighton, *Royalists and Roundheads in Derbs.*; HMC, *Cowper*, i–iii; Glover, *Derbs.*, i.)

*GARDINER, Sir Thomas (1591–1652). IT 10, b 18, B 35; prothonotary and clk. of Crown for Carmarthen, Cardigan, and Pembroke 23. Commendatory verse in W. Browne, *Britannia's Pastorals* (1614). Conveyed Oxon. lands to friend Hugh Audley (for whom, see above), to pay debt to Audley and provide for w. and children. Share of 500 acres in Great Level draining to be sold for w. (Williams, *Welsh Judges*; PCC 369 Berkeley.)

GATES, Thomas (1587–1650), 2 s. Anthony, Churchill, Oxon., by Judith, da. Roger Taverner, Essex. Univ., O, 02; IT 07, b 15, B 32, SL and BExch 48. Mar. Anne, da. Thomas Morley, St Lawrence Jewry, London. Contributed £3. 6s. 8d. to king's expenses 39. (*HS*, xxi; Foss; SP 16/538/84.)

GERRARD, Phillip (*c.*1564–1637), 5 s. William, Harrow, Middx., by Dorothy, da. Thomas Page, Sudbury Court, Middx. Caius, C, 82; GI 84, b 93, B 11; steward of Clare Honour for Duchy of Lancaster. Mar. Frances, da. John Page, Wembley, Middx. (for whom, see below). Requested private night burial without mourning. Inherited Flambard's manor from bro. William (next below). Middx. privy seal assessment @ £20, *c.*1610. Portions of £500 ea. to 4 younger sons and £666. 13s. 4d. to da. (*HS*, lxv; Somerville, *Office Holders*; *VCH, Middlesex*, iv; PCC 15 Goare; Ellesmere 2475.)

GERRARD, William (*c.*1551–1609), 1 s. William, Harrow, Middx. by Dorothy da. Thomas Page, Sudbury Court, Middx. Trinity, C, 65, MA 72; GI 72, b 80, B 96; clk. of Duchy of Lancaster 89; steward and bailiff of Savoy 94. JP; MP 84, 86, 93. Mar. Dorothy, da. Anthony Radcliffe,

London, alderman. Held at d. Flambard's manor and other Middx. lands and reversion of office for s. Gilbert. (*H. of P.*; Greater London RO, Acc 276/315.)

GIBB(E)S (Gipps), Richard (d. 1643), of London, gent. Emmanuel, C, 96 (?); GI 98, b ?, AB 27, and j. of sheriff's ct., London. Mar. Margaret, da. Valentine Pell, Norfolk. (Overall, *Remembrancia*; Smyth, *Obituary*.)

GIBBES, William, (*c.*1536–1616), 1 s. Anthony, Netherbury, Dorset, gent. MT 67, b 75, B 90; steward Bridport ct. *c.*90–00; freeman Poole, *c.*00. Mar. Mary, da. John Newcourt, Pickwell, Devon. Granted arms 01. Requested funeral sermon, but anxious to avoid 'the vulgar imputation of puritanism (which I detest and abhor with all mine heart)'. Leased manor of Court Orchard, South Perrott, held other lands in same area; portion of £600 for 1 da., others provided for elsewhere; assessed £10 in 99 lawyers' subsidy. (*HS*, xx, lxxvi; Hutchins, *Dorset*, i–ii; Dorset RO, B3/D; *APC 1599–1600*; PCC 11 Weldon.)

GILES, John (*fl.* 1594–1637), of Bucks., *gen.* LI 94, b 02, B 18. Clk. to Sir Henry Yelverton, att.-gen., drafting and signing Star Chamber bills 17–20. Mentioned (presumably in error) as 'ancient utter-barrister' 37. Reporter. (Prof. T. G. Barnes, personal communication; LI MS Red Book, fol. 179; Bodl. MS Rawlinson C 647.)

*GLANVILLE, Sir John (1586–1661). LI 03, b 10, B 27; rec. Okehampton *c.*13, Launceston 23; fee'd counsel Liskeard by 18. Verse in W. Browne, *Britannia's Pastorals* (1614); compiled verse paraphrase of Psalms of David. Wealthy; bought land; subscribed £1,800 to Irish venture 42, provided portion of £350 p.a. for da. 42. (R. and O. Peter, *The Histories of Launceston*, 1885; Cornwall RO, B/Liskeard/274; Bridges *et al.*, Okehampton; *VCH, Wilts.*, xii; Egerton 2590; *CCC*.)

*GODBOLD(T), John (*c.*1582–1648), s. Thomas, Tannington, Suffolk. Barnard's Inn; GI 04, b 11, B 27; rec. Bury St Edmunds by 32; CJ Isle of Ely 38. Appointed executor by Richard Sibbes. Assessed @ £400 by Committee for Advancement of Money, 44. (Suffolk RO (Bury), D11/2/2; Harris, thesis; *CCAM*.)

GODDARD, Richard, (*c.*1596–1667), 1 s. Thomas, Clatford, Wilts., by Winifred, da. Thomas Wrothe, Middx. Clifford's Inn; IT 08, b 16, B 33; rec. Winchester 61. JP. Mar. Maria, da. Richard Louis of Cornwall. Raised cavalry troop for king in Hants, but took covenant and negative oath 45–6. Fined @ one-third £862. 10s. 0d.; claimed own lands worth £80 p.a., plus £275 p.a. in w.'s right, £2,000 in debt, with 12 children to support. Cash bequests totalled £1,440. (Not to be confused with royalist namesake of Swindon, d. 50. (*HS*, cv; *WAM*, xxiv; *CSPD 1666–7; VCH, Wilts.*, xi; PCC 1665, fol. 65.)

GOLDSMITH, Clement (d. 1614), 2 s. Francis, Crayford, Kent, by Joanna, da. Clement Newce, Hadham, Herts. GI 74, b 83, B 99. Nominated as sol.-gen. (Ire.) 03. Mar. Joanna Biggs. Accused of taking bribes as commissioner for bankruptcy 07. Assessed @ £20, Middx. *c*.03. Of Clerkenwell, Middx. at d. (*H. of P.*; *HS*, xlii; HMC, *Salisbury*, xii; Haward, *Reports*; Ellesmere 2475; PCC 98 Parker; C33/128/1083ᵛ.)

GREENE, John (1579–1653), 1 s. Thomas, London, haberdasher, by Margaret, da. Lawrence Greene, London. Brasenose, O, 03; LI 05, b 12, B 28, SL 40; counsel to city of Chester 28; j. sheriff's ct. London 34; sjt. of Commonwealth 50. Mar. Anne, da. Thomas Blanchard, London. Inherited Bois Hall, Navestock, Essex. Of Fleet St., and Navestock, Essex, at d. (*EHR*, xliii–iv; *HS*, xv; *VCH, Essex*, iv; *Lancs. & Ches. Rec. Soc.*, cvi; PCC 344 Alchin.)

GREENE, Thomas (d. 1640), 1 s. Thomas, Warwick, mercer, by Isabel, da. Henry Lingen, Hurst, War. Staple Inn; MT 95, b 02, B 21; solicitor Stratford 01, steward 03–17; candidate for stewardship sheriff's ct. Bristol 18, perhaps practising there 21. Edited anti-papal tract (STC 21299), and contributed commendatory verse to M. Drayton, *The Barons' Wars* (1603). Puritan. On leaving Stratford sold property there for £610. Of Bristol at d. (*N & Q*, ccix; *Shakespeare and the Enclosure of Common Fields at Welcombe . . .*, ed. C. M. Ingleby, 1885; Fripp, *Shakespeare Man and Artist*; *Trans. Bristol and Glos. Arch. Soc.*, xcii; PCC 88 Evelyn.)

GWYNN(E), Rice or Richard (*c*.1552–1629), 1 s. John Wynn, Bodfeddan and Ceirchiog, Anglesey, by Margaret, da. John Cooke, Anglesey. IT 83, b 91, B 05, SL 23; steward Norwich 07, rec. Yarmouth 10, Thetford 10, Norwich 12. JP; MP 14. Mar. Mary Thoresby, Bocking, Essex. Bought Bacon's Hall, Fakenham, 93, Walcot and Boles, Little Snoring, 20. Assessed @ £20 for Norfolk privy seal in 04, £5 in 09. (Lloyd, 'Welsh Benchers'; Cozens-Hardy 'Norfolk Lawyers'; *Norfolk Arch.*, ii; Gleason, *Justices*; PCC 51 Scroope.)

HADDE, Edmund (d. 1639), 1 s. Arnold, Canterbury, Kent, esq., by Maria, da. Thomas Hammond, St Alban's, Herts. LI 90, b 98, B 17; freeman of Canterbury by gift 30. JP. Mar. Margaret, da. Thomas Spilman, Great Chart, Kent. Requested burial in St Alphege parish church, Canterbury, 'in the cheapest manner it may be'; if personal estate not sufficient to pay debts and legacies, w. may sell woodlands. (*HS*, xlii; Gleason, *Justices*; Kent AO, PRC, 32/52, fol. 95–95ᵛ.)

HADSOR, Richard (d. 1635), 1 s. Nicholas, Keppocke, Louth, Ire., esq. New Inn; MT 90, b 03, B 17; commr. or 'councell' in England for Irish affairs by 19 at least. Acted for earls of York and Kildare, advised Salisbury on Irish matters. Wrote a 'Discourse on the ancient division of Ireland' 1604. Recommended to Queensborough as MP by duke of Lennox 20; granted Ulster lands 16. Debts of £628, owed as creditor £2,108. (HMC, *Salisbury*, viii–xii, xv, xvi; *Shrewsbury & Talbot, Papers*, ed. Batho, ii;

Cottonian Titus B.x; *APC 1615–16, 1618–19*; Prestwich, *Cranfield; CSP Ire., 1603–6* to *1633–47*; PCC 33 Sadler.)

*HAKEWILL, William (1574–1655). MA, 13; Staple Inn; LI 98, b 06, B 18; fee'd counsel Exeter by 25. Funeral expenses not to exceed £40. Acquired manors of Wyndsgate, Amersham, and Hales in Wendover, Bucks., where he died. (*H. of P.*; *VCH, Bucks.*, iii; Lipscomb, *Bucks.*, ii; Aylmer, *King's Servants.*)

HALES, Sir Charles, (c.1547–1619), 1 s. Stephen, Coventry, War., gent., by Anne, da. Richard Morison, Bucks. ?BA, O, 66; GI 67, b 76, B 92 (not SL, *pace GIPB*, i); counsellor of fee Council of North and ktd. 92. JP. Mar. Elizabeth, da. Walter Fish, London. Dedicatee, works by T. Bell, T. Wilson, and W. Perkins. Will records that he was 'brought up from the tenth year of my age and lived under the gospel of Christ Jesu in the happy days of the most blessed Queen Elizabeth'. Inherited Lascombe, Newland, and Exall manors, War. Assessed @ £12 in 09. (*HS*, xii; Baker, *Serjeants*; *Genealogist*, vi; *VCH, War.*, iii, vi; Gleason, *Justices*; PCC 99 Parker.)

HALL (Haule), Henry (1550–1622), 1 s. George, Wye, Kent, by Joanna, da. Henry Bourne, Sandhurst. Staple Inn; MT 71, b 79, B 95; counsel to Maidstone. JP. Mar. Jane, da. Richard Dering, Pluckley, Kent. Dedicatee, W. Crashawe, *Falsificationum Romanorum* (1606); J. Boughton, *God and Man* (1623). Puritan; challenged authority of ecclesiastical commission Canterbury diocese 89. Assessed £12 in 09. Estate valued at £300 p.a. temp. Jac. I. (*HS*, xlii; *Arch. Cant.*, xi; Clark, *Provincial Society*; Gleason, *Justices*; HMC, *Salisbury*, xxii; Kent AO, U 24823/ZI and PRC 32/45, fols. 281–3.)

HARDING, John (fl. 1594–1627), s. Edmund, Apsley-le-Guise, Beds., gent., by Elizabeth, da. Ralph Potts, Chalgrave, Beds. GI 94, b 00, B 20. JP. Mar. Francis, da. Thomas Cheney, Sundon, Beds., esq. (*HS*, xix; Beds. RO, AD 997, PE 465.)

HAR(R)INGTON, John (1589–1654), 1 s. Sir John, Kelston, Som., by Mary, da. Sir George Rogers, Cannington. Trinity, O, 04; LI 08, b 15, B 33. JP; MP 45. Mar. Dionysia, da. James Ley, earl of Marlborough (for whom, see below). Reporter and diarist. Puritan; parliamentarian; substantial inheritance Corn., Som., Wilts., Dorset. Provided portion of £1,500 for da. and £1,000 for s. (*Som. Rec. Soc.*, lxxiv, and references cited therein.)

HARRIS, John (d. 1625), 2 s. John, Stockton, coroner of Salop, by Pernell, da. John Wynn ap Reignold. Clement's Inn; IT 80, b 90, B 03. JP; MP 01. Mar. Mary, da. John French, Maidstone, Kent, and IT. Declared that 'my sins are scarlet but I am fully assured through the grace that I find working in my inward soul which is the gift of God they shall be made white as snow'. Assessed @ £10 in 09. Left £900 to eldest da. from Essex lands; mentions dwelling-house and other properties Fleet Street, tithes and land in Sheppey, Kent. (*H. of P.*; *HS*, xxviii, xliii; Gleason, *Justices*; PCC 2 Hele.)

HARRIS, Sir Thomas (1550–1627), ?1 s. John, Cruckton, Salop, burgess of Shrewsbury, by Eleanor, da. Thomas Prowde, Sutton, Salop. Clement's Inn (barrister); LI 75, b 84, B 96, SL 03, bt. 23; counsel to Shrewsbury. JP; MP 86, 04. Mar. Eleanor, da. Roger Gifford, London, MD. Dedicatee, T. Gataker, *Of Lots* (1619). Acquired Tonge Castle, Salop, 13. (Not to be confused with namesakes: (i) of Boraston and Onslow, Salop, bt., MCh, and also of LI; (ii) of Corneforth, Devon, and MT, SL 89. *H. of P.*; Wanklyn, thesis; C142/432/22.)

HARRISON, John (*fl.* 1586–1665), y.s. Richard, Finchampstead, Berks., by Elizabeth, da. Thomas Anton. St Mary's Hall, O, 03; Clement's Inn; LI 06, b 13, B 30; rec. or steward Reading 34. Mar. (i) Dorothy, da. Sir Edward Clarke, Ardington, Berks.; (ii) Elizabeth, da. Sir George Carleton of Huntercombe, Oxon. JP. Friend of Elias Ashmole. Appointed commr. of array by Charles I, but no other evidence of public activity during 40s–50s except as bencher and treasurer of LI. (Durston, thesis; *HS*, lvi; *Berks., Bucks. & Oxon. Arch. J.*, xxi. 124.)

HARVEY, Sir Francis (d. 1632), 1 s. Stephen, Hardingstone, Northants, by Ann, da. Richard Greene, Broughton, Herefs., esq. Christ's, C, 83; Barnard's Inn; MT 82, b 91, B 09, SL 14; JCP 24, ktd. 26; fee'd counsel Northampton 02; rec. Leicester 12. JP; MP 97. Cousin of and counsel to sixth earl of Huntingdon. Mar. (i) Elizabeth Heming, of Herts.; (ii) Christian. Will mentions manor of Cotton, alias Ravenscroft; land in Collingtree, Hardingstone, and Northampton. (*H. of P.*; Metcalfe, ed. *Northants Vis.*; Huntington Library, MS Hastings Lit. 3, Box 6, accounts; G. Baker, *The History ... of Northants*, 1822–30, i. 74.)

HATTON (Houghton), Robert (*c.*1589–1661), 2 s. Richard, Long Ditton, Surrey, gent., by Margaret, da. George Evelyn, West Dean, Wilts. MT 06, b 16, B 35, SL 48; rec. Kingston-on-Thames 18. Mar. Alice, da. William Heynes, esq. Parliamentary commr. 43. Sold Kingston manor of Milbourn for £1,000+ in 29; acquired lands at Esher, Surrey, through marriage. Of Thames Ditton at d. (*HS*, lx; *VCH, Surrey*, iii; Aubrey, *Surrey*, i; Surrey RO, 5/1/1/1, p. 385; Manning, *Surrey*, i. 405; *AOI*, i. 116.)

HA(Y)WARD(E), John (*c.*1571–1631), 3 s. Henry, London and Tandridge, Surrey, citizen, by Agnes, da. Thomas Castle, London. Christ's, C, 86; Clifford's Inn; IT 90, b 98, B 13; coroner of Surrey. Mar. (i) Agnes, da. William Wilkinson, London, merchant; (ii) Elizabeth, da. William Angell, London, fishmonger. JP; MP 21, 24. Reporter. Substantial inheritance of manors and lands in Surrey; portions of £500 to 6 das. (Haward, *Reports*; Berks RO, D/EL 1 C1/24, 39–41, 46 *seq.*)

*HEATH, Sir Robert (1575–1649), 1 s. Robert, Sanderstead, Surrey, and

Brasted, Kent, att., by Anne (or Joanna), da. Nicholas Posyer, Guildford, Surrey. Clifford's Inn; IT 93, b 03, B 17; escheator of Kent 96, 99; rec. Guildford 15–19; rec. Rochester 27–37. In 30s drawing £10,000 p.a. from lands; annual income 20s & 30s perhaps £20–25,000. (Kopperman, thesis; papers at Univ. Illinois at Urbana-Champaign.)

HELE, Elizaeus, Elize, or Ellis (*c*.1558–1636), 1 s. Walter, Brixton, Devon, by Jane, da. Thomas Maynard, Brixton. Exeter, O, 75; Lyon's Inn; IT 80, b 90, B 03. JP. Mar. (i) Mary, da. John Hender, Botreaux Castle, Cornwall; (ii) Alice, da. Reginald Bray, Northants. Very wealthy; estate reputedly worth £100,000; left £1,500 p.a. to charitable uses. Of Fardle, Cornwood, Devon, at d. (Prince, *Worthies of Devon*; *Trans. Devon Assocn.*, xvii, xxi; PCC 2 Pile.)

HELE, John (*c*.1557–1611), 1 s. Hugh, Newton Ferrers, Devon, esq., by Cicely, da. Nicholas Cole, Paignton, Devon. Exeter, O, 75; Lyon's Inn; IT 79, b 87, B 01; rec. Plymouth 09–11, rec. Okehampton (?). Mar. da. Fortèscue, Ermington, Devon. Nephew of Sir John Hele, SL (d. 1608). (*H. of P.*; Prince, *Worthies of Devon*; T. Westcott, *A View of Devonshire*, ed. G. Oliver and P. Jones, 1845; R. N. Worth, *History of Plymouth*, 1890.)

HENDEN (Hendon), Sir Edward (*c*.1568–1644), of Biddenden, Kent. Balliol, O, 83; Staple Inn; GI 86, b 91, B 14, SL 16; BExch 39 and ktd.; counsel to Tenterden, steward of lord warden's ct. Dover. JP; MP 14. Reporter. Pious; requested burial 'in decent manner without any pomp or solemnity'. Contributed £50 to king's expenses 39; as assize j. refused to read parl.'s order against commissions of array, and impeached 42; assessed @ £2,000 in Nov. 43, ordered to be levied by distraint Dec., paid portion by 5 Jan., dead by 13 Jan. 44. (*Arch. Cant.*, xxxiii; Chicago MS, f-286; Gleason, *Justices*; Harleian 1331, fols. 1–54; LI MS Misc. 791, fols. 112–167'; Kent AO, PRC 32/53 fol. 417; SP 16/538/84; *CJ*, ii; *LJ*, vi; *CCAM*.)

*HERBERT, Sir Edward (*c*.1591–1657). Queen's, O, 08; IT 10, b 18, B 34; rec. Salisbury. JP; MP 21–9, 40–1. Kinsman and counsel of William Herbert, earl of Pembroke. Wealth unknown. (Keeler.)

*HERNE, John (d. 1649), y.s. Richard, London, alderman and sheriff (but adopted by William Robson, citizen and salter), by Alice, da. John Paske, Cambridge. Clare, C, 08; LI 11, b 18, B 36; fee'd counsel London 28. MP 28. Mar. Susan, da. John Woodward, London, grocer. Will (1649) protested against 'the blockish men of these times [who] have barbarously obtruded upon the people under a pretence of avoiding popery and superstition'; Abp. Ussher to preach funeral sermon. Held manor of Hendon, Middx., paid rent on 32 acres and various messuages Hendon 35; listed as among inhabitants 'of the better sort and best estate', Aldersgate ward, London, 40; left w. £300 p.a. but complained that his 'poor private fortune' was diminished by suretyship for improvident bro., leaving him 'very little to distribute'. (J. S. Watson, *A History of the Salters' Company*, 1963; London Corp. RO, Rep. 42, fol. 70ᵛ; *HS*, xv; *Trans. London & Middx. Arch. Soc.*, vii, pt. 2; Greater London RO, Acc 790/8; PCC 145 Fairfax.)

HERRINGDON (Herronden, Hernden), Anthony (*fl.*1591–1628), of Rutland. LI 91, b 98, B 17; steward of royal manor of Brigstock, Northants, 20. Called in to be SL 23, writ revoked on failure to pay £500. Present at John Barkesdale's reading Lent 28, and appointed keeper of Black Book, Nov. 28. (HMC, *Buccleuch*, iii; Baker, *Serjeants*; HLS, MS 1089, fol. 4ᵛ.)

HESKETH, Sir Thomas (*c.*1548–1605), 2 s. Gabriel, Aughton, Lancs., by Jane, da. Sir Henry Halsall, Halsall, Lancs. Hart Hall, O, *c.*68; also attended Camb. Univ. GI 72, b 80, B 96; escheator Lancs. 88, sjt. and att. at Lancaster 91, rec. Lancaster 97, rec. Liverpool, att. Ct. of Wards 97, vice-chancellor at Lancaster and ktd. 03, member Council in the North 98. JP; MP 86, 89, 97, 01, 04. Dedicatee, works by W. Perkins, and held 'sound' in religion; bought Heslington Hall, nr. York, 01, and Castle Mills on the river Foss. (*H. of P.*)

HETLEY, Sir Thomas (*c.*1570–1637), s. William, Brampton, Hunts., by Jane, da. Richard Worme, Peterborough. Staple Inn; GI 87, b 95, B 18, SL and ktd. 23; rec. Godmanchester 17; learned counsel to Queen Henrietta-Maria. Appointed law-reporter by LdCh Bacon 17. JP; MP 04. Mar. Elizabeth, da. Richard Gore, London, merchant. Requested burial 'without pomp or extraordinary charge'. Inherited lands Brampton and Risley, Beds., bought lands Cambs. Marriage portions of £666 to 3 das. £1,000 to y. s. Overseers Richard Taylor and Edward Wrightington (for whom, see below). (*HS*, xix; *VCH, Hunts.*, iii; *VCH, Cambs.*, iv; PCC 30 Goare; C142/556/104; CUL MS Dd. 3. 64, fol. 32.)

HIGGONS, Richard (*c.*1565–1638), 2 s. Edward, Bury, Sussex, by Juliana, da. Philip Medhurst Surrey. Magds. Hall, O, 78; Staple Inn; GI 93, b ?, B 18. JP. Mar. Elizabeth, da. John Raymond, Appledram, Sussex. Sought burial without pomp, but some religious preacher. Not well off; assessed@ £10 in goods at Chichester 22; lease of farm at Bury plus corn and cattle there to raise 3 portions of £200. (*HS*, liii; W. Berry, *County Genealogies ... Sussex*, 1830; *Sussex Arch. Coll.*, xxiv; PCC 128 Harvey.)

*HITCHAM, Sir Robert (*c.*1573–1636), s. Robert, Levington, or Nacton, Suffolk, yeoman. Barnard's Inn; GI 89, b 95, B 04; att.-gen. to Queen Anne 03; fee'd counsel Camb. borough by 10, Camb. Univ. 14, rec. Ipswich 10, Orford 21. JP; MP 97, 04, 14, 24. Never married. Follower of Sir Robert Cecil? Nominated Bp. Matthew Wren as overseer and Richard Keble (for whom, see below) as executor of his will. Rich; 'he was not born to £200 p.a. and rose to an estate of about £1,500 p.a.'; assessed £30 for loan in Suffolk *c.*1610; bought Framlingham manor for £14,000 in 35.

(*H. of P.*; Mr J. P. Ferris, personal communication; *East Anglian*, 3rd ser., viii; R. Green, *History ... of Framlingham*, 1834.)

HITCHCOCK, Thomas (*c.*1557–*c.*1619), of London. Trinity, O, 74, BA 78; LI 78, b 87, B 02; commr. for depopulation Northants 09. MP 14. Client of earl of Northampton. Familiar with Thomas Gataker at LI. Assessed at £15, as of St Giles-in-the Fields, Middx., *c.*10. Last mentioned LI 19. (Peck, *Northampton*; T. Gataker, *Discours Apologetical*, 1654; Ellesmere 2575.)

HITCHINGS, John (d. 1646), 1 s. Robert, Petrockstow, Devon, gent. MT 06, b 14, B 35. JP. Mar. Anne, da. Roger Fortescue, Buckland Fillegh, Devon, esq. Described himself as 'gent.' in will, 44. Has 'lived and do determine to die a true protestant member of the Church of England, beseeching the Lord to send peace and remove the distractions that are now amongst us'. Named JP from Oxford 43. Of Padstow, Corn., at d. (PCC 86 Fines; *MTR*, ii. 924–5, 940; Black, *Docquets*.)

*HOBART (Hubberd), Sir Henry (*c.*1554–1625), 2 s. Peterhouse, C, 70; Furnival's Inn; LI 75, b 84, B 96; fee'd counsel to Norwich by 91; steward of Yarmouth by 94. Reporter. Kept Richard Holdsworth and Thomas Gataker as chaplains; characterized by John Donne as 'that very good man'; wished burial 'without vain pomp or unnecessary charge', but left £300 'for the performing of my funerals' and £100 for tomb. Very wealthy; left two das. £4,000 each, held at least 33 manors. Overseers Sir Heneage Finch (see above) and Sir Thomas Trevor (see below). (*H. of P.*; PCC 56 Hele; papers at Norfolk RO, esp. NRS 15928, 'A Booke of the Distribution of my Lord Hobarte's Estate'.)

*HOLBO(U)RNE, Sir Robert (d. 1648), 1 s. Nicholas, Chichester, Sussex, esq., by Anne, sister of John Lane. Furnival's Inn; LI 15, b 23, B 39. Tipped as sol.-gen. 40, 'which will be a great rise for him'. Mar. Anne. Devotee of William Lilly, astrologer. Main properties War. worth £80 p.a. (Keeler; C. H. Josten, *Ashmole*, 1966, ii.)

HOLT, William (*c.*1571–*c.*1637), 2 s. Robert, Ashworth, Lancs. Brasenose, O, 86; GI 88, b ?, B 15; foreign burgess of Preston, Lancs., 02; steward of Sir John Byron's ct. Rochdale 09. JP; MP 97, 04. Granted protection from arrest as surety for a bankrupt 18. Attended pension meetings GI until May 37. (*H. of P.*; H. Fishwick, *History of Rochdale*, 1889; *Reports of Cases decided by Francis Bacon*, ed. J. Ritchie, 1932.)

*HOSKYNS, John (1566–1638), 2 s. John, Monnington, Herefs., yeoman. New Coll., O, 85, MA 92; MT 93, b 00, B 20, SL 23; dep.-steward Hereford; j. W. Wales and member Council in the Marches 21. JP. Mar. (i) Benedicta, da. Robert Moyle, Buckwell, Kent; (ii) Isabel Barrett. Bought Morehampton, Herefs., held manor of Do(o)re, messuages in Newton, Hereford and Monmouthshire. (Osborn, *Hoskyns*; Clendinnen; B. W. Whitlock, *John Hoskyns, serjeant-at-law*, 1982.)

*HUDSON, William (*c.*1577–1635), ? of Kent. GI 01, b 06, B 25; under-clk. to att. in Star Chamber 1594, att. *vice* J. Beere 04–8. Leading Star Chamber counsel. Settled freehold estate Moreham-on-the-Hill, Lincs., on 1 s., held leases, rent-charges, tenements, Middx., Oxon., and Herefs. £3,300 to be laid out on lands for 1 s. Overseer Sir John Finch, CJCP (for whom, see above). (Barnes, 'Mr Hudson's Star Chamber', and references cited therein.)

HUGHES, Hugh (d. 1609), 1 s. David, Porthamel, Anglesey, by Anne, da. John Owen, Llanfaethlu, Anglesey. Trinity, C, 64, BA 68; LI 71, b 80, B 94; dep. queen's att. N. Wales 89; sheriff of Anglesey 92, 00; queen's att. N. Wales 96; member Council in the Marches 01; LCJ (Ire.) elected 09, but d. before taking office. JP; MP 97. Mar. Elizabeth, da. Simon Montagu, Brigstock, Northants. 'The real founder of the fortunes of Plas Coch'; built original house there 69, acquired large land holdings. Portions of £300 and £344 to two das. (*DWB; H. of P.*; UCNW, Plas Coch MSS and catalogue.)

*HUGHES, Sir Thomas (d. 1626), ? s. Thomas ap Hugh, Ches. by Catherine, da. Mathew ap Griffith. Queens', C, 71, BA 76, MA 78, fellow 76–82; ? Staple Inn; GI 79 (or 80, if of Staple Inn), b 85, B 06; prothonotary and clk. of Crown S. Wales 16; ktd. 19. Follower of Sir Edward Phelipps (for whom, see below). JP; MP 86. Author. Mar. Frances, da. Nicholas Mynn(ey), Surrey. Reprimanded by Privy Council for signing an 'objectionable demurrer' lodged by Sir John Holles, Lord Houghton, 19. Assessed @ £10 in 09. Of Wells, Som., at d. (*H. of P.*; *APC 1619*; Gleason, *Justices*.)

HUGHES, Thomas (*c.*1601–1664?), 1 s. of above. GI 05, b 23, B 35; prothonotary and clk. of Crown S. Wales 34–64. JP; possibly MP 21–5. Commr. for depopulation Som. 35. Mar. Elizabeth, da. Sir Edmund Ludlow? (Williams, *Welsh Judges*; Hoare, *Modern Wiltshire*, iii: *Heytesbury Hundred*, 15.)

*HUTTON, Sir Richard (1561–1639). GI 80, b 86, B 03; escheator Yorks. 92, fee'd counsel York 03, chancellor of Durham 08, rec. Doncaster 09. Reporter; chronicler. Hoped to partake in the everlasting happiness reserved for the elect; suspected papist 84. Assessed @ £20 in 09; substantial landed estate at Goldsborough, Yorks. (WR). (York City AO, House Book B 33; Carroll, thesis; Hardy, ed., *Records of Doncaster*, iv; HMC, *Salisbury*, xxi; *CSPD, Add. 1580–1625*; Sheffield Public Lib., Wentworth-Woodhouse MSS; PCC 66 Harvey; CUL MSS Add. 6862–3.)

HYDE (Hide), Sir Laurence (*c.*1562–1642), 2 s. Laurence, West Hatch, Wilts., and Gussage St Michael, Dorset, esq., by Anne, da. Nicholas Sibell, Kent. Magd. Hall, O, *c.*79, BA 80; MT 80, b 89, B 08; rec. Bristol 05; att.-gen. to Queen Anne and ktd. 14. JP; MP 86, 97, 01, 04. Mar. Barbara, da. John Baptist Castilian, Benham Valence, Berks. Agent and

counsel for earl of Hertford; acted for Bp. Davenant against Salisbury
Corporation during 30s. Assessed £8 in 09; bought at least three Wilts
manors; venturer in New River and Bermuda companies. Buried Salisbury Cathedral. (*H. of P.*; Clendinnen; Gleason, *Justices*; *VCH, Wilts.*,
xi.)

*HYDE (Hide), Sir Nicholas (1572–1631), 4 s. Laurence, West Hatch, Wilts.,
esq., and Gussage St Michael, Dorset, by Anne, da. Nicholas Sibell, Kent.
Exeter, O, 90; MT 90, b 98, B 17; clk. of assize, Norfolk circuit, 00–3; rec.
Bristol 15. MP 97, 01, 04, 14, 25. Mar. Mary, da. Arthur Swayne,
Amport, Hants. Was left only £30 p.a. at father's d. 90; seised of 6 manors
and other lands in Hants, Devon, Wilts., Som.; £1,200 portion for da.
Member Bermuda and New River companies. (*H. of P.*; Ms V. Moseley,
personal communication; Clendinnen.)

*HYDE (Hide), Sir Robert (1595–1665). Magd. Hall, O, 10; MT 08, b 17, B
39; reversion of common pleadership London 34. Buried Salisbury
Cathedral 'in such decent manner as by the good order of the godly Book
of Common Prayer is directed'; presented silver-gilt altar candlesticks to
cathedral. Inherited Heale estate; composition 48 set at £233, supposedly
2 years' revenue; claimed his Wilts. properties worth only *c*. £100 p.a., and
debts greater than capital value of land. Accumulated more property in
Wilts. post-1660, and also a 'new-built house in Chancery Lane'. (Keeler;
London Corp. RO, Rep. 48, fol. 112.)

IRELAND, Sir Thomas (1560–1625), 2 s. Robert, Frodsham, Ches. by
Margaret, da. Richard Fox, Broughton, Ches. GI 80, b 84, B 08; king's
counsel, Duchy of Lancaster 03; ktd. 17, vice-chamberlain county palatine of Chester 21. JP; MP 14. Mar (i) Margaret Pope, da. London
scrivener; (ii) Mary, da. Sir Thomas Aston, Aston, Ches.; (iii) Susan, da.
Sir Thomas Cheeke; (iv) Margaret, da. William Lloyd, Halton, Flints.,
wid. John Jeffreys, LI, (for whom, see below). Follower and kinsman of
Stanleys, earls of Derby. Puritan? Inventory value £1,065, although 'my
estate is sore burdened with debts', and s. forced to sell Warrington
manor, 28. Left w. £200 p.a. jointure, s. George £150 p.a. rent charge.
(*Chetham Soc.*, lxxv; Somerville, *Office Holders*; *VCH, Lancs.*, iv–v;
Lancs. RO, Sir Thomas Ireland 1625 & DDLi 256; Chester City RO, ML/
6/59.)

JACKSON, Sir John (d. 1623), 1 s. John, Edderthorpe, Yorks., attorney, by
Helen, da. John Wilkinson, Bolton-upon-Dearne, Yorks. IT 82, b 90, B
05; asst. queen's att. in North 97, king's att. 03–8, under-steward of Derby
by 86, rec. Doncaster, Newcastle-upon-Tyne 07, and Pontefract; ktd. 04.
JP; MP 89. Mar. Elizabeth, da. Sir John Savile, BExch. Acquired
numerous properties near Doncaster and Pontefract; left 2 das. portions
of £1,600 each, and £1,000 to grandda. if her father died leaving her
'unpreferred'. Of Edderthorpe, Knottingly, and Hickleton, Yorks., but

buried London. (*H. of P.*; J. Hunter, *South Yorkshire*, 1829–31; *VCH, Yorks* (NR), ii; Ruigh, *Parliament of 1624*; *Wentworth Papers*, ed. Cooper; J. H. Turner, *Biographica Halifaxiensis*, 1883.)

JEFFREY(E)S, John (*c.*1564–1622), s. Jeffrey ap Hugh, Wrexham, Denbighs., citizen, by Catharine, da. Richard ap Richard. Brasenose, O, 80, BA 83, MA 86; LI 87, b 95 (or 98), B 11; king's att. Ches. and N. Wales 08, Council in Marches 16, j. N. Wales 17. Mar. Margaret, da. William Lloyd, Halton, Flints. First to adopt family surname. Consolidated and increased inherited lands around Wrexham. (Williams, *Welsh Judges*; A. N. Palmer, *A History of . . . Wrexham*, 1903; PCC 64 Saville.)

JERM(I)YN(E), John (*c.*1555–1630), 2 s. Robert, Antingham, Norfolk, gent., by Ann, da. Richard Calthorpe, Gunton. Clifford's Inn; MT 79, b 87, B 07; fee'd counsel Norwich 13, Yarmouth 28, steward Norwich 31. Mar. (i) Margaret, da. Thomas Moulton; (ii) Eleanor, sister of Sir Isaac Jermy, Suffolk. Da. Anne mar. Arthur Turner of MT (for whom, see below). JP. Left portion of £1,000 to unmarried da.; kept a coach. (*HS*, xxxii, lxxxv; Cozens-Hardy, 'Norfolk Lawyers'; Manship, *Yarmouth*, ii; PCC 44 St John.)

JERMYN, Philip (*c.*1588–1655), 3 s. Alexander, Exeter, Devon, gent., by Margaret, da. Henry Hill, Lucott, Devon. Exeter, O, 02; MT 05, b 12, B 29, SL 37, JKB 48. JP. Mar. Mary, da. William Gore, London, alderman and draper. Member and counsel of Virginia Co. 20. Parliamentarian committee-man. Rich; portions £2,500 to da., £1,000 to s. Land purchases Devon, including £1,205-worth of dean and chapter lands. Da. Mary mar. 1s. of John Greene of LI (for whom, see above). Left £100 + to provide dwelling for 4 poor boys and master to teach them manual trade. Of Lordington, Sussex, at d. (*HS*, xv; Foss; Kingsbury, *Virginia Company*, i; Fletcher, *Sussex*; PCC 83 Alchin.)

JOHNSON, Edward (*c.*1593–1660), 1 s. Sir Robert, London. Magdalen, O, 07, BA 09; IT 10, b 18, B 35. Commendatory verses in W. Browne, *Britannia's Pastorals* (1614). Nominated director Virginia Co. 23. Member council for regulating trade 50. Assessed @ £100 in 44. Possibly owned house, St Andrew's, Holborn, worth £8 p.a. in 38; buried Temple Church. (A. B. Beaven, *The Aldermen of . . . London*, 1908–13; Kingsbury, *Virginia Company*, i, iii; *AOI*, iii; Dale, *Inhabitants*; A. Brown, *The Genesis of the USA*, 1890; *ITR*, iii.)

JONES, Charles, (d. 1640), 4 s. Sir William (for whom, see below), by 1st w. LI 13, b 20, B 36; reversioner prothonotary and clk. of Crown Denbighs. and Montgoms. 06, rec. Beaumaris 24, fee'd counsel London 29, dep.-rec. 32; rec. Monmouth. MP Beaumaris 24–Apr. 40. Mar. Active in proceedings against Buckingham, 26. Sought burial at St Paul's Cathedral, bequeathing 100 marks to restore south window; recited various mercies and providences, endowed hospital for 12 poor men, Caernarfonshire.

Properties Caernarfon, Merioneth, Anglesey. Overseer John Glynn (presumably LI bencher 41). (*DWB*; T. Nicholas, *Annals . . . of Wales*, 1872, ii. 765; Williams, *Welsh Judges*; London Corp. RO, Rep. 43, fol. 220ᵛ; Lloyd, *Gentry of S.W. Wales*; PCC 153 Coventry.)

JONES, Thomas (d. 1625). Staple Inn; GI 99, b 05, B 17; reversion to offices of town clk., common sjt., under-sheriff London 07; fee'd counsel by 13, common sjt. 14–25. Counsel to Camb. Univ. by 19, to Stationer's Co. London by 17. JP. Dedicatee, H. Overall, *The Prodigal's Teares* (1620). (Overall, *Remembrancia; Guildhall Misc.*, ii; Jackson, ed., *Records of the . . . Stationers' Company*; Cooper, *Annals of Cambridge*, iii.)

*JONES, Sir William (*c.*1566–1640). LI 87, b 95, B 11; rec. Beaumaris, *c.*93. JP; MP 97–14. Granted arms 07, as of Holt, Denbighs.? Dedicatee, J. Trussell, *A Continuation of the . . . History of England* (1636). Although an 'arriviste from hithermost Caernarvonshire', regarded as 'the prime man' in the county by 21; follower of Sir John Wynn of Gwydir. Wealth unknown. (*DWB*; *H. of P.*; *HS*, lxxvi; *Trans. Cymm. Soc.*, 1942.)

JORDAN, Nicholas (d. *c.*1630), of Brasted, Kent, at admission to IT. Lyon's Inn; IT 89, b 97, B 13; recommended by Sir Robert Heath (for whom, see above) as steward, Isle of Wight 24; commr. for martial law Sussex 27. JP; MP 26. Reporter. Described by Bp. Harsnet as 'a grave, staid and temperate gentleman'. Of Chichester, Sussex, at d. (*CSPD 1623–5*; Fletcher, *Sussex*; Hargrave 373; R. F. Dell, *Glynde Place Archives*, 1964.)

*KEBLE, Richard (*fl.* 1609–1660), 7 s. Giles, Old Newton, Suffolk, by Ann Went, Suffolk. Corpus Christi, C, 02, BA 06; GI 09, b 14, B 39, CJ N. Wales 47, SL 48, commr. of Great Seal 49; fee'd counsel Ipswich 34, rec. Orford. 36. JP. Mar. Mary, da. John Sicklemore, Ipswich. (Williams, *Welsh Judges*; Additional 5524, fol. 174; Bacon, *Annalls of Ipswche*; Suffolk RO (Ipswich), Orford Assembly Book 1579–1662, Sept. 1636, Sept. 1647; Bodl. MS Rawlinson C 207.)

KING, Richard, (*c.*1590–1645), 1 s. William, Castle Cary, Som. Oriel, O, 10; IT 12, b 20, B 38; rec. Weymouth and Melcombe Regis 29. JP; MP 40. Mar. (i) Edith, da. Sir Robert Seymour, Hanford, Dorset; (ii) Margaret, da. Robert Harbin, Dorset. Granted arms 41. Royalist, sat in Oxford parl. Assessed on £6 land for 1641 subsidy and @ £1,000 by parl. 44; of Sherborne, Dorset at d. (Mr J. P. Ferris, personal communication; Keeler; Som. RO, DD/PH, 225/64.)

*LAMBARD, William (1536–1601).? Jesus, C, 49 (*or* New Coll., O, 53, BA 61, MA 65); LI 56, b 67, AB 79, B 97. JP; MP 63. Devout protestant. Wealthy; left da. marriage portion £1,300, £105 p.a. for sons' education; held leases and messuages London, manor of Westcombe, Greenwich, and other lands Kent. Bequeathed £10 for plate to LI (*H. of P.*; R. M. Warnicke, *William Lambarde*, 1973; *Index Lib.*, xxxvi.)

*LANE, Sir Richard (1584–1650), 1 s. Richard, Courteenhall, Northants, yeoman. Trinity, C, 02; MT 05, b 13, B 30; dep.-rec. Northampton 15, rec. 28. Dedicatee, T. Randolph, *The Jealous Lovers* (1632). Of Kingsthorpe, Northants at d. (Metcalfe, ed. *Northants Vis.*; J. Bridges, *History of Northants*, 1791, i; *CCC*.)

LANE, Thomas (*c.*1582–1652), 1 s. Robert, Hughenden, Bucks., by Alice, da. Robert Saunders, Hambleden, Bucks. Clifford's Inn; IT 02, b 11, B 27; rec. High Wycombe by 23, feodary Bucks. 29. JP; MP 25, 28, 40. Claimed 41 to have encouraged profanation of the Sabbath; will calls for burial 'without any funeral pomp or vanities'. Parliamentarian. Wealth uncertain, income perhaps £500–£1,000 p.a.; grandniece's portion £500. Subscribed £1,500 to Irish venture. (Keeler; Underdown, *Pride's Purge*; PCC 219 Brent; *Irish Hist. Studs.*, x. 51.)

LAN(E)Y, John (*c.*1549–1633), 1 s. John, Cratfield, Suffolk, esq., by Catherine, da. Anthony Yaxley, Mellis. GI 67, b 69, B 91; rec. Ipswich 84. JP; MP 86. Mar. Mary, da. John Poley, Badley, Suffolk. Wealth uncertain; paid for supply of water to his house 16, will mentions freehold lands Cratfield, messuages and tenements in Basinghall St., London; leaves wife all 'goods, money, plate, jewels and household stuff … wishing they were more because she deserveth more'. Of Ipswich at d. (*H. of P.*; *The Visitations of Suffolk*, ed. W. C. Metcalfe, 1882; Bacon, *Annalls of Ipswche*; G. R. Clarke, *The History … of Ipswich*, 1830, 325; Suffolk (Ipswich) RO, IC/AA2/62.)

LAN(E)Y, John (*c.*1576–1647), 1 s. of preceding. GI 91, b 99, AB 20, B 22; fee'd counsel Ipswich 14, rec. 33; MCh (extraordinary) *c.*19. Mar. (i) Mary, da. John Howe, S. Okenden, Essex; (ii) Elizabeth, da. John Sherman, Ipswich; (iii) da. of one Appleton, Essex. Returned rectory and other church lands to vicar of Cratfield 35. Royalist. Assessed £400 before compounding for delinquency. Will mentions that it 'hath pleased God to increase my estate by unexpected means', noting messuages, tenements, and lands in London and Suffolk, subject to mortgages for younger children. (Metcalfe, ed., *Suffolk Vis.*; Bacon, *Annalls of Ipswche*; *CD 1621*, vii; *CCAM*; Cross, *Justice in Ipswich*; *CJ*, iii; PCC 70 Essex.)

LATHAM (Latho(u)m), Ralph (*c.*1588–*c.*1641), 1 s. William, Upminster, Essex, and London, goldsmith, by Alice, da. Paul D'Ewes, London, esq. Magd. Hall, O, 04; MT 07, b 16, B 36; common sjt. London 25. Mar. Mary, da. Hamlet Clarke. Devout preamble to will; requested burial 'as private as conveniently may be'. Inherited Essex estate, had £10,000 with w. Mortgaged Upminster manor 41, son and heir sold Upminster Hall for £6,640 in 42. (*HS*, xiii; Morant, *Essex* i; *VCH, Essex*, vii; Essex RO, D/AER 20, fol. 194–194^v.)

LAWTON, Thomas (*c.*1558–1606), 3 s. John, Church Lawton, Ches., by Margaret, da. Fulke Dutton, Chester. St Alban Hall, O, 75; IT 76, b 84, B 97; fee'd counsel Chester 96, alderman and rec. 02. JP; MP 84, 04. Mar.

Jane, da. George Spurstowe, Ches. Catholic family ties. Died intestate. (*H. of P.*; Chester City RO, AB/1/246ᵛ, *seq.*; *Chetham Soc.*, 3rd ser., xix.)

LENTHALL, William (1591–1661). LI 09, b 16, B 33. Leading counsel in Exch. Wealthy. (Keeler; Underdown, *Pride's Purge.*)

LEVING(E), Timothy (*c.*1574–1636), 4 s. Thomas, Baddesley, War., by Margaret Freeman, Tamworth, Staffs. Balliol, O, 91; IT 97, b 06, B 22; elected SL but d. before creation; rec. Derby 21. MP 24, 25, 28. Mar. Anna Fairfax, London. Reported on activities of papists Leics. and Derbs. 25. Described as 'a gentleman of good credit' 25. Will mentions properties purchased in Derbs., Notts., and War.; nominal IPM value £6. 3s. p.a. Other lands leased to countess of Devonshire for £100 p.a. Of Derby at d. (*HS*, xii; *Derbs. Arch. J.*, 1966; Baker, *Serjeants*; HMC, *Cowper*, i; PCC 122 Pile; C142/555/80.)

*LEY, Sir James, Earl of Marlborough (1550–1629). Queens', C 71; New Inn; LI 77, b 84, B 00, SL 03; escheator Hants and Wilts. 00–01. Commr. for Ulster plantation 08, grantee of Caribbean lands. Pious but corrupt; gave £20 to poor of Westbury, excluding beggars 'not forced thereto by years or infirmities'. Very wealthy; portions of £2,000 for 2 das.; held some 20 manors, nominal IPM value £130 p.a. (*H. of P.*; Hants RO, 44M69/xl; PCC 27 Ridley; *Index Lib.*, lxxii.)

*LITTLETON, Sir Edward (1590–1645). IT 09, b 17, B 29, SL 40. JP; MP 14, 25, 26, 28. Reporter and legal scholar. Requested 'to be buried decently as a Christian without pomp or worldly ceremony'. Rich; £2,000 marriage portion for da., extensive lands Wales, Salop. (*CLJ*, xxxiii; PCC 165 Fairfax.)

LITTLETON, William (1591–1653), 2 s. Sir Edward, Henley and Munslow, Salop, CJ N. Wales, by Mary, da. Edmund Walter, Ludlow, CJ S. Wales. Broadgates Hall O, 09; IT 12, b 20, B 38; received writ to be SL 48, but not created; rec. Ludlow, j. N. Wales 47, CJ 49. JP. Mar. (i) ?Jane, sister of Simon Rugeley; (ii) Judith Eyton. Parliamentarian committee-man. Bequeathed divinity books and £20 rent charge for propagating the gospel in New England. Parliamentarian commr. for Herefs. and Salop 47. Annual income perhaps £100–250 at d. (*Trans. Salop Arch. Soc.*, 4th ser., iii; Williams, *Welsh Judges*; Baker, *Serjeants*; *AOI*, i; G. E. McParlin, 'The Herefordshire Gentry in County Government 1625–1661', UCNW, Ph.D. thesis, 1981; PCC 247 Brent.)

LLANDEN, Benedict (d. 1632), 3 s. William, Dalby, Lincs., esq., by Eleanor, da. Henry Mainwaring. MT 04, b 10, B 28. Mar. Mary. Claimed his estate 'cannot be expected to be much'; left w. £1,000 in lieu of jointure; £1,500 bond forfeited by his elder bro. to be divided between 2 sons. Of Isleworth, Middx. at d., buried Temple Church. (*HS*, li; STAC 8/242/20; PCC 34 Audley.)

LLOYD, Sir John (d. 1632), 1 s. Ievan, Ceiswyn, Pennall, Merioneths., by

Margaret, da. Maurice ap Owen, Rhiwseason, in Llanbrynmair, Merioneths. Clifford's Inn; IT 83, b 93, B 07, ktd. and SL 24; ? escheator Carmarthens. 96; mentioned as possible LCB (Ire.), 22. JP. Mar. Jane, da. Thomas ap Hugh of Tallyn. Antiquary; dedicatee, L. Owen, *Key of the Spanish Tongue* (1605), and *The Unmasking of all Popish Monks* ... (1623). Wealth unknown. (Lloyd, 'Welsh Benchers'; *Cal. Wynn Papers.*)

LOCKE, Thomas, (1579?–1623). Magd. Hall, O, 85, *or* ?Emmanuel, C, 97; Barnard's Inn; GI 96, b 00, B 21; granted £30 life pension 09 for attendance on Irish commrs.; steward manors of Woodford and Gt. Canfield, Essex, 11, 16. Requested funeral sermon from Dr Sampson Price, noted anti-papist. Mar. (i) ? Helena Hide; (ii) Joyce, da. William Rowe, Higham Hill, Essex; (iii) Susanna, da. Sir William Welby, Lincs. Portions of £66. 13s. 4d. to 2 das. Lands in Cambs. and Essex, nominal IPM value £8. 6s. 8d. p.a. Of Chelmsford, Essex at d. (*HS*, xci; PRO SO 3/4; Essex RO, D/DC/41/499, 23/167; PCC 68 Swann.)

LOVELACE, Lancelot (1563–1640), 2 s. Henry, Chalk, Kent, mercer by Margaret Haman of Crayford, Kent. Staple Inn; GI 81, b ?, B 09; freeman of Canterbury 13, rec. Sandwich 13, Dover 20, Canterbury 21. Steward, Lord Warden's Chancery court at Dover by 32. JP. Mar. Mary, da. William Cayser, Hollingbourne, Kent. Of Canterbury and Hollingbourne at d. (Additional 5507, fols. 207ᵛ–208; *HS*, xlii; Hasted, *Kent*, iii; Boys, *Sandwich*, ii; J. B. Jones, *Annals of Dover*, 1916; Chicago MS f-286.)

LOWE, John (d. 1632), 1 s. Ralph, Herefs. and Erlestoke, Wilts., gent., by Michaell, da. John Gilbert, Maddington, Wilts. New Inn; MT 83, b 91, B 12; fee'd counsel Salisbury Cathedral by 06, steward Baverstock manor by 04. JP; MP 97. Mar. (i) Alice, da. Nicholas Downe, Orcheston, Wilts. (ii) Elizabeth, da. Thomas Hyde, DD, canon of Salisbury Cathedral. Gave plate to Salisbury Cathedral 06. Purchased lands in Wilts., including manor of Orcheston St Mary; lived Salisbury. Assessed £25 for knighthood fine 31 (*H. of P.*; Wilts. RO, 332/24b; PCC 55 Audley; *Index Lib.*, xxiii; *Wilts. N & Q*, i. 54.)

LOWE, Nicholas (d. 1623), ?3 s. Jasper, Derby, by Dorothy, da. William Sacheverell, Stanton, Derbs. St John's, C, 89; Barnard's Inn; GI 91, b 99, B 16; escheator Notts. and Derbs. 02, counsel to earl of Huntingdon 06. Mar. Dorothy. Tithe corn, house at St Ellens, and all land in Derby mortgaged to 'my especial good friend' Sir Edward Henden of GI (see above) for £500. Appointed as overseers four 'loving friends at Gray's Inn', the benchers Sir Henry Yelverton, Sir Euble Thelwall (for whom, see below), Henry Dewell and Thomas Jones (for whom, see above). (Metcalfe, *Derbs. Pedigrees*; *List and Index Soc.*, lxxii; Huntington Lib., MS Hastings Lit. 3, box 6; PCC 19 Byrde.)

LUDLOW, Gabriel (1588–c.1641), 1 s. Thomas, Dinton, Wilts., and Butleigh, Som., by Jane, da. Thomas Pile, Compton Beauchamp, Berks. IT

10, b 20, B 37; receiver for Duchy of Lancaster in Cambs., Norfolk, and Suffolk 29–39; dep.-ranger Selwood Forest 38. Mar. Phyllis. Strong New England and Virginia connections via bros. George and Roger and own children. Examined for possession of tract criticizing ship-money 39. Broke off reading early in 40 because of poverty; lands extended in ct. of Duchy Chamber *c*.40. Last mentioned June 41. (*Virginia Mag. of History and Biography*, liv; Hoare, *Modern Wiltshire*, iii, *Heytsbury Hundred*; *WAM*, xxvi; *Wilts. N & Q*, ii; Bodl. MS Bankes 19/7; Somerville, *Office Holders*; *CSPD 1639–40*; HMC, *Fourth Rep.*, i; *ITR*, ii.)

MAI(Y)N(E), James (*c*.1568–1624), 1 s. Henry, Hemel Hempstead, Herts., by Alice Randolfe, Berks. Magd. Hall, O, 84; GI 85, b 93(?), B 13; bailiff Berkhamstead St Peter *c*.19. Mar. Mary, da. John Andrew(s), Hitchin, Herts., and Sandy, Beds. Wealthy; inherited several Herts. manors; w.'s portion £1,000; also held property Kent and Bucks. Bequeathed 4 das. portions of £1,000 each. (*HS*, xxii; *Trans. E. Herts. Arch. Soc.*, x; Clutterbuck, *Herts.*, i; *VCH, Herts.*, ii; Manningham, *Diary*; Herts. RO, 89/HW/43.)

*MALET, Sir Thomas (*c*.1582–1665), 1 s. Malachi, Luxulyan, Corn., by Elizabeth, da. Richard Trevanion. MT 00, b 06, B and sol.-gen. to queen 26, SL 35. JP; MP 14, 21, 25, 26. Wealthy. (Woods, *Prelude to Civil War*.)

MANATON, Ambrose (d. 1651), 2 s. Peter, Trecarel and South Petherwyn, Lewannick, Corn., esq., by Frances, da. Edward Couch, Houghton. LI 12, b 37, AB 37; rec. Launceston 22, MCh (extraordinary) by 37, mayor of Camelford 40. JP; MP 21, 24, 40. Mar. (i) Anne, da. Piers Edgecombe, Corn. wid. Richard Trefusis, see below; (ii) Jane. Sought private burial at night without mourning, but later funeral sermon on text: 'Blessed are they that die in the Lord for they rest from their labours.' Royalist. Income from lands Corn. and Devon £550 p.a.; left portions of £1,000 and £900 to 2 das. (Keeler; M. Coate, *Cornwall in the Great Civil War*, 1963.)

MANN, Bartholemew (d. 1616), 2 s. John, merchant and mayor of Poole, Dorset. New Inn; MT 69, b 77, B 92; freeman of Canterbury 79? Mar. Mary, da. Paul Johnson, Fordwich, Kent. Of Rochester at d. (*HS*, lxxv; *Arch. Cant.*, xx; Mr J. P. Ferris, personal communication.)

MARSTON, John (d. 1599), 3 s. Ralph, Hayton, Salop, gent., by Joanna, da. Richard Horton. New Inn; MT 70, b 77, B 92. Granted arms 87. Mar. (i) Mary, da. Andrew de Gwerey, merchant or surgeon of London, born Italy; (ii) Mary, da. John Butler, Oxon. Held lands War. and Oxon., dwelling-house Coventry. (*HS*, xxix; *Trans. Salop Arch. Soc.*, 4th ser., ix; PCC 82 Kidd.)

MARTIN, John (*c*.1577–1639), 1 s. Richard, Kirtlington and Witney, Oxon., by Dorothy, da. Ralph Ferne, Lancs. St John's, O, 94; Clement's Inn; IT 98, b 07, B 24; steward of Witney manor by 20. JP. Mar. Anne, da. Roger Bragge, Fleet St., London. (*HS*, v; Oxon. RO, Welch v/1/3, 4.)

*MARTIN, Richard (1570–1618), 1 s. New Inn; MT 85, b 02, B 16. JP; MP 01, 04. Never married. Director Irish and Virginia companies. Left all lands, tenements, leases, and goods to bro. Thomas, mayor of Exeter; miscellaneous cash bequests £45 p.a. and £30. (*H. of P.*; PCC 111 Meade; Rabb, *Enterprise and Empire*.)

*MASON, Robert (1579–1635), s. Stephen, Kingsclere, Hants. LI 92, b 17, B 33; steward Basingstoke 24; secondary of Poultry Compter, London, 16, rec. 34; rec. Winchester 28, Southampton 33. JP. Mar. (i) Edith, da. John Foyle, Dorset; (ii) Hester, da. Edward Richards, Yaverland, Isle of Wight. Acted as counsel for Winchester Cathedral, requested burial there. Bequeathed £300 p.a. jointure to w., portions of £1,500, £1,332, and £1,332 to 2 das. and 1 s. Counsel to and creditor of earl of Southampton. Executors Sir John Glanville (see above) and Sir Edward Littleton (see above). (Ms V. Moseley, personal communication; History of Parliament, 1604–29: draft biography. PCC 13 Pile.)

MEREFIELD, John (1591–1666), 1 s. John, Crewkerne, Som., barrister, by Richarda, da. John Northcott, Crediton, Devon. IT 12, b 20, B 38, SL 60. Mar. Eleanor, da. John Williams, Herringston, Dorset. Dedicatee, R. Herrick, 'The Fairie Temple'. Assessed on £6 lands, 41 subsidy. Royalist, compounded on Exeter articles, fined £500 + £200, reduced on appeal to £200. (*HS*, xi; Som. RO, DD/MR 71; Mr I. Collis, personal communication; *CCC*, 1243; T. L. Stoate, *The Somerset Protestation Returns*, 1975.)

*METHWOLD, Sir William (1560–1620). Lyon's Inn (barrister); LI 81, b 89, B 08, SL 12. Assessed @ £20 for Norfolk privy seal 04. (*Norfolk Arch.*, ii; *Analecta Hibernica*, viii; Additional 4793, fol. 126ᵛ.)

MILWARD, Sir Thomas (*c*.1576–1658), 4 s. William, Eaton, Dovedale, Derbs., by Catherine, da. John Fleetwood, Colwich, Staffs. Balliol, O, 91, BA 95, MA 00; LI 01, b 09, B 27, SL 37, ktd. 38; ?Bailiff Rye 11; CJ Chester and rec. Ludlow 38; ?MCh (extraordinary) 56. JP. Mar. Thomasin, da. Henry Beresford, Alsop-en-le-Dale, Derbs. Royalist at surrender of Ludlow. Not wealthy; fined £360 at one-third in 49; assessed @ £100 in 51. Described in 1638 as 'an obscure man' and client of the marquis of Hamilton. (Metcalfe, *Derbs. Peds.*; HMC, *Fourteenth Rep.*, iv; *List and Index Soc.*, cxvi; Williams, *Welsh Judges*; Dias, thesis; Bright, *Royalists and Roundheads in Derbs.*; Derbs. RO, Okeover 231 M/T730; Knowler, ii. 164.)

MINGAY(E), Francis (*c*.1574–1632), 1 s. William, Arminghall, Norfolk, and Ilketshall St Margaret, Suffolk, mercer and mayor of Norwich, by Winifred, da. Robert Coke, Mileham, Norfolk (sister of Sir Edward, for whom, see above). ?Trinity, C, *c*.92; IT 93, b 00, B 17; justice of the Bridge Yard, Southwark, 14. JP; MP 01, 24. Mar. Frances, da. Edmond Richers, Swannington, Norfolk. Assessed £10 for loan, Suffolk, *c*.10; left portion of £500 to da.; money-lender. (*H. of P.*; *ITR*, i; *HS*, xliii; *East Anglian*, 3rd ser., viii; PCC 64 Audley.)

*MO(U)NTAGU(E), Sir Henry, Earl of Manchester (c.1563–1642), 3 s.; bro. of following. MT 85, b 92, AB 03, B 06, SL 11. Director Virginia and Irish companies. Devout protestant. Claimed that 'latter times have increased me in honours but lessened me in fortune', but still bequeathed £4,676 p.a. to w. and younger sons, plus £4,000 to 2 granddas. Bequeathed gilt cup to MT: 'And at their feasts and readings I wish not my health but my love to that society may be remembered.' (*H. of P.*; Rabb, *Enterprise and Empire*; PCC 47 Rivers.)

MO(U)NTAGU(E), Sir Sidney (c.1571–1644), 6 s. Sir Edward Montagu, Boughton, Northants, by Elizabeth, da. Sir John Harrington, Exton, Rutland. Christ's, C, 88; MT 93, b 01, AB 16, B 20; MReq by 16, MCh (extraordinary) 16. MP 93, 01, 14, 40. Mar. Paulina, da. John Pepys, Cottenham, Cambs. Antiquary. Devout protestant; dedicatee, W. Perkins, *Lectures upon the first three chapters of the Revelation* (1604). Removed from office 40 for refusing Crown loan, but expelled from Long Parl. as royalist Dec. 42. (*H. of P.*; Keeler.)

*MOORE, Sir Francis (1558–1621), 1 s. Edward, East Ilsley, Berks., yeoman. New Inn; MT 80, b 87, AB 03, B 07. Dedicatee, R. West, *The Court of Conscience* (1602). Strong Catholic associations. Challenged in Earl Marshal's ct. 18. Spent at least £10,000 on land in Berks. 1594–1619; left marriage portions of £1,500 each for 2 das. (*H. of P.*; Berks. RO, D/EW/E17; Durston, thesis; *HS*, cvii.)

MOORE (More), John (c.1561–1620), s. John, Mottisfont, Hants. Furnival's Inn; LI 81, b 89, B 03, SL 14; rec. Winchester 96, Portsmouth 00, Romsey 08, steward of Andover 99, Lymington 07, Basingstoke 10. JP; MP 97, 01, 04. Mar. Dousabell, da. James Paget, Grove Place, Nursling, Hants. Dedicatee, T. Gataker, *Of . . . Lots* (1619). Counsel to dean and chapter, Westminster Abbey, by 18. Bought at least 3 Hants manors, left da. portion of £1,600. (*H. of P.*; King, *Old Times in Lymington*; *Southampton Rec. Soc.*, xi; C142/382/30; History of Parliament, 1604–29: draft biography.)

MOORE (More), John (1589–1637), 1 s. John, Bewick, Yorks., by Katherine, da. John Holme, Paull Holme, Yorks. King's, C, 06; GI 06, b 14, B 30. JP. ?Bought land Bridlington 19. (*Her. & Gen.*, viii; Poulson, *Holderness*, i; *VCH, Yorks. (ER)*, ii.)

MOORE, Sir Richard (d. 1635), 1 s. William, Totternhoe, Beds., esq. New Inn; MT 86, b 94, AB 16; MCh (extraordinary) 16, ktd. 19; steward of manor of Gt. Missenden 08. JP; MP 01. Bought Totternhoe manor, 95, sold it 14; bought Presbury rectory, Glos., c.08. Assessed @ £8 in 09. Of Cuddington, Bucks., at d. (*H. of P.*; *VCH, Bucks.*, iii; Gleason, *Justices*; R. Gibbs, *History of Aylesbury*, 1885; Rudder, *Glos.*)

MORGAN, Francis (1547–1612), 1 s. William, Kingsthorpe, Northants, gent., by Elizabeth. New Inn; MT 74, b 81, B 99; j. sheriff's ct. London

04–10; ? feodary of Rutland 09. JP. Mar. Dorothy, da. Ambrose Saunders, Sibbertoft, Northants. Assessed @ £5 in 09. (*HS*, lxxxvii; Overall, *Remembrancia*; *CSPD 1603–10*; Gleason, *Justices*; HMC, *Buccleuch*, iii.)

MOSELEY, Sir Edward (1569–1638), 2 s. Sir Nicholas, London, and Hough End, Lancs., alderman, by Margaret, da. Hugh Whitbroke, Bridgnorth, Salop. Christ's, C, 86; GI 90, b 98, AB 11, B 14; att.-gen. Duchy of Lancaster 03; j. sheriff's ct. London 10. MP 14, 21, 25. Never married. Dedicatee, W. Crashawe, *Parable of Poyson* (1618); R. Sibbes, *The Soules Conflict* (1635). Bequeathed £1 p.a. to morning lectures at St Antholin's, in accordance with father's will. Rich; inherited some lands and £1,450 cash; bought Rolleston manor, Staffs., and corn mills Leeds; held at d. manors and lands in Staffs., Leics., Lincs., Oxon.; bequeathed £1,500 to niece, £40 p.a. to godson. (Somerville, *Office Holders*; Peile, *Biographical Register*; *Chetham Soc.*, xlii; S. Shaw, *History . . . of Staffordshire*, 1798–1801, i; PCC 160 Lee; Leeds District Archives, TN LA 1/8.)

MUTTON, Sir Peter (1565–1637), s. John, Vale of Clwyd and Rhuddlan, Flints., gent., by Ann Wen, da. Griffith ap Ievan ap Llewelyn Vaughan, Plas yn Llanerch, Flints. St Alban Hall, O, 83; Furnival's Inn; LI 86, b 94, B 22; att. Chester and Flint 92, prothonotary and clk. of Crown, N. Wales, 05; att.-gen. Wales 07–14, MCh 14, j. Anglesey 22, CJ and ktd. 22. JP; MP 04, 24. Mar. (i) Ann, da. George Willmer; (ii) Eleanor, sister of Abp. John Williams. Wealthy; held extensive lands Flints. and Denbighs., inherited estate at Llanerch from uncle. (*DWB*; Clendinnen; Williams, *Welsh Judges*; NLW and Clwyd RO, Gwysaney MSS.)

NAPPER (Napier), Sir Robert (c.1542–1615), 3 s. James, Puncknoll, Dorset, gent., by Anne Hilliard. Exeter, O, 59, BA 62; MT 66, b ?, AB 93; CB Exch (Ire.) 1593–1602, ktd. and fee'd counsel Lyme Regis 93, sheriff of Dorset 06–7. JP; MP 86, 01, 04. Mar. (i) Catherine, da. John Warham, Dorset; (ii) Magdalen, da. William Denton, Tonbridge, Kent. Granted arms 76. Bequeathed £2 ea. to 11 Dorset churches, £50 p.a. for Dorchester almshouses ('Napper's mite'); elder bro. and both w.s apparently church papists. Substantial landholdings in Dorset, nominal IPM value £25. 16s. 4d. (Mr. J. P. Ferris, personal communication; *H. of P.*; Clenninden; PCC 108 Rudd.)

*NIC(H)OLLS, Sir Augustine (1559–1616). MT 75, b 84, B 02, SL 03. May have died by poison after being entertained at Naworth Castle, Northumberland, by Lord William Howard. Trustees included Sir Francis Harvey (for whom, see above). (Whitelocke, *Lib. Fam.*; PCC 83 Cope.)

NIGHTINGALE, Geoffrey (d. 1619), s. William, Newport, Essex, gent., by Gonar, da. Geoffrey Thurgood, Ugley, Essex. Christ's, C, 58; GI 67, b 76, B 92; steward of Bassingham and Soham manors for Duchy of Lancaster and of Rickling Hall manor 07. JP. Mar. Catherine, da. John Clamps,

Huntingdon. Among foundation governors Charterhouse School, encouraged setting-up of Newport Grammar School; s. Henry disowned for marrying papist; bequeathed 20s. for funeral sermon from learned preacher. Left £800 portion to da., £3. 6s. 8d. to friend Sir Henry Yelverton (see below); assessed @ £12 in 09. (Peile, *Biographical Register*; Somerville, *Office Holders*; *HS*, xiii; *VCH, Essex*, ii; PCC 29 Soames; Essex RO, D/DB 606.)

*NOY(E), William (1577–1634). LI 94, b 02, B 18. Steward of Savoy manor, Duchy of Lancaster, 29. (Somerville, *Office Holders*; *HLQ* xl (1977).)

OSBALDESTON, Sir Richard (d. 1640), ?1 s. Edward, Altcar and Sefton, Lancs., gent., by Margaret, da. John Molineux, Sefton. GI 04, b ?, B 26; king's att. in Ire. 26, ktd. 37. Mar. (i) Eleanor, da. William Westropp, Brunton, Northumb., and Pickering, Yorks., (ii) Mary, da. Thomas Nettleton, Mirfield, Yorks. Bought manor of Hunmanby 23; left £3,000 to w.; held messuage York, rented by Sir Thomas Widdrington (for whom, see below); nominal IPM value of Yorks. properties £11 p.a.; £788 loaned to earl of Ormonde. Buried at St John's Church, Dublin. (*Dugdale's Visitation of Yorkshire*, ed. J. W. Clay, 1894–1917, i; *VCH, Yorks (ER)*, ii; Sheffield Public Lib., Wentworth-Woodhouse MSS; L. M. Owston, *Hunmanby, East Yorkshire*, 1948; *Historic Soc. Lancs. and Ches.*, lxxxvii; *CSPD 1640–1*; C142/610/94.)

OSBORNE, Edward (1572–1625), 2 s. Sir Edward, London, alderman and lord mayor, by Anne, da. Sir William Hewett, cloth-worker and lord mayor. Trinity, C, 89; Clement's Inn; IT 91, b 00, B 16. JP; MP 21. Mar. (i) Alice, da. William Boteler, Biddenham, Beds; (ii) Francis, da. James Harvey, Dagenham, Essex. Assessed @ £25 in 09; bought Northill manor, Beds., for £3,150 in 10; bought Leics. lands for £5,450; left portions of c. £810 to 3 das. and 1 s., plus unspecified amounts of East India stock. (*HS*, xix; *VCH, Beds.*, iii; Beds. RO, DD HY 92–105; PCC 108 Barrington; History of Parliament, 1604–29: draft biography.)

OVERBURY, Sir Nicholas (1549–1643), 2 s. Thomas, Ashton-sub-Edge, Glos., yeoman. New Inn; MT 74, b 82, B 00; escheator Glos. 94, rec. Gloucester 03; CJ W. Wales 10–37, ktd. 21. JP; MP 04. Mar. Margaret, da. Giles Palmer, Compton Scorpion, War. Bought manor of Bourton-on-the-Hill, Glos., 98, and possibly Oddington c.02. (Clendinnen; Williams, *Welsh Judges*; *List and Index Soc.*, lxxii; *VCH, Glos.*, vi; Additional 34738, fol. 16ᵛ; *Trans. Bristol and Glos. Arch. Soc.*, xvii, xviii.)

PAGE, John (1563–1654), 1 s. John, Wembley, Middx., gent., by Audrey, da. Thomas Redding, Headstone, Herts. Clement's Inn; IT 86, b 95, AB 27; MCh 27. JP. Mar. Katherine. Provided affidavit 48 re damage suffered by John Weaver, MP, for affection to parl. Held manors of Wembley and Tokyngton. (Greater London RO, Acc. 276/367; J. Haydn, *The Book of Dignities*, 1890; *Records of the Cust Family*, i; *CCAM*; Smyth, *Obituary*; PCC 205 Alchin.)

PALMER, Edward (*c*.1589–*c*.1642), 1 s. Anthony, Stoke Doyle, Northants, esq., by Mary, da. William Watts, Blakesley, Northants. King's, C, 06; MT 08, b 16, B 39; escheator Northants 30–1. JP. Mar. Frances, da. Sir Francis Harvey (for whom, see above). Follower of Abp. John Williams; member Company of Mineral and Battery Works. (Metcalfe, ed., *Northants Vis.*; Bridges, *Northants*, i; Hacket, *Scrinia Reserata*, i; Gleason, *Justices*; BL MS Loan 16, ii.)

PARKER, Richard (*c*.1583–1646), 1 s. Henry, Northfleet, Kent, gent., by Eleanor Stoneplace. St Alban Hall, O, 00, BA 04; MT 05, b 14, B 32; steward for Duchy of Lancaster, Essex, 32–5. JP. Mar. (i) Priscilla, da. Robert Edolphe, Hinxhill, Kent; (ii) Dorothy. Will (1640) thanked God he had never been a reprobate sinner and left 20s. for 'some orthodox and honest man' to preach funeral sermon. Held lands Northfleet, dwelling-house with chapel, garden, etc., at Shorne. Cash bequests totalled £569, w. left coach, jewels, etc. (*HS*, xlii; Somerville, *Office Holders*; Hasted, *Kent*, viii; Gleason, *Justices*; *MTR*, ii; PCC 21 Fines.)

PEPPER, Sir Cuthbert (d. 1608), s. Robert, East Cowton, Yorks. (NR), esq., by Marjorie. GI 70, b 78, B 95; rec. Richmond 86, fee'd counsel York 97, att. in the North 98–03, surveyor Ct. of Wards 00, ktd. 04, Chancellor of Durham 05, att. of Wards 07. JP; MP 97, 01. Mar. Margaret, da. Robert Wild, East Cowton. Bought Temple Cowton and lands in vicinity; bequests £135 p.a. and £750 cash. (*H. of P.*; Foster, ed., *Yorks. Vis.*; *VCH, Yorks (NR)*, i; C. Clarkson, *History and Antiquities of Richmond*, 1821; K. Emsley and C. M. Fraser, *The Courts of . . . Durham*, 1984; Borthwick, Reg. 31, fol. 72–72^v; C 142/310/64.)

PEPYS, Talbot (1583–1666), 6 s. John, Impington, Cambs., by Edith, da. Edmund Talbot, Cottenham, Cambs. King's, C, 95, scholar Trinity Hall 01; MT 05, b 13, B 32; rec. Cambridge 24–60, steward Soham Manor for Duchy of Lancaster 23. JP; MP 25. Mar. Beatrice, da. John Castell, Hevingham, Norfolk. Parliamentarian committee-man for Cambridge, 44–5. Rated £4 in lands in 41. Sister mar. Sir Sidney Montagu (for whom, see above). (W. C. Pepys, *Genealogy of the Pepys Family*, 1877; Cambs. RO, Cambridge Common Day Book, vol. 7; F. J. Varley, *Cambridge during the Civil War*, 1935; *East Anglian*, 3rd ser., ix. 172.)

*PHE(A)SANT, Peter (1584–1649), 1 s. GI 02, b 08, B 23, SL 40; steward, ct. baron, Hackney, Middx., 30–41. Pious. Assessed @ £1,000, discharged having paid £50 and lent £350, June 44. One of the 'most ablest' inhabitants of Coleman St. Ward 40. Portion £700 at least to youngest s. Held properties London, manor of Upwood, Hunts., where he died. Overseers Sir John Bramston and Sir Robert Berkeley (for whom, see above). (*HS*, lii; Notts. RO, DD SK, 149/13, 14, 15; *CCAM*; *Misc. Gen. et. Her.*, 2nd ser., ii. 87; PCC 176 Fairfax.)

*PHELIPPS, Sir Edward (*c*.1560–1614), 4 s. Thomas, Montacute, Som., yeoman. New Inn; MT 72, b 79, B 96, SL 03. JP. Described as 'a very great practiser' in Chancery and Star Chamber 96. Rich; built Montacute, 'the most magnificent house of its time in Som.'; landed income perhaps £1,363 p.a., although reputedly some £12,000 in debt at d. (*H. of P.*; Haward, *Reports*; *VCH, Som.*, iii; Clendinnen; Chamberlain, *Letters*, i; Som. RO, DD/PH.)

PHILLIPS, Fabian (d. 1597), 2 s. Robert, Leominster, Herefs., by Elizabeth, da. John Price. MT 60, b ?, AB 90; member Council in Marches 75, j. N. Wales 79–94; rec. Carmarthen by 78. JP; MP 72. Accused of recusant associations, defended by Abp. Whitgift. Acquired Orleton, Herefs., 80, and held other Worcs. lands. (*H. of P.*; Williams, *Welsh Judges*.)

PHILLIPS, William (*fl.* 1587–1625), s. Arthur, Brignall, Yorks. (NR), by Joan, da. William Conyers, Marske, Yorks. LI 87, b 96, AB 20; ? att. in sheriff's ct. London 93; unsuccessful candidate for rec. York 25. JP. Client of Sir Francis Bacon, who requested his promotion as AB. (*Yorks. Arch. & Top. J.*, vi; London Corp. RO, Rep. 23, fol. 107; York City AO, House Book B34, fol. 324ᵛ; *Yorks. Arch. Soc., Rec. Ser.*, iii; *VCH, Yorks. (NR)*, i.)

PLA(O)T(T), John (*c.*1584–*c.*1644), ?3 s. Sir Hugh, Bethnall Green, Middx. Magdalen, O, 01 ('of Wilts.'); Staple Inn; GI 08, b 14, B 34; j. W. Wales, 39–42; sent writ to be SL Dec. 43, but seemingly never created. Mar. Bridget. Friend of Bulstrode Whitelocke on Western circuit 30s. Will dated March 44 mentions houses at Cirencester and Newbury, Berks.; appoints John Whistler (for whom, see below) as overseer. (Williams, *Welsh Judges*; Baker, *Serjeants*; Black, *Docquets*; Additional 53726, fol. 82ᵛ; PCC 90 Rivers.)

POTTS, Nicholas (1546–1623), s. Ralph, Chalgrave, Beds. Christ Chuch, O, BA 61, MA 65; GI 67, b 77, B 94. Steward of Leighton Buzzard manor, Beds. JP; MP 84. Acquired advowson of Chalgrave church 79; assessed @ £10 in 09. (*H. of P.*; *VCH, Beds.*, iii; Beds. RO, CRT/120/18; Gleason, *Justices*; PCC 20 Swann.)

POULTON (Powton), Francis (d. 1642), 1 s. Ferdinando, Bourton, Bucks., and LI, barrister, by Catherine. LI 90, b 00, AB 31. Mar. Susan, da. John Foster. Catholic? In 34 sold Bourton and Durants manors to Sir Richard Minshall, barrister of LI and chamberlain to queen. Will mentions house in Twickenham, manor of Purton, Herts., other lands Herts. & Middx. Portions total £7,232 (8 children). Of Twickenham, Middx. at d. (Lipscomb, *Bucks.*, ii; *VCH, Bucks.*, ii–iii; PCC 77 Cambell.)

POWELL, Andrew (*c.*1565–1631), y.s. John ap David, Howell Trostrey, Monmouths., gent., by Elizabeth, da. Morris David John, of Gwaethfoed ap Cloddien, Monmouths. Hart Hall, O, 81; Clement's Inn; IT 85, b 95, B 10; rec. Brecon 04; j. Brecknock circuit 07, member Council in Marches 17; steward of Caldicot and Newton manors, farmed by Edward, earl of Worcester 27. Mar. (i) Syrophenicia, da. William Mathew, Radyr, Glam.;

(ii) Margaret, da. Mathew Herbert, Coldbrook, Monmouths. Inherited rent charge of £100 p.a. from father, also held numerous properties Monmouths., although lived mainly in London. (Lloyd, 'Welsh benchers'; Williams, *Welsh Judges*; J. A. Bradney, *History of Monmouths.*, 1904–32, iv; PCC 125 St John.)

POWELL, William (d. 1654), s. Richard, Bettws, Glam., Boulston, Pembs. and LI. Furnival's Inn; LI 99, b 05, B 23, SL 48; CJ W. Wales 47–53 (discharged); ? dep. clk. or BExch at Chester 05, 25. Mar. Elizabeth, da. Morgan Meyrick, and, possibly, four other wives. Commr. for assessment Glam., Herefs., 49–50. Said to be worth £300 p.a., 45. (Williams, *Welsh Judges*; G. T. Clark, *Limbus Patrum Morganiae* ..., 1886; Ormerod, *Chester*, i; *CSPD 1652–3*; *AOI*, ii; R. Symonds, *Diary*, CS, 1859.)

PRICE, William (d. 1594), s. John, Barton Regis, Glos., by Alice Brayne, Glos. (and of IT?) IT 67, b ?, B 91; ?escheator Monmouths. 91. Mar. Blanche, da. Nicholas Townley, Royle, Lancs. Will mentions gold rings, plate, lease of close and mill-house, dwelling-house in Barton; cash bequests total £32. (*HS*, xxi; *ITAdmR*; *List and Index Soc.*, lxxii; PCC 87 Dixy.)

PRIDEAUX, Sir Edmond (*c.*1554–1628), 2 s. Roger, Holsworthy and Soldon, Devon, gent., by Philippa, da. Roger York, SL. Lyon's Inn; IT 74, b 84, B 96; sheriff Devon 08, bt. 22. JP. Mar. (i) Bridget, da. Sir John Chichester, Kent; (ii) Katherine, da. Piers Edgecombe, Corn. (iii) Mary, da. Richard Reynell, East Ogwell, Devon. JP. Dedicatee, J. Prideaux, *Eight Sermons* (1621). Patron of Melancthon Thomas Jewell, suspended puritan rector of Thornbury, Devon, 04. Assessed @ £20 in 09. (*G.E.C.*, *Baronetage*; Gowers, thesis; Gleason, *Justices*.)

PROCTOR, Richard (d. 1669), of London. Jesus, C, 07; Barnard's Inn; GI 08, b 14, B 33; granted reversion of town clk., j. sheriff's ct., common sjt. or steward of Southwark, London, 20; MCh 65. JP. Mar. Bridget. Attended GI benchers' meetings throughout 40s; of Clerkenwell, Middx. at d. London Corp. RO, Rep. 35, fol. 66; Haydn, *Dignities*; Smyth, *Obituary*; PCC 164 Coke.)

PROWDE, Lewis (d. 1617), I s. George, Shrewsbury, Salop. burgess. St John's, C, 76; Furnival's Inn (barrister); LI 78, b 87, B 02; steward Westminster College; JKB (Ire.) 04 (but did not act); j. N. Wales 10–14; governor Sutton's Hospital (Charterhouse) 15; under-steward ct. of St Martin's-le-Grand, London. MP 14. Buried Westminster Abbey. (Williams, *Welsh Judges*; Ball, *Judges in Ireland*, i; Whitelocke, *Lib. Fam.*; *Trans. Salop Arch. Soc.*, 4th ser., xii.)

PRYTHERGH (Prydderch, Prothergh), Richard (*c.*1576–1653), I s. Richard, Myfyrian, Anglesey, by Margaret, da. Piers Puleston, Hafod-y-wern, Porthamel, Anglesey. St Edmund's Hall, O, 91, BA 94; Clifford's Inn; IT 96, b 05, B 22; j. Chester 36–47. JP. Mar. Martha. Requested burial without sermon; associate and kinsman of Catholics; claimed that sermon preached by John Donne at the Temple church 15 'had too much learning for ignoramus', but bequeathed an Italian Bible, 'two books of Amesius called Bellarmin Enervatus' (i.e. STC 550 or 551), among other books. Royalist. Bought estate at Llanidan, Anglesey, also held lands Denbighs., Caernarfons. (Lloyd, 'Welsh benchers'; Williams, *Welsh Judges*; SP 30/ 53/7; NLW MSS Chirke Castle 148 and Carreg-lwyd 2408, 2284; PCC Brent 231.)

*PULESTON(E), John (*c.*1583–1659), 1 s. Richard, Kings Worthy, Hants, rector, by Alice, da. David Lewis, Burcot, Oxon. Oriel, O, 01; Clifford's Inn; MT 06, b 16, B 34, SL 48. Devout puritan; fined 19 for serving flesh in MT hall on St Matthew's Day, but accompanied Richard Cartwright to advise Abp. Laud on church law 34. Succeeded to Emral estate on d. of uncle. (*DWB*; *MTR*, ii. 640; *CSPD 1634–5*.)

*PYE, Sir Walter (1571–1635), 1 s. Roger, The Mynde, Herefs., by Bridget, da. Thomas or Walter Kyrle, Herefs. St John's, O; MT 90, b 97, AB 17, B 18; CJ Brecknock circuit 17, att. of Wards and ktd. 21, steward Leominster 23. MP 97, 21–8. Mar. (i) Joan, da. William Rudhall, Herefs; (ii) Hester, da. John Ingland, wid. Alderman Ellis Crispe, London. Wealthy; reputedly left estate of *c.* £2,000 p.a.; IPM shows extensive Herefs. lands, nominal value £27. 15s. p.a. (*H. of P.*; McParlin, thesis; Whitelocke, *Lib. Fam.*; Williams, *Welsh Judges*; Aylmer, *King's Servants*; Knowler, i. 506; Herefs. RO, K79.)

PYNE, Hugh (*c.*1570–1628), 2 s. John (next below). LI 88, b 96, B 14; rec. Weymouth and Melcombe Regis 15; fee'd counsel to Queen Anne. JP; MP 28. Mar. Mabel, da. Henry Staverton, Durley, Hants. Imprisoned after publicly criticizing Charles I at Ilchester sessions 26. Acqd. manor of Cathanger, Som., held other lands Som., Devon, and Dorset; nominal IPM value £37 p.a.; left cash bequests £2,866, including £1,000 to grandda. Said to be worth at least £2,000 p.a. 27. (Mr J. P. Ferris, personal communication; Barnes, *Somerset*; Hutchins, *Dorset*, ii; *VCH, Som.*, iv; WARD 7/78/139; SP16/66/78; PCC 95 Barrington; Birch, *Court and Times of Charles I*, i. 295.)

PYNE, John (d. 1609), of Hants when admitted to LI 73; b 81, B 95. JP. Mar. Juliana, da. John Towse, Swell, Som. Listed as 'lawyer of practice' 99. Assessed @ £20 in 09; purchased lands in Curry Malet, Stowey, and Newport, Som., with w.'s dower, 'since which purchase God hath blessed me with many children, but also with more lands and livings'. Held Pentridge manor, Dorset, and lands in Glastonbury, Long Sutton, and Baltonsborough, Som. Bequests included £10 towards new LI chapel. Of Curry Mallet, Som., at d. (Mr I. P. Collis, personal communication; WARD 7/44/163; J. Collinson, *The History and Antiquities of the County of Somerset*, 1791, i; *APC 1599–1600*; PCC 19 Wingfield.)

*RADCLIFFE, Sir George (1593–1657), 1 s. Nicholas, Thornhill, Yorks., esq. ('bred to the law'). GI 12, b 18, B 32; fee'd counsel York by 31–2; unsuccessful candidate for rec. Doncaster and Pontefract 28. Granted £500 p.a. in compensation for his 'practice and profession of law' 33. (*Radcliffe Correspondence*, ed. Whitaker; York City AO, Chamberlain's accounts 1631–2; *CCC*.)

RAVENSCROFT, William (1561–1628), 2 s. George, Bretton, Flints., gent. by Dorothy, da. John Davis, Hawarden, Flints. Brasenose, O, 78, BA 80; LI 80, b 89, AB 04, B 21; att.-gen. Chester 97, 03; clk. of petty bag, Chancery 98. MP 86, 97, 01–28. Never married. Dedicatee, T. Ravenscroft, *Melismata* (1611); A. Taylor, *Newes from Jerusalem* (1623). Follower of Ellesmere and Sir Julius Caesar. Adjudged able to lend crown £16. 13s. 4d. *c*.11. Engaged as surety for £7,000 to earl of Bridgewater. Cash bequests £622; £100 to LI to pay house debts, bequests to 'dear friends' Christopher Brooke and Nicholas Ducke of LI (for whom, see above). (*DWB*; *H. of P.*; Ormerod, *Chester*, i; Clendinnen; Ellesmere 2942; PCC 99 Barrington.)

*REEVE, Sir Edmund (*c*.1589–1647), s. Christopher, Aylsham and Felthorpe, Norfolk, att., by Martha, da. Edward Grimston, Oxborough. Caius, C, 05; Barnard's Inn; GI 07, b 11, B 32, SL 37; rec. Yarmouth 29, steward Norwich 31. JP. Mar. Mary Corie, Brampton, Norfolk. Son assessed @ £1,000 1647; held manors and lands Norfolk and Suffolk; left rent charges £160 p.a. (*HS*, lxxxvi; Blomefield and Parkin, *Norfolk*, v; Manship, *Yarmouth*, ii; Norfolk RO, Norwich City Records 18(a); PCC 49 Fines; *CCAM*.)

REYNELL (Revell), Richard (d. 1631), 4 s. George, Malston, Devon, esq., by Joan, da. Lewis Fortescue, Fallpit, BExch. New Inn; MT 85, b 94, B 14; ?clk. in office of lord treasurer's remembrancer, Exch. by 93; rec. Bradninch 04–16, fee'd counsel Totnes 01, Exeter 04 (as Reynolds), rec. Totnes by 14. JP; MP 93. Mar. Mary, da. John Peryam, Exeter. Puritan. Acquired manors of Shobrooke (£1,600) and Gunton (£1,200); bequeathed £100 p.a. to y. son, portions of £1,000 ea. to 3 das. Of Creedy-Wiger, Devon, at d. (Not to be confused with namesake, of East Ogwell, who was ktd. 25, nor with the Richard Reynell of Devon ktd. at Theobalds, 23 July 22, *pace H. of P.*; cf. PCC 48 St John and *MTR*, ii. 787. *H. of P.*; *HS*, vi; Devon RO, Z1/15/14, 48/26/1–6, 27/1/28–9, 48/8/1a–c, and ECA, Chamberlain's accounts, 1603–31; PCC 48 St John.)

RICH, Sir Robert (d. *c*.1646), s. Richard, South Weald, Essex, esq., by Rachel, da. Thomas Newborough, Berkeley, Glos. Furnival's Inn; LI 90, b 98, B 18; MCh 18–46, ktd. 19. Commr. for gold and silver thread 36; commr. for scandalous speeches 38. Mar. Anne. JP. Listed as inhabitant of 5 Chancery Lane houses worth £100 p.a. in 38; lent money on recognizance. (Not to be confused with namesake who was knighted by

17 when involved in dispute with Sir Edward Coke.) (Morant, *Essex*, i; *HS*, xiii; Haydn, *Dignities*; Bacon, *Works*, vi. 327; G. Eland, *Shardeloes Papers*, 1947; Dale, *Inhabitants 1638*; *CSPD 1634–5, 1635–6, 1637–8, 1638–9*.)

*RICHARDSON, Sir Thomas (1569–1635), s. Rev. Thomas, Mulbarton, Norfolk, by Agnes. Christ's, C, 84; Thavies Inn; LI 87, b 95, B 10, SL 14. JP. Said to have left estate worth more than £3,000 p.a.; bound to give w. jointure of £300, in fact provided £700 p.a.; portion of £2,000 to da. Named Thomas Bedingfield and Sir Richard Hutton (for whom, see above) as executors. (Cozens-Hardy, 'Norfolk Lawyers'; '*Merry Passages*', ed. Lippincott; *Norf. Rec. Soc.*, xx. 71; Knowler, i. 373; Blomefield and Parkin, *Norfolk*, v, viii, ix; PCC 35 Sadler.)

RIGBY, Hugh (d. 1642), 2 s. Edward, Burgh, Duxbury, Lancs., and GI, esq., by Dorothy, da. Hugh Anderton, Clayton, esq. St John's, C, 05, BA 09; LI 10, b 17, B 33; escheator Lancs. 08–40; co-clk. of Crown, Lancaster 30; rec. Liverpool 34. JP. Married. Bought Travers manor 25; held 2 houses, Sankie and the Hutt, Childwall, nr. Liverpool; inventory valued personalty at £450. 4s. 6d. (Somerville, *Office Holders*; *VCH, Lancs.*, v, vi; *Chetham Soc.*, NS x; Lancs. RO, Inv. Hugh Rigby 1642).

RISDEN, Thomas (*c*.1564–1641), y.s. Thomas Bableigh, Parkham, Devon, IT bencher, by Willmot, da. Thomas Gifford, Halsbury. IT 85, b 95, B 10; fee'd counsel Totnes by 17; rec. Torrington by 20. JP. Mar. Mary Hawkins. Of Sandwell, Devon, at d. (*Trans. Devon Assocn.*, xviii; Devon RO, Totnes borough accounts.)

RIVES, Sir William (d. 1648), 6 s. John, Damory Court, Blandford, Dorset, MT barrister, by Amy Harvey, of Dorset. MT 93, b 00, B 19; j. W. Wales 19–21, ktd. 19, att.-gen. (Ire.) 19–36, JKB (Ire.) 36–42. King's learned counsel (extraordinary), 42. Mar. (i) da. Latham, Latham Hall, Lancs.; (ii) Dorothy, da. John Waldram. Acquired substantial estates in Co. Down, Ire., although described 42 as 'having lost all his fortunes in that kingdom'. Of Dublin at d. (Ball, *Judges in Ireland*, i; Williams, *Welsh Judges*; Hutchins, *Dorset*, iv; Knowler, i; NLW, MS Carreg-lwyd, 1589; PCC 151 Grey.)

ROB(B)INS, Henry (1562–1613), of Matson, Glos. Magd. Hall, O, 81; Clement's Inn; LI 83, b 91, B 09; town clk. Gloucester 03. Mar. Margaret Hyett, Westbury, Glos. Provided 'one corselet' 08. Of Gloucester at d. (M. Robbins, *Gleanings of the Robins*, 1908; Rudder, *Glos.*; Metcalfe, ed., *Glos. Vis.*; *Glos. N & Q*, iv; J. Smyth, *The Names . . . of all the able and sufficient men . . . 1608* (1902), hence *Men and Armour*.)

*ROLLE, Henry (*c*.1590–1656). IT 09, b 17, B 33, fee'd counsel London 36, common pleader 44. JP. Mar. Margaret, da. Thomas Bennet, London, alderman. Signed Devon protest against forced loan 14. Assessed on £10 lands, Crewkerne, Som., 41. Of Shapwick, Som., and London at d.

(London Corp. RO, Rep. 50, fol. 102, and Rep. 57, fol. 240ᵛ; *HS*, xvii; Ellesmere 2504; PCC 366 Berkeley.)

ROLT, Edward (d. 1616), 1 s. Thomas, Bolnhurst, Beds., yeoman. GI 82, b ?, B 10; rec. Bedford 12. JP. Mar. Jane, da. John Baldwin, Great Staughton, Hunts. Requested learned man to preach at funeral. Bequeathed portion of £500 ea. to 4 das., and £300 ea. to 3 das. Lands of £60 p.a. value, plus manor of Pertenhall, to w. Of Pertenhall at d. (*HS*, xix; *VCH, Beds.*, iii; Beds. RO, WG 11; PCC 105 Cope.)

*RUMSEY, Walter (1584–1660), 2 s. GI 03, b 08, B 31; escheator Monmouths. 99, dep.-steward Hereford 23. Owned land in Usk, w. brought estate at Llanover. (Williams, *Welsh Judges*; Bradney, *History of Monmouths.*, iii.)

SALTER, Sir Edward (*c.*1548–1646), s. William, Iver, Bucks., by Alice Sutton, Hunts. ? Queens', C, 77; GI 80, b 89, B 26; ktd., MCh 21, king's carver in ordinary by 25. JP; MP 10, 21. Mar. Ursula, da. Edward Brocket, Herts. Assessed £10 in lands in 09. Acquired Cornwalls manor, Iver, by 17; purchased other lands Bucks. and Middx., leased Whitchurch manor, Dorset. (*HS*, lviii; Haydn, *Dignities*; SP 16/180/16; Gleason, *Justices*; *VCH, Bucks.*, iii; *Recs. of Bucks.*, xv; PCC 41 Fines.)

SARE (Sayer), Adam (d. 1623), 1 s. Thomas, Norton, Kent, secondary in office of prothonotary, CP, by Joan, da. John Ady, Kent. Jesus, C, *c.*90, BA 94; IT 94, b 03, B 19. Mar. (i) Sara, da. Thomas Archdale, London; (ii) Dorothy Bowyer of Salisbury, Wilts. Granted arms 13. Estate valued @ £200, *c.*13. Will prescribes all lands and goods to be sold to pay debts, any surplus divided equally among 5 children. Inherited manor of Provenders, Norton, sold by heirs. Of St Saviour's, Surrey at d. (*HS*, xlii, lxii, lxvi; *ITAdmR*; Hasted, *Kent*, ii; HMC, *Salisbury*, xxii; PCC 30 Byrde.)

SAUNDERSON, Thomas (*c.*1569–1642), 3 s. Robert, Saxby, Lincs., by Katherine, da. Vincent Grantham. Broadgates Hall, O, 87, BA 91; LI 91, b 98, B 17. JP. Mar. (i) Jane, da. Denzil Holles; (ii) Dorcas, da. Sir Julius Caesar, MR (for whom, see below, Appendix F); (iii) Dorothy, da. Richard Maddison, Mablethorpe, Lincs. Learned puritan. Bequeathed silver salt to bench table 'for a seasonable remembrance of my old and never dying duty and love I owe unto my most honoured mother of LI'. Portions of £500 to 2 das., £80 p.a. to w. Of Stratford-le-Bow, Middx., 31, and Gainsborough, Lincs. at d. (*HS*, lii; PCC 128 Cambell; *The Visitation of . . . Lincoln, 1592*, ed. W. C. Metcalfe, 1882.)

SCAMBLER, Adam (1569–1645), 2 s. Edmund, bp. of Norwich. St John's, C, 81, BA 86; IT 87, b ?, B 12; escheator Suffolk 00. JP. Mar. Dorothy, da. John Athow, Brisley, Norfolk. Composed pious verses for own MI at Hevingham, Norfolk. (*DNB*, s.v. Scambler, Edmund; *HS*, lxxxv; *List and Index Soc.*, lxxii; Blomefield and Parkin, *Norfolk*, vi.)

*SELDEN, John (1584–1654). IT 03, b 12, B 33. Will mentions manors and lands in Staffs., and Lincs. (PCC 253 Alchin; *Radicals*, iii; Tuck, *Natural Law Theories*; *Som. Rec. Soc.*, lxxiv.)

SELWYN, Jasper (*c*.1561–1635), 2 s. William, King's Stanley, Glos., yeoman clothier, by Catherine, da. John Clutterbuck, Stanley St Leonard's, Glos. Magd. Hall, O, 80; Clement's Inn; LI 83, b 91, B 10. JP. Mar. Margaret, da. Thomas Robbins, Glos. In 32 recommended by Sir John Bridgeman as commr. for Oyer et Terminer, Glos. Furnished one corselet and musket 08, assessed @ £8 in 09. Bought manors of Matson *c*.00 (£1,700), Bulleyn's and Upton St Leonard 08; held lands in Uley and King's Stanley. Of Matson at d. (*Trans. Bristol and Glos. Arch. Soc.*, ii, xliv, xlvi; *HS*, xxi; *Index Lib.*, ix; Atkyns, *Glos.*; Smyth, *Men and Armour*; Gleason, *Justices.*)

SHEFFIELD, Robert (d. 1602), 1 s. George, Seaton, Rutland, by Elizabeth, da. Robert Harrison, Stow, Northants. Christ's, C, 71; Barnard's Inn; GI 77, b 84, B 02. Mar. Dorothy Boughton, Cawston, War. Bought Downhall, Seaton, 97, inherited Uphall from father; also held mill and lands, nominal IPM value £7. 13s. 4d. (*HS*, iii; *Leics. and Rutland N & Q*, iii; *VCH, Rutland*, ii; C142/270/132.)

*SHELTON, Sir Richard (1578–1647), 2 s. John, mercer. Clement's Inn; IT 97, b 06, B 22; Crown counsel-at-large 41. JP; MP 24, 26, 28. Patron of Paul Micklethwaite as master of Temple Church. Contributed £150 to Staffs. Parliamentary committee 44. Cash bequests totalled £846, plus £100 p.a. Various lands in Staffs. and War., some recently purchased. Trustees included William Booth of MT (for whose father, see above); of West Bromwich, Staffs. at d. (*HS*, lxiii, lxxii; Erdeswick, *Staffs*; *EHR*, lxxiii. 239 n; *VCH, Staffs*, xvii; *Staffs. Rec. Soc.*, 4th ser., i; PCC 82 Essex.)

*SHERFIELD (Shervill), Henry (*c*.1574–1634), 3 s. Richard, of Wilts. (or Walhampton, Hants), by Matilda, da. John Martin. 'Instructed in learning as well in the country schools as afterwards in the university'; LI 98, b 06, B 20; steward of earl of Salisbury 17, rec. Southampton 18, rec. Salisbury 23. Mar. (i) Mary, da. William Hodson, Wilton, Wilts.; (ii) Rebecca, da. Christopher Bailey, Southwick, Wilts. Assessed @ £35 as knighthood compounder Wilts. 31; died some £6,000 in debt. (*Radicals*, iii; Hants RO, 44M69/xxxvi/1, lxv/1, and *passim*; *Wilts. N & Q*, i. 109.)

SHERLAND (Shirland), Christopher (1593–1632), 1 s. Thomas, Milden, Suffolk, and MT, by Anne, da. Sir Christopher Yelverton, JQB. Queen's, O, 07, BA 10; GI 04, b 17, B 27; rec. Northampton 23. MP 24–8. Mar. Jane, da. Edward Oglethorpe, Smithfield, London. Founding member Providence Island Co., Feoffee for Impropriations. Puritan, parliamentary radical. Will mentions properties London and Lincs.; substantial bequests for setting poor to work, buying up impropriations, and to individual godly ministers; cousin John Hampden executor, Richard

Sibbes preached funeral sermon. (*Radicals*, iii; PCC 10 Audley; History of Parliament, 1604–29: draft biography.)

SHIRLEY (Shurley), Sir George (1569–1647), 2 s. Thomas, Isfield, Sussex, esq., by Anne, da. Sir Nicholas Pelham. Clare, C, 87; MT 88, b 97, B 15, SL 20; fee'd counsel Rye 08, CJKB (Ire.) and ktd. 20. Mar. Mary, da. Edward Halffhed (or Halfhyde), Herts. Returned from Ireland (where he bought land) 41, d. Isfield. (Ball, *Judges in Ireland*; *HS*, liii; *CCC*; Boys, *Sandwich*; PCC 246 Fines.)

*SHUTE, Robert (d. 1621). Christ's, C, 99, BA 02, MA 05; GI 00, b 05, B 17; clk. of the Crown, King's Bench 16. JP. Dedicatee, J. Lewis, *Ignis Coelestis* (1620). In debt by 13, when earl of Pembroke a patron. (Whitelocke, *Lib. Fam.*; Calnan, thesis; J. Nicholl, *Some Account of the . . . Ironmongers*, 1851.)

SHUTTLEWORTH, Ughtred (*c.*1589–*c.*1637), 3 s. Thomas, Gawthorpe, Lancs., esq., by Anne, da. Richard Lever, Little Lever, esq. Brasenose, O, 05; LI 06, b 14, B 30 (disbenched 33 for refusing to read and not indicating his intentions or attending council). Manor of Forsett, Yorks., settled on, with others, 96. (*Chetham Soc.*, lxxxviii; *LIBB*, ii; *VCH, Yorks. (NR)*, i; Whitaker, *Richmondshire*, i.)

SKIPWITH, Edward (d. *c.*1620), s. Sir William, South Ormsby, Lincs., by Ann, da. John Tothby, of Tothby. Magd., C, 71; Clement's Inn (barrister); LI 75, b 84, B 00; commr. for gaol delivery Grimsby 92; escheator Lincs. 18–19. JP; MP 01. Mar. (i) Mary, da. Richard Hansard, Biscathorpe; (ii) Elizabeth, da. Richard Death, Gosberton. Requested Christian burial 'honoured with a reverend preaching of that word of truth' which he honoured during lifetime. Rated @ £15 in 09; bequeathed £500 ea. to 2 das. (*H. of P.*; *HS*, lii; HMC, *Fourteenth Rep.*, viii; Gleason, *Justices*; PCC 19 Soame.)

SMITH, Sir Roger (*c.*1561–1655), y.s. Erasmus, Husbands Bosworth, Leics., by da. of one Bidd. Hart Hall, O, 85, BA (from Exeter) 90; LI 94, b 02, AB 19; chamber seized 30, because out of commons since made AB, whereupon he assaulted barrister occupant and failed to appear before LI council; ktd. 35. JP. Mar. (i) Jane, da. Sir Edward Heron, CBExch; (ii) Ann, da. Thomas Goodman, St Botolph's Aldgate, London. Parliamentary commr. for Leics. 45–52. Assessed £400 in 46, as of Clerkenwell, Middx. (Nichols, *Leics.*, ii; *LIBB*, ii; LI MS Red Book, fols. 140–1; *AOI*, i, ii; *CCAM*.)

SMYTH, Robert (*fl.* 1583–1614), 2 s. John, Hundon, Suffolk. ? Caius, C, 78, BA 82; MT 83, b 91, B 11; disbenched 14 for abusing several benchers and Sir Thomas Richardson of LI (for whom, see above); ? clk. or att. outer ct. (i.e. common council) London 93; attendant on alderman in deputation to rec. 07. Mar. ? Katherine, da. Thomas Mantell, Westminster, at St Andrew Hubbert, East Cheap, London, 08. ? Solicitor to Lady

Arabella Stuart and imprisoned 14. (Presumably not the Robert Smyth of Alderton, Suffolk, who mar. Mabel, da. of John Fastolfe, and d. 18; cf. *East Anglian*, 3rd ser., viii; C142/371/139. *MTR*, ii, 580; London Corp. RO, Rep. 23, fol. 130; N. Brett-James, *The Growth of Stuart London*, 1935; *Letters of John Holles*.)

SNIGGE, Sir George (*c*.1545–1617), 1 s. George, Bristol, merchant (? bencher MT). Christ Church, O, 64, BA 66; MT 67, b 75, B 90, SL 03; rec. Bristol 93, BExch 05, CJ Brecknock circuit 08. JP; MP 89, 97, 01, 04. Mar. Alice, da. William Young, Ogbourne, Wilts. Assessed £10 in 99 lawyers' subsidy; Glos. lands nominal IPM value £13. 6s. 8d. (*H. of P.*, but account of parentage given cannot be reconciled with *MTR* or *MTAdmR*; *Trans. Bristol and Glos. Arch. Soc.*; xxxi. 245; Baker, *Serjeants*; *HS*, xxi; PCC 11 Meade; *APC 1590–1600*; C142/377/95.)

*SOTHERTON, John (*c*.1562–1631), 1 s. IT 88, b 97, B 10; fee'd counsel for Norwich by 07. (Norfolk RO, Norwich City Records 17b.)

SOUTH, Thomas (*c*.1574–1636), 1 s. Thomas, Norley, Baddesley, Hants, gent. Hart Hall, O, 89; New Inn; MT 96, b 04, B 22; burgess Lymington 03, rec. 22; rec. Winchester 35. JP. Mar. Abigail. Bought Wimbourne manor, Hants, with William Dunch 19, but perhaps only as agent. Will seeks burial St Clement's Winchester, 'at the least charge that may be'. All lands, personal estate, plate, and money to w. Of Winchester at d. (Richmond, thesis; Woodward, *Hampshire*, iii; *VCH, Hants*, iii; PCC 48 Pile.)

SOUTHWORTH, Thomas (d. 1625), s. Edward, London, merchant, by Jane, da. Edward Lloyd, Salop. GI 87, b ?, B 14; rec. Wells by 13. JP; MP 14, 21, 24; surveyor of Wells Cathedral lands 14. Mar. Jane, da. Nicholas Mynne, Norfolk. Nuncupative will made at Wells in parlour of his dwelling-house: 'I leave all my goods and estate to my w. and am sorry that I have no more to give her.' (*HS*, xi; Barnes, *Somerset*; Gleason, *Justices*; HMC, *Wells*, ii; PCC 139 Clarke.)

STAMPE, Edward (d. 1598), 3 s. Richard, Ilsley, Berks., gent., by Anne, da. Henry Anneslowe, Mapledurham, Oxon. Clement's Inn; MT 71, b 77, B 94; fee'd counsel Henley-on-Thames 90. Mar. Philippa. (*HS*, lvi; *Genealogist*, NS ii; J. S. Burn, *History of Henley-on-Thames*, 1861; PCC 70 Lewyn.)

STAPLETON, Edward (d. 1636), 5 s. Sir Robert, Myton, Yorks.; of Maxstoke, War. at admission to IT 78; b 87, B 01. JP. Mar. Mary, wid. John Coope, London, fishmonger. Solicitor for Sir Richard Gargrave 11. Buried Temple Church. (*HS*, xciii; H. E. Chetwynd-Stapylton, *The Stapletons of Yorkshire*, 1897; STAC 5/S15/18 and 5/S73/40; HMC, *Sackville*, i; *ITR*, ii.)

STEPHENS, Thomas (*c*.1558–1613), 3 s. Edward, Eastington, Stroud and Horsley, Glos., gent., by Joan, da. Richard Fowler, Stonehouse, Glos.

Magd. Hall, O, 75, BA 78; New Inn; MT 78, b 85, B 04; counsel, auditor, and att.-gen. to Henry, Prince of Wales. MP 93. Mar. Elizabeth, da. John Stone, London. Puritan; dedicatee, R. Cleaver, *Foure Sermons* (1613); bequeathed £10 p.a. for 'godly learned preacher' at Stroud. Wealthy; will suggests estate had capital value of over £18,000; substantial purchases in Glos.; portions of £1,000 to 2 das. of Lypiatt and Stroud, Glos., at d. (*H. of P.*; *HS*, xxi; Rudder, *Glos.*; *VCH, Glos.*, xi; Harleian 7007, fol. 144; *Trans. Bristol and Glos. Arch. Soc.*, xiii, xvii, lxxx; PCC 109 Capell.)

STONE, John (d. 1640), y.s. William, Segenhoe, Beds., and London. King's, C, 84; IT 86, b 95, B 12, SL 40; chief clk. to secondary, Bread, Wood and Giltspur St. compters, London, before 09, fee'd counsel London by 09, common pleader by 22. Mar. (i) Cicely Cornwall, Addington, Northants; (ii) Alice, da. Richard Alinery, Chester, alderman. Author of *Reading upon the Statute of . . . Bankrupts* (1656). Bequeathed £10 for restoration of St Paul's Cathedral; £10 to Mr [John] Godwin for funeral sermon. Rich; bought at least 5 Herts. manors by 27; also held lands in Surrey, had £3,880 loaned out upon speciality; assessed among 'most ablest' inhabitants of Coleman St., London, 40; portions of £2,000 for 2 grandchildren. (*HS*, xvii; London Corp. RO, Rep. 29, fol. 119^v; Overall, *Remembrancia*; *VCH, Herts.*, iii–iv; Clutterbuck, *Herts.*, iii; *Guildhall Misc.*, iii. 2; Herts. RO, 73912–73926, 73932–7, 73950–3, 73961–2, 73964–6, 73969–71, 75358–62; *Misc. Gen. et Her.*, 2nd ser., ii. 87; PCC 172 Coventry.)

STRODE, Sir John (c.1561–1642), 2 s. John, Parnham, Beaminster, Dorset, esq., by Katherine, da. Gregory, Lord Cromwell, Leeds Castle, Kent. New Inn; MT 83, b 90, B 11; rec. Bridport 18; ktd. 23. JP; MP 21, 25. Mar. (i) Anne, da. William Chaldecote, Quarleston, Dorset; (ii) Anne, da. Sir John Wyndham, Orchard Wyndham, Dorset. Pious; respected bishops and priests of God, had consecrated chapel in house at Chantmarle. Rich; bought lands worth *c*. £11,000 06–37; assessed on £20 lands in 41; rental £351 in 28. Of Chantmarle, Dorset, at d. (Mr J. P. Ferris, personal communication; Hutchins, *Dorset*, ii; Dorset RO, MW/M4; Aspinall-Oglander, *Nunwell Symphony*; *Wilts. N & Q*, vi. 214; Bayley, *Civil War in Dorset*.)

SWANTON, William (d. 1618), 5 s. Nicholas, Wincanton, Som. New Inn; MT 81, b 90, B 09; ? escheator Som. 11. JP. Mar. Elizabeth, da. Thomas Aubrey, Chaddenwick, Wilts. (Cockburn, *History of English Assizes*; *List and Index Soc.*, lxxii; *Commons 1660–90*, ed. Henning; *MTR*, ii. 628.)

SWAYNE, Richard (c.1556–c.1637), 3 s. John, Blandford Forum, Dorset, merchant, by Agnes, da. Robert Reeves or Ryves, Damorey Court. New Inn; MT 73, b 82, B 97; rec. Poole 92, Weymouth 94, Blandford 06; steward for Dorset, Duchy of Lancaster, 03. JP; MP 97, 01. Mar. Mary, da. William Grove, Ferne, Wilts. Requested burial without pomp. Paid £35 knighthood composition 31. Inherited moiety of Stoke Hyde manor, and messuages in Blandford; all houses in fee simple, Stoke Hyde manor and all goods and chattels to be sold to pay debts and legacies; dwelling-house in Blandford mortgaged for £100. (Mr J. P. Ferris, personal communication; *H. of P.*; Hutchins, *Dorset*, i, iii; E401/2450; PCC 17 Goare.)

TALBOT, Thomas (1585–1642), 1 s. Thomas, Wymondham, Norfolk, civil lawyer, by Katherine Hast. Trinity Hall, C, 01; Thavies Inn; LI 05, b 12, AB 36; ? escheator Norfolk and Suffolk 24–5. JP. Mar. Anne Herne, Tibbenham, Norfolk, where buried 25 Sept. 42. (*CSPD, Add. 1625–49*; Gleason, *Justices*; *List and Index Soc.*, lxxii; Mrs M. Talbot, personal communication.)

*TANFIELD, Sir Lawrence (c.1554–1625), 1 s. Robert, Burford, Oxon., and MT, by Wilgiford Fitzherbert. IT 69, b ?, B 91, SL 03; fee'd counsel to Oxford Univ. 97; rec. Woodstock 02. JP; MP 84–04. Mar. Elizabeth, da. Giles Symonds, Cley, Norfolk. Rich; assessed @ £30 in 99 lawyers' subsidy; bought Burford and Great Tew manors, Oxon., also held lands in Glos. MI Burford. (*H. of P.*; *APC 1599–1600*; *VCH, Oxon.*, xi; Clendinnen; Mr Alan Davidson, personal communication.)

TANFIELD, Robert (1584–1639), 1 s. Robert, Gayton, Northants, and MT, barrister. Emmanuel, C, 99; New Inn; MT 99, b 07, B 24; counsel to Edward, Lord Montagu of Boughton. JP. Mar. Susan, da. Godfrey Chibnal, Northants. Puritan; associate of Simonds D'Ewes, 'assuredly hoped' to be among the 'elect Saints'. Owed £1,000 on mortgage by Lord Fitzwilliam; left manor of Loddington and other Northants lands to cousin Sir Richard Lane of MT (for whom, see above) in trust for 2 das., £60 p.a. to married da. and husband until trustees pay them £1,000 to purchase land. Of Loddington at d. (Metcalfe, ed., *Northants Vis.*; Baker, *Northants*, ii; Gleason, *Justices*; D'Ewes, *Diary*; Harleian 646, fol. 72ᵛ; HMC, *Buccleuch*, iii; PCC 55 Harvey.)

*TATE, Francis (1560–1616). Magd. Hall, O, 77; Staple Inn; MT 79, b 87, B 08; j. S. Wales 04; fee'd counsel Northampton by 02. (*H. of P.*)

TAYLOR, Richard (c.1579–1641), s. Thomas, Bolnhurst, Beds., yeoman, by Elizabeth, da. William King, Chalverston, Beds. Christ's, C, 97, BA 00; LI 00, b 07, B 23, SL 40; dep.-rec. Bedford 17; escheator Beds. and Bucks. 18; manorial steward to Sir Thomas Boteler. JP; MP 21, 24, 25, 28. Mar. Elizabeth, da. William Boteler, Biddenham. Dedicatee, Thomas Gataker, *A Marriage Praier* (1624); said to have defended 'godly men' against the bp. of Lincoln's apparitors 34. Assessed £50 for forced loan in 26; bought Clapham manor 27; assessed £6 in lands for 28–9 subsidy; provided £600 each for 6 younger ss. (*Beds. Hist. Rec. Soc.*, xxv; *HS*, xix; *VCH, Beds.*, ii–iii; *CSPD 1634–5*, 149; Beds. RO, T/53/10 and TW 728, 755; PCC 19 Cambell.)

TEMPEST, Sir Thomas (c.1594–post-1656), 1 s. Rowland, Newcastle-upon-

Tyne, esq., by Barbara, da. Thomas Calverley, Littleburn, Durham. Queen's, O, 10; LI 13, b 20, B 36; king's att. in bishopric of Durham 32, att.-gen. (Ire.) and ktd. 40. Mar. (i) Eleanor, da. William Tempest, Hadham, Oxon.; (ii) Elizabeth, wid. Robert Crewes, St Pancras, Middx. Showed 'abundant religiousness' and exchanged prayers with John Harington (for whom, see above). Returned to England by Feb. 42; royalist, assessed @ £250 in 46; compounded for delinquency (being in king's quarters at York), and paid £134 as his third in 49. Son John nominated knight of the Royal Oak. (Surtees, *Durham*, iv; Additional 40670, fol. 18; *Surtees Soc.*, iv, ci, cxi; *CCC*; *CCAM*; *Som. Rec. Soc.*, lxxiv; *CJ*, iv. 472.)

TERWYTT (Tyrwhit), Thomas (d. 1625), 4 s. Marmaduke, Cammeringham, Lincs., gent., by Ellen or Helen, da. Lionel Reresby, Thrybergh, Yorks. LI 94, b 02, B 18. JP. Mar. Mary. Will mentions messuages and tenements in Gainsborough, plus goods, debts, household stuff, plate, jewels, rings, and utensils, to be divided equally among 6 children. (*HS*, lii; Lincs. RO, Stow Wills 1624–5/232.)

*THELWALL, Sir Eub(u)le (1552–1630). GI 90, b 99, AB 11, B 24; chief master Alienations Office 99; steward and rec. Ruthin 05; reversion, prothonotary, and chief clk. N. Wales 07. Dedicatee, works by W. Crashawe and R. Wright; complained of shortage of preaching ministers, and supported act against scandalous clergymen 28. Substantial properties in Denbighs., and messuage in Theydon Garnon, Essex. (*DWB*; J. Y. W. Lloyd, *History of ... Powys Fadog*, 1881–7, iv. 319; *CD 1628*, iii; NLW Wynnstay MS M1754; PCC 104 Scroope.)

THOMAS, William (*fl.* 1589–1624), 2 s. Thomas ap William, Bettwys, Glam. by Jenet or Catherine, da. Griffith John ap Lewis, of Cilybebyll, Glam. ?Corpus Christi, C, 88; Furnival's Inn; LI 89, b 97, B 13; agent for Viscount Lisle 11; rec. Carmarthen *c*.14. JP; MP 14. (G. T. Clark, *Limbus Patrum Morganiae*, 1886; G.E.C., *Baronetage*; Lloyd, *Gentry of S.W. Wales*; Phillips, *Welsh JPs*; STAC 8/6/11; *Exchequer Procs. Concerning Wales*, ed. Jones.)

THORESBY (Thursbie), Henry (d. 1615), 1 s. William, Leeds, by Anne, da. Lord Scrope. Jesus, C, 67; LI 73, b 81, B 95; escheator Yorks. 88; MCh 07. JP. Mar. Jane, da. John Palmer, Clerkenwell, Middx., esq. Original governor of Charterhouse; left 5 marks towards new LI chapel. Held London properties, plus Borden and Thoresby manors, Yorks., worth at least £440 p.a. Assessed £20 for privy seal, Hackney, temp. Jac. I. and £20 in lands in 09. (Foster, ed., *Yorks. Vis.*; *List and Index Soc.*, lxxii; Gleason, *Justices*; *VCH, Yorks. (NR)*, i; Haydn, *Dignities*; R. Thoresby, *Ducatus Leodiensis*, ed. T. D. Whitaker, 1816; PCC 61 Rudd.)

THORNTON, Thomas (1553–1632), 1 s. Henry, Newnham, Northants, gent., by Anne, da. William Wilmer, Ryton, War. New Inn; LI 75, b 84,

AB 20; fee'd counsel, rec. Daventry from *c*.91. Mar. Elizabeth, da. Henry Acres (or Dacres), Chilvers Coton, War. Pious puritan; thanked God that 'I have been bred up and lived all my days in the flourishing time of his gospel under many religious true and faithful preachers and dispensers of his holy word by which means I have earned my salvation'; bequeathed £40 to Daventry as stock to set poor to work. Purchased lands for some £5,204 in 01–25, plus Brockhall manor 25; rental income ranged between £62 and £288 p.a.; paid 2 das. portions of £300 ea. in 07, bequeathed 1 da. £500 in 29; total income peaked at £651 in 13. Assessed @ £10 for benevolence 25. (Mr T. R. Key, personal communication; *HS*, lxxvii; Metcalfe, ed., *Northants. Vis.*; papers at Northants RO; *Reliquary*, xxiv; PCC 111 Audley.)

THORPE, Robert (*c*.1582–1639), 1 s. Richard, London, vintner. Broadgates Hall, O, 97, BA 00; MT 00, b 08, B 25. Mar. Anne, da. Bryan Jameson, Beaconsfield, Bucks. Left 1 s. (barrister MT 35) £5 only, plus copyhold lands at Witney, Oxon. All personal estate, leases, annuities, rents, farm at North Leigh, Oxon., orchard Beaconsfield, to w. (*HS*, lviii; PCC 47 Harvey.)

THURBARNE, James (d. 1627), s. John, New Romney, Kent. Clare, C, 80; Barnard's Inn; GI 85, b ?, AB 10. Town clk. New Romney by 88; fee'd counsel Cinque Ports 94, Hastings 06, Rye 07, Sandwich by 24, rec. 25; sought to be made MReq 23. Co-patentee with Mompesson for licensing alehouses. MP 97. Mar. Mary, da. Giles Escourt, Salisbury, counsellor of LI. Will witnessed by Sir John Finch, Lancelot Lovelace (for whom, see above), and Richard Sibbes. Of Canterbury at d. (*H. of P.*; HMC, *Thirteenth Rep.*, iv; *Kent Arch. Soc., Kent Recs.*, xix; Boys, *Sandwich*; Hastings Public Museum and Art Gallery, C/A. a. 1, fol. 116; PCC 115 Skynner.)

THYNNE, Sir Aegremont (d. 1637), 8 s. Sir John, Longleat, Wilts., by Dorothy, da. Sir William Wroughton, Broad Hinton, Wilts. MT 97, b 04, B 22, SL 23, ktd. 24. Mar. Barbara, da. Henry Calthorpe, bro. to lord mayor of London. Antiquary, and friend of Sir John Davies. ?Of Broxbourne, Herts., at d. (*HS*, cv, cvi; B. Botfield, *Stemmata Botevilliana*, 1858; HMC, *Hastings*, iv; Hoare, *Modern Wiltshire*, iii: *Heytesbury Hundred*; CUL MS Add. 6863, fol. 88ᵛ.)

TILDESLEY, Sir Thomas (1557–1635), 1 s. Thurston, Wardley, Lancs., by Margaret, da. Sir William Norris, Speke, Lancs. Staple Inn; GI 77, b 84, B 06; king's att. Duchy of Lancaster 04, vice-chancellor and sjt. 06; member Council of North 09; ktd. 16. JP. Mar. Ann, da. Thomas Norreys, Orford, Lancs. Dedicatee, W. Crashawe, *Parable of Poyson* (1618); W. Leigh, *The Dampe of Death* (1618). Father lost Wardley estate; some of w.'s lands sold 31 to pay debts. (*Chetham Soc.*, lxxxii; Somerville, *Office Holders*; Reid, *King's Council in the North*; *VCH, Lancs.*, iii; Hart-Davis, *Wardley Hall*.)

TOPHAM, Henry (d. 1612), y.s. Edward, Agglethorpe, Yorks., gent. Barnard's Inn; GI 82, b ?, B 10; ? member ecclesiastical commission York 03. JP. Mar. Elizabeth, da. John Darley, York. Donated stained-glass window to Ripon Church, *c*.09. Inherited 4 manors oo; also held lands in Hornington and Cornbrough, rectory of Graunton, 2 houses Coney Street, York. Cash bequests £328. (Foster, ed., *Yorks. Vis.*; *VCH, Yorks. (NR)*, i; HMC, *Salisbury*, xvi, xxi; Borthwick, Reg. 35, fol. 471; York City AO, MS Skaife, fol. 241.)

TOWNSHEND, Richard (*c*.1584–*c*.1653), 1 s. John, Warwick, gent., by Christian. Magd. Hall, O, 01; MT 05, b 14, B 31; escheator War. and Leics. 20–2. JP. Mar. Member parliamentary accounts committee, War. Property in Ditchford and Warwick. (*H. of P.*; *List and Index Soc.*, lxxii; *Warwick Quarter Session Order Bk. (1637–50)*; Dr D. Mosler, personal communication.)

TOWSE, William (*c*.1551–1634), of Henham, Essex. Clifford's Inn; IT 72, b ?, B 95, SL 14; town clk. and rec. Colchester by 18; rec. Maldon. JP; MP 86, 14, 21–6. Mar. (i) Jean French; (ii) Katherine. Dedicatee, T. Barnes, *The Court of Conscience* (1623). Assessed £10 in 09; held manor in Bassingbourne, messuages adjoining, lands in Isle of Sheppey, Kent, and Bishop's Stortford, Herts.; nominal annual IPM value £26. 6s. 8d. Buried Takeley, Essex. (*H. of P.*; *HS*, xiii; C142/525/121; Lansdowne 255, fol. 64.)

TREFUSIS, Richard (*c*.1556–1611), 2 s. Nicholas, Landewednack, Corn., by Grace, da. William Millington, Pyngerseck, Corn. New Inn (barrister); LI 79, b 87, B 05; rec. Launceston and commr. to investigate piracy 09. JP; MP 84, 86, 89. Assessed £10 in 09. Held manor of Mutton and properties around Launceston. (*H. of P.*; R. and O. B. Peter, *Histories of Launceston*, 1885; HMC, *Salisbury*, xxii; Gleason, *Justices*; PCC 48 Capell; C142/333/13.)

*TREVOR, Sir Thomas (*c*.1573–1656). Clifford's Inn; IT 93, b 03, B 17, SL 25, feodary of Surrey 03, auditor southern parts of Duchy of Lancaster 04; dep.-steward of honour of Hampton Ct. 10; fee'd counsel Kingston-on-Thames by 15. MP 01–24. Mar. (i) Prudence, da. Henry Butler; (ii) Frances, da. Daniel Blennerhasset, Norfolk; (iii) Ellen Poyntell. Bequeathed £10 to 'Mr Palmer the divine', presumably the puritan James Palmer (see *DNB*), who preached at St Bride's Church, where Trevor erected a 'Monument'. Held extensive properties Denbighs., War., and Middx., part interest in farm of coals by 39. (*DWB*; *H. of P.*; Clendinnen; Greater London RO, Acc 58/12a; Surrey RO, KBA KD5/1/1; PCC 8 Ruthen.)

TRIST, Thomas (1575–1630), 2 s. William, Maidford, Northants, gent., by Agnes, da. Richard Coles, Preston Capes, Northants. Exeter, O, 89; Clement's Inn; MT 94, b 02, B 20. Mar. Margery, da. Edward Pell, Rolleston, Leics. Sought burial without pomp, 'assuredly believing' in his election. Held manor and other properties at Culworth; personal estate (except books) to be sold for maintaining 3 sons at school, university, and inns of court. Of Culworth at d. (*HS*, lxxxvii; PCC 57 Scroope; Additional 25233.)

TROTMAN, Edward (*c*.1580–1643), 1 s. Edward, Cam, Glos., gent., by Ann, da. Richard Watts, Stroud, Glos. Magdalen, O, 94; Clifford's Inn; IT 98, b 07, B 24; escheator Glos. 10. Mar. Anne or Jane, da. Anthony Stratford, Temple Guiting, Glos. Author of *Epitome undecim librorum relationum E. Coke* (1640). Listed 08 as of Mitcheldean, Glos., 'gent., an utter barrister', who furnished one corselet. (*HS*, xxi; F. H. Trotman, *Trotman Family*, 1965; W. P. W. Phillimore, *Collections relating to the family of Trotman*, 1892; Smyth, *Men and Armour*.)

TUCKER (Tooker), Giles (*c*.1565–1623), 1 s. Charles, Maddington, Wilts., yeoman, by Matilda Nipperhead. Barnard's Inn; LI 81, b 89, B 08; fee'd counsel and member of governing body Salisbury 91, rec. 10; rec. Wilton by 23. JP; MP 01–14. Mar. Elizabeth, da. Thomas Eyre(s), Salisbury (sister of Robert and William, for whom, see above). Supported efforts to install presbyterian rector St Edmund's Church, and opposed power of cathedral in Salisbury. Held Wilts. lands, nominal annual IPM value nearly £40, but claimed himself to be worth *c*. £400 p.a. (*H. of P.*; Clendinnen; *VCH, Wilts.*, vi, x, xi; HMC, *Salisbury*, xi; Hoare, *Modern Wiltshire*, vi: *Old and New Sarum*; PCC 4 Byrde; C142/422/39.)

TURNER (Turnour), Arthur (*c*.1589–1651), 2 s. Edward, Canons Green, Essex, MT barrister, by Anne, da. James Morice, Chipping Ongar, Essex, MT bencher. Christ's, C, 03; New Inn; MT 06, b 13, B 24, SL 37. JP; MP 14. Mar. Ann, da. John Jerm(i)yn(e). MT bencher (for whom, see above). Reporter. Testified at Abp. Laud's trial 44; member of Essex committee for scandalous ministers. Listed as resident of Fetter Lane 38, with house worth £16 p.a.; purchased manor of Parndon and other lands in Essex. (Miss E. Henderson, personal communication; Peile, *Biographical Register*; Morant, *Essex*, ii; Cockburn, *Assizes*; papers at HLS; HMC, *House of Lords MSS*, NS, xi, and *Tenth Rep.*, iv; *Essex Rev.*, xlv; SP 16/538/181; *VCH, Essex*, viii; Dale, *Inhabitants 1638*; CUL MS Dd. 5. 51 (i), fols. 64–64ᵛ.)

TURNER (Tourneur), Sir Timothy (*c*.1585–1677), 1 s. Thomas, Astley, Salop, and GI, esq., by Susanna, da. John Farmer, London, grocer. Staple Inn; GI 07, b 11, B 31, SL 69, ktd. 70; sol.-gen. Wales 27, MCh (extraordinary) 30, j. N. Wales 34, CJ W. Wales 37, rec. Shrewsbury 38. JP. Mar. (i) Jane, da. Francis Newton, Highley, Salop; (ii) Ann Johnson, wid. Thomas Johnston. Solicitor to earl of Bridgewater, lord president Council in Marches. Royalist. Income assessed @ £300–£430 p.a. in mid-40s, acquired manor of Winsley, Ford, Salop, by 48; cash bequests total £2,812. (*HS*, xxiv; xxix; University College London, MS Ogden 29;

Williams, *Welsh Judges*; Ellesmere 7386 *et seq.*; *CCAM*; *CCC*; Wanklyn, thesis; *VCH, Salop*, viii; Additional 35397; PCC 25 Hale.)

VALENCE, Thomas (*c.*1523–1601), 2 s. William ap Watkins alias Valence, Abergavenny, Monmouths., by Alice. LI 60, b ?, AB 97 (when described as 'long time a continuer in this house and one who is aged and of a weak constitution of body and of honest and friendly disposition'). Contributed commendatory verse to T. Cooper, *Thesaurus linguae Romanae & Britannicae* (1565). Described as a Catholic by entrant to English College, Rome, 03. Will dated 'the day of the exaltation of the Holy Cross, being 14 Sept. 1600'; executors included John Williams, Lady Margaret Prof. of Divinity, Oxford Univ. (Bradney, *Monmouthshire*, 285; *LIBB*, ii. 50; *Cath. Rec. Soc.*, liv; J. Stow, *The Survey of London*, ed. J. Strype, 1720, i. 257; PCC 83 Woodhall.)

*VERNON, Sir George (?1578–1639). Clement's Inn; IT 94, b 03, B 19, SL 27. MP 26. Engaged in litigation with Sir Randle Crew (for whom, see above); imprisoned by Star Chamber for questioning jurisdiction of Exchequer at Chester *c.*12. Possibly paid cash as inducement for his promotion 27 as BExch; clashed with Wentworth on Northern circuit 33. Family purchased 19 manors between 1578 and 1639; held Haslington manor and other Ches. properties, nominal IPM value £46. 2s. p.a. (*HS*, lix; *English Reports*, lxxii. 926; Whitelocke, *Lib. Fam.*; Baker, *Serjeants*; Knowler, i; Wanklyn, thesis; *Lancs. & Ches. Rec. Soc.*, xci.)

WAKERING, John (d. 1646), 1 s. James. LI 00, b 07, B 23; escheator Staffs. 01. JP. Mar. Mary, da. Dionis Palmer, Felstead, Essex. Cash bequests £300. Licensed to disafforest lands at Kelvedon, Essex, 38; of Kelvedon at d. (Hunts. RO, dd M 16/31, 24b/14, 15; *List & Index Soc.*, lxxii; HMC, *Tenth Rep.*, iv; PCC 168 Twisse.)

WALMSLEY, Edward (d. 1604), 4 s. Thomas, Shelley or Showlay, Lancs., gent., by Margaret, da. Thomas Levesay, Rishton, Lancs. Clement's Inn (barrister); LI 77, b 84, B 01. JP. Mar. Anne, da. William Hawksworth, Otley, Yorks. Inherited lands, Leyland, etc. At d. seised of Darwen or Banester Hall, Walton-le-Dale, Blackburn, and parcels adjoining, nominal IPM value £3. 10s. p.a. (*Chetham Soc.*, lxxxii, NS lxvi, lxxxiv; *VCH, Lancs.*, vi; *Lancs. & Ches. Rec. Soc.*, iii; Lancs. RO, Edmund Walmsley Inv. 1604.)

WALROND, James (1552–1613), 1 s. Roger, Wells, Som., gent., by Agnes, da. John Mauncell, weaver. Clement's Inn; MT 74, b 82, B 01. JP. Twice married, secondly to Margaret. Assessed @ £10 in 99; £20 in 09. Held lands Harrow, Middx., and elsewhere. Of Harrow at d. (Weaver, ed., *Vis. Som.*; *Middx. Co. Rec. Soc.*, i–ii; *APC 1599–1600*; PCC 38 Capell.)

*WALTER, Sir John (*c.*1566–1630), 2 s. Edmund, Ludlow, Salop, CJ S. Wales, by Mary, da. Thomas Hacklett, Eyton, Salop. Brasenose, O, 79; IT 83, b 90, B 05, SL and KSL 25; att.-gen. to Prince Charles 13; counsel to Oxford Univ. JP; MP 21–4. Dedicatee, W. Crashawe, *Querela, . . .* (1622). Made will 'assuredly hoping' to be 'among the blessed souls of the elect children of God'; confirmed gifts for maintenance of preacher at Churchill, Oxon., augmentation of benefice at Sarsden, and maintenance of 10 fellows and scholars at Jesus Coll., O. Rich; portions £3,000 to 2 das. and £80 p.a. until portions paid. Left rings to Sir Edward Coke, Thomas, Lord Coventry, Sir Randle Crew, Sir Edward Littleton, and Sir Thomas Trevor (for whom, see above). (Aylmer, *King's Servants*; PCC 95 Scroope.)

WALTHAM, Richard (d. 1632), 3 s. John, Kenn, Devon, by Elizabeth, da. Richard Stevens, Exminster. New Inn (barrister); LI 82, b 89, B 09; fee'd counsel Exeter by 03, rec. 28. JP. Mar. Ann, da. John Long, Exminster. Sought burial 'without pomp and ceremony'; acted for third earl of Bedford in presenting godly ministers to Devon benefices. Assessed @ £10 in 09; £2 in lands in 29? (*HS*, vi; Devon RO, ECA, Receiver's accounts, 43–44 Eliz.; HMC *Exeter*; Gowers, thesis; PCC 94 Audley; *Devon and Cornwall Rec. Soc.*, NS ii.)

WANDESFORD, Sir Rowland (d. 1652), 1 s. Michael, Pickhill, Yorks., by da. of one Durham. St John's, C, 84; LI 88, b 97, B 14; att. of Wards and ktd. 38 (unsuccessful candidate for rec. Doncaster 23, York 25). Follower of Thomas Wentworth; appointed Lord Cottington as overseer of will 40, but parliamentarian (attended LI council meetings from July 44). Da. mar. Philip, Lord Wharton, to whom passed Newton manor, Burneston, Yorks., and remainder of estate. (Foster, ed., *Yorks. Vis.*; York City AO, Misc. E 34, p. 272; *Wentworth Papers*, ed. Cooper; *VCH, Yorks. (NR)*, i; Jones, *Sawpit Wharton*; LI MS BB VII, fol. 517; *CCAM*; PCC 207 Brent.)

WARD, Rowland (c.1564–1656), 1 s. Thomas, Barford, War., by Martha, da. Thomas Rowley, Idlicote, ?att. MT 00, b 06, B 24, SL 28; steward of Kenilworth 06. JP. Mar. Joanna, da. John Harbourne, Middx. Tried to persuade Warwick corporation to subsidize publication of W. Dugdale, *Antiquities of War.*, 56, but, according to Simonds D'Ewes, a 'dull and easy lawyer'. Presented puritans John Brian and Thomas Dugard to Barford living. Neutral in Civil War. Bought Barford house 20, Pillerton manor 37. (*Trans. Birmingham Arch. Soc.*, lxxviii; *HS*, xii; Hughes, thesis; D'Ewes, *Autobiography*, i; *VCH, War.*, v; Dr D. Mosler, personal communication.)

WARD, William (d. 1648), 4 s. Thomas, Carlton Curlieu, Leics., by Alice, da. William Barton, Braunston, Rutland. GI 10, b 17, B 39. Royalist; compounded August 45. Married. (*HS*, ii; *CCC*; Smyth, *Obituary*.)

WATERHOUSE, David (c.1564–c.1639), 7 s. John, Shibden, nr. Halifax, Yorks., gent., by Jane or Joan, da. Thomas Bosvile, Conisbrough, Yorks. Univ., O, 81; Clifford's Inn; IT 84, b 93, B 05; clk. of Crown, Queen's Bench 96, coroner and att. 97; fee'd counsel York 97–8. MP 89, 01. Mar.

Elizabeth, da. Thomas Craine. Outlawed as bankrupt 14, prisoner in Fleet from ?15, certainly by 27. (*H. of P.*; Dr G. E. Aylmer, personal communication; Leeds District Archives, TN/L 5/6, TN/L 2/1/2; *Halifax Antiq. Soc. Papers*, 1915.)

WELSHE, James (*fl.* 1585–1634), 1 s. John, Barnstaple, Devon. Lyon's Inn; MT 85, b 94, B 13; dep.-rec. Barnstaple by 15. JP. Signed protest of Devon JPs against 14 gratuity. Subscribed £4 to 22 benevolence. The John Welshe whose will was proved in 50 (PCC 83 Pembroke) may be his son. (Chanter and Wainwright, *Barnstaple Records*; Gribble, *Memorials of Barnstaple*; *HS*, vi; Ellesmere 2504; Devon RO, Totnes borough archives, 1579 A/7/1/14.)

*WENTWORTH, Thomas (*c.*1568–1627). LI 85, b 94, B 10; fee'd counsel Oxford 03; discommoned by Oxford Univ. 11 as fomentor of town-gown conflict. Anti-Arminian; expressed assurance that soul and body would be made 'partakers through mere and free grace of eternal glory'. (Clendinnen; Russell, *Parliaments and English Politics*; *Oxford Hist. Soc.*, lxxxvii; *VCH, Oxon.*, iv; PCC 107 Ridley.)

WERE (Weare), Humphrey (*c.*1569–1625), s. John, Bradworthy, Devon, gent. Exeter, O, 85; Lyon's Inn; IT 89, b 97, B 13; nominated as sol.-gen. (Ire.) 03; feodary of Devon by 05; rec. Tiverton by 15. JP; MP 14, 24. Mar. Elizabeth. Signed protest of Devon JPs against 14 benevolence. Inherited lands Bradworthy and Halberton, also held lands Tiverton and rectory of Morebath, nominal IPM value £7. 2s. p.a. (HMC, *Salisbury*, xxiii; W. Harding, *History of Tiverton*, 1847, ii; Ellesmere 2504; PCC 48 Clarke; C 142/417/24.)

WESTON, Sir James (*c.*1573–1634), 3 s. James, Lichfield, registrar of Lichfield diocese, Staffs., by ?Margery, da. Humphrey Lowe, Lichfield. Christ Church, O, 90; Clifford's Inn; IT 92, b 00, B 16, SL, ktd. and BExch 31. Mar. Mary, da. William Weston, Kent. Contributed commendatory verse to W. Gouger, *Ulysses Redux* (Oxford, 1592). Leased manor of Castle Camps, Cambs., from 16. Will mentions leases and lands in Cambs., debt of £200 owed by Catherine, countess of Suffolk. (Foss; *VCH, Cambs.*, vi; PCC 15 Seager; Additional 24607, fols. 66ᵛ–68.)

*WESTON, Sir Richard (*c.*1577–1658), 1 s. Ralph, Rugeley, Staffs., by Anne, da. Thomas Smith, Appleton, Lancs. Exeter, O, 96; IT 99, b 07, B 26, SL 34. JP; MP 21. Mar. Anne, da. Richard Barbour, Hilderstone, Staffs. Reputed papist; in arms for Charles I at Ludlow 51. Inherited Hagley Manor, also owned lands Brereton and Rugeley. Said to have 'lived handsomely but died poor'. (Additional 24607, fol. 66ᵛ; Williams, *Welsh Judges*; *CCAM*; Keeler; *VCH, Staffs.*, v; Erdeswick, *Staffs.*; *Staffs. Parish Reg. Soc.: Rugeley Parish Register Pt. I*, 1928.)

WHATMAN, Thomas (d. 1630), s. Thomas, Hurstpierpoint, Sussex. Hart Hall, O, BA 93; IT 94, b 03, B 20; fee'd counsel Hastings 12, rec.

Portsmouth 15, Chichester 21. JP; MP 21, 24, 26. Mar. Ciceley, da. John
Sackville, Dorking and Bletchingley. Anti-Arminian. Assessed @ £6 in
lands, Chichester, 21–2. Bought manors of Balsden 14, Iping 18, Berwick
23. (East Sussex RO, Act Book B6/38; Fletcher, *Sussex*; Hastings Public
Museum and Art Gallery, C/A a. 1, fol. 157ᵛ; *Sussex Arch. Coll.*, xxiv,
xxv, xliii, lviii; *Sussex Rec. Soc.*, xix.)

WHISTLER, John (*c.*1580–1646), 1 s. Hugh, Little Milton, Oxon. Trinity, O,
97, BA 01; GI 01, b 11, B 28; fee'd counsel and dep.-rec. Oxford 23, rec.
27. MP 24–40. Never married. Requested burial without funeral sermon,
'which for the most part are but empty panegyrics'. Royalist, disabled 44,
although claimed his absence from Westminster involuntary, and arrested
Oxford Dec. 42 after urging citizens not to take up arms. Not rich;
properties in Oxon., Berks., and Hants worth *c.* £140 p.a. (Keeler; *VCH,
Oxon.*, iv; PCC 90 Fines.)

WHITAKER, William (*c.*1580–1646), 1 s. Henry, Westbury, Wilts., gent., by
Judith, da. William Hawkins, Plymouth, Devon. Broadgates Hall, O, 00;
MT 02, b 12, B 27; rec. Shaftesbury 27. JP; MP 24, 25, 26, Apr. and Nov.
40. Mar. Honora, da. Edward Hooper, Boveridge, Cranbourne, Dorset.
Parliamentarian; Associate of John Pym. Inherited mother's lands at
Westbury, Wilts., had £1,000 portion with w., left younger children £400
ea. Of Shaftesbury, Dorset, at d. (Keeler; *Wilts. N. & Q.*, iv. 107.)

*WHITELOCKE, Sir James (1570–1632), 4 s. New Inn; MT 93, b 00, B 19,
SL 20; rec. Woodstock *c.*06. Wealthy; left £2,000 portion to da., and
noted that 'I have plentifully tasted God's blessings though unworthy of
the least of them'. (Spalding, *Improbable Puritan*; PCC 113 Audley.)

WHITFIELD, Sir Ralph (d. 1645), 1 s. Herbert, Tenterden, Kent, esq., by
Martha, da. Robert Shepheard, Peasmarsh, Sussex. Staple Inn; GI 08, b ?,
B 33, SL 34, KSL 35; bailiff and j. Battle ct. of record 25; fee'd counsel
Cinque Ports 34; ktd. 35; king's counsel by 41. JP; MP 24. Counsel and
creditor of earl of Leicester; in Ire. as royal commr. 38–9. Mar. Dorothy,
da. Sir Henry Spelman, Norfolk. Parliamentarian; remained in London
as assistant to HL, applied Aug. 43 for exemption from weekly assessment because 4 horses taken for parl.'s services. Claimed his estate 'much
shortened by the present distractions', but left da. portion of £2,500, and
2 sons £1,000 ea. Assessed among the 'ablest' in ward of Cripplegate
Without 40; bought dwelling-house in the Barbican, manor of Burmarsh,
and other lands, Kent. (*HS*, xlii, cxv–cxvi; *Kent Arch. Soc., Kent Recs.*,
xix; SP 16/493/52; Gleason, *Justices*; Clark, *Provincial Society*; HMC, *De
L'Isle and Dudley*, vi; *LJ*, vi. 178; *CCAM*; Tighe and Davis, *Annals of
Windsor*, i; Hasted, *Kent*, vii, viii; PCC 156 Rivers; *Misc. Gen. et Her.*, 2nd
ser., ii. 108.)

*WIDDRINGTON, Sir Thomas (*c.*1600–1664). Christ's, C, BA 21; GI 19, b ?,
B 39, SL 48 and 60; rec. York 37. Although MP 40–53, attended meetings

of York Corporation as rec. on 15 Jan. and 23 Feb. 44, while king was in city. Requested burial 'without the least funeral pomp ... hoping and believing ... to be eternally saved'; made 'earnest and last request' that his das. should be 'religiously and virtuously educated'. Rich; inherited substantial Northumb. estates, income perhaps £500–£1,000 p.a. in 48. (Keeler; Underdown, *Pride's Purge*; York City AO, House Book B 36, fols. 81ᵛ, 84; Borthwick, Reg. 46, fol. 330.)

WIGHTWICK, John (1581–1645), y.s. William, Tamworth, Staffs., by Mary. Clement's Inn; IT 05, b 14, B 29, SL 40; steward of Coventry. JP; MP 24. Mar. Bridget. Royalist. Inherited Flanders manor 33. Bought Farewell, Staffs., where built 'a very neat house', and held lands and leases Coventry and Derbs. Died Oxford. Wid. claimed her jointure worth only £100 p.a., s. fined @ 1/10, £123. (*Staffs. Rec. Soc.*, 3rd ser., xliv; Hughes, thesis; *VCH, War.*, iv; *CCAM*; *CCC*; PCC 252 Aylett; Dr D. Mosler, personal communication.)

WILBRAHAM, Ralph (1557–1628), 4 s. Richard, Nantwich, Ches., gent., by Eliza, da. Thomas Maisterson, Nantwich. Christ's, C, 79; LI 80, b 89, AB 15 (as 'an ancient utter-barrister'); feodary of Flints. and Ches. 89. JP. Mar. Alice Mainwearing, Nantwich. Desired 'no great dinner at my funeral which time is not fit for feasting, nor painted arms', but burial in parish church with sermon by Mr (?John) Ball, Mr (?William) Hinde (for whom see *DNB*), or Mr Nicholls; 'I have always served the word of God and his messengers that conformably preach the same'. Will mentioned land purchases in Morley and Rugeley; £1,000 to grandson. Assessed @ £10, Herts., 09. Bro. of Roger (next below). (*HS*, lix; Ellesmere 2882; HMC, *Salisbury*, ix, xi; Gleason, *Justices*; Ches. RO, WS 1628.)

WILBRAHAM, Sir Roger (1553–1616), 2 s. Richard, Nantwich, Ches., gent., by Eliza, da. Thomas Maisterson, Nantwich. St John's, C, 73; GI 76, b 83, B 95; sol.-gen. (Ire.) 85, MReq 00, surveyor Ct. of Wards 07, chancellor to Queen Anne. MP 04, 14. Mar. Mary, da. Edward Baber, Chew Magna, Som., SL. Wealthy; said to have left his 3 das. £4,000 p.a. in total; held lands in Ches., Herts., Middx., Northants, Som., and War., nominal IPM value £46. 6s. 8d. p.a., although owing £3,500 to Sir Thomas Pelham; cash bequests over £1,000. Of Hadley, Middx., at d. (*Camden Misc.*, x; Folger MS M.b.42, transcript of original journal; Clendinnen; *Som. Rec. Soc.*, lxvii; PCC 109 Cope.)

WILD (Wylde), George (1550–1616), 2 s. Thomas, Kempsey, Worcs., clothier, by Eleanor, da. George Wall, Droitwich. IT 68, b ?, B 91, SL 14; member Council in Marches 02. JP; MP 84, 93, 04. Mar. Frances, da. Sir Edward Huddleston, Sawston, Cambs. Da. married into Catholic Blount family. Assessed @ £10 in 09; income perhaps £500 p.a. Father of George and John (next two below). (*H. of P.*; Silcock, thesis.)

WILD (Wylde), George (c.1594–1650), 2 s. of preceding. Balliol, O, 08, BA

11; IT 04, b 18, B 35. MP 28, 48. Income perhaps less than £500 p.a. ?Settled at Gressenhall, Norfolk. (Underdown, *Pride's Purge*; W. R. Williams, *The Parliamentary History of Worcs.*, 1897.)

*WILD (Wylde), John (*c.*1590–1669), 1 s. George Wild (1550–1616), next but one above. Balliol, O, 05, BA 07, MA 10; IT 03, b 12, B 28, SL 37; rec. Worcester 40. JP; MP 21–40, 59. Mar. Anne, da. Sir Thomas Harris of LI (for whom, see above). Inherited substantial properties in Worcs., income at least £500 p.a., subscribed £1,400 for Irish venture. (Keeler; Underdown, *Pride's Purge*; Silcock, thesis; *Irish Hist. Studs.*, x. 58.)

*WILLIAMS, Sir David (?1536–1613), y.s. William, Ystradvellte, Brecon, yeoman. MT 68, b 76, B 91, SL 94. JP; MP 84, 86, 89, 97. Reported by Abp. Abbott in 12 to dislike 'all the Lord Coke his courses'. Left £200 for blacks at his funeral, and £4 p.a. to establish 4 annual sermons. Wealthy. (*H. of P.*; *DWB*; Ellesmere 2184.)

WILLIAMSON, Sir Richard (d. 1619), s. John, Gainsborough, Lincs., by Jane, da. Christopher Dobson, Gainsborough. Barnard's Inn; GI 82, b ?, AB 14; member Council in the North 03; MReq 12; steward East Retford, Notts. JP; MP 14. Mar. Mary, da. Thomas Anderson, Castlethorpe. Director Virginia Co. 09. Assessed @ £20 in 09. Sir William Ellis (for whom, see above) his 'dear friend'. (*HS*, lii; Reid, *King's Council in the North*; Gleason, *Justices*; Brown, *Genesis*; PROB 6/10, fol. 34ᵛ.)

WILLIS (Willowes), Thomas (*c.*1576–post-1659), 2 s. Thomas, Horningsea, Cambs., gent., by Jane. IT 98, b 07, B 29; assize clk. Norfolk circuit 14, clk. of Crown in Chancery 29, rec. Basingstoke 35. JP. Mar. Anne Haslewood? Royalist-trimmer; attended king in Oxford, although perhaps only after capture; took covenant 45; in prison for debt by 54, still seeking return of office 59. (*HS*, xiii, xli; Cockburn, *Assizes*; Birch, *Court and Times of Charles I*, ii. 16; Aylmer, *State's Servants*; *CCC*; *CSPD 1658–9, 1659–60, 1660–1*.)

*WINCH, Sir Humphrey (*c.*1555–1625). St John's, C, 70; LI 73, b 81, B 95, SL 06; steward of Newton, Biddenham manor for William Boteler 95; dep.-rec. Bedford 96. JP; MP 93, 97, 01, 04. Sought private burial without heralds, escutcheons, or 'many' blacks. Acquired lands in Beds. and Hunts. Bequeathed gowns, robes, and law books to cousin Richard Taylor of LI (for whom, see above). (*H. of P.*; Ball, *Judges in Ireland*; Beds. RO, TW 726; *VCH, Beds.*, ii; PCC 29 Clarke.)

WOLRITH (Wolrich, Worleche, Worledge, Woolwich, Woolrych), Robert (*fl.* 1607–1661), ? s. Arthur, Ipswich, Suffolk, by Dorcas, da. Thomas Wood, clk. of the Privy Council. GI 07, b 13, B 30. Mar. Attended GI pensions throughout 1640s and 50s; s. and heir Arthur admitted GI 42. Not rich; assessed @ £30 in 43. (Harleian 1560, fol. 214ᵛ; *GIPB*; *GIAdmR*; *CCAM*.)

WOLVERIDGE, Sir James (*c.*1569–1624), 1 s. James, Odiham, Hants, by

Amy, da. John Camm (or Camice). Magd. Hall, O, 82; New Inn; LI 87,
b 96, B 13; MCh 15, ktd. 19. JP. Mar. Bridget, da. William Draper,
Bedenwell, Erith, Kent. Sought burial without pomp; bequeathed £40 for
setting poor of Odiham to work. Acquired manors of Bentworth Hall and
Stepley 09–10. (*HS*, lxiv; *VCH, Hants*, iv.)

WOOD, Toby (d. *c*.1611), s. William, St Botolph's-without-Aldgate, London, mercer. Christ's, C, 69; LI 73, b 83, B 96; att. to Prince Henry; fee'd
counsel London 96; counsel to Coopers' Co., London. JP. Mar. Barbara,
da. William Bowyer, Sussex. Requested burial near father and mother in
St Botolph's-without-Aldgate, 'in full hope and assurance of the resurrec-
tion ... with them and all others the elect children of God'; bequeathed
property for establishment of sermons 'by some learned and religious
divine'. Assessed @ £20 in 09; £1,000 to da., £333 to grandchildren. (Peile,
Biographical Register; London Corp. RO, Rep. 23, fol. 347ᵛ; W. K.
Jordan, The *Charities of London*, 1960; Gleason, *Justices*; PCC 69 Wood.)

WOODROFFE (Woodreeve), Ellis (*fl.* 1611–41), 2 s. Edward or Edmund,
Hope, Derbs. (disclaimed as no gentleman by heralds 11), by Zeno, da.
Ellis Staley, Readstates, Derbs. Clement's Inn; IT 11, b 20, B 37. JP. Mar.
Anne, da. Hugh Browker, IT bencher and prothonotary (for whom, see
below, Appendix F). Presumably d. by 46, when John Selden admitted to
his IT chamber. (S. M. Woodrooffe, *Pedigree of Woodrooffe, with
Memorials* ..., 1878; *Derbs. Arch. J.*, xli. 70; Dias, thesis; *HS*, xlii; *ITR*, ii;
LJ, iv. 275; Hunter, *South Yorks.*, ii.)

WOODWARD, Thomas (d. 1624), 2 s. George, Upton, Berks., esq., by
Katherine, da. Thomas Woodford, Britwell Place, Bucks. ?Clare, C, *c*.93;
LI 97, b 05, B 20; nominated as escheator for Derbs. and Notts. 07;
steward of Windsor. MP 14, 24. (*HS*, lviii; HMC, *Sackville*, i; Ruigh,
Parliament of 1624; PCC 72 Byrde.)

WOTTON (Wooton), William (d. *c*.1632), 1 s. Walter, Inglebourne, Devon,
gent., by Silvester, da. William Gibbes, Venton, Devon. Clifford's Inn;
MT 84, b 96, B 14. Mar. Ann, da. John Giles, Bowden, Devon. Bought
land at Dartington 25; farmed rectory of Ashburton with Bickington 32.
(*HS*, vi; Devon RO, Z 15/18/1/1 and Consistory Court papers, index;
MTR, ii.)

WRIGHT, Euseby (d. 1653), 1 s. Robert, Dennington, Suffolk, clk. (for
whom, see *DNB*), by Joan, da. John Butler, Thoby, Essex. Emmanuel, C,
97; Furnival's Inn; LI 02, b 10, B 27. JP. Mar. Ursula, da. George Digby,
Barnes Elms, Surrey. Attended LI councils June 42, Nov. 45; possibly
practising in Chancery, Easter term 44. Will mentions lands mortgaged
by Sir John Cotton and other properties in Essex; £1,400 to be raised from
moneys owing on mortgage to buy freehold land for bro. Of Great
Totham, Essex, at d. (*HS*, xiii; HMC, *Tenth Rep.*, iv; C33/184, fols. 103–
169ᵛ; LI MS BB VII; PCC 35 Brent.)

WRIGHT, John (d. 1633), ?1 s. John, Wrightsbridge, Havering, Essex, gent., by his 1st w., da. of one Linsell. Emmanuel, C, 85; GI 88, b?, AB 14, B 22; clk. of peace Essex 10–11, clk. HC 12; rec. Maldon 19; dep.-steward Havering. JP. Mar. (i) Martha, da. Robert Castell, East Hatley, Cambs; (ii) da. Sir William Garraway and wid. William Blunt. (Mr J. C. Sainty, personal communication; *HS*, xiii, xvii; Morant, *Essex*, I. ii. 62; *CSPD 1631–3*; Essex RO, D/DB 3/3/217/4; *Inns of Court*; O. C. Williams, *Clerical Organisation of the House of Commons 1161–1850*, 1954.)

WRIGHTINGTON, Sir Edward (c.1580–1658), 1 s. John, Wrightington, Lancs., esq. Brasenose, O, 94; GI 98, b?, B 37; member Council of the North and ktd. 37. JP; MP 21. Protégé of Sir Francis Bacon. Puritan. Royalist, but avoided sequestration. Paid £25 knighthood fine 31. Said to have been born to £800 p.a.; substantial land purchases Lancs.; assessed @ £1,000 in 46. Bequests to servants and poor totalled £1,420, plus £900 to relatives. (*VCH, Lancs.*, vi; Blackwood, thesis; *Chetham Soc.*, ii, xxii; Bacon, *Works*, v. 377; PCC 312 Nabbs; *CCAM*; *CCC*; *Rec. Soc. Lancs. & Ches.*, xcvi.)

WRIGHTINGTON, George (d. 1612), 2 s. Alexander, Enfield, Middx., by Julian, da. William Shenn, Bradley, Berks. Lyon's Inn; MT 78, b 86, B 05. (*MTR*, i & ii; *HS*, lxv.)

YARBOROUGH (Yarburgh), Francis (d. 1595), 2 s. Edmond, Welton, Lincs., esq., by Margaret, da. Sir Vincent Grantham. LI 70, b 79, B 90; recommended by Ellesmere for place at York 92. Mar. (i) Helen, da. George or John Farmery; (ii) Frances, da. Leonard Wray, Yorks., bro. Sir Christopher Wray, LCJ. Cash bequests £1,019, including £400 each to 2 sons. Held land Northorpe, Spridlington, Redbourne, etc., Lincs., also town house Lincoln. Of Northorpe and Welton at d. (*HS*, lii, where mistakenly described as SL, perhaps by confusion with grands. Thomas; Ellesmere 1401; PCC 65 Scott; C 142/242/81.)

*YELVERTON, Sir Henry (1566–1630). Christ's, C, 81; GI ?79, b?, B 07, SL 25. Puritan; largely responsible for inviting Richard Sibbes to GI as preacher, bequeathed Sibbes £5. Rich; portions of £3,000 ea. to 2 das.; owned property in London, Norfolk, Northants, War. (*H. of P.*, Clendinnen; Harris, thesis; PCC 55 Scroope.)

APPENDIX F

Exclusions from Benchers' Sample

Appendix F. Exclusions from Benchers' Sample[a,b]

Name	Inn	Bar	Bench	Office, etc.	Source
BROOKE, Sir John (1575–1660)	LI	—	AB1626	Courtier-politician	G.E.C., Baronetage
BROWKER, Brooker, Hugh (d. 1607)	IT	1589	B1592	Chief prothonotary, Common Pleas	ITR; HS, xliii
BROWNLOE, Richard (1553–1638)	IT	—	B1592	Chief prothonotary, Common Pleas	Aylmer, King's Servants; DNB
CAESAR, Sir Charles (c.1590–1642)	IT	—	AB-B1613	MCh; MR	Levack, Civil Lawyers; DNB
CAESAR, Sir Julius (1558–1636)	IT	—	B1591	MReq; MR	Levack, Civil Lawyers; DNB
CAREW, Sir George (c.1570–1612)	MT	—	AB1602	MCh, etc.	H. of P.; DNB
CHAMBERLAIN, Richard (c.1560–1660)	IT	—	AB1638	Co-chief clk., Wards	Aylmer, King's Servants; Bell, Court of Wards
COMPTON, Sir Henry (c.1584–1649)	LI	—	AB1604	Custos Brevium, Common Pleas	H. of P.; Aylmer, King's Servants
CORY, Thomas (d. 1656)	IT	1638	AB1638	Chief prothonotary, Common Pleas	Aylmer, King's Servants; Smyth, Obituary
CROKE, Sir Henry (1558–1659)	IT	1617 (assoc.)	AB1638	Master, Pipe Office, Exch.	Aylmer, King's Servants
CROMPTON, Thomas (d. 1614)	MT	—	AB1609	Prothonotary, Common Pleas	HS, lxv
CURLE, Francis (c.1577–1626)	GI	—	B1618	Auditor of the Wards	Bell, Court of Wards
DIGGES, Sir Dudley	GI	—	AB1631	MCh; MR; courtier-politician	Aylmer, King's Servants; DNB
DONHAULT, Gregory (d. 1613)	MT	—	AB1612	MCh; Ellesmere's secretary	MTR, ii; PCC 29 Lawe

Name	Inn	Year	Code	Office	Source
FANSHAWE, Sir Thomas (1580–1631)	IT	1666	AB-B1613	Clk. of Crown, King's Bench	Aylmer, *King's Servants*
FARMER, George (1600–70)	IT	1639 (assoc.)	AB1639	Prothonotary, Common Pleas	Nichols, *Leics.*, iv; *ITR*, ii
GOLDESBOROUGH, John (1568–1618)	MT	—	AB1613	Prothonotary, Common Pleas	*VCH, Hunts.*, ii
GRIMSTON, Edward (d. 1610)	GI	—	AB1600	MCh	Keeler; Haydn, *Dignities*
GULSTON, John (fl. 1601–52)	GI	—	B1618	Prothonotary, Common Pleas	Aylmer, *King's Servants*
HARE, John (1546–1613)	IT	1590	B1592	Chief clk., Wards	*H. of P.*; Bell, *Court of Wards*; App. D above
HARE, Sir Ralph (c.1570–1624)	IT	1597	B1605	Co-chief clk. & coroner, King's Bench	*H. of P.*
HENLEY, Sir Robert (d. 1656)	MT	1616	AB-B1632	Six Clerk, Ch; master, King's Bench Office	Aylmer, *King's Servants*
HOBART, Miles (d. 1639)	LI	1618	AB1622	Clk. of Warrants, Common Pleas; s. Sir Henry, LCJ	Norfolk RO, NRS 11078 25 E 3; HS, lxxxv
KEELING, John^c (1576–c.1642)	IT	1618 (assoc.)	AB1638	Clk. of Crown, King's Bench, clk. of Assize	
LEY, Sir Henry (1595–1638)	LI	1616	AB1620	S. of Sir James, LCJ	See App. D above
LITTLETON, James (c.1596–1645)	IT	1639 (assoc.)	B1639	MCh (not master of Temple)	Levack, *Civil Lawyers*; *Inns of Court*
LONG, George (fl. 1623–38)	LI	1631	AB1638	Clk. of Pleas, Exch.	LI MS Red Book, fol. 163
MANN, William (d. 1616)	MT	1604 (assoc.)	AB1608	? Secondary, King's Bench	Bodl. Ashmole MS 824, fol. 224
MEWTIS, Sir Thomas (c.1590–1649)	GI	—	B1626	Clk. of Privy Council	Aylmer, *King's Servants*
MOYLE, Robert (d. 1638)	IT	—	AB-B1627	Prothonotary, Common Pleas	*ITR*, ii; Smyth, *Obituary*

Exclusions from Benchers' Sample[a,b]—continued

Name	Inn	Bar	Bench	Office, etc.	Source
NAUNTON, Sir Robert (1563–1635)	IT	—	AB1616	MReq; master of Wards	HS, lxv
OLDISWORTH, Arnold (fl.1561–1613)	LI	—	AB1612	Keeper, clk. of Hanaper	H. of P.
OWEN, Sir Roger[d] (1573–1617)	LI	1597	AB-B1609		H. of P.; DNB
PAGITT, James (c.1581–1638)	MT	1602	B1631	Baron Cursitor, Exch.	Foss; Lyson, Environs, iii
PENNYMAN, Sir William (1607–43)	GI	—	B1639	Six Clerk, Ch; clk. Star Chamber	Keeler; DNB
RUDYERD, Sir Benjamin (1572–1658)	MT	1600	AB1619	Surveyor of Wards	Keeler; DNB
RUSSELL, Sir Francis (1593–1641)	LI	—	AB1611	Fen-drainer, politician, etc.	DNB
SEDLEY, Sir William[d] (c.1558–1613)	LI	1584	AB-B1589		DNB
SPENCER, Sir Edward (1595–1656)	LI	—	AB1617		Underdown, Pride's Purge
SPENCER, Thomas (c.1547–1630)	LI	1574	AB1615	Custos Brevium, Common Pleas	Finch, Five Northants Families
WALLER, Thomas (d. c.1624)	GI	1591	AB1608	Prothonotary, Common Pleas	VCH, Bucks., iii; GIPB
WASHINGTON, Laurence (d. 1619)	GI	1583	AB1599	Registrar, Ch	Clendinnen
WIGHTWICK, Samuel (c.1592–1662)	IT	1630 (assoc.)	AB1638	Chief clk. of Pleas, King's Bench	Aylmer, King's Servants; HS, lvi

[a] A number of IT and LI barristers called to the bench who were unable, or unwilling, to accept the invitation have also been excluded from this study. They were Charles Gore (LI, *fl.* 1628–46), Luke Norton (IT, d. 1630), Edward Jones (LI, *fl.* 1589–1623), Thomas Oteley (IT, *fl.* 1564–97), Edward Rogers (LI, *fl.* 1604–28), and William Wright (IT, *c.*1565–1613). Finally, Thomas Cheeke (*c.*1566–*c.*1618) was considered for call to the bench at LI in 1610, but not actually promoted (cf. Clendinnen, 269, and *LIBB*, ii. 133), while William Coombes was called only conditionally at MT in 1594, and the condition was not in fact fulfilled (*N & Q*, ccxi, 1966, 286, and *MTR*, i. 347, 349, 353). Christopher Banaster of GI appears to be another 'ghost' bencher; although paying a fine for refusing to read on 15 November 1620, and appointed to the office of pensioner a year later, he never joined the governing body of GI, *pace* Somerville, *Office Holders*, 50; cf. GI MS Order Book, fols. 333ᵛ, 337.

[b] In column 3, (assoc.) = associated to bar, or invited to sit at bar table. In column 4, AB = called to be associate bencher; AB-B = called first as an associate, then to full bench membership.

[c] John Keeling, clerk of the Crown in King's Bench, steward of Hertford, and clerk of assize, Home circuit, 1623–5, is easily confused with his namesake in the barristers sample, who was also an IT member, especially since both were called to the bar (or associated, in the former's case) on 16 April 1618. (See Cockburn, *History of English Assizes*, 314.) However, the office-holder was admitted in 1615, as of Hertford, having previously, in 1604, been granted a reversion of the place of coroner and attorney in King's Bench for life; he married Alice, daughter of Gregory Waterhouse of Halifax, a relative of David Waterhouse, coroner in King's Bench, for whom see App. E above. The practising barrister John Keeling was admitted in 1608, as of Newcastle-under-Lyme, Staffs., married Elizabeth, daughter of William Croke of Chilton, Bucks., and became a common pleader of London in 1640. (*ITAdmR*; *ITR*, ii; *CSPD 1603–10*, 152; *William Salt Arch. Soc.*, v (2), 193–5; Pape, *Newcastle-under-Lyme in Tudor and Early Stuart Times*; Turnor, *History of . . . Hertford*; Appendix D above.)

[d] In *A Discours-Apologetical . . .* (1654), p. 38, Thomas Gataker recalled that while he was preacher at LI (1602–11), 'there lived much in the house, not as practitioners in the law, but as associates with the Bench, two worthy knights of eminent parts for variety of learning and reading, Sir Roger Owen and Sir William Sedley'.

APPENDIX G

Geographical Origins of Bar and Bench Samples

	Bar	Bench
Anglesey	1	4
Bedfordshire	0	11
Berkshire	2	8
Brecknock	0	1
Buckinghamshire	2	14
Caernarfonshire	0	1
Cambridgeshire	1	9
Cardiganshire	0	0
Carmarthanshire	0	0
Cheshire	1	12
Cornwall	0	4
Cumberland	0	3
Denbighshire	1	3
Derbyshire	3	5
Devonshire	4	22
Dorset	4	8
Durham	3	0
Essex	9	14
Flintshire	0	2
Glamorganshire	2	1
Gloucestershire	5	14
Hampshire	1	6
Herefordshire	1	3
Hertfordshire	4	8
Huntingdonshire	1	2
Ireland	2	2
Kent	9	21
Lancashire	1	12
Leicestershire	1	5
Lincolnshire	2	10
London	8	24
Merionethshire	0	1
Monmouthshire	1	2
Montgomeryshire	1	1
Middlesex	1	8
Norfolk	5	16
Northamptonshire	4	16

Northumberland	2	2
Nottinghamshire	0	4
Oxfordshire	2	11
Pembrokeshire	0	0
Radnorshire	0	0
Rutland	0	2
Shropshire	4	12
Somerset	5	13
Staffordshire	4	4
Suffolk	3	14
Surrey	1	6
Sussex	2	7
Warwickshire	2	11
Westmorland	0	0
Wiltshire	4	18
Worcestershire	2	6
Yorkshire	6	16
Unknown	1	4
Totals	118	403

APPENDIX H

Sherfield's Interview with Noy[a]

15 February 1632 Mr. Noye his Majesties Attorney generall having the last night held speech with Mr Richard Taylor of Lincolnes Inne, towching some maner of excusing himself about the proceeding against me Henry Sherfield in the Starr Chamber, which cause was heard and sentenced upon Wednesday 6° and Friday 8° of this moneth, And having told him as Mr Taylor related to me, that the Lord Keeper was to blame in shewing his letter (which he wrote to the Lord Keeper to set downe a day of hearing of my cause) unto Sir Edward Clark, and that he was forced soe to doe, he did in the end (as Mr Taylor told me) entreat him to speake to me to come to him to speake with him. And therefore in this present xvth of February 1632 I repayred to his Chamber, and was after a short stay brought into his Study to him, where I found Mr Mason of this howse; And Mr. Attorney at my first entrance lookt on me smylingly as if there were noe cause of Sadnes in me And said with much glee how dost & used many like Jole passages as he had used formerlie to doe, But then withdrew himself into his lodging Chamber with me to have private Conference with me And then tould me for some excuse of his Replie against me in Starchamber at the hearing (which was [base and (illegible): erased] if noe worse at the least inhumaine) That the king had written his particuler letters to every one of his Counsell Learned who did then plead against me to incouradge them to be well prepared, and to mayntayne the cause against me; That he himself had used meanes to be set aside and not to give Evidance against me in my Cause. That other Counsell were thereupon assigned. But that the king did after that write also a particular letter to him, wherein was mencioned, that he the said Attorney should not desert the cause notwithstanding he had appoynted other Counsell to assist him. And that scinse that his Majestie had by word of mouthe chardged and Enioyned him not to desert him nor his cause for my sake or for any old famyliar acquayntance that had bine betwixt us, but that he should looke into the busynes and mayntayne it on his behalf with his best skill, and thereupon began to offer his excuse, but I tould him he should not neede any such matter I should have bine satisfied without his revealing of any such secreats and prayd him to rest satisfied that I neyther did nor would conceyve amisse of him for urging of any truth against me, and that it was his duty soe to doe, and that he deserved reproof if he omitted any thing of that nature, that concerned the Cause.

He then moved and counselled me to Resigne my Recordership, saying that it would be well taken. I tould him that if it were the kinges pleasure to have it soe I would not only doe it, but lay downe whatsoever I had els at his

[a] (Source: Hants RO, 44M69/xxv/6. Memo Book F (1627–33), unfoliated, 4 leaves from end, reversed.

feet with my life to doe his Majestie service, but I prayed him to lett me knowe whether he thought it fitte thus on the necke of my present disgrace I should encrease it by myne owne acte. He said that as the case now stood, he would not absolutely say it was fitte, but said that he wisht I had surrendered it before my enlardgement out of the Fleete And he then said that it was not well done the Lord Keeper to dischardg me soe soone of myne Imprisonment and that his Lordship had bine blamed for it.

I told him I hoped his Lordship had not done therein any thing but that which he usually did to others, and that Sir Richard Mynshall did not forbeare the barres att Westminster any one daye since he was sentenced, and I trusted that having given security for my Fine there was noe cause for offence given by it.[b] I then prayed him to helpe touchinge my fine which was not mitagated att the last sitting of the Lords. He said it had bene mitigated if I had not bine dischardged of Imprisonment and said that that was the cause of it & that now he knew not how to get any Parte abated and soe I departed praying him to be my Frend still.

On Monday nyght 18 instant February I went againe to the Attorney generall and had much speech with him in his Bedchamber. And prayed him for old acquaintance sake to doe me some good eyther by the dischardge or abatement of my Fine, or els by getting me to be restored to his Majestie grace, which I assured myselfe he might doe if he would but truly informe his Majestie what I am & of what conversacon and that he may take off the false informacons of myne adversaries that he knew well, the same were nothing but falsehoods. But all the Comfort he gave me was that he knew not how to helpe me but said he would have me write to the Mayor and Company of Salisbury to Choose a new Recorder, I pray quoth I if I doe soe would you have me dwell there in the full disgrace of it, noe said he why then I pray will you be a meanes that I may dwell here at London. Noe said he why where then, why said he at your house at Ambrosbury Alas quoth I yt is a poor dwellinge & yet is in a tenants hands which rents my Land there, but he seemed not to regard what became of me, [soe: erased] if he could Ridd me from Salisbury. I yet again prest him to doe me good in letting the King have true understandinge of me, his burden [?] was still then give of your Recordership I seeing him so earnest that way did Imagine that it had pleased the kinges Majestie to expresse himself to him touching me in some respect or other, and therefore I tould him If it were his Majesties pleasure to have it soe that I desired him to take notice that I had neyther that place nor any thing else [of this world: interpolated] which I hold most deare but that I would in all humylity and with other fulnes lay all downe at his feete: And yet I prayed him to take notice that I held it now of soe great Importance to me not to thrust my self into that disgrace That If all [those: erased] the men upon the earth besides his Majestie & without him should desire or presse me to doe it, I would absolutely denye them, & would first departe with my life before I would consent to Leave that place For I sayd that I hold my reputacon much dearer to me then my life. Yet in the end I tould him that if he would please to represent my present state and condicon

---

[b] For the case of Sir Richard Minshall, see Rushworth, *Collections*, II. ii. 49–50.

to his Ma*jes*tie and redeeme my reputacon with him, that I might be recyved into his grace, I tould him I desired his Ma*jes*tie might know that his pleasure declared to me in whatsoever it were should be cherfully obeyed.

[But yet I: erased] He then tould me that he would returne me some answar before Wednesday night next.

But then I doubting that he might mistake my meaning & soe might make some tender of myne owne offer to resygne the Recordership, I desired him to take my meaning aright & not to mistake me, I tould him I did not make any offer nor give any consent to Resigne my place of Recorder of Sarum.

Neyther would I that he should declare any such thing to his Ma*jes*tie for I said I did presume his Ma*jes*tie did not require nor wishe any such thing. And that I did protest against his making of any such overture to his Ma*jes*tie But if it pleased him to represent to his Ma*jes*tie the hearty sorrowe and grief I have by hearing that his highnes is displeased with me, I should thanck him and upon that occasion if he did let his Ma*jes*tie [breaks off]

APPENDIX I

Theses Consulted

Berkowitz, D. S., 'Young Mr Selden', Harvard University Ph.D. thesis, 1946.

Birken, W. J., 'The Fellows of the Royal College of Physicians of London, 1603–1643'. University of North Carolina at Chapel Hill Ph.D. thesis, 1977.

Black, S. F., 'The Judges of Westminster Hall, 1640–1660'. University of Oxford B.Litt. thesis, 1970.

Blackwood, B. G., 'The Lancashire Gentry 1625–1660; A Social and Economic Study'. University of Oxford D.Phil. thesis, 1979.

Brooks, C. W., 'Some Aspects of Attorneys in Late Sixteenth and Early Seventeenth-Century England'. University of Oxford D.Phil. thesis, 1978.

Calnan, J. B., 'County Society and Local Government in the County of Hertford c.1580–c.1630, with special reference to The Commission of the Peace'. University of Cambridge Ph.D. thesis, 1978.

Carroll, R., 'The Parliamentary Representation of Yorkshire 1625–1660'. Vanderbilt University Ph.D. thesis, 1964.

Clark, R., 'Anglicanism, Recusancy and Dissent in Derbyshire 1603–1730'. University of Oxford D.Phil. thesis, 1977.

Clendinnen, T. B., 'The Common Lawyers in Parliament and Society: A Social and Political Study of the Common Lawyers in the First Jacobean Parliament', University of North Carolina Ph.D. thesis, 1975.

Connelly, M. (née Jobling), 'The Godly in Berkshire from the Reign of Elizabeth to c.1642'. University of Reading M.Phil. thesis, 1977.

Cooper, H. H., 'Promotion and Politics among the Common Law Judges of the Reigns of James I and Charles I'. University of Liverpool MA thesis, 1964.

Dias, J. R., 'Politics and Administration in the counties of Nottingham and Derby, 1590–1640'. University of Oxford D.Phil. thesis, 1973.

Durston, C. G., 'Berkshire and Its County Gentry 1625–1649'. University of Reading Ph.D. thesis, 1977.

Everitt, A., 'Kent and its Gentry 1640–60'. University of London Ph.D. thesis, 1957.

Glanville, G. H., 'Aspects of the History of the County of Surrey 1580–1620'. University of London Ph.D. thesis, 1972.

Gowers, I. W., 'Puritanism in the County of Devon Between 1570 and 1640'. University of Exeter MA thesis, 1970.

Harris, J. C., 'Richard Sibbes; A Moderate in Early Seventeenth-Century Puritanism'. University of Melbourne MA thesis, 1979.

Harrison, G. A., 'Royalist Organization in Wiltshire 1642–1646', University of London Ph.D. thesis, 1963.

Heap, P. C., 'The Politics of Stuart Warwickshire'. Yale University Ph.D. thesis, 1975.

Hopkins, E., 'The Bridgewater Estates in North Shropshire in the First Half of the Seventeenth Century'. University of London MA thesis, 1956.

Horton, P. H., 'The Administrative, Social, and Economic Structure of the Durham Bishopric Estates, 1500–1640'. University of Durham M.Litt. thesis, 1975.

Hughes, A., 'Politics, Society and Civil War in Warwickshire, 1620–1650'. University of Liverpool Ph.D. thesis, 1979.

Ives, E. W., 'Some Aspects of the Legal Profession in the Late Fifteenth and Early Sixteenth Centuries'. University of London Ph.D. thesis, 1955.

Jones, M. V., 'The Political History of the Parliamentary Boroughs of Kent 1642–1662'. University of London Ph.D. thesis, 1967.

Kopperman, P. E., 'Sir Robert Heath 1575–1649: A Biography'. University of Illinois at Urbana-Champaign Ph.D. thesis, 1972.

Lake, P., 'Laurence Chaderton and the Cambridge Moderate Puritan Tradition'. University of Cambridge Ph.D. thesis, 1978.

MacCulloch, D. N. J., 'Power, Privilege and the County Community: County Politics in Elizabethan Suffolk'. University of Cambridge Ph.D. thesis, 1977.

McParlin, G. E., 'The Herefordshire Gentry in County Government, 1625–1661', University of Wales, Aberystwyth Ph.D. thesis, 1981.

Mousley, J. E., 'Sussex Country Gentry in the Reign of Elizabeth'. University of London Ph.D. thesis, 1955.

Phillips, C. B., 'The Gentry in Cumberland and Westmorland, 1600–1665'. University of Lancaster Ph.D. thesis, 1974.

Quintrell, B. W., 'The Government of the County of Essex, 1603–1642'. University of London Ph.D. thesis, 1965.

Reed, M., 'Ipswich in the Seventeenth Century'. University of Leicester Ph.D. thesis, 1973.

Richmond, B. J., 'The Work of the Justices of the Peace in Hampshire 1603–1640'. University of Southampton M.Phil. thesis, 1969.

Robbins, M., 'The Agricultural, Domestic, Social and Cultural Interests of the Gentry of South-East Glamorgan, 1540–1640'. University of Wales, Cardiff, Ph.D. thesis, 1974.

Sacks, D. H., 'Trade, Society and Politics in Bristol c.1500–c.1640'. Harvard University Ph.D. thesis, 1977.

Shaller, T. K., 'English Law and the Renaissance: the Common Law and Humanism in the Sixteenth Century'. Harvard University Ph.D. thesis, 1979.

Silcock, R. H., 'County Government in Worcestershire 1603–1660'. University of London Ph.D. thesis, 1974.

Tyacke, N. R. N., 'Arminianism in England, in Religion and Politics, 1604 to 1640'. University of Oxford D.Phil. thesis, 1968.

Wall, A. D., 'The Wiltshire Commission of the Peace: A Study of Its Social Structure'. University of Melbourne MA thesis, 1966.

Wanklyn, M. D. G., 'Landed Society and Allegiance in Cheshire and Shropshire in the First Civil War'. University of Manchester Ph.D. thesis, 1976.
Wilson, B. M., 'The Corporation of York 1580–1660'. University of York M.Phil. thesis, 1967.

INDEX

This index includes references to all individuals who are the main subjects of an entry in Appendices D–F; for further details these entries themselves should be consulted.

422 *Index*

Harris, Sir Thomas 118, 168, 367
Harrison, John 367
Harrison, William, *Description of England* 162, 316
Hartlib, Samuel 220
Harvey, Sir Francis 68–9, 118, 247, 367
Harvey, Gabriel 252
Hastings family 298
Hastings, Sir Francis 32
Hastings, Sir George 309
Hastings, Henry, 3rd earl of Huntingdon 298
Hastings, Henry, 5th earl of Huntingdon 297
Hastings, Lady Mary 32
Hastings, Sussex 55, 297
Hatley, St George, Cambs. 101
Hatton, Sir Christopher 164–5, 212, 320 n.
Hatton, Christopher, Viscount Hatton 198
Hatton, Lady Elizabeth 119, 121
Hatton, Robert 367
Hauslopp, Richard 43 n.
Hauslopp, Thomas 43 n.
Haward, John 25, 42, 303, 367
Hayman, Richard 312
Heath, Edward 119, 201, 221
Heath, Sir Robert 109–10, 119, 170, 173, 177, 221, 268–70, 367–8
Hebrew language 201, 205
Hele, Elize 172, 216 n., 368
Hele, Sir John 53, 124, 175, 247 n., 270, 294
Hele, John 368
Henden, Sir Edward 85, 135, 152–3, 179, 278, 335, 368; *The Perfect Conveyancer* 203
Hengham, Ralph 201
Henley, Sir Robert 86 n., 409
Henrietta Maria 276, 280
Henry I 272
Henry II 272
Henry VI 254
Henry VIII 4, 199
Henshawe, Thomas 69
Hentzner, Paul 201
Herbert family 160
Herbert, Edward 251, 368
Herbert, Henry, earl of Pembroke 160
Hereford 312
Herefordshire 51 n., 168, 410
Herne, John 368–9

Herrick, Robert 304
Herringdon, Anthony 369
Hertford 245, 249, 409
Hertfordshire 120, 134, 198, 410
Hesketh, Sir Thomas 54 n., 305, 369
Heslington, Yorks. 152
Hetley, Sir Thomas 369
Hibberd, Christopher 33
Hicks, John 335
Higgons, Richard 369
High Churchmen 211, 213–14, 217
High Commission, Court of 219
High Court of Justice 282
Hill, Abigail 125 n.
Hill, Adam 109
Hill, Roger 47, 125 n., 221
Hill, Thomas, *The Arte of Gardening* 201
Hilliard, William 53, 307
Hills, Thomas 32
Hindon, Wilts. 64
historical scholarship 195–200, 207
Hitcham, Sir Robert 80 n., 117, 169, 214, 304, 369
Hitchcock, Thomas 266, 303, 370
Hitchings, John 370
Hobart, Sir Henry 98, 118, 170 n., 175, 202, 270, 370; wealth of 129, 155, 177 n., 182–3
Hobart, Miles 177 n., 409
Hobbes, Thomas 304
Hoby, Sir Thomas 300
Holborne, Sir Robert 274, 370
Holbourn, Nicholas 69
Holford, Henry 335
Holland, Anthony 131 n., 204 n., 214, 335
Holland, Edward 336
Holland, John 131 n.
Holles, Gervase 109
Holles, John, earl of Clare 109
Holloway, Charles 275 n.
Holmes, G. S. 2, 94, 324
Holt, William 68–9, 370
Holyday, Barten 11
Honeywood, Sir John 77, 215 n., 336
Honeywood, Sir Thomas 77 n.
Hoskins, W. G. 181
Hoskyns, Benedicta 163
Hoskyns, Sir John 18, 163, 193, 194–5, 206, 254, 269, 370
House of Commons 230, 231, 253–6, 268, 274, 309; speaker of 156, 250, 253
House of Lords 38, 253